309.1
B47h

90803

DATE DUE			
Aug 5 '76			

HUNTERS AND GATHERERS TODAY

A Socioeconomic Study of Eleven Such Cultures
in the Twentieth Century

Edited by

M. G. BICCHIERI

Central Washington State College

HOLT, RINEHART AND WINSTON, INC.
New York   Chicago   San Francisco   Atlanta
Dallas   Montreal   Toronto   London   Sydney

309.1
B47h
90803
nov.1974

PREFACE

For more than 99 percent of the approximately two million years since the emergence of a recognizable human animal man has been a hunter and gatherer. Living in the sedentary, densely populated communities made possible by the adoption of agriculture as a life base is a new condition to which man has only begun to make basic physiological and psychological adjustments. The environment created for man by the industrial age, lasting a mere three hundred years or so, is so recent that we do not know whether man will even survive it, much less adapt to it. The shift from hunting and gathering to agriculture, and finally to an industrial base, is so recent that today there are still human communities living within the framework of each adaptation. The number of hunting and gathering communities is dwindling rapidly. This life form will be extinct within a few more years. It is essential for a balanced view of man to understand the nature of the hunting-gathering adaptation.

Eleven original chapters representing eleven hunting and gathering societies in widely separated parts of the world constitute the body of this volume. A balance has been sought by including papers based on historical reconstruction in addition to those representing the variety inherent in ethnographies based on participant observation. While a general outline has been followed to enhance analytic comparability, each author treats the data somewhat differently, consistent with various approaches in anthropology and with the socioeconomic characteristics of the societies discussed. Each chapter is preceded by a short introduction pointing out its specific character and basic features. A short note on the author accompanies the individual contribution.

The overall significance of these studies is clearly directed at the larger scheme of things human. The main concern of anthropology has been and continues to be the nature of human life, its genesis, development, and future direction. Whether the approach to the question be specific or general, the common concern has been to work toward valid generalizations about man's relation to the give and take of nature, about the way the problem of existence—for the individual as well as for the group—has been solved, and the way in which the persistence of the group is to be assured.

The relevance of the study of small, relatively simple hunting and gathering societies is seen in the light of two major considerations. First, given the fact that the great bulk of man's time on this earth has been spent in a hunting and gathering socioeconomic context, this form of adaptation must be seen as eminently successful. Second, taking as axiomatic that inherent human needs are basically constant, we see that the study of societies without the complexities following upon a sedentary agricultural or industrial adaptation can offer a base for generating hypotheses concerning the elemental features of human social life.

It is not possible to develop anything approaching a basic theory of human life without considering this most enduring form of human adaptation. Within the social sciences the conceptual frame of reference has, for the greatest part, been based on agricultural and industrial societies. This approach is reflected in both the theoretical and the ideological lattice of these disciplines. Even anthropology has, in the past, based much of its observation and generalizations on a sample constituted preponderantly of tribal agricultural socioeconomic systems. With the coverage now provided by systematic studies of food-gathering and hunting societies, we can reevaluate our base data and concepts.

Aside from the direct contribution of data on food collectors to completion of the human record, we can now reconsider ideas relating to population dynamics in their demographic, social, and economic aspects. The relation of populations to their physical environment in terms of optimum sizes for continued and successful exploitation is now seen in a different perspective. The efficiency of various systems of social and economic technology can be evaluated along a wider continuum, and from these evaluations new conclusions can be drawn as to the ecological balance between human populations and their terrestrial habitat. Terminology such as "economic efficiency," "affluence," "standard of living," "advanced technology," and so forth, can be reevaluated.

Ethology, the study of the behavioral process in its evolutionary adaptive sequences, as well as other important phases of research in human behavior must take notice of these data on hunting and gathering adaptations in the development of a consistent theory. Questions concerning territorialism, the handling of aggression, social control, property, leadership, the use of space, and many other dimensions are particularly significant in these contexts. To evaluate any of these focal aspects of human behavior without taking into consideration the socioeconomic adaptation that has characterized most of the span of human life on this planet will eventually bias conclusions and generalizations. If we are to understand human behavior in the light of essential human characteristics and in terms of the whole range of adaptive devices—material as well as social —which have been utilized to adapt to a dynamic environment at different places, then we must reevaluate presently used terms and concepts in the context of a human sample that is as complete as possible.

Within the social sciences we can point to a number of specific areas in which studies of food-collecting societies can be of great import. In the reconstruction of the way of life of extinct populations, which for the most part were food-gathering/hunting populations, it is paramount to have detailed works of similar contemporary groups. The archaeological process of inference, based on the recovery of incomplete assemblages, can be greatly aided by complete studies of contemporary socioeconomic groups which have mediated adaptations to ecological niches demonstrably similar to those of the past. Theories of cultural change can be reformulated, for example, by reassessing the hypothesis that food-gathering societies lived under constant fear of starvation with an enormous expenditure of labor resulting in a meager production of vital materials. We might even be able to challenge the assumption that the "agricultural and industrial revolutions" freed man from the bondage of a laborious, precarious, and unrewarding life. We might, in fact, be able to see these "revolutions" not as great gains in the absolute sense, but rather as necessary "evils" to which man had to submit in order to cope with drastic environmental changes, including a population proliferation resulting from a "successful" hunting and gathering adaptation.

Reassessment of present theories concerning human conflict and group organization can also stem from these studies. The relation between aggression and concern with scarce resources is relatively apparent in ethnographic studies of food-gathering and hunting societies. Not only territorialism and aggression can be studied in this context, but of great relevance to the biologist and the physical anthropologist, consideration can be given to the cultural evolutionary implications of millennia of selective genetic forces directed at maximizing biological adaptive characteristics which are consistent with a hunting and gathering base. A focus on social interaction could concern itself with the web of formal-informal interaction which maintains the functional structure of small, nomadic hunting and gathering social aggregates. There has also been great emphasis given to the analysis of kinship system as derived from the study of tribal-peasant societies. It has been suggested that through time there has been a decrease in the stress on formal kinship relationship as an organizational principle of society. Studies of the kind reported in this volume may prove that such stress is specific for a certain type of tribal-peasant society while being of less significance for many "predomestication" societies as well as for industrial societies.

We have pointed to some of the many new directions that studies of human life can take. For professionals of all disciplines, the increased interest in these types of studies speaks for itself. For those who, living in the world of today, seek directions for the world of tomorrow and who therefore want to have a complete and unbiased view of the human record, it is more than justifiable to read these articles just to educate oneself. A number of stereotypes with which we are enculturated and which are derived largely from folktales and unreliable accounts of culture-bound travelers wll be challenged. We could, for example, dismiss the idea that complexity of technology is a measure of "advancement" and well-being. At a time in which societies are straining under the pressure of upgrading their social technology to meet the heavy demands of extremely complex material technology; at a time in which the city, for long a symbol of the ultimate in "civilization," is crumbling under its own weight and the values of rural living are questioned; at a time in which language is becoming an uncertain means of communication in that meanings are in people rather than in words; at such a time it is vital that we carefully evaluate the solutions devised by "simpler" societies along the course of millennia. It is very possible that in such solutions we might find relevant cues for dealing with some of today's problems.

This book is closely interrelated with other recent events, and derived publications, that are concerned with food-gathering/hunting societies. The National Museum of Canada, Ottawa, held a conference on band organization in 1965, with proceedings published in 1969 (as Bulletin 228 of the National Museum of Canada) titled *Band Societies*; and on cultural ecology in 1966, with proceedings published in 1969 (as Bulletin 230 of the National Museum of Canada) titled *Ecological Essays*. Both of these volumes were edited by David Damas, who has provided a chapter on life among the precontact Copper Eskimo in this volume. These two conferences were relatively small and expressed specialized interests. In 1966 the Wenner-Gren Foundation sponsored a conference on man the hunter attended by students from all over the world working on the various biocultural aspects of food-gathering/hunting societies. *Man the Hunter*, the volume ensuing from this conference and edited by Irven DeVore and Richard Borshay Lee, is an academic cornerstone in the analysis of the ecology of food-collecting populations.

The present volume represents a chronological and supportive follow-through to these conferences and related publications. A collection of contemporary, original studies on the subject of food-gatherers/hunters is essential at this juncture. People intending to work in this and related fields—whether they are just generally interested or whether they are specialized human geographers, historians, biologists, economists, political scientists, sociologists, or anthropologists—must consider these four volumes as a definitive base for this study. The descriptive ethnographies and historical reconstructions, as well as the glossaries and bibliographies of the individual chapters in this volume, will complete the picture for the generalized as well as the specialized reader.

M. G. B.
Ellensburg, Washington
April 1972

CONTENTS

MAP KEY

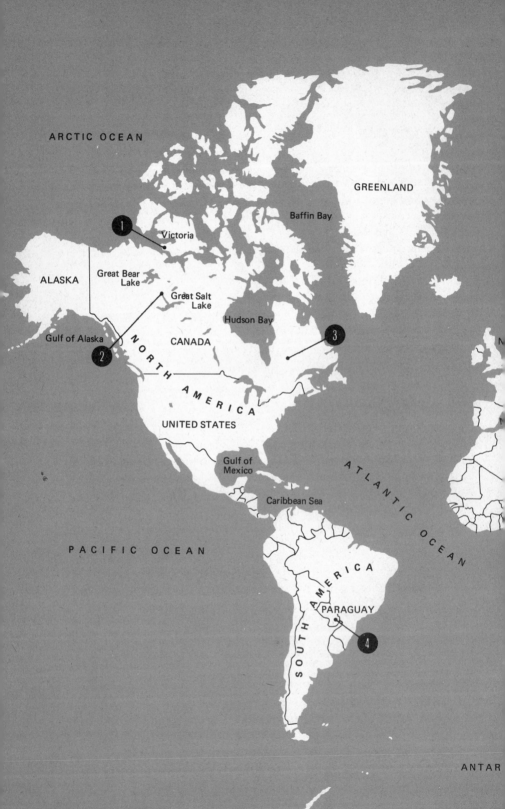

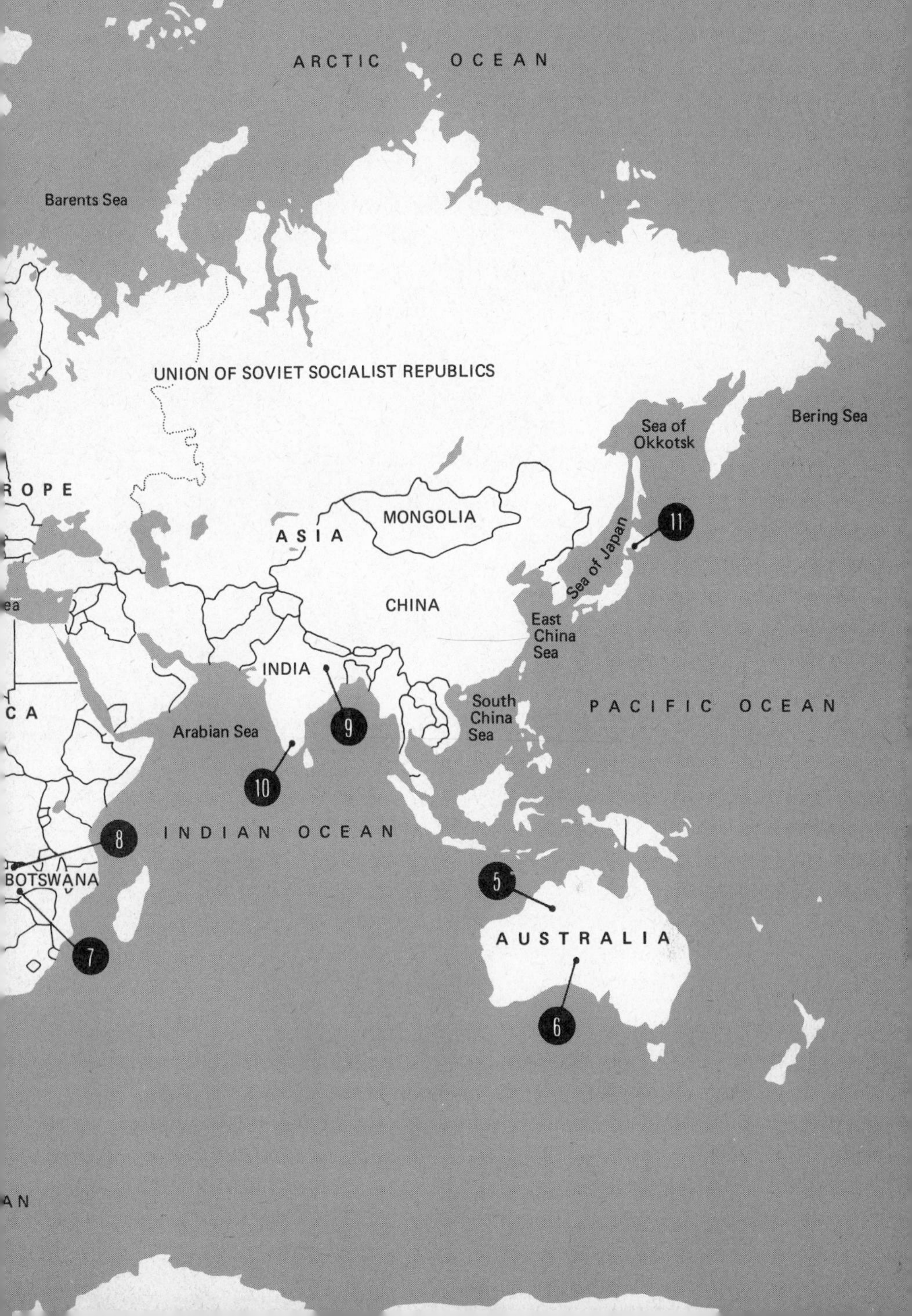

ARCTIC   OCEAN

Barents Sea

UNION OF SOVIET SOCIALIST REPUBLICS

Sea of
Okkotsk

Bering Sea

ROPE

ea

ASIA

MONGOLIA

CHINA

Sea of Japan

(11)

INDIA

Arabian Sea

(9)

East
China
Sea

PACIFIC OCEAN

CA

(10)

South
China
Sea

(8)

INDIAN   OCEAN

BOTSWANA

(7)

(5)

AUSTRALIA

(6)

AN

PART
1
THE
NEW
WORLD

CHAPTER

1

THE COPPER ESKIMO[1]

David Damas

David Damas received his Ph.D. from the University of Chicago in 1962 and is currently Associate Professor of Anthropology at McMaster University. He served as Arctic Ethnologist for the National Museum of Canada in Ottawa from 1962 to 1969 and has conducted field research among the Copper, Netsilik, and Iglulik Eskimo. His fields of investigation have included band organization, the roles of adaptation to environment and history in cultural variability, and the culture change that is taking place among the Eskimo as a result of white contact. He was editor of two bulletins of the National Museum of Canada, Ecological Essays: Proceedings of the Conference on Cultural Ecology *(1969) and* Band Societies: Proceedings of the Conference on Band Organization *(1969).*

EDITOR'S INTRODUCTION

The Copper Eskimo are natives to the central Canadian Arctic area. Their physical appearance, the Arctic Mongoloid type, is like that of other Eskimo populations, and their language has been classified as a member of the Inupiaq group of dialects which are spoken throughout the New World Arctic. Archaeological evidence of all three major stages of Eskimo prehistory has been located in the area, and the modern Copper Eskimo are considered to be descendants of peoples represented by the late Thule culture, which spread from Alaska between A.D. 900 and 1200. Damas believes, however, that many of the distinguishing characteristics of modern Copper Eskimo, such as their extensive use of float copper and their ethnographically recorded seasonal economic cycle, did not develop until the nineteenth century. The climate of their Arctic environment is severe, with long cold winters and short cool summers. Traditionally these Eskimos were hunters, primarily of caribou and seal, and fishermen. Trapping, however, was introduced into the economy with European contact and brought the Copper Eskimo into the marketing system of the "outside world," providing

3

him with new tools, materials, and food resources. The use of such new tools as rifles, nets, and traps led to a more intensive exploitation of the environment, which altered the distribution of game and which, in turn, further altered the traditional economic practices. Recently the Copper Eskimo have been in transition from a hunting and trapping economy in stable contact with Europeans to economic dependence on Canadian government agencies and welfare. This most recent phase in their history has resulted in perhaps the greatest changes in their traditional economic patterns, social organization, and value system.

Damas provides an ethnographic description of precontact Copper Eskimo life and traces the development of their social organization and seasonal economic cycle from that time to the present. Comparison of the Copper Eskimo with their Dogrib "neighbors" reveals, as should be expected, many similarities in their social organization and orientation; the differences are perhaps best attributed to specific demands of both the physical and social environment. More generally, however, cultural themes which have been stressed in both these and other articles in this book, such as the egalitarian ideal and group fission and fusion, methods for the minimization of intra- and intergroup conflicts, can lend insights into what may be functional requisites for the societies organized on the basis of "face-to-face" relations.

LOCATION

The Copper Eskimo inhabit a Canadian Arctic region which extends from southern Banks Island across western, southern, and southeastern Victoria Island and the shores of Dolphin and Union Strait and Coronation Gulf (see Fig. 1-1). They are one of several major groupings or nations of Central Eskimo. A prominent feature of aboriginal Copper Eskimo culture—one that set them off from other groups, and that gave rise to their group name (Stefansson 1913:33)—was the extensive use of float copper for a variety of implements.

PHYSICAL APPEARANCE

Despite an early account that many of the Copper Eskimo had "blond" or European physical traits (Stefansson 1913:182, 191ff.), it now appears that they differ little physically from other Eskimo populations. The Copper Eskimo seem to fit into a generalized Arctic Mongoloid racial type (Oschinsky 1962) which inhabits northern Asia as well as Arctic America.

LANGUAGE

The Copper Eskimo dialect is clearly a member of the Inupiaq or northern group of dialects which are spoken over an area stretching from western Alaska to Greenland (Swadesh 1951). A number of local divergences can be noted, however, perhaps the most prominent being the substitution of "h" for "s," which is used throughout much of the Eskimo area.[2] No convincing affinity has been established between the Eskimo languages and other languages of the New or Old World.

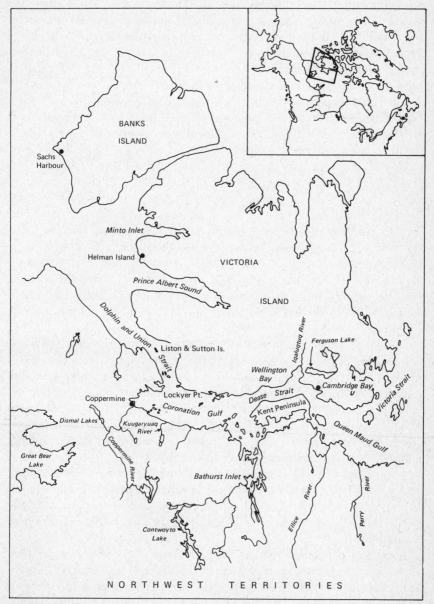

Figure 1–1.   Area of the Copper Eskimo.

HISTORICAL BACKGROUND

All three major stages of Canadian Eskimo prehistory—PreDorset, Dorset, and Thule—are represented in the archaeology of the area. The modern Copper Eskimo culture and the people themselves appear to have descended from late representatives of Thule culture, which originally spread across Arctic Canada from Alaska between A.D. 900 and 1200 (Taylor 1965). Important diagnostic characteristics of early or classic Thule include strong reliance on large whales and the use of whalebone framed houses. Whalebone houses are found only on the periphery of the Copper Eskimo country, and there is little other evidence for whaling in the Thule remains of the area, seal and caribou probably having always been the mainstays of the economy. Comparisons of ethnological and archaeological materials point to a gradual abandonment of certain Thule features and retention of others. Many of the chief characteristics of modern Copper Eskimo culture, including extensive use of copper and probably, as well, the general pattern of the seasonal economic cycle, do not appear to have developed until well into the nineteenth century (McGhee 1968).

Although Hearne visited the mouth of the Coppermine River in 1771, the area was not adequately explored until the nineteenth century when the expeditions of Franklin, Richardson, Simpson, and later McClure, Collinson, and Rae passed through the regions inhabited by Copper Eskimo. Among these early visitors only Collinson's party had much contact with the Eskimo, and none of the early accounts tell much about the people.

During the early years of the twentieth century contact rapidly expanded, and from that period we have the best accounts (Stefansson 1913, 1914a; Jenness 1922; Rasmussen 1932) of the Copper Eskimo—accounts that describe Copper Eskimo culture at a time when it was still aboriginal in most respects. The years from about 1910 until the mid-1920s represented a period of transition leading to the establishment of a society, which was based on a hunting economy, combined with fox trapping, and which was characterized by stabilized relations between the Eskimo and the chief resident Euro-Canadian agencies of traders, missionaries, and police. This adaptation continued for about thirty years and was followed by the contemporary phase of Copper Eskimo history with the appearance of government agencies and programs and the construction of radar sites.

Important population changes have occurred since contact began. One source of change was the influx of European trappers, traders, missionaries, and prospectors. Even though the period of residence for many of these immigrants was short, the area has had a substantial white population since the 1920s. Movement of Eskimo from other areas also occurred.

In the west, beginning in the 1920s, Mackenzie or Alaskan Eskimo moved into southern Banks Island, western Victoria Island, and to a lesser extent, to the entire Copper Eskimo area. Later small groups of Netsilik from Adelaide Peninsula moved into the Perry River region. Although epidemics of the 1920s and 1930s may have temporarily reduced the indigenous populations, the influx of natives from other regions together with improved rates of infant survival in later years have increased the Eskimo population of the area to about 1100 (1963) as compared to the 800–900 given for the early contact period.

ENVIRONMENT

THE LAND

The region of Copper Eskimo habitation is indicated on Figure 1-1. It will be noted that it includes parts of both the northern Canadian mainland and islands in the Arctic Archipelago. Physiographically, the area is divided into PreCambrian Lowland and scarpland of the northern coast of the mainland and part of northwestern Victoria Island and land comprised of sedimentary strata from later geographical ages. The latter is divided into lowland in eastern and southern Victoria Island and upland and plateau in western and southern Banks Island and the southwestern and extreme northwestern tip of Victoria Island.

Most of the region is tundra of various types. Trees, mainly white spruce, grow to the southwest of Dismal Lakes and the Coppermine and actually follow the valley of the Coppermine to within twenty-five miles of its mouth. Vegetation, including groves of willow, is abundant in most places on the mainland, but much of Victoria Island is virtual wasteland, though certain valleys or favorable localities support considerable plant life such as mosses, grasses, and flowers.

CLIMATE

The region lies almost wholly within the Arctic climatic zone, characterized by long cold winters and short cool summers. The following readings over a period of years for the warmest and coldest months give some idea of the severity of the climate:

	February Mean	July Mean
Holman Island	−25°F	46°F
Coppermine	−20°F	49°F
Cambridge Bay	−28°F	48°F

Winter temperatures in the minus forties or fifties can be expected anywhere in the area, while freezing temperatures can occur in any month except perhaps July. Storms may be frequent during the winter, but sus-

Copper Eskimo man.

Copper Eskimo woman.

Hunter waiting at seal hole, Queen Maud Gulf, 1963.

Skinning a caribou, Bathurst Inlet, 1963.

Copper Eskimo clothing styles, 1916.

Copper Eskimo clothing styles, 1963.

Building a new snowhouse village.

Family moving camp in winter.

Summer tent of caribou skin.

tained high winds are confined to only a few localities. Precipitation is light, averaging six to ten inches a year, most of which falls in the form of snow. While snow gathers in deep drifts near obstructions, much of the land is swept virtually bare of snow even during the depth of winter.

A solid sheet of ice forms over the straits and gulfs of the Copper Eskimo region during the autumn months. Little ice remains from the preceding season at the end of summer so that a new sheet covers the surface each year. The dates for the freezing of the sea vary from locality to locality and from year to year, but generally, ice begins to form in the sheltered bays by the end of September or early October, though the center of Coronation Gulf is not solidly covered until November, and Dolphin and Union Strait, Dease Strait, and Queen Maud Gulf are not usually frozen over entirely until December. Lakes freeze over by the end of September in most parts of the area. Dates for break-up of the sea vary from late June around Coppermine in the southwest to mid- or late July in the northwestern and eastern parts of the area. Many of the lakes have ice cover until well into July, and the ground is not free of snow until well into June and is again covered some time in September. These rather extreme climatic conditions strongly influence the life of the Copper Eskimo as well as the game animals upon which they depend.

ANIMAL RESOURCES

The caribou is the chief land quarry of the Copper Eskimo and provides the most desired food and the chief material for clothing. Formerly, the caribou population was divided into two segments, the resident animals, which spent the entire year in the area, and the migratory herds that entered the region from the wooded area to the south in the spring and returned to the south again in late autumn. Resident populations on Banks and Victoria islands were probably always small because of limited winter forage, but numbers swelled each summer on Victoria Island as herds moved north across Coronation Gulf and the straits at either end of the gulf (MacPherson 1961).

Musk oxen appeared in small numbers both on the mainland and on the big islands. A region could be easily divested of this animal because its habit of forming a defensive ring, which while good protection against wolves, was ineffective against armed men using dogs. Only around Bathurst Inlet were musk oxen plentiful enough to comprise a regular part of the diet.

Other land animals such as the Arctic fox and wolves were seldom hunted for meat. The barren ground grizzly is sometimes encountered on the mainland, and moose have begun to extend their range into the country, though aboriginally they did not comprise an expected source of food.

The lakes and rivers of the region supply several species of fish, the most important of which are the lake trout, whitefish, and the Arctic char. The latter descend to the sea for a period each summer before returning inland late in August or early September. Tom cod and sculpins were sometimes caught and served as a stopgap source of food.

The ringed seal was the most important aquatic animal for the Copper Eskimo. It provided a large portion of the food for man and dogs over the year and was, as well, the chief source of fuel, the fat being burned in stone lamps. Seals, which provided material for some summer clothing, are rather evenly distributed in the sea waters of the area, though conditions for hunting them vary from locality to locality.

The bearded or square flipper seal, which weighs six hundred to eight hundred pounds, was a welcome addition to the larder of the Copper Eskimo, but was not often secured. Polar bear are especially numerous off the southeast coast of Banks Island, where they often comprised the chief staple during the winter months. They were also hunted in Victoria Strait and in parts of Queen Maud Gulf.

Small game such as ptarmigan, hare, and wild fowl were important supplements to the Copper Eskimo diet during the warmer months.

OTHER RESOURCES

Wood was the most prized resource of the area. Some groups of Copper Eskimo did not live within easy reach of wooded country, but intertribal trade in wood and wood products and the occurrence of driftwood in much of the country insured them a better supply than was available to the Eskimo to their east. Plant resources were, in general, of little use. While willow provided fuel in summer and sleeping mats when it was available, and berries entered into the diet for a brief season, on the whole plants played only an indirect role in the life of the Copper Eskimo, providing food for some of the chief game animals.

Float copper can be found on the mainland in certain districts of Coronation Gulf and Bathurst Inlet and was important in the tool technology of the Copper Eskimo in aboriginal times. Soapstone is found mainly around Tree River and Bathurst Inlet and provided material for lamps and cooking pots.

ECONOMY

ABORIGINAL HUNTING TECHNIQUES AND THE SEASONAL ECONOMIC CYCLE[3]

From late May until some time in November fish and caribou were the chief game sought by the Copper Eskimo. It appears that caribou were not widely hunted during their spring migration. It has been noted that during May herds migrate across Dolphin and Union Strait, apparently within easy reach of the Eskimo, without any attempt on their part to take the animals. The usual reason given for not hunting them is that during May herds migrated across Dolphin and Union Strait, and the meat was lean and the skin was perforated by warbles during that period. The move from the winter ice began when seals appeared on the surface of the ice. After that tom cod were jigged briefly near the coast or the hunters went directly inland to fish through lake ice for Arctic char and lake trout. Occasional caribou were taken from May to August, but fishing was the chief activity at that time. Beginning in July, when the caribou were again fat and had grown new coats, the principal period of caribou hunting began and extended through the autumn months. As the char returned from the sea in late August or early September, large numbers were taken in stone weirs (*haputit*) set near the mouths of principal streams. In most localities, however, the fish run was only a brief interval of a few days in the season generally devoted to caribou hunting.

Caribou drives were organized as follows: long rows of stones (*inukhuit*) were set on edges along ridges, which were intended to resemble men. Sometimes upright poles were thrust into the ground or held in place with stones and another stick was loosely attached and was sometimes accompanied by long human hair (this arrangement was called *aulaqut*). Together these parts formed a scarecrow of sorts as the loose stick flapped about in the wind. The caribou were driven by shouting women and children between the converging rows of *inukhuit* and *aulaqutit* to the point where bowmen lay waiting in shallow pits.

The other chief method of caribou hunting was carried out from kayaks at crossing places in lakes or streams, with the kayakers thrusting lances at the caribou as they swam.

Wild fowl were secured by bow and arrow or on the ground in weirlike arrangements at the time of moulting.

November was usually the end of the caribou hunting season. The difficulty of stalking in cold clear weather, the problems of using the bow in low temperatures (because of the danger of freezing hands), and the necessity of being close to the sea for sealing to provide fuel were the chief reasons cited by the Copper Eskimo for abandoning caribou hunting in the autumn. However, since rifles came into general use, much of the winter period was spent inland, where caribou hunting and net fishing, together with trapping, were the principal economic activities.

During a period of two to four weeks, usually during November or early December, the Copper Eskimo lived largely on stores while winter clothing was being sewn. These were dried or frozen caribou meat and fat and dried and frozen fish. Occasionally fish were jigged in lakes during this period or caribou were intercepted as they moved to the south.

The move was made to the sea ice after the sewing period. The camps of snowhouses were usually set some distance from the coast,[4] so that a complete circle of about five miles in radius, a convenient walking distance from camp, could be exploited in breathing-hole sealing (*mauliqtuq*). The

Central Eskimo were probably the only people, aside from boat-dwelling Chinese and East Indians, who spent a substantial part of the year actually living on the surface of the sea.

The sealing camps were always set on ice which was formed during the current year, since seals are able to maintain breathing holes by gnawing or scratching with their flippers as the new ice forms during the autumn. As the ice thickens a tube-shaped receptacle is left in the ice, allowing entry for the seal to the small hole in the upper surface, which gives access to the air. Snow usually covers the hole (*aglu*), but the seal can breathe through a surprisingly deep layer. No one seems to know how many breathing holes one seal can maintain during the course of a winter, but at any rate, the holes are so plentiful in most regions of flat new sea ice that the solitary hunter has little hope of success. Indeed, the Eskimo themselves indicate that a large number of hunters is necessary for the successful execution of a breathing-hole seal hunt.[5]

The sealer locates the hole with the aid of specially trained dogs and stations himself, either standing or seated on a block of snow, for the long wait. An assortment of equipment is used, including an especially heavy fur coat, a harpoon with an ice chisel at one end, a knife, a bone indicator, rests for the harpoon, and a fur bag that is used both for carrying the tools of the hunt and as a foot warmer.

When the seal rises to breathe the indicator moves and the hunter thrusts with his harpoon, trying to hit a point as close to the indicator as possible. If he is successful in hitting the hole, which may be quite small, he usually secures the seal. The hole is enlarged with the ice chisel while the seal is held by a lanyard attached to the harpoon head. At times bearded seals are secured by this method, but, generally, a second hunter must be close at hand to help land the large animal.

Another widely practiced method of sealing in other parts of the Arctic was only infrequently used by aboriginal-period Copper Eskimo. This is the method of stalking seals lying on the surface of the ice in spring (*qaqipqayuq*) and killing them with a harpoon. It is puzzling that the Copper Eskimo did not use this method more extensively, because surface, sleeping seals are common in most parts of their area. After the rifle came into common use, this method was employed to a greater extent.

Seals were not hunted from kayaks as was the case in much of the eastern Arctic, but after small skiffs or jolly boats came into use summer sealing became an important activity in much of the area.

Polar bear were usually cornered by dogs, who were cut loose from sleds. While being held at bay, the animal was dispatched with spears or harpoons.

The aboriginal seasonal cycle of the Copper Eskimo, depicted in Figure 1-2, can be divided into two chief phases: (1) the winter period, lasting

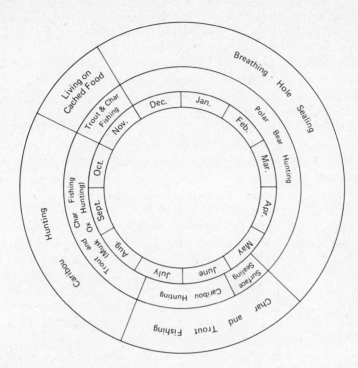

Figure 1–2. Aboriginal Copper Eskimo seasonal economic cycle. Outer circle: *primary pursuits*; inner circle: *secondary pursuits*.

roughly from December through much of May, when breathing-hole sealing was the chief activity (though supplemented in some regions by polar bear hunting), and (2) the period from May to November, when caribou hunting, fishing, and some small-game hunting and fowling were carried out. As noted above, economic activity was virtually at a standstill at the beginning of winter.

The seasonal pattern of exploitation had a far-reaching effect upon the dispersal of population throughout the area. The relation between the yearly cycle and settlement pattern will be discussed under "Social Organization."

MATERIAL CULTURE

The Copper Eskimo employed a number of implements during the year's hunting cycle. Wooden and musk oxen horn bows, copper and bone, antler, and iron-tipped arrows, harpoons, lances, knives, leisters, the kayak, and many minor implements made up the inventory of equipment of the typical Copper Eskimo hunter.

In addition to these tools of the hunt, other important artifacts were used, including snow knives, snow shovels, drills, adzes, sewing equipment, stone lamps and pots, and the *ulu*, or woman's knife.

The archaeology of the area has revealed the existence of permanent houses of stone and sod, framed either with whalebone (these are rare) or with driftwood, but they all belong to the prehistory of the Copper Eskimo, snowhouses and skin tents (at times with snow walls) being the only dwellings known to the ethnographic era. The snowhouse of the Copper Eskimo was a domed structure built of blocks cut from the floor area. Snowhouses in this area resembled ones used further east by the Netsilik and Iglulik Eskimo, except that composite dwellings were less common[6] and the porches were straight-sided passageways rather than the series of domes found further east.

In early spring when the roofs of snowhouses began to thaw, heavy caribou skin ridge or conical tents were set in place, surrounded by a wall of snow, with the usual passageway. The summer tent was a much smaller affair, with a caribou or sealskin covering. In a country where wood is always at a premium, the poles were ice chisels, harpoons, fish spears, walking sticks, and so on.

The individual Copper Eskimo had a rather extensive wardrobe comprised mainly of caribou skin garments. Each man wore a light inner suit of coat, trousers, and stockings with fur inside as the main dress in summer and as underwear in winter. He also possessed a ceremonial coat, tailored with a high waist in front and a swallow tail and elaborately trimmed with stripes of white fur. Winter trousers were similarly trimmed. The heavy fur coat (*qulitaq*) made from late autumn skins was used for cold weather travel and for hunting seals at breathing holes. Outer stockings or boots of caribou skin, with slippers of either caribou or sealskin, completed the man's winter suit. Sealskin raincoats were also used. All coats except for some ceremonial garments were hooded.

The woman's dress featured exaggerated shoulders and hoods and combination leggings and boots. While caribou skin clothing is a close to ideal material for the Arctic climate, certain features of the Copper Eskimo costume sacrifice comfort to style (Jenness 1946). The features of cut, but more especially trimming and the higher development of a special ceremonial costume, set off the Copper Eskimo wardrobe from that of other Central Eskimo.

The material culture of the Copper Eskimo was indeed an impressive feature of the total culture. With the occurrence of native copper, which could be used for projectile points, knives, and other implements, steatite for lamps and cooking utensils, and driftwood and occasional stands of timber on the mainland for material for sledges and kayaks, the Copper Eskimo was far more fortunate than the Netsilik or Iglulik Eskimo to the east.

Dogs

As with most Eskimo groups, the Copper Eskimo were reliant upon their dogs to an important extent. It should be noted, however, that the burden of keeping dogs was a great drain on the family resources, so that one or two was the usual number owned by the typical Copper Eskimo nuclear family; three was the maximum number in the aboriginal period. Although dogs were valuable in moving camps in winter by hauling sledges and in summer by carrying packs, their primary function was their use in hunting. The importance of dogs in breathing-hole sealing has been mentioned—indeed, this was their most important job—but they were also used in hunting polar bear and musk oxen.

Economic Life, 1925–1955

Rifles, traps, and fishnets were the important hunting tools that were introduced into the area in the period after about 1910. It was not until the mid-1920s, however, that these implements were abundant enough, or their use understood well enough, that they produced a marked influence on the round of economic activities. By about 1925, alteration was firmly established in the seasonal cycles of most of the Copper Eskimo groups.[7] In the western part of Coronation Gulf and in Dolphin and Union Strait the period of winter sealing was shortened as the Eskimo began to move inland, some time in March, to hunt caribou with the rifle. Also, after 1925, migration of caribou to Victoria Island ceased and a number of Victoria Island Eskimo moved to the mainland for their spring and summer hunting. Around Bathurst Inlet the people began to spend winters inland or based on points and bays of the inlet, hunting caribou and trapping as well as setting nets in lakes and streams. For heat they burned willow in iron stoves, caribou fat in stone lamps, and occasionally primus stoves, which burned kerosene, but generally these were used for cooking only, as the weight and price of the fuel was prohibitive. In March they returned to the Inlet for breathing-hole sealing until some time in May, when they began to intercept the spring herds of caribou. In this period a greater and greater part of the year was spent inland.

In any year when the supply of caribou became scarce, reversion to the winter breathing-hole sealing was apparent anywhere in the area. In general, informants testify that whenever possible this method was avoided because of the exposure and monotony it entails, though in most places at least a short period in the spring continued to be devoted to this practice.

In the extreme northwest, with the Eskimo of western Victoria Island and Banks Island being cut off from the formerly large herds of caribou, the economy focused more strongly on the seal. These were hunted from boats in the summer, and during the winter steel hooks were set in the holes, which were visited at intervals. This procedure eliminated the need for waiting, but numbers of seals escaped, often in a badly wounded condition. The method spread further east, but only around Coppermine was it carried out regularly. Fishing, which had always been an important Copper Eskimo activity, increased in importance and in productivity with the general use of nets. On the other hand, the Copper Eskimo have never adopted net fishing in a systematic way. In order for that method to be efficient it is necessary to lift nets at least once a day. Whether it is due to failure to understand that principal or because of the multiplicity of tasks that are undertaken together with fishing, few Copper Eskimo lift their nets frequently enough.

Fox trapping occupied a considerable part of the Copper Eskimo's energy and time from November to mid-April. Correct trapping technique includes burying the trap in a depression in the snow and then covering it with a wafer of snow. A chain from the trap is fastened to a stick, which is frozen fast in the snow and acts as an anchor. Bits of fat and meat are scattered on the snow in the immediate area. A fox prowling the area, after being attracted by the odor of the fat and meat, will usually step through the wafer and catch a leg in the jaws of the trap. Frequent visits to traps are required in order to insure that the wafer is not either eroded by wind so that the trap is exposed or buried by drift so that it will support the weight of the fox. It is to a large extent the failure to visit traps frequently enough which accounts for the rather mediocre trapping results that most of the Copper Eskimo experience. Only in the west (around Sachs Harbor and Holman Island) is fox trapping carried out with appropriate energy, and the leading trappers in that part of the country appear to be immigrants from the Mackenzie area.

Just as in the case of net fishing, failure to establish and properly maintain long trap lines cannot wholly be attributed to sloth. Rather, the Eskimo were involved in a number of activities during the trapping season. Some of these were lifting nets, hunting caribou or seal, and visiting caches. In addition, trapping is a solitary pursuit which necessitates long periods away from one's family—one that certainly must be disagreeable to a seemingly gregarious people such as the Copper Eskimo.

The period 1925–1955 saw the disappearance of a number of traditional artifacts which had been associated with aboriginal hunting techniques. The kayak and the bow and arrow fell out of use with the rise of caribou hunting with the rifle. In general, caribou hunting became a much more individual pursuit, with the need for drives being obviated by the ability to secure caribou at long range with the rifle. Caches of caribou meat became important focal points for activity, since they served as bait for the fox, many of the traps being set around the sites of summer or autumn caribou kills.

Dog team travel became more important, since with the establishment of trap lines, greater mobility was required. Each man now owned five or six dogs. The traditional fan hitch with each dog leading an individual trace was replaced by the western Nome hitch with pairs of dogs attached with short lines to a central trace. Dog feed became a vital consideration, as the man's team might actually require as much as or more meat than his family.

In summary, the period 1925–1955 saw a number of significant changes in the economic life of the Copper Eskimo. The rise in importance of trapping drew the Eskimo into the marketing system of the outside world, providing him not only with goods useful in exploiting the environment, such as rifles and ammunition, small boats and nets, and the traps themselves, but also with food, tobacco, tea, canvas tents, and clothing. Important changes in the seasonal round of economic activities characterized the period.

With the failure of the caribou migration from the mainland to Victoria Island, readaptations in economy were necessary for those Copper Eskimo who lived around Prince Albert Sound in the west and Wellington Bay and Cambridge Bay in the east. Hunting of seals in summer, as well as fishing (which had always been important in the east), largely replaced the caribou hunt, except for the easterners, who made excursions to Kent Peninsula, and those who lived on the western part of the island, who managed to secure a few of the resident animals each year.

People who lived on the mainland moved in another direction in their adaptation, with caribou hunting becoming the most important activity. For example, as late as the winter of 1952–1953, five thousand caribou were reported to have been taken in the Bathurst Inlet trading area as compared to only three hundred seals. It was estimated that 80 to 90 percent of the dog food in the area was caribou meat at this time, the remainder being fish,[8] though fish appear to have been underexploited in that region at that period.

Changes in the Copper Eskimo economic cycle in the years 1925–1955 brought about greater diversity in that area than had prevailed in the aboriginal period. Some of these changes were due to a changed technology and the introduction of new techniques of exploitation. In the wake of these changes alterations in distribution of game followed, which in turn affected economic practices.

In general, winter sealing became less important, although it persisted to some extent throughout the region for periods of each year, usually in the spring. Hunting of surface, sleeping seals in spring expanded somewhat after rifles came into general use, but certainly it has not been as highly developed as in the eastern Arctic.

ECONOMIC LIFE IN THE CONTEMPORARY PERIOD[9]

By the mid-1950s the decline in caribou forced further economic changes on the mainland Copper Eskimo groups. Around Bathurst settlement, the shift was more to the shores of the inlet where seals could be hunted the year round, and less reliance was placed on caribou, with fishing also gaining in prominence. The Copper Eskimo of Bathurst generally were able to survive without outside help, but there were several incidents of famine during the 1950s which were alleviated by drops of buffalo meat by the government.

In the Perry River region, natives continued to gather in the spring for breathing-hole sealing, reminiscent of the aboriginal pattern. However, most often settlement was concentrated inland in winter at sites of caribou caches and fishing places. In lean years when caribou were scarce, the Perry River people resorted to winter sealing on Queen Maud Gulf.

The people who had lived in the interior along the Coppermine and its tributaries moved to the coast when the caribou failed to appear in numbers in about 1954. Most of them concentrated in the settlement at Coppermine itself, though several satellite camps also grew up along both shores of Coronation Gulf. The Contwoyto Lake area continued to support two groups of Eskimo (one originally from the Coppermine area and the other from around Bathurst), mainly on caribou, which continued to be plentiful in most years. Occasionally small groups from Coppermine or Bathurst would attempt to spend a winter in the interior, and a number of forays for caribou were also made inland from each of these places, but the interior has been largely uninhabited during the period since 1955.

Centralization at Cambridge Bay stemmed mainly from 1955 when a large number of young men were recruited from Bathurst Inlet and Perry River and eastern Victoria Island for building radar sites. Missions, a Department of Transport, weather observing personnel, Royal Canadian Mounted Police, and a trading post had already been established at Cambridge, so that a sizable native population was already present, but with the advent of the DEW line, employment opportunities expanded substantially. At the same period a government representative (Areal Administrator) and a school became established there to swell both the white population and the number of employed natives. Employment possibilities were far greater than was the case at Coppermine; a comparison of sources of income between the two communities for the year 1962–1963 is revealing in this regard. At Coppermine approximately $60,000[10] was earned in casual or permanent employment, $58,000 came from relief and social legislation, and $17,000 was derived from fur and $9000 from handicrafts. At Cambridge (including the DEW line station) about $135,000 was earned in wages, about $29,000 came from relief and social legislation, and $17,000 derived from local resources, including fox furs and sealskins and profits from the native-run fishing cooperative. Even though large sums of money entered the Cambridge economy from wages, social legislation and relief monies were proportionately smaller than at Coppermine, but everywhere local employment opportunities did not keep pace with income needs.

A third site of centralization in the Copper Eskimo area has been

Holman Island near the mouth of Prince Albert Sound. At that place the contact-traditional hunting-trapping economy was still carried on in earnest in the early 1960s, with income from furs being the single largest source, exceeding that from relief and social legislation combined. Casual employment was fifth on the list, following handicrafts. Nevertheless, relief payments of $10,000 in 1962–1963 indicate that the economy is not flourishing as it should, despite rather energetic efforts by some of the men in sealing and trapping.

At the smaller trading centers of Bathurst Inlet and Perry Island income from fur and social legislation contribute about equal amounts to the economy. Relief issuances account for $35 and $50 per capita, respectively, at these places, compared with $65 for Coppermine and $76 for Holman Island for the same period (1962–1963). Although neither the Perry Island nor the Bathurst Inlet people display much energy in exploiting their environment, their communities are closer to being self-sustaining than most of those of present-day Copper Eskimo. This is accomplished at a much lower standard of living than is typical in the centralized communities.

The inlanders, who live in two groups at either end of Contwoyto Lake, are more fortunate in securing large numbers of caribou, which remain as their chief source of food to this day, despite attempts to develop the fishing industry. Furs (mainly fox but also some exported caribou skins) and casual labor with prospectors or other mining concerns comprise the chief sources of cash income, though mineral exploration may not continue in the area.

Even in the centralized communities game provides a very substantial portion of the diet. Hunting activity is mainly restricted to the warmer seasons around Coppermine and Cambridge, but during that period of the year a number of outlying camps develop and daily excursions are made to the neighboring countryside for fish and fowling from the centers themselves. Every fine day in late spring or in the summer will find most of the adult population that is not permanently employed at Cambridge Bay scattered to nearby lakes and tundra.

Fox prices and the supply of that animal have always shown marked fluctuations in the area, but by the 1960s far less energy, time, and personnel were devoted to fox trapping, though in the winter of 1966–1967 the price of fox increased, and untypically enough, the supply of fox was also good, so that a larger number of trappers than usual for recent years established trap lines running out from the centralized communities.

In 1963, the popularity of sealskin handicraft objects and items of clothing in the United States and southern Canada raised the price of sealskin from three to five dollars to fifteen to twenty-eight dollars and inspired more intensive sealing throughout the area. By 1966, the prices had fallen and the boom appeared to be over.

In the same period the price of polar bear offered to the Eskimo rose from a rather stable average of about fifty dollars to one hundred fifty and two hundred dollars. Apparently one of the reasons for this increase was the rising number of bear skins sold to private individuals such as DEW line personnel, Department of Transport workers, and the growing number of tourists entering the country. This market shows no signs of falling off, but certainly the supply of polar bear in this and other Canadian Arctic regions will not allow an indefinite expansion of this source of income.

The prospects for long-term reliance on furs, either fox, seal, or polar bear, as a dependable source of income is not promising. Another program that has shown some promise as a provider of income for the Eskimo around Cambridge Bay has been the Ekaloktotsiak (Iqaluqtucciaq) Eskimo Cooperative, Ltd., an organization devoted to fishing in the Ferguson Lake-Iqaluqtuq River region.

This program has three phases: (1) trout taken in winter on the lake (frozen) and used by the natives for food; (2) trout taken in summer on the lake and sun dried also to be used locally; and (3) Arctic char, taken in the Iqaluqtuq River and off its mouth in Wellington Bay, which is stored temporarily in a freezer which was located first at Cambridge and later at the fishing site. The char is flown to markets in the south, profits from the operation going to the members of the cooperative. It was estimated that in 1963, a net of about five thousand dollars was earned from this operation.

Tourism was beginning to develop in much of the area by the mid-1960s. Private firms established fishing lodges at several places in the region, and government-sponsored sport fishing began to expand. Chartered aircraft transported sportsmen to remote lakes in the interior of the mainland and Victoria Island where they were guided by government tourist offices. Little of the income from the fishing enterprises came into the hands of the Eskimo, but, particularly at Coppermine, sale of handicrafts and art objects to tourists was a significant source of money for the community.

In summary, the twentieth-century economic history of the Copper Eskimo has been characterized by two major changes. The first was the alteration of traditional hunting practices to a hunting-trapping economy. Generally, this meant greater prosperity and comfort for the Copper Eskimo, although they were still dependent upon variable game resources both with regard to food animals and with regard to their cash animal, the white fox. Even though periods of food shortage continued to occur, actual death from starvation was less imminent than had been the case in the aboriginal period, for white agencies were at hand to assist. The new techniques for exploiting the country were not always developed as highly as possible in the period 1925–1955, but that period represented an essentially stabilized economic era which began to disintegrate because of the shortage of caribou and the immigration to new white-Eskimo communities.

The second major change was the alteration of a hunting-trapping economy to a limited cash-income economy with the development of some minor industries always backed by substantial government subsidies. This most recent period finds the Copper Eskimo exploiting the game resources to a much lesser degree than at any earlier period.

SOCIAL ORGANIZATION[11]

DEMOGRAPHY OF THE ABORIGINAL SOCIETY

Famine was not uncommon in the aboriginal period, and the demography clearly parallels the basically marginal subsistence and the nomadic seasonal cycle. An over-all census (Rasmussen 1932:70, 78–85) for 1923–1924 reveals that males outnumbered females about three to two in the area. This disproportion reflects the practice of female infanticide. Informants admit the earlier practice of infanticide and justify it on grounds of economic necessity or on the basis of the difficulty of caring for newborn infants while traveling. It would appear that many or most Eskimo groups practiced infanticide on the march, but it is doubtful that the exposure of children under these circumstances was selective according to sex. For the Netsilik and Copper Eskimo, however, it is clear that a greater rate of infanticide was called for than elsewhere and that the additional cases seem to have been mostly female infants.

Rasmussen (1932:17) has posited the shortage of females as one of the factors leading to a high rate of homicide among the Copper Eskimo. In many cases the rivalry over women seems to have set off a series of killings.

THE ECONOMIC CYCLE AND THE SETTLEMENT PATTERN

It was indicated in the preceding section that a large number of persons was required for breathing-hole sealing. This factor had a strong influence on the aggregation of people during the winter months. Winter aggregations ranged in size from about fifty to perhaps two hundred persons, with the average being about one hundred. This range might have represented the optimum number of hunters that could adequately or profitably exploit a circle five miles in radius around the camp. Ideally the camp was moved a distance of about ten miles about once a month, and thus a fresh area was exploited for a period. Larger aggregations were fleeting in duration, and smaller ones also did not seem to have a long life during the *mauliqtuq* sealing season.

In the spring, dispersal into smaller groups probably also had its economic motivations, for caribou were generally scattered into small herds, and fish, which were the most important source of food at that season, were also not highly concentrated but spread more evenly in lakes and streams. Larger aggregations occurred at the sites of the late summer fish runs. The number of good fishing sites was not great, so that factor alone may have accounted for the tendency to aggregate at those times. Another aspect of that situation is that the acquisition of a large number of fish enabled more people to live together for a time. Whatever the interpretation, both the larger groups in the winter and those that aggregated at the fish runs during the summer phase of the season had an economic component in their existence. This does not seem to be the case for the autumn sewing aggregation, which took place in the relatively idle period before winter sealing commenced and after the principal caribou hunting ceased. While social factors may have influenced the size and location of summer and winter groupings, they must have been preeminent in the autumn aggregations; that is, after a period of fragmentation the desire to expand social contacts must have been the overwhelming motive for aggregation, since there was certainly no economic advantage at a period when economic activity was almost at a standstill.

SHARING PRACTICES

While the cooperative units usually corresponded to local units, the sharing units were more complexly organized. Indeed, the most important economic components of Copper Eskimo social organization involved sharing and commensal practices. In one sense the minimal economic unit was the nuclear family. Each man owned his hunting equipment, each woman her household fittings. There was no automatic sharing among close relatives as was the case further east in the Netsilik and Iglulik areas. A definite system of sharing partnerships involved kin and nonkin for each man. This system of *piqatigiit* was based on the division of the ringed seal. Fourteen major parts of the seal were designated, and each was represented by an individual who would receive that part from successful partners. When the seal was hauled home the partitioning took place in the house of the successful hunter, and children from each partner's immediate family received the designated share in a skin bucket and carried it home. The killer of the seal received only the skin, entrails, and fat, if all of his partners were present in the village at the time of the kill. However, he received a share whenever one of his partners caught a seal. Most of the food sharing in the winter camp was regulated along the lines of *piqat*, though voluntary gifts of food were made as well.

Supplementing the rather wide dispersal of meat through the winter village through the *piqat* system was the general practice of communal eating. It appears that most of the meals were taken with a large number of the people of the village eating in common. Apparently by prior arrangement, a constant round of visiting in the evening occurred, with meals being served in shifts at one or several of the houses. During the day, women joined in common meals while men were absent at the hunt, but otherwise men and women ate together.

Even though each household may have had its source of food in excess of current consumption, the bulk of meat caught was consumed on a village-wide basis during the winter.

During the summer when settlement was scattered into small groups, the seal-sharing partnerships are said by some informants to have been extended to division of fish and caribou meat, especially in cases of unequal success, and again meals were taken in common throughout the local settlement. All food that was taken in excess of immediate needs was cached in individual lots.

Another form of sharing took place during the autumn sewing period and occasionally later in winter when caches were visited. The owner of the meat that was brought into the village generally was expected to share, though this form of sharing (*payuktuq*) was actually voluntary. At times *paaqaqtariik* (those who shared composite snowhouses), who may have been relatives, spouse-exchange partners, or not related, and those who were not *paaqaqtariik* would share food during the duration of their co-residence period.

While it is stated by informants that persons other than *paqaqtariik* or their families received only very small amounts of an individual's kill, the systems of voluntary sharing and communal eating extended food sharing quite broadly throughout any local grouping, so that together with the various other forms of meat sharing, a nicely meshed system existed which insured a wide passage of food. This operated to adjust for the uncertainties of the hunt—the vagaries of individual luck and differences in skill.

Aboriginal Social Units

Earlier ethnologists have remarked on the fluidity of personnel that comprised the various groupings and have decried the difficulty of isolating definite social units among Central Eskimo groups, including the Copper Eskimo. Indeed, statements of informants indicate that during a lifetime a man is affiliated with the people of several regions within the Copper Eskimo area. In the majority of cases, however, one regional group is acknowledged by most men as being their chief focus of alliance.

One difficulty inherent in identifying local units arises in the uses of the postbase -*miut*. This element translates as "natives of," such as do the English suffixes "ers," "ians," "ans," and so on. The term -*miut*, however, has several levels of reference. For example, the entire people of the Copper Eskimo area are known by the Netsilik Eskimo as the Killinirmiut. Within the Copper Eskimo area itself, the term applies to the Eskimo who spent the summer period on southeastern Victoria Island and the winters on the ice of Dease Strait. These people regard themselves as Kuugmiut, Nuvugmiut, and Iqaluqturmiut, according to their more specific regions of summer hunting. Similarly, the groups at the western end of Coronation Gulf were known collectively by the eastern groups as Ualliarmiut, though they knew themselves by such names as Nagyukturmiut and Quqluqtur-miut. It is thus apparent that among the Copper Eskimo three general uses of -miut were apparent. First, groups other than Copper Eskimo were classed globally with that term; second, -miut was used to designate those who share a summer hunting district; third, those groups that merged into a large sealing village were also usually designated by that postbase.

Another source of confusion relates to the circumstance of a hunting area being abandoned, with the nucleus of people who had hunted there together shifting to a new district and taking its name. This situation became more frequent in postcontact times when shifts in faunal distribution occurred or hunting techniques changed, but these movements also occurred earlier.

A genealogical reconstruction of Rasmussen's (1932:78–85) census for 1923–1924 indicates that members occasionally spent summer hunting periods outside the territory of their name groups. Generally, however, the small summer groups, which varied from three to about twenty members during most of the period, merged at the *innakharviit*, or fishing places. In some cases two of the name groups, for example, the Kuugmiut (Paliryuarmiut) and the Iqaluqturmiut, merged at a common sewing place each year. The sewing group varied from about twenty to perhaps sixty or seventy persons, with the usual range being from thirty to sixty. The groupings associated with the sewing period at times began the winter sealing period alone, but later merged with other such units, so that through the bulk of each winter the aboriginal population of eight or nine hundred was divided into about eight major sealing villages. This picture appears to have persisted until about the early 1920s for the area as a whole.

In comparing these units with similar ones described in the ethnographic literature of North America, it appears that the term *"band"*[12] has been most often used in this context. The band has the qualities of having a name associated with a territory, fusion and fission over the year's cycle, a large core of the same personnel returning each year, genealogical continuity within, and, usually, aggregation as a whole at some point during the cycle. This designation fits the winter sealing aggregation quite well (see the discussion of band composition below), but also applies in large measure to the groups named for summer hunting districts. It might be useful to regard the winter groupings as *maximal bands* and the lesser -miut as *minimal bands*. Figure 1-3 depicts aboriginal Copper Eskimo local groups.

Those small units of three to twenty persons that made up the local groupings during a large part of the summer phase of the cycle are regarded as *hunting groups* for the purpose of this discussion.

The Copper Eskimo as a whole, a total population which did not aggregate, did form a unit with regard to dialect and genealogical discrete-

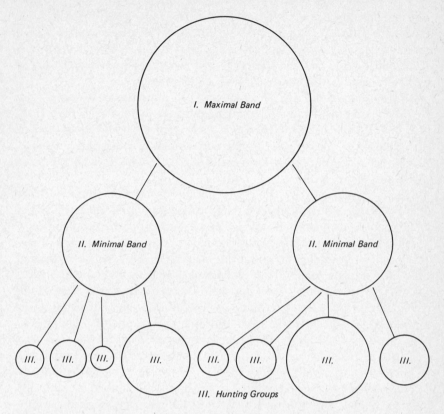

Figure 1–3. *Aboriginal Copper Eskimo local groups. I, maximal band: average of 100 persons assembled on sea ice during breathing-hole sealing, December–May. II, minimal band: 30–60 persons assembled at points of land during sewing period, November–December (also occasionally at fish runs in summer). III, hunting groups: highly mobile groups May–November, 5–20 members each; fluctuate in size and composition. The maximal band (I) is at times split during the season, but not necessarily along the lines of II.*

ness and a number of shared distinctive cultural traits, but not a political unity. Perhaps the term "nation" best describes this unit.

Composition of the Social Units[13]

With reference to internal composition, the smallest unit, the *hunting group*, was the least regular and the least stable. Alternate associations appear to have been exploited by each nuclear family during the course of one year or from year to year. Making up the core of these groups were close kin ties such as father-son or brother-brother, more distant kin ties, or specially formalized partnerships such as spouse-exchange associations. At times there does not seem to have been any formalized or kin relationship existing between family heads making up the nucleus of the hunting group. Occasionally, as well, the nuclear family separated and operated for short periods as independent units. During the course of a summer season these units met and separated, and a certain amount of shifting of personnel appears to have taken place among them.

Each hunting group was generally made up of personnel recruited from within the minimal band. However, some breaks in continuity of primary kin bonds usually existed at this level. That is, there was a certain amount of shifting from year to year to different summer hunting districts, movements that served to disrupt continuous kinship connections in the minimal band.

The maximal band showed a greater degree of kinship continuity. Charts of some of the eastern Copper Eskimo bands show that primary kin ties alone could be demonstrated among 80 to 90 percent of the band, and with a slight extension of charts, to include secondary relatives, ninety-five percent or more of the persons within the maximal band could be connected on a chart. Membership stability was also greater than in the smaller units, with at least two thirds of the members of one year's winter aggregation returning the following year. Aside from indicating the continuity of kin links among members of the maximal band, analysis of these bands indicates a pronounced slant toward predominance of male-male ties over male-female ties. One could accordingly characterize the maximal bands as bilateral entities with a pronounced slant toward "viri-orientation."

The nation was the most stable group, forming as it did a practically discrete "deme" with at least 95 percent of the marriages occurring within that unit. Thus there was little fluctuation in membership from one year to another, except with respect to births and deaths. Continuity of kin ties was probably as great or even greater than in the maximal band, though genealogically detached units were present at times in cases of immigration (though the gaps created this way were often quickly obliterated with marriages in descending generations) or isolation through death of connecting kin.

KINSHIP TERMINOLOGY AND BEHAVIOR

The Copper Eskimo share a number of kinship terms with other Central Eskimo and even Western Eskimo groups, although several Copper Eskimo terms are absent or obscure in the other regions. Differences are more apparent in the arrangement of terms.

Copper Eskimo cousin terminology can perhaps be classed as "Eskimo," in that cousin terms are separate from sibling terms. However, there is a distinction between patrilateral parallel cousin (*angutiqat*) and all other cousins (*arnaqat*) that would set off the system from a classical "Eskimo type."

Older and younger siblings of either sex are distinguished both by male and female Egos, making a total of eight separate sibling terms.

In the first descending generation Ego's children are set off from col-laterals. The terms for brother's child (M Ego = *qangiaq*; F Ego = *nurraq*) and sister's child (M Ego = *uyuruk*; F Ego = *angngaq*) are extended respectively to the children of male cousins and female cousins. Common terms are used for everyone on each of the first and second descending generations. In Ego's as well as all descending generations, in-marrying males are *ningauk* and females *ukuaq*. These arrangements follow generalized Central Eskimo patterns.

In the parental generation the boundaries between affines and consan-guines is crossed. For example, *pangnaaryuk* refers to both FB and FZH and *angak* is used for both MB and MZH.

While members of the grandparental generation are separated by sex, there is no distinction between consanguines and affines. One term applies for all great grandparental generation members.

The patterning of kinship behavior and its expression in the arrange-ments of terms is not as highly developed, for example, as among the Iglulingmiut. One pattern of terminology that does emerge, and one that seems to imply behavioral correlates, is the system of dyads, indicated by the postbase *-riik* or *-giik*. Consistently only the term for one of the two members of the dyad is used to form the base. Thus father *angut—son—irniq* is *irniriik*; older brother *angayuk*; younger brother *nukaq* is *nukariik*. This system is extended widely throughout the total terminology. It would seem to imply a principal of subordinance and dominance with the be-haviorally subordinant member being indicated by the postbase of the dyadic term. Behavioral ideals are, however, very difficult to derive from informants. Only a few of the kinship statuses in the system appear to bear with them specific directives for behavior. Among those that are expressed are avoidance ("shyness") relationships between *aigiik* (brother-in-law—sister-in-law) and father-in-law—mother-in-law and mother-in-law—son-in-law relationships. There appears to be a general feeling that younger siblings should obey older ones regardless of sex. None of the behavioral directives appear to be as highly structured or as frequently actualized as the writer found to be the case around Iglulik.

Kinship and Naming Practices

The narrow scope and weakness of behavioral directives is paralleled by the preference for use of given names over kin terms in reference or in address. This is true even between small children and aged persons. Naming proceeds along the lines of a system known over much of the Eskimo area. Children are usually named after recently deceased people, usually relatives. Thus it is common to find in genealogies that a name is repeated in alternate generations. Today, with an expanding birth rate, it is common to find a number of persons sharing the same name in the same age range. The supernatural implications of the naming practices, specifically whether or not there is soul transferral, is vaguely known by the Copper Eskimo, and it does not appear that behavior is influenced by shared names as may be the case for other Eskimo groups (Stefansson 1913).

Expansion of the Kinship Network

The universe of kinship is expanded by several mechanisms—marriage, which is common to all peoples, and adoption and spouse exchange, which were highly institutionalized and widespread practices throughout the Eskimo area.

Child betrothal was widely practiced. Marriages were usually contracted early in the childhood of the pair. Due to the practice of selective female infanticide, the assignment of brides to young men was, of course, crucial. Marriages were contracted between both unrelated and related persons. Cousin marriage appears to have been common but most often second, third, and fourth cousins were involved. Kinship was acknowledged and there was no prohibition against any sort of cousin marriage. At the same time it is not clear that there was a stated preference for marriage between cousins. A number of marriages took place between members of adjacent generations, though usually in such cases the mates were near the same age.

The young man commonly joined his future father-in-law's household a year or two before the girl reached puberty and stayed on as a servant (kivgaq) until the girl was "ripe," after which he established a separate household. This was thus a form of bride service. The practice was by no means universal, however, although it survives to some extent today.

Adoption was rather widely practiced, as it is in most Eskimo areas. Two main patterns of adoption occurred in the Copper Eskimo area. First, older couples often adopted grandchildren. Both affectional and practical factors were involved in this practice. The closeness felt between alternate generations in many societies is expressed in actual absorption of grandchildren into the nuclear family of the grandparents. The grandparents also capitalize on help provided by the grandchildren in old age or after their own children have married and formed separate households. This form of adoption is based on obligation, and cases examined show that the relative fecundity of the parents of the adopted child did not seem to enter into consideration. Ideally each elderly or mature couple would adopt one grandson and one granddaughter. In that way both the man and the woman would have assistance in the varied tasks of the hunt on the one hand and of the household on the other.

The second main pattern of adoption relates to redistribution of population. Childless couples or those with only one child would seek to adopt, again for both affectional and practical reasons. Those with larger families would often adopt children out as a happy alternative to infanticide. Case histories show that the recipient couple would adopt children of either sex if they were childless, or a child of the sex opposite of their own offspring.

The donor parents would generally adopt out children of the sex which was in surplus in their family.

Usually the natural and adoptive parents involved in this second type of adoption were related to one another, the most common situation being the adoption of a brother's or sister's child. Adoption of unrelated or distantly related offspring was accompanied by payment such as knives or sledges, or later, rifles. I am uncertain as to what degree of collaterality of kinship formed the break-off point beyond which payment was required.

There are a few cases of adoption which appear to be anomalous to these two main patterns. Detailed examination of each of these cases would have to be undertaken in order to sort out the motives or obligations involved.

The adoptive child was absorbed into the adoptive family and his primary loyalty rested in the sociological family. Assistance and residence (at least on the level of the maximal band) was usually oriented toward the adoptive family even though a separate household was formed in most cases when the adoptive child reached adulthood. Exceptions to that pattern occurred when the adoptive parents were already quite helpless, in which case they were actually absorbed into the new household of the adoptive child.

Another means of extending the network of kinship was through spouse exchange, a practice found throughout most of the Eskimo area. This traditional practice appears to have served several purposes in the social life of the Copper Eskimo. During travel it was advantageous for men to exchange wives when visiting foreign camps, especially those in which the traveler had no kin. At other times a man might leave his wife behind on a journey while being accompanied by another's wife. In these cases the traveler would be visiting the band of the latter woman's kin. It is also probable that an unattached male who served as a *kivgaq* or servant for another might also share the favors of the latter's wife. The sociological result of the formalized spouse exchange relationship was extension of kinship both terminologically[14] and behaviorally, as spouse exchange occurred exclusively between nonkindred. Psychologically there was undoubtedly a release of tensions inherent in monogamous mating, though at times this solution backfired, as sexual jealousy is by no means unknown to the Copper Eskimo. Another psychological benefit is suggested in that a more intimate sort of friendship developed between the two men and between the two women involved than was characteristic even among siblings.

OTHER PARTNERSHIPS

Another sort of relationship that occurred among nonkindred (*adlagiit*) was partnerships in dancing, or *numiqatigiik*. Pairings could be contracted between members of the same sex or across the sexes. Frequently this relationship developed when small or large segments of different maximal bands or even different nations encountered one another. A ceremony took place in the dance house (*qadgi*) on these occasions. An individual dancer, beating the skin drum in the center of the circle of bystanders, would call out the name of one of the bystanders to dance around him. The indicated individual would run around the drummer, first in one direction and then in the other, thus establishing the *numiqatigiik* relationship. Examination of evidence from informants indicates that almost always the "dancing associates" were unrelated to one another and each member of the pair would be a member of different maximal bands, the association thus serving as a mechanism to extend associations beyond the group within which one most commonly resided. While informants state that a man or woman might have dancing associates of either sex, my data shows that most often men paired with men and women with women.

A less formalized sort of relationship was *ingiuqatigiik*, or song fellows. Duets appear to have been formed on a voluntary basis and had little significance beyond the period of singing.

Joking associates (*kipaqatigiik*) joked roughly with one another, the joking being characterized by banter, irony, and sarcasm. A number of these partners were also spouse-exchange partners. The relationship is said to grow from close friendship and is said never to occur between relatives. At times it appears to be a four-cornered relationship, that is, especially in the case of spouse exchange, a man or woman would be *kipaqatigiik* with both the exchange husband and his wife or the exchange wife and her husband. While most joking partnerships obtained between persons unrelated by blood or marriage (aside from the secondary marriage of spouse exchange), some partners appear to have been distantly related.

Paralleling the joking relationships were formalized respect or avoidance relationships, or *illinuariik*. In this situation the partner can be spoken to only through a third person and cannot ordinarily mention the name of his *illinuariik*. This feature appears to be a more strict and more formalized relationship than avoidances between certain classes of kin. Some informants say that some of these partnerships, especially *illinuariik* and the earlier-discussed *piqatigiit*, are inherited from father to son, that is, a young man's partners will be the sons of equivalent partners of his father. Some cases support this contention, but many more run counter to it.

LEADERSHIP AND LAW

Persistent questioning of older informants failed to reveal any structurally defined institution of leadership.[15] All informants stressed egalitarianism. To be sure, certain men were more respected than others on the basis of personal qualities. There is also a term *ataniq*, which appears to indicate the organizer of a hunt. No one had the authority of the *isumataaq* of farther east, a position determined largely by kinship considerations, but also at times extended in some regions to cover a large local settlement such as the winter sealing encampment.

On the other hand there were individuals who were feared rather than respected and who often violated personal liberties. Many of the shamans fell under this category. They held the threat of witchcraft over others and were, for the main part, not highly susceptible to vengeance because of their presumed supernatural immunities.

Another sort of menace to the community was the aggressive, strong man who often took what he liked (including women) by force. Such men often met with violent ends, either through simple vindictive homicide or through execution-type killings, agreed upon perhaps by the offenders' relatives. But while they lived they were a constant threat to the peace and harmony of their community.

Mechanisms for settling disputes or righting wrongdoings were not highly developed in the Copper Eskimo area. Insult singing was known, but contests of fisticuffs, which are well known in the Netsilik area, do not seem to have been commonly practiced among the Copper Eskimo.

Without the existence of strong leaders or village councils, settlement of grievances became largely a private affair and often homicide was the only solution available. Some support from kindred can be seen in the existence of blood vengeance, which seems to have been rather highly developed in the area. The frequency of homicide, due to one cause or another, can be appreciated from Rasmussen's (1932) survey of an encampment of fifteen families, where he found that "there was not a single grown man who had not been involved in a killing one way or another."

To summarize, aboriginal Copper Eskimo social organization was characterized by systems of kinship and partnerships and the facts of shared locality generating cooperation, sharing, and emotional closeness.

Kinship factors were important in betrothal, adoption, residence (at least on the band level), blood vengeance, and aspects of interpersonal behavior, but in the last analysis, considering the nucleation of families, the narrow scope of behavioral directives, and the subordinate role played in economic affairs, kinship was not as highly developed an integrating mechanism as it generally is in most hunting societies. Under such circumstances the several systems of partnerships assume greater importance.

Egalitarianism was the keynote of interpersonal relations, and mechanisms of social control had a hollow reality in a society in which there was no council, few sanctions, and a high rate of homicide.

Social Organization, 1925–1955

It was indicated earlier that rather significant changes took place in the yearly cycle after the introduction of the fur trade, principally the adoption of fox trapping, winter hunting of caribou, and summer hunting of seals from boats, as well as fishing with nets. These changes were paralleled by changes in settlement pattern and certain features of social organization.

After about 1925, the mainland population from Perry River to Coppermine was scattered in camps strung along river valleys by lakes or on points of land on the coast which were accessible to the interior. Locations were determined in part by proximity to good fishing sites and also by closeness to caches of caribou killed in summer and fall. Census data indicate that occasionally these camps were made up of single nuclear families, but most often they ranged in size from ten to fifty or sixty persons during much of the year. The duration of these camps was variable from year to year and probably, as well, from locality to locality. In some places a descent was made to the sea for a period of sealing as early as January; in others this form of hunting was restricted to the period beginning in March and ending in May. Reports of large sealing aggregations continued to appear in the records of the period following 1925. A village of thirty snowhouses was seen off Bathurst Inlet in 1929, another group of approximately twenty-five families was gathered on the ice at the mouth of the Kuugaryuaq River in 1929 and 1930, a village of twenty snowhouses was located off Lockyer Point in 1931, and twenty-one families were gathered for sealing in Minto Inlet in 1932. After that period such aggregations appear to have been less frequent as inland adaptation became more marked, though a sealing camp of indeterminate size was visited by Harrington in 1949.[16]

It is likely that many social and ceremonial activities which had been principally associated with the large winter aggregations also persisted throughout much of this period. Generally, however, population tended to be dispersed for longer periods, especially in good caribou years when it was not necessary to come down to the sea to secure seals. Additionally, presence of European agencies in the country doubtlessly had effects on native social practices.

During the 1920s and 1930s an impressive number of trading posts, operated by representatives of large firms or by free traders, opened and many of them closed. The locations of these posts had some effect on the distribution of population. Although the traders tried to establish themselves in the heart of traditional hunting areas, location had to be influenced by considerations of availability of drinking water and accessibility for supply ships. The posts became focuses for travel. Interregional trade among the Copper Eskimo bands all but died out, though visiting relatives seeking wives or trying out new hunting areas continued to motivate some movement outside of the trading area. In general, however, group identity became associated with the trading community, and membership in each of these entities was more stabilized than it had been in the aboriginal maximal bands.

Within each trading area there was considerable movement of people from season to season and from year to year. Examination of personal histories reveals that two or three men might form associations, based either on kinship or partnerships of formal or informal nature, that would endure over a period of years. That is, they would habitually share a locality and relocate together; other men would alternate their residential associations much more freely. In these cases a man might have shared a camp with his father-in-law in October and with his brother in January, and in March he might have lived in a camp where no close kin ties were apparent. The typical fluidity of group membership of the aboriginal hunting group appears to have found its corollary in the organization of the hunting-trapping camp of the later period.

As winter sealing became less significant in most of the area, the seal-sharing practices which had provided such an important mechanism of distribution began to fade in importance. Data taken from informants in the eastern Copper Eskimo regions in 1962–1963 indicates that men in their sixties could generally name the full fourteen *piqat*, men in their fifties could name four to eight, men in their forties, one to seven, and those under forty, one or two. One explanation that was given for the virtual disappearance of the *piqat* system was the death of a large number of older men in the epidemics of the 1920s and 1930s, but the point remains that even though many of the partnerships may have been inactivated by death, the nature of the economy and the dispersed settlement pattern did not inspire continuance of these practices.

With the fading of the *piqat* network, various sharing arrangements were established. To judge by the current practices seen in camps around Bathurst and Perry River and Victoria Island, communal eating continues as perhaps the most important medium of sharing. In addition, the larger villages were segmented into sections that would "trade together" or cooperate in net hauling, as well as sharing caches. These economic partnerships were at times based on kinship, and true extended family organizations appear to have existed in terms of economics during the period after 1925 in a few cases, though others were based mainly on friendship.

Almost invariably tents or snowhouses (which remained as the chief dwelling types) were occupied by only one nuclear family.

Other traditional practices appear to have been retained in force during the period 1925–1955. Child betrothal was still common and began to fade only in the centralized communities of the contemporary period. Adoption continued to be an important social feature. Spouse exchange also undoubtedly continued.

While many of the traditional elements of social organization continued and others underwent gradual change or abandonment, relations with European agencies became more or less standardized in the period 1925–1955. Although communities tended to remain all native in composition, influence of outside authority was definitely felt. The economic destiny of the Copper Eskimo now depended to a large extent upon the traders. Credit was extended according to the judgment of the trader, and traps were sometimes given on credit at the beginning of the season in order to encourage greater trapping activity. The character of the trader's relation with the Eskimo depended to a great extent upon his individual personality and judgment. Intermarriages between Copper Eskimo and immigrant western Eskimo or with white free traders and trappers did occur, and often these outsiders would exercise a certain degree of authority over small segments of the native population.

Clothing began to change both with respect to material, with the adoption of cloth for summer and inner garments; and, with the influx of western Eskimo, with respect to style including the use of wolverine trim for hoods.

Missionaries appear to have met with indifferent success. Neither Anglicanism nor Catholicism was strongly embraced, and at least one nativistic religious movement occurred, though most of the natives were nominal Christians. Services were irregular, occurring mainly when the trade-mission community was visited or when catechists or missionaries traveled to outlying camps; the sabbath was usually not observed.

Representatives of the Royal Canadian Mounted Police had some effect on social control in Copper Eskimo society. No longer did grievances remain a private matter, but rather Eskimo behavior fell under the legal system of Euro-Canadian society. The high rate of homicide in the aboriginal society continued for a number of years after the establishment of police detachments in the area. Police records show that nearly every year an investigation of murder was one of the chief motives for dog sledge patrols. The suspects were usually tried at courts of special magistrates. Eskimo were hanged in the 1920s, but later more usual sentences for manslaughter were on the order of one to two years in prison.

The police also discouraged infanticide. At first this practice was openly admitted, but after lectures by the police the people talked less of exposing children, but in comparing sex ratios in the eastern part of the Copper Eskimo area, it is apparent that the practice of female infanticide continued until at least 1940.

Killing of musk oxen had been outlawed since 1917, but around Bathurst Inlet, at least, reported slaughters were investigated every few years, though usually the cases were designated as hardship situations.

In general, police control can be said to have been paternalistic, but not severe.

The chief white agents in the area—police, missionaries, and traders—served a valuable function as lay medical practitioners.

SOCIAL ORGANIZATION IN THE PERIOD SINCE 1955

The general trend toward centralization after 1955 brought further change in social features. The small all-native community persisted in parts of the area, and satellite camps appeared each summer with membership recruited from personnel of the centralized communities. The exodus to Cambridge Bay and to Coppermine thinned the populations in the outlying regions of Bathurst Inlet, Perry River, and the interior of the area south of Coronation Gulf (largely uninhabited except for the Contwoyto Lake region after about 1954). Camps seldom exceed twenty-five persons, and generally the populations of these settlements are in the range of seven to twenty persons. The number of sites occupied around Perry River and Bathurst are not noticeably smaller than in the preceding period, but the size of local groupings shrank.

My observations around Perry River and Bathurst in 1962–1963, together with supplementary information from Bathurst for the following year,[17] suggest that sites are usually occupied continuously from about August through March. The spring and early summer are the periods of greatest relocation and wandering. At times, settlement in that period resembles closely the aboriginal pattern of up to six camp relocations in a month, though this is not general. From one year to another favorite sites are often occupied by a core of the same personnel, though there are a number of individuals in these areas who are quite mobile from year to year as well as over much of each year's cycle.

Associations among family heads appear to be showing a trend toward regularity. At Bathurst, for example, three men have habitually shared a locality for a number of years even though they are not closely linked by kinship ties. At the same time, kin ties are becoming firmly established through marriage linkages on the following generation. In general, it seems to be true around Perry River and Bathurst that such linkages, in addition to primary kin linkages, seem to be increasing in groupings which show greater persistence over the year's cycle. Considerable variability can, however, be found in the social organization of the small camps that comprise the chief settlement in the Perry River-Bathurst-Cambridge Bay areas. In at least one case a rather highly developed patrilocal extended family usually operates as the local group, and even when combined with other units, persists as the economic unit. In still other cases, two men might form partnerships in trading, sharing the fox profits. In other cases, the local group does not form a close kinship unit, but does form a trading partnership and to some extent a cooperative unit. As far as I was able to determine, these examples appear to represent the diversity in these areas that characterized the preceding period.

In the early stages of the development of the centralized communities, place of origin and, correlatively, kin ties as well, were expressed in neighborhood organizations. At Cambridge Bay, for example, the native houses were separated into three main neighborhoods—one for the people from Bathurst, another made up of Ellice River people, and a third composed of local Victoria Island natives. Later, intermarriages among these groups tended to break down the distinction as new houses were built. Government housing programs more completely disrupted this quasi-band neighborhood arrangement. One group of houses was constructed for welfare cases, usually blind, aged, or crippled Eskimo; another was set up for steady-wage employees of the various agencies. By the mid-1960s few of the original native-constructed shacks (built from scrap lumber) were occupied, and the arrangement of the town into such neighborhoods had largely broken down, though patterns of visiting could be discerned which revealed a relation to place of common origin or kinship ties.

Decision-making is to a great extent in the hands of Euro-Canadian agencies. Relief issued by government representatives, credit extended by the Hudson's Bay Company, and wages earned in employment are important economic components of the activities of outside agencies. Decisions concerning schools (although in the beginning, at least, schools were supposedly voluntary), assignment of housing, and hospitalization (including transportation of patients south for treatment) all remain out of Eskimo hands.

More recently two agencies have developed which are designed to give a certain measure of political and economic responsibility to the natives of Cambridge Bay. These are the fishing cooperative and the community council.

The economic aspects of the fishing cooperative have already been discussed. With regard to organization, it should be mentioned that although the cooperative is purportedly an all-native organization, the important functions of arranging for shipping, soliciting a market, and selling are largely in the hands of various Euro-Canadian persons.

Another move that has been made toward self-determination for the Eskimo of Cambridge Bay has been the growth of the community council. The constitution of the council, drafted in 1962, provides that the council shall "consider itself constituted for the betterment of the whole community and for the advancement of understanding between various sections and interests within the community," although its powers are recognized as being only advisory. Each non-Eskimo agency is allowed one representative, and the constitution provides that Eskimo and non-Eskimo membership be equal. Bimonthly meetings are held and each member's term of office is one year. From the beginning, language difficulties, plus the customary reluctance of most of the Eskimo members to speak out at meetings, have hampered native participation. The council has, however, played an increasing role in ironing out difficulties among the various interest groups as well as serving as an important panel for diffusion of information regarding everyday problems in Cambridge. Undoubtedly, this body has contributed much to bridging the communication gap between the Eskimo and non-Eskimo populations of the community.

ETHOS[18]

RELIGIOUS BELIEFS AND DEITIES

The chief deity of the Copper Eskimo was Arnakapfaaluk, or "the big bad woman." Arnakapfaaluk dwells in the cave at the bottom of the sea and controls the activities of the sea animals. She is the famous Sedna of Boas, who is also known variously throughout the Eskimo areas as Nuliayuk or Arnaluk-Takanaaluk. Hila inua, the spirit of the air, governs the weather, but is in turn influenced by Arnakapfaaluk. The celestial bodies are regarded as departed peoples, and other natural phenomena like thunder and rainbows are endowed with supernatural significance.

An elaborate system of taboos and observances comprise the main parts of Copper Eskimo religion. Many of these have to do with special customs regarding sea mammals, their separation from land animals, and their significance as the creatures of Arnakapfaaluk. The rules separating land and sea mammals are somewhat less stringent than is the case farther east, but a substantial body of prohibitions still exist in the area. For example, fresh caribou meat must never lie on the side platform of the snowhouse together with seal meat; cod must never be eaten with the blubber of a bearded seal; products of the land and the sea must never be cooked in the same pot at the same time; seal blood cannot be used for splicing arrows intended for caribou hunting; sealskin may not be sewn at the fishing creeks while the char are still running. Above all, caribou skin clothing cannot be sewn on the sea ice during the dark period of winter.

These taboos are observed in order to keep from incurring the displeasure of Arnakapfaaluk, who would either withhold the animals of the sea from the Eskimo or influence Hila inua to bring bad weather which would interfere with hunting.

A dead seal must be handled with special precautions. No woman can sew on the day her husband catches a seal, rime must not be scraped from the ice window of the snowhouse while a seal lies unflensed in the house; people hunting the seal while based in snowhouses on the sea ice must not work in soapstone, and so on.

Handling of the caribou is also surrounded with ritual. Special skinning procedures must be followed. The head of a newly shot caribou must be laid out in the snow when a camp is deserted, the head being set with its snout pointing in the direction in which new game will be sought.

Other rituals accompany important events such as birth, a boy's first kill, and death. Some of these procedures will be referred to later.

SHAMANISM

The shaman (*angatkuq*) acts as intermediary between the spirits and the people. The shaman can be a man or a woman, but special experiences are usually attributed to those who are trained for shamanism. The shaman's dreams have special significance as omens, and he is thought to be visited from time to time by his helping, or familiar, spirit, which is the source of his special powers. The functions of the *angatkuq* were (1) to cure the sick; (2) to quell storms and bad weather; (3) to attack and kill evil spirits; and (4) to procure animals for hunting. Each of these aims was served by special seances, but only the curing of the sick was done for a fee. The shaman had to stage special tricks periodically in order to provide proof of his powers, although it is likely from descriptions of performances that the bystanders were somewhat gullible and the tricks of the shaman were often obvious deceptions.

Perhaps one of the most common procedures used to seek supernatural aid was the divining ceremony of *qilaniq*, or raising and lowering the head of a supine Eskimo with a belt. This procedure could be carried out either by a shaman or a layman.

MYTHOLOGY OR FOLKLORE

A fair number of Copper Eskimo tales deal with the spirits. The Sedna tale has special versions which actually vary within the Copper Eskimo area. Hila inua is the subject of other myths. There are epic tales as well. One deals with the pan-Eskimo hero Kiviuq. The myth of the origin of the white men from a dog mating with a woman is known in the area. A number of other tales depict animals or animals mating with humans or animals appearing in human form. Murder and vengeance are subjects of other tales.

The songs of the Copper Eskimo are a particularly prominent part of their oral culture. Most songs are sung in accompaniment to the drum dances. An eastern group of Copper Eskimo, the Umingmakturmiut, were described by Rasmussen (1932:16) as the most poetically gifted group of Eskimo he had known. Every man or woman in that group was said to have had his own compositions. Some of the subjects of the songs were man's impotence in the universe, hunger, songs of the hunt, songs of lust, the fear of loneliness, and death. There were also spirit hymns sung by the shaman in the course of his performances.

The language of the songs as well as that used by the *anqatkuq* in seances is specialized, symbolic, and poetic. The musk ox, for example, is known as *Huqhuqtuq*, or "the one with the conspicuous weapon of defense"; caribou may be called "the one with branching antlers"; and a seal, "the animal that supplies hot broth."

Although Christianity has been adopted on at least a nominal basis, it is likely that many elements of native belief still persist. Shamans are known to exist today and at times may actually exert considerable influence. The drum dance still took place at Bathurst Inlet and Perry River at the time of my visits to those places (1962–1963) and usually occurred at the times of largest gathering—which, incidentally, take place at the Christian holidays of Christmas and Easter. These events provide opportunities to keep alive the old songs. It is doubtful that the view of the universe depicted in these songs and other oral tradition has been drastically altered in the minds of older and middle-aged Copper Eskimo. It is probably only with school attendance, especially when schooling requires relocation for ten months of the year, that the old beliefs are rejected. To be sure, the Copper Eskimo of today has been exposed to a variety of technological changes and more recently has been drawn into the mass media of Western civilization, but for the most part he lacks the scientific foundation to understand the universe in a more sophisticated fashion.

THE LIFE CYCLE

By following the career of the individual Copper Eskimo, the operation of principals of social organization and the belief system can be examined in dynamic perspective.

Birth and Childhood

Childbirth was aided by a group of women. The child was delivered with the mother kneeling and gripping a rod. The baby was received by one of the women, who was careful to keep the head from touching the skins on the platform. One of the women, the *uaqti*, washed the afterbirth from the child. The child was then named, and a number of ritual activities took place shortly afterward. A male child's arms were drawn into the position of a bowman and the body was cleaned with a bull caribou skin or the skin of a loon gull tern. These procedures were meant to insure skill in hunting and fishing. A girl's body was cleaned with the skin of a ground squirrel to bring beauty. A loon's bill might be inserted into the mouth of a child to give him that bird's singing ability.

A taboo on work was imposed until the umbilicus was healed. If the child was male, the mother followed this taboo, if female, the father followed it.

Nursing often continued until the age of three or even five. This custom is related in part to the difficulty of providing suitable food for infants. The indulgence to children that is attributed to the Eskimo is quite apparent among the Copper Eskimo. I have seen children being allowed to leave and enter a snowhouse four or five times in the course of an hour even though closing and opening the door has a considerable cooling effect in the house. The mother patiently dresses and undresses the child as often as he wishes in these cases. Certain disciplinary training is also apparent. If a child is hurt, he or she might be picked up, but will quickly be put down again when he or she stops crying. Stern disapproval is given children who behave roughly toward others, and they are quickly separated when they physically abuse others.

Toilet training is patiently but persistently pursued. The child is removed several times during the day and stimulated to urinate. The child is never reprimanded for defecating or urinating inside the mother's coat when he is carried.

During childhood the adult pursuits are gradually and indulgently taught to the child. Children are never ridiculed for failure in adult pursuits, at least not by their own parents.

PUBERTY AND MARRIAGE

For a boy, an important transitional event was the ceremony accompanying the first kill. When the first seal was killed and pulled from its breathing hole, it was dragged over the body of the successful young hunter. The seal was then apportioned by a close relative (usually an uncle) and given to the predetermined seal-sharing partnership. The *piqatigiit* system was thereby activated. The boy also usually wrestled in a mock battle with his father, the winner throwing the other onto the body of the dead seal.

A man might be as young as fourteen or as old as his late twenties when he married. Often but not always he resided with the prospective father-in-law, working as a servant (*kivgaq*) until the girl reached puberty. No special ceremony took place at that time, but the couple usually moved into separate quarters. They might remain in the hunting group of the wife's parents or shift to that of the husband's father or join that of less closely related or even unrelated persons. Generally, during the winter the young man would reside in the band aggregation, which included either his father, his father-in-law, or both while they are still living.

Copper Eskimo women usually married at about age twelve to fourteen. In cases where bride service was followed, the actual marriage was considered to have occurred when the girl reached puberty, but in other cases the girl often took up residence with the husband before puberty. Because of the rather late age of puberty and a period of adolescent sterility, girls seldom gave birth until age seventeen or eighteen. Despite the apparently small families of Copper Eskimo, it is evident that the women were fairly fertile. It was not unusual for a woman to give birth to six or eight children, though it was not likely with the occurrences of miscarriage, infanticide, death in childhood, and adoption of children out to others that half of those born would actually be reared to adulthood in their natal family.

ADULTHOOD

The Copper Eskimo began to make an economic contribution in his teens and usually remained active until after sixty. During this period of active life the hunt and talk about the hunt were his favorite occupations, though companionship, cohabitation, song, dance, and games were all sources of joy in his life. He might separate and remarry several times during these years, become involved in a vendetta, live through especially hard winters during which some of his older friends and relatives might die, and travel outside the normal hunting grounds of his band or even outside the Copper Eskimo area. He would relate to his fellows on an egalitarian basis and no great honors would accrue to him, though he might gain some reputation for being an especially skilled hunter or organizer of hunts.

The female Copper Eskimo would devote much of her time to child-rearing and lighter household tasks such as cooking, preparing skins for clothing, and trimming the wick of the seal oil lamp. In addition, she was expected to carry out jobs that called for physical labor. Pitching and breaking camp, pulling sledges with the dogs, and backpacking considerable loads in summer were all occupations the women were expected to share with the men. During the winter much of the day was spent in visiting and gossiping with the other women while the men were away sealing. At other times of the year women were expected to fish and to act as beaters at the caribou drives.

Old Age and Death

Exposure of the sick and aged was occasionally practiced but was by no means as common as infanticide. Usually the period of old age was one of no little discomfort in a nomadic society such as that of the aboriginal Copper Eskimo. The moves between campsites would become more and more difficult for the old to negotiate, but usually they were taken care of patiently by children or adoptive children. It appears that the stress of cold weather and the dampness accelerate aging. During the periods of famine the old would suffer most, and many of the deaths at those times were among those already weakened by old age.

Death was surrounded by a number of procedures and taboos. The corpse was dressed in a sack of skin over the inner garments and was left in the house for three days if a male and four days if a female. The body was then removed through a hole in the back of the snowhouse or through the rear of the tent. The corpse was interred in a circle of stones in summer or a small snow hut in winter. Articles of the hunt, or at least miniature replicas of such tools, were left with deceased males. This practice indicates some belief in an afterlife, although these beliefs are only poorly conceptualized by the Copper Eskimo themselves.[19]

These observations on the individual life cycle refer specifically to the aboriginal period but apply in most respects to the period after 1925. With the establishment of family allowances and old age and disability pensions in the 1940s, some of the burden of supporting children and unproductive adults was eased, and the apparent disappearance of population control measures seems to be in part related to this income.

Currently, with the provision of special housing for aged and invalid

Eskimo, together with medical aid, greater comfort is experienced in old age. Also with the establishment of centralized communities, we have noted that the status of both the young and the old has somewhat improved. The young have gained new importance through their knowledge of English and, at times, other skills they have learned.

CHANGE

If viewed from the broad perspective of the history of human culture, such a relatively short-term cultural development as that of the modern Eskimo could perhaps be viewed as a virtual continuum of change. However, in considering the history of one specific group such as the Copper Eskimo, at least, two periods of stability can be noted which can be contrasted to two shorter periods of dramatic change.

For about a century, from the late archaeological into the contact ethnographic period, exploitation, elements of material culture, and settlement pattern probably remained essentially unchanged. At the same time, a number of local variations in these features (from neighboring nations), as well as other cultural distinctiveness, indicate that historical processes were at work. Local adaptations to conditions (including use of local raw materials) together with isolation from other nations may have accounted for the occurrence of some of this distinctiveness, although with the present state of our archaeology of the area it is not possible to rule out a later movement of peoples in the area (as compared to groups farther east). Thus despite an apparent common heritage of a large part of Eskimo culture and the likelihood of diffusion between nations, divergent change apparently occurred, though this change took the form of slow unfolding of distinctive cultural features and focuses.

During the period following first intensive contact (roughly 1910–1925), with the introduction of new technology and the adoption of new hunting techniques, important economic changes took place. Rifles, nets, traps, small boats, and so on, made significant impact on the seasonal economic cycle, and these changes in turn affected the dispersal of settlement, which in turn affected features of social organization that are associated mainly with larger gatherings, which had become rarer and shorter-lived. The influx of Euro-Canadians into the area also affected social and cultural activities and components in a dozen tangible and intangible ways.

Shortly, however, another period of relative stability began. White agencies were rather limited in function, and, for the most part, relationships were defined and specific. Many of the aboriginal ways and views of the world continued essentially unchanged for another thirty years. Neither missionization nor education was highly successful or (in the latter cases) systematically presented to the Eskimo. The people of the all-native community, which was still the principal form of settlement, continued to live in a narrow universe. Native institutions still persisted, although many were weakened by change.

Since 1955, a second period of highly accelerated change has been occurring. Change in game supply, influx of new elements of Euro-Canadian society, increasing government interest and intervention, growth schools within the area, all of which accompanied the move of natives away from the all-native communities to white-native communities, are ingredients in a picture of intensive contact and realignment of economic aims, social goals, and psychological viewpoints. While the first flush of intensive contact in the period 1910–1925 brought about changes that were mostly external in nature, further changes during the recent period of centralization have involved problems of adjustment to a new scale of values and confrontations with a sharply broadened universe as a result of abrupt exposure to the mass media of the outside world. The chief medium of information will continue to be the program of education, which will undoubtedly expand the horizons of the present-day youth and that of future generations and eventually supplant much of the Eskimo's view of the world and strongly affect his system of values.

The latest phase of Copper Eskimo history has not yet run its course. A new period of relative equilibrium will probably follow, but its eventual character is still conjectural.

NOTES

1. My field work with the Copper Eskimo extended from September 1962 to September 1963 and was supported by the National Museum of Canada. I have drawn heavily on the early sources (Stefansson 1913, 1914; Jenness 1922; Rasmussen 1932) in my portrayal of the aboriginal society.

   Conversations with Dr. Diamond Jenness, L. M. LeMer, O.M.I., Louis Men'ez, O.M.I., and Duncan M. Pryde and John Stanners of the Hudson's Bay Company have been helpful in my attempts to fill out the picture of the past and present Copper Eskimo society and culture.

   Records that were made available to me by Mr. Stanners and Father Men'ez were very valuable to my study as was the linguistic assistance and service as an interpreter provided by Mr. Pryde. The orthography used here is based on one used by Mr. Pryde, but does not correspond in all particulars to his.

   I was especially fortunate in having Dr. Jenness available for critical reading of the manuscript.

2. In phonetic terms "h" is a voiceless glottal fricative while "s" is a voiceless palatal spirant.

3. This description is based on Stefansson (1914) and Jenness (1922) for the western part of the area and on Rasmussen (1932) and my own data from informants for the eastern portion of the Copper Eskimo country.

4. Jenness (personal communication) indicates that snowhouses were built on Liston and Sutton islands and were occupied until February because the

strong currents in Dolphin and Union Strait made for uncertain ice conditions. He also suggests that in localities where the water is moderately deep near land, seals might be found in greater abundance closer to shore, in contrast to conditions along shelving coasts.

5. Work in other parts of the Canadian Arctic has indicated that in certain localities such as Thom Bay in the Netsilik area and possibly as well Arctic Bay and Pond Inlet in the Iglulik Eskimo area, where seals are for some reason or other more easily secured, this principal is not as crucial as it appears to be in most or all of the Copper Eskimo regions. However, during the spring of 1963, observations of Copper Eskimo hunting with the *mauliqtuq* method on Queen Maud Gulf convinces me of the importance of a large number of hunters being available.

6. Jenness (1922:65–76) has illustrated various types of composite snowhouses, but adds "single houses are as common as two-roomed huts or huts joined in their passages," and "it is not true of these Eskimos that the hut contains at least two platforms and two lamps" (Jenness 1922:77).

7. Sources for this period include Hoare (1927), Annual Reports of the Royal Canadian Mounted Police, a diary kept intermittently at the Bathurst Inlet post of the Hudson's Bay Company, records of the Roman Catholic mission at Bathurst, and the popular accounts of Finnie (1940) and Harrington (1954).

8. These figures were taken from the files of the Northern Administration Branch of the Department of Indian Affairs and Northern Development (formerly Northern Affairs and National Resources).

9. I have used my own field notes for the main part of this section, but Jenness (1964) and Abrahamson *et al.* (1964) and the file of the Department of Indian Affairs and Northern Development have also been helpful.

10. These figures are from Abrahamson *et al.* (1964).

11. This section is based mainly on my field notes, but Jenness (1922) and Rasmussen (1932) provided much valuable data on social organization as well.

12. I have applied the concept of the band to Copper, Netsilik, and Iglulik Eskimo groupings in another paper (Damas, 1969).

13. The procedure used in analyzing the structure of these bands is presented in Helm's article, "Statistical Method of Analysis of Community Composition: Quantification Intensity and Kind of Primary Relative Bands in Community Co-Residence," to appear in *Band Societies, Proceedings of the Conference on Band Organization*, National Museum of Canada, Bulletin No. 228.

14. I am uncertain as to whether the network of terms is developed in cases where the exchange occurs only once, as is suggested by Jenness (1922:85).

15. Jenness (1922:93–94; 1964:162) describes two very influential Copper Eskimo men in terms that might belie these statements by natives and his own assertion that the Copper Eskimo were without chiefs. Nevertheless, I believe that such men were rare and that leadership was certainly not institutionalized to the extent found further east.

16. This information on sealing villages comes from the Annual Reports of the Royal Canadian Mounted Police and from Harrington (1954).

17. Information on the 1963–1964 groups was kindly provided by Father Louis Men'ez.
18. I have relied heavily on Jenness (1922, 1924b, 1924c); Roberts and Jenness (1925); and Rasmussen (1932) in this section.
19. Rasmussen (1932:33–34) thought that this vagueness regarding the afterlife and some rather bizarre versions of the afterlife that he received were the result of the influence of a missionary, but Jenness does not specify Copper Eskimo views of the afterlife, and his visit was contemporaneous and previous to that of the first missionary to have any influence (Jenness 1922:11).

REFERENCES

Abrahamson, G., et al, 1954. The Copper Eskimo: An Areal Economic Survey, Ottawa: Department of Northern Affairs and National Resources.
Contains information on contemporary Copper Eskimo economy.
Bird, J. B., and M. B. Bird, 1961. Bathurst Inlet, Northwestern Territories, Ottawa: Department of Mines and Technical Surveys, Geographical Branch Memoir 7.
A survey of the physical, biological, and human geography of the Bathurst Inlet area.
Birket-Smith, K., 1945. Ethnographical Collections from the Northwest Passage, Copenhagen: Report of the Fifth Thule Expedition, 1921–1924, 6 (2).
A study of Copper and Netsilik Eskimo material culture with comparisons with other Eskimo groups.
Damas, D., 1966. "Diversity in White-Eskimo Leadership Interaction," Anthropologica 8:45–52.
A comparative study of aboriginal and contemporary leadership patterns among the Copper Eskimo of Bathurst Inlet and the Iglulingmiut.
———, 1969. "Characteristics of Central Eskimo Band Structure," in Band Societies: Proceedings of the Conference on Band Organization, National Museum of Canada Bulletin No. 228.
Portrays Central Eskimo groupings, including Copper Eskimo, in terms of the concept of the band.
Finnie, R., 1940. Lure of the North, New York: David McKay Company.
Gives a brief glimpse into the life of the Copper Eskimo of the early 1930s, a period which is otherwise not represented in the literature.
Harrington, R., 1954. The Face of the Arctic, London: Hodder & Stoughton.
This popular account contains information about the inland-dwelling Copper Eskimo of 1949.
Hoare, W. B. H., 1927. Report of Investigations Affecting Eskimo and Wild Life, District of Mackenzie, 1924–1926, Department of the Interior.
Depicts the readaptation of economy in the Copper Eskimo area that was taking place in the 1920s.
Jenness, D., 1921. "The Blond Eskimos," American Anthropologist 23:257–267.
A critique of Stefansson's hypothesis regarding Norse elements in physical anthropology of the Copper Eskimo.

————, 1922. *The Life of the Copper Eskimo*, Ottawa: Report of the Canadian Arctic Expedition, 1913–1918, Vol. 12A.

————, 1923a. *Physical Characteristics of the Copper Eskimos*, Ottawa: Report of the Canadian Arctic Expedition, 1913–1918, Vol. 12B.

————, 1923b. *Osteology and Dentition of the Western and Copper Eskimos*, Ottawa: Report of the Canadian Arctic Expedition, Vol. 12C.

————, 1924a. *Eskimo String Figures*, Ottawa: Report of the Canadian Arctic Expedition, Vol. 13B.

————, 1924b. *Myth and Tradition from Northern Alaska, the Mackenzie Delta and Coronation Gulf*, Ottawa: Report of the Canadian Arctic Expedition, 1913–1918, Vol. 13A.

————, 1924c. *Eskimo Folktales*, Ottawa: Report of the Canadian Arctic Expedition, 1913–1918, Vol. 13A.

————, 1928. *Comparative Vocabulary of the Western Eskimo Dialects*, Ottawa: Report of the Canadian Arctic Expedition, 1913–1918, Vol. 15A.

————, 1944. *Grammatical Notes on Some Western Eskimo Dialects*, Ottawa: Report of the Canadian Arctic Expedition, 1913–1918, Vol. 15B.

————, 1946. *Material Culture of the Copper Eskimo*, Ottawa: Report of the Canadian Arctic Expedition, 1913–1918, Vol. 16.
These volumes together with Roberts and Jenness (1924) provide the most complete ethnography of any aboriginal Eskimo group.

————, 1964. *Eskimo Administration: II. Canada*. Arctic Institute of North America, Technical Paper No. 14.
Contains much valuable information on and analysis of the period since contact for the Canadian Eskimo in general, with some reference to the Copper Eskimo area.

McGhee, R. J., 1968. *Copper Eskimo Prehistory*, unpublished doctoral dissertation, Department of Archaeology, University of Calgary, Calgary, Alberta.
Discusses evolution of Copper Eskimo culture using archaeological, linguistic, physical anthropological, and ethnographic data.

Macpherson, A. H., 1961. "On the Abundance of Certain Mammals in the Western Canadian Arctic Islands in 1958–1959," *The Arctic Circular* 5 (1).
Covers distribution of land mammals in the Copper Eskimo regions of Banks and Victoria islands.

Oschinsky, L., 1962. "Facial Flatness and Cheekbone Morphology in Arctic Mongoloids: A Case for Morphological Taxonomy," *Anthropologica* 4:349–377.
Northern Asiatic racial types are linked with the Eskimo.

Ostermann, H., 1942. *The Mackenzie Eskimos*, Copenhagen: Report of the Fifth Thule Expedition, 1921–1924, 10 (2).
This collection of posthumous notes of Rasmussen contains a valuable census of western groups of Copper Eskimo for 1924.

Rasmussen, K., 1932. *Intellectual Culture of the Copper Eskimos*, Copenhagen: Report of the Fifth Thule Expedition, 1921–1924, Vol. 9.
An important source for the final phase of the aboriginal period. Contains 1924 census data for eastern groups of Copper Eskimo and lengthy treatment of oral tradition.

Roberts, H. H., and D. Jenness, 1925. *Songs of the Copper Eskimos*, Ottawa: Report of the Canadian Arctic Expedition, 1913–1918, Vol. 14.

Complements Jenness (1924a, 1924b) and Rasmussen (1932) in the area of oral culture.

Stefansson, V., 1913. *My Life with the Eskimo*, New York: Macmillan.
This first significant account of the Copper Eskimo contains a substantial amount of ethnographic data for the popular reader. Raised the question of the "blond Eskimos."

———, 1914a. *The Stefansson-Anderson Expedition: Preliminary Ethnological Report*, New York, Anthropological Papers of the American Museum of Natural History, Vol. 14.
Ethnographic detail upon which Stefansson (1913) is based. Important for its early period and uniqueness in being an account of first contact of an Eskimo group being established by an anthropologist.

———, 1914b. "Prehistoric and Present Commerce among the Arctic Coast Eskimos," *Geological Survey of Canada*, National Museum of Canada Bulletin No. 6.
Outlines Eskimo trade routes from Alaska to Hudson's Bay.

———, 1921. *The Friendly Arctic*, New York: Macmillan.
Contains a brief account of the Minto Inlet group of Copper Eskimo (1915).

Swadesh, M., 1951. "Kleinschmidt Centennial III: Unaaliq and Proto-Eskimo, Comparative Vocabulary," *International Journal of American Linguistics* 17:241–256.
Discusses dialects of Eskimo-Aleut family of languages.

Taylor, W. E., Jr., 1965. "The Fragments of Eskimo Prehistory," *Beaver*, Spring 1965:4–17.
Reviews current picture of archaeological background of Canadian Eskimo.

GLOSSARY

GENERAL

aglu: seal's breathing hole

angatkug: shaman

Arnakapfaaluk: the Eskimo goddess of the sea, also known by other names, as noted in the text

ataniq: Copper Eskimo term for leader of a hunt

aulaqut (pl. *aulaqutit*): scarecrow-like structure used in caribou drives

haputit: stone weirs built in streams for intercepting Arctic char

Hila inua: the spirit of the air

Huqhuqtuq: shaman's name for musk oxen

illinuariit (dl. *illinuariik*): persons forbidden to name one another

innakharvik (pl. *innakharviit*): place where Copper Eskimo gathered for the period of sewing winter skins

iniuqatigiit (dl. *inuiqatigiik*): song fellows

inukhuk (pl. *inukhuit*): stones set in converging rows for caribou drives

iqaluqtucciaq: "the fair fishing place"; Copper Eskimo name for Cambridge Bay

jigged: to catch a fish with a jig

kivgaq: "servant," usually prospective son-in-law working his bride service

Kiviuq: an epic hero known to most Eskimo regions

mauliqtuq: method of hunting seals at their breathing holes

-miut: postbase indicating area usually frequented by groups of Eskimo

numiqatigiit (dl. *numiqatigiik*): associates in dancing

paagagtariik (pl. *paagagtariit*): men whose snowhouses shared a common entry

payuktuq: voluntary sharing system

piqat: literally "partners"; also specialized postbase used to indicate seal-sharing partners (dl. *piqatigiik,* pl. *piqatigiit*)

qadgi: community house; large snowhouse used for dancing and other ceremonial

qilaniq: ritual of raising head of patient with belt

qulitaq: heavy caribou skin coat used in winter

uaqti: woman who assists at birth; also washes afterbirth from baby

ulu: semilunar woman's knife

Kinship Terms

ai: husband's brothers, wife's sisters, female's sister's husband (extended to husband of male cousin), male's brother's wife

aliqa: older sister of man

amauq: great grandparent

anaanacciq: grandmother

angak: MB and MZH

angayuk: older sibling, same sex

angayunnguk: spouse's older sister's husband and older brother's wife

angut: literally, "man" or "male"; Copper Eskimo father

angutiqat: FBch

ani: older brother of female

anngak: female brother's child (extended to children of male cousin)

aqqaluaq: female's younger brother

arnaaryuk: FBW, MBW

arnaq: literally, "woman" or "female"; Copper Eskimo mother

arnaqat: FZch, MZch, MBch

arnarvik: MZ

ataataciaq: grandfather

gangiaq: male's brother's child (extended to child of male cousin)

haki: parent-in-law

hakiaq: wife's brother, husband's sister

iluliarut: great grandchild

ingnutaq: grandchildren

nayak: younger sister of man

ningauk: man's sister's husband, son-in-law

nukaq: younger sibling, same sex

nukaunnguk: spouse's younger sister's husband and older brother's wife

nurraq: female's sister's child, extended to children of female cousin

pangnaaryuk: FB and FZH

ukuaq: female's brother's wife (extended to wife of male cousin)

CHAPTER

2

THE DOGRIB INDIANS¹

June Helm

June Helm is Professor of Anthropology at the University of Iowa. She received her Ph.D. from the University of Chicago in 1958, and since 1951, has made a dozen field trips to the Athapaskan-speaking Indians of Canada's Northwest Territories. Dr. Helm has published a number of articles on folklore, kinship, and political and territorial organization in several tribal groups, as well as a general study of a community of Slave Indians, The Lynx Point People *(1961), and in co-authorship with Nancy O. Lurie, an analysis of the* Dogrib Hand Game *(1966). Both are monographs in the National Museum of Canada Bulletin series. She is the editor of the volume on the Indians of the subarctic in the forthcoming* Handbook of North American Indians *(Smithsonian Institution) and has been the editor of the publications of the American Ethnological Society (1964–1968) and president of the Central States Anthropological Society (1970–1971).*

EDITOR'S INTRODUCTION

The Dogribs of the northwestern Canadian subarctic are a group of Athapaskan-speaking "Treaty Indians." Like the Copper Eskimo, the Dogribs were traditionally hunters and fishermen, but they have been exposed to a long period of limited Western contact and now support themselves through federal aid and occasional wage labor as well as through hunting, fishing, and trapping. In their harsh climate and natural domain of boreal forest, streams, marshes, and lakes, the Dogribs, as other hunting groups, moved camp with the changing seasons, their exploitative techniques varying with the time and place. The household, which in the past included wives, offspring, and occasionally other dependents, was and is the daily food-producing sharing unit. Because of the physical environment, which necessitates cooperation, and the external social control demanding conformity to the dominant Euro-Canadian life pattern, the Dogribs attempt to foster physical welfare and social harmony among group members, whose prospects for other means of livelihood are poor.

51

Helm outlines some of the changes in Dogrib life that have taken place since Western contact, but emphasizes their exploitative techniques, both social and material, as they have been in recent times. Her interest is primarily in a social order which is maintained by kinship ties and divisions of socio-territorial groups. Comparison of the Dogribs with the Copper Eskimo and Mistassini Cree demonstrates similar responses to culture change resulting from the coming first of missionaries and traders and more recently of Canadian government agencies and welfare. Such a comparison also demonstrates the range of variability in adaptations of economies and social systems in somewhat parallel environments.

LOCATION

The Dogrib Indians exploit a vast subarctic forest land in Canada's Northwest Territories. Lying between the 62d and 65th parallels and between 110 and 120 degrees of longitude, the Dogrib range encloses roughly 45,000 square miles. (See Fig. 2-1.) The bulk of the Dogribs trade into the "fort" of Rae, near the North Arm of Great Slave Lake. A smaller segment lives near the town of Yellowknife.[2]

POPULATION

The government "band rolls" for the Rae and Yellowknife administrative areas listed 1496 "Treaty Indians" in the year 1965. This count makes the Dogribs perhaps the largest "tribal" population in the Northwest Territories.[3] The Dogribs living in or trading into Rae, on whom this study concentrates, numbered about 1200 in 1965. Comparing this figure with Mason's (1946:14) estimate of 700 in 1913 and Petitot's (1884) count of 788 in 1864 demonstrates the effectiveness of the medical services brought to the Dogribs in the last twenty years in controlling epidemics and tuberculosis and, especially, in reducing infant deaths.

LANGUAGE

The Dogribs speak an Athapaskan language, as do the other Indian populations of the Northwest Territories, the Yukon, and interior Alaska. To date, the relation of the Dogrib language to other languages of the widespread Athapaskan family has not been adequately assessed. The phonemes of Dogrib are presented by Robert Howren in the Appendix to this chapter.

Most Dogribs under twenty have English as a second language as a result of the intensified school program of the last fifteen years. In the older generations, only a few Dogribs have even moderate fluency in English.

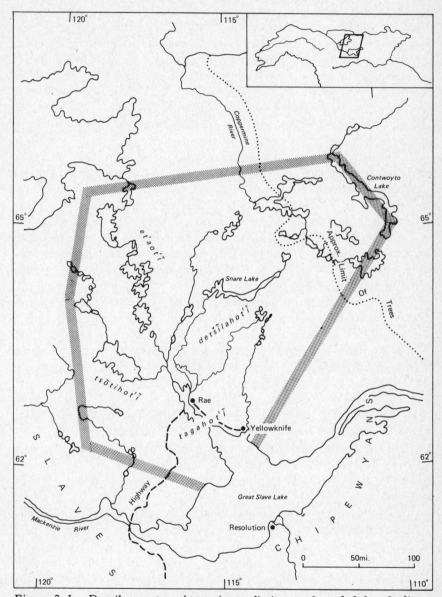

Figure 2–1. *Dogrib country. Approximate limits are bounded by shading. Regional band areas are designated by italics.*

PHYSICAL APPEARANCE

There have been no anthropometric studies of Dogrib populations.[4] Some of the more characteristically Asiatic facial features of the Dogribs are prominent cheekbones, flaring gonial angles, and, in many children, an inner epicanthic fold which tends to disappear as they grow older.

The Dogribs are a gracile people. Measured against an ethnologist standing 5 feet, 5 inches, almost all of the women are several inches shorter and many of the men are no taller, although a few attain a slim six feet.

HISTORICAL BACKGROUND

In the early 1700s, a few trade goods from the Hudson's Bay Company forts on the west side of Hudson Bay were probably reaching Dogribs through Chipewyan middlemen. The first trading expedition into Dogrib country was in 1789 when LeRoux, a clerk of the Northwest Company under Alexander Mackenzie, visited Lac La Martre (Mackenzie 1911).

For several decades, the Dogribs were under attack by an Athapaskan people of Chipewyan affinities.[5] The period of warfare ended in 1823 with the destruction of a sizable segment of these people by the Dogribs (T. Simpson 1843:318).

Until the twentieth century, Dogrib contact with Western culture was almost solely through two kinds of agents: the Hudson's Bay Company fur traders and the Oblate (Roman Catholic) fathers, the latter entering Dogrib territory in the 1860s. Fort Rae (as it was then known) became the point of trade for the Dogribs.[6] A small number of the Dogrib people were included in the treaty between indigenes and the Canadian government signed at Fort Resolution in 1899. The bulk of the Dogribs, however, did not "take treaty" until 1921. Only after the treaty was a Royal Canadian Mounted Police detachment established at Rae.

By taking treaty, these Dogribs relinquished title to the land, but were accorded access to their traditional resources of flesh and fur and the payment of $5 per head per year, plus a few items of goods, such as fishnets.

The Indians of the Northwest Territories differ from most of the Indian populations north of Mexico in that they are not on reserves. Game regulations, however, restrict their full use of the land's fauna and are much resented.

The Northwest Territories are just entering what may be termed the "government-industrial period" in the Canadian North (Helm and Leacock 1971). It is characterized by the development of extractive industries, accelerated communication and transportation facilities, and expanded government agencies and services, most of the latter revolving about the native populations. Whatever the future holds for the younger Dogribs, the ways of their parents exemplify the "fur and mission period" of the

Canadian North, when the thinly spaced trading "forts" and missions were the only significant points of acculturative press for over 100 years (Helm and Leacock 1971; Helm and Damas 1963). Only in the last twenty years have the trader and missionary begun to abdicate their preeminence to the schoolteacher and the government official.

ENVIRONMENT

The Natural Domain

Terrain and Climate Dogrib technology and exploitative techniques are adapted to the northern "bush." The bush is composed of stands of boreal forest interspersed with thousands upon thousands of lakes, streams, and swamps. The waters of the last glaciation are still draining from the land.

From the north arm of Great Slave Lake to the southeasternmost shores of Great Bear Lake extends a chain of lakes that mark a geological and forest-cover break line. To the west of the chain of lakes are the Mackenzie River lowlands. In these lowlands, glacial, alluvial, and lacustrine soils, laid down during the Cenozoic, support good-sized trees: white spruce, poplars, and birch, with black spruce and tamarack in the swamps and jack pine in the sandy soils.

The greater amount of Dogrib exploitation is east of the axis of lakes. Here lie the low hills and granite and basalt outcrops of the Precambrian Shield; the forest cover is a stunted growth and is found chiefly in alluvial flats or on well-drained river slopes. Beyond this "rock country," as the Dogribs call it, lies the barren grounds, or tundra, which Dogribs penetrate only briefly and intermittently.

This interior continental land is marked by long, cold winters and short, warm summers. Through the Dogrib country runs the mean January isotherm of -20 degrees F. The mean July isotherm cutting the region is 55 degrees F. Annual precipitation is slight, averaging only about 15 inches per year. This includes an annual mean snowfall of about 50 inches, most of it falling in early winter and not melting until spring (Kendrew and Currie 1955).

Regional Band Areas The drainage pattern of the Dogrib country is the key to human movement and exploitation and thus to the traditional regional band areas. (See Fig. 2-1.) One drainage route is that chain of lakes lying on the south-north geological axis. Brief portages carry one across the height of land that separates the southward drainage to Great Slave Lake from the northward drainage to Great Bear Lake. This is the traditional "road" of the *et'aot'ı̄*, People Next to Another People.[7]

To the southeast of these lands is the Lac La Martre country, where some of the *tsõtihot'ı̄*, Feces Lake People, still reside. They are now clustered in a hamlet of about twenty families at the southern outlet of Lac La Martre, whose waters eventually flow into Great Slave Lake. The *tagahot'i,* Follow the Shore People, exploited the lands lying on both sides of the north arm of Great Slave Lake itself. Today, besides the concentration of population from all areas in the trading fort of Rae, there are two small camp-hamlets which are occupied year round within this region. The final regional domain is that of the *detsilahot'i,* Edge of the Woods People. It extends northeast from the North Arm along river and lake routes that lead toward the barrens.[8] Along these routes Dogrib hunters of caribou (and in the past, musk oxen) sometimes push northeast as far as Contwoyto Lake, where they occasionally encounter Eskimo following the caribou herds inland.

THE SOCIOCULTURAL ENVIRONMENT

Euro-Canadian Installations The Dogrib people exploiting these four regions trade into the settlement of Rae on Marian Lake, which is separated by a narrow channel from the North Arm of Great Slave Lake. The Euro-Canadian installations at this fort, as trading settlements are known in the North, have grown from two trading posts and the Roman Catholic mission to include a mission hospital, doctor, and nursing sisters; an RCMP detachment of two men; in recent years, a game officer and an Indian Affairs officer; and an ever-expanding school complex. The lure of services at Rae—especially the post office with its monthly distribution of family allowance and old age pension checks—has in the last two decades increasingly pulled the people into residence at the fort.

In the governmental organization of Indian "bands," the "Dogrib Rae Band" represents a single political unit. The Rae Dogribs, who make up the bulk of the Dogrib people, are thus separated administratively from those Dogribs residing at Old Yellowknife Village and in the gold-mining and administrative town of Yellowknife.

Yellowknife, founded as a boom town in the mid-1930s, is 70 miles by road from Rae and has a population of 5000 persons, predominantly Euro-Canadians and recent European migrants. Yellowknife is the terminus of the single all-weather road, the Mackenzie Highway, that links the Northwest Territories with southern Canada. In 1961 Rae and Yellowknife were joined by the final segment of this road. The highway, with its thrice-weekly bus service, allows the Rae Dogribs easy access to fellow-Indians in Yellowknife, as well as to its stores, bars, and government liquor outlet.

Other Indian Populations Except where Dogrib lands impinge upon Eskimo country to the northeast in the barrens, the Dogribs are surrounded by other Athapaskan-speaking peoples: Chipewyan groups on the south side of Great Slave Lake, the Slave Indians (or Slaveys) to the west along the Mackenzie River, and the Bear Lake Indians to the north.[9] Occasionally intermarriage occurs with these Athapaskan groups.

ECONOMY AND ECOLOGY

For survival in the subarctic man requires fire, clothing, and shelter as surely as he requires food. With the advent of the European—which is the same as saying with the advent of the fur trade—came superior implements for the struggle for existence. Iron ice chisels, knives, files, axes, firearms and ammunition, and flints for fire enabled the Indian to pursue his age-old survival tasks more easily. The obtaining of these tools, however, forced a redefinition of the exploitable environment, natural and sociocultural: the fur trader was incorporated into the necessary dealings in life, and fur-bearing animals became a resource by means of which the Indian could obtain the coveted tools from the trader. Moreover, as the decades of the fur trade advanced, the Indians' "felt needs" moved beyond simply the tools for basic subsistence pursuits to desire for European food, shelter, clothing, and transportation items.

Men in their sixties recall living in caribou skin tipis in their childhood, traveling in birchbark canoes, and hunting waterfowl with bow and arrow. But, even in the early years of this century, canvas was more and more a substitute for caribou hide and birchbark, adult hunters were using guns rather than bows, and tea and tobacco were as necessary to the Indian as to the Englishman. Some Indians had also built log cabins, either at the mission and trading post site or in the area they exploited for trapping.

The hunting and trapping Dogrib of today is poised between two economies. He does not and cannot rely entirely upon money-making activities for his livelihood, nor can he gain all of life's sustenance directly from the land. To maintain his present level of living, he requires many purchased goods and foodstuffs, but he must also take much of his food and some materials for clothing and shelter from the land.

LEVEL OF LIVING

MATERIAL GOODS

A survey of major household and personal goods reveals the extent to which the level of living of the contemporary Dogribs is based on the products of Western technology.

The few families who do not own a permanent dwelling live the year round in a canvas wall tent. The permanent house is a one-room log cabin, modeled on the white man's frontier dwelling, except where in the last few years government housing has been supplied.[10] Only the squared logs that form the outer walls of the log cabin and the mud and moss for chinking are local materials. All of the finishing requires commercial products. Outbuildings may include board latrines and doghouses and small log warehouses and stages for storing goods and frozen fish.

Household furnishings are sparse by Euro-Canadian standards. Most households have a metal frame bed in addition to board bunks, and at night bedding of blankets and homemade quilts may also be laid on the floor to provide additional sleeping accommodations. In most houses, there are one or two straight chairs, a table, plates and cups, and some silver, though much eating is done with the fingers. Small trunks hold extra clothing, sewing equipment, mementos, and the like. Some families own a gramophone or battery-powered radio. All houses have clocks and religious pictures. Generally, living spaces are kept as bare as possible. Items not in immediate use are tucked away in trunks or stored in lofts. The heating unit may be a commercial tin stove or the lower third of a 45-gallon oil drum with the top replaced and used as a cooking surface. Seasoned logs for fuel are brought from the bush by raft in summer and by dogsled in winter.

Tools once made from bone, antler, and stone have been almost completely replaced by metal items. For construction and the daily maintenance needs of the household, tools in general use include axes, files, ice chisels, cross-cut saws, carpentry saws, hammers, planes, levels, and T-squares. Housewives have hand-cranked sewing machines and other sewing equipment, cooking utensils, basins and scrub boards, pails, brooms, and scrubbing brushes.

For travel and the pursuit of livelihood, all major items with the exception of snowshoes—canoes, outboard motors, dog toboggans, rifles (.22 and .30-.30s) and shotguns, traps, gill nets (in part supplied today by Indian Affairs)—are purchased ready-made or made of manufactured materials.

Except for moccasins and mitts, the same is true for clothing. Women wear commercially manufactured or homemade cloth dresses the year round, accompanied by bloomers, lisle hose, and a cardigan sweater. Men dress in long underwear, heavy cotton or woolen pants, shirts, jackets, visored caps, and cloth parkas. The parkas may be decorated by fringed and embroidered or beaded yokes made by the wife of the household. In the summer, rubbers are worn over the moccasins of native manufacture.

Although the bulk of goods used by the Dogribs of today are products of the Western world, some items are still derived from the resources of the bush. Spruce is the most versatile of the plant species. It is the main building material for cabins and stages. It is shaped and bent into snowshoe frames, drum frames, and ice-scoop frames and was formerly used for making toboggans. Wooden "needles" for making nets and boards for drying peltry are sometimes carved of spruce or birch, but thin-milled board is preferred if available. Spruce boughs are replaced every few days as flooring in the canvas wall tents, if these do not have a board floor. Spruce boughs also serve for overnight camp bedding. Many men make canoe paddles of spruce; these paddles have round shafts and thick, narrow blades, being so designed to withstand the shock of striking or pushing against boulders in the streams. Rotten spruce is required for smoking hides. Spruce is the main fuel for the woodburning stoves or the open campfire.

Birchbark is still sewn with spruce root to form a variety of containers, particularly those for carrying and storing berries. The birchbark canoe has been abandoned for almost half a century. Bowls and spoons were once carved from birchwood, but these have long been replaced by commercially manufactured utensils.

Today willow is seldom used, except for the hoop on which the beaver pelt is stretched. The most important uses of willow in former times were for bows and for twisted fishnet cordage made from willow bast.

Caribou and moose are the source of hides for footgear and mitts. The usefulness of the hide mitt and of the hide moccasin (in its variant forms of ankle-wrap and slipper styles, and as the boot or "mukluk") remains undiminished. The process of hide preparation is lengthy and toilsome for the women. Hides must be dehaired, fleshed (bone fleshers are still used), soaked and scraped (usually done three times for moosehide), and finally smoked, which keeps the suedelike leather flexible through repeated wettings.

Although sometimes commercial twine is used, the sinew from the back of the caribou is preferred for sewing leather. Caribou rawhide is required for drum heads and for the netting of the snowshoe. Its many uses as lashings have largely been superseded by manufactured products.

Dressed, furred hides are used today only for the furred caribou parka, which not all men possess, and for furred caribou-hide bags. (Although the latter are considered superior storage bags for drymeat, the housewife of today mostly uses cardboard boxes or flour sacks.) Strips of unprepared beaver and wolverine fur decorate slipper moccasins, mukluks, mitts, and parkas. The netting of furred-hare cordage to make blankets and undergarments has been abandoned. Hare skins formerly served, as did sphagnum moss, for packing in the moccasin; these have been replaced by wool socks or duffel (blanket) boot packs.

Commercial Food

In the bush camp or hamlet, a relatively small proportion of the diet consists of commercial food. The common ones are tea, sugar, salt, oatmeal, rice, bannock bread made of flour, lard, and baking powder, and canned or powdered milk for infants. These foods (except tea) can be, and often are, foregone at intervals between trips to the fort.

Extended fort living requires that these items become true staples of diet, as sufficient wild-flesh foods cannot be obtained. The two stores at Rae provide a variety of canned goods, breads, frozen commercial meat, and storable fresh vegetables to those who can afford them.

Income

The foregoing accounts give some idea of the extent to which the present-day Dogribs are committed to the consumption of commercially manufactured products and thereby to the money-and-market economy of the Western world. Increasing federal aid and services give a partial, though inadequate, financial floor to the economy of the Dogrib household. The Canadian family allowance provides $6 to $8 per month for each child (to the age of sixteen) in residence with his parents. Widow's and old-age assistance and tubercular's allowance, as well as other welfare aid, also provide direct or indirect income for some households. Occasional wage labor, usually in the summer, for such work as the clearing of bush for roads and power lines is a welcome but unpredictable financial boon for a few families. For many families, the "baby bonus" may provide one fourth to one half of the total annual income; fur trapping provides the rest. A successful trapper with four young children is (by crude estimate) unlikely to have more than $800 to $1000 in annual income, unless he has the rare windfall of a wage-labor job for a month or more. About eighteen full-time jobs were held by Dogribs (twelve by men and six by women) in Rae in the fall of 1967.[11]

It must be emphasized that fur trapping is the predominant source of *earned* income in the Dogrib community. And, like subsistence hunting and fishing, fur trapping is a direct exploitative operation upon the resources of the land. In fact, the taking of furs for the market and direct subsistence activities interdigitate in the daily and seasonal exploitative cycle.

It is, then, animal life that provides, through direct consumption or through sale in the market, most of life's necessities for the contemporary Dogrib. The interweaving of exploitative activities around fur and food resources are best seen by following the Dogrib in his yearly round. But, first, there follows a survey of the species involved in the total economy of the Dogrib.

BIOTAL RESOURCES

ANIMAL RESOURCES FOR INCOME

Beaver, mink, and marten bring the best prices. Colored foxes (*Vulpes fulva*) and lynx are common in the area, but their price has been low in recent years.[12] Weasel (ermine) and squirrel bring even less. Of the cheap furs, muskrat can be taken in large numbers (two to three hundred pelts in a season for a good hunter) in portions of the Dogrib country. Otter is one of the better-priced furs, but is not taken in much quantity. Wolverine is valued locally for trim on parkas, as it does not frost from the breath. Wolf is seldom trapped.

Fur prices fluctuate markedly, both within the trapping season and through the years. The last great fur boom was during World War II. Since then, the total picture has been one of a ragged decline in prices. For example, "blanket beaver"—that is, largest and finest grade—brought about $50 a pelt in 1944, $30 in the spring of 1959, and $10 to $7 in the spring of 1967. In 1951, top-quality muskrat brought $2 a pelt; it brought about 75 cents a pelt in the spring of 1967. Indians have excellent recall of past fur prices and are painfully aware that the same amount of toil on the trapline may from one year to another yield the same amount of furs, but perhaps one half the monetary return.

The heyday of trade for the Dogrib was in the last decades of the nineteenth century. In that era, the Dogribs were uniquely situated to exploit, for trade, the great herds of caribou and musk oxen. Dogrib hunters, equipped with firearms, supplied bale upon bale of caribou dry-meat to the Hudson's Bay post at Fort Rae. This meat was used to provision other trading posts the length of the Mackenzie River. The heavy kill of barren grounds caribou in that period by Dogribs, other native populations, and Europeans initiated the decline of the caribou population. Today, their survival as a self-sustaining population is in doubt (Banfield 1957).

So, also, for a generation or more, the Dogrib profited from the trade in musk ox robes to the Hudson's Bay Company. The unparalleled slaughter of these animals, defenseless against the rifle, reduced the herds to a few remnants far in the barrens, and the trade was halted about 1915. To the young men, the musk ox is only a memory of their grandfathers; they have never seen one.

FOOD RESOURCES

Viewed from the perspective of the hunting-gathering cultures which occupy the warm zones of the world, a striking feature of Dogrib subsistence ecology is the remarkably few species exploited.

The indigenous plant foods of the Dogrib are limited to about ten species of edible berries.[13] Only blueberries and cranberries are consumed in any quantity. For most families this means, at best, a few quarts per year. Berries are available only during the month of August, with the exception of the cranberry, which stays on the bushes into the fall. Their restricted availability negates the food value of berries in the Dogrib diet.

Life for the Dogrib has depended upon the flesh of animals. The flesh foods are comprised of nine species of fish, four species of small mammal, four species of large mammal, and about sixteen species of birds identified as edible by informants. Birds, mainly ducks, grouse, and ptarmigan, are but a supplement to the diet. The Indians rely upon the combination or alternation of fish with the flesh of three main mammals: snowshoe or varying hare, moose, and barren ground caribou.

The fish species are the whitefish, the lake trout (salmon trout), the great northern pike, the loche (burbot), two species of suckers, the pickerel, the inconnu ("connie," *Stenodus leucichthys*), and the Arctic grayling. Not all species are found in all waters. Whitefish, trout, pike, pickerel, and suckers are most widely distributed through the waters and are taken in the greatest quantities.

Of the four small mammals eaten by Dogribs, porcupine is enjoyed, but is taken only occasionally. Muskrat is eaten during the spring "ratting" season, but probably was seldom eaten aboriginally. Beaver meat is prized when fat, but, like muskrats, beavers are today taken only in conjunction with the fur quest. (Squirrel is eaten only "when we are really starving".)

The varying hare, locally called rabbit, is the important small food mammal. The hare population, however, not only varies in the quality of the fat and flesh by season but rises and falls in roughly a ten-year cycle. The Dogribs are aware that the hare disappear and then "come back," but apparently do not recognize the regularity of the cycle.

> When there are no rabbits, the people say, "No rabbits, funny!" And then a man from Hislop Lake comes in and a man from Rae Lake and another from Lac La Martre, and they all start to say the same thing: "The rabbits are coming back." So we hear the news from all over. And that's the truth. When the rabbits come back, it is like thunder hits the ground, there is a big noise. . . . And when you tell the old people, "I heard the sound of the rabbits drop," they say, "Thanks, thanks, thanks, the rabbits are coming back!"

Of the large food mammals, black bear is only an occasional kill, and the woodland caribou are limited to the southwesternmost section of the Dogrib country. The moose and, even more, the barren land caribou, are the two game animals of great importance in the Dogrib subsistence economy. The markedly different life patterns of these Cervidae carry different implications for Dogrib ecology. The moose is a solitary, non-migratory forest animal. The barren ground caribou migrate in great and smaller herds seasonally from the calving grounds in the tundra near the Arctic coast into and through the Dogrib country and back to the coast again in the course of each year. The movements of the caribou affect the movements of the Dogrib hunters, and, in former days especially, the great herds encouraged concentration and coordination of the human population.[14]

Of all the Indian peoples north of Great Slave Lake, the Dogrib are the most strongly committed to the exploitation of the caribou. In the ten-year period from 1943 to 1952, the Fort Rae Dogribs killed 53,595 caribou, averaging 36.7 caribou per hunter per year (Kelsall 1957:96, 97, 99).

In former days, the great "Rae herd" of caribou yearly crossed the North Arm of Great Slave Lake by the thousands in early winter. Today, should a sizable number of caribou appear anywhere in Dogrib country word is quickly sent to other Indians. In March 1966, word came to Rae that the caribou were passing near Hardisty Lake (perhaps 150 land miles north of Rae). About a dozen hunters left the fort by dogteam; they killed over 100 caribou. The government arranged transport of the carcasses by winter truck road back to Rae, where the meat was stored for the people in the government-operated freezer.

THE YEARLY ROUND

SUMMER

By the first of July, summer, in Indian terms, has truly arrived. The waters are clear of ice and only a few sheltered crevices in the land hold snow. The July days are warm, the thermometer not uncommonly going over 80 degrees F. Although the summer solstice has passed, night is no more than a twilight interlude between the long hours of sunshine. Treaty has just been paid at Rae, so most of the Dogribs are assembled in the fort.

Most of the Indian families remain in Rae throughout July. More often in recent years, there has been construction work or other wage labor available for a minority of the men, and those called must respond to the draft to fight the forest fires brought on by the hot, dry weather. For most families, however, it is a lean time. The income from the spring beaver and muskrat hunt is gone, and there is little food in the land.

The fish catch begins to decline about the first of July as the fish seek the deeper, colder water of the lake. Fish are taken by the stationary gill net, into which the fish swim and are entrapped by their gills. The standard net used today is 150 feet long and 8 feet deep, with a 4-inch mesh.[15] With weights and floats attached, the net is extended between poles driven into the bottom of the lake or stream. Fishing is considered good when the net yields thirty or more fish per day. Some families own more than one net.

Fish taken in excess of daily needs must, in warm weather, be quickly converted to dryfish. A dryfish is prepared by a set of ingenious slashes on the body of the fish so that head, spine, ribs, and entrails are removed and the flesh is opened out into a single broad, thin slab.[16] These splayed fish are then draped over horizontal poles, flesh side up the first day and skin side up the second. With sunny weather and perhaps some auxiliary smoking, two days suffice to produce a condition of preservation that will last many months. Bundles of dryfish are then hung on top of high poles out of the reach of dogs. The dryfish preparation is women's work. Each fish takes a little under ten minutes to prepare: preparing a catch of thirty fish, therefore, consumes about four hours of a woman's work day. The residue of dryfish preparation (entrails, heads, and so on) is fed to the dogs.

The furred caribou robe has been cured and is ready to be used in making a winter parka.

At the "free trader's" store in Rae.

Tenting at Rae during Treaty Time. Dryfish hang from the horizontal pole.

Frozen fish in storage stage, November, Lac La Martre.

Ice fishing.

Starting out on the trap line from Lac La Martre hamlet.

Carrying the baby in the shawl.

Dogrib hand game, summer 1962. Each player holds a hidden object in one fist. Moving in rhythm to the drums, the men await the guess of the captain of the opposing team.

Families who have canoes and nets continue to tend their nets daily, during July. Besides food for the human members of the household, the five or six dogs of the team must be fed. At this season the dogs are not working and are continually staked. They are fed lightly, one two-pound fish each per day if the family is fortunate in its catch. Otherwise, dryfish put up in June or earlier is brought out of reserve to feed the animals; this supply is often exhausted by the first of August. As the fish continue to "get poorer," more and more Indian families begin "bumming" fish from their kinsmen and neighbors. For these folk it is hand to mouth, and their dogs are starving.

Rabbits are not plentiful in this season, especially around the fort. Some of the old people and the widows set snares, but at best will get but three or four hare a day, and those young ones. There are few ducks all summer, and, although current game conventions declare waterfowl out of season, men take ducks when beyond earshot of the fort. Duck hunting is often carried out while visiting the fishnets. A man is always alert for sight or sign of moose. Moose hunting is done along the waterways rather than overland in this season, because men are usually traveling by canoe and also because moose, plagued by mosquitoes, are likely to be half submerged in the small lakes. The Indians say that this time of year is good for moose hunting, as they are easily approached. Moose are nonmigratory, so the population is stable year round, but in recent years moose have not been plentiful around the fort. Should any caribou or moose hides be left unprepared from spring, or any fresh moose hides taken, the housewife must be prepared to begin work on them at once, because the hot weather causes them to rot quickly.

Families begin to leave the fort by the end of July, either dispersing temporarily to fishing stations or returning to the region that is their home base for winter hunting and trapping.

August is "berries ripening month."[17] Women and children form picnic excursions for berrying. Usually they travel to the berry patches by canoe, accompanied by a youth to run the "kicker" (outboard motor). He also serves as protection against *nahgā*, the mythical bush prowlers who roam the forest in the summer and kidnap women and children.

Two important subsistence activities begin about the middle of August, as fall approaches. "In August, we eat mostly fish": a two-week run of fish allows the people once again to rely on fish for their daily food. The prime excitement in August, however, is the fall caribou hunt.

FALL

In August, the barren ground caribou approach the tree line, coming in small bands from their summer pasturage in the tundra. Dogrib hunters head for the edge of the woods to arrive in the barrens about the 18th or 20th of August. They are eager to meet the caribou as soon as possible, because only on the August skins is the hair right, "not too thick and not too light," for making furred caribou parkas. Hunters travel in several "crews." A crew may consist of ten or twelve men in two or three canoes or five or six men in a single canoe. There are two alternate water routes leading to Snare Lake and another that follows the Emile River. These routes take the hunters northeast from Rae to the edge of the trees along the lakes feeding the Coppermine River.[18] Crews going the same route travel together until they approach the hunting grounds.

The journey to the hunting grounds involves many portages, which the men cross at a fast dogtrot, carrying canoes, outboard motors, gas, and other supplies. Each portage usually requires a couple of trips by most of the men to get all the gear across. Dogribs take pride in being "good travelers," starting early, traveling long and fast, sleeping little. The Snare River–Snare Lake route to the hunting grounds has 47 portages and is over 100 air miles from Rae, probably almost 200 overland. It is sometimes covered in five days, all upstream.

Each crew has a *k'awo*, or "boss." While a set of crews are together, one *k'awo* is in charge of all. A *k'awo* decides when to camp and travel and, once caribou are encountered, determines the directions in which small parties of two and three hunters fan out.

> When a bunch goes on a caribou hunt, they work just like they are own brothers. If one man is short [of supplies], they help one another until they get back. They don't charge nothing. And if some poor man is too loaded [on the portages], the *k'awo* is going to tell them, "He's pitiful. He's a poor man to work, so you might as well give him a hand."

A successful hunter may be directed by the *k'awo* to hunt with a man who has killed little. If one group of hunters encounters many caribou, word is carried to the *k'awo*, who in turn sends word to the other scattered groups.

Once enough caribou have been killed, or the season has advanced, the *k'awo* directs the groups of men to spread out in various small bays and creeks where there are sufficient stands of willow to make drymeat. By reducing the water content, much more meat can be transported home. Drymeat is made by slicing chunks of flesh into thin slabs. The slabs are then hung over poles and turned every hour. A smoldering fire of willows and moss under the meat hastens the drying process and drives off flies. From a successful hunt each man takes home a "bale" of drymeat as heavy as he can carry, a "bale" of skins, and perhaps some marrow encased in a sewn birchbark box.

The fall caribou hunt lasts but three or four weeks. The Dogrib hunters hurry back to their families awaiting them at the fort or in fishing camps.

It is now September, and if the men delay at the edge of the woods they may get caught in the early freeze-up there. The drymeat brought home by the hunter lasts only a few days, for custom calls for the hunter to serve cooked meat in his home to those who come and to give away portions.

In September, living is good. The hare begin to turn white and are easily seen against the ground, to be dispatched with a .22. September is also the month that the moose breed. This means good hunting, for the rutting bulls respond to the lure of the moose scapula scraped against a tree.

September's major activity is fishing. The Dogrib term for this period is "hanging up fish month." After the two-week fish run in August, the fish supply drops down to four or five a day per net until about the 10th or 15th of September, when "the fish come back again and run pretty near till Christmas." By now the weather is cold enough that fish for dog feed need not be dried. The fish are simply strung through the tails or gills onto a slim pole. The people reckon in terms of "sticks" of fish. There are ordinarily ten fish to a stick, unless, as at Lac La Martre, the fish are so large that the pole will support only six. These poles with their pendant fish are hung rack fashion from a stage made of logs. About 1000 ordinary-sized fish (two to three pounds each) are needed to feed a dog team for three months.

Freeze-up   Nets must be taken up just before freeze-up, or they will be lost. Ice usually starts to form the first week of October. Within a week lakes may change from open water to ice thick enough to support men and dog teams. Running streams and rivers, however, remain open longer, and even after ice covers the streams, overflow onto the ice, hazardous to dog teams, continues through most of November.

As soon as the ice is thick enough to walk on, nets are set under the ice. The operation requires sending a cord under the ice the length of the net and then using it to pull the net, complete with weights and floats, under the ice. The cord is attached to a long pole which is guided and shoved along through holes chopped in the ice at intervals almost the pole's length apart. At this season, the ice is thin and clear enough that the progress of the pole can be seen.

Once set, the net is usually tended every day. The ice chisel is used to break through the fresh ice at the holes at either end of the net. With the ice scoop, a raquetlike device, the chopped ice is cleared from the hole. The net is then drawn out and the fish removed. They freeze quickly upon reaching the air. To reset the net, the cord attached at the opposite end is pulled, drawing the net back to its original hanging position under the ice.

The ptarmigan turn white with the first snows of October and, migrating from the barren grounds, cross the North Arm of Great Slave Lake by the thousands to spend the winter in the thick bush to the west. Hunters take them with shotguns, if they own them, or .22s. Nets can also be rigged for ptarmigan at this season. Now, also, every household sets rabbit snares. The ten-year cycle permitting, rabbits are in fair supply until the deep cold of January.

After freeze-up, life begins again for the dogs. Their ration goes up to two fish per day as they start their working season. They greet any sign that they are to be taken from their chains and put in the traces with joyous yelps. Five or six dogs is the usual complement of the team. In the forested terrain and deep snow of Dogrib country, the tandem hitch, one dog behind another, is used to draw the runnerless "sleigh," or toboggan. (Aboriginally, the toboggan was drawn by hand; dog traction is a post-contact introduction.) The long, slim toboggan is surmounted by a cariole, a long, baglike arrangement, open at the top, in which goods are carried or a person may ride.

Winter

The trapping season opens November 1. November and December are the best trapping months: it is not too cold or dark for men to travel easily, and the fur animals also are "traveling" (that is, more in evidence and easier to take). Mink, marten, fox, otter, and lynx are trapped in this season.

> The more traps, the more better. If you got 40 or 50 traps, you can't go far. If you have 80 or 100 you can make a long trip. You do not get fur in every trap. If you use 80 traps you might get 10 or 12 furs.

The Dogrib trapper tends to follow the same route or set of routes year after year, becoming familiar with those locales where different kinds of fur are likely to be found.[19] By December, the snow is soft and deep in the bush. Winter trails follow lakes. Where they cross the land, they become ruts of packed snow from the passage of toboggans. Off the trail, snowshoes must be used. The narrow snowshoes, with up-turned toes, are made in roughly three sizes. The 'atšo ("big snowshoe"), such as used for moose hunting, may be almost five feet long. A man usually has at least a smaller and a larger pair of snowshoes and selects among them according to the nature of the snow and the task.

To tend a trapline alone is an unnecessary hardship. Men customarily go in groups of two or three. They can thus spell one another in camp chores and hunting. Four or more men trapping together would require too much country to cover for an adequate yield of fur. The partners set their traps, usually in alternation, wherever there is "sign" of fur. Men own perhaps two or three sizes of traps. Number 1½ size is useful for most animals from fox to muskrats. Various baits are known to be effective for the different animals. Deadfalls are usually used for wolverine, and sometimes for marten.

The men are continually alert for rabbits, shooting them while on the trail. If there is "sign" of large game, usually moose in this season, one man follows the sign on snowshoes, perhaps carrying a few traps with him. His dogs go on ahead with the other men, the partners agreeing where the hunter is to seek the night's camp.

Although men owning few traps would ordinarily not go as far as others, the time spent and the distance covered on each trapline trip is governed primarily by the amount of food for men and dogs. Besides their bedrolls and other gear, men must start out carrying some food for themselves and some fish or commercial dog feed for the team. Twenty-five pounds of dog feed, costing $6 to $8, lasts four or five days for six dogs. Nowadays, because of low fur prices, the traders grant little credit to trappers going out in the fall. As a result, the Indians say, many trappers based in the fort cannot go far, because they do not have enough "groceries" to keep them on the line.[20] In such a case, the trapper hopes to take enough fur quickly to be able to purchase supplies for a longer trip. One man with equipment and money for supplies may offer to share with one who cannot outfit himself.

After Christmas the hardest times of the year are upon the people.

In January and February the people are just trying to save their lives. They can't do much. They just try to get some food, that's all. The trappers are still after marten, mink, and fox, but the fur doesn't travel much in the cold.

The fish are not "traveling" either. They have retreated to the deepest portions of the lakes, often beyond the reach of nets. Also, lake ice by now may be over three feet thick, and it refreezes so quickly and solidly that it is almost impossible to clear holes daily with the ice chisel. Hunting and fishing are cruel work in this season, when temperatures may drop to minus 50 degrees F.

When it is real cold you cannot get close to caribou. The sound comes from a long distance. By the time you get close, the caribou are running away. It is the same thing with moose.

The people await the lengthening, warming days of March, when the fish and fur animals "start to travel again." By the middle of March the people get perhaps fifteen, twenty, or twenty-five fish in a net each day. The caribou are moving toward the barrens, following the lakes.[21]

Spring

Known of old as snow-blindness month, April is now called Easter
month. Families that have been wintering in a bush camp return to the
fort for the Easter celebrations of the church and for Indian festivities.
By the middle of April, the caribou have returned to the barrens. It is
nearing the time for the spring beaver and muskrat hunt. The snow begins
to melt toward the end of April. Men planning an extended beaver hunt
will usually start about that time, traveling by dog team and toboggan.
(In a good fur year, a group of men sometimes charter a ski plane.) It is
feasible for a larger group of men to go together on the spring fur hunt;
often a group numbers four or more. Men may travel 100 miles to reach
good beaver grounds; by the time they arrive it may be near the middle of
May.

Break-up May is "following open water month." The ice is clearing
from the smaller streams and bays. The men far in the bush on the spring
beaver hunt now abandon their toboggans. If the terrain or distance is
such that the dogs cannot follow the canoes, the hunters may kill their
dogs (in which case they will have taken only their "poor" dogs). The
hunters build small canoes from the canvas, paint, and nails they have
carried with them by toboggan, using local spruce wood for the framing.
The hunt is usually carried out by shooting the "rats" and beavers from
the canoe, with one man paddling, the other shooting. The kill is divided
evenly. If it is late spring, and therefore there is not much open water,
traps must be set through holes chopped in the ice. This method is not
favored, as it is a hard job. In a good season, a man may take at least two
or three dozen beaver and 200 or more "rats."

The spring fur hunt, when for weeks the men are without shelter and
are traveling amid the melting snows, is often cold, miserable work. The
men may have to depend upon beaver and muskrat flesh for food, unless
they are fortunate enough to kill a moose. The fishing is good in May, and
if the men on the hunt are not traveling too fast, they set nets.

Once break-up is really completed, that is, all the waterways leading
home are open, the men return from the spring hunt. The last usually
arrive in the fort with their furs by the middle of June; by this time the
days are approaching their greatest length and the mild nights have begun.
Trappers whose wives have been in bush camps bring their families to the
fort. Only a couple of permanent bush hamlets maintain their population
at this season. Everyone else is in-gathering for treaty. A brief run of fish
in the last half of June enables the people in the fort to hold their own
into July, when once again the fish catch starts to drop.

THE SOCIAL ORDER

Dogrib social organization is without cults, sodalities, or clans. Social identities derive from bilateral kin reckoning and spatial-territorial locus. To distinguish kin-based groups from spatial-territorial groups is a matter of contrastive emphasis rather than of opposable categories.

KINSMEN AND KIN BEHAVIOR

Dogrib kin reckoning strikes a familiar chord in a Euro-American. A Dogrib's "relations" (*sehot'ī*, "my people") embrace a rather flexible range of consanguines, reckoned bilaterally from Ego and the spouses of those consanguines.

Primary relatives—one's parents, siblings, spouse, and children—ordinarily command continuing allegiance and concern throughout one's life. There are, however, no "rules" as to which sorts of relatives the adult male, notably, must work with or by. There is no inheritable title to status or to possessions—territorial, material, or ritual—to bind the individual to any form of family line.[22]

"The young kids growing up now, going away to school, are different than before," but some older Dogribs still observe traditional manners and modes of behavior between kinsmen.[23] There are no avoidance rules in Dogrib society, but a man should practice reserve toward his sister and her husband. A man and his sister should not look directly into one another's face. A man who wishes to express his pleasure upon a reunion with his sister may joke with others in her presence, to make her laugh, but without looking at her. A man should not joke directly with his brother-in-law or allude to sexual matters in his presence.

The traditional reserve between sister's husband and wife's brother does not prevent these affines from living in the same domestic unit and frequently working together. One Dogrib explains a preference for trapping with one's brother-in-law:

> With your dad, you kill yourself to do all the work. Going with your older brother is just like going with your dad. He won't work hard. He expects you (as the younger brother) to do most of the work. So you don't take your own brother very often (as a work partner). You take your brother-in-law most of the time. Brothers-in-law do the work just the same (that is, they share the labor equally).

As with his brother-in-law, a man feels somewhat "shy" in the presence of his father-in-law. Furthermore, the father-in-law has the same right to command the energies of a young man that his father and older brother have.

Young persons are expected to be obedient and helpful toward older persons, including, of course, their own parents. With the grandparents, however, or any elderly person, the relationship is one of easy affection. So also with aunts and uncles. Similarly, a man is "not shy" with his sisters-in-law (WZ or BW) or with cousins of either sex.

MARRIAGE

In the pre-Christian past, polygyny was permitted, but probably only a handful of superior providers had multiple wives. In those days, also, wives might change hands through wrestling contests or gambling. Today the marriage bond is sealed by the Roman Catholic ceremony and is enduring. No Dogrib has had recourse to legal divorce, and desertion is rare.

The conservative ideal is that a young man should seek in marriage a hard-working girl who stays home and does not chase after boys. The youth should prove his capacity for hard work by serving for his prospective bride—daily bringing water and firewood for his future mother-in-law and hunting and trapping under the direction of his father-in-law. A young man and woman should not marry without parental approval, which is largely contingent upon parents' mutual regard for the working standards of each young person and that person's family. But, here, too, "the young kids growing up now . . . are different than before."

In pre-Christian days, courtship (occurring as the bride service mentioned above) apparently usually involved the assumption of sexual relations, thus merging into a *de facto* marriage relationship.[24] Marriages today are not uncommonly precipitated by the girl's pregnancy. The older generation decries the loose morals of today's young people—"too many babies without fathers"—but premarital and even extramarital sexual relations bring no harsher sanctions than gossip and "tut-tutting."

THE NUCLEAR FAMILY AND THE DOMESTIC GROUP

If for several generations now marriage has been a lifetime matter, life often has been short. Many persons today who are sixty years of age have lost one or more spouses through death. Remarriage expands the sibling bond within the nuclear family to half- and step-siblings. A couple burdened with many children, especially if one of the parents is in the hospital, is apt to "give" a child to another conjugal pair for an indeterminate or permanent period. The adopting pair is often the grandparents or aunt and uncle of the child.

Temperament and compatibility factors being equal, Dogribs regard stepparents, stepchildren, adopted children, and half- or step-siblings as they do their "own." Effectively, the "family" thus includes step- and half-relationships, as well as adoptive ones.

The domestic unit, the household, is the daily food-producing and sharing unit. It is often composed of a single nuclear family—a conjugal pair and their unmarried children. This is not to say that the household may not include aged dependents, unmarried siblings of the conjugal pair, or a married offspring with his or her spouse. Also, the mobility of the people frequently brings related nuclear families into relatively temporary co-residence in one dwelling.

CHILD CARE AND TRAINING WITHIN THE DOMESTIC GROUP

The domestic group provides the child with basic physical care and the model of the adult male or female role that is to be his or her own. There is little explicit training of children in work tasks. The child is simply expected and encouraged to assume tasks as his or her physical development permits.

Babies are the household pets. They are fed, cuddled, and comforted whenever they cry. Not only the mother and the older female siblings give the baby much attention. Adult and juvenile males express their affection for infants in kissing and fondling.

Weaning is apt to be abrupt only upon the arrival of a new baby. Nursing bottles have been in use for a few decades now and are frequently used to supplement the breast. In the recent past infants were laced into a soft bag padded with sphagnum moss. Nowadays babies are heavily swaddled in blankets and carried as little packages in the shawl on their mother's back.

In families where babies come at frequent intervals, the toddler is rudely supplanted as the center of household affection and attention when the next baby appears. Supervision of the toddler passes to the older sister.

Both boys and girls are called on to bring water, saw wood, and help with other household maintenance tasks. The boys spend much of their day ranging over the camp or village. As girls are more likely to be near home, they often get assigned the chore at hand.

Boys who attend school are not initiated into trapping and hunting as early and as fully as before. However, a father is likely to take his preteen son on short trips, where he learns the routines of bush life. By the age of twelve he has probably had experience in most of the adult male pursuits: setting and tending nets, traps and snares, hunting small game with a .22, harnessing dogs, making camp.

Dogrib culture never formally acknowledged the entry of the male into puberty. Sexual contact with girls was proscribed, and even casual interaction discouraged in order to guard the youth's hunting powers. After marriage, sexuality is no longer a threat.

Menstrual blood menaces children's health and men's hunting capacity. Women are not to move about much or approach men's gear during menstruation. Conservative families continue to isolate their daughters upon the menarche for the period of the menstruation. The girl is put in a shelter apart from the camp or village and is attended only by her mother. She is to keep busy at tasks in this interval, the rationale being that she thereby learns to be a hard worker.

Socio-Territorial Groups[25]

Four general sorts of Dogrib socio-territorial groups may be distinguished analytically: the task group, the local band, the regional band, and the people or tribe.

Varieties of task groups were described in the section on the yearly round. The task group is of brief duration and is explicitly created for exploitative activities. It is sometimes composed of households (for example, a multifamily fishing camp), sometimes of persons of a single sex (for example, a men's hunting party). At the other extreme the Dogribs (*tłįtšõ*) as a people or "tribe" exhibit the greatest duration, and recruitment, in the sense of a conscious decision to affiliate, is at a minimum. One joins a task group temporarily; one is born into, and ordinarily remains a member of, the tribe.

Sometimes a small group of related nuclear families, usually focused around a dominant set of siblings, endures for a few or many years as a community body resident in one settlement or, formerly, in a series of relatively compacted camp areas. Such a local group, or local band, may comprise as few as two or three conjugal pairs and their children.

The regional band has tribelike characteristics. Enduring generation after generation, it "recruits" much of its personnel through birth. The four regional bands of the Rae Dogrib were specified in an earlier section. Some of the constituent members of the regional band may be spatially and socially oriented into a local group. But the total constituency of the regional band is larger (dozens of nuclear families) than a local band, and it lacks continual nucleation of settlement. The region and the regional band are defined in terms of the "road" (the main routes) of summer and winter movement. The regional band's territory thus has an axis rather than boundaries or edges. Moreover, there is no sense of the territory as a band "holding." It "belongs" to no group; any group is free to use its resources.[26]

Traditionally, from the patterns of human ecology that the region imposed upon the Indians exploiting it, the region and its people were socially defined. To some extent today, but more so in the past, as part of the region and the regional band, task groups and local bands camp regularly or settle at certain locales. At any moment in time, any individual —let us call him Joe Dene—can be placed by any knowledgeable Dogrib in several socio-territorial identities. As a member of one of several households currently hunting muskrats at the locale *kwekateli*, Joe and that task group are *kwekatelihot'i* (Water over Rocks Place People) on the basis of their temporary residence at that site. Since Joe has a cabin in a local-group hamlet on Snare Lake, he will, in appropriate context, be identified as one of the *ts'ikakogolahot'i* (House Place at Ghost Channel People). He is equally *detsilahot'i*, or Edge of the Woods Man, thereby specifying his regional identity. He is, of course, also *tłitsŏ*, a Dogrib. Joe Dene's multiple territorial-group identities demonstrate how misleading a simplistic definition of "*the* Dogrib band" must be.

Dogrib bands or communities, of whatever sort, are neither exogamous nor endogamous. Propinquity and convenience encourage marrying in. Too close consanguinity between many community members encourages the seeking of a mate from beyond the group. After marriage, the residence choice of the conjugal pair is essentially bilocal, and the decision is not necessarily permanent. The relative dominance, solidarity, and energy of the husband's versus wife's set of male siblings and/or father seem to be important factors affecting decisions of the pair.

The Dogrib People and Polity

The language of the Dogribs, the marriage universe that encompasses the people in a web of kinship, and the free access to all the Dogrib domain regardless of regional identities buttress the sense of being a single people.[27] Moreover, within the span of memory culture, the Dogrib people have had the germ of polity in their recognition of a prime leader of all the Dogribs among a set of lesser leaders.

We have already met the *k'awo* in the form of the "boss" of the fall caribou hunt. *K'awo* is a generic term applicable to any man enacting a leader role. It is specifically applied to the temporary traveling or hunting "boss" selected by group consensus, and to an executive officer, either temporary or "permanent," appointed by chief or headman to organize and direct group events. The chief or regional band leader in his total capacity may also be called *k'awo* (Helm 1965b).

The Canadian government recognizes and treats with—but accords no powers to—a set of leader representatives, who derive directly from the indigenous leadership pattern operative before and at the advent of treaty. The seven "councillors" (*gwatia*, "little chiefs") of the Rae Dogrib are the direct successors of men recognized as regional or subregional band leaders before treaty. The present chief Jimmy Bruneau (*gwati*, or *gwatinde*, "big chief") succeeds from Mohwi, "the headest man of all" among the Dogribs for many years, before and after the signing of treaty, and from Mohwi's predecessor, Ekawi Jimmy (the father of the present Chief Bruneau). The chief is the head of *all* the Dogribs, and, in that capacity, is beyond a regional identity. As one Dogrib puts it, "The chief is for the whole band (people); he's not really on one road."

The "authority" of the councillors and head chief rests solely in the respect and deference granted by their followers. A councillor can be thrown out upon the consensual decision of his people, as could the

regional headman (*denegak'awo*) of pre-treaty times. The selection of his
successor proceeds in the same manner—by the achievement of consensus
by the responsible males of his group.

The councillors and the chief are men over fifty years of age (in 1967),
monolingual "bush Indians," respected and chosen on the basis of character and of being hard workers and "good talkers." Their roles have
undergone continuing frustration and attenuation since the signing of
treaty. The leader whose moral authority once embodied group discipline
and morale, whose word brought supplies from the trader, who sent the
young hunters to kill caribou for all to share is now called on by his
followers to extract "welfare" from the government. "My people come to
me for help, and I have nothing to give them but my fingernails," says
the oldest councillor.

Treaty Time

The official events of treaty time include a public meeting of representatives of Indian Affairs and other branches of the Canadian government
with the chief and councillors and an Indian audience. After what are
often mutually unsatisfactory exchanges regarding government regulations
and Indian needs and complaints, treaty is paid. Each man, woman, and
child registered on the band role receives five dollars. The councillors
receive fifteen. After treaty payment, most of the Indians line up for X-ray.
Inoculations are also often given to children at this time.

After transactions between Indians and government are over at Rae,
Indian-organized festivities follow. The feast, which may occur that same
evening or within a day or two, is the first event. The chief's *k'awo* visits
the two trading establishments, soliciting contributions of food for the
feast. Men have been dispatched by the *k'awo* to gather firewood for
cooking, and the food and firewood are distributed to various households
where the women begin their work. Several tents are joined together to
make one large shelter for the feasters.[28] When all is ready, a rifle is fired
to notify the people that the feast is to begin. Each person brings his
own eating utensils. The people seat themselves upon the tarp-covered
ground, closely packed side by side under the shelter and around it. The
men locate centrally and the women and children on the outskirts.
More than 250 people may be served by the several dozen men who make
up the serving crew. A speech by the chief and by the eldest councillor and
prayers precede the feasting.

The feast is followed by a "tea dance." The people join in a dancing
circle, facing inward. They accompany their side steps with melodious,
pulsating songs. The dance sometimes continues until five or six o'clock in
the morning. In ensuing days there may be more sessions of dancing as
well as of the hand game. The hand game is a hidden-object guessing
game played to the accompaniment of vigorous drum beats and chanting.
Traditionally, the men of regional bands contested against one another in

the hand game, and when in contact with alien groups, the Dogribs formed a team against other tribes. Feasting, dances, and hand games are also features of the ingatherings at Christmastime and at Easter. Along with treaty time, these are also the occasions when multiple weddings of several couples occur.

One hears the echo of Durkheimian precepts as thoughtful Dogribs struggle to express the ethnic and cultural reaffirmation that they sense to be inherent in the enactment of these collective "ceremonies" of feasting, dancing, and games.

SOCIAL CONTROL AND RELIGION

The slacker, the womanizer, and other transgressors of the norms were traditionally subject only to the controls of family disapproval and pressure, of adverse public opinion and gossip, and, perhaps, a public tongue-lashing by a group leader. Wrongdoing might also incur the visitation of supernatural illness. Direct coercive powers were vested in no persons or institutions.

Upon occassion traditional intrasocietal sanctions have been imposed, first, the moral authority of the Roman Catholic missionaries and, for less than fifty years, the police power of the "Mounties" backed by government legal and punitive action. The two Royal Canadian Mounted Police stationed at Rae have not had problems with major crimes. Most of their arrests are for public drunkenness.[29] Once in a while youths indulge in drunken physical aggression, but, past or present, there is no evidence of homicide. Occasional hunting infractions and, very rarely, theft from whites may bring arrest.

The Dogribs seem generally to be contented communicants in the Roman Catholic Church, to like their priests, and to accept the latter's authority in matters of moral and social behavior.[30]

Conservative Dogribs adhere equally to the Church and to belief in the waning guardian spirit complex. Some of the oldest generation of Dogribs command shamanistic powers. Gaining his "medicine" or power from tutelary spirits, a man could be adept in divining the future, in controlling game and weather, and in curing. Curing includes talking with the spirits, extraction of foreign objects from the body, and sometimes nowadays, handing out Catholic holy pictures. Sickness was often diagnosed as a supernatural consequence of sexual transgression. Only confession, and this meant public confession with the group gathered around, could effect a cure. The practitioner manipulated the fears and emotions of the ailing person, aided by the importunations of the onlookers, until confession occurred.

The easy travel allowed by the recent opening of the Mackenzie Highway has since 1966 brought Dogribs into contact with the preachings and presence of Athapaskan (Slave) "prophets" from northern Alberta.

Preachments of the major prophet against drinking, coupled with three drink-induced deaths at Rae within a year, have been taken much to heart. Even hardened drinkers aver that there has been a pronounced drop in drunkenness and liquor consumption. In 1967, several Dogribs began to practice prophet dances and songs borrowed from their mentors to the south. The dancing and songs in praise of Christian divinities aim to bring a better life and more moral behavior to the practicants. The exclusion of the white man, counseled by the southern prophets, from witnessing or participating in these activities is perhaps the first organized and overt expression of anti-white sentiment among the Dogribs.

CHARACTER VALUES

The qualities of character and temperament valued by the Dogribs are those that foster the physical welfare and social harmony of the group. The ethos ideal embraces generosity, emotional equanimity, egalitarianism, and the commitment to hard work and physical endurance as a complex of characterological means toward the goal of group well-being.

The man who by his effort has good tools, a full fish stage, a well-built house, and a well-stocked woodpile, "that's what we call smart." It is the pragmatic demonstration that he is a "rustler." Such a man must then expect, in fact, take pride that his relatives and the members of the local group turn to him for material aid, especially food.

The temperamental and physical capacity to drive oneself while cold, exhausted, and hungry for a few more hours on the hunt, or to set a pace ahead of the dogs for hours on end, is another mark of the "rustler," and, by the same token, an asset to the community. Endurance as a Dogrib virtue contrasts with the male European disposition toward physical bravery or bravado as a personal exploit. Risk for its own sake has no connotation of manliness to the Dogrib.

The egalitarianism that pervades Dogrib social values has its own distinctive cast: because all men are equal, they should equally agree. Dogribs should "listen to one another." Thereby is achieved the ideal of consensus in group affairs. To ignore the interests and opinions of the members of the group or pit one's will against them is antipathetic to Dogrib ethos.

So also is ego aggrandizement at the expense of others (as in Latin *machismo*). Indulgence in arrogance, anger, sexual jealousy, or other such self-assertive behavior threatens group well-being. The Dogrib emotional style stresses equanimity. A proper Dogrib, for example, is shamed should he act in a way—such as dancing beside his wife in the dancing circle—that can be construed as showing sexual possessiveness.

Perhaps it is simplest to say that the principle of generosity underlies all aspects of the Dogrib ethos ideal—in the sense of magnanimity of spirit in all human dealings, in which openhandedness with material things is only one part.

Those men who serve as leaders are chosen for all the major virtues, plus that special ability of being a "good talker." The good talker is he who can richly and forcefully express the wisdom based in commitment to and concern with group needs and values. Without this ability, a man may be much esteemed, but he is recognized not to have the full complement of qualities needed for leadership.

CHANGE

The Dogribs today face a world of new and often conflicting experiences unparalleled in the history of the people. The highway now allows easy access to the beer parlors and other urban delights of Yellowknife; it also leads south to contact with the stirring of pan-Indian movements among more acculturated and depressed tribal populations. The many, changing government programs, federal and territorial, exert a continual push-pull on the Indian. As one example, the education program, by conforming to the southern Canadian school year, holds families in Rae during the trapping season, thereby frustrating the efforts of game officials to encourage long trapping tours.

The older generations of Dogrib recall the good old days of high fur prices. The new generation faces a future in which trapping can, by present living standards, no longer provide even the modest rewards that their parents have known. In any case, the wholesale removal of the children into day school and hostel takes them not only from parental control and influence but from knowledge, ability, and commitment to bush life. Yet the prospects for other means of livelihood are poor. The threat of proletarianization hangs over the people—as rural welfare cases or, at best, casual laborers on the fringe of Canadian society.

In the face of onrushing change, older Dogribs fear for the survival of Dogrib freedom, virtue, and morale as they have known it. A man in his sixties talks to his peers:

In the old days, Resolution (the Chipewyan settlement on the south shore of Great Slave Lake) was just like us. They had *k'awos* and chiefs steady. And they listened to them. They had hand games, dancing and lots of fun. Now they're changing councillors and head chief. No more hand game, no more dance, no more feast, no *k'awo*. Everything is mixed up. That's on account of pretty near' every year, they change councillors and chief.

All these young fellows are just like they are lost. They won't listen to one another. That's what spoils the whole band. [*Translation from tape*]

Another says:

What are we going to do after the old man (Chief Bruneau) dies? It's pretty hard to find a man like him. Even if he is pretty deaf, he's still going strong. He's got a good head. Now we can hunt, and we are free, just like our fathers. And it's because of this old man. [*Translation from tape*]

Chief Bruneau speaks to men gathered to ponder what a meeting of chiefs, called by white officials, portends:

> I'll be glad if they don't make any change in this treaty-signing. That's the only thing I'm worrying about. No matter if I'm going to die, the next man who comes in my place is going to keep my word. That's the way I've been, since old Mohwi (the previous head chief) died. I've kept the same road as Mohwi. I've been holding this job for over thirty years. I don't care for money. I want us to be free for hunting on the land. I don't want money for land. If everything comes out all right I'll thank them. [*Translation from tape*]

A high official in the government of the Northwest Territories states his view: "(Chief) Bruneau rules that community with the fear of ghosts and hobgoblins."[31]

NOTES

1. Of the many Dogribs who by their words and deeds have contributed to this report, Vital Thomas must be accorded special mention. I am grateful equally for his patient commitment as a teacher of the Dogrib ways and for his friendship.

   Nancy Oestreich Lurie has been my field partner for three of the many periods I have spent with the Dogribs. We have shared field experiences and exploration of their meanings so fully that I cannot in many cases distinguish her contributions to this report from my own.

   My field work among the Dogribs has been supported by the Northern Coordination and Research Centre of the Department of Northern Affairs of Canada, by the National Museum of Canada, and by the University of Iowa.

2. The Dogribs of Rae and those of the Yellowknife area are in frequent contact and interaction, including marriage. The Yellowknife Dogribs, known before the settling of the town of Yellowknife and the Connie River People, are considered to speak a "mixed-up" language of Dogrib with Chipewyan infusions. Dogrib occupation, say Dogrib informants, once extended along the east arm of Slave Lake and is represented by persons of Dogrib ancestry today trading into the forts of Resolution and Snowdrift on the south side of the lake. These people now speak Chipewyan. Before 1928, some Dogribs were localized in small groups between the mouth of the Yellowknife River and Gros Cap, the southeastern tip of the north arm of Great Slave Lake. Most of them are said to have perished in the 1928 flu epidemic. The survivors deserted the area.

3. The "band rolls" kept by the Canadian Indian Affairs Branch do not designate the "tribal" or linguistic affiliations of persons listed, so estimates of different "tribal" populations must remain provisional. Furthermore, an individual's assignment to one administrative band roll is apt to continue years after he has moved to another area. For example, Dogribs who have

lived their adult life in the Rae area are still listed on the band roll of the Yellowknife area where they were born.

By the 1961 Canadian census, the total Indian population of the Northwest Territories was 5256; Eskimo, 7997; all others, 9745.

The forbidding climate and physiography of the Canadian North, unamenable to agriculture, have forestalled the swamping of the native population by people of European descent. Compare the Soviet Union today north of the 60th parallel, with a population of five million people and a million acres of land under cultivation, to Canada's comparable latitudes—comprising all the Northwest Territories and the Yukon Territory, plus the northern tip of Quebec—which have a total population of 32,000 (Phillips 1967:289).

4. Gates (1929) took blood samples from seven Dogribs encountered at Fort Norman, beyond the Dogrib domain proper. Four were of blood group O and three of blood group A. The absence of blood group B and blood group AB in this inadequate sample corresponded to the absence of those groups in samples from the Dogrib's Athapaskan neighbors, the Slave and the Hare Indians. According to Dr. T. Jayachandran, resident physician in Rae (1967), tests on fifty pregnant Dogrib women produced only A and O types (personal communication).

5. This people is known in the literature as the Yellowknife Indians, Red Knife Indians, or Copper Indians. Dogrib legend calls them *tedzõt'i* (the term used today for Chipewyans), or *eketšo wetšeke* ("Akaitcho's Bunch"), after their leader of the 1823 period. According to Dogrib informants, they should not be confused with the "Dogribs" presently living near the modern settlement of Yellowknife.

6. The site of Fort Rae, today simply Rae, has been moved several miles from its original location. There was also an earlier point of trade in Dogrib country. A complete account of the trading "forts" contacted by Dogribs cannot be given here.

7. In times past, a portion of these people, under the trading chief called the Bear Lake Chief, ranged the southern shores of Great Bear Lake. They intermarried with the Bear Lake Indians proper and, using Fort Norman as their point of trade, became disassociated from the main Dogrib population (see Osgood 1932).

Since 1962, two hamlets, under government auspices and with government-built houses, have been established in *et'aot'i* country. An older, native-built hamlet at the mouth of Marion River still has a few year-round occupants. The bulk of the *et'aot'i*, like most of the other Dogribs, are based in Rae.

8. A government-sponsored hamlet of nine houses has been established on Snare Lake in *detšilahot'i* country.

9. The Hare Indians and the Peel River Kutchin exploit the forest lands north and west of Great Bear Lake. Both groups are Athapaskan speakers.

10. The government housing program for the Indians and Eskimos of the Northwest Territories began in the 1950s and accelerated greatly in the 1960s. It has varied from providing finishing materials for new log cabins to prefabricated units brought in from southern Canada. In 1962, most of

the permanent Indian dwellings in Rae were old log cabins. By 1967, the majority of families were living in milled lumber houses with electric lighting. Bush hamlets also have new housing.

11. Full-time jobs included three interpreter-helpers for government agencies, six store clerks, two janitors for government installations, and two clerks and five truck drivers (water and garbage detail) for the Co-op. The history of the Co-op has been brief but so tumultuous, being caught in the cross fire of white politics, that it cannot be encapsulated here.

12. Good prices formerly drew trappers to the range of the white Arctic fox in the eastern reaches of the Dogrib domain.

13. Rock tripe, sometimes spiced with a piece of moccasin, was the starvation fare of the early explorers of the region. A lichen, rock tripe is no longer eaten by Dogribs. Old-timers recall scraping the growth of rock tripe off boulders, "pounding, pounding, pounding till it comes like flour," followed by boiling.

14. As indicated earlier, musk oxen have not been killed for many decades. In any event, the exploitation of musk oxen was probably seasonal and not of much importance to the Dogrib until the trade in musk ox robes arose in the nineteenth century. According to the earliest records, on the south shore of Great Slave Lake (in Chipewyan country) and in the southwesternmost portion of the Dogrib country the woods bison could once be found. There is no memory of exploitation of these animals among Dogribs.

15. In some areas of the Dogrib country mesh up to 5½ inches may be used; it will not serve for areas where fish are smaller.

16. There are two variant methods of slicing for dryfish: one technique yields fillets which may be dried and pounded to produce storable fish flour.

17. In the present day, the Dogribs divide the year into twelve months which correlate with the European months. It seems unlikely that aboriginal reckoning corresponded so closely to the European system.

18. Another route was common for the Yellowknife Dogribs, but apparently today they are likely to join the mixed Chipewyan-Dogrib populations along the east arm of Slave Lake on yet another route, more southerly, to the barren grounds. Sometimes a crew or two from the Rae join them.

19. The Dogribs are not restricted as groups or individually to any set routes or areas of trapping. In other words, there are no "registered traplines," as obtain in other parts of Canada.

20. All the contingencies affecting trapping tours cannot be considered in this condensed account. Not many trappers now follow the practice of establishing a bush camp with their families in August, building up a supply of fish and firewood, and trying to live off the land until the Christmas trip to the trading fort. Low fur prices allow little or no credit for an initial grubstake. An equally discouraging factor is the removal of the children from the Rae school that this necessitates. Government officials at some distance from the scene stress that there is (1) an allowance from the game warden's office to grubstake trappers and (2) government payment available to Indian foster homes to take in school-children. In fact, (1) the trapping allowance is a revolving fund that, as of fall 1967, has been largely eliminated through non-repayment of loans, and (2) practical and emotional considera-

tions cannot allow any great number of children to board in already crowded Indian homes.

21. In the old days, before the rifle was common, the Dogribs at Snare Lake in this season built brush fences at the eastern extremity of that long, thin lake. Interspersed in the fences were snares, slip nooses of caribou rawhide, in which caribou were caught, to be dispatched with spears.

22. Inheritance of personal possessions occurs casually within the nuclear family according to need and appropriateness. The surviving spouse has rights to the cabin and any other goods useful or appropriate to the sex. Older children of the appropriate sex may take some of the other articles of the deceased. Personal eating utensils and certain similar possessions are often destroyed at the grave site.

23. Another traditional set of manners regards the use of personal names. One should never, in the old custom, address another person directly by his name. A kinship term may be used or teknonymous address ("So-and-so's Father," and so on). "Nowadays," however, "they just throw your name at you."

24. It is said that in the old days girls were sometimes married before puberty. In such cases the husband did not assume sexual relations with his wife until after her menarche.

The nineteenth-century literature on the northern Athapaskans notes the practice of female infanticide. This practice may lie at the base of the stories told by older Dogribs of the days when girls were scarce and female infant betrothal was sometimes practiced. One reputedly true story, told with much amusement, is of the Dogrib who did bride service for an unborn child, only to be confronted, after months of labor for the household of his "father-in-law," with a baby boy.

25. For fuller analysis and documentation of the socioterritorial organization of the Dogrib and neighboring Athapaskans, see Helm (1965a), Helm (1968), and Helm and Damas (1963).

26. A notable example of the right of free access by all to a region was in the mustering in the old days of Dogribs from all regions, and even of the Slavey from Fort Simpson, in the Snare Lake area for the fall caribou hunt. Snare Lake is in the detšilahot'i, Edge of the Woods People, territory.

27. Whether or not the people in precontact times had a comparable sense of ethnic unity and of polity is problematic. Several conditions resulting from the intrusion of the Western world are likely factors in the development of the Dogrib people and polity. These include the hostilities with the Chipewyan, stimulated by the fur trade, around the beginning of the nineteenth century; the development of the ekawi, or "trading chief," as negotiator with the monopolistic Hudson's Bay Company during that century (Helm 1965b); and the advent of the mission for Dogribs in the 1860s and the establishment of Rae as the single point of trade and missionization.

28. A community hall, administered by the white-dominated community club, was completed a few years ago. In regard to its use by Indians, policy has varied; at some periods they have been required to pay rental if they wish to hold their celebrations indoors.

29. Before 1959, it was illegal for Indians to possess or consume alcohol. The

making of home brew was common in that period and was a major cause of arrest. Brew making is still illegal, but the accessibility of liquor in Yellowknife has reduced that activity greatly.

30. The Oblate fathers (*Oblats de Marie Immaculée*) are the only group of whites in the Athapaskan North who speak the native languages. Usually recruited from France and Belgium and standing apart from the Anglo-Protestant community, their comprehension of and involvement in Indian life is far deeper than that of any other class of Euro-Canadian.

31. Since the writing of this chapter in 1967, the pace of change continues to accelerate for the Rae Dogrib community. Only a few major events can be enumerated here.

As of December 1971, the Old Chief is still alive. However, he retired from office a couple of years ago in favor of his son. In July 1971, for the first time the Rae Dogribs held an election for the office of chief (rather than choosing the chief by male consensus). Like his predecessors, the new chief is a respected monolingual "bush Indian."

Under government instigation a Community Council of white and Indian members has been elected at Rae. The Indians boycotted the first election, subsequently declared void, because the traditional leaders feared that the Community Council (designed to deal with the "municipal" problems of the fast-growing town) would obliterate the role of the Band Council as the representative body of the Indian community.

Although still few in number, the young Dogribs who have begun to return from residential school with advanced (tenth to twelfth grade) education are providing active and articulate workers in pan-Indian causes such as the Canadian Indian Brotherhood movement. In February 1971, one of these young Dogribs assumed his seat in the Territorial Council (the governing body of the Northwest Territories) as the elected representative for the District of Mackenzie North.

A few miles from Rae a new townsite, Edzo, has come into being. It is the location of the new school, which opened in the fall of 1971. In its administration and curriculum the school is modeled on the Navajo Rough Rock Demonstration School. This means that a significant portion of the instruction is to be in the native language by Dogribs (who need not meet usual professional training requirements for teachers), that Dogrib traditions are to be part of the instructional content, and that the parents of the pupils are to have power to determine curriculum content and school policy.

APPENDIX

THE PHONEMES OF DOGRIB

Robert Howren

The phonological system of Dogrib (or, more accurately, of the conservative form of the Rae dialect of Dogrib) may be described in terms of thirty-four consonant phonemes and four vowel phonemes, the latter extended by pitch and nasality modifications.

The consonants are:

	Lenis	b	d	dl	dz	dž	g	gw	
Occlusives	Fortis		t	tł	ts	tš	k	kw	
	Glottalized		t'	tł'	ts'	tš'	k'	kw'	?
	Lenis	w		l	z	ž	g		
Spirants	Fortis	w		ł	s	š	h		
Resonants		m	n		r	y			

The lenis occlusives are phonetically voiceless or weakly voiced and differ from their fortis counterparts mainly in lacking aspiration. The fortis occlusives are strongly aspirated. The lenis and fortis spirants are voiced and voiceless, respectively. The glottalized occlusives are characterized by simultaneous glottal and lingual closure, with lingual release slightly preceding release of the glottal closure. The labialized velars are phonetically velar stops with simultaneous lip-rounding.

The basic vowel system is defined by two binary contrasts in tongue position, high versus low and front versus back:

$$/i \qquad o$$
$$e \qquad a/$$

plus a diphthong /aⁱ/. In addition, each vowel may be modified by either one of two contrasting tones (low, marked /'/, and high, unmarked) and by nasalization. Thus the basic vowel system with modifications of pitch and nasality yields twenty distinctive syllabics. For the high-back position, for example: /tło/ smoke, /tłŏ/ much, /libò/ cup, /dahmŏ/ roof. (Pitch has not been indicated in the Dogrib words presented in the text—J. H.)

REFERENCES

Asterisked items are cited as references in the text of the chapter.

Ethnographic studies and reports, based on field data except where indicated.

Helm, J., 1965a*. "Bilaterality in the Socio-Territorial Organization of the Arctic Drainage Dene," *Ethnology* 4:361–385.

———, 1965b*. "Patterns of Allocation among the Arctic Drainage Dene," in J. Helm, ed., *Essays in Economic Anthropology*, Annual Proceedings of the American Ethnological Society, Seattle: University of Washington Press, pp. 33–45.

———, 1968*. "The Nature of Dogrib Socio-Territorial Groups," in I. DeVore and R. B. Lee, eds., *Man the Hunter*, Chicago: Aldine Press, pp. 118–125.

———, and D. Damas, 1963*. "The Contact-Traditional All-Native Com-

munity of the Canadian North: The Upper Mackenzie 'Bush' Athapaskans
and the Igluligmiut," *Anthropologica*, n.s., 3:9–22.

————, and E. B. Leacock, 1971*. "The Hunting Tribes of Subarctic Canada,"
in E. B. Leacock and N. O. Lurie, eds., *North American Indians in Historical Perspective*, New York: Random House, pp. 343–374. Combines historical material with field data to chart the course of culture contact and change
among northern Athapaskan and Algonkian groups since the advent of the
European.

————, and N. O. Lurie, 1961. *The Subsistence Economy of the Dogrib
Indians of Lac La Martre in the Mackenzie District of the Northwest
Territories*, Northern Co-ordination and Research Centre, Department of
Northern Affairs and National Resources, Canada.

————, and ————, 1966*. *The Dogrib Hand Game*, Ottawa: National
Museum of Canada Bulletin No. 205.

————, and V. Thomas, 1966. "Tales from the Dogribs," *Beaver*, Autumn
1966:16–20; Winter 1966:52–54.

MacNeish, J. H., 1956. "Leadership among the Northeastern Athabascans,"
Anthropologica 2:131–163.
A reconstruction from historical sources.

Mason, J. A., 1946*. *Notes on the Indians of the Great Slave Lake Area*, Yale
University Publications in Anthropology 34, New Haven, Conn.: Yale
University Press.

*The major explorers', missionaries' and travelers' accounts from which ethno-
graphic and historical material on the Dogribs may be culled. These accounts
are often partial, casual, and impressionistic.*

Duchaussois, R. P., 1928. *Aux Glaces Polaires* (nouvelle édition), Paris:
Editions SPES.
See pages 291–306, featuring the missionization of the Dogribs, and page
432 for identification and location.

Finnie, R., 1940. "Dogrib Treaty," *Natural History* 46:52–58.

Mackenzie, A., 1911*. *Voyages from Montreal through the Continent of
North America to the Frozen and Pacific Oceans in 1789 and 1793*, Vol. 1,
Toronto: The Courier Press.

Petitot, E. F. S., 1891. *Autour du Grand Lac des Esclaves*, Paris: Nouvelle
Librairie Parisienne.

Richardson, Sir J., 1851. *Arctic Searching Expedition*, Vol. 2, London: Longmans, Brown, Green, and Longmans, pp. 1–31, 395–402.

Russell, F., 1898. *Explorations in the Far North*, Iowa City: University of Iowa.

Simpson, T., 1843*. *Narrative of the Discoveries on the North Coast of
America*, London: Bentley.

Wheeler, D. E., 1914. *The Dog-Rib Indian and His Home*, Bulletin of the
Geographical Society of Philadelphia, 12 (2).

*Miscellaneous materials. Works of use primarily in regard to historical problems
of identification. Designation and location of Dogrib populations are indicated by (I) following the entry. Works cited in the text which provide*

*nonethnographic background information relevant to Dogrib life are indi-
cated by* (N) *following the entry.*

Anonymous, 1910. *Thlingchadinne,* Bureau of American Ethnology Bulletin
No. 30, Part 2:744–745. (I)
Banfield, A. W. F., 1957*. "The Plight of the Barren-Ground Caribou," *Oryx*
4 (1):5–20. (N)
Gates, R. R., 1929*. "Blood Groups of Canadian Indians and Eskimos,"
American Journal of Physical Anthropology 12:475–485. (N)
Jenness, D., 1932. *The Indians of Canada,* Ottawa: National Museum of
Canada Bulletin No. 65:392–393. (I)
Kelsall, J. P., 1957*. *Continued Barren-Ground Caribou Studies,* Ottawa:
Canada Department of Northern Affairs and National Resources, Wildlife
Management Bulletin Series 1, No. 12. (N)
Kendrew, W. G., and B. W. Currie, 1955*. *The Climate of Canada,* Ottawa:
Queen's Printer. (N)
Morice, A. G., 1926. "The Great Dene Race," *Anthropos* 1:229–278. (I)
Osgood, C., 1932*. *The Ethnography of the Great Bear Lake Indians,* Ottawa:
National Museum of Canada Bulletin No. 70:31–34. (I)
———, 1936. *The Distribution of the Northern Athapaskan Indians,* Yale
University Publications in Anthropology No. 6, New Haven, Conn.: Yale
University Press, p. 11. (I)
Petitot, E., 1884–1885*. "Athabasca District of the Canadian Northwest
Territory," *The Canadian Record of Science* 1 (1):27–53. (I)
Phillips, R. A. J., 1967*. *Canada's North,* Toronto: Macmillan. (N)

GLOSSARY

'atšo: snowshoe worn when moose hunting; very large—almost five feet in length
denegak'awo: regional headman of pretreaty times
detšilahot'ĭ: Edge of the Woods People
et'aot'ĭ: People Next to Another People
gwati/or gwatinde: head chief
gwatia: councillors—"little chiefs," representatives from the regional groups to
the tribal council
k'awo: boss of the hunting crew; also, chief of a regional band
kwekatelĭhot'ĭ: Water over Rocks Place People
nahgā: the mythical bush prowlers who roam the forest in the summer and
kidnap women and children
sehot'ĭ: my people, my relatives
tagahot'ĭ: Follow the Shore People
tłĭtšo: Dogribs as a tribe
ts'ĭkakōgolahot'ĭ: House Place at Ghost Channel People
tsōtihot'ĭ: Feces Lake People

CHAPTER
3
THE MISTASSINI CREE

Edward S. Rogers

Edward Rogers is currently Head of the Department of Ethnology, Royal Ontario Museum, University of Toronto. He received his Ph.D. in anthropology from the University of New Mexico in 1958 and has conducted ethnographic research among the Mistassini Cree, the Apache of the Mescalero Reservation, and the Ojibwa of Northern Ontario. In addition, he has conducted archaeological survey and excavation in Quebec. The outcome of his ethnographic research has been summarized in several articles concerned with economic patterns, social organization, and cultural change in hunting groups, which have been published primarily in Arctic and through the National Museum of Canada.

EDITOR'S INTRODUCTION

The Mistassini Cree, natives to the Labrador Peninsula of Canada, speak a Cree dialect of the Algonkian language family. Their natural domain is similar to that of the Dogribs, with forests inundated by lakes and streams. The climate too is extreme, with long, cold winters and short, although warm, summers. The Mistassini have been exposed to long but, until recently, limited contact with the Western world. Like the Copper Eskimo and the Dogribs, they were involved for many years in the trapping and trading network of the northern fur companies, and during that time trapping played a major role in the economy alongside traditional hunting and fishing activities. Only within the last ten years has the introduction of roads, railroads, and air facilities brought them into intensive contact with tourists, industries, and government agencies.

Rogers takes as his ethnographic present the period of a fairly stable hunting, fishing, and trapping economy. His emphasis is on the yearly cycle of food getting which revolved around the movements of big game, primarily caribou, bear, and, more recently, moose, and the availability of fishing sites and fur-bearing animals. An analysis of Mistassini exploitative techniques shows strong similarities to other hunting groups, most notably the Dogribs, in the organization of their socioeconomic units and their definitions of territory. Their adaptation to the introduction of fur trade is also similar to that of the Dogribs and the Copper Eskimo, with the perhaps significant exception of the development of strong leadership patterns in well-defined hunting territories.

THE "BIG HUNTERS"

The Mistassini Cree represent one group of "Big Hunters" of the Labrador Peninsula.[1] The Mistassini have had contact with Europeans for over three hundred years, being first mentioned by the Jesuits in 1642–1643. And yet only very recently has contact with the outside world become intensive. No doubt this long period of limited contact was due to the fact that the Mistassini were located deep within the interior of the peninsula, a rugged land difficult to penetrate. Their old way of life of hunting, trapping, and fishing, persisted, little changed, until about ten years ago. With the advent of a road and railroad to the southern part of their lands and increased air facilities, they no longer were able to maintain their traditional way of life. Indications are that soon this will be only a fond memory.

To the Mistassini, the search for and successful capture of big game—caribou, moose, and bear—was a prime purpose of life and entitled the successful one to the title of Great Hunter. But this is a most difficult country from which to gain a living. Game is scarce and usually widely dispersed, the winters long and extremely cold, and the land, if not mountainous or hilly, rugged.

LOCATION

The Mistassini inhabit a large tract of land in the southwestern portion of the Labrador Peninsula, inland several hundred miles from James Bay and similarly from Lake St. John (see Fig. 3-1). Their territory encompasses the upper drainage of the Rupert River, roughly between latitudes 50 and 52 degrees north and longitudes 71 and 75 degrees west.

POPULATION AND PHYSICAL TYPE[2]

In 1953–1954 there were over 600 Indians who gathered at the south end of Lake Mistassini. It was here that trading posts were located. The Indians of Lake Mistassini exploited 42,500 square miles. Not all of them are Mistassini Cree, but represent other bands or parts thereof (see Fig. 3-2). Only an estimated 450 are Mistassini.

The Mistassini are of moderate height. In a sample of Montagnais-

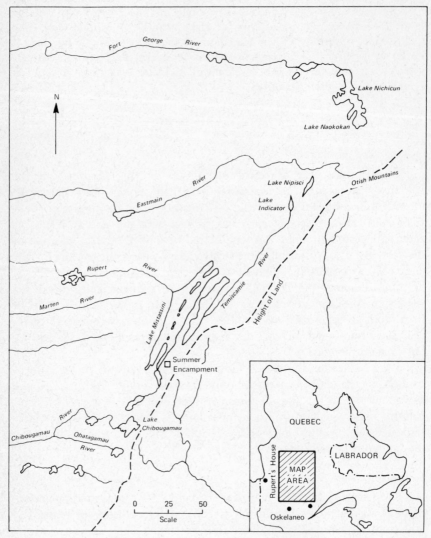

Figure 3–1. The area of Lake Mistassini.

Naskapi, which included Mistassini, the mean height for males was 66 inches and for women, 61 inches. Both sexes tend to be brachycephalic, with the women slightly more so than the men. The Indians are of a relative homogeneous physical type. The hair is predominately straight and black. Skin color is dark, due in part to exposure to the elements. Eye color tends to be dark brown and the epicanthic fold generally lacking.

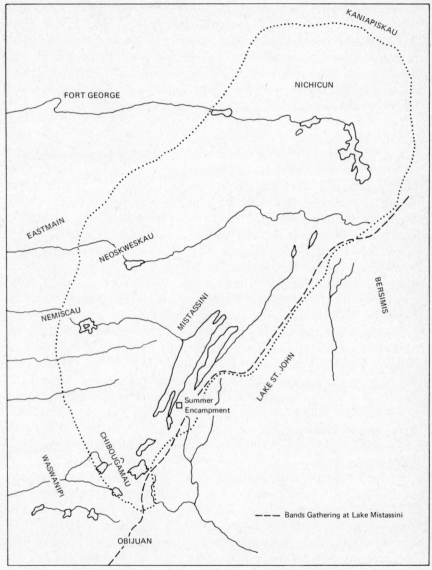

Figure 3–2. Bands inhabiting south-central Quebec.

LANGUAGE[3]

The Mistassini speak a dialect of Cree, a branch of the Algonkian linguistic family. Phonemes are of two types: consonants and vowels. Stress differences are slight and non-phonemic. Consonants are of four types:

stops, spirants, nasals, and semivowels. Vowels occur in normal and short length. The dialect contains three major word classes: verbs, nouns, and particles. Verbs and nouns are inflected, but particles are not. The major verb types are inanimate intransitive, animate intransitive, transitive inanimate, and transitive animate, distinguished by sets of inflections for person, number, and gender of subjects and objects, within a complex system allowing for discrimination of tense, aspect, and mode. Nouns are inflected for possession, number, and animate or inanimate gender.

HISTORY

The Mistassini have had a long history of contact with Europeans. The first mention of them was in 1642–1643. Eventually the French made contact with the Mistassini on their home grounds. Jesuit missionaries pushed up the Saguenay to Lake St. John, reaching there in 1647. In 1663, Guillaume Couture and two other Frenchmen, with a party of Indians, went from Lake St. John to Lake Mistassini and thence to Lake Nemiscau, where they turned back. Then in 1672, Father Albanel reached Lake Mistassini, where he met Mistassini on his way to James Bay to investigate the Hudson's Bay Company's new operations. Contact continued to increase for a time, but during the 1700s, interest in the country decreased. In about 1725 a trading post, possibly the first one, was established among the Mistassini, but it was soon abandoned. For trade goods, the Mistassini traveled to the French at Lake St. John or the English at Fort Rupert.

When the British took over rule from the French in 1763, the Hudson's Bay Company began expansion into the Labrador Peninsula. About 1787, they built a post at Neoskweskau and thereafter additional posts were established. By 1800, there may have existed a post on Lake Mistassini. It has been in continuous operation to this day. For a few years in the early 1800s, the Northwest Company had a post at the south end of Lake Mistassini in opposition to the Hudson's Bay Company.

During all but the early years of the 1800s, the Hudson's Bay Company was undisputed master of the area. Each summer the company supplied trade goods by means of canoe brigades manned by Indians. The goods were transported from Fort Rupert, but only in limited quantities. This was probably of little concern to the Mistassini, since their numbers had been greatly reduced through disease and game was probably still in sufficient amount to supply their wants. By the end of the century, however, the Mistassini had increased in numbers and game was becoming scarce.

During the last forty years, accelerating contact with Euro-Canadian culture has taken place. In 1926 the post at Mistassini was transferred from the James Bay District to the Lake St. John District, and, accordingly, the supply route was changed. Now fur brigades operated between Mistassini and the town of Oskelaneo, on the Canadian National Railroad to the south. This lessened the distance goods had to be transported by about 150 miles. Most bulky and inexpensive goods were transported in this manner until the early 1950s. Other goods were flown in from the south.

Beginning some fifteen years ago, considerable prospecting took place about Lake Chibougamau, located in the southern part of the area. At this time, the Hudson's Bay Company opened a post on Lake Chibougamau that lasted only a few years. Eventually the mining industry became established, with a number of mines coming into operation. These soon necessitated a road, and during the late 1940s the Quebec government built one from Lake St. John. Then a railroad was constructed from Senneterre and another from Lake St. John. Now a road is being built northward past the Indian settlement at the south end of Lake Mistassini toward iron deposits on the Temiscamie River, in the heart of Mistassini territory.

Today, goods of all kinds, in quantity, are available to the Mistassini. Yet as late as 1913–1918 a family might be allowed to take only fifty pounds of flour for the winter and depend on the land for support. Informants recalled that in the 1920s store food was exhausted by Christmas, and even in the early 1950s it was often consumed by early spring. In 1953–1954, the Matoush hunting group still took 70 percent of their food from the land.

THE ENVIRONMENT

PHYSIOGRAPHY

The land of the Mistassini is flat, between 1000 and 2000 feet above sea level, with the average about 1300 feet. The highest elevations occur on the east side of the territory in the Otish Mountains, which are nearly 4000 feet high. These mountains trend east-west and are located just south of the headwaters of the Eastmain River. The land dips slightly to the west toward James Bay. Although the country is termed flat, this does not mean to imply that it is plainslike. It is rolling topography of gravel and bedrock hills, between which are extensive areas of muskeg as well as many lakes and ponds, both shallow and deep and all linked together by a network of streams and rivers.

Pleistocene glaciation produced this land configuration. In some areas it stripped the bedrock bare and in others it left drift, moraines, eskers, and outwash plains of gravel and sand. The process disrupted the drainage pattern, which accounts for the extensive areas of muskeg and the many lakes and ponds that exist today.

The lakes within the area vary greatly in size. Lake Mistassini is the largest, being approximately 100 miles long with a maximum width of 16 miles. The lake covers an area of 840 square miles. Another large lake is

Albanel, located to the east of Lake Mistassini. Lake Albanel is approximately 60 miles long and has an average width of 5 miles.

The major portion of the area drains west into James Bay. The Rupert River is the major drainage system and flows out of Lake Mistassini. Many rivers flow into Lake Mistassini, of which the most important is the Temiscamie, flowing southwest into Lake Albanel and thence into Lake Mistassini. Others are the Waconichi, Chalafor, Takwa, Papaskwasate and Wabbissinon rivers. To the north, the headwaters of the Eastmain River drain a segment of Mistassini territory.

The water, in all but the most shallow lakes and rivers, is cold year round. Temperatures probably do not rise above 40 to 50 degrees F. Most, if not all, of the bogs and muskeg are acidic. Here and there the shores of lakes and rivers consist of sandy beaches, but, more generally, the shores are bedrock or coarse gravel and boulders. The soils are thin and mostly podzolic, but are not everywhere present.

Climate

Climatic conditions are extreme. A distinctly continental climate prevails with long, very cold winters and short, warm summers. The low temperatures are due to the prevailing westerly winds which sweep in from across the cold wastes of Hudson Bay. December, January, and February are the coldest months. January has a mean temperature of −3.2 degrees F. The lowest temperature recorded at Lake Mistassini during the winter of 1953–1954 was −45 degrees F, and at Lake Nipisci, at the southern edge of the Otish Mountains, during the same winter the maximum low was −64 degrees F. The lowest ever recorded for Lake Mistassini was −56 degrees F. These extreme temperatures occur during the early hours of the morning when outside activity by the Mistassini is curtailed. As a rule, temperatures rise during the day and reach a maximum by early afternoon. In 1953–1954, on the coldest day of the year at Mistassini the maximum temperature there was −18 degrees F and at Lake Nipisci, −25 degrees F. Since the Mistassini, as a rule, carry on outdoor activities only during the daylight hours, the rise in temperature is important to them. There is a rather large diurnal range in winter temperatures, less during the summer, and large seasonal variations. Summer temperatures range between 40 and 90 degrees F during the day, and usually drop somewhat during the night. July is without frost and usually so are June and August.

Winter is the longest season of the year. Snow generally covers the ground by late October or early November. At this time, the smaller lakes and streams freeze over. By December all water bodies are frozen and the ice continues to thicken through February and sometimes into March. By then, the ice is several feet thick. Sometimes during the winter there are warm spells, at which time it may rain, and a crust is apt to form on the surface of the snow. These occurrences are rare; normally the snow is light and powdery, accumulating to a depth of several feet.

Winter draws to a close toward the end of April. Leads of open water begin to appear, and throughout April and May the upper levels of the snow thaw during the day and saturate the lower levels. At night the temperature drops below freezing and, accordingly, a crust forms on the surface, not to thaw again until late in the morning. The Mistassini take advantage of this crust to travel in the early morning hours. Under these conditions travel can be rapid, but later in the day it is almost impossible. By mid-May the snow has usually all melted except at higher elevations. The last snowfalls occur during this month, although they have been known to occur in June. Because of the rapid melting of the vast accumulation of snow, the lakes and rivers are in flood condition. Initially the melted water overflows the ice, but as soon as the latter becomes rotten it breaks away from the shores; winds break up the ice and it is soon rafted downstream. The high waters begin to recede and continue to do so for a time.

It then warms up rapidly and summer begins, continuing for three months. In September frosts may occur and snow falls in the mountains; within a short period winter begins again.

Although this is a land of abundant water, total yearly precipitation only amounts to about 30 inches. Rainfall almost every day during the summer accounts for about two thirds of the total annual precipitation. It falls in the form of drizzles, although there are occasional thunderstorms. Lightning, which accompanies these storms, occasionally starts forest fires. These fires, if not too intensive and extensive, are of benefit to the Mistassini. Sere stages are initiated, the early ones being the prime habitats for moose, bear, beaver, and blueberries. If the fires are widespread and burn deeply, however, they destroy the land for caribou, porcupine, squirrel, and marten. Large tracts within the territory of the Mistassini show the effects of recent fires.

Winter snowfall is heavy. Between 100 and 125 inches fall, although generally only three to five feet accumulate on the ground at any one time. At higher elevations, such as the Otish Mountains, the winds blow away much of the snow. Since the snow depth is less in such places, caribou move to these areas during the winter in search of lichens. Snowstorms are the result of fronts produced by eastward- and northeastward-moving cyclones. The ground, since it is snow covered, freezes only to a depth of several inches.

Windy weather is frequent, sometimes of high velocity, with prevailing winds from the northwest, west, and southwest. Southwesterly winds tend to be most common during the summer. Often at this time of year,

The Mistassini Cree: Physical type.

The clothing and climate of the Mistassini Cree.

Log cabins.

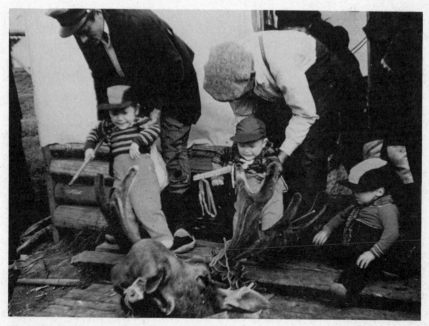

Game secured—moose.

House types.

Woman's work around the camp.

especially during early summer, they are accompanied by drizzling rains and cool winds from the north. In winter, northwest winds are frequent, bringing with them clear weather, very low temperatures, and a dry atmosphere. During this season, winds from other quarters are often accompanied by storms, higher humidity, and a rise in temperature. January and February are very windy months. These winds are feared by the Mistassini because they are associated with low temperatures, and therefore the wind-chill factor is very high and there is a constant danger of freezing when outdoors.

FLORA

Most of the country of the Mistassini is covered with forests; the exceptions are recent burns and the higher elevations, such as the Otish Mountains, where a tundralike vegetation exists. The forest is part of the circumpolar boreal forest formation. White spruce, black spruce, balsam fir, Banksian pine, and larch represent the small number of species that compose it. Cedar grows only as far north as the southern end of Lake Mistassini. White spruce is considered the climax forest, although 80 percent of the trees are black spruce. The hardwood trees form sere stages that are composed of white birch, aspen, balsam poplar, willows, and alders. Generally no trees reach more than 50 feet.

In recent burns, fireweed, Labrador tea, blueberries, and sheep laurel occur. In time, white birch and aspen grow up to form a subclimax with an undergrowth of the above plants, the original colonizers. On the crests of sandy ridges grow Banksian pine, with an understory of ericaceous plants and reindeer moss. This assemblage may represent a fire subclimax.

Along the shores of the lakes and streams are usually found thick stands of willows, alders, and ericaceous shrubs. These form the transition to the forest proper, but are so thick and tangled that they are almost impossible to penetrate. In the sphagnum bogs grow larch and stunted black spruce along with willow, alder, Labrador tea, and laurel.

The ponds and lakes in general lack much vegetation. Lake bottoms are mostly rocky, the waters are acidic, and there are great fluctuations in the water level. Presumably, due to these factors, there is little plant growth and because of limited plant growth, fish are not especially numerous.

There are some differences between the forests of the southern and northern parts of Mistassini territory, but botanists have not yet divided these into associations. However, several structural types have been suggested; some of these are not climax, but sere stages. One has been called the closed forest type. The vegetation consists of black spruce, balsam fir, numerous mosses, and some typical herbs. A second is the lichen-woodland type, with open stands of black and white spruce and occasionally larch and Banksian pine, and the ground cover is lichen. A third is the

muskeg type, occurring on poorly drained ground. Black spruce and occasionally larch grow in this type, as well as sphagnum moss and certain
shrubs.

North and west of Lake Mistassini is found the lichen-woodland type,
and this is part of the open boreal forest. To the south and east, within
the basins of Lakes Mistassini and Albanel, and to the west, occurs the
closed-forest type that forms the main boreal forest.

Berry bushes are scattered throughout the area. The most common are
blueberries, but others occurring in limited numbers are mountain ash,
bird cherry, and raspberry.

FAUNA

Like the vegetation of the area, the fauna is restricted in the number of
species present; furthermore, nowhere within the area is any species common, except for insects. Caribou, once so basic to the life of the Mistassini,
have decreased greatly in numbers and are now found only to the north
and east of Lake Mistassini, primarily about the Otish Mountains. Moose
entered the area shortly after the turn of the century and are found mostly
in the southern part of the territory but are continuing to move northward. Bear inhabit the area, but are not numerous; they are most often
encountered during the fall around berry patches. To the Mistassini,
they are of extreme importance because of their religious significance and
the amount of fat they yield, which is important in the diet as a source
of energy and heat. Beaver, in spite of the fact that aspen and willows are
common, are rare, apparently due to overtrapping. The greatest numbers
are found in the western part of the area. Otter occur, though not in
abundance; in contrast to some other species, they do not fluctuate greatly
in numbers from year to year. Mink are not uncommon, their numbers
varying from one section of the country to another. Marten, inhabitants of
dense coniferous forests, are rare, most likely because of the destruction
of such forests by fire. Muskrats occur in limited numbers, probably because of the lack of adequate aquatic vegetation and overtrapping. Hares,
important not as a source of food but rather of clothing, fluctuate greatly
in numbers from year to year. They reach a peak of overpopulation every
few years and then practically disappear. Furthermore, their numbers vary
from one district to another.

Mammals inhabit the area the entire year and therefore are always
available, though often difficult to find. Most are active throughout the
year and, accordingly, can be detected because of their movements. Others
restrict their movements during the winter, making finding them much
more difficult. Bears, for example, go into hibernation and are hard to
locate, while caribou, which are constantly on the move, betray their
presence by their tracks.

Birds, in contrast to mammals, are not necessarily confined to the area
year round. Most species leave for the winter months, although a few

remain throughout the year. These include the gray jay, spruce and ruffed grouse, chickadee, pine grosbeak, and white-winged crossbill. Only spruce grouse can be considered at all numerous and of importance in the diet. In addition, willow and rock ptarmigan and snowy owl migrate in from the north during the winter. Rock ptarmigan move into the northern half of Mistassini territory, while willow ptarmigan are found throughout the region.

During spring and fall, rather large numbers of waterfowl are a source of food. Most of these pass through the area, few nesting within it. Those that generally do not remain for the summer are the Canada goose, snow goose, brant, green-winged teal, old-squaw, white-winged scoter, surf scoter, American scoter, and red-throated loon. These waterfowl arrive in May. By September, those that have been north make their temporary return, and by the end of October or early November all have left the area for the south.

Besides these transient visitors, some waterfowl arrive from the south, nest within the area, and leave again with the approach of fall. These are the black duck, American goldeneye, American merganser, red-breasted merganser, common loon, osprey, spotted sandpiper, greater yellowlegs, herring gull, common tern, great horned owl, nighthawk, kingfisher, crow, and a variety of songbirds.

Fish, although present, are by no means abundant. Some species have a very limited distribution and few bodies of water are productive. Within any lake or river there are restricted areas where fish may be obtained; in part, this is seasonal, since during the spawning period certain species move to particular areas, and, also, informants contend that during the winter, fish move into deep water. Fish that occur in the area are lake trout, speckled trout, whitefish, pike, walleyed pike, common and red sucker, burbot, and sturgeon. Suckers are the most common fish. Walleyed pike are confined to the southern part of the area and are most likely absent from the headwaters of the Eastmain River. Sturgeon are found only in the southwestern part of the territory.

Invertebrates are the most numerous of all fauna. Those of most concern are the moose flies, deer flies, black flies, sand flies, and mosquitoes. They appear as early as late May and remain until September, but are most numerous in early summer. Their habit of biting causes some discomfort to the Mistassini. Head lice and fish tapeworms are also present.

ECONOMY

INTRODUCTION

The Mistassini Cree, over the years, became immersed in a fur-trapping economy, an extractive industry rather than the purely subsistence activities formerly engaged in. Although fur trapping played a part in the economy, it still meant that the Mistassini were essentially dependent upon the environment. And in the case of one hunting group, not atypical, 70 percent of the food was derived from the land. Accordingly, the Mistassini remain primarily hunters and, to a certain extent, fishermen. The gathering of vegetal foods is minimal.

Because of the meager resources available within the eastern subarctic, the Mistassini, of necessity, utilize almost everything they can. The only limitations are due to their technology and culturally determined prohibitions. Securing sufficient food is a constant problem and a never-ending concern. Times of starvation are vividly remembered and countless tales are told concerning such events. It is perhaps because of this that so much of Mistassini religion revolves about the quest for food.

Big game (caribou, moose recently, bear, and beaver) are most inten-

TABLE 3-1

NUMBERS AND POUNDS OF GAME SECURED FROM THE ENVIRONMENT BY THE ALFIE MATOUSH HUNTING GROUP

Game	Numbers Taken	Pounds of Edible Food
Fish	1,582	3,165
Mammals		
Moose	10	4,000
Caribou	12	1,500
Bear	1	210
Beaver	55	2,120
Hare	76	114
Muskrat	120	240
Porcupine	6	60
Mink	132	33
Squirrel	33	8
Marten	5	5
Otter	11	110
		8,400
Birds		
Loon	11	44
Geese	12	67
Ducks	132	231
Duck eggs	23	
Ptarmigan	301	150
Spruce grouse	75	38
Ruffed grouse	2	1
Owl	2	1
		532
Vegetal foods	5 large pails of blueberries	
Grand total		12,097

sively sought. This was especially true in the past, because these animals supplied a substantial proportion of the food. Big game is still eagerly pursued whenever possible. At the same time, small game, birds, and fish are a necessary supplement to the diet, without which the Mistassini would not be able to survive. Big game is not numerous enough to be the sole support. Table 3-1 gives the game taken by one hunting group for the winter of 1953–1954.

Species utilized or not utilized are given in the following sections.

THE LAND

To the Mistassini, the land is not "real estate." Rather, it is a part of the total environment within which they live, including not only the physical realm but also the supernatural. The land, as such, is not a commodity that might be sold. Rather, it is something that is given and yields, in terms of natural resources, the means whereby the Mistassini can exist. It is the products of the land that are of importance for food, clothing, fuel, shelter, means of transportation, and all the rest that is necessary to maintain life. These are secured later. The resources derived from the land, so essential to life itself, are also not private property but available to all Mistassini, to all men to harvest for the survival of themselves and their families.

Although the above is the philosophy of the Mistassini, they do have means whereby the "land" is distributed so that all may have a fairly equal chance of survival. Under the impact of the fur trade, they developed hunting territories, areas that were exploited for both subsistence and commercial gain by individual hunting groups. These territories were utilized from fall until late spring (Fig. 3-3). If the territory was sufficiently large, the hunting group would establish two or more base camps from which the men radiated out in search of game. These camps were usually placed well within the territory, upon the shores of a prominent body of water. The group returned year after year to these lakes and rivers, but new campsites were chosen each year, since supplies of firewood and boughs were depleted during the course of one winter.

Boundaries to the hunting territories are but vaguely known, within a limit of several miles. Each territory is conceived of as a series of interlocking lakes, streams, and rivers. It is along these that the hunting group travels and builds camps. One elderly informant stated that the men from adjacent territories discuss among themselves just how far each group will go.

The size of the hunting territories varies greatly, due, in part, to game densities, size of hunting group, topography, and population pressure. Sizes range from 300 square miles to 2000 square miles. The former is exploited by two married men and the latter usually by three married men and two teenage boys. This territory is larger than could be exploited in any one winter, given the means of transportation at the disposal of

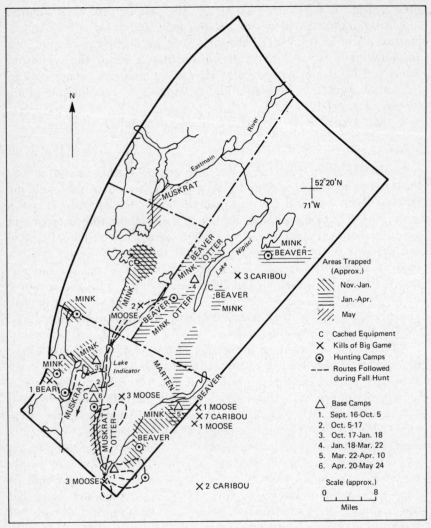

Figure 3–3.   Matoush hunting territory. Areas and game exploited, 1953–1954.

the Mistassini. In fact, only 1500 square miles can be effectively exploited in any one year.

From a sample of five hunting groups, the area each man theoretically exploits varies from 130 to nearly 500 square miles. The average area for each hunter who gathers at Mistassini is approximately 260 square miles.

As a rule, each year the same families return to the same territory, but there are exceptions. After marriage, a man and his new wife are expected to spend a year of the first three of their marriage living with the wife's parents. Sometimes this develops into a permanent-residence pattern.

Furthermore, illness might necessitate winter residence elsewhere, or the depletion of game on the home territory might force families to move elsewhere.

No system of naming the territories exist. Rather, the areas are known by the same names as the lakes and rivers that form the core of the territory.

The resources found within the territory are of two types, those over which the hunting group has exclusive rights and those that are free goods and may be exploited by any Mistassini. Exclusive rights are held by the hunting group over those resources used in trade, primarily fur bearers. All resources used directly for subsistence are free goods. Direct observations indicate that fishing grounds, berry patches, firewood, boughs, waterfowl, wood, hare, moose, and, no doubt, caribou are considered free goods. Apparently, muskrat are free goods also, since they are an exception to the rule that fur bearers are the exclusive property of the hunting group. The very low value of their pelts may be the reason.

Ideas regarding trespass are not clear-cut; furthermore there are no remaining mechanisms whereby a trespasser can be punished. It is contended that only in cases of extreme starvation would hunting take place on another's territory. In practice, however, hunting and trapping excursions are undertaken within the margins of neighboring groups' territories. Permission is not obtained, but no complications arise.

In a sense, the leader of the hunting group "owns" the land, but he has no right to prohibit any member of his group from exploiting the land to his advantage. It appears that, in general, the hunting territory passes to the oldest male, usually a son of the previous "owner."

The Yearly Cycle

Since the Mistassini Cree live by hunting and, to a certain extent, by fishing, they have to be often on the move. The year is divided into the six periods shown in Table 3-2. Nevertheless, from direct observation eight periods can be designated: *fall travel, fall hunt, winter camp construction, early winter trapping, late winter hunt, spring trapping, spring travel,* and *summer activities.* These terms are used for descriptive purposes in this account.

Fall Travel

Toward the end of summer, activities within the summer encampment intensify as different families prepare to leave for their winter camps. Supplies and equipment have to be purchased and canoes and motors repaired. After a week or so of feverish activity, family groups begin to leave the settlement. By mid-September, all have left. Some must travel up to 300 miles to reach their winter camps. Travel is by freighter canoe, one or more of which is generally powered by an outboard motor and which tows one or more canoes. Travel is usually undertaken only during

TABLE 3-2

SEASONAL ACTIVITIES AND MOVEMENTS OF THE MISTASSINI INDIANS

Periods of Activities	Summer Activities			Fall Travel	Fall Hunt	Winter Camp Construction	Early Winter Trapping		Late Winter Hunt			Spring Trapping	Summer Trapping
Mistassini Seasons	Nipin				Ahkuwacin	Miciskasic	Pipun					Sikwan	Miyuskamu
Months	June	July	Aug.	Sept.	Oct.	Nov.	Dec.	Jan.	Feb.	Mar.	Apr.	May	
Snow					Freeze-Up							Break-Up	
Travel and Transportation	Canoe		Periods				Sled	of Toboggan		Snowshoes	Travel	Canoe	
Fishing													
Hunting	Waterfowl			Bear Moose		Grouse			Moose Caribou			Waterfowl	
Trapping			Muskrat		Mink		Beaver		Marten		Muskrat Otter		
Establishing Winter Camps													
Feasts				X	X		X				X	X	

fair weather because of the small children. Fishing is conducted at the end of each day and rabbit snares are set and waterfowl hunted. Occasionally stops of several days' duration are made during which big game is sought.

FALL HUNT

Upon reaching the hunting grounds, the hunting group establishes a base camp composed of canvas tents, one for each family. This is the start of the fall hunt, which lasts from late September until mid-October.

As much game as possible is secured and dried for winter use during these months. Trips of one to several days' duration are made by the men from the base camp in various directions in search of bear, moose, and caribou. If a kill is made at any distance from base camp, a move is made to the kill, where the meat is brought into the camp. Once a kill has been made and processed, or if, within a short time, no game has been sighted, camp is moved to another part of the territory and the search continues. This is true only for the large hunting territories. At the same time, fishing is intensified, a duty primarily of the women. Muskrat are trapped and waterfowl shot. This is a crucial period of the year, since game must be secured if the winter is to be passed without hardship. The elder males frequently drum during the evenings to ensure success in hunting.

WINTER CAMP CONSTRUCTION

As freeze-up approaches, a more permanent camp is erected, which in the smaller territories might be inhabited all winter, but on the large ones is abandoned in early January. This period lasts about two weeks. More substantial dwellings—log cabins with canvas or pole and turf roofs—are built which are large enough to house the whole hunting group. Cache racks and drying racks have to be set up and canoes stored. Again there are evenings spent in drumming, in order to learn what the winter promises for the group.

EARLY WINTER TRAPPING

At freeze-up, the men prepare their equipment and get ready to start intensive trapping. Fishnets have to be brought in so they will not freeze in the ice. Then, the men leave for trips of a week to ten days. On these trips they set out their traps and erect trapping camps to which they will periodically return. While the men are away, the women hunt spruce grouse and ptarmigan, snare hare, and trap fur bearers around camp.

When the men are in camp, which is usually for only a few days at a time, they help their wives set and tend the fishnets and, in addition, set and inspect traps in the vicinity. They also manufacture snowshoe frames and toboggans. In addition, quantities of firewood have to be secured. This is, obviously, a period of intensive activity.

LATE WINTER HUNT

In early January, as a rule, the hunting group abandons its early winter camp and moves into canvas tents or traditional lodges. Food is scarce and game in the vicinity has been killed, scared away, or is nonexistent. All of January might be spent in moving to a more productive area. The distance to be traversed might not be too many miles in total, but only a few miles can be covered each day. This is due to the shortness of daylight hours, the hours necessary to erect an overnight camp, and the discomfort the young children have to endure at the extremely low temperatures that occur at this time of year. Once a new locale has been reached, a semipermanent camp is built. Fishnets are set, and then the men leave to hunt big game. At the same time, they engage in limited amounts of trapping, although at this time of year, fur bearers tend to remain dormant and are difficult to secure. The major emphasis is on the hunting of big game. (Whenever secured in quantity and at any distance from the camp, the hunting group moves to the site of the kill, where the animals are processed.) These activities continue until about the middle of April, just before break-up. It is then time to move back to where the canoes had been left the previous fall, since without them travel would soon be impossible. Furthermore, food is again limited. The canoes were left where there was good spring fishing. Although there is some urgency, hunting is continued as the group travels.

SPRING TRAPPING

Once the Mistassini arrive where the canoes were cached, a new semipermanent camp is erected. Muskrat are the major fur bearer sought. Food is low after the long winter and, therefore, constant search for game is necessary. Waterfowl and fish are the main game available at this time of the year and as many as possible are taken. Once a sufficient number has been secured, a feast is held in thanksgiving for having survived the winter. As this period draws to a close toward the end of May, preparations are made for the return to the summer settlement. Excess waterfowl, fish, and muskrats are dried and smoked for food, new equipment is made and the old repaired, and winter equipment is cached for use the next winter. Finally, any bear skulls and caribou antlers that were secured during the course of the year are ritually erected in order to appease the spirits of the slain animals.

SPRING TRAVEL

As the ice in the rivers and lakes begins to disappear and water levels drop, making it easier to navigate the rapids, a sharp watch is kept to determine the moment of leaving. As soon as conditions are proper, camp is dismantled, canoes are loaded, and the trip back to the settlement begins. This occurs late in May. The trip takes a minimum of time, since loads are light and the securing of food does not, as a rule, have to be considered. Usually enough has been secured during the spring trapping to last the group for the trip.

SUMMER ACTIVITIES

Summer activities last from June into August. It is a time when the men relax after the exhausting work of the winter. They aid their wives in tending fishnets, but fishing is quite unproductive. Occasionally, short hunting trips are undertaken. The women, of course, have the usual household tasks to perform, as they did during the winter. As summer draws to a close, a new yearly cycle commences.

SUBSISTENCE AND FUR TRAPPING

HUNTING

The Mistassini Cree are dependent on hunting in two ways, to secure large game animals for subsistence and small game animals whose pelts can be exchanged with the traders for food and equipment. The greater part of the year is spent in these pursuits. The equipment and techniques used in hunting, whether for fur or meat, are similar.

Caribou are not only a source of meat but the bones and antlers are used for tools and the hides for clothing and containers. Caribou may be killed at any time of the year, but it is during the fall and late winter hunts that they are actively sought. Occasionally a chute and pound may be erected in which to snare the animals, although usually they are shot with 30-caliber rifles.

Woodland caribou are a herd animal. Several—up to as many as thirty—are usually found together. Accordingly, all the men of the hunting group cooperate to most effectively exploit them. Once a herd has been located, the men split, each half going to one side of the herd. As the herd moves off, the men race to the front in a pincer movement; those animals that escape are immediately pursued in the same fashion.

Moose supply the Mistassini with the same commodities as caribou. Moose are killed with rifles whenever they are encountered, but are actively sought only during the fall and late winter hunts. Since moose are usually solitary animals, no more than two men, as a rule, are involved in the hunt. During late winter, however, when several moose yard because of the deep snow, all the men of the hunting group may be involved in their capture.

Bear are greatly desired as food, especially because of the large amount of fat they yield. They are taken at every opportunity, but are eagerly sought during the fall when they are fattest. The Mistassini take bear in baited and unbaited deadfalls and upon occasion in steel traps, and often they are shot with a rifle. Formerly, a small hunting dog was used to find bear during the winter when they were in hibernation; at the time of field work, not over a half dozen of these small hunting dogs remained.

Beaver rival bear as an item relished in the diet because of their high fat content. Beaver are captured in deadfalls and occasionally in nets, but more commonly in steel traps. In the past, the small hunting dog was also used to locate the burrows of the beaver.

Hare are another source of food, although of limited importance, except in years of abundance. In effect, they are starvation food, since they possess very little fat. On the other hand, their hide is of extreme importance in the manufacture of blankets and some items of clothing. Hare are taken in stationary wire snares and occasionally, if ammunition is low, shot with bows and blunt arrows.

Other animals taken for food, although of much less importance than the above, are otter, porcupine, lynx, muskrat, and mink. These are taken in snares or steel traps. Otter are sometimes taken in nets, marten in Sampson post deadfalls, and porcupine are clubbed to death.

Birds are of some importance to the Mistassini as a source of food. Spruce grouse are sought, especially during the fall, with slingshots. During the winter willow and rock ptarmigan, if available, are captured in snares and shot with bow and blunt arrow. During the fall, though predominately in the spring, waterfowl—loons, ducks and geese—are sought. Geese are sometimes taken in nets, but more frequently they are killed with shotguns, usually from behind blinds placed on the shore or on the bow of a canoe. Infrequently, decoys are used. Ducks and loons are secured with shotguns and the latter also with 30-caliber rifles.

FISHING

Fishing is undertaken throughout the year, except during freeze-up. Fish are important as supplementary food and therefore basic to the diet. They are, however, taken in only limited quantities.

The gill net is the principal means used in the capture of fish. There are indications that this device is not aboriginal in these northern areas; rather, the net and the technique of its manufacture were derived from Europeans. Whitefish, lake trout, pike, walleyed pike, and ling are secured in this manner. Whitefish and lake trout are taken in the spawning grounds during the fall and walleyed pike during the spring. The few ling secured are taken during the winter. Lake trout are taken with set lines and, on rare occasions, by trawling with commercial spoons. Sturgeon are netted or speared during the period of open water. Jigging for fish is done on occasion.

GATHERING

The collection of vegetal food is minimal. Berries are gathered in season, but the quantity is limited and few, if any, are preserved for the winter. Blueberries are the major crop sought. Other berries are usually eaten immediately when found.

TRAPPING

A variety of fur bearers are taken for exchange for Euro-Canadian products with the traders. The techniques of exploitation have been given above. Suffice it to say that the most important pelts are those of beaver, with mink ranking second. Otter often brings a high price, but the animals are so few in numbers that they are rather insignificant. Marten are also in this class. Muskrat must be abundant before much income can be derived from them. Ermine and squirrel are insignificant as a source of fur, while fox are occasionally important as an income source.

PROTECTION, MOBILITY, AND EQUIPMENT

HOUSE TYPES AND SETTLEMENT PATTERNS

The Mistassini utilize a variety of house types. Most provide shelter for only the nuclear family and dependents. Since the Mistassini are often on the move, their shelters have to be relatively small, easily and quickly erected, and of materials readily available. During the greater part of the year, canvas tents are used, both when the Mistassini are traveling and for more permanent camps, both in the bush and at the summer encampment. In the latter case, the tent is often erected on top of low log walls and is stretched over a frame superstructure. Cabins made of boards and roofed with tar paper also exist in the village, but they are few. Log cabins are frequently built for the early winter trapping period and are generally used only for the one season. The roof is of poles covered with turf or canvas.

Several aboriginal types of lodges are occasionally used. One is the ridge-pole lodge, which has an A-frame at either end supporting a ridge pole. Additional poles are leaned against the frame and covered with birchbark or canvas. At one end is a doorway. In the one observed, two fireplaces and a stove had been placed in a row down the center. Such a lodge is approximately 14 by 18 feet and houses two to three families. Also in use are dome-shaped lodges covered with canvas instead of the hide or birchbark formerly used. The conical lodge is rarely, if ever, used today.

A form used until quite recently was the earth-covered conical lodge, which was made of poles placed close together and covered with moss and turf. This type apparently was developed late as a result of the introduction of steel axes.

The lodges in any one camp vary in type, number, and location, depending upon the season of the year. This variation produces a distinctive settlement pattern, further distinguished by various types of camp equipment, which might or might not be present.

During the summer, the Mistassini reside in an encampment at the south end of Lake Mistassini. Here, there is fairly high ground upon which the lodges, tents, tents on frames, and cabins are located. The dwellings are laid out in several rows parallel to the shore and parallel to each other (Fig. 3-4). The Mistassini reside here for only a few weeks each year. For the greater part of the year they are scattered throughout the band territory.

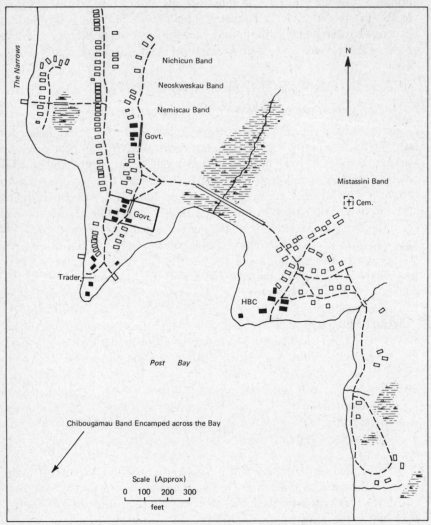

Figure 3–4. Post Bay summer encampment.

When the Mistassini are not living in the summer encampment, they occupy travel camps or base camps, the latter located within the hunting group's land. These are small establishments composed of a few lodges (Fig. 3-5), usually tents and sometimes cabins. Camps are usually erected on the shore of a lake or river, occasionally somewhere along a portage trail, but still within easy distance of water. At base camps, the lodges are placed with the entrance facing east to southeast. Otherwise, there is no prescribed order, although they are always placed quite close to one another. There are few additional structures. Travel camps are located within a few

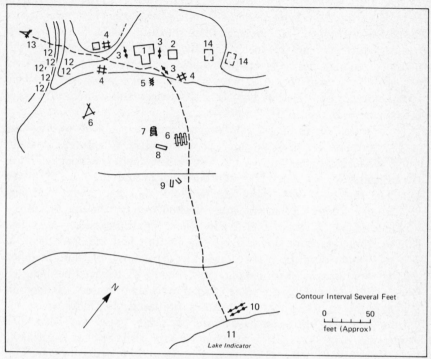

Figure 3–5. A base camp. 1: *Communal log cabin.* 2: *Supply tents.* 3: *Bedding racks.* 4: *Moose hide stretchers.* 5: *Saw frame.* 6: *Cache racks.* 7: *Moose drying rack.* 8: *Toboggan planing log.* 9: *Beaming logs.* 10: *Canoe cache rack.* 11: *Water hole.* 12: *Dog houses.* 13: *Cache rack for bones.* 14: *Author's camp.*

yards of the shore. For base camps, the distance is often 100 yards. The distance is much more if the camp is located on the east shore of a lake or river, where it would be exposed to the full blast of northwest winds during the winter.

TRAVEL AND TRANSPORTATION

Mobility is essential to the Mistassini. Of necessity, they have to traverse long distances in their never-ending search for food and furs.

Basically, transportation has to be adapted to two seasons, winter and summer. Each poses its own problems. During the winter, when the land is covered with snow and the lakes and rivers frozen, overland travel is possible, but only with the proper equipment because of the deep, powdery snows. During the summer, on the other hand, overland travel is restricted because of the forest found almost everywhere and the extensive areas of muskeg. At this time of year, the waterways are the highways.

In winter, the men and women wear snowshoes so they are able to move easily over the light, powdery snows. The women wear swallowtails for the entire season. The men use them also, but only during the first and last parts of the season. When the snows are deepest and most powdery, the men wear beavertail snowshoes, which have a finer mesh than the other style and, therefore, have a better bearing surface. In recent years, the pointed snowshoe has been adopted by the western Mistassini from their neighbors to the west.

To transport their supplies, toboggans and sleds pulled by dogs are used. Toboggans are made of larch or white birch. Sometimes, aided by a dog, men draw them, with women also pulling them occasionally. There are basically two sizes of toboggan—the freighter and the hunting toboggan. The former is 12 or more feet long and the latter about half that length. The hunting toboggan is used when out on the trapline or in search of game. Sleds are a relatively recent innovation. They were first derived from traders on James Bay, who in turn had acquired them, as well as Eskimo dogs, from the north. The Mistassini, in time, modified the sled and dispensed with Eskimo dogs. They were replaced by mongrels from Lake St. John. Dogs are named, but they were not formally trained for driving. Only a few simple commands are used. In addition to the Eskimo sled, the Mistassini have taken over the "prospector" sled. The men make both types of sleds. One type of sled that is most likely aboriginal is the "canoe sled." It is composed of two narrow and thin runners, each having two uprights the tops of which are connected by crossbars. These sleds are used in the spring to move canoes and supplies when the snow is slushy. To load them, poles are laid the length of the sled to form a bed on which the goods will be placed. This type of sled keeps the load raised above the slush and melt water.

Another item that should be mentioned is the hunting bag carried by the men when out for a day. Made by the women from tent canvas, the men carry it slung across their backs with a supporting strap crossing their upper arms and chest. In it they carry food, trapping equipment, and other sundries.

During the summer, water transport is the principal means of movement; for this canoes are used and, on the rare occasions when no canoe is available, a raft is built. Formerly, birchbark canoes were built by the Mistassini. A number of years ago they were replaced by canvas canoes secured from the traders. These are of two types. One, the freighter canoe, has a square end for the attachment of an outboard motor. It is used primarily for freighting supplies and people to and from the hunting territories. The other type of canoe, the paddler, is much smaller and is pointed at both ends. It is used in hunting, primarily when the group is on its hunting grounds. Canoes are ideal, since they are light and can be easily portaged about the many rapids and between water systems.

Tumplines are used when moving goods, slain game, and canoes overland. Another item so used is the *nimapan*, or ceremonial drag line. Made of four strands of caribou hide plaited to form a long cord, it is used to drag beaver and otter into camp. Also the bear's head, when the carcass is being portaged, is held in place with one of these. Porcupines are also carried with the aid of these drag lines.

CLOTHING AND BEDDING

At the time of field work, most clothing was of European style, purchased from the traders. Often, however, children's clothing is homemade, as are women's dresses. A limited amount of clothing is worn both summer and winter. In the latter season, out-of-doors warmth is maintained by rapid movement and by frequent stops, at which times a fire is built and food rich in fat is consumed, which effectively maintains body temperature. The diet of the Mistassini is high in fat content and is designed to combat the cold and to provide the necessary calories needed for hard work.

Although most of the Mistassini clothing is obtained from the traders, several items are still in use which are indigenous. These latter the women make. Moccasins are still worn, made from either smoked moose or caribou hide. "Puckered" moccasins are the most common, although on occasion "pointed" moccasins are made for children. In the past, several other styles were in use. Mittens are made from smoked moose and occasionally from caribou hide. Mittens may not be an old item, but rather derived ultimately from the Eskimo. The Jesuits made no mention of this item of clothing when discussing the dress of neighboring Indians. Furthermore, the Mistassini have still to master the technique of manufacture, which suggests that mittens are not an ancient trait.

Rabbit skin parkas are made, but, according to available information, only for children, probably because of the paucity of hares in the area. Such items of clothing are extremely warm. Rabbit skins are also used as socks. No preparation other than drying the skin is necessary.

Formerly clothing was of skins, primarily caribou. Unfortunately, very little is known about this aspect of Mistassini culture. No doubt there were parkas, breech clouts, leggings, sleeves, and dresses.

Bedding is derived from European sources and consists mostly of woolen blankets and occasionally sleeping bags. Nevertheless, the Mistassini still produce some of their own bedding. Rabbit skin blankets are more important. Sometimes these are encased within canvas to preserve the skins, since the hairs rapidly fall out. Small pillows are another item enjoyed by the Mistassini. No doubt these too are a European innovation. They are quite small, of cotton cloth stuffed with the down and feathers of ducks and geese. Ground cloths are of canvas and bear skin, although in the past caribou hides were no doubt used. Infants are placed in moss sacks and sleep in hammocks. The latter are most likely a European inspiration. Cradle boards are known and said to be occasionally used, but none were seen. There is one in the collections of the National Museum of Canada said to be from the Mistassini.

EQUIPMENT

In order for the Mistassini to survive in the harsh environment of the eastern subarctic, a number of other items of equipment are necessary. Among these are wooden snowshovels, used to clear away the snow when setting up permanent camps and setting and tending traps. Ice chisels with wooden handles and metal points obtained from the traders are used to cut holes in the ice in order to set gill nets and to obtain drinking water. Specialized tools exist for lacing and unlacing snowshoe frames. These consist of bone needles and mesh eveners. To unlace snowshoes, the unmodified lower jaw of a lynx is used. For working wood, the Mistassini have the crooked knife, which has an iron blade, purchased from the traders or are made by the men from files. In addition, there are awls, drills, chisels, saws, and axes. Wooden wedges are made as the occasion demands. In working hides, several bone tools are used, such as beamers, fleshers and flencers, and also steel needles. A wooden and, sometimes, bone needle is used in "weaving" rabbit skin parkas and blankets. In addition, there are wooden grease ladles and fish spoons made by the men. Containers are usually obtained through trade, although bags are still being made from the skins from the lower legs of caribou. Birchbark boxes, although remembered, are a thing of the past. Guns are kept in decorated cases. Shells are carried in pouches supported by a bandolier.

SOCIOPOLITICAL ORGANIZATION

THE DOMESTIC GROUP

The nuclear family with dependents is a basic socioeconomic unit among the Mistassini. Marriage is the desire of all Mistassini and one is not considered adult until married. At the time of field work, all marriages were monogamous, although in the past polygamy has been allowed. Only one woman over thirty was unmarried and she was a hunchback. The age of marriage is, as a rule, quite young with males marrying in their early twenties and females in their late teens. As a rule any one individual, if he or she lives long enough, has two or more spouses, due to the death of the previous spouse(s). Of 92 married men, each had an average of 1.3 wives, and this figure is low, since many were young men.

Parents usually arrange for the marriage of their offspring. If the parents are deceased, other relatives look after the matter. In practice, it is the boy's parents who initiate the negotiations at the request of the boy, who names his choice. It is not often that the girl's parents make the arrangements. The basis for the selection of a mate depends upon practical considerations as well as upon kinship and geographical proximity. The capabilities of the individuals to conduct the normal tasks of survival is of considerable importance. In addition, bilateral cross-cousin marriage is a consideration, since it is and has been practiced to a certain extent. In the past, the sororate was allowed, but it is not known how often it occurred. Often, two brothers married two sisters or brother-sister exchange took place. The former was the more common.

Neighboring hunting groups tend to intermarry slightly more frequently with each other than with those more remotely located. Nevertheless, marriages take place even outside the band, the latter not being either endogamous or exogamous. Somewhat more than 20 percent of the wives are from outside groups.

If a marriage is arranged and the boy is dissatisfied, he is not compelled to comply with the desire of his parents. A girl may do the same, although not so commonly.

No information could be secured as to any type of marriage ceremony before church weddings were introduced by the missionaries. Now, marriages take place during the summer, with from two to four couples being married simultaneously in the Anglican Church. The ceremony is followed with a feast and sometimes with a dance.

The preparation of clothing and food for the wedding and accompanying feast is not allowed until the actual day of the event. If this procedure is not followed, it is thought that bad luck will result.

Generally, the couple spends the first night or two in the boy's father's lodge and then erects one for themselves nearby. Accordingly, a tendency exists for the men of one patrilineal line to be closely associated spatially. This is countered by the fact that the members of one hunting group often live side by side and that the members are not necessarily related patrilineally. As a rule, the couple lives in their own lodge, but during the early winter, at least, all the families of one hunting group live in a large communal lodge.

With marriage, the young couple has to adjust not only to each other but to their in-laws as well. No parent-in-law avoidance is practiced, although they are shown respect, most likely simply because of their seniority. Siblings-in-law exhibit no special behavior patterns.

Cooperation in marriage is the norm, although there is occasional strife between a man and his wife. Affection is often expressed and this intensifies with age. The nuclear family is a unit bound tightly together emotionally, more so than any other group. Marriages are stable, being disrupted only through death and the marriage of children. Only one separation has been recorded. The almost total absence of separations may be due to church influence, although this is doubtful.

The nuclear family is the most important social unit in Mistassini society; as an economic unit it is of equal importance to the hunting group. The husband hunts and traps while his wife takes care of the camp. The younger children and girls help their mother, and the older boys aid their father. The man and his wife often tend fishnets together and, on occasion, go on what might be termed "picnics" to gather berries or other produce. The family is also the commensal unit, except for feasts.

The husband is the legal authority, although from behind the scenes the wife wields considerable power. Often they jointly discuss various matters; in such cases, the wife gives her comments, which may or may not be heeded. No matter what the result, no conflicts occur.

The Hunting Group

The hunting group is the largest unit engaged in the exploitation of the environment. From late August until early June, it is the only economic, political, social, and religious unit in Mistassini society. This is a period of isolation, each group being 10 to 50 miles from its nearest neighbors.

All winter long the hunting group works, lives, and travels together. All members of the group join together for feasts, religious rituals, and games. The men, in pairs or all together, hunt and trap in association, especially when away from camp for more than a day. Organized hunts for caribou include all the adult males of the group. Except for caribou hunts, where cooperation is essential for a successful hunt, the main purpose of association is for companionship and for the education of the younger members. There is not, on the other hand, the degree of cooperation between the women of different households, except within the household.

As mentioned, the hunting group is of equal importance to the nuclear family as an economic unit. All ages except the very young are expected to contribute to the well-being of the unit. Although each individual is capable of performing nearly all tasks essential for survival, there is a sexual division of labor.

There is limited economic cooperation in securing food and furs, but the members of the hunting group aid each other through the distribution of foods secured from the land. A man is expected to give of both his time and food to others, especially those in dire straits; children from an early age are instructed to be generous. Country game and hides destined for domestic use are the main products shared most equitably. This is done by direct giving and through feasts. Food produced from the stores is not exchanged. Store food might be given away, but the understanding is that it must later be replaced. Furs are rarely given to others. Equipment is lent on occasion, and the men sometimes tend each other's traps and fishnets. Widows and their children are cared for by other members of the group who are able. Of course, the elders are cared for by their children.

The hunting groups are small, ranging in size from ten to twenty individuals, rarely larger or smaller. Each group is composed of three to five nuclear families. The desired composition is four families, so that the four married males could hunt and trap as a group or in pairs. The composition of any one hunting group is affected by residence rules and sex ratios. Ideally, patrilocal residence is the norm, a father with three married sons. But this is not always possible, since there might be a preponderance of girls in the family. Furthermore, within the first three years of marriage, the couple must reside for one year with the girl's parents. The family might also increase greatly in size, necessitating a split. Accordingly, various combinations are found. The flexibility of residence allows for the equitable distribution of land and resources so important for survival under the extreme conditions of the eastern subarctic.

Usually one of the males of the hunting group is somewhat older than the others and acts as leader. It is interesting to note that in 1953–1954, there were 35 males over fifty years of age and 126 males between the ages of twenty and fifty. This gives a ratio of one elder to 3.6 junior men and approximates the ideal and the actual hunting group composition.

The leader and his family form the core of the hunting group. Generally, each year the same families join the leader, but on occasion they may not, and some other family may join the group. Fission may be temporary or permanent.

Cooperation between the women of the different households is limited; it exists more for sociability than for cooperation in economic pursuits. On occasion, all the women might go berry picking together, but the berries are not shared. The same is true when they gather spruce or balsam boughs together. They aid each other in sickness and tend the children if one of the mothers is away.

The hunting group is the largest political unit for the greater part of the year. From late summer to late spring it is supreme. Yet, the leader has little real authority except over his immediate family. Other families are dependent upon him, but only when on the hunting grounds. Because of his age, the leader is considered to have the greatest spiritual powers and therefore is thought to be best able to guide the activities of the group. Furthermore, an able leader looks after the interests and welfare of the group. Usually leadership is not assumed until a man has reached at least the age of forty. If there are two men of about equal age, the more aggressive male assumes leadership, and the other either follows or splits, with his family, from the group. Policies are discussed by all the men, but usually the leader's course of action is followed. There have been times when the leader has relinquished his position. Whenever a man other than the leader kills big game, it is the hunter who is then in charge of butchering, bringing the meat back to camp, and distributing it. Also, when one of the males other than the leader has a dream revelation, this might affect the course of action to be taken. The leader may, on the other hand, choose to ignore the revelation. The weakness of leadership allows the men to retain a high degree of sociability.

The members of the hunting group have a community of interest, especially during the winter months. Conversation, companionship, and mutual aid are important aspects of intragroup relations. Definite conventions apply within the lodge as to sitting and sleeping arrangements. Arrangements are on the basis of age and sex. The place of honor in a single-family dwelling is at the rear of the lodge. This is generally reserved for the family head. Other males are next to him. The women are toward the door, with teenage females just inside the door; it is they who tend the fire. Teenage boys are toward the rear and separated from the girls. In communal dwellings families are on each side, with the men toward the rear.

Community interests for the hunting group also involve various forms of group recreation. There are a variety of games, which some or all members of the group engage in occasionally. These consist of the cup and pin game, muskrat-skull divination, breaking a beaver tibia, and cards, derived from Europeans in recent years. In addition, there are social visits, where conversation is of importance. Generally, visits are made to the leader's lodge; only on rare occasions does the leader make visits to other members of the group. Feasts are another form of social interaction.

Religion among the Mistassini is, for the most part, an individual affair, yet the hunting group is a religious unit as far as certain native and assimulated Christian practices are concerned. Christian rituals which involve the entire band occur in summer and include Sunday services and marriage rites.

The hunting group has a high degree of continuity, despite the fact that the composition of the group varies to a certain extent. The factors responsible are not fully known. Overt aggressive behavior cannot be considered a factor, since it was never observed. Yet, interpersonal hostilities of a covert nature did exist. This in part may explain the process of fission. There might be jealousy between men as to their competence, generosity, leadership ability, and shamanistic powers. Furthermore, a leader, to maintain a group, has to prove himself constantly as the senior religious expert and most competent hunter and provider.

The Band

The term "band" has been used in various ways, but primarily to denote the largest assemblage of Indians that occurs within the eastern subarctic (and elsewhere). Yet, this definition has not always meant the same sociopolitical unit over the years. With time, the largest aggregation has altered in structure and, therefore, there have existed a variety of band types.

The Mistassini band has been no exception to the above remarks. Formerly, there were aggregates of hunting groups during the summer at favorable fishing locales. Then, after the establishment of a fur-trade economy, the hunting groups began to congregate during the summer about the trading posts, whether or not there was good fishing in the vicinity. Finally, came the government band, established for administrative purposes, which might include several former bands.

The Mistassini band is of the second type merging into the third. It comes into existence only during the summer months, but is not a strongly organized political, social, economic, or religious unit. Although other Indians of other bands reside at the trading posts, the Mistassini tend to settle in one particular neighborhood. The government imposes upon all those Indians who gather at Mistassini an elected chief and councilor system, but they have no real power or authority and were merely ineffective intermediaries with the government.

The band in no way holds title to the land its members exploit. There are hunting territories exploited by hunting groups. Even here it is not the land itself but rather the resources of the land that are considered the property of the group, although not in absolute terms. A man has a right to take game whenever he finds it if he and his family are in need. The combined hunting territories form the territorial extent of the band. But alterations take place if a group on the margins journeys elsewhere to trade. Then, their territory is incorporated into that of the band where they then trade. In recent years, this practice has been possible only with the consent of the federal government.

Although the band is weakly organized politically and not a cooperative economic unit, it does have some social functions. It joins together for wedding feasts and dances. The former is a rather formal affair, often with several couples being married at the same time. The latter is a much more informal affair.

In summary, the band is of limited significance in the lives of the Mistassini except for the social interactions it allows during the summer and the opportunity to secure marriage partners.

THE LIFE CYCLE

Age and marital status are the criteria by which the Mistassini establish four stages in the life of an individual. These are, as follows: a very small child, *AwAsIs*; an unmarried boy, *napesIs*, or an unmarried girl, *IskwesIs*; a married man, *napew*, or a married woman, *Iskwew*; an old person regardless of sex, *cIsenIw*. An individual proceeds gradually from stage to stage except at marriage, when adult status is automatically conferred.

For presentation, however, several rites are added which do not coincide with any of the changes in status implied in the above stages. *Infancy* is considered as lasting from birth until the "infant's rite." *Childhood*, the next stage, starts with the "infant's rite" and for boys ends with the "first kill rite" and for girls with the "puberty rite." Although life does not basically alter, both boys and girls are expected to assume a more adult role. *Adulthood* is fully assumed at marriage. There is nothing to initiate *old age* unless it is the beginning of general physical debilitation.

Socialization is continuous almost throughout life, and only in old age is one free of the advice of elders. During infancy, a child has considerable freedom except for that imposed by being kept in a moss sack for the first year or so. As the infant matures he or she tends to become somewhat aggressive and independent. This occurs about the age of five or six, at which time social pressures begin to be brought to bear on the child. These continue over the years until teenagers are under the complete domination of their elders. No breach of conduct is tolerated. In late teens, an individual is competent in most matters related to the exploitation of the environment. Upon entering adulthood, he is still guided by his elders and continues to learn the various skills deemed important in Mistassini society. He may, as he advances in years, aspire to the leadership of the hunting group and shamanism. Old age is a respected position and elders are honored for their superior wisdom. Elderly males have the greatest religious knowledge, which is most beneficial to the group, since it is primarily related to the securing of food from the land.

A prime goal of all Mistassini is to have children. For example, when the wife of an elderly male dies, he often marries a younger woman so as to have more offspring.

Before the birth of a child only minimal arrangements are made, such as collecting sphagnum moss to thaw and dry in advance of a winter birth. As the moment approaches, the husband usually remains near camp so as to be of assistance. The woman gives birth within the lodge and is assisted by her husband and another woman of the camp. As a rule, younger members of the family leave and remain in a neighbor's lodge. Delivery takes place in a kneeling position. Once the baby is born and the navel cord is cut, the child is placed in a moss sack. The mother is secured in an abdominal binder and spends about three days resting, with the lodge kept very hot. The binder is tightened each day for about a week so as to restore her internal organs to proper position. After the birth, females and children are allowed to visit, but all men are excluded except the husband.

A few days after the child is born, the mother requests a female relative or friend to name the infant. Male offspring frequently are given the name of their father, and usually one child in the family is named after a grandparent. The one who names the child is expected at some later date to give the child a present. In addition to the formal name, an individual often receives a nickname because of some unusual event.

For the first few days, the infant is not nursed but rather given "fish liquor." When the colostrum is gone from the mother's milk, she begins to suckle. After about two months, additional foods are fed to the infant.

Feeding occurs whenever the child cries. Weaning does not take place until the child is at least a year old.

Toilet training is a gradual process. No undue pressures are brought to bear on the child; he is merely encouraged to conform, although by the age of four any mishaps may be sternly scolded.

By the time infants can walk to a slight degree, they are given commands and sent on errands and are even told to put firewood in the stove. Infants also attempt to help their older siblings while they are performing some task.

The "infant's rite" is given as soon as a child walks or crawls out of the lodge. When this occurs, a feast must be given even if only bannock and fish are available. The desire, however, is to have big game, so an eye is kept on the child until such food is available. The rite symbolizes the future adult role of the children involved. Only one rite was observed in which three boys and two girls took part. The children were between one and a half and two. The boy ritually "killed" and then brought the meat into camp and gave it away. The girls carried in firewood and boughs, which were deposited inside the lodge. This is a festive affair and the children are dressed in new clothing. Afterwards the feast is held.

Childhood follows the "infant's rite" and lasts for boys until the "first kill rite" and for girls until the "puberty rite." Socialization is continued, but there are no outward signs of rebellion, except among four-year-olds, who might have tantrums, directed always against the mother. It must be remembered that this is the age when pressures to conform are initiated. As the child matures, more and more time is spent in work and less and less in play. By the time a boy is thirteen, full days are spent in work during the fall and spring travel periods and winter hunt. Girls are somewhat younger when they start full-time work, being about ten years old. There is, however, considerable variation in the amount of work required, depending on the number of children, their relative ages, and the health of the parents.

Generally, the responsibility for the care and training of children lies with their parents. Sometimes in very large families a child or two lives with the grandparents and aids them during the winter. The grandparents may or may not belong to the same hunting group. A widower who has to care for an infant might give it to another family until the child is four or five, then he is returned to his father. Older siblings frequently care for the younger ones in the same manner as the parents. Of course, other relatives are, on occasion, instrumental in training children.

During the period of childhood, the youth learns to obey without question. This is accomplished through repeated commands. Rarely is corporal punishment used and then only with young children. Threats of supernaturals, laughter, ridicule, and, as a last resort, ostracism are other techniques of social control applied to children and even to adults.

Children are consciously trained by their parents in everyday tasks.

They also learn through imitating their elders, whether parents or siblings in play activities. Also, they are generally with their elders and learn by direct observation.

Entrance to adolescence for a boy is marked by the "first kill rite." As a boy approaches puberty, he spends more and more time hunting in the neighborhood of camp, sometimes accompanied by an older person. Eventually, the youth kills some game animal, after which a feast is held and the meat distributed. He is now considered a hunter and spends more time with the men on their hunting excursions.

A girl enters adolescence at menarche when she undertakes the "puberty rite." During the puberty rite the girl spends her time in isolation. She lives in a special lodge out of sight of the main camp. Here she cooks her own food, uses her own dishes, and gathers her own firewood. A young girl may sleep with her, but no males may even see the menstrual lodge. The period was said to have lasted ten days, but at the time of field work isolation was two to three days. There is no feast at the conclusion, since this is not a public celebration.

This change from childhood to adolescence is not a sharp one. It means, though, that the work load is continuously increased as the years go by. It is a time when adolescents are expected to thoroughly master the skills needed for adulthood. No longer is there time for play; rather, the winter days are spent fully occupied in work, depending on the physical strength of the individual.

During adolescence, the sexes are rigidly separated. A boy and his sister, who had played together and slept side by side, must now remain apart. There is, however, no avoidance taboo in that they should not see or speak to one another. This also applies to those who are unrelated. Love affairs do occur and may result in marriage.

Marriage marks the entrance into full adult status. Until this time no one is considered a "true" man or a "true" woman. Marriages are monogamous, a situation dictated by the church. Marriage is solemnized by a church wedding followed by a feast and, occasionally, a dance.

With marriage, a man and woman assume new duties and obligations, uniting their combined skills in order to make survival possible in the subarctic environment.

The main economic duties of the men are hunting and trapping. Together the men butcher large game and bring it into camp. The men, often aided by the women, work the larger hides. Only occasionally do they prepare the smaller pelts. During the winter, the men set gill nets under the ice and sometimes are assisted by their wives when tending the net. Heavy loads are moved by the men; they also erect the tents, log cabins, and stoves. On most occasions they run the outboard motors. Wooden articles are made by the men, and men secure some of the firewood and boughs for flooring.

Women's work is much more restricted to the vicinity of the camp. Here they gather boughs and seek firewood, which they transport to camp, saw, and split. They catch fish on set lines, trap fur bearers, and hunt small game. This latter activity is of extreme importance, since it often supplies supplementary food when the men are out of camp. At times, this is the only food available. Besides this work, there are innumerable jobs within the lodge such as cooking, doing the laundry, placing down boughs several times a week, lacing snowshoes, making and mending clothing, and preparing pelts. Also, children must be tended. In all these tasks the women are aided by older girls.

SOCIAL CONTROL

Social control throughout adulthood is similar to that which has brought conformance in the early years of life. No doubt it is as effective, except that now a transgressor has the opportunity of moving elsewhere.

With advancing years, physical debility sets in, but at the same time religious knowledge generally increases; thus, for a man and for a woman old age is initiated. The woman gains in wisdom, as does the man, but not necessarily in religious power. Yet, both are respected and always cared for, and their advice is usually followed.

Death is disturbing, no matter what the person's age. When it occurs, the deceased is dressed and placed in a coffin, which is interred in the cemetery at the summer settlement or, at other times of the year, near the encampment. Prayers are said over the corpse, the grave is filled in, and a picket fence is built about it. A man's possessions are stored for a year and then distributed and sold. His name, especially if old and respected, is mentioned only with reluctance. On anniversaries of the death, feasts are sometimes held in honor of the deceased and the next day a pilgrimage is made to the grave.

RELIGION

Religion to the Mistassini is a personal and individual affair. As a Mistassini, especially a male, grows in age, he gains religious experience. And, it is the elders who have the most religious knowledge over and above what others know to be considered shamans and the religious practitioners of the group.

The primary concern of Mistassini religion has to do with the pursuit of game animals to insure survival. A variety of practices are carried out, such as divination practices and the supplication or honoring of game animals.

Mistassini religion also incorporates interpersonal relations of a ritual nature, modified Christian beliefs and practices, and various miscellaneous beliefs, such as those concerning constellations. In addition, a number of different spirit beings inhabit the world of the Mistassini, which might or might not be of harm to them. Some rituals are used for a variety of purposes. Accordingly, rather than organizing the latter according to functions, the various practices will be described. These consist of the "shaking tent rite," "the sweat lodge," bear ceremonialism, the treatment of game remains in general, feasts, drumming, dreaming, scapulimancy, and, finally, the Church. Following this, supernatural beings will be mentioned along with the various omens in which the Mistassini believe.

The "shaking tent rite" is performed for at least two reasons—to destroy the *wihtIko*, a cannibal giant who eats people, and to determine the results of future hunting. There is limited evidence that it was used in witchcraft. According to informants, only "old men" (mostly shamans) know how to perform the rite.

The "tent" is constructed of six poles, each about 1½ inches in diameter and from 7 to 8 feet long. One pole is of larch, two of birch, and three of black spruce. The poles are placed upright in the ground about the circumference of a circle with a diameter of several feet. They converge slightly at the top. A birch pole is placed on either side of the larch pole. The three spruce poles complete the circle. Several inches below the top on the outside of the poles a hoop is placed. A second hoop is placed on the inside of the frame about halfway between the top and the ground. The poles are tied to the hoops with roots. Formerly the "tent" was covered with bark and probably also with hide, but later canvas came to be used. The top is left open. The place of entrance can face in any direction, although it must be located between a larch and a birch pole.

The structure is not erected by the performer. Rather, he delegates the task to any man present in the group who knows how to do so. The "tent" is placed inside the lodge in winter and outside in summer. As mentioned, "the shaking tent" is used against the *wihtIko*. If a *wihtIko* is near, one of the old men is expected to feel the cannibal's presence and know he will come during the night. When this happens, the old man tells several of the men to get the proper poles before dark and to erect the "tent." That evening the old man enters the "tent" and soon his spirit helpers arrive. These include *ciwetInIsIw*, *sawInIssIw*, *NipIn InsIw*, and *wapAnIsIw*. Eventually the old man returns to the "tent" and emerges. He announces his success by showing parts of the *wihtIko* which he and his spirits have killed.

The "shaking tent" is also used to find the location of game and to give other prophesies. The old man enters the "tent" and his spirit helpers arrive. People sit around outside near the "tent" watching and listening. The performer talks of hunting and sings; as he does, the poles of the lodge shake. Through these actions, the shaman discovers where game might be found. In addition, the onlookers, if they so desire, ask questions of the old man, who discovers the answers for them.

The "sweat lodge" is employed for divination and for treating the sick.

A "sweat lodge" is constructed just before a hunt, often during the fall, to determine the outcome of the winter hunt. The lodge is a small dome-shaped structure made of arched spruce poles. The door faces in any direction. On the right as one enters, a number of sticks are laid on the ground parallel to one another.

After the lodge is built, stones are heated in a fire outside; they are then brought inside and placed on the stick platform; next, the man performing the rite enters and closes the doorway securely, sealing the lodge. He then places water on the heated stone and then sits on the side of the lodge opposite the stones and sings. He continues singing as the heat increases in intensity. If he is able to withstand the heat, it means that soon he will kill an animal, such as a bear or a caribou. On the other hand, if he is forced to leave the lodge, he will kill little or no game during the coming winter.

The bear is of extreme importance in the religious thought of the Mistassini. The special treatment accorded the bear consists of speaking to the animal before and after slaying it, giving it tobacco, dressing it inside the lodge, drawing a mark on the skull, preparing a chin skin "charm," erecting the skull and paw bones on a tree trunk and sometimes painting the skull, placing the other bones on a special cache rack, giving a bear feast, and not using the hide for one year.

When a bear is located, the hunter talks to the animal, especially if it is in winter hibernation, saying that he is sorry he has to kill it. After the animal has been slain, it is placed on its back and pipe tobacco placed on its chest. Then the hunter sits back and smokes over the bear. The carcass is then carried back to camp. If it is carried overland, it is portaged on the back of the hunter with a tumpline and the head secured over one shoulder by holding it there with a *ninmapan*. On arrival in camp, the carcass is taken immediately inside the lodge, where it is then dressed. After the hide has been taken from the skull, a black charcoal mark is placed over the eyes of the bear.

Several days after the bear has been killed, a feast is held. The meat, except the head and forelegs, is smoked for one day, then boiled the day of the feast. The ceremony is held in the evening, and everybody assembles at the leader's tent, each bringing his own plate, cup, and knife. After everyone arrives, the leader passes tobacco and everyone smokes. After smoking, the leader arranges the pans of meat in front of him. Small pieces are cut from various sections and placed in the bowl of a grease ladle, after which the contents of the ladle are emptied into the fire in the stove. The meat is divided and each person is given a share on his plate. Next, the leader rubs bear grease in his hair and drinks a ladle full of grease, which is now passed on to the others who repeat the performance. The women do not receive any meat from the forelegs. Afterwards, every-one eats. At the conclusion, the remaining food that has not been served is carefully taken away. Each individual who has any remaining on his plate will take it home with him.

The hide is carefully prepared and then stored for one year before being used. This is done in honor of the bear. The chin skin is made into a charm by one of the women of the group. The *liguum frenual* of the bear is sewn to the center of the chin skin, which is then folded around it. This symbolizes a bear.

In the spring, the skull is secured to the trunk of a tree overlooking a body of water. Occasionally, it is painted with red designs. The bones of the forepaws are wrapped in birchbark and attached to the trunk of the tree. All other bones, except the tibia, are placed on a special bone cache reserved for important animals. The tibia is made into a flenser for removing the hide from beaver.

There are a number of observances regarding the treatment of the remains of other slain animals. Caribou antlers are erected on horizontal poles, moose antlers are placed on stumps, and the scapulae of both are hung in a tree. In addition, a ceremonial hide of caribou is on occasion prepared and a caribou feast given.

Other observances are the suspending on a pole or in a tree of beaver skulls, duck wings and upper bills, loon breast bones, and large trout mandibles. Bones placed on special cache racks are caribou, moose, otter, beaver, lynx, mink, duck, loon, and large trout. Most bones except hare, partridge, and fish are not fed to the dogs. It is said that if these observances are not attended, the hunter will not be able to secure game in the future.

Feasts are another form of objective religious behavior. Not all feasts, however, have religious content. Some are purely social, though these may be recent innovations, such as marriage feasts. Others, such as the beaver "eat-all feast," are divinitory or were given in honor of a slain animal. Christmas and Easter feasts are recent innovations.

Feasts are regarded as either *mAkUsan*, "feast proper," or *ApIsis mAkUsan*, "little feast." In the former case, all the families of a hunting group, as a rule, gather together for a joint ceremony. Each family usually contributes a share of the food. When a "little feast" is given, the families do not eat together. Rather, the family giving the feast sends food to each family in the camp.

Feasts are given on many occasions. They can be conveniently placed in three groups: animal feasts, seasonal feasts, and life-cycle feasts. Animal feasts include otter feasts, moose feasts, bear feasts, rabbit-grouse feasts, and large lake trout feasts. Seasonal feasts consist of two fall feasts, a Christmas feast, a midwinter feast, an Easter feast, and a spring "thanksgiving" feast. Life-cycle feasts are those given for a child's "first step rite," when a boy kills his first game, occasionally on a child's birthday, at marriage, and sometimes for deceased hunters. These feasts are not always given exclusive of one another. For example, several moose might be killed in the fall and a moose feast given. This might coincide with one of the fall feasts and could conceivably be in honor of a child's birthday.

The future is also predicted by drumming. This is of special importance in the fall, since that is the time to determine the prospects of killing game for the coming winter. The performance is always, as far as known, given in conjunction with a feast.

Generally, it is the "old men" who drum. Several men in their thirties, however, were observed using drums. It is claimed that a boy first begins to drum when in his twenties, generally after he is married, and is taught by his father.

The drum is hung before the leader by a suspension cord. This is attached to a large pin thrust through the roof of the lodge. The bottom of the drum is raised above the floor from three to four inches. The leader drums first, singing his hunting songs in a very low note hardly audible. After he has performed, the drum is passed to the next oldest man until all have had an opportunity. During the performance, the drummer stops and smokes. During any performance, other members of the group might listen intently, carry on conversations in low tones, or even play games, as the children often do. Each man might drum for an hour or two. When all have performed, the leader puts the drum away.

Another important means used to foretell the future is the interpretation of dreams. Both men and women are said to dream and to see the future. One informant said that "somebody" spoke to them in their dreams, describing the future. Dreaming occurs at any time of the year, but is most common after the fall feast and during the winter. A man often dreams of the coming winter and whether or not his luck will be good. Women also dream of the coming winter. A man's dreams indicate to him the presence or absence of game, its location, and whether or not he will kill it. When he arises in the morning, he tells about his dream.

Other forms of divination are associated with bear patella; beaver tail bone, leg bone, and pelvic bone; caribou and moose scapulae; caribou lower jaw bone; mink carcass; muskrat skull; otter game; caribou game; otter forepaw and tail bone; grouse sternum and frucula; and match.

The Mistassini are considered "converted" to Christianity, and most are listed as Anglicans. They have a resident Indian-Anglican catechist, who holds Sunday services and performs the marriage ceremonies, aided by his twin brother. Also, during the summer months, there are sometimes evening services. During the rest of the year, the individual hunting groups perform their own Christian services, such as having a Christmas and Easter feast in which hymns are sung and prayers said. These feasts are simply a modification of the feasts of the past with trimmings of Christianity; nevertheless, Sunday hymns are sung and occasionally services are held.

Supernatural beings include *sawInIsIw*, *wapAnIsIw*, *nipIn InIw*, and *ciwetInIsIw*. The first is the spirit or person of the south wind and comes from that direction. The second is the east wind and comes from that direction. The third is "summer man," the warm weather. The last spirit is "winter man," the snow, the wind, the cold, and the ice. In addition, two other spirits are identified but apparently never called upon for help. These are the *wihtIko* and *WapAlAhkiwAc*. The former, also known as the *Atus* and *mACAwen*, is a cannibal being who kills people and lives by eating them. The Mistassini are very much afraid of this spirit. *WapAlAhkiwAc* take human form and are of a mischievous nature, going around at night with a candle, untying tent ropes, and committing similar acts. While informants at times talked freely of these spirits in a lighthearted manner, they still feared them.

The Mistassini have a number of omens. For example, it is considered bad luck for children to count the lodge poles. If a squirrel or Canada jay is heard near the lodge at night when the occupants are asleep, it means that someone will die. It is bad luck to find the eggs of the Canada jay. If a person finds the eggs of a spruce grouse, someone will be visited with misfortune. If a spruce grouse lands on the tent, it means that one of the occupants will soon die. When the cleithrum of a pike is found which has a large growth in the center of the concave side, it is a sign that the hunter will kill big game.

Two charms are recorded. One, the lower incisors of a caribou strung on a string, was suspended about a child's neck so that the wearer might have good teeth. A second charm was a small disc secured on the front of a baby's moss sack to protect the child from harmful influences.

Groups of stars, not necessarily corresponding to our constellations, are named. One consists of Ursa Major with additional stars in surrounding groups. It is referred to as *wucelAtItihkU*. According to several informants, it represents an animal having the forelegs of a caribou and the hind legs of a moose, with a tail formed by the handle of the dipper. Women and children cannot see this "constellation." Men, however, on reaching maturity are able to see varying amounts depending on their age and experience. In old age, they can distinguish all of it. A second "constellation," perhaps Corona Borealis, represents a drum and a rattle. Only old men can see this one.

Change

Over the years, tremendous changes have taken place in the life of the Mistassini Cree. These are the result primarily of contact with Euro-Canadians.

Environmental changes have occurred, but the extent and intensity of these are difficult, if not impossible, to determine precisely. There has been a decrease in caribou and beaver, and no doubt among other species as well, but to offset this, around the turn of the century, moose began to enter the area and have become fairly common. During the last century vast forest fires swept through most of the Labrador Peninsula, affecting much of the territory of the Mistassini.

The environmental changes that have transpired have not been as forceful in altering the Mistassini's way of life as contact with Euro-Canadians. At first, it was the fur trade, then the missionary, and, finally, the tourist and industrial personnel. During the present century, this contact with outsiders has increased tremendously, and soon the way of life of the Mistassini will be totally altered, becoming much closer to that of the West.

Changes in material culture were initiated early. Native materials utilized for tools and other equipment, such as bone, antler, wood, bark, and hide, were rapidly replaced. Iron was perhaps one of the most important of the early trade items, but soon came cloth and canvas, guns and steel traps, and many other items brought by the traders. In time, the Mistassini became dependent upon the trading companies for much of their material equipment and recently all or much of their food. New forms of housing were introduced, such as log cabins. There have also been alterations in the transportation system, with the introduction of large dogs and sleds and outboard motors. The fur trade allowed for the development of hunting territories. It also gave impetus to the establishment for a time of a relatively strong leadership pattern. These were charismatic individuals who were allied with the trading companies and were in charge of the fur brigades. Leadership formerly did not appear to be exceedingly well developed and these leaders did not remain long in power. As soon as the trading companies began to lose control over the fur trade, these leaders were no longer encouraged. Instead, the government imposed upon the people a system of elected chiefs and councillors and other institutions such as schools. At the same time, the independent bands began to gather together about the trading posts and no longer at their favorite summer fishing camps. As this pattern developed, the result was an acephalous community. Much more time was then spent in the community than in former days when hunting and trapping were of prime importance. In addition, there are now other economic outlets such as wage labor, the tourist industry, and commercial fishing. At the same time, the hunting group was losing its central position in the sociopolitical system and the nuclear family was emerging as a relatively independent social and economic unit. As this transpired, there were accordingly changes in the kinship structure. Kin terms were becoming much more restrictive. Finally, the religious system has undergone considerable alteration. Christianity was introduced by missionaries and the people were "converted." Nevertheless, the former religious practices, although altered and weakened have not disappeared, even though shamanism is no longer the power that it was in previous years.

NOTES

1. The data on which this paper are based were secured during a year's residence with the Mistassini in 1953–1954. Most of the time was spent with the Matoush hunting group on their lands, some two hundred miles north of the posts on the south end of Lake Mistassini. We left in late August and returned in early June. The group was composed of thirteen individuals.

   I wish to thank the Arctic Institute of North America, which sponsored the field work, the Office of Naval Research, Washington, which made funds available, and the Royal Ontario Museum, Toronto, which made possible the preparation of this paper. Many individuals made the work possible, but especially Mr. and Mrs. Wilfred Jeffreys, then manager of the Hudson's Bay Company post at Lake Mistassini, Alfie Matoush and the members of his group, and above all my wife, who accompanied me.

2. The data here are based on Hallowell (1929).

3. The data here are based on J. Rogers (1960).

REFERENCES

Hallowell, A. I., 1929. "The Physical Characteristics of the Indians of Labrador," *Journal de la Société des Américanistes*, Paris, n.s., 21:337–371.
This paper is a preliminary outline of the physical characteristics of the Indians of the Labrador Peninsula. It is based primarily on metric measurements of a relatively small sample of individuals.

Lips, J. E., 1936. "Trap Systems among the Montagnais-Naskapi Indians of the Labrador Peninsula," *The Ethnographic Museum of Sweden*, Stockholm: Smarre Meddelanden, No. 13.
Various types of traps used by several Indian bands of the southwestern part of the Labrador Peninsula are described. It is a purely descriptive article.

———, 1937. "Public Opinion and Mutual Assistance among the Montagnais-Naskapi," *American Anthropologist* 39:222–228.
Lips has contributed in this article exceedingly important data dealing with the ways in which the Indians of the southwestern part of the Labrador Peninsula aid one another, especially when on the traplines. It details the types of signs employed to attract or gain help.

———, 1947a. "Naskapi Law: (Lake St. John and Mistassini bands) Law and Order in a Hunting Society," *Transactions of the American Philosophical Society*, n.s., 37, Part 4:379–492.
This work deals with social control among two bands of Indians in the southwestern part of the Labrador Peninsula. It is a rather detailed account, but unfortunately it attempts to portray an aboriginal situation, which, of course, could not be done on the basis of memory recall from informants. It, in fact, pertains to the period 1875–1900.

———, 1947b. "Notes on Montagnais-Naskapi Economy," *Ethnos* 12 (1–2).
Here Lips gives a descriptive account of the technology and subsistence patterns of several Indian bands living in the southwestern part of the Labrador Peninsula.

Martijn, C. A., and E. S. Rogers, 1969. "Mistassini-Albanel: Contributions to the Prehistory of Quebec," Centre des Etudes Nordiques, No. 25, Univ. Laval., Quebec.

Rogers, E. S., 1963a. "Notes on Lodge Plans in the Lake Indicator Area of South-Central Quebec," *Arctic* 16 (4):219–227.
An account which describes the earth-covered conical lodge and suggests that it was a late development, occurring after the introduction of iron tools.

———, 1963b. "The Hunting Group—Hunting Territory Complex among the Mistassini Indians," National Museum of Canada Bulletin No. 195, Anthropological Series No. 63.
This work attempts to show that the hunting territory is a late development in response to the fur trade.

———, 1966. "Subsistence Areas of the Cree Ojibwa of the Eastern Sub-arctic: A Preliminary Study," National Museum of Canada Bulletin No. 204, paper No. 3. *Contributions to Anthropology*, 1963–1964, Part II.

———, 1967. "The Material Culture of the Mistassini," National Museum of Canada Bulletin No. 218, Anthropological Series No. 80.
An account which describes the material culture of the Mistassini as it existed in 1953–1954 and in the past, where possible based on testimony of informants. An attempt has been made to place the changes that have occurred in the context of the acculturation of the Mistassini.

———, and J. H. Rogers, 1959. "The Yearly Cycle of the Mistassini Indians," *Arctic* 12 (3):130–138.
This article recounts a year's economic activities among one hunting group of Mistassini Indians.

———, and ———, 1960. "The Individual in Mistassini Society from Birth to Death," National Museum of Canada Bulletin No. 190. *Contributions to Anthropology*, 1960, Part II, Anthropological Series No. 60:14–36.
A descriptive account of the life cycle of the Mistassini which details the various stages an individual passes through from birth to death.

Rogers, J. H., 1960. "Notes on Mistassini Phonemics and Morphology," National Museum of Canada Bulletin 167. *Contributions to Anthropology*, 1958:90–113.
The linguistics of the Mistassini are presented in preliminary form in this paper.

Rousseau, J. J., 1945. "Chez des Mistassini," *Revue d'Institut Français d'Amérique Latine* 2:64–91.
Here is described the life of the Mistassini Indians.

———, 1946. "Autour de la marmite des Mistassini," *Gastronomie* No. 8:9–12.
Rousseau here discusses food among the Mistassini.

———, 1947a. "Le Dualisme Religieuse chez les Mistassini," *Annales de l'Association Canadienne-Française pour l'Avancement des Sciences*, Quebec, 13:118–119.
The religious system of the Mistassini is portrayed, and the author discusses how it has developed into two phases or aspects. The Christian aspect is carried on during the summer months at the trading posts and the aboriginal pattern is practiced during the winter months when the Indians are living in isolation on the hunting territories.

————, 1947b. "Ethnobotanique des Mistassini," *Annales de l'Association Canadienne-Française pour l'Avancement des Sciences,* Quebec 13:118.
The utilization of plants by the Mistassini is discussed here.

————, 1948. "La Crainte des Iroquois chez les Mistassini," *Revue d'Histoire de l'Amérique Française* 2 (1).
An account which describes how the Mistassini Indians still fear the Iroquois and use it as a means of controlling their children.

————, 1949. "Mistassini Calendar," *Beaver,* Outfit 280:33–37.
Rousseau here gives a general account of a summer visit to the Mistassini.

————, 1950. II. "Chez le chef Peter Matoush," Montreal: *La Patrie,* Dec. 3:32, 33, 35.
The story of Peter Matoush, a noted Mistassini Indian whose hunting territory was at the head of the Tamiscami River, is presented here.

————, 1951a. XXXII. "L'ours chez les Mistassini," Montreal: *La Patrie,* Feb. 18:32.
This paper documents the importance of the bear among the Mistassini Indians.

————, 1951b. "Chez les Indiens de la forèt et de la Toundra Québecorses, Les Resources du Laicat Missionaires," pp. 237–251, in *Le Laicat et les Missions,* Vol. 1 of Les Editions de l'Université d'Ottawa.
A short account which presents the differences that existed between the northern Indians of the tundra and those to the south within the boreal forest.

————, and J. P. Currier, 1947. "Notes sur le folklore zoologique des Mistassini et particulièrement la pêche," *Annales de l'Association Canadienne-Française pour l'Avancement des Sciences* 13:117–118.
A short account which describes the knowledge the Mistassini possess regarding the fauna of the area.

Rousseau, M., and J. J. Rousseau, 1947. "La Cérémonie de la Tente Agite chez les Mistassini," *28th International Congress of Americanists,* pp. 307–315.
A description of the shaking-tent ceremony among the Mistassini is given in this paper.

Speck, F. G., 1923. "Mistassini Hunting Territories in the Labrador Peninsula," *American Anthropologist* 25:452–471.
This paper presents details of the hunting territories and their locations and an account of the individuals who hunt in each territory.

————, 1930. "Mistassini Notes," Museum of the American Indian, Heye Foundation, *Indian Notes* 7 (4):410–457.
Games and material culture of the Mistassini Indians are depicted in this paper.

————, 1935. "*Naskapi, the Savage Hunter of the Labrador Peninsula,*" Norman, Okla.: University of Oklahoma Press.
The religious system of the Indians of the Labrador Peninsula is presented in detail. This study deals primarily with those Indians living in the southwestern part of the peninsula, including the Mistassini. It is an analysis of the religious thought of these Indians in relation to the supernatural and the environment, especially as it concerns the big game so necessary for survival.

Speck, F. G., and G. G. Heye, 1921. "Hunting Charms of the Montagnais and the Mistassini," Museum of the American Indian, Heye Foundation, *Indian Notes and Monographs*, Series 2, No. 13.
Speck here gives a description of the charms employed by the Mistassini for hunting luck.

Thwaites, R. G., ed., 1896–1901. *The Jesuit Relations and Allied Documents*, Vols. 1–73, Cleveland: Burrows Brothers Company.
Early missionary accounts of their work, with a considerable amount of information on the Indians of eastern Canada.

GLOSSARY

AhlcUwacin: early fall

ApIsis mAkUsan: feasts held at the winter camp; food is distributed to each lodge rather than all members assembling in the leader's tent to participate

Atus: see *wihtIko*

AwAsIs: very small child

band: aggregate of Indians who gather together around a trading post and exploit a continuous tract of territory, which consists of all the hunting territories exploited by the band

cIsenIw: old person

ciwetInIsIw: spirit of winter

IskwesIs: unmarried girl

Iskwew: married woman

mACAwen: see *wihtIko*

mAkUsan: feast which everyone at the winter camp is invited to attend

miciskasic: late fall

miyuskAmu: late spring

napesIs: unmarried boy

napew: married man

nimapan: ceremonial dragline or carrying string for beaver, otter, and other game made of four strands of caribou babiche braided together and decorated with colored yarn or thread. These are usually made in response to a dream experience.

nipin: summer

nipIn InIw: spirit of summer

pipun: winter

sawInIsIw: spirit of the south wind

sikwAn: early spring

WapAlAhkiwAc: spirit believed to take human form and at night walk through the camps engaging in mischievous acts.

wapAnIsIw: spirit of the east wind

wihtIko: a giant cannibal spirit who is believed to roam the forest during the winter

wucelAtItihkU: constellation Ursa Major along with additional stars from surrounding groups; it is said to represent an animal having the forelegs of a caribou and the hind legs of a moose.

CHAPTER

4

THE GUAYAKI

Pierre Clastres

Pierre Clastres is currently attached to the Centre National de la Recherche Scientifique in Paris and received his doctorat de troisième cycle in 1965. His experience as a field researcher has included work among the Guayaki, Guarani, Ashluslay, and Yanomami Indians of South America. His publications include articles which have appeared in Journal de la Société des Américanistes, L'Homme, Critique, *and* Les Temps Modernes. *He is presently preparing a thesis on the problem raised by political power in South American Indian societies.*

EDITOR'S INTRODUCTION

The Guayaki inhabit the tropical forests of Paraguay and speak a dialect of the Guarani linguistic stock. Historically, they have lived in purposeful isolation from Paraguayan plantation owners and their Mbya neighbors in order to avoid hostile contact. The physical environment provides ample resources for hunting, gathering, and, in some areas, fishing. Hunting, however, provides the focus not only for their economic activities but for their ritual life, group ethics, and individual prestige as well. Unlike many tropical climes, temperature, not rainfall, is the basis of seasonal change; rainfall being fairly constant year round. The Guayaki are organized into territorially based autonomous tribes, which are further subdivided into allied bands comprised of four to five nuclear families each. The cyclic wandering of each band within its own territory follows a pattern organized around the harvest and preparation of *guchu* larvae beds, a sort of semi-cultivation activity.

Clastres has emphasized Guayaki material and social techniques used to exploit their physical environment and demonstrates the close adaptive relation between economic and social organization. The Guayaki's strict definition of tribal territory stands in contrast to definitions of territory given by the North American and African groups represented in this book. Their formalization of food distribution through the rule that a hunter cannot eat the game he has taken, increasing group interdependence, finds counterparts to a greater or lesser extent in other societies, such as the Copper Eskimo with their system of sharing partnerships, and the !Kung distribution of large game. The evasive mobility that the Guayaki found necessary to maintain may be paralleled, perhaps, only by the Paliyans; and the effects of this necessity, such as in limiting the number of band members and in placing a premium on self-sufficiency, are similar in both cases.

HISTORICAL BACKGROUND AND GEOGRAPHIC LOCATION

For centuries, or at least since the conquest of Paraguay by the Spaniards, the Guayaki Indians have occupied the same territory in the thick tropical forest which covers most of the eastern section of the country. The historical habitat of these Indians is therefore inclusive within the right bank of the Paraná to the east, the Sierra de Mbaracaju to the north, and the Andean Belt of Caaguazu and the Sierra de San Joaquin to the west. This region is the watershed between the tributaries of the right bank of the Paraná and the tributaries of the left bank of the Paraguay (see Figs. 4-1 and 4-2). Many streams and brooks run through the forest, thereby assuring the inhabitants a ready supply of water.

The climate of the area is not dominated by the opposition of the dry and wet seasons, as in the Chace, but rather by the alternation of winter and summer. Rainfall occurs regularly throughout the year. Therefore, it is the variations in temperature and not the system of rainfall which exert a greater influence on the life of the Indians. The winter months are characterized for the Guayaki by a serious shortage of food resources, such as larvae, honey, and small animals. The months of October through March are very hot; those from April through September are cooler, and it is in June and July that the temperature drops the most. On certain mornings in June, the clearing where the Indian camp was situated was entirely covered with frost, allowing the unusual sight of nude Guayaki children running over the whitened grass.

Because of their very small number, the Guayaki obviously do not occupy all of the territory defined above. They live only in the most central part, where the forest is least penetrable; the mountainous regions also serve as a natural refuge for these Indians. To demarcate the territory of this tribe, therefore, means really to fix the boundaries to which their ceaseless travels take them. The eastern section of Paraguay was a Guarani-speaking area in the sixteenth century; it remains in part Guarani in the

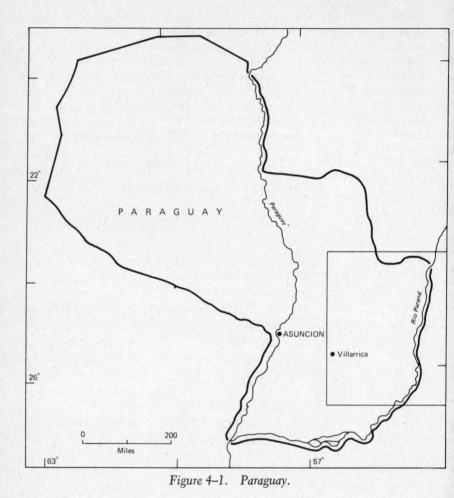

Figure 4–1.   Paraguay.

eastern section. The tribes belonging to this large South American linguistic
stock were very numerous, and it was in the Guarani area that the Jesuits
set up their famous missions.

The Guarani Indians who populated the eastern section of Paraguay
were sedentary farmers. Of course, hunting, gathering, and fishing provided
a substantial complement to agriculture, but farming constituted the basis
of their economy. Their plantations, established by the burning of sections
of the forest, furnished the Guarani with manioc, maize, beans, bananas,
and tobacco.

The social life, rituals, and mythology were grounded largely in farming.
The Guarani had developed in the Guaira a relatively high level of civilization. But the Guayaki know nothing of agriculture; their economic life
depends entirely upon natural resources. These Indians are purely hunter-
gatherers and as such spend the entire year wandering. It is this endless

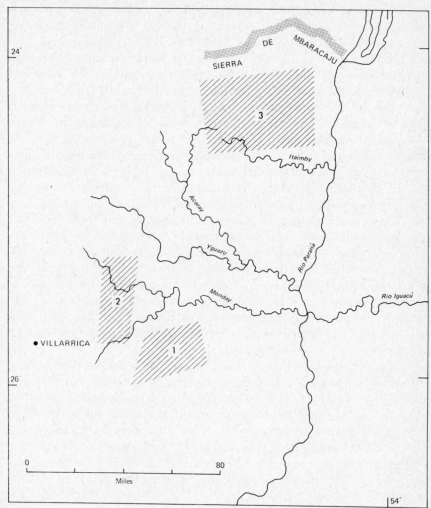

Figure 4–2.   Area of the Guayaki.

shifting about that has always made it nearly impossible to have a non-hostile contact with the Guayaki.

What is more, these Indians belong to the Tupi-Guarani linguistic stock. The similarity of the Guarani and Guayaki languages has been noted since the eighteenth century. Recent studies of the Paraguayan scientists Leon Cadogan (1960, 1965) and B. Susnick (1961) confirm the identification of the Guayaki language as a Tupi-Guarani dialect. It is essential to emphasize the linguistic appurtenance of the Guayaki. For now we can see them as a tribe of nomadic hunters whose area of wandering is located right in the middle of the traditional territories of the Guarani, who are settled farmers. This ethnological situation is exceptional, because we find, side by side, two completely different "samples" of the vast Tupi-Guarani whole: nomadic hunters with a very low cultural level surrounded on all sides by settled farmers of an incomparably superior cultural level. This strange coexistence of the Guayaki and the Mbya-Guarani was probably established in the remote past. The Mbya-Guarani live in a territory contiguous to the forest where the Guayaki find refuge. If Indian America is an area of "primitive" societies—a very general determination which in no way excludes a "hierarchy"—there are, in effect, certain Indian cultures more primitive than others. However, one cannot overlook the fact that a large majority of these societies practiced farming while a small number ignored it completely, depending upon hunting, fishing, and gathering. It should be noted, too, that certain of these latter populations live in climates that make all forms of agriculture difficult—as, for example, the inhabitants of the Tierra del Fuego or of the southern part of the Argentine pampas. But if one remains within tropical America, that is, within this huge zone which is almost completely capable of cultivation throughout, it may be seen that nearly all the tribes that occupy this region depend upon the cultivation of sweet or bitter manioc, numerous varieties of maize, sweet potatoes, beans, and so on, in varying degrees. Some of these peoples cultivate in a cruder manner than others. There are inequalities in know-how and in the quantities produced, but one can say that all these societies are at a neolithic level.

Nomadic peoples are rare in South America; they constitute something out of the ordinary there. Such is the case of the Guayaki. Strangely enough, they have survived to present times—an inaccessible primitive stream—without contact with their powerful Guarani neighbors. Even more paradoxical is the fact that this tribe, while knowing nothing about agriculture, belongs to the Tupi-Guarani class through many cultural traits other than language; one notes particularly their similarity of ritual and mythology. The Guayaki are an almost unbelievable combination: both Guarani and nonagriculturalists.

It is here that they pose a decisive problem to ethnology, a problem beyond their particular case, one that concerns the whole of South America. Should one consider the nonagricultural Indian peoples as survivors of a period prior to the appearance of cultivated plants, and therefore very ancient, or as the result of cultural regression? In the case of the Guayaki, one cannot avoid this question, and it should at least be tackled without prejudicing the answer which the analysis of the ethnographic material may bring.

HISTORICAL DATA

One can now turn to tracing a brief historical outline, not of a history fairly well destined to remain hypothetical but of the history of these Indians in ethnological literature. There is not an abundance of information here. A. Métraux and H. Baldus recall in the *Handbook of South American Indians* (Vol. I, p. 435) that until very recently, the Guayaki were among the least known of the tribes of the continent. They first appear with this name in the eighteenth century in the work of the Jesuit priest Father Pedro Lozano. An historian of the conquest of tropical South America, he used in his work the remarkable archives of the company. In this way, he was able to gather an abundant amount of ethnographic information concerning not only the tribes that accepted the "protection" of the priests but also those that preferred to follow their lives freely in the Brazilian and Paraguayan forests. From the missionaries Father Lozano obtained the first data on the mysterious tribe, the Guachagui (as he named it), a tribe feared and hated by their Mbya neighbors. To them, the Guayaki were only barbarians, differing very little from the wild animals of the forest. From what Lozano says, one can readily see that since the eighteenth century the relation between the Guayaki and the Guarani was strictly a hostile one. It is necessary, moreover, to note that the Guarani were most likely the attackers, for the very timid Guayaki thought only of fleeing at the approach of strangers. In effect, then, the Mbya tried to exterminate the Guayaki, and considering the reciprocal terms by which these two tribes designate one another, it is clear that these terms simply translate the type of relation maintained between them. The word "guayaki" comes from the Guarani dialect spoken by the Mbya and would appear to signify, according to Cadogan (1960), "the ferocious rat." As for the Guayaki, they name their adversary the *machi-tara*, and the literal translation of this term is "many-arrows." It should be stressed that this climate of hostility and hatred that always surrounded the Guayaki explains, in great part, why it was impossible to study these people for such a long time.

It seems that after the fruitless attempts of the Jesuits in the seventeenth and eighteenth centuries, contact with the Guayaki completely stopped until the beginning of the twentieth century. In any case, their name is only occasionally mentioned in traveling accounts.

It was therefore necessary to await the coming of the twentieth century for a peaceful contact with the Guayaki to be realized. F. C. Mayntzhusen (1911, 1924–1926), a German stock breeder, was the first European able to observe and describe these Indians. He settled along the border of the Paraná and spent many years following traces of Guayaki bands in the forest. Finally, in 1908, he was able to establish friendly relations with some of them, even convincing about twenty-five individuals to come and settle down on his estancia. These people, though very well treated, soon fell victim to epidemics, so that a few years later there were only a very few survivors. Mayntzhusen, however, used the time he spent living with Guayaki profitably to gather valuable ethnographic material, all the more useful, since almost nothing was known about this tribe. Certain work of the German researcher was the essential source for the chapter of the

Handbook devoted to the Guayaki. Unfortunately, most of his notes are still unedited.

Mayntzhusen's later attempts to enter into contact with other Guayaki groups failed, and almost half a century passed before a group of about twenty individuals appeared, in August 1959, around Arroyo Moroti, 9 miles from the village of San Juan Nepomucena. They placed themselves under the protection of a native of the region in order to escape professional Guayaki hunters. These men tracked down Indians in the forest, attacked their campsites, and captured their children to sell as slaves to the farmers of this region. The man at whose home the Indians sought refuge had at his service two Guayaki adults who had been captured several months before. He succeeded in winning their confidence, for they disappeared one day and turned up again a few weeks later, accompanied by the band to which they belonged. They had been able to convince them to abandon a free but now impossible existence in order to accept the sedentary life beside a "good" Paraguayan. The experience was deemed favorable by the Indians, for a while later the rest of this tribe rejoined the first group. Thus, for the first time in the history of the Guayaki, a whole tribe (even though it consisted of only some thirty-five persons) agreed to live with the enemy. Thereafter, it was easy for the Paraguayan who had brought these people together to look for another tribe situated in the cordillera of the Yvytyrusu, near Villarrica. And in June 1962, almost all of this group established itself with the first in Arroyo Moroti. Only a few Indians refused to leave their forest. But they finally decided to do so, and by strange coincidence, they appeared at the encampment of their brothers on the very day of our arrival among the Guayaki. It is these two groups which are the object of the present study. The two tribes are made up of about one hundred individuals. The first will be called the Yñarö group and the second, the Yvytyrusu group, after the territories from which they came. The name Guayaki give themselves is Aché, signifying "people." Other than these two groups, which are rapidly becoming extinct, there exists a third, more northern, tribe. These Guayaki are still completely hostile, and at the time of this writing, contact with them appears unlikely. It is therefore impossible to evaluate their numbers, which are probably not great.

TECHNOLOGY

The Guayaki Indians are purely nomadic hunters. Consequently, their technology is strictly adapted to a roving existence, in which moving is an almost daily affair. These journeys last the greater part of the year, with certain periods involving many hours of difficult walking, even for the Indians, because of the density of the vegetation. It therefore is immediately apparent that the quantity of goods and instruments the Guayaki can use is limited by what the women can carry. All the basic goods of each family are packed into the carrying basket, the capacity of which is only slightly limited by their great physical strength. In addition, the time spent in any one encampment is always so short that it is possible to devote only a little time to the fabrication of tools. Too, the Indians are continually exposed to diverse dangers such as the approach of another presumably hostile band, and more frequently, Paraguayans with clear intentions. All of this incites the Indians to remain ready to flee as soon as the danger has been spotted. Within only a few moments the women must assemble and pack up all the goods scattered around them in order to quickly disappear into the protection of the forest. This is another reason for owning only a few things and for never completely unpacking the basket.

If the Guayaki are poorly equipped, it is because they are nomads and their technology hinges on this form of life. Even if destitute, they are no less capable than any other tribe of satisfying the needs that their lives demand. And one could even say that, devoid of agriculture and wholly dependent as a result upon natural resources, the Guayaki, by surviving under such harsh conditions, show a remarkable capacity to adapt technically to the environment. If the equipment of these Indians is strictly in accord with an economic life based upon hunting and gathering, it nevertheless includes certain characteristics that seem to be in disagreement with the life of a hunter-gatherer. This point will be examined later.

Equipment of the Men

The principal activity of the men revolves almost entirely around hunting, and each Guayaki adult owns a bow and a set of eight to fifteen arrows. The dimensions of the bows and arrows are impressive. Without a doubt, there are few bows, at least in South America, that attain or surpass their height except those of the Sirione of Bolivia. The size of the bows varies from 6 feet, 4 inches to 7 feet, 8 inches, and it is a curious sight to see these small men manipulating gigantic weapons, which are sometimes as much as 3 feet taller than they are.

The bow (*rapa*) is made from the wood of *toi*, the pindo palm (*Cocos romanzoffana*), or the wood of the *jyvyté* (*Hiocalyx balansae*). Huge and somewhat irregularly polished, they are hewn from almost circular sections or from very flat sections. The string (*paa*) is simply hooked by a loop to the top end, and the extra string is wrapped around the bottom end in reserve. Generally, the string, consisting of three strands, is made from fibers of the pindo palm mixed with fibers of *pyno*, the nettle plant (*Urera baccifera*) and of *dyvi* (*Bombax*). The women make the strings for their husband's bow by rolling fibers with their hands.

The Guayaki have owned iron tools stolen from the Paraguayans for a long time. Thus, the sectioning of the wood is done with an old knife.

But the fine work of polishing is done with the hard shell of a large snail (*tyta*) which abounds in the forest. After the shell has been pierced, it is used as a plane. Because of their size and the hardness of the wood, the bows of the Guayaki are heavy and powerful; a hunter can easily shoot his arrow over 100 yards, and he can hit a game animal at 45 or 55 yards. Though the string is made by the women, they cannot touch the bow itself for fear of bringing their husbands *pané*, bad luck, in the hunt.

Arrows The arrows (*machi*) are as large as the bows, from 5 feet, 8 inches to 6 feet, 8 inches. They consist of two parts: the head, which is made of very hard wood (*jyvyte*), is between 2 and 4 feet long; it is joined to a reed shaft (*kyti*) of between 1 foot, 8 inches and 4 feet long. A small cord of nettle fibers (*gary*) or a binding of tiana bark (*bupi*) holds the head in the shaft. The feathering is tangential; the feathers (*pepo*) are simply fastened into a tight binding of *bupi* bark, which is itself then glued to the reed tube with *ganchi* wax. The exceptional length of these arrows is understandable, in that they must be in proportion to the bow in size and also because the head, even though it is of very hard wood, breaks frequently. Each time this happens the hunter resharpens the head and its length diminishes. When the head is too short for the initial shaft, it is fitted to a longer reed to obtain an arrow about the same length as the old one, causing the head and the shaft to vary inversely to their size. The making of arrows requires such patient labor that the head is used as long as possible; an arrow that goes astray or that is shot into the high branches of a tree is always salvaged. The feathers most often used for arrows are those of the *briku* (vulture), the *kimira* (a bird of prey), and the *jaku* (a type of pheasant). Generally the feathers of predatory birds are preferred because feathers from other birds, it is believed, might bring bad luck to the hunter.

Each Guayaki owns an average of twelve arrows, one of which is specially designed for small and middle-sized birds. The latter is not really an arrow, and it is called *rapia*, not *machi*. It consists of a reed tube into which is stuck a piece of hard wood with a large rounded point. This makes it possible for the hunter to stun birds without tearing them to shreds.

There are three types of true arrows, or *machi*. One type, consisting of a head which is barbed on one side, is used for large birds, monkeys, and middle-sized game (coatis, pacas, iguanas, and so on). A second type is barbed on both sides and is used to kill large animals (anteaters, capivaras, jaguars, and so on). Finally, there is the arrow the head of which is a long blade of wood without barbs, which is used on the crocodile (*jacaré*) and the jaguar. Only two or three men owned these last two types of arrows, probably because of individual specializations: one of these hunters very much enjoyed the killing of *jacaré* and therefore used arrows suited to piercing the hard shell-like skin of the animal.

Stone Hatchet This is the only tool used by the Guayaki for felling trees. For several decades, however, the Indians have known how to use iron stolen from the Paraguayans, and they use it more and more in place of the older stone hatchet (*itajy*). The Guayaki are probably the last people in South America to continue to use this neolithic hatchet. They find the stone in stream beds, and the polishing gives to this "diabase" a nearly cylindrical shape. One end is made thinner to use for cutting. Actually, this hatchet is not sharp; it mostly crushes the fibers of the tree to be felled. The other end is rounded off and embedded in a hollow area of the handle, which is made from the wood of the wild orange tree (*turi*). No other fastening technique exists. The theory that the Guayaki fit handles to their hatchets by driving the stone into a stock that unites itself to this rock as it grows is pure legend.

The hatchet is used to cut down pindo palm, the wood of which serves as raw material for arrows. It is also used for widening the openings of beehives, which are hidden in the hollows of trees, in order to extract honey. Curiously, the women are the ones who polish the stone and attach it to the handle, the men being satisfied with cutting and hollowing out the wood. When traveling, it is the woman who carries this heavy hatchet. And so strong is this division of the sexes in carrying obligations that the modern metal hatchets, even though used only by the men, are always carried by the women.

Boar Spear This is a long piece (about 6 feet) of very hard wood tapered at both ends, one of which is sharpened to a point. This instrument, (*bairakwa*, or *pypé*), used only by the Yñarö group resembles a lance, and although designated as a boar spear, it is essentially used to kill the jaguar and the capivara.

Digging Stick This instrument consists simply of a piece of bow wood (*rapa chonga*). When a bow is too old, it snaps in the middle, and the two parts are used by their thinner ends to dig up the ground. They are used for digging roots, for enlarging a hole in order to trap armadillos, for digging deep pits for trapping tapir, and, finally, for digging graves.

Only two tools are used for making arrows, the snail shell and the chipping chisel. When a long, thick splinter of wood has been obtained with the hatchet, it is thinned and polished and filed down with the *tyta* shell. Once the wooden blade is straight and smooth, teeth are carved upon it by using a chipping chisel made of a capivara incisor mounted on a monkey bone, which serves as a handle. This is the extent of the equipment of the Guayaki hunter.

Equipment of the Women

The tools of the women, in effect, constitute the household goods and therefore serve both the man and his wife. But since it is the wife alone who makes them, she is the owner in the same way that the man is the owner of his bow and arrows.

This equipment is obviously more varied than that of the men because it encompasses almost all the objects of the Guayaki technology except for weapons—namely baskets, pottery, and woven goods, the making of which are all women's tasks because of the sexual division of labor.

Baskets The most important container is the carrying basket (*nako*), which is made from one or two palm branches of the pindo and has a rather large load capacity. When it is worn out, it is thrown away and a new one is made; Guayaki women work quickly, and they need very little time to replace the basket.

The basket is carried across the back, hooked onto a wide frontal headband (*nako chä*); the head, therefore, supports most of the weight. Only married women own and make these baskets, although a mother can give a small one to her little girl who wants to imitate her. Besides the basket, each woman owns two or three mats (*davé*), also made of pindo. Forty inches long and 20 inches wide, they are used both to sit on and to lie on. In addition, each household has two or three fans (*pekä*), which are used to stir up the fire during winter and to chase mosquitoes away during summer.

The feathers the husband keeps in reserve for the feathering of his arrows are kept in a container 12 inches long and 4 inches wide. Besides this, one often finds a small sack containing vulture's down (*viju*), which is used for medical and ritual purposes. The *kromi piaa*, carrying headbands which the Aché Gatu use for carrying young children, also belong to the category of basketry, for they are made in the same way as the carrying headbands for the baskets; indeed, they constitute a larger replica of the latter. Made of very tightly braided fibers of *dyvi* (*Bombax*), the child-carrier and the headband for the basket are quite solid and can be used much longer than the implements made from pindo palms.

Pottery The two groups are familiar with the making of earthenware (*kara*) from soft clay (*moo*) that is found in certain parts of the forest. This clay is mixed with charcoal in powder form, and the Indians say that this is the cleansing process used "to insure that the pottery is good and black." The pots are made by the coiling technique.

The polishing is done with the aid of the snail shell already mentioned and with a kind of forest "bean" (*proaa*). When this work is finished, the piece is dried in the sun and then baked. Its bottom is slightly pointed. The dimensions of these containers vary, the largest having a diameter of 10 inches and a depth of 5 inches. Some of the pottery is decorated with three or four lines of fingerprint impressions along the upper part, a type of decoration typically Tupi-Guarani.

These small pots, which are made by married women, have diverse uses. First, they are used in cooking when meat or pindo flour is boiled, but they are also used to store honey and to search for water. The presence of earthenware in a nomadic group such as the Guayaki is unusual, and one is tempted to say that under most circumstances they would not have it.

It is important to remember that the Gé, of an infinitely higher cultural level, do not have earthenware.

Other Containers There is also a container made from a waterproof weaving. This is the *daity*, a large basket of ovoid shape made of fine layers of *takwarembo*, tightly braided, and whose exterior surface is covered with a thick layer of beeswax (*ganchi*), which makes it completely waterproof. Water, and especially honey, are carried in it. Actually, it is the principal container in which liquids are carried, as it is provided with a woven handle attached to a net wrapped around it. Water can also be carried in a bamboo tube (*krachira*).

The Guayaki also use turtle shells in which honey and water can be mixed; a sort of gourd called *biru*, which is stolen from the Paraguayans or the Mbya; and the underside of the armadillo shell, in which a beeswax called *ychy* is stored for medical and ritual use.

Weaving The use of the term "weaving" is actually not correct, because the Guayaki know nothing about the use of the loom. Their weaving is actually a very tight braiding of plant fibers, which resembles crochet work, that the Indians call *tyru*. The Guarani Indians used the same raw material to make a fabric that is also called *tyru*.

From the *tyru*, the women of the second group make headbands for carrying children, mats, and also small, square pieces of fabric to be used sometimes by the old people to cover their shoulders in winter or to cover a basket when it is overloaded.

Rope-Making Included first of all in the category of rope-making is the bow string. Also included is a rope made of plant fibers, women's hair, and monkey hair, which the men roll around their left forearm to protect themselves from the bite of the coati. This rope (*pavwä*) may also serve as a sign of prestige for the hunter. Finally, there is the thin string (*gary*) which is used for threading teeth to make necklaces.

Other objects one might find in the women's baskets include a fibula of a monkey (*piju*), sharpened on one side and used as a needle; slivers of bamboo (*kyti*), which are used as knives and as razors; and pieces of pindo wood, which are frayed at one end so that they resemble a brush. This instrument (*koto*) is used to drink liquid food. It is soaked in the pot and the juice drunk by sucking on the brush. There also may be found a reserve of *ganchi* wax in the form of a large blackish ball. Another *ychy* wax is applied to the face and the body of a sick person with a well-polished wooden blade (*pétö*). Finally, there might be a small sieve (*vava*), made from intercreased thin pieces of bamboo, which is used for cleaning the coarse pindo flour in the women's baskets.

MISCELLANEOUS EQUIPMENT AND DOMESTICATED ANIMALS

In connection with the rudimentary esthetic activities of the Guayaki, the pan flutes (*mimby*), made of three or four reed tubes, must be mentioned. These are foreign to the Yvytyrusu group, which has only a hunting whistle made from monkey or vulture bone. It is also necessary to point out that the teeth necklaces, some of which can be very long and can carry several hundred teeth, are owned by all married women. The women make them by saving the teeth of the animals killed by their husbands. Sometimes, as a symbol of prestige, the men wear a headdress (*ambwa*), consisting of a piece of jaguar skin and a bunch of tails, either of the coati or the howling monkey, which hangs from the shoulders.

One must, in terminating, indicate that the Guayaki have domesticated animals. Each family almost always owns one or more coati. Used in the place of watchdogs, they are distrustful and they immediately signal the approach of strangers or other animals. They also serve as a food reserve and are often eaten after having been fattened. In addition, the Indians sometimes raise monkeys, but they mostly serve as children's playthings and are the butt of their games.

SETTLEMENT PATTERNS

The camp is rapidly organized because it is always temporary. The Guayaki almost never stay in the same spot more than two or three days. In choosing a favorable resting place for the band, several factors are taken into consideration. The site should be close to a spring or a brook, but at the same time far enough away from the water to be free from the swarms of mosquitoes which infest the humid zones. Second, the noise of the water must not cover the eventual approach of a jaguar or an enemy. Finally, a place in the forest is chosen where there are mostly ferns and where the trees are not very tall, thus reducing the chance of attracting lightning. The ideal site is a spot equally near some pindo palms, so necessary to the lives of the Guayaki, and other sorts of vegetation that have either a real or imaginary use, such as the genipap tree (*tarë*), the leaves of which fall and crack under the feet of the jaguar, thus forewarning the Indians. The encampment (*enda*) is in the form of a circle, the diameter of which is determined by the number of families making up the band, the average being about 40 feet. The men carefully clear this area of shrubs and parasitic vegetation which congests it. The Guayaki campsite is very small. It is, moreover, impossible to locate because it is surrounded by a forest wall, and unless a child starts to cry, one could pass within 40 or 50 feet of a band without even knowing it. Once the campsite is cleared, the men build the shelters, which consist of four uprights and a grass roofing. Four forked posts are staked into the ground about 5 feet away from each other. When possible, the trunks of small trees are used as roof supports, since this saves both time and energy. A fragile latticework of thin branches, sometimes bound with the liana plant, is placed on the framework, which consists of the four mountings. Finally, a good thickness of pindo palms is placed upon the latticework. The Guayaki house (*tapy*) is therefore limited to a simple roof about 4 feet, 4 inches high. There are no walls, and the house serves merely as protection from the rain and for resting and sleeping between excursions into the forest. It is also important to note that the Indians do not even bother to set up such shelter when there is no fear of rain and when the night is not too cool. Each family occupies a shelter; therefore, there are as many families in each camp as there are *tapy* arranged in a circle around the cleared space. It is difficult to imagine more rudimentary living conditions than those of the Guayaki, but at the same time, it is easy to understand why they do not spend more time and effort on their huts, since they live in these shelters only a short time.

FIRE-MAKING

The Guayaki make fire by friction—the nearly universal method of South America. A piece of the shaft of an arrow pressed against a piece of tender and very dry wood (*chäka*) is turned as rapidly as possible between the palms of the hands. If the wood is in the least bit damp, the operation can be long, and many men take turns, because the making of the fire is a man's job.

Making fire is also a grave, almost religious, act, and if someone laughs during the act, the fire will refuse to appear. Moreover, women should not watch the operation. Actually, fire-making occurs very rarely because the Guayaki never let the fire go out, and during the period of travel, each woman, in addition to her burdens described earlier, carries a piece of live coal which will allow her to light the fire without effort at the next stopping point. The Guayaki are naturally expert in discovering the best wood to burn, or at least which wood gives off the most heat. The fire is situated at the edge of the hut, just within the limits of the roof. Three or four large logs feed the fireplace, and at night the whole family lies on the ground in the little space left between the basket and the fire. The children nestle against their parents, facing the flame, with the adults behind them. As the heat diminishes, the father or mother gets up and replenishes the logs. Since the nights are often cool, each one in his sleep tends to draw nearer the fire, and the morning reveals a pile of naked bodies half covered with ashes.

FOOD PRACTICES

There is no apparent order in the hour of the Indian meal. One eats when one is hungry. It seems, however, that the evening meal is the most consistent of the day. This is understandable, since the day is generally spent hunting for food that will be eaten in the evening.

Cooking is, of course, a task that falls to the women. It is rudimentary, and the meat is either boiled in earthenware pots or roasted. Monkey meat, for example, is always boiled (*baku*); venison or wild pig is always roasted (*kai*). The game is sometimes poorly cooked, and often the repugnant odor of half-spoiled armadillo meat comes from the women's baskets. When some large game is killed (deer, jaguar, horse, or cow), it is cut into quarters to be roasted on a large wooden grill (*byta*), under which a fire burns. Moreover, the cutting up and dismembering of the game is subject to numerous prohibitions, depending upon the animals. For example, a man cannot without great danger cut up an armadillo—his wife must do it. Likewise, each person eats only certain meats or certain parts of the animals. Thus a woman pregnant with her first child should not eat the meat of the howling monkey; or a man in his prime should not suck from the head of an animal, which is reserved for old people. As for the huge larvae of certain large insects, they are not only eaten raw but also alive. The meat is torn with the bare hands, and the juice which flows down the fingers is sucked with pleasure. The delicious marrow of the pindo palm is generally eaten as soon as it is obtained, but the women also know how to make a kind of thick soup out of it (*bruéé*), to be eaten with the larvae. The Guayaki know nothing about salt, fermented drinks, or tobacco. Their food is marked by one great contrast: the sweet, or sugared (*eë*), and the bitter (*iro*). The Guayaki hate the ·bitter and are very fond of sweets, of which honey is an example.

THE ECONOMY

FOOD RESOURCES

The economic life of the Guayaki is a continual food quest. Nomads and not agriculturalists, they do not provide themselves, as do other tribes, with food reserves in manioc, maize, beans, sweet potatoes, and so on. Since they depend entirely upon natural plant or animal life, this search for their "daily bread" must start anew each day of their existence. Certainly they succeed in surviving, but only at the price of an incessant effort and of an intensive exploitation of the forest (relative to their technical level). But the Guayaki confront the observer with a level of civilization (not a historic era) that is extremely primitive. For this reason one should take particular care to study their economic life. Besides, if the vital necessity of spending the greatest part of their time hunting for food perhaps hinders the Guayaki in attaining more complex forms of socio-religious life, the weight of the economy is, in turn, felt at all levels of group life, and that weight pervades all social activities. In fact, the quest for food is the guideline for those activities; it becomes their reference point, the goal of their existence. Almost all rituals—the taboos (those associated with foods, as well as others), the songs, and naturally the social organization—are celebrated, respected, and instituted in terms of the economic life, more in terms of its repetition than its development. And so existence, economically defined, is all the more oppressive because it is less secure. But even the insecurity of the economic life of the Guayaki finds its compensation and its point of honor in the effect it has on their various modes of life.

To begin with, an error should be pointed out that most of the few books dealing with the Guayaki have perpetrated. The point in question concerns the description of the economic life of these Indians and the relative importance of hunting and food-gathering in their subsistence. In his book, Vellard (1939) writes: "The Guayaki have not yet truly become hunters: remaining in the most primitive stage, they rely especially upon gathering the products of the forest vegetation for their subsistence" (p. 78). Baldus (1943), in agreement with Vellard on this point, asserts in a short resumé of the Guayaki culture: "The fruit and vegetable matter from *Cocos romanzoffiana* in addition to honey or larvae constitute, rather than hunting, the subsistence base for the Guayaki" (p. 147). Finally, the chapter of the *Handbook* devoted to the Guayaki expresses this same point of view (Vol. I, p. 436). Consequently, according to these authors, the Guayaki depend more upon gathering food than upon hunting, and for Vellard, these Indians still live in a stage not only preagricultural but also prehunting. But my observations contradict the preceding statements in all respects.

Hunting is not only the business of Guayaki life (that is, the activity to which they give the most time and that yields the greatest quantity of their food) but it also is a Guayaki preoccupation. They give it great symbolic importance—to the point that, directly or indirectly, most of the "profane" or "sacred" acts that they perform turn on the hunt.

The Guayaki have a veritable hunting complex in the two meanings of the term. It is a complex in the concrete, physical sense because the men spend most of their time either in the forest tracking and killing animals or in the camp making or repairing arrows and bows. It is a complex in the psychological sense because to be a good hunter, to bring in a great deal of game, to be *paña*, is what the Guayaki think about without end—almost to the point of obsession. And how can it be otherwise when this obsession is simply preoccupation with self-preservation and the survival of one's children? So, as will be amply verified later, the hunt, the principal activity of the Guayaki, is also a focus for their ritual life. Hunting is so important to them that it pervades their socioreligious life. For the Guayaki the hunt serves the same organizational function that agriculture does for neighboring tribes. The destiny of a Guayaki, from birth to death, is almost completely dominated by the hunt (*bareka*), because it is by hunting that he lives, both in nature and in culture. The hunt serves to satisfy the material needs of the body, but it also affects individual prestige, group ethics, and metaphysical thought.

The Guayaki are therefore much more hunters than they are gatherers; to say otherwise is to indicate an ignorance of their entire religious and ritual framework. Before approaching these problems, it is necessary to describe the economic life of the Indians and to take an inventory of the resources the forest furnishes them. The resources are gained very unequally from hunting, fishing, and gathering.

HUNTING

It is superfluous to stress the ability of the Guayaki to interpret the tracks or the cries of animals, their skill in approaching game, the accuracy of their shots, or their physical strength.

Likewise, it will suffice to indicate that these Indians are experts in their knowledge of the forest and of the ways of wild animals. Their knowledge of the environment is so vast that unfortunately only a small part of it can be collected. The life of the Guayaki depends directly upon a familiarity with their natural habitat, and it should be added here that these Indians eat all animals of the forest, almost without exception. Only a small number of birds which serve an important mythological function are not used for food.

When a jaguar is killed, for example, it is eaten, without any other ritual, as ordinary game. At the beginning of our inquiry, the Guayaki assured us that they ate frogs quite readily, but that they disliked toads: "*Iro puté*," they explained, "very bitter." We believed at that time to have found the one food not eaten, until one day a Guayaki was seen in the process of stunning an enormous toad. He was asked, "Do you want to eat it?" He said yes, that he was going to boil it, and though it was very bitter, he said he was very hungry. Toad skin is evidently very distasteful, but when there is nothing else, it is eaten. The animals killed most often by the Guayaki, be they big or small, are wild pigs, deer, coatis, armadillos, iguanas, capivaras, agoutis, jaguars, ant nests, and monkeys. Various sorts of rats, serpents, lizards, and most types of birds which are found in such large numbers throughout the South American forest are also killed, such as birds of prey, partridges, pheasants, vultures, and even small birds, which when plucked in the wink of an eye and quickly roasted are crunched in one mouthful. It is nearly useless to give a complete list of the animals the Guayaki kill because they eat everything. And, in respect to this, it should be indicated that the *Handbook* gives some surprising information: duck meat is forbidden to Guayaki women (Vol. I, p. 442). However, these Indians all bear the names of animals the mother eats during her pregnancy, and we found in both Indian groups the name "duck" (*chimbégi*). They therefore do not have a taboo on the eating of duck. But since the information given by the *Handbook* comes from Mayntzhusen, it is worthy of respect: perhaps it is a question of a taboo of a particular band or of the High-Paraná group.

A great number of the animals mentioned above are killed with the bow and arrow, which is the most essential hunting weapon among the Guayaki. Other techniques are used for some animals. The armadillo, blocked in his hole, which is then enlarged to the dimensions of a veritable pit, is either held to the ground with the left hand while his neck is wrung with the right, or he is stabbed with one end of the bow. Arrows are shot at trees upon whose branches the coati takes refuge, and as a result he is generally forced to come down, whereupon he is seized by the tail and with the left hand is banged against the tree trunk while the left forearm is protected by the thick roll of *pavwä* rope, which neutralizes the effect of the dangerous teeth of this animal. The Aché Gatu also sometimes use the *pypé* spear to bring to bay the jaguar or the capivara. Of course, all of this does not occur without accidents, and most of the men bear on their bodies numerous deep scars from claws and fangs. Indeed, they are very proud of these scars, which promise their souls an easier climb toward the sun after death. One thing left strangely unlearned by a people as tributary to game animals as the Guayaki is trap or snare hunting, at which the neighboring Mbya tribe is expert. The trap technique is used only in the capture of the tapir. Mayntzhusen mentions, however, a rather complex jaguar trap that neither Guayaki group knew anything about. Once a habitual path of a tapir has been discovered, a fairly deep pit is dug, narrower toward the bottom than at the top. The opening is hidden under fragile latticework of branches and leaves, which collapses under the weight of the heavy animal and sends it hurtling into the pit, from which it cannot escape. The hunter then stuns the beast with heavy blows of the bow; he does not kill it with an arrow because the hide is too thick. The tapir trap (*brévi ityty*, "make the tapir fall") is only rarely made, and several days can pass before the beast comes along that same path again. The Guayaki do not wait such a long time, so often it is a jaguar that profits from the windfall.

Even though the hunt is the center of the socioeconomic life of the Guayaki, its technical description is limited here; the social incidence of the hunting economy will be examined later with the social organization. It is simply to be indicated here that the Guayaki make meat their principal food, and if they are deprived of it for three or four consecutive days, they fall into a state of apathy and sadness which is almost comical.

FISHING

Fishing is secondary because the streams that flow through the Guayaki territory are poorly supplied with fish. It is important to point out, however, that there are differences from group to group. It seems, for example, that among the Guayaki of the High-Parana, studied by Mayntzhusen, fishing is much more important than it is for the two groups considered here. Among these two groups, few individuals are named "Fish" (*Piragi*), which demonstrates the slight importance of fishing. Since the waters are shallow and clear, fish are either speared or caught by hand. When fish are particularly abundant in a stream, the Guayaki build a sort of reed dam against which they push the fish, catch them by hand, and throw them up onto the river bank. This is a collective type of fishing in which women and children participate. The Guayaki know neither net fishing nor pole fishing, although the liana vine is abundantly used in ritual.

GATHERING

According to certain authorities, it is gathering that constitutes the most important economic activity of the Guayaki. But the undeniable truth commands attention from the outset: it is a fact that the Paraguayan forest is actually poor in types of consumable vegetation. There are fruits, generally small, found on some dozen trees; wild oranges are succulent but rare. These oranges come from trees planted by the Jesuits in the sixteenth and seventeenth centuries and which have since grown wild. As for the native wild orange trees, the Guayaki do not eat the fruit, which is very tart. Finally, they eat the marrow of the pindo palm and the large terminal bud of the tree. It should be pointed out that the fruit from *kybwé* (*Chrysephyllum lucimifolium*) appears only during the hot months, the fruit from the *pypö* tree (*Myrciaria baporeti*) appears only in cold months, and the oranges (*turi-ia*) appear only for a few weeks. The only permanent plant collecting is gathering the marrow of the palm tree (*kraku*) and the fibers from the trunk of this tree, from which is extracted a coarse flour which is sifted through a small sieve (*vava*). The boiled mixture of this flour (*toi wii*) with larvae makes a sort of soup which is well liked by the Indians, *bruéé*; it is drunk with the *koto* brush. As for the terminal buds, which, are most often eaten raw, they are a very good-tasting food, and very nutritious. This is about all the picking the Guayaki do. It is really limited to a few items, because in this forest there is nothing else to pick. Game animals always exist, however, and if not in abundance, they appear at least in large enough quantity to feed the band.

Honey Honey plays an important role in the subsistence of the Guayaki, but it is not as decisive in importance as Vellard (1939) notes:

> These different types of honey, especially the Mellipones, so numerous in the Paraguayan forest, give the Guayaki an abundant supply of highly nutritious food which is much more important to them than is the hunt or even the plant products . . . honey forms the food base of these Indians. (p. 80)

This caution having been given, one still must not underestimate the role of honey.

First, it seems that honey can be found year round, though less is available during the winter than during the summer. The Guayaki are very fond of it, as they are of everything mild and sweet. They also spend a great deal of their time and effort hunting for it, and they are skillful in discovering the hives sheltered in tree hollows and at extracting this precious food. Using the hatchet, the men enlarge the opening to the hive and the bees are smoked out. Once this is done, an arm is stuck down the hole to catch the heavy shelves of wax, flowing with magnificent golden honey. All this is done despite the hundreds of insects furiously buzzing about, sticking to the hair and to the junction of the lips and getting into the ears, but these bees are not dangerous, as they never sting. When the Guayaki are provided with only a stone hatchet, they climb a tree to the level of the hive; but when they have metal hatchets, they knock the hive down and extract the honey from the ground. The wax shelves, the honeycombs, are pressed with the hand, and the honey flows into the *daity* basket and the residue wax is carefully sucked and chewed to gain every drop of honey (*ai*). Moreover, as has already been pointed out, the wax of two types of bees is saved: one (*ganchi*) is used as glue and the other (*ychy*) is used for medication. Honey is never eaten pure for fear of a serious, indeed, deadly, illness (*ai baivwanvé*). It is always mixed with water in a turtle shell or in an earthenware pot.

Numerous taboos are associated with the eating of honey, depending on the sex, age, or the particular situation of the individual. The prohibitions vary as to their causes and effects; a pregnant woman, for example, should not consume the honey of the *myrynga* bee or her child's body will be covered with "serosity"; and an uninitiated boy must not drink the honey of the *taré* bee or he will have no pubic hairs. The Guayaki are acquainted with thirteen different types of bees that are apparently nontoxic. Besides the bees, the Guayaki know of eight types of wasps which do not make honey or make so little that the Indians are satisfied simply to eat handfuls of the young larvae (*tay*) of these insects, of which they are very fond. There are food taboos on three types of wasps.

Can one speak of the Guayaki culture as a culture based on honey? For the Guayaki, honey is not in the least the basic food. They eat a great deal of honey, but the quantity consumed is still less than the amount of meat eaten. Honey is, in a manner of speaking, a dessert which is served very often. The technology of the Indians is certainly not centered solely around honey collecting, as exemplified by the fact that the stone hatchet, the *daity*, and the earthenware pots are not equipment especially made for the gathering and consuming of honey.

As for the quantity of honey consumed by the Guayaki, it is certainly less than the amount eaten by the Chaco tribes, for example. The Guayaki have no more of a culture centered around honey than any other

Men's equipment.

A Guayaki man using a machete to make a digging stick out of a broken bow.

Guayaki under a thatch-roofed shelter. Carrying baskets (nako) are in the foreground.

Women and children under a shelter.

Guayaki children.

A Guayaki man.

159

tribe, and, as a matter of fact, one could say that the Guayaki are far less concerned with honey than are other tribes. While many Chaco or Tupi-Guarani tribes have rituals and annual festivals centered around honey, the Guayaki have no such thing, and should they happen to have a honey festival, it would simply be a very weak copy of what other tribes do. For the Guayaki, moreover, game animals, not honey, constitute gifts to the parents-in-law. If classified, the Guayaki could be thought of much more accurately as a civilization of the pindo palm, because this tree is an essential source of raw materials and sustenance for the Indians, as can be seen in Table 4-1, which shows the various uses of this tree. In any case, what such authors as Vellard (1939) and Baldus (1943) have misunderstood is that, above all, the Guayaki are hunters, that game is their primary source of food, and that the acquisition of game is the governing factor for their entire socioeconomic life.

Larvae The Guayaki recognize numerous varieties of larvae, and they know at first glance how to spot a half-rotten trunk which is likely to have some in it. With a quick blow from the hatchet, the soft area in the wood hollowed out by the larvae is opened. The larvae have the appearance of being more or less long, fat, and whitish, and they are eaten as soon as they are found. By far the most important variety for the Guayaki is the one that produces the eggs of the very large coleoptera (*Mynda*). This insect lays its eggs in the trunk of the pindo palm, and the resulting larva (*guchu*) is enormous, sometimes growing to 4 inches in length. It is a sort of flabby sack filled with an oily, yellowish material extremely rich in fats. The Indians eat it with relish in large quantities, cooked or raw. Everyone, including the very young children, eats *guchu*. When it is to be fed to a baby still at the breasts, the larva is pushed into the child's mouth after the hard head is removed with the fingernails.

The interest in the *guchu* larvae is not limited solely to its food value. The Guayaki consider it more than a food gathered by chance in the forest; rather, it is the product of a sort of cultivation. The Indians knock down the palm tree, leaving a stump about 3 feet high. They then generally cut the fallen trunk into sections 10 or 12 feet long, preparing the wood for the insects, who can then lay their eggs more easily both in the stump and in the round sections on the ground. The larvae then reproduce and grow while feeding on the fibers of the wood. Each man is the owner of his larvae bed, since he alone cut and sectioned a certain number of palm trees. This private property is almost always respected and no one touches the larvae of another. Later, the harvest is divided and eaten collectively. Thus the Guayaki distribute a relatively abundant supply of food, which they can easily gather when returning to the larvae plantation after the beds are judged "ripe." It seems that the Indians eat larvae year round, but they actually do the harvesting in the summer, between October and March. The felling and preparation of the palm tree

Table 4-1

Various Uses of the Pindo Palm

Eating utensils	Brush (*koto*) for sucking liquid food
Food	Buds (*kraku*), flour (*wii*), larvae
Hunting	Wood for the bow, fibers for the bow string
Shelter	Covering for the roof
Weaving	Baskets, matting, fans, case for feathers

occurs preferably at the end of the summer and during the winter, in view of the summer harvest which the women gather after the men have split open the trunks and the sections of the trees. It is of great interest to see that the Guayaki, despite their being nomads, establish a fixed source of food to be gathered much later. In doing so, they are obliged to return to the cultivation area after many months of traveling, which can easily take them far from the site. This cultivation of *guchu* therefore exerts a profound influence upon the wandering habits of the Guayaki in that it gives an order to their travels.

Undoubtedly, few societies offer as good an illustration as that of the Guayaki of a close adaptive relation between economic and social functions. It is impossible to envisage the social dimension of Guayaki life without describing the economic life at the same time. Thus, the ethnology of the Guayaki gives complete significance to the idea of a socioeconomic organization, because this category of social anthropology becomes both pertinent and heuristic when applied to the study of the Guayaki. The economic existence and the social organization mediate each other reciprocally.

THE SOCIOPOLITICAL UNIT

There is no community that groups all the Aché so that an individual feels conscious of himself as a member of one group with a political significance encompassing all the Guayaki. Consequently, the very profound cultural homogeneity (implying similar language, technical development, way of life, religion, and so on) contrasts with the political division of this cultural unit into several tribes. These groups or tribes make up the largest sociopolitical unit with which each individual identifies.

The social units correspond to territorial units. All the Indians who wander within the boundaries of a certain territory recognize their attachment to the same group. The Guayaki population is therefore split into three or four tribes whose sociopolitical unity is determined territorially. Each of these units, whose subdivisions will be examined later, jealously guards its economic area, signifying that intertribal relations are either nonexistent or hostile. Every violation of the frontiers of one group's territory by members of another group is equivalent to a declaration of war. This economically based protectionism fosters a "nationalistic" spirit which gives a special mark to each sociological unit. Thus the Yñarö Guayaki are somehow different from the Yvytyrusu group. The political isolation of each group, tied to the general necessity to protect the area of the forest which furnishes its food resources, is further reinforced by the fact that each tribe is endogamous. This inbreeding does not occur because of some explicitly stated rule of marriage, but more simply for lack of political intertribal relations, which`alone would allow for matrimonial exchange and group exogamy.

The protection of economic space therefore involves a political exclusiveness for each territorial unit, which in turn sets the foundation for group endogamy. By culminating these effects, these various determinates finally succeed in transforming each group into an ensemble of consanguineous relatives, thus constantly reaffirming and reinforcing the spirit of solidarity which animates each tribe. Moreover, the vocabulary reflects very clearly this total autonomy of each sociopolitical Guayaki unit on the economic and political level as well as on that of marriage. This vocabulary also clearly reflects the nature of the relations that maintain these units. There are, in fact, two terms for designating members identified with the group—the *irondy*, those who come from the same tribe, and the *iröiangi*, the Guayaki of other groups.

An analysis of these terms is extremely interesting. Both are built on the same word, *irö*, which means "comrade." *Irondy* can be broken up into *irö-ty*, which literally means "comrade custom," that is, those in the habit of being comrades. The word *iröiangi* can be broken into three parts: *irö* = "comrade," *ia* = a negative idea, and *gi* = a suffix indicating that it concerns people. The translation is thus "comrades not people," or those who are not comrades.

All the members of the same tribe maintain a relation of *irondy*, or friendship, mutual aid, and solidarity. Opposing this, with foreign Guayaki, with the *iröiangi*, relations are always negative: meetings between the two groups are either avoided or risk being hostile.

For each tribe or group of *irondy*, the members of the other groups are *iröiangi* Aché, foreign Guayaki, potential enemies. Even if a general political organization gathering all the tribes together does not exist, each Indian knows how to recognize another Guayaki. Outside of the language, which is the same for all except for small differences, there is a physical type particular to these Indians and also, of course, specific cultural traits such as perforation of the lip and ritual sacrifices. But this consciousness of a deep cultural identity, which forces all the Guayaki to think of themselves as Aché, thus asserting their difference in relation to the whites (*berú*) and to the Mbya Indians (*machi-tara*), does not in the least lead to an institution of intertribal solidarity.

Practically speaking, this means that each Guayaki tribe holds feelings of distrust, fear, hatred, and disdain for the others. Each tribe considers the others as dangerous cannibals, and if two strange bands meet by chance in the forest, they either try to massacre each other or flee in opposite directions. It must be added here that bloody encounters are rare, because the various bands take care not to cross paths. The moment a traveling group discovers the tracks of a foreign band, it goes back the way it came. One can thus see that relations between Guayaki tribes is marked by the same hostility that exists between the Guayaki and the Guarani or the Paraguayans. The two groups we studied were not acquainted with each other before being captured by the Paraguayans and placed in the Arroyo Moroti encampment. Both groups were aware of the existence of the other. However, since their respective hunting territories were adjacent, they had always avoided meeting or going into the "foreigners'" area. The Yñarö Guayaki, while journeying, had often noticed traces left by the other Aché bands, but they always quickly changed their direction of travel. When asked why they changed direction, they answered, "The *iröiangi* Aché would have shot us with arrows." It goes without saying that if the bands attached to different tribes generally respect this law of ignoring each other, certain circumstances can occur where there are peaceful encounters and sometimes even fusions of foreign bands, of which there are some examples. But the fundamental principle of the political organization of the Guayaki at this time is that of solidarity of the *irondy* and of open or latent hostility toward the *iröiangi*.

Subdivisions of the Sociopolitical Unit

As just discussed, sociopolitical subdivisions are economically determined, since a unit is defined as a group of persons living in the same section of the forest. The Guayaki are nomads and the natural resources of the forest are not abundant. This forces the Indians to do their traveling in small groups, usually comprising no more than fifteen or twenty persons (an average of four or five families). The scarcity of food resources and the difficulties involved in hunting necessitate the dispersal of the sociopolitical unit and, consequently, its fragmentation into bands. Incidentally, if these bands are made up of about twenty people, it is most likely not the product of chance but rather that this number is no doubt the most favorable. In effect, the band is, before everything else, a traveling unit. All the families in a band travel together and therefore also live in the same economic area. It seems that as soon as a band has more than twenty persons, it has serious problems satisfying the need for food. This is true since complete dependence with regard to natural resources forms a quasi-mathematical relation between the exploited area and the number of persons living off that area. The larger a band, the more space it needs to be on the move. Occupying a larger territory, the band would have at its disposal a more abundant food supply, but these resources could not be obtained precisely because of their being too greatly scattered.

The main problem of the Guayaki is finding food in the forest, but it is also obtaining the maximum amount of food in the least amount of time. Since these people are nomadic, it is necessary to consider not only the relation between the economic area and the number of inhabitants that live within it but also the relation between this area and the time necessary for a determined number of individuals traveling across it to exploit it. That is, the Guayaki have an obvious interest in situating themselves not too far from a hunting or gathering area; or, in other words, the demographic-surface relation is greatly modified by the time factor.

Twenty persons is a maximum number, and at the same time the most favorable number. As a traveling group, a Guayaki band is an economic unit of production and consumption of food. As such, its major problem is assuring each of its members a sufficient daily quantity of food. It is therefore necessary that journeys be limited; that is, the area of wandering must be both large enough to contain the necessary food resources for some twenty people and small enough so that those resources can be found and gathered regularly each day. Forty people could not live off a territory sufficient for only twenty because there would not be enough game or pindo palm trees; nor could these people survive on a territory twice as large, because then they would not have enough time to gather the minimum amount necessary for each person. Thus it is the distance covered and the time necessary to cover this distance which makes it imperative for the Guayaki to limit their bands to some twenty individuals.

It should also be noted that a band cannot have less than fifteen people. A single elementary family, for example, would have great difficulty in surviving alone in the forest. In fact, the same reasons that keep a band from being larger than twenty people also keep it from being much smaller than this number. Since the resources are scarce and scattered over a vast area, twenty persons have a better chance statistically than ten persons of getting what they need, because the cooperation among the members of a band is the principal determining factor of its unity. There is also the problem of security, since every Guayaki band should be able to participate and eventually repel the attacks of other Guayaki, of the Mbya-Guarani, and especially of the Paraguayans.

This self-defense is effective only when the responsibility rests with seven or eight hunters; a band of ten or twelve individuals which has three or four men would be very vulnerable. Therefore, units of about twenty people are those best able to defend themselves and are best suited to the forest environment, which is their economic area.

In summary, let us recall that these Indians are divided into socio-political units or tribes; these are territorially defined groups which are generally hostile toward one another. The members of these groups have a spirit of solidarity among them and, in addition, these units are endogamous. For the economic reasons cited above, the sociopolitical units must be divided into smaller groups averaging twenty people. These bands are veritable socioeconomic units, because though also endowed with specific political functions, they exist and function as groups of production and consumption of food. Following from this, the cooperative spirit is affirmed even more clearly at the level of the members of the same band than at the level of the tribe, even though all the bands that make up a tribe recognize each other as allies whose solidarity can be called upon at every moment.

Moreover, the allied bands meet at regular intervals or upon the occasion of certain ritual happenings. To express this in a formula, one could say that the principle of the social organization of the Guayaki is built on the division of sociopolitical units or tribes into socioeconomic units or bands.

THE STRUCTURE OF NOMADISM

If one wants to examine the way a band functions socioeconomically, it is necessary to analyze the way in which the journeying takes place, since the economic and social life occur through nomadism. The first fact to be considered is that band movement, far from being unorganized and left to chance or to the fancies of each member, is quite strictly regulated.

The bands that make up the tribe wander only within the tribal territory, showing great care when approaching land belonging to neighboring groups. On the other hand, the bands tend to travel only within the habitual area of their own movement.

Certain indications lead one to believe that each socioeconomic unit owns its own hunting and gathering territory and that therefore a tribal territory is divided into as many sections as there are bands. Of course, the relations between bands are friendly, since no band of one tribe considers another of the same tribe as *iröiangi*, or foreigners. If a band lives for a while within a territory that ordinarily is inhabited by another band, this latter group will certainly not seek retaliation. It is simply that each band tries as far as possible to respect the boundaries of neighboring sections, in order to avoid taking food resources that belong to *irondy*. It must be noted that such an occurrence is very unlikely. Except in exceptional circumstances, such as when a band is under attack and must flee far from its wandering area, each socioeconomic unit owns a sufficiently large territory to never have to enter neighboring areas. A band of twenty persons moves within a surface area of at least 300 square miles.

In other terms, the vast reserve of space allows each unit to look for food only within its own territory, thus assuring the continuity of good relations between bands of the same tribe. The dimensions of the territory serve both an economic and a political function. By allowing for the material autonomy of each band, they eliminate the major war risks, thereby founding the solidarity of all the bands of the tribe. In this way the division lines of the tribal territory are decided.

It is necessary now to examine the way in which the movement of each band occurs and the rhythm and structure of its wanderings within the section of the forest it exploits. The traveling of the band within the area given is determined by economic factors. The wandering pattern of the Guayaki, as explained earlier, largely turns on the gathering of the larvae of the coleoptera, which lays its eggs in the trunk of the pindo palm. The trunk is cut and prepared beforehand by the men in such a way that it is possible to leave these plantation beds as long as is necessary for the larvae to be laid and to grow. For each band there are, therefore, a large number of small food deposits, in the form of bunches of felled palm trees, scattered throughout the forest.

It seems that the "population" of these trees is divided into clusters, which may group from four to five or from ten to fifteen, making a considerable storehouse not only of marrow but also of larvae, and the Indians never fail to cut down the palm trees which they encounter in the course of their trek. One can therefore see the immediate relation between the fixed larvae beds and the constant traveling of the Indians. Leaving behind them the felled palm trees and knowing very well the location of the deposits, they will return in due time in order to gather the rich *guchu* which will have flourished there. The band's march is therefore guided in one direction by the preparation of the palm trees and in an opposite one by the collection of the larvae. The same route is covered twice, since it is always necessary to return to the point of departure at harvest time. Consequently, the nomadism of the Guayaki can be defined as a circular and periodic movement linked to the anticipated preparation of the palm trees and to the ultimate necessity of returning to gather the larvae.

The Indians prefer to go from grove to grove, collecting the terminal buds and the marrow and, at the same time, preparing the trees for the future egg laying of the insects. Following this, they retrace their steps and visit locations of previous halts where they believe the growth of the larvae is sufficient. Thus, the nomadism of the Guayaki is most certainly a circulatory one, determined by the necessity of seasonal returns to larvae beds. Even if the Guayaki are nomads primarily because they are hunters, it is to a great extent the gathering of larvae that organizes their journey.

The movements which are directly connected to the gathering of larvae take place especially during the hot months of summer, from November to February. Since this season lasts, in effect, five or six months, it takes in a large part of the annual economic cycle of the Guayaki. Hence, it seems that their primary activity—hunting and tracking down game—is organized in reference to the twofold work demanded by the harvest of larvae. The importance of the gathering of *guchu* in the economic and food supply of the Guayaki is evident, and it should never be underestimated. It is not, however, so significant that it can be given a place more important than hunting, as Baldus (1943) and, seemingly, even Mayntzhusen (1911, 1924–1926) have done. In truth, one must not confuse the quantity of food furnished by the larvae with the incidence of their collection during the movements necessitated by the hunt. Hunting, while making up the principal and permanent source of food, turns out to be tributary to the collection of larvae—at least as far as the structure of nomadism it implies. This is true even though the amount of *guchu* consumed is less than the amount of meat.

Even if the organization of the hunt is partially adapted to the harvest of larvae, it does not necessarily follow that the latter is of greater importance than the former. It simply means that the Guayaki choose to hunt in areas where pindo palm trees are plentiful. This is probably the reason that led Mayntzhusen to describe the Guayaki as principally collectors rather than hunters. Indeed, this author says that the Indians are able to resolve the problem of food thanks to the pindo palm tree. In fact, the existence of this tree and its use as an "incubator" for the insect's eggs simply help to structure the area and the nomadism of the Guayaki. In any case, the material life of the Indians, as well as their ritual life, attests to the economic prominence of the hunt.

THE EXCHANGE OF GOODS

It would be possible to state *a priori* that the scarcer the resources available to a society, the more rigorously organized and regulated are the production, allotment, and consumption of food; or that for a living society, the world of law is all the more constraining the more precarious the material conditions of its existence. This is the case, with the Guayaki.

The search for food and its distribution are essentially collective activities. On the economic level, the band functions as a whole. For this reason, it is among members of the same band that the feeling of solidarity is most intense. Of course, one should not, while recognizing an autonomous ensemble of "producers-consumers" in the band, neglect the role played by the constitutive elements of this unit, the elementary families. These operate as such at certain important junctures of economic life; but they are obliged to rely upon the band in order to assure the greatest part of their subsistence.

First, the question arises, who among the Guayaki is in charge of the economic life? The answer is implicitly contained in the preceding developments, since almost all the elements of the problem have been discussed, but most important is that the food producers are essentially the men. It is curious, but at the same time easily explicable, to see how limited is the economic role of women among the Guayaki.

There is a division of work in regard to the fabrication of objects and tools. In this area, the women do almost everything (rope-making, weaving, pottery-making, and so on), but they play almost no part in the search for food. This is above all because the Guayaki depend mostly upon hunting, and this activity is obviously a man's job. But even when one considers gathering activities as such, it can be seen that the role of the women is of no real importance. If one wants to get the heart of the palm tree or make pindo flour, it is necessary to fell the tree, and this too is men's work. As for the honey, the men extract it after having enlarged the entrance of the beehive or, more simply, after having downed the tree. These happen to be the four principal food sources of the Guayaki —game animals, the marrow of the palm tree, larvae, and honey—and we see that it is the men alone who supply these things. Therefore, if the women play an economic role, it can only be secondary; as a matter of fact, it is almost entirely limited to the picking and gathering of fruits from some ten or twelve types of trees, but this food source represents only a very small part of the Guayaki economy. Hence, the economic function of the women is quite limited. And how could it be otherwise, since the Paraguayan forest is poor in edible types of plants, thus making very minor the ordinary collecting activity of the woman in primitive societies. The heavy, agonizing task of feeding the community therefore falls on the men, and it is up to them to establish an exchange by which each individual asserts at one and the same time his dependence upon others and his hold over them. Simple in its formulation but admirable in its effects, the basic law of the Guayaki society assures the survival of its members by instituting among these members a total reciprocal dependence. This occurs through a food taboo which dictates that a hunter cannot eat his own take from the hunt. Neither he nor his parents are allowed to eat the meat he brings into camp; he gives it to his family (wife and children) and to other members of the band to whom he belongs. This taboo is strictly respected because it is basic to the spirit of these Indians.

If a hunter, the Guayaki explain, were to eat his own game, he would become *pané*, that is, he would have bad luck in hunting. This is the worst thing that can happen to a Guayaki, since to be *pané* is to be incapable of feeding one's family, of giving to others, and, therefore, of receiving. It is consequently to be incapable of feeding oneself. The fear of *pané* is a veritable anguish, and one scrupulously avoids taking any risk that might cause it. On the contrary, the Guayaki unceasingly dwell, as if to ward off that always possible evil, on their hunting exploits, on their *paña* (which equals *pané-iä*, "bad luck not"). For a woman, the ideal husband is a *paña* man, and every young boy aspires to become a great hunter, a *paña*, a man of good luck.[1] The *pané* for the Guayaki is therefore extremely dangerous, and one understands the importance of a food taboo that when broken will lead to it. The Guayaki know this very well, they are perfectly conscious of it, and they have an explanation for it. The way in which Guayaki thought envisages the necessity of exchange is expressed in their language as a condition that makes possible the existence of the social life of the group. But anthropology cannot be content with the indigenous explanation; it should look beyond the explicit and conscious speech of the Indians to what is said and done unconsciously. In the present case, it is necessary to identify the decisive social consequences and the structural implications of the food taboo. It will be seen, in effect, that the social life of the Guayaki is organized around this taboo, and that if the fear of the *pané* partly determines the individual psychology of each Indian, the methods used to avoid it refer us back to the world of exchange.

A hunter who returns to the camp after a hunt in the forest, not being able to eat the meat of his own game, gives some of it to other families in the band. When he has killed a large or average-sized animal, he in effect gives the largest part of the meat to his comrades, since his wife and children need only a small amount. On occasion two hunters were seen arriving in the camp with ten monkeys, which probably represented at least 50 pounds of meat. Of the ten animals, eight were given to other Indians. The hunter made a gift of his take; but in this case, what is he himself going to eat if he cannot touch his own meat? It is precisely here that the counterpart of the gift, the compensation of the food taboo, enters into play. This is where the exchange of goods occurs. All the hunters are in the same situation; all of them must make a gift of the fruits of their hunt to the band. In other words, each hunter gives his game to others, but, in return, the others offer their own game to him. Each Guayaki is therefore permanently a potential giver and receiver. When he gives away his own meat, he knows he can count on the meat of his comrades, because the same obligation of giving away the meat falls on all the hunters without exception. This giving associated with the food taboo (*bai jyvömbré ja uéméré*: "the animals that one shoots should not be eaten by oneself") finds its necessary complement in the receiving and thus forms the basis of this uninterrupted exchange (*pepy*), the heart of Guayaki life. One cannot overemphasize the great importance of this obligation to give, consciously perceived by the Indians as a food prohibition. The taboo is the positive form of the prohibition. This obligation admirably creates a complete dependence of each hunter, since it is others who give him his food. In this way, by the absolute reciprocal interdependence of all the hunters, the world of exchange is created. That is the essence of Guayaki social life.

The Guayaki example is remarkable because it allows us to observe directly, only slightly marred by the representation that indigenous thought creates, the founding and constituent function of exchange. If there is a human group built as a society upon the institution of a general rule of exchange of economic goods, it is the Guayaki society. Each of its productive members is totally defined by the relation of dependence which the obligation of the gift puts him in. Therefore, there is no individual autonomy, since the social group is constituted as such only through the alienation of the individual. In the obligation of the permanent gift of the gains from the hunt, every hunter renounces an uncertain economic independence, but he gains in return the security offered by the support of the entire group. At this point, the intense solidarity that exists among the members of the same band and the reasons for which it is this type of group that plays the socioeconomic role become understandable. A band is an ensemble of individuals who carry on among themselves the exchange of food. Therefore very strong threads of mutual aid and cooperation are woven, threads valuable not only in terms of economic life but in social and ritual life as well.

Thus, one can speak of a fundamental law of the Guayaki society, articulated in a food taboo, which requires every hunter to include his game in the cycle of food circulation. Obviously, if this taboo were placed upon some food resource other than meat, the gift and the consecutive exchange would be much less important and much less compelling. These Indians are hunters par excellence, and it is precisely the gain from the hunt that is put under the taboo and is made to circulate as a gift and in the flow of exchange. Thus it is that each adult Guayaki male spends his life hunting for others because the others spend their lives hunting for him. This gives the law of exchange of game an inestimable formative value which marks every level of Guayaki social life. For example, it excludes the autonomy of the elementary family, because this would literally condemn a man to starve to death since he cannot eat the meat from his catch. Thus the Guayaki are grouped in a band which averages six or seven families, because only a group of this size is capable of assuring a minimal material security to each of its members. Consequently, if from time to time individual families leave the band, it can be only for a short time—two or three days at the most. Likewise, though other food resources are not placed under the same taboo that meat is, the obligation of giving and, consequently, of exchanging, are still implicit.

In any case, this is what occurs among the Yvytyrusu and the Yñarö Aché. The latter group, quite wrongly, looked down somewhat upon the first group, especially for following to the letter the law of food exchange, correctly interpreted as a right for them to share in the resources of the others. Often the Gatu Aché were relieved in a split second of their yield of honey, pindo, or larvae. "The foreign Aché eat much, and they ask without cease!" cursed the givers, who were made to give against their will. These latter, in return, always accepted the offerings that their comrades never failed to make to them.

The Guayaki ethic of exchange therefore touches all aspects of their daily life. Each one is for the other a permanent promise of a gift, something offered or something received. Beyond the inevitable material necessity, the exchanged food is not only the vehicle of bodily substance but also the symbolic food of fraternity expressed with force in the certitude of *ure Aché*, "we Guayaki."

Parents are examples by which the spirit of exchange touches the young children. Expressed in this ethic of exchange which dominates the adults' world is a pedagogy of exchange by which the Guayaki society teaches the children by giving to them the model of their own relations. Observed a thousand times was the adults' desire to train the children, to teach them the spontaneous meaning of giving and consequently the innocent feeling of receiving and the tranquillity of asking. For example, a little girl, in the process of chewing on a piece of meat, passes by an old woman seated by her fire; the old woman holds out her hand: "Give me some!" The little girl does so immediately. There are multiple examples of this kind: everything converges on interpreting to the children the idea that food is, above all, a good that circulates.

Particularly suggestive were the relations observed between a group of children from six to twelve years old and one of children from three to six. The two play groups were autonomous, the small ones not being able to follow the games of the older ones. They did, however, do certain things together—bathing, for example. More than once we saw a ten-year-old boy literally take a larva out of the mouth of a younger boy without the younger boy protesting in the least. Likewise, when a young child demands food from an older child, the latter offers it to him. Sometimes this is done with a certain condescension, but it is never refused. And, of course, the adults unceasingly encourage these exchanges.

The method of distribution of food conforms to the principle of kinship, though it is not limited by it. A hunter first gives part of his game to his own family (wife and children); he then gives some to his closest relatives (siblings), but excluding his mother and father, who are under the same taboo he is. Then he gives to Indians with whom he has particularly close relations (to whom he is "related," for example, through a ritual that followed his birth or his initiation); finally, the last to be served, but never forgotten, are the Indians the hunter is tied to neither by blood nor artificial kinship. These are *picha*, "friends." In fact, however, the *picha* of an individual are not any less his blood relatives than are other Indians, because the weak demographic dimension and the inbreeding of the socio-political units makes all the members blood relatives. Normally the number of persons a hunter gives food to should be proportional to the amount of game he brings in, so that if there is less meat, only the closest relatives will benefit. Small animals, such as lizard, small snakes, and small birds, are not shared. It is probable, however, that if food were more abundant in the forest, the division would always follow the pattern just given. The scarcity of resources obliges the Indian to divide equally, not so much the food itself as something material, for there is often too little of it to satisfy anyone's appetite, but rather as a sign that one is part of a circle of exchange: a fraternal society.

Since the whole band collectively spends its time hunting food, it is in this sense truly a socioeconomic unit. This signifies that hunting expeditions generally include several hunters, and almost never less than two.

Nothing prevents a solitary hunter from shooting animals he finds in his path and that he can succeed in killing alone. But generally the habits of the animals themselves necessitate collective hunting. Many of the animals that are important in the food supply of the Guayaki live in "societies," the two varieties of wild pigs and monkeys being good examples. If an individual tries to kill a certain beast, more often than not the discovery of the herd, the hunting departure, and the organization of the shooting are collective. The hunt is conducted in this manner because a single hunter, for reasons of the taboo already explained, could not survive alone. If the hunters of a band go on a collective expedition, each one has a better chance of bringing in more game than do one or two individual hunters.

Central to the economic life of the Guayaki, there is, then, a clear opposition between the production of food, which is collective, and the consumption of food, which is private. The band is a unit of production, and the family is the unit of consumption. It is only in a passive activity such as the consumption of food that each individual unit regains an autonomy impossible in the production plan.

NOTES

1. There were two *pané* men among the Guayaki. They did not hunt, nor did they own a bow; they did certain women's tasks.

REFERENCES

Baldus, H., 1943. "Sinopse da cultura Guayaki," *Sociologia*, Sâo Paulo, 5 (2): 147–153.

Cadogan, L., 1960. "Algunes Textes Guayaki del Yñarö," Part 1, Soc. Cientifica del Paraguay, *Ethnolinguistica* 4.

——, "Les Indiens Guayaki de l'Yñarö," Part 2, Bulletin de la Faculté des Lettres de Strasbourg. Tilas IV (mai–juin):21–54.

Clastres, P., 1966a. "La Civilization Guayaki: Archaism ou Regression?" *Supplemente Antropólógico de la Revista del Atenco Paraguayo* 2 (1).

——, 1966b. "L'Arc et le Panier," *L'Homme* 6, Cahier 2.

Lozano, P., 1873–1874. *Historia de la Conquista del Paraguay, Rio de la Plata y Tucuman*, Vol. 1, Buenos-Aires, pp. 412–421.

Mayntzhusen, F. C., 1911. "Uber Gebráuche bei der Geburt und die Namongebung der Guayaki," Congr. Int. Ameri, session 18, London, pp. 408–412.

——, 1924–1926. "Guayaki-Ferschungen," *Zeit. Ethnol.* 57:315–318.

Métraux, A., and H. Baldus, 1963. "The Guayaki," in J. Steward, ed., *Handbook of South American Indians*, Vol. 1, The Marginal Tribes. New York: Cooper Square Publishers, Inc.

Susnick, B., 1961. "Estudios Guayaki," Part 2, Soc. Cientifica del Paraguay, *Ethnolinguistica* 5.

Vellard, J., 1939. *Une Civilisation du Miel*, Paris: Gallimard edition.

GLOSSARY

Aché: Guayaki word for all Guayaki as a people
ai: honey
ai baivwanvé: a serious illness believed to result from the consumption of pure honey
ambwa: a prestigious headdress worn by men
bai jyvoṁbré ja véméré: "The animals that one shoots should not be eaten by oneself"—the Guayaki verbalization of the food taboo that enforces their interdependence
bairakwa or *pypé:* a wooden "lance" designed as a boar spear but used primarily to kill jaguar and capivara
baku: the process of boiling
bareka: the hunt
béru: white men
biru: a type of gourd used as a container
brevi ityty: a tapir trap; literally, "make the tapir fall"
briku: a vulture
bruéé: a thick soup made from *guchu* larvae and the marrow of the pindo palm
bupi: bark of the tiana tree
byta: a large wooden grill
chäka: dry wood used as tinder
chimbégi: a duck
daity: a large ovoid basket used to carry liquids
davé: a mat made of pindo palm branches
dyvi: a plant (*Bombax* sp.)
eë: sweet
enda: the circular encampment of a Guayaki band
ganchi: beeswax used for waterproofing and as a glue
gary: a cord of nettle fibers used in binding arrows and stringing necklaces
gi: a suffix connoting people as opposed to animals or things
guchu: the larva of the coleoptera *Mynda*
ia: a negation
iro: bitter
irö: comrade
iröiangi: members of foreign Guayaki tribes
irondy: members of one's own tribe
iro puté: very bitter
irö-ty: "comrade custom"; those in the habit of being comrades
itajy: a stone hatchet
jacaré: a crocodile
jaku: a type of pheasant
jyvyté: a hardwood tree (*Hiocalyx balansae*)
kai: the process of roasting
kara: earthenware
kimira: a bird of prey
koto: a "brush" made from frayed pieces of pindo wood; used to drink liquid food

krachira: a bamboo tube used in carrying water
kraku: the marrow and buds of the pindo palm
kromi piaa: headbands used in carrying young children
kybwé: a fruit tree (*Chrysephyllum lucimifolium*)
kyti: a reed shaft or sliver
machi: an arrow
machi-tara: Guayaki word for the Mbya; literally, "many-arrows"
mimby: a pan flute made of three to four reed tubes
moo: a soft clay
mynda: the large coleoptera that produces *guchu* larvae
myrynga: a type of bee whose honey is taboo to pregnant women
nako: a carrying basket made from pindo palm branches
nako chä: the headbands hooked to the carrying basket
paa: a bow string
pabwä: a rope made of plant fibers, women's hair, and monkey's hair, which
    men wear around their left forearms as protection from coati bites and as a
    sign of prestige
paña: to have good luck in hunting
pané: to have bad luck in hunting
pekä: a fan
pepo: feathers
pétö: a polished wooden blade
picha: friends
piju: a labret made from the fibula of a monkey
piragi: a fish
proaa: a type of forest "bean"
pyno: a nettle plant (*Urera baccifera*)
pypö: a fruit tree (*Myrciaria baporeti*)
rapa: bow
rapa chonga: a piece of bow wood
rapia: a small arrow designed to kill small and middle-sized birds
takwarembo: a plant fiber used in making baskets
tapy: a Guayaki house
tarë: a type of bee whose honey is taboo to uninitiated boys
tay: young larvae
toi: a pindo palm tree
toi wii: a coarse flour extracted from the fibers of the trunk of the pindo palm
turi-ia: wild oranges
turni: a wild orange tree
tyru: a type of Guayaki weaving of plant fibers that resembles crochet work
tyta: a large snail
ure Aché: "we Guayaki"
vava: a small sieve
viju: vulture's down; used for medical and ritual purposes
ychy: a beeswax rolled in a cone and stored in the underside of an armadillo
    shell; used for medical and ritual purposes

PART
2
AUSTRALIA

CHAPTER

5

THE WALMADJERI
AND GUGADJA

Ronald M. Berndt

*Ronald Berndt is Professor of Anthropology and Head of the Depart-
ment of Anthropology at the University of Western Australia. He received
his Ph.D. from the London School of Economics and Political Science in
1955 and has conducted extensive field research in Australia and the Eastern
Highlands of New Guinea since 1939. His principal fields of emphasis in
research have been social order and control, social organization, culture
contact and culture change, myth and ritual, and art. His numerous publications include articles, monographs, and volumes concerning these and other
subjects as they pertain to the Australian Aborigines and the New Guinea
Highlanders. Dr. Berndt's other professional activities include membership
and positions of leadership in the Australian Institute of Aboriginal Studies
and in professional associations in the United States, Great Britain, and
Australia and the general editorship of Anthropological Forum. He has
been awarded the distinctions of the Royal Society of New South Wales'
Edgeworth David Medal for Anthropology in 1950 and the Royal Anthropological Institute's Welcome Medal in 1958.*

EDITOR'S INTRODUCTION

The "bush" people from the Balgo region of Australia, represented in this
chapter by the Walmadjeri and Gugadja, share one broad culture pattern,
which has been distinguished as the Western Desert culture. Their physical
type is similar to other Australian Aboriginal groups and they all speak dialects of Mandjildjara as a *lingua franca*. Each group of desert people traditionally roamed over a particular stretch of territory in a determined pattern,
exploiting the faunal and floral resources of their "desert" environment.
Actually, this environment contains a wide variety of foods and encompasses
different types of terrain, so it is not a desert in the classic sense. The tracks

of the Aborigines follow the main waters and incorporate all topographical features that are economically and spiritually significant.

European influence in Australia has resulted in a changing pattern of life for the Aborigines; their tribal areas today are becoming depopulated due to the different forms of socialization now available, their old values are coming into question, and their seminomadic existence is losing popularity.

Berndt emphasizes here the direct bearing that myth and ritual have on social and economic organization. He focuses specifically on the desert "lines of communication" that mythologically based movements propagate, the people following the courses taken by the spirit beings in the Dreaming era. These beings are the creators and sustainers of the land's fertility, the mediators between the land and the people; and this bond between mythic and actual is both individual and social, providing physical and emotional direction and security.

Comparison of the Walmadjeri and Gugadja with the Pitjandjara in Chapter 6 discloses, of course, more similarities than differences, since they are all groups within the greater Western Desert culture type. Such a comparison is more useful perhaps in that the two chapters complement each other in emphasis; this chapter is most concerned with the interaction between myth and ritual and the social and economic organization, while the following chapter examines the interaction between social and economic organization and the physical environment. Within the societies represented here, the high formalization of relations between man and nature through ritual and myth, such as found among Australian Aborigines, is somewhat paralleled in Ainu social organization—two areas with divergent physical and social environments.

THE COUNTRY AND THE PEOPLE

The area we are concerned with here is located in the southern Kimberley of Western Australia, south of Hall's Creek township and Sturt Creek pastoral station. In 1958 and 1960 my wife (Dr. Catherine Berndt) and I carried out field work at Balgo Hills, southeast of Billaluna and east of Gregory Salt Lake, a Roman Catholic Pallottine Mission settlement. This was established in the 1930s to serve as a buffer between Aborigines from the southern and southwestern Desert and the pastoral stations to the immediate north. (We were on several of these stations in 1944–1945, mainly in the Victoria River district, and in the Hall's Creek area in 1962.) Balgo itself is in a strategic position. It faces the great Western Desert, which extends eastward into the Northern Territory and includes within its perspective the Canning Stock Route, running north and northeast from Wiluna. Jigalong, another fringe settlement, lies west of Lake Disappointment, and to the southeast of Balgo are Lakes White, Hazlett, and Mackay. (We visited Wiluna and Jigalong in 1957, in the course of a larger survey.) Some of the Desert people to the south have come into Balgo. Others have remained in the Desert or are dispersed among the pastoral stations and townships to the west and north.

This Desert, however, is not a desert in the true sense. It is not uniformly arid. It includes low undulating ridges and sand dunes covered by spinifex grass and mulga scrub, claypans, and shallow creek beds, some edged with eucalypts and acacias, as well as stretches of dry sandhill country, expanses of pebbles or gibber, and occasional rocky outcrops. During good seasons the whole area abounds in game and edible roots and plants. In fact, heavy rain transforms the countryside dramatically from its generally dry aspect. Unless a period of drought has been considerably protracted, the supply of food does not become a serious problem, although shortage of rain inevitably means that both quality and quantity suffer and hunting and food-collecting parties must go farther afield. Generally, the annual rainfall is rather erratic. The over-all pattern consists of a good season followed by several dry ones; if these continue for too long, a condition of drought ensues, and this can bring considerable hardship. Under these circumstances, people are forced to congregate near permanent waters, with the danger of exhausting local resources. Severe drought can bring death for the old, the physically unfit, or the very young: a party can be caught "in between waters" in its search for a more rewarding area. Normally, then, the Desert contains a relatively wide variety of foods, but the difficulties inherent in an extended dry period should not be underestimated. Water is of basic importance for Aborigines and for all the natural species. It is no exaggeration to say that a great deal of their (traditional) everyday as well as religious life is focused on this particular theme—and it is this that will be explored presently.

The Desert people distinguish eight kinds of physiographic features which are water-producing: soak (*djunu*), subsurface water, for which they must dig; rockhole (*waniri*), some virtually permanent; spring (*windji*), fairly rare; creek or river (*giligi*), which fills only occasionally, but sometimes leaves waterholes which last for varying periods; billabong (*walgir*), which fills up after heavy rain; swamp (*baldju*), which results from rain and does not last long; claypan (*waran*), a temporary receptacle for rain water but usually a plain; and salt lake (*baragu*), which can be relied on to produce drinkable water, at least in parts and during good seasons. In addition, emergency water can be obtained, for example, from some trees and/or their roots or from underground deposits of coagulated frogs. In summer, when rain can be expected, temperatures vary from 90 to 120 degrees F; in winter, the dry period, they range from 45 to 85 degrees F, with extremely cold nights. Traditionally, these people went naked but occasionally wore pubic tassels; today, on settlements, they wear clothing.

The Balgo population is a fluctuating one. In 1960, approximately 150 adults and children were more or less permanently resident there. The official (Native Welfare Department, W. A.) figure for 1966–1967 was 268, including 149 children under 16. The reservoir of "bush" or Desert people has now been almost entirely depleted. There are probably no more than 50 or so persons remaining outside the orbit of European influence. The pre-European population of the *whole* Desert region (excluding Yuendumu, in the Northern Territory), including parts of the Northern Territory and Central Australia as far south as the transcontinental railway line running through South Australia and Western Australia, an area of approximately 250,000 square miles, could have been about 10,000 persons, or .007 person per square mile. Today, the same area holds up to 3200 persons, or .00128 person per square mile (Berndt 1959:85–86). The population of the area, shown in Figure 5-1, including Balgo and Billaluna, the "lakes area" on the Northern Territory-Western Australian boundary, and southwest to Lake Disappointment and Jigalong mission is approximately 856, but no more than 900 persons.

The "tribal" composition of this region is mixed, especially on mission settlements and in and around the townships. These and the pastoral

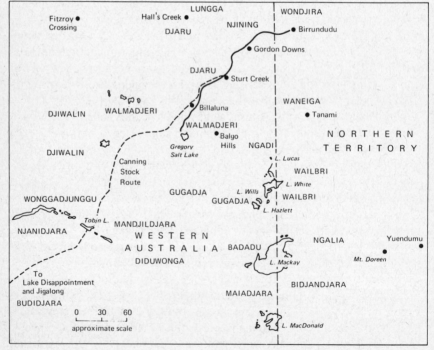

Figure 5–1. Northern section of the Western Desert tribal distribution from the perspective of Balgo.

stations have been attracting small groups of people out of the Desert for more than forty years or so now—initially, it seems, through simple curiosity; but the majority have remained for various reasons, not all associated with a reaction against the rigors of their own home territories, because life was in some respects easier in the Desert than on the settlements. Many came only for short visits, but the usual tendency has been for such visits to grow shorter until they became virtually permanent residents. However, those who came in as adults do retain some ties with their own countries, or territories, and parties still set out occasionally for the bush, where they stay for varying periods. But except in a few isolated cases, they no longer envisage remaining there: they do not travel as far afield as they did, and the waterhole routes mentioned later do not have the same economic significance as they did in the immediate past.

At Balgo, for instance, the population includes Walmadjeri (called Wolmeri by Kaberry 1939), Gugadja, Mandjildjara, Wonggadjunggu, and Ngadi, with Gugadja and Walmadjeri predominating, the latter being, originally, the local people. The Gugadja and Ngadi (Kaberry 1939 also mentions the Ngadi), particularly, are closely linked with the Wailbri (Meggitt 1962:41–43, Walbiri) and less so with the Waneiga. There is evidence to suggest that the Gugadja were spreading into Wailbri territory around Lakes White and Hazlett less than a decade ago. (My tribal positioning differs quite considerably from that of Tindale 1940. For instance, from the Balgo perspective the Pintubi, or Bindubi, are not a tribal entity, but *bindubi* is simply an exclamation of tiredness or boredom. However "Pintubi" does represent a "tribe" from the perspective of people living in the Warburton-Giles areas to the south.) To the west and northwest of the Walmadjeri are Gunia (Kaberry 1939, Kunian) and Djiwalin, while along the Canning Stock Route to Lake Disappointment, from north to southwest, are Walmadjeri, Wonggadjunggu, Mandjildjara, Njanidjara, and, at Jigalong, Budidjara (among others). South and southeast are the central Desert people, the Diduwonga, Badadu (on the western side of Lake Mackay), Maiadjara, Ngalia, and Bidjandjara. The linguistic-cultural break occurs immediately north of Balgo, with the Djaru, Njining, Lungga, and Wondjira. At the same time, the break is not too pronounced culturally, as research at Hall's Creek and Birrundudu has demonstrated (1944–1945, 1962); at Birrundudu and Gordon Downs stations there were Ngadi, Walmadjeri, Waneiga, and Wailbri as well as Walmala, Buniba, Njining, and Wondjira.

All the groups from this region share one broad cultural pattern, which has been distinguished as the Western Desert culture. This is the largest cultural bloc in Aboriginal Australia. There are striking similarities throughout the area in terms of social organization, behavioral patterns, and ideology in general, despite many variations. Especially, methods of gaining a livelihood from the natural environment, domestic arrangements, and mytho-ritual activity all have an essentially common core and can easily be identified from one part of the region to the other, sometimes hundreds of miles apart. An example of transmission over a great distance is given by R. Tonkinson (1966:162), who shows the remarkable similarity between songs I recorded at Ooldea in 1940 (R. and C. Berndt 1945) and songs he obtained at Jigalong in 1963, a direct distance of some 750 miles, but much further if Aboriginal tracks are taken in account. Numerous such examples could be given from my research at various fringe settlements throughout this cultural bloc. The cultural break is more apparent to the southeast with the Wailbri, but not with the Ngalia. The Walmadjeri, for example, were possibly less Desert-oriented in the past than they are now, and like the Gugadja probably have today a fairly "mixed" culture. In terms of language, there is considerable dialectal variation—perhaps more apparent among the Walmadjeri and Gugadja. However, all recognize that they speak as a *lingua franca* Mandjildjara, which is regarded as being a "type" dialectal unit for the Desert region. Mandjildjara is closely allied to Bidjandjara, which is another "type" indicator. In actual fact, it is misleading to speak of "tribes" in this region (R. Berndt 1959:81–107), since the names on Figure 5-1 really stand for dialect units that have some recognized mutual intelligibility—that is, recognized by the people themselves. Each such dialect unit derives its name from the way its members pronounce some everyday common word: Mandjildjara, for instance, is derived from *mandjila*, "to pick up (something)"; see R. Berndt 1959:92 for other examples.

RELATION TO THE NATURAL ENVIRONMENT

From the perspective of adult Balgo men of mixed dialect origin, the positioning of units on Figure 5-1 represents a traditional view. It also indicates what representatives of those units regard as their own territories, together with their identification of groups adjacent to them and others further away, all considered to fall within their sphere of interaction. This means that all the units distinguished on Figure 5-1 are (were) recognized by adults now living at Balgo, and that representatives of these are acknowledged at the personal level. Actually, their social perspective is much more extensive than the map suggests: it extends southward to Wiluna and even to the Warburtons.

People identify specific land as their "country," not in terms simply of a stretch of territory with clear-cut boundaries, but much more intimately and precisely on the basis of local sites—waterholes, hills, ridges, claypans, camping grounds, and so forth. It is the significant areas within a particular stretch of territory that define the territorial range of a dialect unit, rather than its over-all composition. Specific sites are claimed as belonging to one such unit rather than to another, and the sum total of these constitutes its particular territory. But people do not restrict themselves to these regions any more than to their local group territories (see below), and traditionally they wandered over areas claimed in the same way by members of other units. All these people were/are seminomadic; they move across limited regions, but not unrestrictedly so. The main factor here is the exigencies of hunting and food-collecting. During good seasons, as noted, they are not obliged to move too far: as the seasons change or if a dry period becomes prolonged, economic necessity forces them to go considerable distances from their own local group territory and out of the land relevant to their dialect unit. But such movement is nearly always circumscribed. Traditionally, they probably did not go much beyond 180 to 200 or so miles as the crow flies from their local group territory and less from the region claimed for the dialect unit. One social implication of this is the creation of interactory zones which cut across these dialect units and overlap with others.

On the other hand, it means also an extension of knowledge relevant to that country. The whole Western Desert, like many other parts of Aboriginal Australia, is crisscrossed by tracks which follow the main waters. They extend in every direction, from one site to the next, and incorporate all topographical features that are economically as well as spiritually significant in Aboriginal terms. Such lines of communication are mythologically based and follow the tracks taken by mythic and spirit beings in the Dreaming era (the *djugurba* or *djumanggani*).

Strong emotional ties link man with the land—not simply because of its economic potentialities or the utter dependence of man on what is produced, but more directly through the mythic beings themselves, the creators and sustainers of the land's fertility, the stimulators of natural increase of the species. These beings are seen as mediators between the land and the people. The assumption, articulated in varying degrees, is that without their abiding presence people could have no real security and no vision of continuity. Consistent with this concept of the Dreaming, throughout Aboriginal Australia, many such mythic beings were shape-changing: their corporeal forms were sometimes human, sometimes not. They are eternal: they continue to exist in spirit form, although in the creative era they traveled across the country, and after various adventures eventually turned into something else. For example, they were metamorphosed as rocks or trees, or went into the ground at a particular place, perhaps to reappear at another. This association with one site or territory rather than another is not fortuitous. It is an association that is defined in personal terms, in terms of social relationships with members of specific local groups.

It was mentioned before that the tracks of some of these mythic beings, or "ancestral" beings, are very extensive indeed, traversing the full width and breadth of the Desert region and embracing a number of local groups and dialect units, while others are quite localized.

To illustrate this, we can look at one small "slice" of this region. Figure 5-2 is a reproduction of part of a series of Aboriginal "maps" obtained from Balgo. They are not drawn to scale, but this example gives some idea of the total picture—with the proviso that this is only a small segment of country showing three major tracks: between them and crossing them are more tracks, not included here.

In Figure 5-2, sites are indicated by numbers. The following list notes only "big names," but at each of these there may be other smaller names. Some mythical associations are also given for each site; but again, to simplify presentation, additional mythic-clusters are omitted.

1. Balgo hills: Gideri waterhole. Associated with a small boy, Jarangu, who traveled from the east.
2. Malan (European name "Kamit"). Here the *djugur(ba)* dog "dived" into the ground and made a soak.

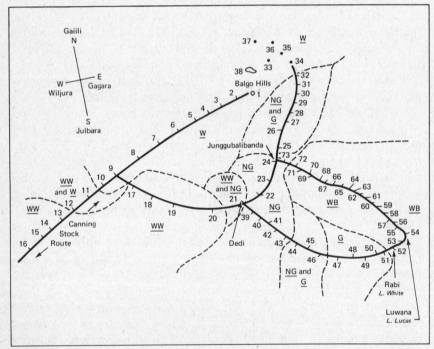

Figure 5–2. A small segment of country showing three major tracks. W = *Walmadjeri;* WW = *Wonggadjunggu;* NG = *Ngadi;* G = *Gugadja;* WB = *Wailbri.*

3. Banggubidi (windmill here). The *djugur* frog, Gaidjama, "dived" into the ground.
4. Lake Baragu. Here, *djugur* star (Gigi) fell down.
5. Lake Gudu. Associated with water *djugur*.
6. Gilanggilang lake (or Delivery Camp). The great Rainbow Snake, Guleii (also called, generally, Wonambi), emerged.
7. Djigan well. Guleii "dived" into this well.
8. Lambu well. No mythical associations.
9. Ganingara rockhole. Guleii made rain here. He was a man, called Wadi (man) Guleii.
10. Gadalabaru soak. The Dadjal snake lived here.
11. Gudjuwari soak. A *djugur* man dug a hole here in search of Dadjal.
12. Djindidjindi soak. Increase center for Logudi (Lugidi), a witchetty grub.
13. Djinberinggara well. No Dreaming.
14. Gadeidjilga well and soak. Here Guleii lives.
15. Guleii rockhole. Guleii entered here. This section of his travels ends here.
16. Drio well and soak. The *djugur* turkey, Gerangalgu, entered here.
17. Djidir hill. In the mythical period, men (*dingari*: see below) stood in a row on this hill when the *djugur* Fire blazed up.
18. Ngulu rockhole. A large group of *dingari* men (associated with sacred ritual: see below) clapped their hands as they sang.
19. Budja billabong. The Wadi Dingari are here with the Gadjeri Mother (see below).
20. Badi rockhole. No Dreaming.
21. Dedi rockhole associated with Wilbin, wild cat.
22. Dalabundu claypan. Lingga snake *djugur* place.
23. Balgubalgu creek. Fire *djugur* was burning here.
24. Junggubalibanda rock and rockhole. Jaldji, bush potato, lived here as a man. The Wadi Gudjara (Men/Two) passed through this place; these two mythical characters, white and black goanna men, are important throughout the Desert area.
25. Ngana claypan. Wadi Gadjeri (male counterpart of the Gadjeri Mother) was (were) burnt here by Fire.
26. Jilijili claypan, where Wadi Gadjeri (*dingari*) opened arm veins to obtain blood for ritual purposes.
27. Nandalara claypan. Wadi Gadjeri made a waterhole.
28. Jeijar soak associated with (group of) Wadi Gadjeri.
29. Ngali creek: same associations as 28.
30. Djidjiwari creek: same associations as 28.
31. Lundi soak. Gadjeri defecated here.
32. Gia soak. Site for *djugur* Mala (kangaroo rat).
33. Walwia rockhole. *Djugur* site for Guldji (louse).
34. Gagu rockhole. Frog (see 3) lives here.
35. Diring rockhole. Also associated with frog.
36. Gana hill and water, associated with Minma (woman) Gaidjama, frog.

37. Djumundur creek (near Balgo airstrip). *Djugur* Gaidjama place.
38. Gideri (Balgo mission billabong). *Djugur* Giwilji made this place. (Same as 1.)
39. Wandidjara rockhole. Lingga went inside.
40. Nguragudjara ("two camps") soak and rockhole. The Gadjeri group lived here, singing.
41. Berbiga rockhole: same association as 40.
42. Merinmerin rockhole, where Gadjeri women obtained *djudjun* grass seeds and put them into wooden dishes.
43. Gandawara rockhole, where there are Wadi Gadjeri paintings left by *djugur dingari* men.
44. Junin rockhole, associated with the *dingari*.
45. Gangunung rockhole and hill. Guleii *djugur*.
46. Lirawilji rockhole and spring. Ngindaga, white goanna, lives here.
47. Waldjabanda creek and rockhole. Guleii *djugur*.
48. Gidjaral rockhole. Associated with Guleii.
49. Ngurdjir soak. As 48.
50. Djireribanda soak. Wadi Mingaduru, bandicoot, lives here.
51. Wamugawanu soak. Group of *djugur* women called Wadanuma (from their dancing) live here.
52. Rabi salt lake, or Lake White. Associated with the Wadi Gudjara.
53. Gabululangga sandhills: no water. The two *djugur* Gabulula sisters entered these.
54. Luwana spring, or Lake Lucas. Associated with the Wadi Gadjeri.
55. Gunamanara spring. Guleii defecated here.
56. Dildi spring and rockhole. The *djugur* place of Julububu, dove.
57. Bulbur rockhole and spring. Associated with Budeia, bandicoot, who lives in a hole here.
58. Wagilbi soak. Guleii passed through this place.
59. Djilgudjara river. The *djugur* Baba (dog) lives here.
60. Nindiwara rockhole. Baba was born here.
61. Ngalgu spring. Baba walked about here.
62. Biring well (made by Europeans). *Djugur* site of Wadi Gangga, crow.
63. Wongganbeli rockhole and spring, associated with Gangga.
64. Riljirilji creek. Also associated with Gangga.
65. Gilelji soak. *Djugur* Mingadu, bandicoot.
66. Ngiril rockhole, associated with the Minma Ganabuda group (of the Gadjeri-*dingari* tradition).
67. Luldu rockhole. Wadi Djilgamada (echidna) site.
68. Walubun rockhole. As 67.
69. Ruru rockhole. On the Wadi Gudjara track.
70. Lunggara rockhole. As 69.
71. Liga soak. The *djugur* Ganu lizard lives here—a large group of Ganu men and women.
72. Jireribi soak, associated with Wadi Bira (moon), who is sitting here.
73. Mandabanda soak. Moon rested here as he traveled by himself, followed by his *djugur* dogs.

From this example, it should be clear that the whole country is full of signs—signs that are framed in mythic terms. Almost every site shows some such association. The list refers only very briefly to the particular *djugur* characters, in either their human or their animal guise. Their spirits are linked in some way with these sites: for example, they may be concerned with one or more sites and then move on to others on other paths.

The Aboriginal cartographer has set about drawing a "map" that shows a line of waters along which a person can move from, for example, point A to point B, from Balgo to Lake White, as the case may be. In doing so, he must pass through the Dreaming areas of a fairly wide range of mythic characters and through the local group territories of several dialect units. However, the *actual* mythic tracks cut across the "line of waters," because the characters concerned did not go directly from one such point to the next: in moving across the country, they did not adhere to the principle of taking the shortest distance between two points. Mythically they were not interested, it is assumed, in getting from point A to point B in the shortest possible time. Therefore, over and above these direct lines of communication, as set out in Figure 5-2, are the links between specific sites on a mythical basis, representing further tracks along which those characters traveled. And it is along these, rather than by the direct routes, that contemporary people move in their quest for food and spiritual sustenance, because these two elements are irrevocably linked. Apart from the miraculous and magical actions of some of these beings, the flexibility of their bodily forms and their superhuman powers, their life as set out in the myths did not differ radically from the life of traditionally oriented Aborigines today. Both depended on the natural environment for sustenance and for emotional security, and both adopted special attitudes toward that land and everything within it. There is a striking parallel between them, one that needs to be underlined, especially in terms of the value orientation and basic assumptions on which their particular social order depended. According to this, mythic man existed in the creative era in much the same way as Aboriginal man does today, but with one major difference. The mythic beings were shape-changing, and they left their spiritual essence at particular sites, whether or not they passed on to other sites or disappeared in some way. Contemporary people hold part of that spiritual essence because they are believed to be physically and spiritually linked with those beings—their living nonmythic representatives—and are fundamentally dependent on them. This association, in traditional terms, is of overriding significance for these Desert people, just as it is, or has been, for other Aboriginal Australians.

These tracks crisscrossing the Desert region represent the essential fabric of social living, but they are also significant economically in several ways. Each site is, in fact, the visible and tangible expression of a segment of a myth, and this segment, through story and/or song, provides contemporary people with information that is vital to their survival. For one thing, it specifically locates in space the sources of fresh water, which they cannot do without. Also, the myths indicate the characteristics of a site or local area: the main features of the immediate environment and what it contains and whether or not extra measures must be undertaken to ensure their continuation, for example, through increase ritual. The various segments together with the total myth of much wider spatial relevance, are guides to action without which Aboriginal man could not easily have existed in this region. They represent a corpus of information on economic resources, certainly one that is couched in mythic terms, but no less significant on that account in mundane terms. Some of this information is transmitted during early childhood or in the course of initiation; but a great deal of it is mediated through the myths—as narratives or in their song form during the performance of sacred rituals. They represent in toto the experience and heritage of the people concerned, a basis for social as well as economic living. In this sense, myth is by no means nonrational or rooted in fantasy: on the contrary, it is highly practical, directly relevant to ordinary everyday living.

As lines of communication that extend in all directions, the mythic tracks also represent channels along which trade items are passed, but not necessarily by trading parties coming from, say, Jigalong to Balgo, or from the Warburtons to Balgo. Trade goods are passed, so to speak, from one interactory zone to the next. When large ceremonies and rituals are held, some of the participants come from places a great distance apart; they provide, therefore, an ideal opportunity for bartering. Trade takes place within the context of ritual and often is not seen as being something separate. Items that change hands at such times include red ocher, spears, and native tobacco. (Two major varieties of tobacco are found in the vicinity of Balgo: *binggiwanu*, which grows in caves, especially at Namalu, not far from the Balgo settlement; and *managaridja*, the large-leafed variety found under trees in sandhill country.) But the most important "goods" are pearl shells and sacred boards (see below). Pearl shells are highly valued, especially those that have been incised with designs. They are ritually presented to postulants after subincision and worn as pubic coverings; they are also used as chest ornaments during ritual and for magical purposes. Many are secret-sacred and are not displayed publicly. Pearl shells from the Kimberleys are found as far south as the transcontinental railway line.

A point to be borne in mind here is that knowledge of the economic resources of the country is not enough in itself. To be effective, it must be translated into action, and this means the development of hunting and food-collecting skills. Training begins informally in early childhood and continues throughout active adulthood. Skill is especially necessary because the technical equipment of these people is not particularly complex. Men must depend on their spears and "throwers," women on their digging sticks; formerly stone axes were important for both. These are the essential tools of each sex, supplemented by such things as simple traps, grinding stones, stone knives, and women's large wooden dishes for carrying food and water and small belongings.

THE SOCIAL BASIS OF LIVING

Two kinds of social units reflect what are actually the two basic issues of this Desert life. One is the economic, the other the religious, and in this situation they are more than usually interdependent (see R. Berndt 1964:264–266). The first is the local group, or, more correctly, the local descent group; the other is what has been called, in Australian ethnography, the horde, but could just as easily have been referred to by some other label, such as the band. Each is related to the land in a different way, one through descent and the other through usage.

The local descent group is an exogamous unit, and its members are closely bound to the myth-oriented sites they hold in trust, in perpetuity. This land-owning group varies in size, both spatially and in terms of population. The territory is not "owned" personally, but is held on a corporate, nonindividual basis by virtue of its members' relationship to the mythic beings that are spiritually represented there. It is nontransferable and not in any sense, traditionally, a commodity that can be marketed or exchanged. This is not so much "ownership" as trusteeship, established through a "real" or putative relationship to the mythic beings, substantiated by rights over and responsibilities toward that territory—not specifically the land per se, except insofar as the mythic beings are manifested through physiographic features, in what they left, including representations of themselves, and what they made.

The members of such a unit are related by patrilineal descent; the men are expected to attend to the sites within their area and to perform appropriate rites on appropriate occasions, while women retain emotional ties with their own "country" even in circumstances where marriage takes them very far away from it. Local descent group territory, like dialect-unit territory, is defined by the actual sites it contains. Ideally, each local descent group has control over its own sites. Looking at Figure 5-2, we see that a large number of site names is provided for three routes. One or more of them, involving several mythical traditions, may be regarded as belonging to one local descent group—as constituting its territory. However, each site noted in the list on page 184 can be regarded as a "big name," encompassing a number of other smaller names that are no less significant mythologically. In fact, demarcating local descent groups exactly is something of a problem. There is no specific local term for such a unit; in referring to it, people speak primarily of "country" and only secondarily of the persons associated with it. When they do this, they first designate a "big name" and then, within that, define several other sites that collectively make up the "country." I shall take one such example, without going into the details of actual membership on a personal basis.

At Balgo in 1960 there were twelve male members (A to L) of "one country," Luwana, near Lake White and probably part of the area around Lake Lucas (noted in Fig. 5-1). Figure 5-3 shows Luwana, with its "small names" (numbers are used to indicate these). Eleven sites are noted; ten men each claimed a different site within this area, while the other two claimed one site.

> Site 1 is a soak and rockhole, Lalwiri. It is associated with Wadi
>   Bududjuru, a small kangaroo rat who sits within a hole at this place,
>   and is now represented by a stone into which he turned. A, who
>   claimed this site, said that his father ate a *bududjuru* he had caught
>   here. As a result, he (A) "got up"—that is, the *djugur bududjuru*
>   was manifested through him (A). A's *djugur* and conception totem
>   (*djarin*) coincided (see below).
> Site 2 is a rockhole, Bulgu. It is mythically associated with the Didji-
>   gudjara (children/two) or Didji-nanari, who were orphans. This was
>   B's *djugur*, but his *djarin* was the *gunia* or *djerin* carpet snake.
> Site 3 is a rockhole, Mingu. The Wadi Gudjara made fire here by twirl-
>   ing one stick on another. However, they lost these sticks, which be-
>   came rocks at this site. The Wadi Gudjara traveled northward. This

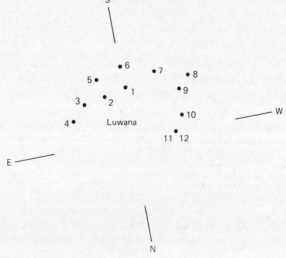

Figure 5–3. Sites within vicinity of Luwana.

was C's *djugur*, but his *djarin* was *gudedji* (singing), relevant to circumcision.

Site 4 is a soak, Gura. The *djugur* Water came from Gulbulundu, in the east, and camped here, leaving water behind when he continued on his travels. D's father drank water from this place and felt sick: later, D was born—Water was manifested through him, as his *djarin*. However, he claimed the *mundun*, black snake, as his *djugur*.

Site 5 is a rockhole, Jalala. This is the mythical site of Warana, a red lizard man who entered this place. E's father killed a *warana* here: it was manifested through E, as his *djarin* and *djugur*.

Site 6 is a creek, Gundindi. The *djugur* Mala, kangaroo rat, lives here. F, who claims this site, says it is his *djugur* and *djarin*.

Site 7 is a claypan and billabong, Dulgul, mythically associated with Wadi Lingga, white snake, who came from the east and entered this site, where he left his skin; then he continued on. G's father killed a *lingga* here and ate it, but vomited soon afterward. Later, G was born: the *lingga* "became" G, "it turned." To demonstrate this affinity, G showed the marks under his chest which were, it is said, in the same position as the wounds on the *lingga* killed by his father. This was G's *djugur* and *djarin*.

Site 8 is a rockhole, Budubudu. Wadi Lunggada, blue-tongued lizard, saw a spreading bush fire: he thought of a repository of sacred ritual boards (*darugu*) in the vicinity of this place and went in search of them to save them from being destroyed. When he found they had already been burnt, he ran back to Budubudu and entered the rockhole, where he still remains. H claims the *lunggada* as his *djugur* and *djarin*.

Site 9 is a billabong, Jabaru. Minma Baba (or Djandu), a bitch, brought food for her young. The puppies fought over it; one of them ran into a hole at this place, where it still remains. I, who claims this site, says, "That pup turned into myself." It is his *djugur* and *djarin*.

Site 10 is a rockhole, Lirawilji. The mythical kangaroo slept here in a hut, after traveling from the west, and still remains at this site. J's father killed a kangaroo here: its spirit "turned into" J at birth: it is his *djugur* and *djarin*.

Sites 11 and 12, a rockhole and soak, Jugulbali, are associated with the mythical thin bush potato, *djirilbadja*. Wadi Nundangidjara (small lizard) was carrying this potato, but it was too heavy for him: consequently, he remained at Jugulbali. Also associated with this place is the bush tomato, *wirga*, a mythical man who came underground from the east. Two men claimed this site: one, K, acknowledged the tomato as his *djugur*, but had the *gunia* or *djerin* snake as his *djarin*; the other, L, had the potato as his *djugur* and the *ngalameri* (bat) as his *djarin*.

This material points up several aspects which express a constant theme in Desert culture. Among these is the linkage with the mythical era, mediated through contemporary representatives of that era. Some creature or plant, when killed or eaten, "turns into" or is manifested through or becomes a living, contemporary human being. This bond and identification draw together both man and nature in such a manner that it is clear they are not conceived of as being qualitatively different. Also, an economic basis is created, and mythically substantiated.

In the Luwana example, a number of *djugur*, or "totemic," associations are provided, linked with specific sites, and these in turn are integrated with a series of mythical tracks which bring in further mythic beings. In other words, the mythical associations do not end with those mentioned here. Luwana, in Figure 5-2, site 54, is said to have Wadi Gadjeri associations; in Figure 5-3 no site is specifically allocated to the Gadjeri. However, some of these sites, most notably 8, are connected with the *darugu* boards that were destroyed by fire: these *darugu* were owned by the *dingari*, a mythical ritual traveling group, identified with the Gadjeri. There is, therefore, no inconsistency in this context: Gadjeri is selected as an "all-embracing" referent.

In this example, too, we have both the separation of the *djugur* (cult lodge or local group totem) from, and its identification with, the *djarin* (conception totem). In the southern part of the Desert, it is the *djugur* that is significant (R. and C. Berndt 1945:370–374). Kaberry (1939:194–197) distinguishes *djering* (*djarin*) from (for example) the *waldjiri* (cult totem). At Jigalong (R. Tonkinson 1966:209–211) the conception totem is *djarinba*, and "a person's 'cult' totem depends usually upon his area or place of conception or birth."

As far as the personnel for the Luwana sites are concerned, these twelve men (A to L) share among them six subsection labels (see below). This automatically rules out identifying Luwana as a single local group territory, since father-son paired subsection affiliation would ideally constitute a local group: that is, only two subsection labels would be found in one local group, or—allowing for alternative marriages—only four subsection labels, or two father-son pairs. What we are actually faced with here are four local groups focused on Luwana. Following Figure 5-3, men belonging to sites 5, 6, 8, 10, and 11 belong to one local group; 2 and 4 to a second; 3, 7, 9, and 12 to a third; and 1 to a fourth. Conceivably, the first and fourth could be regarded as constituting one group and the second and third the other.

However, Luwana is regarded as "one country." It is therefore quite likely that, through depopulation of the Desert over a long period, local groups have coalesced to form common membership units based on a constellation of contiguous sites all concerned with aspects of an inter-related mythology. They form what can be called a community, but not in the same way that Meggitt (1962:69–70) uses the term. It is not such a large unit as in the Wailbri case. Nor is it synonymous with the horde (see below). But marriage within the "community" is possible. It is also likely that this was the case traditionally. The population was always, probably, rather sparsely distributed throughout the Desert, and actual sites of sacred or of generally mythic significance were far in excess of living-person allocation. This meant that, although all sites were "tribally" or linguistically claimed, they did not all have at any one time formally specified caretakers. Many were never likely to have any; others could expect to obtain them through *djarin-djugur* identification, or through ordinary *djugur* extension—that is, through the principle that what was relevant for one particular local group, mythically, could also be relevant to other areas associated with the same mythic beings, by track linkage alone.

The "community," then, consisting of one or more local groups, was the land-renewing or land-sustaining group (see R. Berndt 1964:265): its adult male members looked after the sites and performed the rites in order to maintain a supply of the natural species and to ensure the continuation of the seasons. They came together with members of other similarly constituted units for major ritual performances, and in doing so formed what we can call a religious unit (see R. Berndt 1959:99). However, the unit we have called the horde (or band) was of different structure. Usually, it consisted of members of more than one community, more than one local group: it was made up of men and women related as spouses and their families, not necessarily linked in terms of patrilineal descent. This is the land-occupying or land-utilizing or land-exploiting group, concerned with hunting and food-collecting—that is—the economic unit. It has no fixed membership: its members vary according to the seasons as well as to other circumstances. It does not restrict itself to the "community" territories of its members, but moves over wider areas and across the land of other "communities." It is the main functional unit throughout the Desert, as it is (or was) in many other parts of aboriginal Australia.

These two groups, the community and/or local group and the horde, are complementary: much the same personnel are involved in both, and in being so are committed to two basic forms of social action. On one hand, in the first context, they are involved in maintaining the basic machinery of living—taking the proper ritual steps to release the power inherent in the various spirit beings, so ensuring the continuation of the way of life that they themselves know, socially as well as economically. Their duties and responsibilities in this respect are predominantly religious. On the other hand, the horde fulfills economic functions. The contrast between the two units underlines the division of labor between the sexes as a major structural feature. In the first, men have the main organizing and executive role in ritual action, including the handing on of knowledge, whereas women's role is submissive: they are intermediaries rather than activators. The heavy Desert emphasis on patriliny shows up in the examples (in the material relevant to Figure 5-3), where it is men's initiative, not women's, that is said to have instigated the spirits of particular creatures to "turn into" or be manifested through their sons. In many other areas, women are reported to play a more positive part in causing this to come about; but, to balance this, material obtained by my wife from Desert women gives a fairly equal weighting to women's responsibility in regard to conception totemism. In any case, women have the important task of producing children (*cum* spirits), and this is ritually recognized. In the horde, men and women make up a cooperative food-collecting unit, bound by broader social commitments *vis-à-vis* other persons than is the case with the local descent group or the "community." Each sex has its specified field of economic operation, but in all instances these fields are seen as being essentially complementary: men depend on women, as women depend on men.

Within the horde, relationships are proliferated much more widely than is the case in the local group, with its narrow range of genealogically defined patrilineal descent. The Balgo concept of the "community," which is wider than the local group, mirrors relationships found within the horde.

One way of approaching the wider social situation is to look briefly at the subsection system. Table 5-1 shows the pattern generally accepted.

In the north of the Desert, subsections have been in fairly general use for many years: the forms closely resemble the Wailbri (see Meggitt

TABLE 5-1

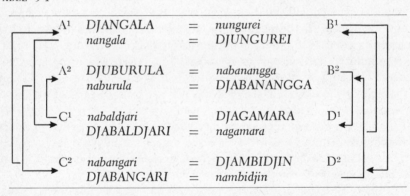

A^1	DJANGALA	=	nungurei	B^1
	nangala	=	DJUNGUREI	
A^2	DJUBURULA	=	nabanangga	B^2
	naburula	=	DJABANANGGA	
C^1	nabaldjari	=	DJAGAMARA	D^1
	DJABALDJARI	=	nagamara	
C^2	nabangari	=	DJAMBIDJIN	D^2
	DJABANGARI	=	nambidjin	

Key

a. The system is arranged schematically, in a conventional pattern. See R. and C. Berndt (1964:50–53) for variants.

b. Subsection labels are given in male and female versions (male in block letters), but conventional symbols are provided for reference—A^1, B^2, and so on.

c. Subsections are sections divided into two: for example, A^1 and A^2 represent one section made up of two subsections.

d. = signifies marriage; arrows point to offspring.

e. A^1-A^2, B^1-B^2 are arranged to form one generation level; C^1-C^2 and D^1-D^2 the alternate level.

f. Two matrilineal cycles are an intrinsic part of the system: those on the left make up one exogamous moiety; those on the right, the other moiety.

g. Patrilineal exogamous moieties are also inherent in the system and are arranged diagonally: the two parts of A and D form one, the two parts of B and C the other.

1962:61) and Jigalong (Tonkinson 1966:97) rather than the northern variants (see Kaberry 1939:117; C. Berndt 1950:19). At Jigalong, however, the section system is more popular. The section system is used at Balgo, too, but the labels vary from those at Jigalong and are closer to those we recorded at Ooldea in 1941. They are given in Table 5-2.

Traditionally, throughout the whole Desert as far as we know, alternating generation levels were an important structural element (see R. and C. Berndt 1964:45–46). They are still significant at Jigalong (Tonkinson 1966:103), but not especially so at Balgo, even though the same terms (*marira* and *jinara*) are in use there. Their function has been usurped by the subsections, since the subsection system itself incorporates alternating generation levels: in one level are persons classified as being of one's own and one's grandparents' and grandchildren's generations, in the other persons classified as belonging to one's children's and parents' generations (see key to Table 5-1, *e*). The division of generations on this basis means that two cooperative, nonexogamous categories are available for the general purposes of work—especially ritual work. Also, the subsection system divides each of the two generation levels into four further categories— two matri-moieties (arranged vertically in this schematic representation) and two patri-moieties (arranged diagonally), which incorporate both generations; but in the Balgo area there is no recognition of moieties by name. Subsections categorize everyone within a given person's perspective, for example, everyone within the "tribe" or language unit; each person acquires such a label at birth (actually, before birth) and gradually learns where he stands in relation to people classified in the other seven. In other words, the range of kin terminology (consanguineal, affinal, or classificatory) relevant to this area, and used in address or in reference, is spread over the eight subsections according to the kin orientation of any one person. Also each category is associated with a general but fairly flexible behavioral pattern, or cluster of patterns. A man of subsection A^1 knows, broadly, what his rights and obligations are *vis-à-vis* a man or woman of, for example, subsection D^1, and so on. Such labels are used for general purposes. They do not define exactly or specifically the kin relationship, if any, between two persons of different subsection labels. For that one must resort to genealogy, and genealogical kinship takes precedence over the nominal or formal kinship reckoning which is all that the subsections can provide.

The subsection system, further, not only points to but actually stipulates

TABLE 5-2

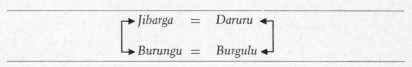

preferential forms of marriage and the subsection affiliation of offspring. In the first instance, cross-cousins are separated from other persons in a man's or woman's generation level. A man of A^1 subsection would preferentially marry a woman in subsection B^1, classified from his point of view by the general term *njuba*, "spouse"; but A^1's cross-cousins, both maternal and paternal, his *banggu*, are in subsection B^2. In the second instance, all subsection systems are structurally based on indirect matrilineal descent: a child's subsection label depends on its mother's, not on its father's, but is not the same as its mother's. The arrows in Table 5-1 indicate the subsection labels of offspring. Three principles are involved in determining a child's subsection affiliation: (1) the child is in the matri-moiety of its mother and, ideally, the patri-moiety of its father; (2) it is not in its parents' generation level but in the alternate one—the generation level of its parents' parents and parents' children; and (3) it is of the same section as its mother's mother, but not of the same subsection. No matter whom a woman marries, her child's subsection will generally not vary. On this last point, the local model is in the form of two closed matrilineal cycles— for example, a B^1 woman has D^2 offspring, a D^2 woman's children are B^2, a B^2 woman's are D^1, a D^1 woman's are B^1, and so on; the same is the case with the other matri-cycle.

Over and above their use of subsections in classifying kin, people now at Balgo have acknowledged relatives, close or distant, as far south and southwest as Carnegie Station, Wiluna, and Jigalong and as far southeast as Lakes White and Hazlett among the neighboring Wailbri. On the north, they have relatives scattered among the pastoral stations—including Djaru, Lungga, and Njining speakers. Cultural variation in and around the Desert region is especially pertinent in regard to kinship. Here only a few points will be mentioned.

In the Great Victoria Desert around Ooldea, far beyond the social perspective of the Balgo people but still broadly within the limits of the Western Desert culture, the partners in a conventionally preferred marriage are related to each other as "mother's mother's brother's son's daughter" and "father's father's sister's daughter's son": spouse, *guri*, is classified separately from a man's matri- and patri-cross-cousins, *narumba*. At Jigalong, the term for a man's spouse is *madungu* (Mandjildjara: or *njuba*, Gadudjara) and she is a "long way" cross-cousin, while *narumba* (or *njarumba*) are parallel cousins (Tonkinson 1966). In one sense, this is similar to the Ooldea situation, although some of the terms differ. A man's wife should be a daughter of a woman he calls *jumari*—this *jumari* is his classificatory mother's brother's wife or father's sister. He should not marry the daughter of a woman he calls *gundili*, father's sister, because her daughter (as in the Ooldea area) is classified as a sister to him. But according to Tonkinson (1966:112), marriage with an actual mother's brother's daughter is possible. On the other hand, the Wailbri system (Meggitt 1962:tables to Chapter XII; 85–86) stipulates that a man should marry a classificatory "mother's mother's brother's daughter's daughter," or a *gandia*; his actual "mother's mother's brother's daughter's daughter" and "mother's mother's brother's daughter's son" are classified as *jabila* and *ngumbana*; cross-cousins are *bangu*. However, he may marry his "mother's brother's daughter," provided she is not his actual mother's brother's daughter, or a father's sister's daughter. The Jigalong people and the Wailbri have only a few terms in common.

The situation at Balgo is composite and is dominated by the Gugadja and Walmadjeri kinship systems. The first is close to the Wailbri system, but not an exact parallel; the second is closer to Mandjildjara, but varies somewhat. A Walmadjeri man's spouse is *njuba*, a woman's husband is *ngumbana*; a wife's brother is *gandia*. Patri- and matri-cross-cousins are *banggu* in Walmadjeri; Gugadja use *banggu* for matri-cross-cousins, but distinguish between male and female patri-cross-cousins, the former being *banggu*, but the latter *djudu*, a term used for a sister; from a female's point of view, *djudu* is elder sister. At Jigalong, too, *djudu* is elder sister. Children of a man's mother's brother's daughter are his *jundal* or *gadja* (daughter and son), but the reciprocal is not *wabira* or *mama* (father) but *ngamini* (equivalent to a mother's brother) in Gugadja, or *gaga* in Walmadjeri. The Gugadja classify a man's father's sister's daughter's children in the same way, but classify his father's sister's son's children as *ngamini* (males) and *jibidja* (females: "mother"), each with the reciprocal *ngunjai*, equivalent to the Wailbri *nguniari*, "sister's son." The Walmadjeri also make a distinction here. Marriage between a man and his actual cross-cousins is prohibited, although (as at Jigalong) he may marry a distant mother's brother's daughter—not a distant father's sister's daughter. Preferentially, a man marries a woman whose mother and father he calls, respectively, *jumari* and *wabudju* (or in Walmadjeri, *lambar*, equivalent to "taboo"): *jumari* is used for wife's mother and daughter's husband, wife's mother's brother, and sister's daughter's husband; *wabudju* for wife's father and daughter's son, wife's father's sister and brother's daughter's husband, son's wife and husband's father, daughter's husband and wife's father. In conventional terms, a man's spouse (*njuba*) is related to him as a classificatory "mother's mother's brother's daughter's daughter," as in the Wailbri example; the terms used for spouse are different, but the Gugadja use the same term for wife's brother, *gandia*, as do the Wailbri, who also use that term for spouse: the Wailbri use the term *ngumbana* (Gugadja, *ngumbana*) for mother's mother's brother's daughter's son and wife's brother. In the subsection system (Table 5-1), if a man were A^1, his preferential spouse would fall within the B^1 category and be related to him as a classificatory mother's mother's brother's daughter's daughter. However, the system would also permit, under certain circumstances, classificatory matri-cross-cousin marriage by (for example) allowing an A^1 man to marry a woman of the B^2 subsection.

Just as each subsection is associated with a generalized pattern of behavior, from the perspective of a person in any one of them, so the kin terms themselves codify and also evoke behavioral responses. Each in use has associated with it (or the term itself symbolizes) certain attitudes and mutually expected actions which are acknowledged between those using the relevant terms: the degree of response varies according to the closeness of the relationship—whether, for example, this is genealogically demonstrable or classificatory. Superordination-subordination is clearly defined between generations, and especially between succeeding generations. Generally speaking, men and women in a parents' generation have authority over those included in the generation of their children; in the first, for instance, are found the *jumari* and *wabudju* relatives who are most obviously linked with avoidance. Within a person's own generation, too, are relationships of circumspection, even restraint (for example, between brother and sister, between a man and his sister's husband, a man and his brothers' wives, and close cross-cousins), as well as relationships that allow a fair degree of freedom (for example, between spouses, parallel cousins, and brothers). But relations between grandparents' and grandchildren's generations show the greatest flexibility and permissiveness in interpersonal affairs. There are some exceptions to this broad construct, but they will not be dealt with here, since each relationship should be looked at separately.

Enough has been said to emphasize that the basic fabric of Desert society is, as for other Aborigines, the network of social relations expressed through the medium of kinship. It is relevant to every aspect of living. Particularly, in this context, it is significant in two ways. First, all relationships involve responsibilities and commitments of one kind or another. Some are in imbalance, a few are quite tenuous, but others entail more or less explicit obligations of reciprocity and gift-giving, rights to circumcise, rights to sexual access, duties to supply a hairbelt at an initiation, to provide a wife, to give support in times of trouble or dispute, and so on. It is, however, in the patterning of marriage relationships, in the sealing of a betrothal arrangement, that the economic element is of greatest importance. This comes out quite conspicuously in the kind of behavior expected between a man and his prospective parents-in-law. Apart from treating them in a general way with deference and respect, he must provide them with visible and tangible assistance on a continuing basis— giving them food and other gifts, helping them in building their camp, and so on.

Second, these Desert people are economically dependent—not only on their country and its resources, not only on the religious ritual complex which they believe makes it possible for these resources to continue, but on their kin. They are dependent on knowing what to expect from others— and kinship particularly and subsections secondarily provide this knowledge. The horde or band is not just a group made up of nucleated family units, even though superficially the presence of some polygynous families may give this impression. It is more than this. It is a cooperative unit, with each member caught up in an intimate network of responsibilities and obligations, depending on others as others depend on him. And this is the social basis of Desert economics.

THE LIFE PATTERN

A sketch of Desert social living and of the place of man in his natural environment has already been provided. This final section focuses on two major aspects: the mytho-ritual basis of life and the process of socialization. These two are not sharply distinct. At one level, the level of belief and values, they are two sides of the same coin, but in the sphere of overt action, also, they coincide at various points. The revelatory rituals of adulthood are still part of the religious socializing process that continues (right through) until death. Even the simplest initiation series are not designed just for the benefit of novices, but add up to a social event of deep religious significance. It is useful to look at socialization, therefore, under the aspect of religion. Certainly, there are other ways of approaching it, but this provides a basic—or, actually, *the* basic, framework.

In the Balgo environment, as on other fringe settlements, European contact through the mission itself, Native Welfare administration, and the school has brought about changes in some quite crucial aspects of initiation. One of these is the physical operation itself: in recent years, several boys have been sent to a Kimberley coastal town to be circumcised by a medical practitioner. Also, the great rituals are no longer performed regularly or in full sequence. Often this is because these are frowned upon by the local representatives of European society. More tellingly, many men and women are employed in tasks that are essentially nontraditional, and the leisure time they have available is becoming increasingly restricted.

Nevertheless, in spite of these pressures, much of the traditional life proceeds almost uninterruptedly, although much less energetically and obviously more spasmodically. The authority system that rested on kinship on one hand and on religious sanctions on the other is still significant, but, again, it is more limited in terms of executive action. Kinship provides a series of checks and counterchecks which ensure that internal affairs run in a reasonably smooth fashion, if only because people are committed to certain forms of social activity involving rights and dues of a mutually sustaining kind. These cannot be evaded.

However, there are plenty of areas in which dissension can occur. In traditional terms, these are mainly related to women, religious matters, and sorcery accusations. Conflict arising from any or all of these can take the form of minor quarrels or more serious fights that bring injury or death to one or more of the participants. The line-up in such disputes

A camp scene at Balgo mission station, 1969. The traditional windbreaks are in evidence alongside European clothing.

Meditating over sacred boards, Balgo, 1969.

Jigalong desert men decorated with lightening designs for rain-making dances to welcome an incoming group, 1965. (Photo courtesy of R. Tonkinson)

Girl leaving a soak with a wooden dish of water, Western Desert, 1964–1965. (Photo courtesy of R. Tonkinson)

Collecting seeds. Beside the woman are a wooden dish, a digging stick, and an emu feather head pad for carrying the dish, Western Desert, 1964–1965. (Photo courtesy of R. Tonkinson)

The man prepares a fire for cooking kangaroo while the children play with the carcass, Western Desert, 1964–1965. (Photo courtesy of R. Tonkinson)

is not only or not always on the basis of kinship, but kin relationships are certainly important in any question of "taking sides": whether and when, and in what circumstances, to support or oppose someone—and whom. Such choices are made easier in one way, more complicated in another, by the fact that nearly all grievances are aired openly and nearly all quarrels take place in public. The traditional arrangement of the camps, with their open windbreaks, lends itself to this practice, and the absence of any premium on privacy as such reinforces it. In an ordinary camp fight, women are as active as men and often noisier; in fights between women, men usually try to keep out of the way; in fights between men, there is more likelihood of someone being badly hurt.

One point that is significant in containing or limiting disputes is the recognition of certain rules or norms that qualify the ordinary kinship rules—such as the rather weakly developed notion of "fair play." Also, not only in the religious sphere but, at least potentially, in mundane affairs, leaders of local groups and/or communities, men who are leaders in religious terms, may intervene to separate the combatants and settle the dispute (see R. Berndt, in R. and C. Berndt, eds. 1965:Chap. 7). Trouble centering on sorcery accusations and elopement can involve a great deal of protracted discussion; but in all instances where settlement is effected, payments are made in compensation to an injured party. There is (and was) no fighting on a group basis, such as there used to be in Arnhem Land. However, small parties of men would go out after an eloping couple, as they did in the case of a death attributed to sorcery where divination had supplied an answer to the question of who was to blame. In the Balgo region, as at Jigalong (Tonkinson 1966:300), among the Wailbri (Meggitt 1962:133, 262–263, 300), and elsewhere in the Desert, penis-holding is a significant rite connected with the settling of disputes (see R. Berndt, in R. and C. Berndt, eds. 1965:187–190) and, more specifically, with subincision. Between the individual participants in this rite, previous grievances are wiped out and gifts are exchanged to ratify or confirm the settlement.

Social control in the broadest sense, however, commences from early childhood. Parents are especially indulgent and rarely or only spasmodically discipline their own children—and never, or virtually never, the children of others, not unless they are prepared to become embroiled in a general argument. Restraint is a major principle that the young are expected to learn, and according to some adults, this is best taught by example. On the whole, boys have maximum freedom from responsibilities until the onset of their initiation rites. Girls, on the other hand, quickly learn to participate in the activities of their mothers and older women. There is no formal instruction for girls in the Balgo area, although farther south there was, in the past, hymen-cutting (see R. and C. Berndt 1945:227–230). Women also have their own secret-sacred rites from which men are excluded. Much of this ritual-song complex has to do with fertility and love magic, among other things. (See C. Berndt 1950: C. Berndt, in R. and C. Berndt, eds. 1965:Chap. 9.)

At initiation, the situation for boys changes quite radically. Precircumcision rites usually commence when a boy reaches puberty, roughly between about fourteen and eighteen years old, with some leeway on either side. Among the groups now gathered at Balgo, the traditional emphasis was on the younger age brackets, but now, as noted, boys are (or have been) sent by the missionary to be circumcised in Broome or Derby, so that the actual physical operation is no longer the prerogative of the religious leaders. However, novices still participate in the relevant rites; they must still become social adults. All initiation includes instruction: novices are guided and the rituals are revealed to them, section by section. They are supported by their immediate kin, but particularly by brothers and cross-cousins, as well as by their grandparents.

To put it briefly, a youth is seized and taken to a secluded camp. He is now classified as a *malulu*, is continually under surveillance until the termination of the initiatory sequence, and conventionally he must keep silent. Traditionally, he is taken by his prospective circumcisers on a trip to various sacred sites, which may last for several months. This is in a sense a pilgrimage, during which he is shown and presumably learns about a wide range of mythology. All initiation ritual, incidentally, is substantiated by mythological accounts: the situation in which a novice is involved is intended to be a replication of what was done, in the Dreaming era, by particular mythic beings. Once he returns to his "home camp," the people there are organized into two groups, or sets, each with a different assortment of tasks to perform. There are the "active" and "executive" participants, including those directly involved in his initiation. In this active category are, for example, prospective parents-in-law and grandparents. The others have mainly the more passive role of wailing for the novice and preparing gifts for the initiators; they are the novice's own parents, brothers, and actual cross-cousins. During the circumcision proceedings, women and children come on to the sacred ground and dance: the novice is regarded as ritually dead—he is said to have left his "old life" behind and is emerging as a social adult. The women and children then go ("are sent") back to the main camp. Once they have left, the actual cutting takes place, formerly with a stone flake, but in these days with a razor blade: or, if the novice has already been physically circumcised, the cutting is done symbolically. Immediately afterward, the youth is given his first bullroarer (*darugu*, "sacred").

From this point, until his subincision, a youth is called *bugudi*. Shortly after being circumcised he is involved in a blood rite: he is given arm blood to drink, and some is also spurted over him. Right through this period, various rites are performed. Episodes from certain myths are dramatized, and the relevant song cycles are sung and explained to him.

Sacred objects are also displayed, but he is not yet permitted to look at them properly or to see the full range, and when he is present on the dancing ground he is usually covered with blankets.

Some months later, he re-enters the main camp. Traditionally, he should now devote much of his time to attending rituals and learning the songs, until he is seized for subincision. However, these days he either returns to school or goes to work, and it may be some time before an opportunity arises for his subincision. After that rite he is again shown "higher" revelatory rites, along with sacred boards, and, especially, the "thread-cross" hair-string object called *wanigi*.

Over and above his specifically ritual instruction, his guardians emphasize, in ideal terms, how he should interact with others in the course of everyday activity. He is repeatedly told to be good—not to go contrary to custom, not to quarrel, to conform; to pay attention to his elders, particularly ritual leaders; to shoulder his responsibilities and fulfill his obligations; to supply food and to look after those who perform ritual; and not to be promiscuous. These injunctions form a special part of his formal education, and the rites impress on him, or are designed to impress on him, the importance of conforming. He is no longer a boy or youth for whom excuses will be made, but an adult on whom others will depend; he is now a functional member of his community, his society, incorporated actively in its network of social relations. And behind instruction, supported by ritual, is the threat of religious sanction.

After subincision come several other rites. For instance, in one he is presented with a pearl-shell pendant after he has seen the sacred repository of *darugu* boards, when their incised designs are explained to him. About this time, he is permitted to marry. He has, of course, been formally betrothed long before this, but it is not until after subincision that his betrothed wife comes to his camp openly and they are regarded as married. There is no actual marriage rite: the fact that they are living together publicly is sufficient, following a properly arranged betrothal which was already a matter of public knowledge.

Throughout his life, an adult man is involved in the rituals of his cult "lodge," either specifically in relation to them or more generally in participating with others in the re-enactment of the great mythic cycles. Associated with these are poetic song cycles made up of hundreds of verses. The rituals themselves involve the use of sacred objects and emblems, including wooden boards of varying size. These boards are also known collectively as *darugu*, "sacred" or "set apart," taboo. They vary from a diameter of 1 inch to a length of some 15 to 18 feet. All are incised with sacred designs referring to the actions and travels of mythic beings, and some are regarded as their actual "bodies."

There are many mythical characters, but probably the primary ones for this region are the Ganabuda (or Gadjeri, the Old Mother or Woman, or group of women, sometimes with male counterparts), the Wadi Gudjara

(Men/Two), and Wadi Malu (Man/Kangaroo). There are also several traditions that have been diffused into the Balgo area. The Wadi Gudjara and Wadi Malu are more typically of the Desert and are associated with a whole range of other characters of varying importance. Many of the beings who traveled along the various tracks through the Desert or were localized at specific sites are ritually significant. As far as the Ganabuda is/are concerned, there are at least two traditions. Both can be incorporated under the Gadjeri complex, and Petri (1960) mentions two traditions that are relevant to the people now living around Anna Plains. The Balgo Ganabuda-Gadjeri is identified with the northeastern myths and rites of that name; and these, in turn, are associated in part with the Kunapipi, which is very widely distributed throughout the north of the Northern Territory and into the Kimberleys (see R. Berndt 1951). Meggitt, discussing the Gadjeri (or Gadjari) among the Wailbri, observes that it was Waneiga (Woneiga) and northern Wailbri (Walbiri) men who were "the 'true' organizers of, and repositories of knowledge about, the Gadjari" (1966:5). It seems likely, however, that the Balgo Ganabuda-Gadjeri is derived from two sources—from the Waneiga-Wailbri on one hand and from the northern Kimberley via, for example, the Djaru on the other. Whatever the source, both traditions are now rooted in the natural environment of the Desert and have associated with them a large number of subsidiary myths. Furthermore, the Gadjeri, in its ritual manifestation (and not necessarily in terms of its mythology), has spread widely over the Desert into Jigalong and south to the Warburtons. These ritual expressions, more or less substantiated by the Gadjeri mythology, are primarily the *dingari* and *gurangara*. Petri (1960) links these together: *dingari*, according to him, refers to the Dreaming (the *djugurba*) and *gurangara* (or *kuranggara*) to the ritual cycle. The *gurangara* is also discussed by other writers, notably Piddington (1932:81–82—that is, as *kurangada*), Lommel (1952:82–88) and Petri (1954:243). In the *dingari*, Petri says, parties of fully initiated spirit beings moved across the country carrying sacred boards; they were followed by women and novices. This was, incidentally, the conventional traditional picture—the whole initiation sequence never taking place, as it does today, in one particular camp or area. Meggitt (1966:3–4) mentions that *malulu* novices are included, but that in the Wailbri Gadjeri this term is used loosely to apply to all males participating in the rituals.

Tonkinson (1966:224–226) distinguishes between the *dingari* (the *dingari-maligi*, the latter term being synonymous with *malulu*, see above) and the *gurangara*, although they are closely identified. In agreement with Balgo material, the Jigalong *dingari* refers to groups of people, for example, "*dingari* mobs," who move across the country, performing ritual and having adventures. The Gadjeri, as such, as the great Fertility Mother in Kunapipi terms (see R. Berndt 1951), does not specifically appear, although her name is mentioned from time to time and much of the ritual concerns fertility. The Balgo Ganabuda is, primarily, a group of women possessed of magical powers who originally, in the creative Dreaming era, had ritual knowledge that was denied to men. They traveled either alone or with a *dingari* ritual group who were also the food collectors.

At Balgo, too, the Ganabuda are associated with various "totemic" characters, among them Lundu or Lon, the Kingfisher man (regarded by some as the *dingari* leader). R. and C. Berndt (1964:224–225) give two versions relating to *dingari* "mobs." In the first, the Ganabuda originally possessed all ritual power, which they kept under their armbands; but this was taken over by the men, one of whom succeeded in stealing it. In the second, *dingari* leaders reveal to novices the meanings of the sacred *darugu* boards, and the novices, in turn, must "pay" them with meat. The following excerpts give some idea of the nature of these myths, and their association with the land as well as with ritual. I shall not attempt to give an over-all view, because these myths are extremely detailed and contain much symbolism that is not easily summarized.

EXCERPT 1

The Ganabuda move across the country as a *dingari* group. The men spread out to hunt and the Ganabuda (Gadjeri) come behind, in this case with one novice named Marumaru. They perform the precircumcision tossing rite.

SONG

jalgiri	*marumaru*	*wandinjani*
"sky"	(novice)	"falling" (after being tossed)

They leave Marumaru at Rabi (Lake White, noted on Figure 5-2), where he, or one manifestation of him, remains in spirit form in the middle of the lake. A mythical fire appears, burning some of the Ganabuda; others escape into a hole. Afterward, they get the novice and continue on their journey, carrying him.

SONG

guljari	*bibiri*	*jambujambu* . . .
"uncircumcised"	"youth"	"carrying"

The next song provides an explanation of the fire. The *dingari* were at Jabuna (Lake Hazlett) first, before coming to Rabi.

SONG

wilgungarala	*djanmuwandinja*	*bulingga*
"Wilgungara"	"erecting in the ground"	"on the hill"
	lira	*gulugulu* . . .
	darugu	*darugu*

The traditional name of Jabuna is Wilgungara, a term also used for the local people. It refers to the Ganabuda, who are "like salt"—that is, shining like the salt plain; they are identified with the widely known Mungamunga (see R. Berndt 1951; C. Berndt 1950). The Ganabuda erect *darugu* ritual boards on a hill. The boards are secret-sacred and so powerful that fire issues from the apex of the hill. This is the fire that burns some of them at Rabi.

To escape the fire, the women make a deep pit at Rabi and most of them go into it.

Song

ganindjara	*lirinmannguni*	*nanggurula*
"inside" (*ganala* hole)	"entering"	"*nanggaru* hole"

badubadula . . .
"shallow pit"

Ganala and *nanggaru* are the names of two ritual pits used in the Kunapipi (see R. Berndt 1951 for their symbolic significance). In this case, the Ganabuda shelter in them to escape the fire, but because there are so many of them the pits become "shallow" or filled up. Young novices are with them.

They leave Rabi

Song

wanajalindjunu	*gadababadjura*	*bagana . . .*
"carrying on shoulders"	"long lengths"	"lifting them"

The Ganabuda lift on to their shoulders the long *darugu* sacred boards.

Song

gadababa	*djurunggadjurungga*	*wanajalindjunu*
"long lengths"	"running quickly"	"carrying on shoulders"

The Ganabuda are hurrying, because of the weight of the *darugu*.

Song

walalajani	*bingawolidjara*	*walalamana*
"sun's heat"	"too far"	"sun shining"

jurungunbana   *walalajani . . .*
"cool time"   "sun's heat"

They are hot and tired from the sun, but another reason for hurrying is that they have so far to go. It is the cool of the evening when they again reach Wilgungara (mentioned in the second song). The Ganabuda go into the ground here, but they come out at Djawuldjawul soak and rockhole to dance the *bandiri* (or *bandimi*), the northeastern version of the women's circumcision dancing. One man also emerged here. He was a *djalbandjeri* lizard man named Gadadjilga, of the *djungurei* subsection. The Ganabuda women belonged, between them, to all eight subsections. When they saw Gadadjilga, they ran away. He chased them, using *djarada* love magic (see C. Berndt 1950) and caught one girl, Guwalia. She was of the *nabangari* subsection, and this meant that she was related to him as *jumari*—an avoidance relationship (for example, between a mother-in-law and son-in-law): but he had sexual intercourse with her. This was *wadji* (wrong), and punishable. She escaped from him during the night and rejoined the other Ganabuda. In the morning, Gadadjilga followed her tracks and found her sitting in the shade with the other Ganabuda. They killed him (but, apparently, not her).

This is the opening section of the long myth, which follows a defined track incorporating many sites and provides an "explanation" or statement on each one of them.

Excerpt 2

The *dingari* men begin their travels at Warawara on the Canning Stock Route, between Gudjuwari and Djindidjindi (nos. 11 and 12 of Figure 5-2), and head eastward. On the way, they cut wood to make long *jarindal darugu* boards and carry these on their shoulders until they come to a good watering place called Waran. Here they shape the boards and incise them with sacred designs relating to this country. Then they fix eagle feathers to the "heads" of these *darugu*. Lunggar, a small cave-euro, is frightened of them, thinking the feathers belong to a real eagle that is about to swoop down on him: he goes into a hole at Waran and becomes *djugur*. The *dingari* men stand one *darugu* on top of the hill, Liraganila, which is also the name of a big rockhole (probably at Mt. Stewart). This ridge runs toward Bilu-ulu, where there is another rockhole (probably at Mt. Fothringham). The *dingari* men assemble along the ridge, camping at Gimari soak. They are still there, in one spirit manifestation of themselves. Gimari is named after the stone-flake blades the *dingari* made for their spears.

They continue eastward to Maiada-maiada, a rockhole where they swing a *madagi* bullroarer. Later, they meet two old men at Djalberidjalberi soak. These two are unmarried brothers, both of the *djagamara* subsection, one bearing the same name as the soak and the other named Dingga. They own a large number of *darugu* objects.

The Gadjeri (or *dingari*) throw a long *darugu* board at the two men, killing them. After hitting them, the *darugu* flies onward through the sky until it "comes down" at Djilbir, farther east, leaving a "mountain ridge" (probably Roberts Range) resembling a long *darugu* board. The *dingari* come after it, to Djilbir, and pick up the *darugu*. Lon (the Kingfisher man) is there: he is their leader. Carrying the *darugu*, they go farther east to Lon, a waterhole named after this mythical man, and then on to Djidir (no. 17 of Figure 5-2; the relative positioning, however, is wrong: the mythical version given in that context refers to another incident involving the same *dingari*). Djidir is a big hill, with a soak, and a painting of Lon. During the night, the *dingari* swing their bullroarers. Then they go on to Wiladulgudulgu rockhole, where they set up a tall *darugu* board. Near here is Ngulu (see no. 18 of Figure 5-2), from which they had begun their travels. Approaching this place once more, they see their old tracks. They sing and make more *darugu* there, and also paint novices. After that, some *dingari* go to Jarinbir soak, and others to Nganjagudjara or Nguragudjara rockhole and soak (no. 40 of Figure 5-2). The first group go a little south and continue to Mandjabunda rockhole; they are looking for a grinding stone for their *balgurba* grass seeds, but when they cannot find one they are forced to use their *darugu* for this purpose. They travel on eastward to Mudjun soak, and at Didjinanar they meet up with the others who have come northeast from Nganjagudjara. At Mudjun they mount their big *darugu* and fly into the sky, traveling northward to Ngalgildjara soak, where they dance and sing: they then go on to Jilijili (no. 26 of Figure 5-2).

These examples provide a mythical background to ritual action. The major characters performed rites, including initiation rites, and had in their possession sacred objects endowed with great magical power. These objects could be used to fly through the sky and are, in fact, still believed to be used in this way, as well as in the more conventional ritual contexts —or as a weapon of death, as in the case of the two brothers at Djalberidjalberi; in hunting for game; or to make waterholes or soaks or alter some physiographic feature. The *dingari* rituals are re-enactments of mythical incidents: the performers participate in the identity of these mythic beings—they are ritually transformed. These particular *dingari*-Gadjeri rites are secret-sacred to men. Bullroarers are swung and various "totemic" creatures are danced, with the use of decorated *darugu* boards. And novices sit in a shallow pit while fire brands are ritually thrown over them: this represents the *djugur* scene at Rabi.

In the *gurangara* rituals, which are closely linked with the *dingari* and mythologically are not always separable, men sing over sacred *darugu* boards and posture with them in dancing. Also, *darugu* are handed over to visitors who take them to other areas for ritual performances. In the *dingari*, as in the *gurangara*, women have complementary rites that they carry out in the main camp. In the *gurangara*, women not only attend but also participate in certain sections of the men's ritual. Probably the most important feature in this context is the ritual *midajidi* or *mididi* feast (see also Petri 1960; Piddington 1932:65; Tonkinson 1966:189–190). This feast is prepared by specific women. Since the *gurangara* is concerned with initiation, the meal is eaten by men or boys seeing the sacred *darugu* boards for the first time. According to Petri (1960), this takes place after circumcision and the *mididi* is the novice's first ceremonial meal: this, he says, is linked with the Wadi Gudjara tradition. According to Tonkinson (1966), the *mididi* meal of meat and damper takes place about two years after subincision, and it is at this time that the meaning of designs on the *darugu* is explained to the youth. This is similar to Balgo custom.

There are several other ritual cycles that I shall not mention here: I have simply selected two of the most important, each with a wide range of myth-rituals clustered around it. Also under the broad heading of magico-religious belief and behavior come a number of increase rites for the natural species which are performed at local sites and are not necessarily occasions of collective action.

Several points stand out clearly. In the first place, myth and ritual, together or separately, have a direct bearing on social living, in specific and general terms. There is no compartmentalization of religion in this context. We can, of course, speak of the division of labor between the sexes, secret-sacred ritual, limitations on access to certain areas of knowledge, and so on, but religious action is something that is relevant to everyone. Boys and youths are initiated into the preliminary levels, and then begins the long task of mastering traditional material—a process that normally leads to active participation in ritual and, in some cases, to leadership. This process is actually an intrinsic part of social living. All men participate in it to a greater or lesser degree, just as they do in gaining a livelihood from the natural environment. These areas of activity are not mutually exclusive. The same is the case with women, but in a different way. What they do in ritual is complementary—whether this is dancing in the main camp, preparing the *mididi* feast, making parts of objects to be used by novices, singing love magic songs, or performing their own secret-sacred rites. Even though they are excluded from certain aspects of male ritual, their contribution is important to the over-all picture. The two facets are interdependent and mutually reinforcing.

These myths and rituals emphasize a special kind of relation to the land: a religious and essentially personal relation, in which man is part of nature and not in opposition to it. But, although there is this apparent identification, religion creates a buffer between man and nature. Man is seen as not being alone in his struggle for existence, because he has the spirit beings as intermediaries. In one sense, in this view of the religious life, ordinary mundane living is sacred too. On the other hand, there is the formal division of the sacred, the *darugu*, with its connotation of "set apart," "sacred," a term usually applied to the secret-sacred activities of

men, less often or less consistently to the secret-sacred activities of
women. But we could equally well say, from looking at the content of the
mythology and the ritual, that the *darugu* symbolizes the mundane life of
the people, their getting to grips with their environment and their almost
ceaseless search for food.

In fact, there is a tremendous stress on the socioeconomic, as, of course,
there must be in this context. The idea of compensation permeates all
social undertakings, whether or not they are of a sacred nature. Most
conspicuous, perhaps, are the kinship obligations where reciprocity is an
essential ingredient. Or, looking at this from the angle of situation or
circumstance, we could take as an example the economic aspects of ritual
—where kinship is also directly as well as indirectly significant. The
preparations for any ritual sequence that is intended to continue for several
weeks (as most of them were, traditionally) include the collection of a
fair amount of food, meat as well as vegetable. But, this basic necessity
apart, there are the economic issues that surround the making of ritual
objects. As we saw in regard to the passing on of *darugu* boards in the
gurangara, it is the custom in this part of the Western Desert for men to
make small sacred boards on which are incised designs relevant to the
maker's *djugur* and/or *djarin* site or sites. They are made to "show" specifically chosen persons "what a particular site or stretch of country looks
like and what it means." Such boards are exchanged, and with them go
certain mutually recognized obligations. An exchange of boards means also
an exchange of gifts, the cementing of a particularly close relationship—
because each board is said to contain within it not only the essence of the
mythic being whose site is depicted but also part of the person to whom
that site "belongs," or who "belongs" to that site.

The traditional life of the people now centered on Balgo was one
deeply concerned with survival—not necessarily in terms of struggle but
survival in their *own* terms, according to their *own* formula. An elaborate
cultural superstructure had been developed to deal with the problems
facing them in everyday living, a superstructure held together by the
network of kin relationships, linking man to man in an essentially cooperative scheme. However, it was not simply this. A further network of
relations incorporated the mythic beings, who were linked not only to
one another but directly to Aboriginal man, in a bond that was both
individual and social. *In toto*, it was a well-integrated pattern that, as far as
it went, seems to have provided a reasonable measure of physical and
emotional direction and security.

The coming of Europeans to this region, the establishment of pastoral
stations to the north and of fringe mission settlements at strategic points
around the Desert, inevitably meant the depopulation of "tribal" areas. It
meant, too, the partial destruction or at least the modification of the way

of life I have been describing. Different forms of socialization are available now, especially with the establishment of schools; pressures toward finding new avenues of employment are increasing and have, in fact, become imperatives; the "old" values are in question and new ones are taking their place, though rather slowly. The patterns of living are changing. The attractions of a seminomadic existence are giving way to life in a static camp that is now being transformed into a conventional housing settlement, where food can be obtained in a different and sometimes less arduous way than before. Much of traditional life still persists—or, rather, much of the content remains—but in a less coherent and consistent shape; the structure, the over-all system, is becoming very different indeed. How long it will continue in this way is open to speculation. But one thing can certainly be said: the balance of traditional existence has been drastically upset. Practically speaking, for these people, survival is no longer conceptualized in traditional Aboriginal terms. The basis of their religious life and of the values manifested through it has been undermined, though not entirely. They are no longer dependent—as they were only a few years ago, and notwithstanding the fact that some of them still believe they are—on the mythic beings and on what those beings symbolically stood for: they are no longer directly dependent on their natural environment. And, except in retrospect, most of them are no longer Desert people.

REFERENCES

Berndt, C. H., 1950. "Women's Changing Ceremonies in Northern Australia," *L'Homme*, No. 1, Paris: Hermann.
———, 1965. "Women and the 'Secret Life,' " in R. M. and C. H. Berndt, eds., *Aboriginal Man in Australia*, Sydney: Angus and Robertson.
Berndt, R. M., 1951. *Kunapipi*, Melbourne: Cheshire.
———, 1959. "The Concept of 'the Tribe' in the Western Desert of Australia," *Oceania* 30 (2).
———, 1964. "The Gove Dispute: The Question of Australian Aboriginal Land and the Preservation of Sacred Sites," *Anthropological Forum* 1 (2).
———, 1965. "Law and Order in Aboriginal Australia," in R. M. and C. H. Berndt, eds., *Aboriginal Man in Australia*, Sydney: Angus and Robertson.
———, 1970. "Traditional Morality as Expressed through the Medium of an Australian Aboriginal Religion," in R. M. Berndt, ed., *Australian Aboriginal Anthropology*, Perth: University of Western Australia Press.
———, and C. H. Berndt, 1945. "A Preliminary Report of Field Work in the Ooldea Region, Western South Australia," *Oceania Offprint*, Sydney. (Also see *Oceania* 12 [4] to 15 [3].)
———, and ———, 1960. "Report on Survey of the Balgo Hills Area, Southern Kimberleys, Western Australia, University of Western Australia," Department of Anthropology, mimeographed.
———, and ———, 1964. *The World of the First Australians*, Sydney: Ure Smith. (Second printing, 1965; paperback, 1968.)

————, and ————, 1965 (eds.), *Aboriginal Man in Australia*, Sydney: Angus and Robertson.

Kaberry, P. M., 1939. *Aboriginal Woman, Sacred and Profane*, London: Routledge.

Lommel, A., 1952. "Die Unambal," *Monographien zur Völkerkunde*, Hamburg: Museum für Völkerkunde.

Meggitt, M. J., 1962. *Desert People*, Sydney: Angus and Robertson.

————, 1966. "Gadjari among the Walbiri Aborigines of Central Australia," *Oceania Monographs* No. 14, Sydney.

Petri, H., 1954. *Sterbende Welt in Nordwest-Australien*, Braunschweig: Limbach.

————, 1960. Summary of a talk entitled "Anthropological Research in the Kimberley Area of Western Australia," Anthropological Society of Western Australia, mimeographed.

Piddington, R., 1932. "Karadjeri Initiation," *Oceania* 3 (1).

Tindale, N. B., 1940. "Distribution of Australian Aboriginal Tribes," *Transactions of the Royal Society of South Australia* 64 (1).

Tonkinson, R., 1966. "Social Structure and Acculturation of Aborigines in the Western Desert," M.A. thesis in anthropology, University of Western Australia.

GLOSSARY

baldju: a swamp

bandiri: northeast version of women's dancing in a circumcision ritual

banggu: (1) Walmadjeri—matri- and patri- cross-cousins; (2) Gugadja—matri- and male patri- cross-cousins

baragu: a salt lake

bindubi: an exclamation of tiredness or boredom. Also a "tribal" name

binggiwanu: a variety of tobacco that grows in caves

bududjuru: a small kangaroo rat

bugudi: the name for an initiate between the rites of circumcision and subincision

darugu: sacred or set apart, taboo. Applied to secret-sacred ritual activities of men (in some contexts, of women), including ritual boards (*darugu* boards) and other emblemic objects: also relevant to actions of mythic beings

dingari: groups of mythic beings who moved over the country performing ritual; also contemporary rites associated with them and/or with the Gadjeri or Fertility Mother concept

djarin: a conception totem

djirilbadja: bush potato

djudu: (Gugadja) a female patri- cross-cousin, a sister; and from the female point of view, an elder sister

djugur: local-group totem; refers to Dreaming era

djugurba or *djumanggani:* the Dreaming era (noun or adjective)

djunu: subsurface water; a soak

gadja: (1) Walmadjeri—son and male ego's Mo Bro Da So; (2) Gugadja— son, male ego's Mo Bro Da So, and male ego's Fa Sis Da So

Ganabuda: a group of mythical women who originally possessed all ritual power, later taken over by men. Associated with the Gadjeri Fertility Mother concept, and inspiring the *dingari* and *gurangara* rituals

ganala and *nanggaru:* two pits used in *dingari* ritual

gandia (Walmadjeri and Gugadja): a wife's brother

giligi: a creek or river

gudedji: special singing associated with circumcision

gunia or *djerin:* a carpet snake

gurangara: one ritual expression substantiated by Gadjeri mythology, closely associated with the *dingari*

jibidja (Gugadja): equivalent to "mother," or male ego's Fa Sis So Da

jumari (Walmadjeri and Gugadja): avoidance relationship; wife's mother and daughter's husband; also, wife's mother's brother and sister's daughter's husband

jundal: (1) Walmadjeri—daughter and male ego's Mo Bro Da Da; (2) Gugadja —daughter, male ego's Mo Bro Da Da, and male ego's Fa Sis Da Da

lingga: a white snake

lunggada: a blue-tongued lizard

malulu: a youth in the first stage of his initiatory sequence; a circumcision novice

managaridja: a variety of tobacco found under trees in sandhill country

Mandjildjara: a "type" dialect spoken as a *lingua franca* by Walmadjeri and Gugadja; derived from word *mandjila* "to pick up (something)." Closely allied to Bidjandjara (or Pitjandjara)

mididi or *midajidi:* a ritual feast in connection with the *gurangara* ritual cycle

mundun: a black snake

ngalameri: a bat

ngamini (Gugadja) or *gaga* (Walmadjeri): mother's brother and male ego's Fa Sis So So; reciprocal of *ngunjai*

ngumbana (Walmadjeri and Gugadja): a woman's husband

ngunjai (Gugadja): sister's son and reciprocal of *ngamini* and *jibidja*

nguba (Walmadjeri and Gugadja): a man's wife

Subsection labels:

males	females
djangala	nangala
djungurei	nungurei
djuburula	naburula
djabanangga	nabanangga
djabaldjari	nabaldjari
djagamara	nagamara
djabangari	nabangari
djambidjin	nambidjin

wabudju (Gugadja) or *lambar* (Walmadjeri; literally, "taboo"): wife's father and daughter's son; wife's father's sister and brother's daughter's husband; son's wife and husband's father; daughter's husband and wife's father *wadji:* "wrong": referring to a breach of the rules governing marriage and ordinary sexual relations

walgir: a billabong; a small lake that fills after heavy rain

wanigi: "thread cross" hair-string object; a sacred emblem used in ritual generally, but especially during initiation

waniri: a rockhole that contains water

waran: a claypan that serves as a temporary receptacle for rainwater; usually a plain

warana: a red lizard

windji: a spring

wirga: bush tomato

ADDITIONAL COMMENT

This contribution was written in August 1968. Since that time, the Balgo settlement has been moved to its new site at Ngarili, where a new missionary is now in charge. Further field research was carried out there in 1969. For a study of the *dingari* as a moral system, see R. M. Berndt (1970:216–247).

Two further comments. In this chapter, vernacular words are in simple anglicized form—except that in Aboriginal place names, j equals y. Also, Aborigines and Aboriginal are spelled with a capital "A" in accordance with a general ruling made by the Australian Institute of Aboriginal Studies, to distinguish Australian Aborigines (singular, Aboriginal) from aborigines in other parts of the world.

CHAPTER

6

THE PITJANDJARA

Norman B. Tindale

Norman Tindale is currently Visiting Professor of Anthropology at the University of Colorado and received his B.Sc. at the University of Adelaide. He is a D.Sc. (Honoris Causae) of the University of Colorado. He began his scientific career in 1919 as an entomologist for the South Australia Museum, in which capacity he had the opportunity to gather considerable data on previously undocumented human populations in addition to entomological information. In 1928 his position of Assistant Entomologist, which he held until 1933, was coupled with that of ethnologist, which he retained until his retirement in 1965. Throughout his museum career and since his retirement, Dr. Tindale's archaeological and ethnographic field research in Australia has resulted in numerous publications in those fields. He served as a special delegate to the Pan Pacific Science Congress in Honolulu in 1961 and has held positions of leadership in the Royal Society of South Australia. He was awarded the distinctions of the Verco Medal in 1956 and the Australian Natural History Medallion in 1968.

EDITOR'S INTRODUCTION

The Pitjandjara of Australia's Western Desert speak a dialect of Kukatja and have been aptly categorized as Desert in physical type. Isolation in the Desert's belt of maximum aridity rendered them somewhat unique as a Western Desert-type population, most notably in the absence of complex section terms and matrilineal moieties. This situation, however, was changing due to increasing contact with other aboriginal populations during the early phases of the movement of Europeans into Australia. The Pitjandjara, like the Walmadjeri, Gugadja, and other Australian bush peoples, utilized a myth and ritual complex to link men to nature and to other men, as well as a less formalized, flexible system of socioeconomic groups for exploitation. Today the traditional Pitjandjara patterns of organization and exploitation

217

are changing through influence from Euro-Australian government agencies, missionaries, and teachers. Government schools offer new means of socialization, and medical and financial support has reduced the necessity for population controls, resulting in a rapid rate of population growth.

This article emphasizes the interrelations between the physical environment and Pitjandjara social organization and economic activities. Besides being valuable for students of human ecology in general, it contains clues that may be of particular interest to archaeologists.

Comparison of this chapter with the preceding one on the Walmadjeri and Gugadja is advantageous primarily in that, as was previously noted, the emphases of the two authors are complementary. On a more general level, contrast between these Australian groups and the G/wi and !Kung Bushmen of the Kalahari should be noted within the context of variation in adaptation to extremely arid environments.

The Pitjandjara are a simple hunting and food-gathering people who live in the northwestern corner of the state of South Australia, with their territory extending westward just over the West Australian border and northward into the Northern Territory of Australia. Figures 6-1 and 6-2 show the limits of their country together with a few of their key waters.

Their homeland is far from the sea, lying within the bounds of the vast area of the interior known to South Australians as the Western Desert, but to the people of Western Australia as the Eastern Desert. Each of these names registers its aridity. A third name, Gibson's Desert, applies strictly to a particularly desolate area west of Pitjandjara territory. The name recalls the death of one of the Western explorers who ventured into its unknown vastness.

The name Pitjandjara (Pitjandjadjara, Pitjantjara) is applied to one of the major tribal units in the Western Desert. Its people are of peculiar interest because their traditions assert that they came to their country from the south, the direction of the sea. They knew it only as a vast salt lake. Their migrations took them northward to the area around Mt. Sir Thomas, where they lived securely in a focal area, known as Kalaiapiti, or the "Emu Rockhole," which, according to tradition, long remained the heartland of their territory. From this area they spread north and northeastward into the Tomkinson and Mann ranges, as well as northward to the Petermanns, with several hordes traveling eastward and claiming water rights at Oparinna (the native name is Aparina or Ngaparina, place of *Melaleuca* tea trees) in the Western Musgrave ranges.

This was their territory during the nineteenth century, when they first came to the casual and brief attention of several Western explorers. None of these visitors—Giles, the Elder exploration party, or the surveyor Carruthers—were able to record their tribal name, and it is from aboriginal

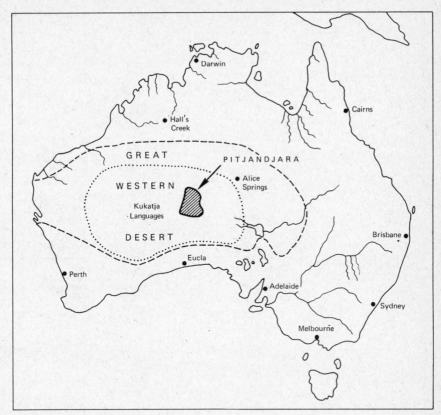

Figure 6–1. Map of Australia showing the location of the Pitjandjara in the Great Western Desert and the general distribution of Kukatja-type languages.

sources that we learn that their parents and grandparents were the ones who first encountered white strangers.

During the almost country-wide major drought of the years 1914–1915, lack of water became so great a problem that the Pitjandjara were forced eastward. In desperation, and by reason of power of superior numbers, they drove the rightful inhabitants of the Eastern Musgrave ranges, the Jang-kundjara, out of part of their territory, forcing them to move down Officer Creek toward the southern limits of their territory, in the Everard ranges.

When the rains came again and the pressure was relieved, not all of the Pitjandjara returned within their former bounds. Instead, they remained in the Musgraves, usurping the country as far east as Ernabella, which became one of the important summer watering places. Shortly after World War I, white men as settlers began to penetrate the area from the east. A few of the Jangkundjara then returned to Ernabella under white protection, as native assistants, working out from Moorilyanna Sheep Station (ranch),

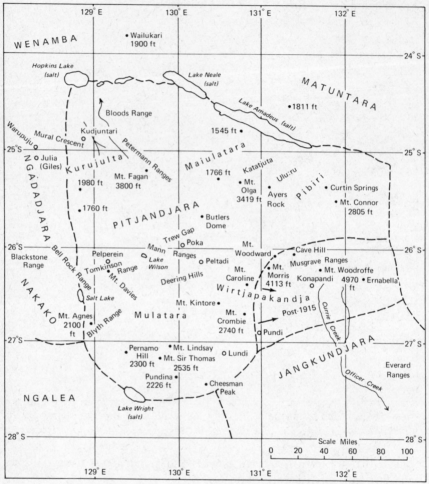

Figure 6–2. Homeland of the Pitjandjara.

which lies on a western tributary of the Alberga River. Ernabella station was founded by Stan Ferguson and Alan Brumby. A shed, an open kitchen enclosure, and a sheep yard introduced a small measure of European influence, which at first had only minor effects on these people. Another small station house, built of adobe, was erected near Officer Creek by a man named Brown, who lived with an aboriginal wife until his accidental death, brought about during a violent rainstorm by the sudden collapse of an adobe wall of his house.

The westernmost horde of the Pitjandjara lived east of Mt. Hinckley and claimed the area just to the north (which is now becoming known because of its outcrops of nickel and cobalt ore) at Wingelina.

The senior male of this western horde, whose white-man–given name is Peter, had made an intertribal marriage with a Ngadadjara woman. Her hordal country lay between Mt. Hinckley and the Blackstone Range. This marriage was the oldest western intertribal contact remembered by the Pitjandjara, and it was to become important to them for several reasons.

The Ngadadjara people possess a classificatory system of social organization with four named classes or sectional terms. This system came to their country from Kaieli, that is, from the north. Such terms were foreign to the Pitjandjara, who used only a series of kinship terms divided by nameless recognition of alternate generations above and below. The *nganandaruka* term was applied not only to one's own generation but equally to grandparents and to grandchildren. Pitjandjara at one time also lacked possession of large wooden *tum:a* boards. These were objects like large *tjurunga* (*churinga*) marked with carved designs and were much treasured by the Ngadadjara as well as by men of the tribes to the west and north. The first *tum:a* boards, or as they came to be called *inma tjukurupa*, at first were an embarrassment, and even in 1933 the secret handing on of boards associated with a Ngadadjara woman's clan was a predicament to her Pitjandjara husband. Even though a woman would not be aware of the existence of these secret boards, her brothers and her father had the duty of passing them into her husband's possession and he then became responsible for them. These foreign contacts had other effects we will mention later.

The aborigines' fear of *ngatari*, or strangers, often unfamiliar natives displaced from their normal waters by drought or other causes, is very evident in all their dealings with persons unknown to them.

The fears are often expressed in song. A western Pitjandjara example is:

SONG

> *walmala katu katu merarara*   *ngilji*
> "strange people looking down deadly"
> "silently"
>   (like eagles) *mere* = "dead" or "death"
> *ma:nu*
> "stealing"
> "sneaking"

This song tells of their fears of unknown people from the southwest. Dramatic evidence of this fear was apparent at a night camp in the Blyth Range in 1957, after the two-week-old remains of a camp of about fifteen persons, unknown to the Pitjandjara, were seen at Makurapiti (Mt. Agnes) on the southwestern edge of Pitjandjara territory. Our men woke and shivered in fear. Only the firing of Verey lights and the discharge of a rifle by members of our party set their minds at rest for the night.

There are fears of such contacts even when members of two tribes have been in communication. One of the two Pitjandjara men referred to was one who many years previously had taken a Ngadadjara woman, of an adjoining horde and tribe, as his wife. Therefore, he said, he had no personal fears about going to his wife's birthplace at Ero:tjo (Mt. Hinckley), just over the border in Njadadjara territory. Nevertheless, when we approached the place he was noticed to be singing the above song to himself, indicating a certain unease, even though it was known that there were no Ngadadjara people in the area.

The term *walmala* mentioned in the song means "stranger" or "strange people." There is a similar term, *warumala* or *warmala*, which perhaps had a different origin, since it appears in the form Wati Warumala (Man Warumala), an invisible avenging being who upholds the rights of those who require protection and need to hold inviolate their own tribal territory. There is a ceremonial place belonging to this being at Malaranja or Malara (Teizi Spring) in the Tomkinson ranges. This is an important water which possesses a *'wanambi*, or snake, and is therefore considered to be permanent. The Wati Warumala strikes those who do wrong, as with a spear, and gives them mortal wounds (*'walpuru pungu*). Songs about the Wati Warumala of Malaranja are as follows:

Song

>   *I:para   i:para   jilui   itja:tja   lal':awa: kanui*

Song

>   *Ngilpa   kona   jai   nun:i   tji:ta   koruparu   nga:la   wan:ala*

The physical form of the Pitjandjara falls into the group which has been loosely labeled Desert, being seemingly a mixed type compounded of all three of the racial types: Barrinean negrito, Murrayian Australoid, and the Carpentarians, all of whom have been postulated as having entered the Australian region from the direction of Asia during the past fifty thousand years. A recent statement by Birdsell (1967), based upon the study of many individuals of all three types in all of the Australian states, is authoritative and should be consulted for details.

The generality of Pitjandjara are linear, often rather tall and usually spare. A few individuals show a marked tendency to dwarfism. Their skins, from exposure, are relatively darker than the Murrayian people of the coast tribes, the Mirning and Wirangu to the south, and similar people in southwestern Australia. The Ngalea and the Kokata, who live immediately to the south, appear intermediate. Murrayians of the south have a high tendency toward hairy bodies in both sexes. The Pitjandjara have relatively hairless bodies.

A striking characteristic of these people and of their western neighbors, the Ngadadjara, is the prevalence of blond hair in children, ranging from 90 percent in the Warburton ranges to 50 percent among the eastern Pitjandjara.

The Pitjandjara language is a dialect of a widely spoken Western Desert language, first made known in any detail as Loritja, to use the improper Aranda name for the Kukatja tribe of the Western MacDonnell ranges. Pitjandjara as a central form of it is rapidly becoming a *lingua franca*.

Speakers using recognizable dialects of the Kukatja language are to be found as far away as Lake Waukarlycarly, 700 miles to the west-northwest, and among other people at an almost equal distance toward the southwest. The whole area is occupied by Kukatja-type languages, as indicated in Figure 6-1. Elements in Pitjandjara suggest that it is a rather old Australian speech which has persisted long in its desert environment. Community of vocabulary has been maintained by the need for periodic sharing of waters and the forced fraternal contacts necessitated by the hazards of great local variations in water supply and food. An overlay of northern language terms appears to have entered the area principally from the north and northwest following trade routes from the general inland vicinities of Hall Creek, Fitzroy Crossing, and Roebuck Bay.

The underlying southern influences are even more strongly evident among the Ngalea and Pindiini, who live to the south and southwest of the Pitjandjara. Indirectly their language and culture reveal links with the Kokata, whose present-day territory extends southeast to Pimba in South Australia.

Both desert and range country were important. In the proper seasons, man and animals often had to seek food away from the mountain refuges and gamble on the presence of water remote from more assured supplies.

The Pitjandjara were, in a sense, committed to an annual cycle of movements, controlled and haphazardly modified by the vagaries of the rain showers upon whose seasonal comings their whole life depended.

As we have seen, the whole population of the Pitjandjara is divided into a series of smaller groups with patrilineal descent. These groups are called clans. The basis of their clan organization is a ceremonial one and is linked with a patrilineal and patrilocal inheritance of the totem of a specific locality, and inheritance shared by all men who are directly descended from a common paternal ancestor. Only the initiated men share the secret parts of the stories associated with the totem; children begin to learn of the less secret aspects from early childhood, and in very early life learn also of the dangers of going near forbidden places associated with the totemic being. All of these prohibitions are forced also on the older girls of the clan. They usually learn only part of their own totemic story before they are given away to men of other clans in marriage. Girls imported to the clan in exchange as wives at first know very little of their husband's clan story and are never allowed to share in its deeper secrets. Drastic punishments fall on women who pry into men's secrets.

Brothers are of the one clan and therefore possess the same territory. Since an essential element in a Pitjandjara hordal territory seems to be the presence of rocks or mountains (*japu*) to hold up and provide permanent waters and springs, it is said of two brothers that they are:

japuwara kotjodjara
"hill" "one possessing"

The normal living unit or local group likely to be found exploiting the area around an important totemic locality is a different one than the clan and is to be known as a horde. It tends to be composed of male members of the clan minus the older girls and women who have been sent away as wives to other clans, but plus the girls and women who have been brought in as brides for local clansmen. To these persons may be added a few casual visitors and some odd persons who for one reason or another have become attached to the local group from other clans. Such persons through the passing of time may become a part of it. Thus the local group or horde constitutes the usual agglutinative group which traverses a hordal territory in the seasons favorable for such activities.

The obtaining of accurate information on the numbers of such hordes present among the Pitjandjara has been difficult, and the decline and dispersal of some hordes in recent years has not made the task easier. It seems likely that there were originally thirty important hordal groups together with remnants of several less successful family lines which were at the point of disappearance at the time when inquiries first became fruitful. If these figures are correct, the mean size of the Pitjandjara hordal group was around twenty persons, varying from less than ten to more than forty persons. Since marriage usually results from the interclan exchange of women, the mean size of the clan was also around the same figure of twenty persons. The larger clans were often more successful in arranging marriages than were the smaller ones, a factor that tended to extend somewhat the range in numbers in different hordes, since a youth of a lesser horde, or his parents, often had to accept the promise of a bride in a rather remote future rather than a more tangible offer of a girl already of about equal age, such as could be obtained by a youth belonging to a clan possessing evident power through force of numbers.

As an example of a western Pitjandjara clan of relatively large size, we may take the kangaroo totemic clan of Malupiti at Mt. Davies in the Tomkinson ranges. Counting their sisters who have been sent away in marriage to other clans, we find there are about forty people who are of this *malu tjukurupa* clan. Not all of the men live in the area centered in Mt. Davies. Some of them have gone to live elsewhere and return only occasionally to take part in gatherings and to perform their increase ceremonies. At an increase ceremony at Konapandi in June 1933, no fewer than eleven Malu men were present. The *malu inma* or *malu tjukurupa* was, in 1957, the emblem still of nine adult men who were related as *kurta* and *malanji* (elder and younger brothers). They, together with their fathers, most of whom were dead, were all *kondanu* and all were *wilano*—that is, had been initiated. They had sons and daughters who also were of the *malu inma*, but their younger offspring were not active as members of the clan in its ceremonial aspects, although the boys would become active after initiation.

The increase ceremony for the kangaroos of Malupiti is conducted in a circular area close to the main water at Pelpereing, which is near a cave shelter (Pulpa teteara) west of Malupiti, a flat piece of ground surrounded by rocks and trees.

The Malu increase ceremonies may be held at places other than at Pelpereing and, as indicated above and described in detail later on, were performed at Konapandi in June 1933. Each of the nine men today possesses a share of the songs which together make up the whole story of the activities of the ancestral being. Thus one man, who is the present *maijada*, or leader, for this ceremony at Pelpereing, has a series of twenty-two songs describing the movements of Malu before he came to Pelpereing. Another of the nine men possesses a song series of thirty songs, of which only a few are the same as those of the *maijada*. They tell of a western journey by Malu, after he had been at Malupiti. When all nine men are present at a ceremony, the song series becomes very long and the associated activities are drawn out. Figure 6-3A shows, the *wanigi*, or thread cross, which Mundjandji, one of these men, prepares and displays when his song series is being sung. The ancestral Malu made the original *wanigi* at the place Erinatja (not identified) and brought it to Malupiti. This thread cross is of human hair string: the inner turns are of red ocher and the outer ones of black or naturally colored hair. This hair is provided by members of the clan. When the Malu Being arrived, he possessed a boomerang, or *kali*, which is depicted beside the *wanigi*. The Pitjandjara today know the boomerang only in their legends.

Taking the song series of Mundjandji Malutjukurupa, as depicted by him in Figure 6-3B and using it as an example, we see that the Malu Being was newly initiated at Malupiti. He traveled south and west to a place called Nganawara, where he displayed his newly cut and still-bleeding penis. The song called Nganawarawara recalls this place. He then went to Wipiala, where he encountered an emu (*kalaia*) and to Kalawari, where he met a lizard being (*ngintaka*), and so he journeyed on; at Julangu he heard dogs howling, and at the next stopping place he had the septum of his nose pierced. At Kandibatala he obtained *kandi*, or chert, for stone tools and learned how to sharpen the cutting stones by striking them. Continuing his journey to Tjitjitjitjintjito, he saw many little children (*tjitji*) and put them in his pouch. At Malu wiputjara he saw another kangaroo being who was carrying a large phallus. At the next watering place the song Muluru poropateno tells how Malu smelled the smoke of

Figure 6–3A.   Wanigi of the Inma Wati Pampul, Konapandi, June 23, 1933.

a great fire and ran away to Letaratara, where he danced and saw that he
had a large group of small children around him. He now turned to travel in
an easterly direction and continued the dancing at Wipultu pungu, which
means "striking the penis." He danced in such a way that his subincised
penis flapped up and down. The boy children that he had been carrying in
the pouch all the way from Tjitjitjitjintjito now came out. There is confusion here between the male and female kangaroo; this is not uncommon.
Actually, the beings have all the attributes of men. Malu traveled along
slowly with his children to Mananari. At Mungarundu he saw his first
wardaruka (*Acacia ligulata*) shrub and made a song about it. At Banaralka
he saw a *warilju*, or misteltoe (*Lysiana murrayi*), growing on a tree. He
approached the eastern end of the Blackstone Range in Western Australia,
a place now in the territory of the Ngadadjara tribe. At Patinidjaranja in
this range he gave blood from his arm to feed a little boy. The bleeding
took away his fat, so that at Nanja naranu he fell down with weakness
and loss of blood. But the next song at Tjiwana reruki records that he
revived. He traveled over the sandhills, or *pila*, and when approaching

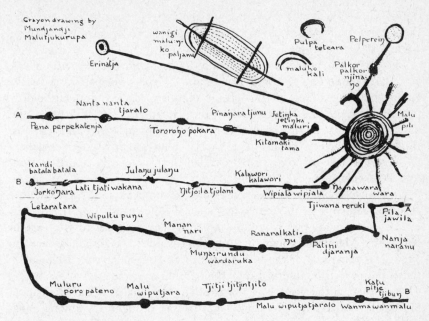

Figure 6–3B. Wandering of an ancestral being, the kangaroo man, linking place names and song outlines, as drawn by a man of the western Pitjandjara at Mt. Davies in the Tomkinson ranges, South Australia.

Pena perpekatenja he heard footsteps and fled in fear. He ran out onto a plain, where he saw a tall *korukara*, or desert oak (*Casuarina decaisneana*). At Tororongo he saw *pokara* shrubs (*Thryptomene maisonneuvii*) and sampled the honey water which hangs from the leaves early on dewy winter mornings.

Then he saw *tjuta*, white bark gum trees (*Eucalyptus* sp.), at Pinangaratjunu; coming to rocky ground, he found *Triodia* grass (*tjandi*) with the resin called *keiti*, which is used for making the resin handles of circumcision knives. And so he returned to Malupiti.

The singing of the increase songs of the Malu is a task shared by the clan members, and each clan has responsibilities for the increase of one or more totemic animals or plants. The list of totemic beings covers the principal food and water interests of the people, and there tends to be a recognized degree of importance commensurate with the likely availability of the totemic animal as food. In 1963, men of the Malu totem were very anxiously attempting to increase their subsidiary *inma waro,* or rock wallaby totem, having become concerned that this species had rather suddenly become so rare that they feared it had left their country.

Pitjandjara tribespeople recognize five named regional units, which are separate and tend to live in different parts of their whole territory except during the annual season of drought in early summer when several of them may congregate in the Western Musgraves where there is a virtually assured supply of water.

The Kurujulta hordes were generally to be found in the north of the tribal area extending eastward from Patupiri, the principal water in the Kathleen Range. Many of the people of this area, including the oldest-remembered person, Patupiri, are dead. Imandura, an unmarried girl about eighteen years of age who was at Giles Pinnacle in 1963, is almost the only known survivor still living in her country, along with Ngadadjara persons who have for some years extended their living area into the Western Petermann ranges as the Pitjandjara have withdrawn to the east to live nearer to civilization. The ceremonies of the bat totem (*patupiri*) are therefore remembered by only a few men of other bands.

The Maiulatara were a group which frequented areas to the east of Kurujulta. Many years ago they moved eastward to Tempe Downs to Areyonga, being one of the first groups to make contact with white men; they are now partly absorbed into the Matuntara. Some are at Areyonga. The mother of the aged F_1 half-caste Tommy Dodd was a Maiulatara. She spoke Pitjandjara; her son Tommy was brought up among Jang-kundjara people in the Everard ranges.

The southeastern groups, many of whom are now living near Oparinna and Musgrave Park, are the Wirtjapakandja. It was this portion of the tribe which commenced the movement into the Eastern Musgraves, after the 1914–1915 drought, and usurped the country just to the west of them, extending south to Kalaiapiti near Mt. Sir Thomas and west to near Mt. Hinckley. The term Wirtjapakandja has a meaning akin to "displaced persons."

The Pibiri were the northeasternmost group living west of Mt. Connor and claimed Ayers Rock and Mt. Olga. Their hunting areas adjoined the tribal bounds of the Matuntara tribespeople, who possess a different dialect, which the Pitjandjara call Aluna. The Pibiri and Maiulatara were a little different from other Pitjandjara in speech and in behavior, and the Mulatara who lived rather far away from them considered them to be almost a separate people. It must not be considered that these are true subtribal groupings. Rather, they are generalized names associated with smaller regional groups within the whole tribal area.

CLIMATE AND SEASONS

The whole of the area inhabited by the Pitjandjara lies within the Australian Desert region and within the belt of maximum aridity, which runs east and west across Australia between general limits of latitudes 20 degrees south and 30 degrees south. The center of this broad belt passes to the north of the Musgrave ranges and runs through the Petermanns, and only in the Musgrave ranges and on some higher plateaus to the west does increased altitude cause some slight amelioration of this arid condition. In the classification of climates by Thornthwaite (1931) the whole region falls into his EB', which is an arid, warm climate. In Koeppen's system (1932) the whole area lies within his dry climate, with dry winter and warm annual mean temperature (B w h).

The northwest monsoonal rains begin to influence the area usually in December, there being a lag of several weeks as the winds move south from the northern coast. Heavy rains fall along parts of the north coast, but the clouds become less water laden as they move southward. Effective rainfall is both low and highly irregular and often occurs in local showers, so that one area of country may be fertile and green after a heavy rain and an adjoining one may still be desert. It is possible sometimes to step, in a few feet, from a dry, vegetation-lacking belt to one luxurious with flowering ephemerals and annuals.

The summer rains replenish the water table storage, fill the rockhole catchments, and place water in the sandy beds of creeks, especially where there is a rocky bar to hold up the flow of water. The whole Pitjandjara area is without flowing rivers. In general, there are few recognizable drainage channels or creeks away from the vicinity of the low mountains. The major exceptions are the Alberga River, in the extreme northeast of Pitjandjara territory, and a few ill-defined stream channels, including the Giles, the Docker, and the Armstrong, which lead away to the north.

Much of the tribal area is a plateau of a general height of 1600–1800 feet, with low mountains rising rather suddenly from low slopes into which run-off water sinks with some rapidity. The slopes near the ranges generally support more vegetation, especially on the southern side, where the influence of mountain shade sometimes permits what is called, in northern parts of the United States, an augmented "steptoe" type of vegetation, or what is known in the deserts on the border of Arizona and California as *bajada*. In such situations in the Western Desert, *Callitris* pines may be present. Where the hills are low and rocky they are usually covered with porcupine grass (*Triodia*). Granite outcrops often have native fig trees (*Ficus platypoda*) rooted in crevices and growing in a luxuriant spread over the rocks, especially where there is a chance for water supply in the crevices and some shelter from the full effects of the sun. Higher summits, such as Mt. Woodroffe, are heavily covered with *Triodia* grass, with occasional low thickets of *Melaleuca corrugata*, a tea tree. Traces of many fires set in the driving of euro (*Macropus robustus*) are evident.

The piedmont is often covered in open scrub, but this may have been eliminated by the constant firing which takes place when aborigines are traveling along the margins of the ranges. Large areas of plain, especially where water may temporarily flood after rain, are covered in mulga (*Acacia aneura*) scrub. Sandy areas usually bank up into parallel dunes, usually

Entakutji, a male, 48 years, Pitjandjara tribe, Mann ranges, 1933. His body is decorated with red ocher and fat.

Man dancing around circles of men, preparing to embrace his puruka. Konapandi (June 1933.) (Photo courtesy of C. Hackett)

A Pitjandjara husband taking a drink from a mulga grass-filled water-carrying mimbu brought from the rockhole water at Poka, Mann ranges, July 1933.

A *Pitjandjara hunter returning with a dingo as kill. He carries native tobacco* (Nicotiana excelsior) *under his arm. Mann ranges, 1933.*

A Pitjandjara woman carrying her dishes, digging sticks, fire sticks, and female infant. Mann ranges, 1933.

A *Pitjandjara boy, an* ulpuru, *with freshly killed dingo pup. White burn scars cover his chest. Southwest of Kona-pandi, 1933.*

View looking northwest from Poka, Mann ranges, July 1933.

232

with southeast to northwest, and these dunes tend to be growing at their northern ends by movement of the sands in the direction of transport by the southeast trade winds, which prevail during the fall and winter months of the year (April to November). Most sandhills to the south of the Mann ranges are vegetated with a species of porcupine grass (*Triodia*), and often there are shrubs, including poison bush (*Duboisia hopwoodii*) and tea trees (*Melaleuca glomerata*).

In a traverse of thirteen miles northeast commencing at Mt. Crombie on July 21, 1933, we crossed twenty-eight sand dunes, each about 50 feet high and rather regularly spaced, a half a mile apart, and often with a moving crest. Occasionally twin dunes lay close together. At Mt. Crombie we saw *Callitris* growing on the southwestern slope; the northeastern face had only *Triodia* grass and an occasional spiny shrub (*Acacia tetragonophylla*).

On the northern piedmont there was chiefly *Triodia* and *Duboisia*, while on the level plateau *Melaleuca* appeared commonly on the first few dunes and then became less evident, while mulga scrub (*Acacia aneura*) appeared in most interdune areas, with broad belts of only *Triodia* grass lying in some swales. Five miles out mallees (*Eucalyptus* spp.) began to appear and several other species of *Acacia*. The mallee roots yield water and the wattle tree roots have *mako ilkoara*, that is, larvae of a species of Cossid moth (*Xyleutes*). The mallee belts between the sandhills continued for about four miles, with a few desert kurrajong trees (*Brachychiton gregorii*) yielding food seeds and edible flowers and roots. Mulga flats reappear, then some *Melaleuca*, with an occasional *Codonocarpus* or native poplar, in the roots of which beetle grubs are abundant. Camp was made in sandhills west of Mt. Harriet (Penandi).

This route is one constantly traveled by aborigines moving from east to west and gives an idea of the kind of trail they follow. On a similar traverse, in almost the reverse direction on the following day, water was obtained at a rockhole in the face of a large gneissic granite outcrop called Itjarango, holding 30–35 gallons of liquid, after they had called at a smaller granite outcrop at Pitjil and had found the rockhole there to be dry. Near Itjarango there is an oval outcrop of granite, part of a large buried boulder 25 feet long. On one side of it had been arranged fourteen dark spherical stones, each 2–4 feet in diameter, with the fourteenth stone smaller than the others. This is a totemic spot on the track of the ancestral emu and marks the line of travel of Kalaia tjukur. The stones represent the fourteen eggs usually laid by an emu, and the smallest stone represents the last-laid egg, which in Pitjandjara mythology, as in stories elsewhere in Southern Australia, is a runt bird smaller than the others that generally runs behind the others when a flock of young are disturbed. Rock carvings in many places depict the fourteen eggs of this bird and show the same runt egg. The companions with me were not yet fully initiated, and therefore it was only later that I learned the full significance of the place. Itjarango is on the line of travel of Kalaia men as they journey southwest to their clan territory at Kalaiapiti, near Mt. Sir Thomas.

North of the Musgrave ranges, the sand dune trend is to northeast and southwest, where the vegetation changes to dense mulga flats between the dunes, many of which are covered only with *Triodia* grass.

Westward on the southern and northern sides of the Mann ranges are open forests of large desert oaks (*Casuarina decaisneana*), generally on plains covered with porcupine grass. Some of these trees are of great size, with trunks 2–3 feet in diameter. They give a strangely fertile look to the country, belied by its general sterility as an area for native foods.

Venturing away from the ranges, people can sometimes extend their tours in winter when southwestern rains blow up from the southern coastal areas and replenish supplies in rockholes, so that their water-carrying life is extended into spring. At such times the remoter bounds of their country may be visited. The winter rains have no effects on vegetation growth, which seems to be stimulated only by the coming of summer heat and showers of the northwest monsoon. The winter rains are a mixed blessing. The rain wets the supplies of dry figs lying on granite rocks and may render them useless as food, but the hard, ripe kurrajong seeds, deposited in the dung and coughings of ravens around rockholes, may be washed clean of their coatings of dung and so are freed for human consumption, either after being roasted in hot ashes or pounded into a meal between stones and baked as a cake.

Figure 6-4 illustrates the general cycle of the seasons as it appears to the Pitjandjara. The rising of the star cluster of the Pleiades in the dawn sky during May is an important event. The appearance of the Kung-karungkara, or unmarried girls, who flee everlastingly from the attentions of men, represented by the wandering planets, seems to mark their nearest concept of a beginning of the year. It is the beginning of Njenga, or the cold season of frost, of water turning to ice, of cold winds and sometimes drizzles of rain from the south, and at long intervals of time a storm which blankets the earth with snow.

The appearance of the Kungkarungkara, who in their belief are accompanied by many dogs, marks the time when dingo puppies begin to be born in lairs in the country, especially in places far from the main ranges. As a result of the performance in May and June of increase ceremonies for *papa* (the dingo), during which period dingos are not hunted, these unmolested dingo puppies become fat and soon provide a rich food for the winter months. At this time of the year water supplies usually have been well replenished by summer rains, and it is the time for dispersal of the several different hordes. The hordes tend to depart along the an-cestral trails of their totems to exploit the peculiar resources of their clan territories, feeding along the routes by which their country is best ap-

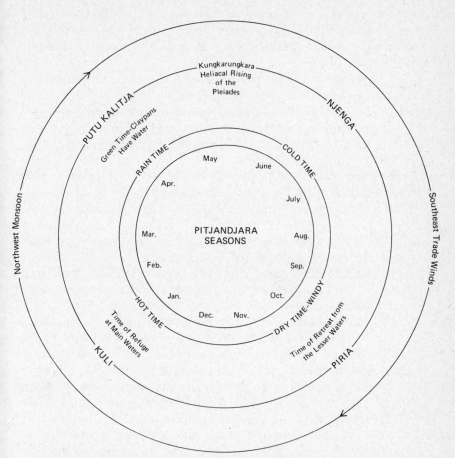

Figure 6–4. Cycle of the seasons as viewed by the Pitjandjara.

proached and later along those by which it will be necessary to retreat as
the time of abundance of water passes. At this time of the year, small
Pitjandjara hordes tend to appear as near the limits of their tribal territory
as is possible in the light of the amount of rain that their particular part
of the country has enjoyed over the previous summer. There are attractions
in going there. In remote cave mouths they often can glean a harvest of
mingul (*Nicotiana excelsior*), the native chewing tobacco which grows
best near the entrances to old caves and rock shelters where enriched
soils, shelter from the wind, and the higher humidity of south-facing cave
mouths enables this luxury plant to grow to perfection. In better rainfall
years the remotest areas are highly attractive, since the absence of exploitation has left undisturbed many of the small animals which do not
need open supplies of water. Often, vegetable products are also abundant.
In dry years, venturing into and leaving such areas is often a matter

requiring great skill in planning to make the best use of the yield of various lesser water supplies without entering a cul-de-sac from which escape would be difficult, or impossible, as could happen when waters dry up.

Thus, the period from May to September is one of greatest dispersal, a time when humans are most widely and thinly spread over Pitjandjara territory. This is a time when a horde approaching its territorial limits may see signs of other people, who also are exploiting their territory toward its limits. It is often a "smoke" on the horizon which influences a decision to turn back, unless earlier experiences have been such as to encourage temporary contact with the "strangers" for the chance to obtain wanted materials in trade such as millstones, red ocher, flint for knives, pearl shells, and glistening wad (manganese dioxide) for blackening the forehead.

Since the territorial limits usually have come to be at places least likely to sustain life for long periods of time, contacts are usually of short duration, and in many instances fear of unknown strangers leads to a quick retreat as soon as signs of their presence is evident on the horizon.

The Pitjandjara recognize the advantages that come with winter rains, especially in replenishing water supplies, even though such rains have little effect on vegetational growth, which is in general determined by the northern rains and the heat of summer. There are magical practices associated with special rain sticks. Men also wave *Eucalyptus oleosa*, water mallee branches, in the air to fetch cold, rain-laden southerly winds. Occasionally in the western part of their country men of evil intent are believed to cause *njenga*, or cold weather, taking the form of icy showers of hail and, even more rarely, a blanket of snow. Such visitations and heavy ground frosts sometimes kill the mulga scrub over wide areas, but as one observant man indicated, this provides much ready firewood and so is not an unmixed evil. Njenga, the Ice or Snow Man, is a totemic being of the Ngadadjara tribe, about whose adventures and actions men sing songs.

With the coming of Piria, the windy period of equinoctial gales and the gradual drying up of all but the most reliable waters, people turn back toward their summer refuges on the main waters and their mountains. This is a period when knowledge of waters is most important, for a mistake in leaving a dwindling water supply to go to one already dry may in the extreme case cause the death of a whole horde of people and at least cause great anxiety, suffering, and thirst, especially for women and children. It is then that a man may rush ahead, carrying a wooden water dish to obtain water for his lagging family. In the extremity in which he finds his family he forgets that normally this is a woman's task.

Falling back on the main waters enables temporarily a return to easy living, since many of the larger game animals and birds and all the tiny parrots, doves, and finches are increasingly compelled to seek water also

and so may fall ready victims to hunters lying in ambush near water and
even to little boys and girls who, armed with sticks, strike down thirsty
birds by the hundreds as they come to water. As Piria time merges into
Kuli, the time of heat, life can still be easy. Swimming in the shallow
pools of larger waters is a joy for some at this time, but there is great fear
of deep cold pools which drown people, and often hunters object to
children who make noises and so frighten emus and kangaroos that may
be seeking water. At this time some forms of vegetable food are scarce, but
there are other ways for women to obtain food. Wherever nutgrass
(*Cyperus*) has grown up after summer rains, the resting nuts or corms are
to be found by digging in the soils along the banks of creeks. Acres of
ground at a time may be turned over to obtain the nuts buried a few
inches down in the soil. The Desert kurrajong trees (*Brachychiton gregorii*)
are in fresh green fruit and edible flowers, and well-thrown stones bring
down showers of food.

At this time, the men engage in ceremonies to hasten the coming of
the full force of the northwest monsoon, with its chances for thundershowers and for the occasional joy of a real rain. In these ceremonies
pearl-shell ornaments from the northwest provide white powder scrapings
which help to create the rain clouds. At this season increase ceremonies
for other foods such as *anumara* are performed. Since this food, the dark
larvae of one of the large hawk moths (*Celerio lineata livornicoides*), is
gathered by women, the increase ceremony is a *laka*, or half-secret one,
in which women and children share in the singing and the men of the
anumara clan perform their part by engaging in secret all-night rituals in a
separate camp, shut off from the singers by a fence of brush and by a
distance of several hundred yards.

Showers at this time cause the growth of many plants, and if there is
enough rain to form open-water pools, most of the game animals disperse.
At this season there is often a period of semistarvation, because the new
growth takes a while to develop edible quality, and animal food has disappeared. Small lizards may be a staple food. Up to this time people have
slept in the open behind simple breakwinds of mulga branches and
Eucalyptus boughs. The increasing number of showers leads to the making
of round huts, covered with porcupine grass in such a way as to ward off
all but the heavier showers and so protect cooking fires from being
drenched with water. Smoke-filled round huts also deter the mosquitoes,
which may appear even in this arid environment. If the rain-making ceremonies have been successful, heavy rains may have put out all fires. The
oldest women, whose duties and skills should have protected the flames,
are scolded or punished by beating, and the men have to repair to caves
and rock shelters in whose dry depths they have wisely stored sticks and
grass as tinder so that new fires can be lit—often a difficult task when
everything is damp.

The first showers cause the rapid growth of plants such as the low-creeping vine *Boerhavia*, which spreads over the ground and is soon covered with small black *anumara* larvae. These grow in about a month to be two-inch long caterpillars. Hundreds of these are gathered into wooden dishes, covered with bark or confined until they have passed all of the *Boerhavia* leafy matter through their bodies and ejected it as frass. The women then separate the larvae from their dung by rocking them in their wooden dishes and cook the grubs by shaking them along with hot ashes, and so good food is available once more. The great heat and rain also ripen the native tomatoes (*Solanum ellipticum*), for the increase of which men of the Koilpuru clan have already performed their *inma laka* rites. The half-inch green and yellow fruits may be eaten raw in handfuls, and so any temporary dearth of food is overcome. Where there are sand and sandhills near water, unusual sources of food become apparent. The after-rain seal of water on the sand causes the marsupial mole (*Notoryctes typhlops*) to work its way to the surface of the ground and for the moment leave traces of its presence on the surface of the sand. In the same way, the blind, wingless mole crickets, *Cylindracheta*, also break the surface and are captured by children, who find in them a tiny source of food. After rain has flattened the sand, every visible animal track is a fresh one, and even to the trained eye of the aboriginal hunter this is a pleasure, since he can now scan large areas at a glance and so know at once where food is likely to be found.

Rain time is good time—everywhere is a camp. Big rains fill every claypan and so there is little need for planning. One can camp anywhere. Soft, wet ground is difficult to walk over for long distances, and the great humidity and heat discourages long-distance travel. The need for food is less; it is a time of laziness and of minimum activity. In the cool of a rock shelter or the shade of a tree there is work in repairing weapons, preparing for the good hunting days. Idle time may lead to the carving of designs on the bark of trees, the telling of stories, or the painting of pictures on the walls of the shelters, or it is a time for doing "nothing."

As the days pass and cooler spells break the great heat, women spread further afield to gather vegetable foods, which now are in abundance. The green herbage has attracted kangaroos, euros, and many small mammals, and in later days rabbits, so that the rewards of hunting are increased.

During the hottest times when the ground is soft and wet, young men have a special method of hunting kangaroos. Two men will follow a kangaroo's track and set it in motion, one running after it while the other circles to head it off, knowing the animal will turn as it runs; he takes up the chase, both continuing until the exhausted animal gives up and suffers the fate of being killed with a stick. Young men can outlast a kangaroo, but they are so exhausted that they rest for several days after such an effort, being supplied with food by others.

PREHISTORY OF THE PITJANDJARA AREA

There has been little archaeological work done in the Pitjandjara area. A few inches of deposit has been noted in several cave shelters and deeper deposits in others, but the difficulties of remaining for periods long enough for proper excavations have not yet been overcome.

Elsewhere in Australia, in Victoria, the archaeological record goes back at least 31,000 years, and more detailed evidence is available on the eastern fringe of the Western Desert, at Lake Menindee, from 26,000 years ago. There is also evidence for the presence of man near the coast south of Pitjandjara territory 18,000 years ago. Mulvaney (1966) and Tindale (1968) give summaries of the data available up to the present. Late discoveries at Mungo Lake, New South Wales, carry early occupation back to 39,000 years ago.

The living Pitjandjara make and use resin-hafted *tjimari* knives (Tindale 1965), which are similar in form, size, and modes of manufacture and technique of sharpening to those found in the Tartangan culture of the Murray Valley in South Australia and dated there to between 6000 and 11,000 years ago. Similar ones were in common use in Tasmania until recent times. Archaeological sites showing *tjimari* knives of the same kind as in the living culture have been reported by J. E. Johnson from Pitjandjara territory; they probably have had a long history there.

The people also still use a hand chopper which bears considerable resemblance to the "horsehoof" implement characteristic of the Tartangan and earlier Kartan cultures of other parts of Australia. They also use simple, resin-hafted flakes for circumcision knives and as blood-letting instruments (Fig. 6-5). Culturally the living people seem to have retained in postclimax fashion older forms of stone tools. Unifacially flaked leaf-shaped projectile points of the so-called "pirri" type have been found in at least two places in Pitjandjara territory. In the Murray Valley these have been dated to between 4000 and 5000 years before the present and to 1860 years ago near Lake Torrens. The same types occur, however, in the living culture some 700 miles to the west and also about the same distance north of Pitjandjara territory. On the tentative assumption that

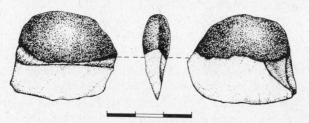

Figure 6–5. Circumcision knife used at Konapandi, June 23, 1933 (scale in centimeters).

there is a culture gradient from southeast to northwest, it could be that "pirri" spear points are less than 1000 years old in Pitjandjara territory. One site where they occur is south of the Musgrave ranges in sandhills surrounding a lake bed which no longer fills with water. The aborigines do not know of any present-day watering place near it.

The principal present-day methods aborigines use in recording events of the past is by word of mouth, by rock paintings and carvings, and in mime and song.

At least one historical event, a struggle between two people, is accurately registered to a date, because it is linked to a specific hill and tied to an eclipse of the sun at a specific time of the day.

Some historical happenings become reoriented, incorporated into, and linked with their increase rites for totemic animals and plant species. Thus the rock carvings and paintings often serve as reminders of certain events, but the clues are soon lost. The continuity of the Kunkarungkara or Pleiades story in the rock shelter at Owalinja (Tindale 1959) is preserved by the annual renewal of the paintings of these women in the cave. Otherwise the story might have been lost. Many rock carvings are so old that no link now remains with the present. A few are self-explanatory, and others offer broad possibilities for interpretation.

Fortunately, we have a few rock paintings executed within the past one hundred years which indirectly are documented through Western sources, and so we are able to understand the general character of older ones like them, even when they are not vocative in themselves.

The tracks made by the horses of Giles the explorer and the silhouettes of the camels and their riders of the next few groups of explorers have already been mentioned. A white man once tried to cycle across Australia shortly after World War I and disappeared. A drawing at Fort Mueller shows him walking beside a bicycle and indicates he passed that way. In similar fashion, the early explorations of the Woomera patrol officer W. B. McDougall, in a four-wheel drive motor vehicle and trailer, are chronicled with a silhouette of his vehicle to show he passed that way in the 1940s.

The movement of Pitjandjara folk from the Tomkinson ranges into the Central Musgraves is indirectly chonicled by the sudden appearance of paintings in yellow cobalt ocher as overlays on older red, black, and white paintings in the magnificent rock shelters at Owalinja, in the area the Pitjandjara usurped in 1915 (Tindale 1959). The absence of earlier yellow ocher paintings is a strong indication that the Pitjandjara had not previously entered into trade contact with their eastern neighbors, the Jankundjara.

Finally, we may indicate that ancient archaeological carvings of the tracks of the extinct giant bird *Genyornis*, carved at Eucolo Creek, show by their intimate detail that the aborigines who lived south of the Pitjandjara were the earliest known local scientific recorders: they accurately

depicted the traces of the three large, downwardly directed claws of this
bird in contradistinction to the anteriorly directed claws of the emu (Hall,
McGowan, and Guleksen 1951), observation which has been confirmed by
palaeontologists who have recovered the bones of this bird.

EFFECTS OF PITJANDJARA ACTIVITIES
ON THEIR ENVIRONMENT

The presence of man in the Western Desert, as in other areas of Australia, has had profound effects on the plants and animals which inhabit
this environment, although it is only in recent years that observers have
been convinced that this is so (Tindale 1959:43). Some others have
considered that as a late Pleistocene newcomer, in ineffectually small
numbers, man had merely scratched a few holes, destroyed some forests,
and made alterations which could be dismissed as insignificant. One observer considered that despite many thousands of years of occupation,
aboriginal man had not caused any profound modifications and that it
was the recent arrival of Europeans, with sheep, cattle, rabbits, and the
bulldozer, which caused the first major changes.

Because of the Pitjandjara man's simple tool kit—hand-held choppers
of chipped stone, hafted *tjimari* stone knives, and his simple *kandi* adze—
his major weapon in the attack on his environment is the fire stick, whether
it is used for setting fire to great sheets of grassland with intentions of
driving kangaroos toward an ambush area or for the simple act of felling
a tree by burning lesser timbers against its butt. Broad swathes of fire-
modified vegetation mark the line of normal travel across the country. It
should be indicated that the vegetation of Australia in many areas is a
fire-succession one, but the Pitjandjara, by lighting fires at all seasons
of the year instead of only at times when lightning and thundershowers
work in company to kindle and then douse fires, have caused the wastage
of many seeds and so have changed the character of the landscape.

Figure 6-6 shows the different effects which may result from brief and
from long occupation of the area around a native watering place. Where
the water hole is an important one (Fig. 6-6B), it is usually surrounded by
an open area extending outward in a radius of nearly one and a half miles.
Here the larger natural vegetation has been largely obliterated by past
generations of visitors; sometimes one or two large shade trees are the
only survivors. There is little comfort in living here, and the camps may be
as much as two miles from the water source in still open country, but
with dead trees and firewood in relative abundance a little beyond. The
normal method of sleeping behind a low breakwind of branches placed to
windward of sleeping fires means that many trees and shrubs are much
injured by the breaking off of their lower limbs. A little further away the
trees are relatively intact save for a few that show scars of the removal of

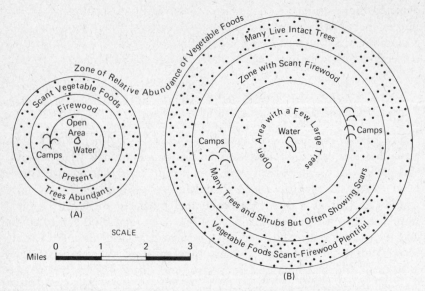

Figure 6–6. Different effects which may result from brief and from long occupation of the area around a native watering place.

slabs of wood wedged off from their trunks in the making of weapons. In this zone the search for vegetable foods, roots, and corms has depleted much of the small plant cover except for the *Cyperus* plants, which seem to thrive from the turning over of the soil in the search for the nuts: this act thus becomes a form of unconscious cultivation. One may have to travel at least three miles from the water before finding vegetation that is sufficiently unaltered to produce a relative abundance of vegetable foods. A little-used or small water hole visited only in passing reveals these features to a lesser degree (Fig. 6-6A).

The choice of relatively open country for camping is governed by two factors. First, light timbering means that the breezes will tend to blow more steadily from one direction, and thus the breakwinds do not have to be reconstructed many times as the wind makes slight changes of direction, changes which are, of course, accentuated in hilly and more heavily vegetated country. The other consideration is that the people of a horde or even a larger group want to have warning of the approach of strangers so that they have sufficient time to grasp their weapons and prepare for an emergency. A camping area with one elevated place from which there is a general view of the surrounding country is considered desirable even though the young men who live near it are subject to wind changes in their camp. Such outcrops of rock and hilltops are natural resting places and lookouts for a hunting people such as the Pitjandjara, and they have a special term, *tarnda*, which describes the act of standing on top of an eminence such as a granite boulder. Men often rest at such places, either as they watch for euros and other game or to observe and interpret the smoke fires they see on the horizon. Consequently, one will often find rock carvings (*walka*) which have been hammered into the rocks. These register something of the men's thoughts of kangaroo and euro tracks, of weapons, and of female sex organs, and there often will be depicted concentric circles representing the living places of the food animals about which they are thinking.

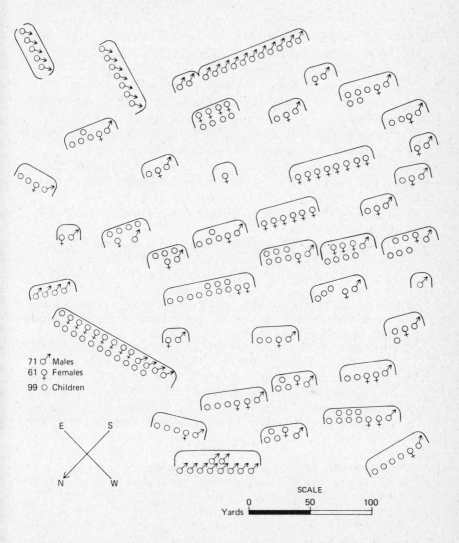

Figure 6–7. *Sketch plan of camp at Konapandi, June 22, 1933. Shelters are oriented to shield people from southeast breezes.*

Figure 6-7 illustrates the general layout of a big camp, the camp of June 22, 1933, at Konapandi in the Western Musgrave ranges, with the positions of 231 of the over 256 persons who were present on the occasion of the holding of Pitjandjara initiation and increase ceremonies. The area was in open mulga scrub with some low hills at the eastern end. The great majority of the camps were oriented to have shelter from the southeast trade winds.

Konapandi had not been used for initiation ceremonies for some years previously, and there was dead mulga nearby for firewood, but after a week of ceremonies the women began to complain about the great distance they had to trek to gather vegetable foods for the idle men. Even though young men were sent out to get euro meats in the mountains to the north, the ceremonies had to be brought to an early conclusion.

We have already indicated the food advantages which cause dispersal of the several bands as soon as general rains have built up water reserves in outlying places.

The above examples show the general way in which population pressure and the activities of Pitjandjara have modified their country.

The factors, in general order of importance, that determine choice of campsites by the Pitjandjara can thus be summarized as follows:

1. The presence of water in spring, soak, well, rockhole, or (least attractive) tree roots.
2. A supply of firewood. A rough measure of the importance of native water is given by the radius of the ring of woodless country around it. A one-hundred yard ring indicates casual occupation; a half a mile or more places it as a well-recognized camping area. A major site may have an open area of more than a mile radius around the water. The chosen camping area is on the cleared side of the wood-providing area, where visibility is greatest.
3. View sufficient to prevent close approach of strangers (*ngatari*) without visual warning for the last one or two hundred yards of approach. This factor operates very strictly in hilly or undulating country; it may be less important on open plains.
4. Texture of ground. Warm sandy ground is first choice; rough rocks and clay are avoided if possible. Granite boulders are favorable for their warmth when the sun has been on them and they give coolness in their shade. Thus an isolated rocky knoll on a rise, with a long-lasting pool of water, can be a place of special significance.
5. In many parts of arid Australia an important factor is the presence or absence of the spiny seeds of *Calotis hispidula*, the *tjilka* of the Pitjandjara, the Bogan flea of Australian sheepmen. It is often difficult to find a camping place where none are present, and in some places it is virtually impossible to make a comfortable camp because of the abundant presence of these seed pests.
6. Presence or absence of features such as rocks and other obstructions

which preclude a steady flow of air. The almost hourly reorientation of windbreaks in camps on some nights during the seasons when people sleep between fires behind a brush barrier is a response to the many changes in wind direction which can occur even when there are few obstructions for the even flow of the wind; aborigines for reasons of this kind instinctively avoid places where wind eddies are prevalent.

7. A factor considered by men is the ready presence of game within walking distance; the distance of a kill from camp often determines whether food is cooked at a temporary camp or whether it is carried back to base, and whether or not the group should move and camp in the vicinity of the area where game is more abundant.

8. A factor important for women is the presence of adequate supplies of the basic root-stem and leaf vegetables and the small animals such as lizards and insects which they must provide as their share of the family food supply. They expect to travel a mile or two, since previous visits and other days' activities are likely to have depleted supplies much nearer to the chosen camping place; a walk greater than three miles is sufficient to induce grumblings and cause scoldings of their husbands. As we see in another section, even the duration and scale of the most important of the men's initiation ceremonies are likely to be determined by the revolt of women following the exhaustion of ready supplies of woman-gathered foods within a radius of three to four miles of the chosen place of meeting.

As Figure 6-6 indicates, the immediate area around a watering place is free of brush. Thus animals coming to drink are very evident and can be trailed and speared. Often low ambush blinds of brush are placed near the water and men hide behind them. Traps and yards of brush fencing, leading animals to water along specific trails, are often built, and remains of stone arrangements of similar kind around some waters testify to the occasionally ambitious scale of these traps in past times.

DIVISION OF LABOR AND THE GATHERING OF FOOD

The Pitjandjara have very definite ideas about what is women's work and what a man should do and equally decided ideas on what tools the sexes may utilize.

Men fight and hunt with spears. No females over about two years of age are allowed to touch a spear or even pretend to throw one. Boomerangs are known only in the traditions of their ancestral beings. It is a man's work to make weapons and to chop out and fashion wooden dishes, shields, spear-throwers (*atlatls*), and most other wooden implements except the digging stick. Women are expected to make digging sticks by chopping off a suitable length of mulga wood from a living tree, using the sharp edge of a large core or block of stone. They then sharpen the working end by half burying it in the fire hearth in such a way that an obliquely pointed digging edge is developed. The differential charring process is controlled by rubbing and scraping off unwanted wood, using the aforesaid sharp-edged block as a tool. The fire also hardens the tip of the stick. In its most developed form a crude stone implement of the type used by the women resembles the so-called "horsehoof core" of the archaeologists; however, only those that have been used, discarded, and then resharpened and reused many times approach this "ideal" type, which after all is one which has reached its ultimate form and is therefore virtually a discard.

The most important and difficult manufacturing task of men is the making of the deep *Eucalyptus* wood dish (*mimbu*) for use by women in carrying water. One of these containers is a treasure and not easy to obtain. The basis of each is a swelling or bole which appears on some species of *Eucalyptus* trees. Certain lake-like depressions, margined by *Eucalyptus* which have germinated together when the lake at some time in the past filled with rain water, have a reputation for yielding trees with such swellings. Each such place tends to be a hordal possession. The bole is chopped off the living tree with a sharp-edged block of stone similar in size, shape, and weight (roughly 18–22 ounces) to that used by women in making their digging sticks. To hollow out the bole the *kandi* adze is used. This tool is made with a stone flake set in *Triodia* (porcupine grass) resin (*keiti*), either on the handle end of a spear-thrower or on one end of a cylindrical, slightly curved throwing club. The *kandi* stone, originally a naturally flaked random piece, after being set in position, is sharpened by knapping the edge to develop a unifacially worked semidiscoidal cutting margin. The chipping out of the bowl takes a long time, often needing three to four hours of steady work. Fire is not used to burn out the interior.

The photograph on page 231 shows a Pitjandjara woman setting out on a day's trek to gather vegetable food with two digging sticks and several shallow winnowing and scooping bowls carried inside her empty wooden water container. Armed with two burning fire sticks held behind her, a girl child on her back, and her two older boys wandering with her, she has all her material possessions with her and is fully equipped for her role as a food-gatherer.

Her husband's equipment is almost equally scanty. He has several spears and a spear-thrower and usually carries a *kandi* chisel tucked into a waist belt of several turns of two-ply string made of animal fur or human hair. This club comes to rest in his crutch as he walks. Sometimes it is dispensed with, especially if he is in country where he will not be able to use it as a throwing club. At such times the *kandi* stone on his spear-thrower is all he requires, especially if he is engaged in his most interesting and important pursuits, the stalking of the plains kangaroo, a euro on the hills, or emus. If he is staying in a camp for several days, he may make a new throwing club. When stalking the special kind of kangaroo which lives in the southern parts of his country, the *kulbiru*, he may need it to give the *coup de grâce* to the animal, for this species, when wounded, attempts to grapple with its assailant and to rip out his gut or gash his legs with the claws on its hind legs while gripping him in its arms. When dingo dogs are used to hunt this animal they are frequently injured in this way.

A man wears his hair long and tied over a parcel containing secret objects, such as magical stones, a few simple *kandi* flakes for new adze blades, a piece of red ocher stone, or even a marine shell traded from hundreds of miles away. The parcel is bound with two-stranded fur string, forming an oval ball over which his hair is pulled at the back of his head and bound with a further length of fur string. A bone skewer or two and a wooden head-scratching pin passed through his hair bun completes his dressing. Usually a few lengths of the sinews of a kangaroo's leg are caught in the final turns of the string, which holds his headdress in place. Sinews are essential for repairing the spears he breaks during the day's hunt. He may carry from one to four spears, depending on his estimate of current needs. Spearing euro on a stony hill is more wearing on his spears than stalking kangaroos on sandy ground.

If he is a young man, he will be very active at hunting larger game, so he will go lightly equipped, an older man will often travel with his wives and may carry, under his arm or in a parcel held in one hand, other treasures, such as tapping sticks (*kondala*) for beating time at dances and perhaps a bullroarer or other secret objects used in men's ceremonies. He also may have a supply of *mingul*, his native chewing tobacco leaf. With this equipment and a burning pair of fire sticks in his free hand, he also is fully prepared for the activities and normal emergencies in his life.

Gathering vegetable food and most activities which are repetitive and laborious are women's work. A woman digs for roots, excavates deep holes in sandy creek beds to get water, and turns over acres of ground to get out worms and the nuts of such plants as *Cyperus*. She carries firewood, winnows, mills, and cleans grains and seeds, and gathers great armfuls of *Triodia* grass, necessary for beating out the resinous dust for the making of a man's tool-haft splices. The man does the technical work of melting the resinous dust into a cake of resin, but the woman rocks the dust in her wooden dishes to separate the good resin from the pieces of porcupine grass, stem, sand, and grit which would impair its quality. She also goes to the source of water, prepares the filter basin at the water's edge, and fills her wooden dish with water, placing dry mulga grass in it to prevent its slopping about while carrying it to the camping place. Her most painful job is perhaps making the early morning journey in winter over frosty ground at dawn to fetch water for her family. Another difficult task is going from bush to bush before dawn on dewy mornings to catch precious drops of the honey sweet water which hangs heavily on certain kinds of shrubs such as *wapiti* (*Thryptomene maisonneuvii*), a bush which grows in sandhill country where water is often scarce.

Hunting animals the size of a rat and smaller, digging out various types of insect grubs from the ground, and similar repetitive chores are women's work, as is caring for children. In all of these activities the woman must bear the burden of her youngest infant, either straddled on her neck or clasped to her hip. The gathering of seeds of all kinds and their winnowing, milling, and cooking are all tasks inevitably assigned to women.

Men use stone tools, make and use spears, spear-throwers, clubs, wooden ceremonial objects, and, in secrecy, the objects of string, blood, and feathers used in their secret ceremonial activities. They hunt the larger game, thus enjoying the fruits and excitement of the chase, the periods of tense activity, and the preparation of major game animals for eating. Men gather to eat native fruits and search for vegetable food for their own immediate needs while walking out to stalk game, but they neither gather it for their families nor carry such products back to camp. Of course, they note the presence of unusual quantities of any vegetable food and direct the women to the area, at times even taking small youths with them to act as messengers to their wives when foods are noted.

In the male-oriented society of the Pitjandjara, it is the men who decide the direction of travel and the watering places they will touch, although their wives will recall and emphasize the merits of certain areas where vegetable foods are likely to be found.

By choice, the Pitjandjara seem to live at the lower end of the scale of adequate nutrition. Above this level, their food-gathering efforts soon slacken and are replaced by other, more exciting, activities. Men are quick to remember the need for performing ceremonies and preparing new weapons. In idle time they even use their energy in making trinkets, small weapons for their children, and carved or decorated weapons for their own enjoyment. Thus, they are not fat people.

Women who realize they have enough food to satisfy the immediate needs of their families at this level of nutrition tend to enjoy the leisure of doing very little—perhaps resting, talking, decorating the ends of tufts of hair on their heads with gumnuts (*Eucalyptus* seed capsules) wedged in with sticks, or just doing nothing.

In the following paragraphs we will discuss some principal foods, arranging them roughly in the order of their importance. Few attempts to assess the quantitative aspects of native foods have been made and have not been very informative when done.

The Pitjandjara consider the best meats to be kangaroo and euro, making little distinction between them. They are selective with such animals. When killed they immediately feel the body for evidence of the presence of caul fat. If the animal is *njuka*, or fatless, it is usually left, unless they are themselves starving. These meats are not the staple ones,

however. Prior to the coming of the rabbit, the several species of bandi-
coots and the hare wallabies were staple items of diet, but by the beginning of the third decade of the twentieth century rabbits had become
the virtual replacement. A Pitjandjara man sitting in his camp for an
entire afternoon in expectation of others fetching him kangaroo meat may
resign himself suddenly to another meal of rabbit. With a resigned look
on his face, he may stand up, walk a few steps, and, stamping on the
ground, break into a burrow, reaching down to draw out one or more
rabbits. He obviously had observed the burrow earlier and assessed where
to dig, but had hoped for better fare.

In the following paragraphs further reference will be made to particular
foods. Some of the comments should be of particular interest to archaeologists who may in the future attempt to interpret the ecology of long-dead
subjects.

The role of children in food-gathering starts as soon as they can sit
up and take notice. By the time they are ten years old they are capable of
satisfying perhaps as much as a fourth of their daily requirements while
following in the wake of their mother's wanderings in search of vegetable
food.

We have already mentioned the gathering of *anumara* hawk moth
caterpillars on *Boerhavia* vines as food. In the dry days of the Piria the
growing tips of *Boerhavia diffusa*, called *uruba*, are often covered with a
viscid substance. Children spread quantities of it about to entangle finches
and other small birds when they come to water and then lie in wait behind
small shelters to strike down the birds with sticks. Handfuls of the small
carcasses are cooked by them and eaten.

Even the tiniest tots squat on the ground and dig with sticks for *Cyperus*
nuts while small boys and girls dart here and there in the wake of the
great grass fires the women light, picking up the scorched small life which
emerges from each burning clump.

The Pitjandjara are, of course, keen observers of all aspects of nature
which affect their food supply or which lead them to food. Thus, places
where the shrub *waljuwalju* (*Prostanthera baxteri*) grow are remembered
because caterpillars (*milpali mako*) appear on the leaves at certain times
of the year and attract the attention of large V*aranus* lizards (*milpali*),
which can be readily killed while they are feeding.

In the south of the Pitjandjara country is a particular species of kangaroo
which they call *kulbiru*. Its favored food is one of the bluebushes (*Craty-
stylis conocephala*), and they particularly seek out places where the shrub
occurs when hunting for this animal.

Turkey bustards are attracted to places where the liliaceous herb *Anguillaria dioica* is abundant in spring; thus, it is appropriately named *keipara
mai* (turkey food). The roots of the plant are used as a vegetable by the
Pitjandjara.

Few parts of a kangaroo are wasted, and even the rib cage, a share often given to women, is not discarded. After the flesh has been stripped off and eaten, the bones, if young and tender, are pounded into a bone meal called *mungara*; this word is compounded from the word *munga*, meaning "evening" or "night," and suggests the preparation of bone meal as an evening occupation for women and children who work and play for hours making both mincemeat and bone meal by pounding and grinding the leavings from the day's take of kangaroos.

Women are so much concerned with the milling of seeds, using millstones and hammerstones, that a Pitjandjara men's term for woman generally is *mirigadjara*, that is, those concerned with *miri* (hammerstones or upper millstones). The seeds of *itawara* (*Acacia notabilis*), a tall shrub, are gathered, ground between stones, and made into a form of bread by mixing them with water and baking in hot ashes; the result, called a *konakandi*, is like the several types of grass-seed cake similarly prepared. The seeds of *wardaruka* (*Acacia ligulata*) are similarly treated. The *mai kurara*, or seeds of the *kurara*, one of the needle bushes (*Acacia tetragono-phylla*), so treated is an important food. The seeds of some other *Acacia* species are avoided as causing stomach upsets.

Pitjandjara women gather great quantities of *kandilkandilpa*, purslane or pigweed (*Portulaca oleracea*), which grows abundantly on flooded flat ground after rain, especially where there is a trace of salt in the soil. They use the succulent taproot as a vegetable and stack the plants into great heaps, often enclosing an area of hard ground with a ring of stones 6–10 feet in diameter. The fermentation of the heap in a day or two ripens the seed pods, and the small black seeds which have been shed are then swept up. Since several women may work together, a series of stone circles may occur together, and some Australian archaeologists, unaware of their real purpose, have imagined these rings to be ceremonial places. The seeds are oily and constitute an important food. The mode of eating them in a large area of the Western Desert has caused the development of a special form of upper millstone (*miri*), which has been given the name of licking or lick stone. The seeds, cleaned after cooking by being shaken with hot ashes in a wooden dish, are placed, a small pile at a time, on a lower millstone. The lick stone (*miri*), dampened with saliva, is rubbed over the pile, away from and then toward the seated diner, with a rolling motion of the wrist, anti-clockwise and then clockwise; the crushed seed adheres to the stone, is transferred to the mouth, and licked off. The action gives rise to the verb *mirini*, meaning "to slide off" or "to peel." Women eat in this way. In an alternative method the crushed seeds are compressed into a cake and heated in the ashes. A woman presents such a cake to her husband and may share one among her children. It is of some interest that purslane is almost universal in its occurrence, and upper millstones of characteristic lick-stone shape have been noticed archaeologically, for example, in the San Dieguito culture of southern California (personal observation). The oily seeds of *wakati*, also called *parukeilpa* (Parakeelya)

(*Calandrinia balonnensis*), succulent plants with purple flowers, are among the important foods used by the Pitjandjara. The seeds on their drying stems are very tiny and are shaken out of the seed capsules. Sometimes, like those of *Portulaca oleracea*, the ripening plants are piled together within an enclosure so that the heat of semifermentation dries and opens the capsules. The seeds are treated similarly, being crushed and eaten by the same method of using a lick stone (*miri*) as is described for *Portulaca*.

The native peach or quandong (Pitjandjara name *walku*) (*Santalum acuminatum*), a small tree, has an edible red fruit with a deeply pitted round stone. The fruits are usually ripe in November and December. The fruit itself, *mangartu*, is prepared by compressing it into a cake after mashing it to a pulp, using a hammerstone in a heavy wooden dish. The stones are broken to extract the kernel. When other food is abundant the stones are discarded in great quantities around their camp, it being too much trouble to break them, but they often serve as a standby food, eaten when people might otherwise have to go hungry.

A small kangaroo mouse called *talkuwara* is considered unfriendly because it nibbles holes in the hard, pitted *walku* stones and so destroys their food value. The fruit is the subject of increase ceremonies, and there is an important *walku tjukurupa* place at Immuruka, a water some distance (perhaps 20 miles) south of Mt. Lindsay.

The *koparta* (*Santalum lanceolatum*), or native plum, is also an important fruit. The Pitjandjara sometimes use the term *koparta* loosely for the quandong and also have the term *kombalba*.

At least three species of native mustard grass, called *enmurta* (*Lepidium oxytrichum*, *L. rotundum*, and *L. muellerferdinandi*), are used as steamed vegetables by placing masses of them on a bed of fleshy *Zygophyllum* branches on a fire with hot stones or hot ash in a hole, the whole being blanketed by further *Zygophyllum*, grass, and a covering of sand. When steam breaks through the seal the food is considered cooked. The leaves are stripped and eaten, and the stems are often hammered to a meal on stones and also eaten.

The plants of the family Zygophyllaceae, besides their uses as coverings in the steaming of greens, provide two genera, *Nitraria* and *Zygophyllum*, which have Cossid moth larvae boring in their stems. These grubs provide important foods. Thus, *Zygophyllum aurantiacum*, sometimes called native hop, is known to the Pitjandjara as *pijarpiti*. It is a low shrub with slender, rigid stems and yellow flowers with four petals. It frequently grows in places where the soil contains traces of salt. The grubs boring in the stems are called *mako biarpiti* at Ooldea and are the larvae of a yellow and black spotted moth (*Xyleutes biarpiti*), the female of which has only partly developed wings and so cannot fly. The larvae are abundant where they occur and children spend many happy hours hunting for them. The moth of this species and several other forms are described in Tindale (1952).

Nitraria schoberi, the niter bush, which lives on saline soils, also provides *Xyleutes* larvae, which bore in the stems and are an important source of food. The shrubs occur near some of the larger dry lake beds which margin the southern border of Pitjandjara territory. On certain nights in summer thousands of the moths, white-winged with black spots, fly into fires, but as they generally come at a time when better food is available, they are not always eaten. On the other hand, the grubs and pupae boring in the base of the stem of the shrub earlier in the season are eagerly sought-after items of food.

Two plants of the family Asclepiadaceae are of particular importance as edible greens. One, called *puji* or *puja* (*Pentatropis kempeana*), is a slender twiner with long, delicate leaves and tender stems. The whole plant, including the root, may be eaten, either raw or after brief cooking in ashes. The native pear or banana (*Marsdenia australis*) has long, thick leaves and bears an elongate fruit with thick endocarp, which is eaten while still green, together with all the tender young growths of the vine. Pitjandjara claim that when they can eat these plants in quantity they are never sick, and it seems likely that they are useful as antiscorbutic foods. They are certainly tasty and healthy, since the eating of these and other native foods enabled Dr. C. Hackett and myself to spend three months in the Western Desert without signs of malnutritional sores such as used to plague western Europeans in the arid central Australian deserts before the important role of vitamins was generally known.

Lerp scales occur on several species of *Acacia* and *Eucalyptus* and provide a source of sugar as food upon which all may need to feed. The *wama wanari,* or lac scale of the mulga (*Acacia aneura*), is found infesting large areas of mulga and then may be absent over equally wide areas. Western Pitjandjara may live for days on this substance, breaking off the twigs covered with scale and drawing them through the lips sore and bleeding from the rough sticks drawn across them. The lerp scale of the *ngarukalja* (*Hakea francisiana*) yields a similar *wama,* which is of sufficient importance that it is the subject of an increase ceremony (*inma tjukur*).

As an example of an insect clan totem, we may note the *purara,* or honey ant (*Melophorus inflatus*). The ancestral being originator of this clan, was the Wati Purara or the Man Purara. He came into being at a place called Wamajununja (*wama*—anything sweet or honeylike) and traveled to Wamapiti, a ceremonial place and the clan center, where he was initiated into manhood. This place is situated close to Oparinna (Apari or Ngaparina), a spring in the Western Musgrave ranges near Mt. Morris. He then went south to another place, also called Wamapiti. This is a low quartzite dome southwest of Meiti and east of Mount Caroline. There he went *tarupango,* that is, he changed state, went down into the ground, and became a large stone. Therefore he had become *tjurungaraka.*

The term *wamapiti* is often used as a term for any form of lerp sugar as well as honey. Honey ants occur only in mulga scrub. After big rains they harvest the flow of honey from flowers and the sweet sap from glands on the growing tips of mulga twigs. It is stored well below ground level in the inflated abdomens of certain worker ants. These living stores of honey, each the size of a pea, tide the ants over lean years during which lack of rain prevents the flowering of the mulga. Thus honey ants are one of the buffer food supplies for natives in dry years. Usually women dig for honey ants using a digging stick and wooden scoop. Sometimes when other food is in short supply men join in the search. Holes as deep as 3 and 4 feet may develop, often several yards in diameter, as they search for storage holes and their living sacs of sweetness.

In times of drought and hunger many lesser foods are eaten by the Pitjandjara, for example, the seeds of *pitalpital* (*Erodium cygnorum*), a form of wild geranium. At other times it is called *malu pumpunju*; when newly developing the plant is an attractive food for kangaroos (*malu*).

When all else fails the hairy colonial larvae of the bag shelter moth (*Panacela*), which occur in frass-filled silken webs on *Eucalyptus*, are gathered and eaten. Their irritating hairs are singed off by heating them with hot ashes. The hairs of the caterpillars cause intense irritation to the lips and throat and also cause a skin rash. The Pitjandjara concept of abject misery is to be under the necessity of eating such larvae.

An important standby food is the black seed of a grass known as *juninba*, of which I do not have a good identification. It is a good *mai*, or vegetable food, but the seed is protected with fine, stiff hairs. These spicules cause intense skin irritation and have to be rubbed off the dry seed heads. Women are very much afraid of inhaling the dust and husks and take great care in winnowing the grain by keeping well to windward. They call it *mamukata*, "devil's son," *mamu* being the term for an evil spirit which comes and kills in the night.

Water-bearing frogs (*ngangi*) may be found by observing round holes, often under the shade of *wanari* (*Acacia* sp.) shrubs. Women use a digging stick and wooden scoop, making an oval hole about 18 inches deep, to reach the frog. The frog does not appear to have any cell but to be entirely encased in the red sandy earth of the mulga tree plain. Each frog yields a small share of water through squeezing and is then cooked in ashes as a morsel of food.

PLANTS YIELDING MATERIAL PRODUCTS

Many plants are used for making products of economic importance. Others serve as items of adornment. The latter are many, ranging from the strong-scented flowers of *Cassia eremophila*, *enondji* (Western dialect), and *undunu* (Eastern dialect), which they wear in their headbands, to the *Eucalyptus* seed pods which the women attach to the tips of their hair.

Of great importance is the shrub *urutjan* (*Pandorea doratoxylon*), which provides the butt part of the shaft of the composite spear. Whole spears may be made of it for the hunting of small game such as the introduced rabbit.

The resin (*keiti*) of the *Triodia* grass which grows on hill slopes and the even more valuable resin of the grass tree (*Xanthorrhoea thorntoni*) are essential in the hafting of stone tools and in joining the oblique splices necessary in making the three-piece spears with their lashed-on, single wooden barb.

Of particular interest to men are the chewing tobaccos, of which there are several species. The best in this area is *mingurpa* (*Nicotiana excelsior*). Different men have preferences in the types of *Acacia* phyllodes they burn to make the ash, which is an essential ingredient in the chewing bolus. The best tobacco grows in the shadows near cliffs and at the mouths of rock shelters. An inferior tobacco, called *tawal*, grows in the sandhills, but is chewed only in emergency.

The leaves of the *kuramaru* (*Duboisia hopwoodii*), or poison bush, is used to poison emus by steeping them in the watering place of the birds. The Pitjandjara do not use it as a chewing narcotic, as do the aborigines of Lake Eyre, although its highly narcotic properties are known.

SOCIAL ORGANIZATION

Brief reference was made in the introduction to the kinship system of the Pitjandjara.

Their scheme is notable for the complete absence of class (section) terms; they have become aware of the existence of these among other Australian people only since their increasing contact with other aborigines after 1933.

First acquaintance with section terms came to the western Pitjandjara by reason of contact and an intertribal marriage with a Ngadadjara woman in the early years of the twentieth century. After many years their information was amplified by contact with the Wenamba and Pintubi in the 1930s. Now six separate terms belonging to four differing class systems are known to them.

Strehlow (1965:30) has discussed the southward movement of section systems without giving dates and infers that the harsh environment was a cause of the absence of section terms among some of the Western Desert tribes.

In my opinion, the reason for the absence is purely a historical one and one due to isolation. Class terms were spreading south and southeast-ward in the Desert only during the late nineteenth century and had not reached the Pitjandjara, who thus were aware only of an older system.

The Pitjandjara system is one based entirely on kinship terms and on the recognition of the different roles played by alternate generations of people. Figure 6-8 shows the system as arranged on a H. K. Fry framework. Un-

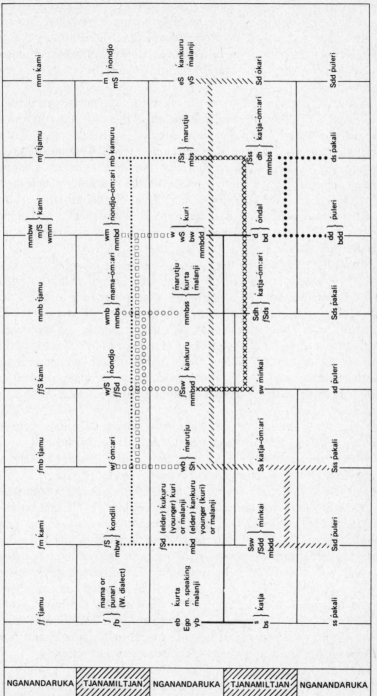

Figure 6–8. Pitjandjara kinship terms.

like several other Western Desert tribes who use the alternate-generations system, the Pitjandjara lack any fixed name applied to these generations. Instead, they use two terms, *nganandaruka* and *tjanamiltjan*. The first is for their own generation, the other for that above and below an individual. One's grandparents' and grand children's generations are also termed *nganandaruka*.

In the Ngadadjara tribe to the west the successive generations are alternately and formally *tjindulakalnguru* ("those who sit in the sun") and *wiltjalanguru* ("those who sit in the shade"). Recognition of alternate generations in this manner is a very ancient and widespread Australian classificatory device and is recognizable not only as far as the western Australian coast but is seemingly present in the east among such people as the strange Barbaram (or Mbarbaram) tribe of the Atherton Tableland in Queensland, where we find *anggormok* ("sun men") and *annomok* ("night men"), who function with differing roles at ceremonies (Tindale and Birdsell 1941:6).

Normal marriage among the Pitjandjara is by the taking of a *kuri*, who is a mother's mother's brother's daughter's daughter or falls into the niche in the Fry framework. As an alternative, a man may have as wife a father's sister's daughter or a mother's brother's daughter who is a junior, but he is forbidden to take either *kukuru* or *kankuru*, those who are elders. He may marry only his *nganandaruka*, and no marriage is permitted with his *tjanamiltjan* generation. When there is difficulty in obtaining a regular marriage, compromises may allow selection of an older woman in the earlier *nganandaruka* generation or even a young person in the second generation below his own.

There are no hints of the matrilineal moiety divisions *kararu* and *matari*, as found in the Kokata and Pangkala and other tribes to the southeast, although there is a trade route leading to the Kokata which brings manganese dioxide pigment which is traded for pearl shell ornaments coming from the northwest. Another term, *tjundal*, is said to denote both northwestern cumulus clouds and the white clouds that come from the southwest. The only word that has resemblance to *kararu* is *karar*, or *kararba*, the name of the white pearl shells received by the Pitjandjara in trade from the northwestern coast of Australia near Broome. Such shells are highly treasured and are of importance, since scrapings of the edges, mixed with human semen, are employed in rain-making ceremonies designed to hasten the coming of the rains of the northwest monsoon. Whether the seeming association of both of these matrilineally inherited moiety terms with rain clouds has a historical significance or not must be left for further study and a more detailed search for evidence.

The selection of a wife or wives is made for a growing youth by his male parent. It is a matter of arrangement between the boy's father and some man who is of the boy's *tjanamiltjan* generation and stands in the relationship of *ommari* (also called *waputju*) or *mama-ommari*. This man promises a daughter. On acceptance by the boy's father, the lad who is living in exile from the camp is taken and circumcised by the *ommari* with the aid of men of both generations, who play differing roles as guardians and supporters. The father of the boy customarily attends the initial meetings, at which increase ceremonies are sung and dances are performed. There is a formal interlude when the proposed marriage arrangements are discussed and confirmed, whereupon the parent sits aside and weeps for a while and then returns to his camp. The youth is then operated on. In the next part of this account the proceedings at an initiation ceremony witnessed in June 1933 at Konapandi on the south side of the Western Musgrave ranges will be described. After a period of isolation while his wounds are healing the youth is taken, with a companion or two, on a journey or tour to important ceremonial places and the watering places of his and kindred clans. He is under a ban of silence for much of the time and may talk only by hand signs. He listens to accounts of the totemic beings of the places he visits and thus comes to be inculcated with the intimate geography of his country. As many as three hundred places may be visited during a year of seclusion. Following this period of education the boy is brought back into the society of his horde as a "half man," or *wankar*.

The return of the initiated youth is a special occasion accompanied by a series of all-night dances, during which women and children lie down near a barrier or fencelike structure while men sing songs, dance over ground which has been strewn with red hot charcoal, and spin bullroarers under cover of darkness, indicating the approaching return of the boys. They then pass the boys through a smoking rite, *punjunju*, during which the hair on their foreheads and their pubic hair is plucked out and spun into two-stranded string with which a tiny pubic tassel is made and tied to a few pubic hairs left long for that purpose. A dense smoke fire of *altarupa* leaves (*Eucalyptus*) and *pundi* (*Cassia phyllodinea*) is created in a pit, and the youth is held over the smoke so that the volatile oils smooth and cleanse his skin. His hair is freshly tied up with a *pokoti*, or head bun, and manganese dioxide (or *wad*), traded from the southeast, or charcoal and grease, is rubbed over his forehead. At dawn, armed with spears and spear-throwers, the youth walks through the main camp to his father's camping place, ostentatiously ignoring the small children who vigorously attack him as he approaches, using spears of cane and reed.

After a year or two the time comes for a youth to pass from the half-man (*wankar*) stage to being a full man. This requires the operation which has come to be known as subincision. In the nineteenth century it was called the dreadful rite. The youth is laid on a table of bodies of associates of his own generation who already have undergone the rite and is held down by a man who is called his *puruka*. The youth's prospective wife's father (*ommari*), using a small, primary stone flake which may be inserted in a handle formed of a piece of *Triodia* resin, splits the urethral pipe down to the scrotum, cutting along the ventral midline. Since few blood vessels cross this line, there is relatively little bleeding, except when mistakes are made. An operator who is skilled is often chosen for the role in place of the *ommari*, since it is considered a dangerous operation and young men have been known to bleed to death. Because this might happen and a dispute would ensue, men come to the subincision ceremony well armed and keep their spears close by. The youth returns to seclusion while his wounds heal. He is now a full man (*wati*). One further operation, the evulsion of an upper-central incisor, stands between him and his marriage. This operation is of high significance in some matrilineal societies to the south and east. Among the Pitjandjara it is a minor event, performed by men but without ritual seclusion. The tooth is hammered out using a bone skewer to loosen the gums and a stick frayed at the end as an instrument to pass on the hammer blows.

Shortly after the wound is healed the youth is free to claim his bride. When he is about to ritually take his promised wife from her father's camp he walks through the camp carrying his spear-thrower under his arm as a sign that he is about to possess her. This rite is called *meru nakolba*, meaning "letting the spear-thrower be seen."

The girl's mother or another female relation helps her prepare a new camp; a fire is lit and the girl sits beside it. Her husband arrives and sits down by the fire without comment. The girl soon after rises and disappears. She may do this again the next night, but usually she stays and the union is complete. Shortly afterward the man returns to his own horde unless circumstances have been such that she has already been "growing up" in her husband's horde, as sometimes happens.

LIFE CYCLE OF A PITJANDJARA

A woman carrying a child may feel birth pangs as she and her family are traveling from one place to another. She drops behind, either alone or with another woman, and when the child is about to appear she rests briefly. As soon as the afterbirth appears she buries it, places the child in the flat wooden dish she uses for cleaning grass-seed foods, and follows on to the proposed camping place, where she may arrive two or three hours later than the others. It is not considered necessary that she should rest.

The first decision has to be whether to keep or to dispose of the infant. Since there are no supplementary weaning diets available, a child born while an older one is still suckling cannot be kept, and a few handfuls of sand solves the problem. So socially acceptable is this custom that the inquiring anthropologist sometimes has difficulty in getting a decision

as to whether a given child was disposed of between the births of B and C
or between C and D. The act itself is not concealed.

A woman may give birth to as many as nine children in the course of
her fertile period. Her first menstruation may come at about the age of
fifteen, and her first child is most often born in her eighteenth or nineteenth year. Her husband will usually be about three years older at his
marriage. The birth of a child before marriage was rare until well after
the period of first contact with Europeans.

The infant is suckled for at least two years, usually for longer, being
given *mako witjuti* (Cossid grubs of *Acacia kempeana*) and other insect
foods to suck from an early age. Since most adult women remain constantly lactating, an older child may be comforted and fed by more than
one person. Infants are born with skin a little darker than Europeans.
It takes several weeks to develop full pigmentation, and the child has to
be covered with grease and charcoal to protect its tender skin from the
sun. It is at first carried in a wooden dish. A support made from several
turns of a double twist of opossum or kangaroo fur is passed around the
dish and over the woman's shoulder to assist in carrying this cradle. At
about six to eight months the child is considered old enough to be held
astraddle the mother's neck or be supported with one arm while riding
astride her hip. The woman soon learns to anticipate the bowel movements of her infant; accidents are a constant source of amusement and
comment.

As soon as it can crawl the child learns by experience to avoid hot
coals and imitates its mother as she prepares food by winnowing and
rocking it in her wooden dishes. Small children, as soon as they can
walk, play at throwing spears, but at a very early age girl children are
forbidden to throw spears and they thereafter play at digging with sticks.
A favorite girl child's game is to make a small breakwind of a few twigs,
place pieces of bark as men and women behind it, and then take the role
of a man and beat the women dolls with a switch, playing out the game
of punishing the woman for wrongdoing.

From this earliest age children learn to dig with sticks in the ground
for *Cyperus* nuts and other foods which are eaten as they are unearthed.
Boys soon learn to track and dig out small lizards, which they cook and
eat. Women spur the tiniest of children into tracking beetles over the
sand and reward them with praise when they find the insect at the end
of its trail. Children accompany their mother on her daily foraging for
food. By the time they are six boys and girls may move away, even out of
sight of their parent, while searching for morsels of food and for ripening
fruits. Their sharp eyes often are the ones that see clumps of grass with
seed heads, ripening *kamburarupa* (native tomatoes), and the developing
native banana fruits (*Marsdenia*).

Boys of seven are active at throwing toy spears, soon graduating to using a hooked stick as a spear-thrower, an aid in propelling the weapon. A circular piece of *Eucalyptus* bark thrown like a wheel along the ground becomes a moving target—in their mind's eye a kangaroo, a euro, or a fast-moving hare wallaby.

At a little older age they love to play at spear fighting, with reeds as spears, courting attack so that they can divert the spear with a touch of their spear-thrower or elude it by a quick move to one side or the other.

At the first indications of puberty and of giving attention to girls, the women of the horde suddenly turn on the boy and he is driven from his mother's camp. He has now to live outside the main circle, an outcast, with others of his age, to await the day, perhaps a year or two ahead, when he is seized and made into a half man.

During this period a boy learns to forage for much of his own food and may accompany young men on their hunting expeditions, acting as an assistant in such tasks as firing swathes of grassland in endeavors to drive game toward ambush. Outcast boys dig for animals whose tracks they observe, and cook them, generally behaving, within their knowledge, as if they were already young men.

A girl continues with her mother, assisting in the care of younger children, caring for small dingo pups, and performing such chores as leading an old blind relative by holding the end of the old lady's digging stick. Often she is seen as an irresponsible, active person with few fixed chores other than helping her mother in the inevitable digging, winnowing and pounding of food, fetching firewood for her father's kangaroo-cooking oven hole, and similar activities. In her father's horde she is safe from sexual molestation, and she will very likely go to her husband without having given birth to a child.

While she is still young she will be taken by men and decorated with body paints, with rites which even today are kept very secret, her body is rubbed against certain painted stones whose merit, passing into her, cause the swelling of her breasts. Long before this she will have played such games as clamping ant lion larvae, with their powerful jaws, on her nipples and pretending they are swelling up.

After the beginning of menstruation a girl generally sleeps along with other young girls and an older woman behind a separate breakwind. At the conclusion of each menstruating period she paints her forehead, and sometimes her breasts with dabs of yellow cobalt ocher from Wingelina.

Usually a year or two later she is claimed by her *kuri* and she takes up her life in a new environment and learns from the older women the characteristic foods of a different hordal area and acquires there afresh the nuances of food gathering.

It is of interest that it is the woman who in the Desert areas has to face the unknown and explore new places for vegetable food. In this she is undoubtedly helped by the general distribution of the several plant associations which extend throughout the Western Desert with but little variation. However, she still has to learn much, and quickly, from her husband's parents and the older wives of clansmen who earlier passed through similar experiences.

The adult life of a Pitjandjara woman is bounded by the constant tasks, often lasting from four to six hours a day, of walking and digging, gathering and cleaning food, gathering firewood and carrying water, varied only by such minor interesting chores as using one of her wooden dishes as a pump to force smoke down an animal burrow to smoke out an opossum (*Trichosurus vulpecula*), using her fire stick to burn the nest made by *tjuijalpa*, twig mound-building rats (*Leporilus apicalis*), or working to secure a *koka tjirili*, or porcupine (*Tachyglossus aculeata*). She also may have the pleasure of tracking a female dingo and trying to read the import of its various movements to determine if and where she has hidden her pups.

With the coming of children her chores are multiplied, and she often welcomes a second wife to share her work. Often this wife is a younger sister and so a companion from her earlier life.

Jealousies and quarrels with other women and beatings from her husband when she disagrees with him may in time leave scars on a woman's body; and in play she may also have induced keloid and burn scars. With increasing age she passes the age of giving birth to children, sees her daughters go elsewhere to live, and becomes old and wrinkled. With the death of her aged husband, if he has managed to survive the many vicissitudes of middle age, she often becomes a querulous old widow, entrusted only with the duty of keeping alight a fire so others will not have to rekindle a flame by other means. Old and often cold, she surrounds herself with dogs, using their warmth to sustain heat in her wasted and wrinkled body. She may live to a relatively great age— exactly how old cannot be known, for there are no birth records to consult. Too old to follow her folk, she may at the last be left, feeble and sick, to die alone.

A young man who has passed into manhood and marriage assumes many responsibilities as time goes on. Commencing in the days when he was still only a half man, or *wankar*, he has been shown the secret dances and heard and sung with vigor the songs of the many totemic beings whose stories dominate men's thoughts. Following his father, or even his father's father, he has attempted the movements of the dances of his clan ancestor, trying to perfect his movements so that they will copy exactly the ancient pattern of activity which is considered so vital in the act of increasing the clan totem. As he grows older, his aging father, father's brothers, and father's father will entrust greater secrets to him, so that in course of time he becomes the fount of knowledge of his own country and its lore. With this knowledge, if he is an astute individual, will come influence which will enable him to bend others to his wishes, even though, in his society, there is no accepted leader. By possession of the intimate knowledge of the totemic songs of his clan and the rites, he will come to be a *maijada* and so direct the activities of his fellow-clansmen. Thus his influence will tend to remain so long as he is active in mind and clear in his thoughts and keen of tongue. With increasing age he will allow his son to perform the definitive dances of his clan totem. He is considered as becoming again a child; his body bends and finally he dies.

Death in middle age is considered due to magic or sorcery and the activities of malicious persons living at a distance. There are detailed inquests which vary from area to area. In the only one of which I have some direct knowledge, a cleanly swept area with a radius of about 12 feet was ringed with small stone, and relatives, keeping an all-night watch, lay around it, without fires, and cried. Insect tracks passing over the cleared ground were thought to indicate the direction in which the person responsible for the death was living, but in this case the result was indeterminate.

Burial is in a side chamber in a hole up to 6 feet deep. The hole itself is filled with timber and sticks and then the sand is replaced as a mound. There is no fixed orientation of the grave, and the body is usually placed in the tomb in the extended position, unlike the people farther south who flex the bodies of the dead and bind them in the prenatal position.

PITJANDJARA IN THE MODERN WORLD

The horizons of the Pitjandjara have been greatly widened since their first contacts with the Western world. The change began with the coming of settlers to the country east of the Musgraves. There were initial successes on the sheep and cattle runs as their stock fed on the virgin vegetation, which was soon depleted, causing soil erosion and the creation of naked stony plateaus where once had been shrub-clothed plains. Having depleted their capital of vegetation and drained their wells of the accumulated ground water of centuries, some of the stations, such as Moorilyanna and Mt. Connor, were abandoned.

The effects on aborigines were drastic in that the sheep and cattle ate their food plants down to ground level, eliminating the normal indications upon which women relied for finding food, and by eliminating flowerings the cattle prevented the regeneration of plants. Such valuable greens as *Marsdenia*, for example, were virtually eliminated, and the cropping of mulga scrub by cattle, to a height of 7 or more feet, left the roots exposed to erosion. Numerous seedling plants and shelter vegetation which originally grew in the partial shade and among the leafy debris under the trees also disappeared. Killing of sheep and cattle, the first attempted solution to the problem of starvation, led to the jailing in Port Augusta of younger Pitjandjara men who tried this way out.

The concern of the South Australian government, stimulated by public interest and pressure, led to the formation of the Native Reserve in the northwestern portion of the state and to the founding of a Presbyterian mission on what had been Ernabella Station in the Eastern Musgraves.

Early policies led to the use of Pitjandjara as the primary medium of teaching. The immediate results were good, and Pitjandjara children of eight and nine were becoming able to write fluently in Pitjandjara using a simplified version of the International Phonetic Alphabet. Instruction in English was not at first emphasized; in the late 1940s this led to some difficulties when outside employment was sought for the young men who were growing up. A decade later many Pitjandjara had migrated from their own country, some to other missions in the MacDonnell ranges, others to the vicinity of the small towns on the Central Australian Railway, for example, to Finke Crossing, where in 1962 there was a sizable school population receiving instruction in English.

Pitjandjara men wandering south discovered opportunities in digging for opal at Coober Pedy, and arising out of this their attention was directed to the surface mining of chrysoprase in their own reserve areas, an activity which has produced some real wealth for them. This move to exploit their own country has had some advantages in keeping alive knowledge of the main travel routes and waters in their territory, but they are becoming increasingly dependent on automobile transport. A few of the older, more conservative aborigines use the camels discarded by Afghan camel men in the late 1930s when the general introduction of four-wheel-drive vehicles drove them out of competition. Camels probably will soon be abandoned as the older aborigines die, since the young men are not interested in this mode of travel. As a result, wild camels are already roaming in such places as the Arunta Desert and are multiplying to the extent of becoming a minor problem.

Medical care and better feeding have halted the formerly accepted fact that contact with civilization meant a rapid decline in numbers of aborigines through sickness and the malnutrition accompanying the ignorant use of Western foods in place of their own vitamin-rich, although often meager, food resources.

The granting of Commonwealth pensions at the same rate as for others in the Australian population, which began to affect the Pitjandjara with the formation of the Musgrave Park settlement in 1961, has made each Pitjandjara aged person a relatively wealthy individual as compared with his earlier condition. In addition, the support offered to native mothers, in common with others in the white population, also has led to a rapid rise in numbers.

The Pitjandjara birth rate is now higher than that of the white population, approaching 4 percent a year. Nearly half of the Pitjandjara population is now under the age of seventeen, and their total number is approaching 1000 persons.

The education of Pitjandjara people as well as of all other aboriginal persons is now receiving the special attention of the Commonwealth of Australia under the direction of the Minister for Aboriginal Affairs (Mr. W. Wentworth), and there should be marked developments in their status in the next decade.

The few Pitjandjara aboriginal and part-aboriginal persons who have, by chance, received advanced education have established themselves in the community at large in positions of responsibility. One is a teacher and another is charged with the care of aborigines. Their success foreshadows what may be an outcome of changing conditions.

ACKNOWLEDGMENTS

The field work in 1933 which forms the background of this contribution was made possible by a grant to the Board for Anthropological Research of the University of Adelaide by the Rockefeller Foundation through the then National Research Council of Australia. Later expeditions were in part supported by the Wenner-Gren Foundation for Anthropological Research. The South Australian Museum in Adelaide, on whose staff I was Curator of Anthropology, under several different titles, from 1928 to 1965, afforded opportunities for the work to be done. Grateful acknowledgment is made for the companionship of Dr. Cecil Hackett, my associate on the field work in the Mann ranges in 1933, to Professor Victor McFarlane for including me in his field team in 1963 and 1966, to the authorities of the Woomera Establishment for allowing me to take part in extensive journeys with the Native Patrol Officer, and to Mr. W. B. MacDougall, whose knowledge and advice on many matters was of paramount help. Mr. Peter Aitken, an associate in my later work, kindly checked the names of mammals for me. Finally, I am grateful to the many Pitjandjara aborigines whom we met and worked with and who were the principal contributors to the work. The youngsters whom we followed in their initiations who now are grown to middle age still claim friendly relation because of the bonds so forged, and continue to be helpers. Errors I may have made are due to my inability to follow their leads and not to their lack of knowledge. No work is perfect, and one can only hope that some morsels of truth in it will help the Pitjandjara, a friendly Desert people, become better known.

REFERENCES

Birdsell, J. B., 1967. "Preliminary Data on the Trihybrid Origin of the Australian Aborigines," *Archaeology and Physical Anthropology in Oceania*, Sydney, 2 (2):100–155.

Black, J. M., 1943–1957. *Flora of South Australia*, 2d ed., Adelaide: Government Printer.

Cleland, J. B., and N. B. Tindale, 1959. "Native Names and Uses of Plants at Haast Bluff, Central Australia," *Transactions of the Royal Society of South Australia*, Adelaide, 82:132–140.

Douglas, W. H., 1959. *Illustrated Topical Dictionary of the Western Desert Language. Warburton Ranges Dialect.* Perth.

Eichler, H., 1965. *Supplement to J. M. Black's Flora of South Australia,* Adelaide: Government Printer.

Finlayson, H. H., 1961. "On Central Australian Mammals." Part IV: "The Distribution and Status of Central Australian Species," *Records of the South Australian Museum,* 14 (1):141–191.

Hackett, C. J., and L. J. A. Loewenthal, 1960. *Differential Diagnosis of Yaws,* World Health Organization Monograph No. 45.

Hall, F. J., R. G. McGowan, and G. F. Guleksen, 1951. "Aboriginal Rock Carvings: A Locality Near Pimba, South Australia," *Records of the South Australian Museum,* Adelaide, 9 (4):375–382.

Koeppen, W., 1931. *Grundriss der Klimakunde,* Berlin: Gruyter.

Mulvaney, D. J., 1966. "Prehistory of the Australian Aborigine, *Scientific American* 214 (3):84–93.

Strehlow, T. G. H., 1965. *Culture, Social Structure and Environment in Aboriginal Central Australia,* in R. M. and C. H. Berndt, eds., *Aboriginal Man in Australia,* Sydney: Angus and Robertson, pp. 121–145.

Tindale, N. B., 1933. "Report on Field Trip," Oceania, Sydney, 4:101–105.

———, 1935. "Initiation among the Pitjandjara Natives of the Mann and Tomkinson Ranges, South Australia," *Oceania* 6(2):199–224.

———, 1939. *Vocabulary of Pitjandjara,* preliminary limited edition, typescript, Adelaide.

———, 1941. "List of Plants Collected in the Musgrave and Mann Ranges, South Australia, 1933," *South Australian Naturalist* 21 (1):8–12.

———, 1952. "On Some Australian Cossidae, Including the Moth of the Witjuti (Witchety) Grub," *Transactions of the Royal Society of Southern Australia,* Adelaide, 76:56–65.

———, 1959. "Totemic Beliefs in the Western Desert of Australia." Part I: "Women Who Became the Pleiades," *Records of the South Australian Museum,* Adelaide, 13(3):305–332.

———, 1963. "Totemic Beliefs." Part II: "Musical Rocks and Associated Objects of the Pitjandjara People," *Records of the South Australian Museum,* Adelaide, 14 (3):499–514.

———, 1965. "Stone Implement Making among the Nakako, Ngadadjara and Pitjandjara of the Great Western Desert," *Records of the South Australian Museum,* Adelaide, 15 (1):131–164.

———, 1968. Nomenclature of Archaeological Cultures and Associated Implements in Australia," *Records of the South Australian Museum,* Adelaide, 15 (4):615–640.

———, and J. B. Birdsell, 1941. "Results of the Harvard-Adelaide Universities Anthropological Expedition, 1938–1939. Tasmanoid Tribes in North Queensland," *Records of the South Australian Museum,* Adelaide, 7 (1):1–9.

——— and B. George, 1971. "Australian Aborigines," Sydney: Golden Press.

Trudinger, R. M., 1943. "Grammar of the Pitjantatjara Dialect, Central Australia," *Oceania* 13 (3):205–223.

Wood-Jones, F., 1923–1925. *Mammals of South Australia,* Adelaide: Government Printer.

GLOSSARY

anumara: the larvae of a large hawk moth (*Celerio lineata*)

atlatl: a spear-thrower (American Indian term)

enmurta: native mustard grass; includes at least three species (*Lepidium oxytrichum, L. rotundum, L. muellerferdinandi*)

enondji (Western dialect) or *undunu* (Eastern dialect): a flower of *Cassia eremophilia* which is worn in the headband for adornment

inma waro: rock wallaby totem

itawara: a tall shrub (*Acacia notabilis*)

japu: a rise; that is, a hill or mountain

juninba: a grass whose seed is an important standby food

kalaia: an emu

kali: a boomerang

kamburarupa: native tomatoes (one of a dozen native species of *Solanum*)

kandi: chert

kandi adze: an adze made by setting a stone flake with resin into the handle end of a spear-thrower or into one end of a cylindrical, slightly curved throwing stick

kandilkandilpa: purslave or pigweed (*Portulaca oleracea*)

karar or *kararba*: white pearl shells obtained by trade from the northwest Australian coast

keipara mai: a liliaceous herb (*Anguillaria dioica*); literally, "turkey food"

keiti: the resin of porcupine grass

koka tjirili: a porcupine (*Tachyglossus aculeata*)

konakandi: a bread made from the seeds of *itawara*

kondala: tapping sticks used for beating time at dances

koparta: the native plum (*Santalum lanceolatum*); may also be used loosely to refer to *walku*, native peach

korukara: a desert oak (*Casuarina decaisneana*)

kukuru or *kankuru*: female cross-cousin older than ego

kulbiru: a type of kangaroo that lives in southern Pitjandjara country

kuli: hot season

kuramara: poison bush (*Duboisia hopwoodii*)

kurara: a needle bush (*Acacia tetragonaphylla*)

kuri: "wife"; may be Mo Mo Bro Da Da; or Fa Sis Da or Mo Bro Da who are younger than ego

kurta: elder brother

laka: a "half-secret" ceremony; that is, includes some participation by women and children

mai: vegetable food

maijada: leader

mai kurara: the seeds of *kurara*

mako biarpiti: the *biarpiti* species of Cossid moth (*Xyleutes*)

mako ilkoara: the larvae of the Cossid moth (*Xyleutes*) in *Acacia excelsior* roots

mako witjuti: Cossid grubs living in *Acacia kempeana* roots

malanji: younger brother

Malu: the ancestral kangaroo being

malu tjukurupa or *malu inma*: kangaroo totem

mamu: an evil spirit that kills at night

mamukata: "devil's son," said of a species of grass with irritant spicules

mangartu: a native peach

meru nakolba: "letting the spear-thrower be seen"; the ritual whereby a man takes his promised wife from her father's camp

milpali: a type of large lizard (*Varanus* sp.)

milpali mako: a caterpillar

mimbu: a deep *Eucalyptus* wood dish used to carry water

mingul: native chewing tobacco

mingurpa: a type of native chewing tobacco (*Nicotiana excelsior*)

miri: hammer stones or upper millstones

mirigadjara: "those concerned with miri"; Pitjandjara men's term for women

mirini: "to slide off" or "to peel"

munga: evening or night

mungara: kangaroo bone meal

nganandaruka: a generation term applying to ego's own as well as his grand-parental and grandchildren's generations

ngangi: water-bearing frogs

ngarukalja: a plant (*Hakea francisiana*) whose lerp scales yield a sweet juice

ngatari: strangers

ngintaka: a lizard

njenga: cold weather

ommari or *waputju* or *mama-ommari*: ego's prospective wife's father; theoretically the man who performs ego's subincision at initiation

papa: the dingo (Australian wild dog)

patupiri: bat totem

pijarpiti: a low shrub (*Zygophyllum aurantiacum*) whose stems are often bored by Cossid moth larvae

pila: sandhills

pitalpital or *malu pumpunju* ("kangaroo food"): the seeds of wild geranium (*Erodium cygnorum*)

Piria: the season of equinoctial gales and the drying up of all but the most reliable water sources

pokara: a shrub (*Thryptomene maisonneuvii*)

pokoti: head bun

puji or *puja*: a twining plant (*Pentatropis kempeana*) which is an important edible green

punjunju: a smoking rite; part of the initiation ceremony

purara: honey ant (*Melophorus inflatus*)

puruka: the man who holds the initiate during subincision

talkuwara: a small kangaroo mouse

tarnda: the act of standing on top of an eminence (that is, to "look out")

tarupango: to change state or form

tawal: a low-grade native chewing tobacco

tjanamiltjan: a generation term applying to ego's parental and children's generations

tjandi: porcupine grass (*Triodi* sp.)

tjilka: the spiny seeds of *Calotis hispidula*

tjimari knives: resin-hafted stone knives used by the Pitjandjara; they are similar to knives well represented in the archaeological record and which date to 11,000 B.C. and earlier

tjitji: young children

tjuta: white bark gum trees (*Eucalyptus papuana*)

tjuijalpi: twig mound-building rats (*Leporilus apicalis*)

tjundal: northwest cumulus clouds and white clouds from the southwest

tum:a or *inma tjukurupa*: sacred ritual boards (also known in accounts as *churinga* or *tjurunga*)

uruba: the growing tips of *Boerhavia diffusa*, a vine

urutjan: a shrub (*Pandorea doratoxylon*)

wakati or *parukeilpa*: a succulent plant (*Calandrinia balonnensis*) whose oily seeds are an important Pitjandjara food

waljuwalju: a bush (*Prostanthera baxteri*)

walka: rock carvings

walku: the native peach tree (*Santalum acuminatum*)

walmala: strange people

walpuru pungu: mortal wounds

wama: sweet or honeylike

wamapiti: any form of lerp sugar or honey

wama wanari: the lerp scales of mulga (*Acacia aneura*) which are a source of sugar

wanambi: a snake

wanari: a shrub (*Acacia aneura*)

wanigi: thread cross made of human hair and used in ritual

wankar: "half-man"; a youth who has completed only the first stage of initiation

wapiti: a bush (*Thryptomene maisonneuvii*) that secretes a sweet juice and grows in sandhill country

wardaruka: a shrub (*Acacia ligulata*)

warilju: mistletoe (*Yysiana murrayi*)

wati: a fully initiated man

PART

3

AFRICA

CHAPTER
7
THE G/WI BUSHMEN

George B. Silberbauer

George Silberbauer received his B.A. in African studies from the University of Stellenbasch and an Honors degree in social anthropology and linguistics from the University of the Witwatersand, South Africa. He was employed by the British Colonial Service as District Officer in the Bechuanaland Protectorate (Botswana) from 1953 to 1967, and he served as Bushman Survey Officer from 1958 to 1966. Since that time he has held the position of Senior Lecturer in the Department of Anthropology and Sociology at Monash University, Clayton, Victoria, Australia. He has done ethnographic field research among the Bushmen and, more recently, among the Aborigines of central Australia. His research has been summarized in numerous articles and monographs as well as in his ethnographic overview of the Botswana area, the Bushman Survey Report *(1965).*

EDITOR'S INTRODUCTION

The G/wi Bushmen of the Kalahari Desert are one among many groups of Bushmen which comprise a virtually unique physical and linguistic group. Their physical type has been termed Khoisanoid, and their language, characterized by a series of "clicks," has been likewise classified as Khoisan. Historical evidence indicates that these peoples once inhabited all of southern Africa and that their numbers were reduced first through assimilation or extermination by European immigrants and their pastoralist practices and then, more recently, by movement of Europeans into the area. The G/wi lived in relative isolation, saved by their severe climate, until the foundation of Bantu ranches in the nineteenth century. Today there is a "continuum of acculturation," from Bushmen employed by Bantu and European ranchers to Bushmen following traditional ways of life on the Kalahari Reserve.

In their desert environment the movements of G/wi bands are primarily

determined by the availability of water in its natural form or in the form
of esculent plants. Such bands are rather loosely organized through kin and
marriage relationships, real or invented, which permit frequent fission or
fusion if necessary. Silberbauer notes that the object of life in this demanding environment is not, as one would expect, the amassing of surplus for
the lean years but rather the enjoyment of good company.

Emphasis in this chapter is on the material and social technology utilized
by the G/wi to exploit the resources of the desert. Silberbauer notes in
particular the loose structure of a social order in which band recruitment is
based on congeniality.

Comparison of the G/wi and !Kung Bushmen is illuminating in stressing
such factors as the flexible organization of bands based more on "good
company" than on strict rules of kinship, the functional importance of the
egalitarian ideal, which was also emphasized in the chapters on North
American aboriginal societies, and the amount of time and labor that is
actually spent by hunting and gathering groups in food-getting.

THE WIDER CONTEXT

The Bushmen of southern Africa are generally identified, together with
the Hottentots, as belonging to the Khoisanoid race. This type is characterized by short stature, yellow-brown skin color, woolly "peppercorn"
hair, and prominent forehead and cheekbones above a small, pointed
chin. The type locality of this description was historically the northwestern Cape Province of South Africa and was, as can be seen from the
excellent life models in the Cape Town Museum, essentially accurate
with respect to the Cape Bushmen. The surviving Bushmen in southern
Africa depart from the standard type in their larger stature and, because
of a long process of hybridization, in the other features mentioned;
however, it is true that they still resemble the Cape Bushmen more than
they resemble any of the other racial groups in the subcontinent.

There is ample historical evidence that Bushmen and Hottentots
formerly lived in most of what is now South Africa, South West Africa,
the Republic of Botswana, and the southern parts of Angola, Zambia,
and Rhodesia. Their distribution in more northerly areas is less easily
determined. From the sporadic finds of skeletal remains, the evidence
of rock art (Summers 1955), and the rather garbled Bantu accounts
recorded by early European travelers, we can assume that the Khoisanoid
population once extended to the Congo and Tanzanian borders. (The
case for a relation between Bushmen and Hottentots and the Sandawe
and Hadza peoples of East Africa is, in this writer's opinion, not proved
and the question remains open.)

The early history of Khoisan and Bantu contact is obscure, but the
evidence suggests that there was a period of symbiosis during the Iron Age

from about A.D. 900 onward (R. Mason personal communication). It is probable that this led to a measure of absorption of local Bushmen by the iron-working Bantu in the region of the Magaliesberg mountains in the central Transvaal. In the last two centuries, however, the Bushman population was greatly reduced by the depredations of immigrant Bantu and European pastoralists who grazed their stock on Bushman hunting grounds. This competition was exacerbated by the Bushmen's hunting the introduced stock. In the punitive raids which followed, the Bushmen resisted with courage and cunning, but were eventually beaten by the superior numbers, organization, and armament of their foes. This, together with the ravages of smallpox epidemics, led to their eventual extermination in most areas. Today Bushmen remain only in Botswana, South West Africa, and Angola, with remnant groups in South Africa, Zambia, and Rhodesia.

Many authorities have assumed the surviving Bushmen to be refugees from the punitive raids of European and Bantu, that they were driven into the less hospitable parts of southern African, which nobody else wanted, where their foes were not prepared to follow them. Although it is true that the Bushman's present habitat is mostly inhospitable country, the above-mentioned assumption is contradicted by the historical records of Bushmen having fought to the death in the areas where they became exterminated. There is no evidence of migrations of refugees. The linguistic evidence in the form of loan words occurring in adjacent Bantu languages and the dialect gradation between Bushman groups speaking languages of the same family indicate that their occupation of their present habitat is more ancient than the period of genocidal conflict. This view is supported by the extent of cultural adaptation to the present surroundings of the Bushmen. In this writer's opinion, the surviving Bushmen are not refugee remnants but a people who have occupied their present habitats for considerable periods of time.

The latest serious estimate of the numbers of surviving Bushmen is that made by Lee (1965:13), who, drawing on various sources, computed a total of 44,100, of which 24,600 are in Botswana. The Botswana figure probably ought to be nearer 30,000.

THE SPECIFIC CONTEXT

The G/wi[1] number about two thousand and speak a common, distinctive language. This group has a sense of its own identity, but does not constitute a tribe with a central organization having recognized authority over the members of the group, as is the case with Bantu tribes. It is, rather, a loose confederation of smaller communities, termed bands, each of which is autonomous, having its own territory and organization. The links between bands are maintained by the kinship system and intermarriage, by sporadic visiting between bands, and by the flow of goods along a network of gift-exchange and trading operations.

The country of the G/wi stretches southeastward from the eastern Ghanzi ranches to include about half of the Central Kalahari Reserve. The ranches are owned and managed by Europeans, who employ Bantu and Bushmen as stockmen and laborers. G/wi living on the ranches have become acculturated to this way of life and have abandoned, for the most part, the hunting and food-gathering existence of the "wild" G/wi in the reserve. However, in the wet season, some ranch G/wi "go walkabout" and visit their friends and kinsmen of the nearer bands in the reserve, temporarily returning to their way of life. In years of bad drought, these visits are reciprocated by the nearer reserve G/wi, who move in on their kinsmen on the ranches. On the ranches, with what is to the reserve G/wi a relatively plentiful supply of food and water, they escape from the discomfort and, sometimes, the danger of the drought-stricken reserve.

There is thus a continuum of acculturation between the ranch G/wi and those who inhabit the remote parts of the reserve, whose only contact with the outside world has been secondhand from the accounts of others who have visited the ranches.

HISTORY

G/wi country lies far out in the desert, east of the comparatively well-watered route from the Okavango Swamps to Gobabis in South West Africa. Their desert isolation protected the G/wi from Bantu and European incursion until the end of the nineteenth century when the Ghanzi ranches were settled. Prior to that, nothing is known of their history. There are no legends of migrations into their habitat, not even of their own ancient entry into this part of the country, and, as far as they are concerned, they have been there ever since man was created.

LANGUAGE

The G/wi language, together with the other Central Group Bushman languages, belongs to the same family as the Hottentot languages. The affinities of vocabulary and structure are unmistakable. Like all Khoisan languages, that of the G/wi has a preponderance of "click" consonants and is a tone language. The great majority of morphemes are monosyllabic. There are three grammatical numbers: singular, dual, and plural (numerals are restricted to one, two, and three). There are masculine and feminine genders and, in dual and plural nominals, an agglomerative gender comprising both masculine and feminine objects. Number and gender are signified by nominal suffixes (number-gender suffixes, here termed NGS). The NGS is modified according to whether the nominal has subjectival or objectival status in the utterance. There is a full range of pronouns which discriminate not only person, number-gender, and subjectival-objectival status but also inclusion-exclusion in the action of the principal clause of the utterance. The genitive is signified by infixing *-gi-* before the NGS.

Adjectives that qualify nouns are formed by a number of adjectival stems, by noun and verb stems functioning adjectivally, and by numerals, enumeratives, and demonstratives. To all of these is suffixed the NGS appropriate to the qualified noun.

There are two sets of demonstratives: definitive, where the position referred to is known to the person addressed, and the indefinite, where the position is unknown to the listener. G/wi demonstratives distinguish three positions, including two refinements of the third position. There is a parallel series of referential demonstratives, signifying "this/that/yonder," and so on, to which reference has already been made.

There are several nonadjectival noun constructions which have adverbial, or quasi-adverbial, functions—for example, locative, instrumentative ("by means of"), associative ("together with"), and comparative forms.

Verbs are subject to modification by adverbs and by extension suffixes. All forms may be negated by means of negative formatives. There is an extensive range of temporal adverbs functioning as tenses other than the perfect stative, and other adverbs of time, manner, duration, and intensity. The adverbial suffix *-si* enlarges the range of adverbs by permitting the use of many noun and verb stems as adverbs. The verbal extensions include the perfect stative (functionally a tense), neuter, passive, causative, reciprocal, and intensive-extensive constructions.[2]

There are two series of copulatives, but the distinction between them has escaped this writer.

It will be clear from the foregoing that the amount of mandatory information in any utterance is considerable. Consider, for instance, the complexity of the pronoun system, which is employed mainly in reference to humans, and which requires specification of the sex and number of the person(s) to which pronominal reference is made and whether or not the person so referred to is or is not party to the action of the utterance.

The vocabulary of the language is rich in relation to the environment and is constantly being enlarged by the coining of compound words which express new or different concepts.

TOTAL ENVIRONMENT

As its name makes obvious, the Central Kalahari Reserve is part of the so-called Kalahari Desert, which stretches from about 30 degrees south northward up the western side of southern Africa, covering nearly one third of the subcontinent (see Fig. 7-1). The Kalahari is a sand-filled basin dissected by the three major river systems, the Okavango-Botletle, the Cuando, and the Zambesi. For the rest, it is devoid of permanent surface water. The mean annual rainfall varies from over 40 inches in the north to about 5 inches in the south. The 20-inch isohyet approximately coincides with the twentieth parallel of south latitude (Wellington 1955:Vol. I, Map III). The change in rainfall is reflected in the vegetation, which varies from dense forest in the north to the sparse scrub and grass of the south.

The Central Kalahari Reserve, 20,115 square miles in extent, is itself divided into three regions: the northern dune woodlands, the central scrub plain, and the southern scrub woodlands (see Fig. 7-2).

The dune woodlands consist of 60- to 70-foot sand dunes covered and stabilized by a comparatively rich variety of trees, shrubs, and ground-layer plants. Large acacias stand in the flats between the dunes, surrounded by dense thickets of smaller trees and shrubs or open stretches

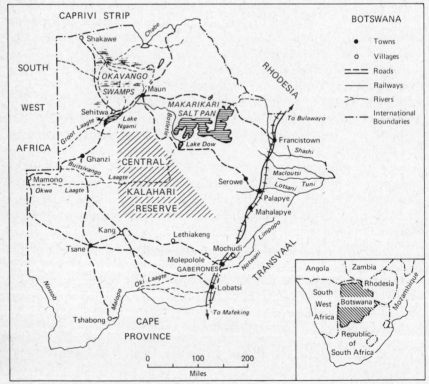

Figure 7–1. Botswana.

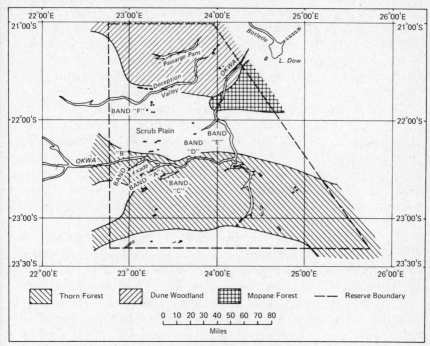

Figure 7–2. Central Kalahari Reserve.

of waist-high grass. This vegetation supports a large population of grazing and browsing animals. These have trodden out hollows in the depressions and flats between the dunes and, in the wet season, these hollows hold reasonably good supplies of water for several weeks. Despite the attractions of good water and the large game population, the dune woodlands are not permanently inhabited by Bushmen. The range and amounts of plants edible by man are evidently not sufficient to furnish a reliable food supply in all seasons. The woodlands therefore contain only satellite territories, which are visited during the season of particular food plants not occurring further south. The importance of this area to the Bushman population also lies in the fact that it is a vital staging area for the great herds of game which migrate across the reserve at the beginning and end of summer.

The almost flat, gently undulating central plain is covered by low shrubs and sparse, short grass. Its monotony is relieved by spinneys, a few acres in extent, of close-growing small trees and by numerous hard-floored pans. Hollows in the relatively impervious floors of these pans hold pools of rainwater for six or eight weeks in the wet season. Seeds drift into the hollows and, in time, establish small, localized plant communities around the waterholes, giving shelter and sustenance to a variety of animals and birds. The short *Cynodon* grass which covers the pans attracts grazing game animals, which, because of the absence of cover through which their predators can stalk them, also enjoy a greater measure of security on the pans than out in the plain. The pans thus become focal points of the activities of many animal species, and for that reason and because of the presence of water, they are of great importance to the G/wi, whose country reaches across much of the plain.

The thorn woodlands of the south are to the G/wi the richest part of the reserve. The hard-floored tributary valleys of the Okwa and the pans of this region, although less numerous than those of the plain, hold fairly good supplies of water during the rain season. There is a greater variety of food plants than in the two northerly regions, and the grass, although less plentiful than on the plain, supplemented by the foliage of the many species of trees, shrubs, and ground-layer plants, can support a large game population.

The topography of the southern region is flat except near pans and valleys, where dunes have developed to the leeward of the depressions. Except for occasional almost impenetrable thickets of *Acacia mellifera* and other small-thorn trees, the forest is fairly open. Fine-leafed genera (*Acacia, Albizzia,* and *Boscia*) predominate and average about 25 feet in height. *Combretum* and *Zizyphus* are found growing in the calcritic soils around pans. *Lonchocarpus* and *Terminalia sericea*, normally of a shrub habit, occasionally grow to tree size. In the forest the shrub layer consists of *Acacia, Dichrostachys, Terminalia, Lonchocarpus, Grewia, Bauhinia, Rhigosum, Commiphora,* and *Catophractes* species. These also grow out in the open, covering extensive areas between forest patches.

The plants of the ground layer are almost all annuals or deciduous tuberous and bulbed species, including several vines and creepers. The grasses tend to specialize according to soil type and degree of competition from trees and shrubs.

The climate of the reserve is typical of the southern Kalahari. Winters are dry with bitterly cold nights.[3] On still days the weather can be pleasant and mild, but when the cold south wind blows, it seems to cut right through to the marrow. The chilling nights are accompanied by frosts which blight the sappy portions of plants; overnight the stock of food plants may be depleted, leaving only underground tubers, bulbs, and roots for man to eat.

The cold weather persists through August. Apart from intermittent cold snaps, the return of hot weather is apparent by the middle of September. Then begins the most trying season for man and animal; the air is very dry and the blustering spring winds bombard one with stinging, choking sand. Plant foods are scarce, the diet is monotonous; hunger and thirst are the common lot. The heat of the sun is intensified by reflection off the sand, bared by the withering winter cold and the scouring winds. Temperatures measured under appropriate screens reached as high as 48 degrees C (119 degrees F) and are higher in the filigree shade of the bare trees. Sand-surface temperatures rise above 72 degrees C (161 degrees F) (Cloudsley-Thompson and Chadwick 1964:15).

The wet season begins with a few premonitory flurries of light rain from the west toward the end of November. It is not until late December or after the new year that the cyclonic depressions of the Indian Ocean acquire enough momentum to carry their moisture-laden air across the subcontinent to the Kalahari, and it is only then that the proper rains begin. Widespread, set-in rain is rare; most precipitation is from localized, short-lived thunderstorms. As much as 3 inches of rain may fall in forty minutes, but the benefit is often confined to a narrow strip along the storm's path, and for this reason the rainfall is erratic; one place may receive a good shower and then little or nothing for weeks on end, while more rain has fallen a dozen or fewer miles away. There is great variation in annual falls and also between the falls received by different places in the same year. The mean annual rainfall for the southern part of the reserve is probably about 16 inches, but yearly totals can be as low as half that amount. The median fall is probably between 12 and 14 inches.

The vegetation, particularly the annual species, responds with almost startling rapidity to the first good rain. Within a few days, the bare sand is brushed with green and, after a week or ten days, is well covered by grass, vines, and fast-growing forbs, which greatly ameliorate the heat of the sun. A half an inch of rainfall is enough to fill a waterhole to a depth of a few inches, providing relief from the thirst tormenting man and animal. Due to the erratic distribution of rain, a waterhole may dry out and be refilled several times during the wet season; and the water supply is intermittent and lasts a total of only six to eight weeks, leaving no water for the remaining 44–46 weeks of the year.

Ground water lies deep below the surface in the reserve, and the only water available is that which falls as rain. Rain is the most significant variable in the life of the reserve, leading to considerable local annual variations in the plant and animal life upon which the G/wi depend. The G/wi have no reliable staple plant food, such as the mangetti nuts of the !Kung, but exploit a wide spectrum of annuals and other species which are comparatively drought sensitive. The number of esculent species available for exploitation is greatest in the autumn months, by which time the rain has fallen and already determined the plant food resources of each locality. For this reason the herbivore population which each locality can support is largely determined by rainfall. The route of the migrating antelope herds follows a broad trend diagonally across the reserve, between its northeast and southwest corners, but is subject to great local variation in the numbers and species passing though, the rate at which they pass, and the numbers that interrupt their migration to

Kinama, a young G/wi girl. Her "peppercorn" hair, prominent forehead and cheekbones, flat nose, and heavy lips are typical Bushman features. Her lobeless ears with their folded upper margins are also characteristic. Note how, even at her young age, her teeth have been worn by chewing sandy food. (Photo courtesy of the Silberbauer Collection, S.A. State Library, Adelaide)

The band winds its way across its territory, migrating to the next campsite. Such moves take place at intervals of about three weeks, when the local resources around the old campsite have been exhausted. (Photo courtesy of the Silberbauer Collection, S.A. State Library, Adelaide)

Hunters leaving for a day's sortie from the band camp. Their weapons are carried in the satchels; bow, quiver of arrows, digging stick, club, and spear. (Photo courtesy of the Silberbauer Collection, S.A. State Library, Adelaide)

A hartebeest hide is pegged out in the sun to dry before the fat and other tissue are scraped off. When this has been done the hide is softened and tanned by treatment with rotted brains, plant juices, and urine. (Photo courtesy of the Silberbauer Collection, S.A. State Library, Adelaide)

A hut built toward the end of the wet season, when a waterproof structure is still needed, though it need not be as substantial as those built earlier in the wet season to withstand the buffetings of the severe storms of that time. (Photo courtesy of the Silberbauer Collection, S.A. State Library, Adelaide)

There is always an elderly man or woman to keep an eye on the children when their parents are away from the band camp. Informal classes are conducted in whichever activity interests the children. (Photo courtesy of the Silberbauer Collection, S.A. State Library, Adelaide)

remain static for weeks or months. The state of the vegetation is apparently the main factor determining the numbers and species which do not make the return migration, but remain in the reserve until the following wet season.

ECONOMIC FEATURES

SUBSISTENCE BASIS

Plant Foods Esculent plants are the basis of G/wi subsistence. They are the source of the major portion or even, at times, the whole of the daily diet. During the months when no water is available plant juices are the main substitute.

Table 7-1 and Figure 7-3 show the periods of availability of plant foods and the seasonal variation in the number of species of food plants to be

TABLE 7–1   G/WI PLANT FOOD—PERIODS OF AVAILABILITY

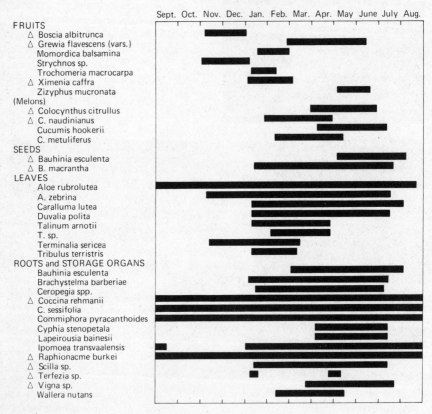

NOTE: △ denotes a species of major importance; bars denote the period when the plant food is available.

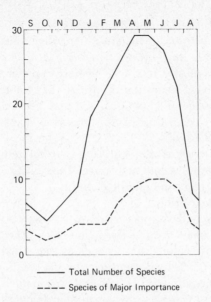

Figure 7–3. Monthly variation in number of species of food plants available.

had. This is not a reflection of the amount of plant material gathered; because of their reliance on plants for fluid as well as for food, each person must maintain a daily intake of between six and eight pounds at least. A smaller number of species available means that the plants are more widely dispersed. The smaller the choice and the wider the dispersal, the greater the work of gathering plants. Conversely, when there is a greater variety of species of plant food to be had, the amount of plants required to fill daily needs can be collected in a smaller area with correspondingly less effort spent on searching for them.

Among the food plants the G/wi exploit, only thirteen species are gathered in sufficient amounts to give them major dietary significance. Three of these species are available for short periods only: Witgat berries (*Boscia albitrunca*), truffles (*Terfezia* sp.), and wild plums (*Ximenia caffra*). Two tubers, although available throughout the year, are conserved for exploitation during early summer when they are the main source of food and fluid. They are *Coccina rehmanii* and *Raphionacme burkei*. Morama beans (*Bauhinia esculenta*) are confined in their distribution to the dune woodlands and the northern fringe of the central plain and can be gathered only by the G/wi of the more southern regions when the climate and the supply of food en route permit travel to the north in autumn and winter.

Of the seven remaining species of food plants, an abundance of tsama melons (*Colocynthus citrullus*) is preferred above all other plant foods, but a plentiful supply of *Vigna* roots is preferred to a small or widely dispersed growth of tsamas. Raisin berries (*Grewia* spp.) are preferred to wild cucumbers (*Colocynthus naudinianus*), which, in turn, are preferred to *Scilla* bulbs. Bride's Bush beans (*Bauhinia macrantha*) are available for a long season, but in most years the G/wi seem to prefer to exploit the crop intensively and briefly, exhausting the supply in a short time, usually between the end of the raisin berry season and the height of the tsama season. Bride's bush beans thus have a brief ascendancy over *Vigna* roots, cucumbers, and *Scilla* bulbs.

Even in a good tsama season, the G/wi do not restrict themselves to a diet of one species only, but supplement the seasonal staple with whatever other plants can be found. In choosing from among a number of available species, their criteria of preference are, in order of importance, the thirst and hunger-allaying properties of the plant food, the ease with which it may be exploited, and, lastly, its flavor. The first two are self-explanatory. Ease of exploitation depends on the situation of the edible portion of the plant, whether lying deep or shallow in the sand, on the surface, or above the surface. The size and weight of the portion that is taken are also factors to consider; the greater the amount taken at one time, the easier is exploitation, since fewer plants have to be located and exploited (which may or may not involve digging) than if the yield per plant is smaller. Delicacies exist among plant foods and are enjoyed and valued, but not to the extent of sacrificing carrying space for them at the expense of a sufficiency of staples to feed the household.

Animal Products   Animal products provide a supplement to the vegetable basis of the G/wi diet. The meat of antelope and springhares (*Pedestes caffer*) is by far the most important of the animal products eaten, but the meat of other mammals and of birds and reptiles, the eggs of birds, and a number of edible insects are also regularly included in the diet, and in their seasons of availability, assume considerable temporary importance.

Figure 7-4 indicates the seasonal variation in meat intake. This is, however, no more than a seasonal pattern, within which great irregularities occur. The high mobility of many animals, notably of the migratory antelope, makes their occurrence in an area somewhat unpredictable. Hunting is everywhere subject to uncertain fortune, and if G/wi hunters should be deserted by the antelope herds or by their own skill or luck, their band may go with little or no meat for weeks at a time.

The species hunted by one band are shown in Table 7-2, together with the writer's estimate of the annual kill of each species.[4] No estimate was made of the numbers of small birds and reptiles taken, as these are seldom brought back to camp (except in times of great food shortage), but are eaten as a snack out in the veld, and many are taken by children.

In the second half of summer an unidentified species of hairless caterpillar, three inches long in its full form, is enthusiastically sought, and

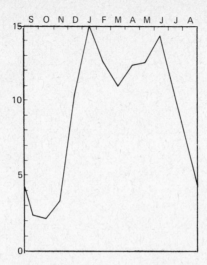

Figure 7–4. Estimated monthly meat intake (pounds per person).

large numbers are eaten in the occasional and brief periods when it is superabundant. Its distribution is sporadic and localized, but a report of a good swarm brings a band hastening across country to camp in the vicinity for five or six days, during which the caterpillars form a major part of the diet.

Ostrich nests are commonly robbed. A small hole is made at either the apex or the midline of each egg and the contents (equivalent to two dozen hen's eggs) extracted for eating. The shells are later used for carrying and storing water during the wet season. The average annual take is three eggs per household, which is surprisingly small considering the popularity and the nutritive value of ostrich eggs and the fact that these birds lay in October, when food is scarcest. The explanation probably lies in the sparse distribution of nests, the difficulty of making an extensive search in October when travel is full of hardship, and the effective concealment tactics of the nesting birds.

Nests of other birds are haphazardly robbed of eggs and young, but apparently play no significant part in the diet of the G/wi.

When termites swarm in the wet season they are caught in large numbers, but this is not a precisely predictable event and it is a stroke of luck for a band to be camped near enough to a swarming nest to be able to take advantage of the occasion. Termites provide one or two big meals a year, on average, and their catching provides a great deal of fun and excitement.

Honey is a rare delicacy which the G/wi take no trouble to seek out. It is taken when they happen to cut down a tree containing a hive. As the African honeybee is notoriously aggressive, and the Kalahari variety

Table 7-2 Estimated Monthly Totals of Animals Killed by ǂXade Band

Species	Meat Yield (lb)	Sept.	Oct.	Nov.	Dec.	Jan.	Feb.	Mar.	Apr.	May	June	July	Aug.
Giraffe	300					1							
Eland	190				1	2	1		1	3	1		
Kudu	100								1	1			
Gemsbok	150				3	2	4	2	1		3	3	2
Hartebeest	80				1			2	1	2	2	2	1
Wildebeest	80				1	1		3	2		2	2	1
Springbok	25				1	4	2	6	6	4	6	2	1
Duiker	10	12	10	12	4	5	4	3	7	2	3	1	2
Steenbok	8	8	10	15	3	3	4	3	6	8	2	4	2
Springhare	1½	3		8	32	30	24	28	30	26	22	15	4
Porcupine	10							1		1			
Warthog	35								1				
Fox	4	2	1	4					4		3	1	3
Jackal	5	4						2		1	2	2	3
Rodents	⅛	15	15	30	30	20	30	30	30	40	20	20	15
Birds	½	16	16	20	8	18	22	13	14	6	12	4	12
Tortoises	¼			50	90	90	90	80	40				
Snakes	½			6	4	8	4		8	10	8	2	
Ants	(pints)			1	1	1	1	1					
Termites	(pints)				4	8	4						

particularly so (or thus it seems to this allergic observer), one would not deliver more than two axe blows against a tree containing a hive without becoming aware of its presence. All that follows must therefore be deliberate. Informants maintain that trees are not cut to rob hives; rather, the G/wi rob any hives they find in trees which they fell. This seems to be true, as the location of every hive in the vicinity of a campsite is known.

Snakes are usually avoided rather than hunted, but occasionally one is killed and given as a delicacy to an old man or woman. Snakes are taboo to all but the elderly.

Water   Water, in the form of rainwater which has drained into depressions on pans, is available only for some two weeks after each heavy fall of rain. Although the wet season lasts for about three months, not all falls are of sufficient intensity to cause runoff and, in most years, water is only intermittently available for a total of six or eight weeks. For the rest of the year the G/wi must find substitutes for water. The most common substitute is the fluid content of plant foods and the contents of the rumens of large antelope killed by hunters. The hydrochloric acid in the rumen contents might have an effect in helping the G/wi to maintain their internal salt balance. There is no natural salt in their diet and, apart from rumen contents, their only supply of salt is in the fresh blood of prey animals which they drink and in the leaves of a species of *Tallinum* which they eat in its season.

SUBSISTENCE TECHNOLOGY

Plant Foods   Most of the food plants are gathered by women and girls in the course of their daily foraging within a five-mile radius around the band campsite. Where the useful portion of a plant is a root, tuber, or bulb, it is dug out by means of a pointed digging stick, which is used to break up the sand before scraping it out by hand. This method is slow but efficient in that the equipment is light and easily portable. Furthermore, there is no call for sudden exertion; rather, there is a slow, steady expenditure of energy, which better suits the small, lightly muscled women. A woman carries her gathered plant food in the lower portion of her skin cloak, caught up and knotted to form a bag. Here also there is an economy in the lightness and easy portability of equipment and in the many uses to which the cloak is put.

As most food plants are distributed rather thinly, there is an unavoidable waste of time and energy in searching for them and in moving from one patch to the next. This wastage is minimized by the expertise in field botany which is possessed by G/wi adults and which is passed on to girls while they are out gathering with their mothers and the other women of the band. They learn to identify esculent and other useful species, their seasons of availability, and the types of locations and plant associations in which each is found. Any individual moving about the band's territory, whether a man on a hunting trip or a band member migrating to a new campsite, takes note of the state of growth of food plants and passes this information on to the others in the band. This constant updating of intelligence more narrowly defines the possible areas in which food plants might be found.

Men gather plant foods for themselves while out on hunting trips and join their wives and daughters in collecting for the household during early summer when little or no hunting can be undertaken and when the work of gathering is made more difficult by the harshness of the season and the scarcity of esculent plants. The men's technique of gathering is similar to that of the women.

While some plant foods, such as berries, may be eaten without any preparation, they are sometimes cooked to vary the otherwise rather monotonous diet, or mixed with other foods. There are also some species of esculent plants which are poisonous when raw and must therefore be cooked before they can be eaten. G/wi cooking is versatile and takes advantage of what is seasonally available. There is a variety of salads and gruels. The preparation of some plant foods involves ingenious processes, but the cuisine is restricted by the perishable nature of the foodstuffs, by the absence of salt and fat in the diet, and by the shortage of water. Cooking is limited to the processes of roasting in coals or ash pits or boiling in a pot. The necessity for a family to limit its possessions to what can be carried when the band moves camp restricts the number of utensils, thus inhibiting the versatility of G/wi food preparation.

Cast-iron pots have almost completely replaced the clay cooking vessels the G/wi previously obtained from the G//ana people along the Botletle River. Enamel bowls, mugs, and plates have also been imported, but have not yet replaced the wooden articles the G/wi still make and use, nor the cleaned carapaces of smaller tortoises which serve as ladles and mugs.

Wooden mortars and pestles are used to pulp berries, wild cucumbers, and other fruits and to grind roasted tsama seeds into a coarse meal. A woven grass sieve is used to winnow the seeds from the ashes in which they are roasted.

Animal Products: Hunting Most animal products utilized by the G/wi are obtained from animals hunted or trapped by the men. Most hunting is done with bows and poisoned arrows.

The G/wi bow is a light, single-curve stave made from the wood of the raisin bush (*Grewia flava*), with a bowstring made from sinews taken from the back muscles of eland. The stave is bound at both ends and in the middle with flat sinews of gemsbok. A short stick in the form of a "thumb" is let into the foot of the bow and bound fast. An eye is spliced into one end of the bowstring and, looped over the head of the bow, anchors that end of the string. The other end is passed between the "thumb" and the bowstave and is wound around the foot of the bow. The string is tightened by twisting the windings and pushing them against the "thumb," which pinches the string and prevents its slipping. The correct tension of the string is recognized by its musical pitch when plucked. A tuned bow has a weight (pull) of about twenty pounds at its draw of some eight inches, which will carry an arrow beyond the hundred-yard mark. However, accurate range is limited to about 25 yards by the design of the arrow.

The arrow consists of four parts: head, sleeve, link shaft, and main shaft. Heads may be piles (simple point) or broadheads (barbed). Heavy-gauge steel fencing wire is the material from which broadheads are usually made today, although the art of making them from bone has not been lost. A five-inch length of wire is heated in a pit of coals, raised to their maximum temperature by means of a blowpipe, and is then beaten into shape on a block of quartzite, another piece of quartzite being used as a hammer. More and more commonly, a heavy piece of steel, such as an abandoned kingpin, is being used as the hammer. Some men have files for finishing their arrows, but most can manage to give good points and edges to their arrows with the crude quartzite anvils and hammers. Fencing wire is a more durable material than is bone and, because of its malleability, takes a sharper edge. It is therefore the preferred material and is a valuable exchange commodity.

The sleeve of the arrow is a short tubular section of reed which fits over the shaft of the arrowhead and over the point of the link shaft, connecting the two. To prevent its bursting under the force of impact, the sleeve is bound with sinew.

A two-inch spindle of hard wood or bone forms the linkshaft. Its rear point fits snugly into the bound main shaft, but not so tightly as to prevent its being detached, for the function of the link shaft is to allow the main shaft to come away from the arrowhead once it has struck home. The precious main shaft can then be recovered intact, and the animal is also prevented from levering out the arrowhead and its load of poison.

The main shaft is about seventeen inches long and of reed or the thick culm of one of the suitable grasses. As neither of these is common in the Kalahari, wands of Grewia flava are sometimes used as substitutes for the preferred main shafts. The G/wi arrow is not fletched or flighted in any way. As it is very light, therefore having small momentum and impact energy, it is necessarily a short-range weapon. It is doubtful whether the increased accuracy of flights would increase the efficiency of these arrows. The purpose of the arrow is not to inflict a mortal wound in a hunted animal but to inject into it a load of poison. The poison is made from the intestines of the larval grubs of a beetle, Diamphidia simplex. G/wi men dig up the larvae, gently squeeze and roll them to break up the intestines of the insects without breaking the skins, nip their heads off, and then squeeze the now pastelike insides out onto the shafts of their arrowheads. The poison is placed behind the barbs; in order to minimize the chances of accidental poisoning, the sharp parts of the arrowheads are not coated with the poison. Eight larvae are used to arm each arrow and this dose is lethal to most animals. To place his arrow effectively a hunter must hit his prey in a fleshy part where the arrow may penetrate to a depth of three or four inches so that its poison may be dissolved by the animal's bloodstream.

To achieve this with a weapon of the limited accuracy and range of the G/wi bow and arrow requires considerable ability. Most game animals range too widely and shift their grazing grounds too frequently to allow G/wi hunters to predict their movements accurately enough to enable them to organize beats in which the herds may be driven toward bowmen concealed at a prearranged spot. The game must be taken where it is found, and to find it at all depends on luck and knowledge of the country and of the habits of the various species of game animals, as well as on up-to-date intelligence of their movements gained from others' observations and the hunters' own interpretation of the signs of the animals' movements.

Parties of men up to twelve strong make two or three protracted "biltong"[5] hunts during the year. On these hunts, the parties cover most of their band territory, hunting as they go and cutting up the animals which they kill, drying the meat and hanging it in the sun to preserve it and also to make it lighter and easier to carry on their journey back to camp. During these patrols of the band territory the state of growth of food plants is noted and the information passed on to the rest of the band to guide future decisions concerning the location of campsites.

Most hunting, however, is done by men working in pairs, making sorties of a day or less from the band's camp. Before going out, the hunters discuss their intentions and arrange their plans so as to avoid interference of one party by the others. There are seldom more than four pairs in the field on the same day, and there is usually more than one area in which game is to be found within the fifteen-mile operational radius of a daily hunting party. Conflict of intention is therefore unlikely and is, in any case, resolved by according precedence to the most-skilled hunters.

No informant was able to give a connected, coherent account of the theory and rationale of hunting tactics. What follows is derived from discussion and postmortems of hunts and from the writer's own observation of G/wi hunts. It is necessarily of a generalized nature, since the differing circumstances of each hunt make it a unique event.

A hunter carries his arrows, ready poisoned, in a quiver sewn into his steenbok-hide hunting satchel. The satchel is slung over his left shoulder and also holds his bow, club, digging stick, and a smaller quiver containing a repair kit of spare portions of arrows, lengths of sinew for replacing broken bindings, bowstring, a small supply of poison grubs, and gum for fixing bindings (which has a modern substitute in the shape of pieces of rubber cut from old tires; when heated the rubber makes a prime serving pitch). Loops and a small sheath sewn to the hunting satchel hold his spear, and a knife is carried in a sheath strapped to his waist.

A pair going out to their chosen hunting ground walks out at a good pace, the second man treading exactly in the footsteps of the first to minimize noise and to avoid thorns. If the two speak at all, it is in muted tones. Most communication is by hand signals. Tracks encountered on the way are commented on by gesture; the direction taken by the animal is shown by a wave—a fast wave for a gallop and a slow, wavering sweep of the hand for a grazing animal. The distance traveled by the animal since it made the tracks is indicated by the extent of the follow-through of the wave. A flick of the fingers shows a very fresh spoor, with the animal still nearby, while an old or fruitless spoor is indicated by turning the palm upward. There is a hand signal for each of the species hunted or frequently encountered, the fingers being held in positions imitative of the shape of the horns or heads of the animal thus identified.

Hunters expecting to find game in a particular vicinity unobtrusively scout the land ahead, climbing into trees or edging over the tops of dunes and peering through the covering vegetation, always taking care not to betray their presence by sound, sight, or scent. In reconnoitering, they note the size and position of the herd, whether it is resting or grazing, quietly or nervously, the disposition of sentry animals, and many other factors. The preferred target is an animal on the flank, somewhat on the downwind side of the herd. The hindmost beast is usually wary and difficult to approach closely enough for a good, telling shot. Herds generally move into the wind and the foremost animals are also difficult targets, since the hunters' scent is likely to be carried down to the rest of the herd, which would raise the alarm, scaring the animals away before a close approach could be made. A lamed but not emaciated animal is favored, since it cannot run as far as a healthy specimen. Whether a male or female is easier to hunt depends upon the species; kudu bulls are more alert than are cows in mixed herds, but cows often run farther when wounded. A hartebeest cow may run a short distance after being wounded and then stop and stand, giving the hunters a chance for a second shot.

The hunters plan their approach, taking into account the wind, the state of the herd, and the cover lying between them and the herd. G/wi hunters can stalk almost invisibly through the sparsest cover at surprising speed. Bodies bent almost double, they advance in short stages, taking advantage of any disturbance of grass and shrubs by wind to mask their movements.

The usual approach is a pincer movement, which allows both hunters a chance for a shot. Ideally, each shoots an arrow into the target to increase the amount of poison injected and to reduce the chance of an animal's escaping through the arrow falling out before the poison has been absorbed. They do not shoot simultaneously, but try to remain hidden in order to get in successive shots. Unless backed by many helpers, hunters will not shoot more than one animal, since to follow the spoor of a single animal with reasonable chance of success is all that one pair of hunters can manage alone.

Helpers are called if the hunters return to the band camp for the night or after the animal is killed to assist in cutting up the carcass and in carrying the meat back to camp.

Bow and arrow hunting is restricted to those months when poison grubs are available and from four to six months after, beyond which time the poison is either weakened by age or the supplies have run out. The early months of summer are usually too hot for this type of hunting even if some men still have supplies of good poison. Instead, hunters take to trapping.

Animal Products: Trapping Although most trapping is done by men, whose prey is steenbok and duiker (solitary territorial antelope), adolescent boys and girls also set traps for small mammals and gallinaceous birds. All use the same type of spring-loaded noose made of *Sansevieria* twine. This is pegged out around the bait (for birds and small mammals) or the concealed pit (for steenbok and duiker), anchored by the triggerpeg, and the free end of the twine is tied to a stout stick or small sapling, bent over to provide the spring to close the noose. When an animal releases the trigger peg by taking the bait or by stepping into the concealed pit, the spring flies up, tightening the noose about the neck of the animal drawn to the bait or around the pastern of the small antelope, and jerks the unfortunate creature into the air.

A trap is baited with a ball of *Acacia* gum and set in a place frequented by the bird or animal it is intended to catch. Snares for steenbok or duiker are set across the paths of these antelope. Unobtrusive barriers are erected to guide the antelope onto the snare.

G/wi hunters occasionally club small animals and birds to death. They either stalk up to their prey or throw their clubs to knock them down as they run. A club is cut from the straight stem of a shrub which has a suitably shaped and sized portion of root. When trimmed to shape, the weapon weighs about two pounds.

Spears are seldom used as primary weapons, but to give the *coup de grâce* to animals already *in extremis* from the effects of arrow poison. The G/wi make a composite spear consisting of shaft and head. The shaft of *Grewia* wood is about 53 inches long and tapers from ¾ inch in width at the front end to half this thickness at the butt. The front six inches, where the tang of the head is inserted, is bound with sinew to prevent its splitting. Spearheads are beaten out of ⅜-inch rods of soft iron 18–24 inches by the same technique of forging used for making wire arrowheads. The spear blade is leaf-shaped, about five inches long, with a slightly raised midrib to give it greater strength. Both edges are sharpened and meet in a sharp point.

The remaining length of rod forms the tang, which may be squared to prevent its turning in the wooden haft, or left in the round.

Springhare sticks are made from several straight, peeled lengths of *Grewia*, lashed together to form a supple rod twelve to fifteen feet long. One end of the rod is barbed with a sharp steenbok or duiker horn, pointing outward and backwards and lashed fast. This weapon is used to impale springhares in their burrows and immobilize them while they are dug out by the hunters. As springhares can dig faster than can a man using only a digging stick, they would be able to escape were they not held fast.

Quivers for holding arrows, and a smaller version for holding a repair kit, are made from tubes of root bark of *Acacia giraffae*. The lower ends are blocked with a formed leather cap and the tubes are bound with sinew to prevent their splitting.

The satchels in which men carry their hunting weapons, food, and smaller kills are made of steenbok hide. The G/wi make a variety of leather satchels, bags, and purses, their sizes and shapes depending on the nature of their intended contents.

Axes, adzes, and chisels are interchangeable in that they all have the same blade, a drawn-out triangle beaten from a ⅜-inch iron rod, the sharpened edge forming the base of the triangle and the tapering tang its apex. This blade set in the plane of the wooden haft makes an axe; set transversely it is an adze; and set end on, is a chisel. All three tools have a wide range of uses, from butchering animal carcasses to cutting and carving wood.

Knives are also made from a ⅜-inch rod forged into much the same shape as a spear blade, with the tang set in a short wooden handle. The double-edged, pointed blades are between two and six inches in length.

Clothing is made from cured hides of antelope. The curing process consists of repeatedly moistening the cleaned skin with a variety of fluids (plant juices, urine, rumen contents), wringing it out to expel the moisture and soften it, and then allowing it to dry, and again kneading it by hand. Boys and men wear breechclouts of steenbok hide, which, when cured, is as soft as fine kid leather. Women and girls wear two fore- and one hind skirt of steenbok, duiker, and other antelope skins. Both men and women have leather blankets made from the hides of larger antelope. These also serve as blankets and as carrying bags. Children go naked until the age of six or seven.

Shelters vary in design with the seasons. In winter and early summer they are no more than screens of grass, leaves, and branches to give shelter from the wind. As summer advances the increasing heat brings a need for shade, and the shelters are roofed over. They are still flimsy, shapeless, and rather haphazard improvisations on the natural framework of the tree or large shrub against which they are set. Their purpose is to give shade and peace from the tormenting wind-driven sand of the burning early months of summer. It is only when the sky is full of promise of rain, toward the end of December, that the G/wi seriously get down to building something that could be called a hut.

The framework of a wet-season hut is made of branches set in a rough circle in the sand and meeting at the top to form a firm structure in the approximate shape of a cone, five or six feet in height and diameter. This frame is thatched with clumps of grass wrenched or dug out of the sand, complete with roots. To shed rainwater the clumps are successively layered from the ground level upward, their tops pointing downward. For greater strength, the G/wi prefer to build their huts against trees or large shrubs, but a campsite seldom has enough trees for each hut, and even those that stand free are proof against the great squalls of wind and the torrential rain of the wet-season thunderstorms.

The setting of huts in a band's camp is dictated by the current segmentation of the band. Each group of kin and friends builds its huts close together, even touching one another. The positioning of the triangular entrances depends as much on social factors as on climatic factors. Most people prefer not to face their hut entrances to the northeast into the prevailing wind, but will position them in any other direction in order to face the other huts of the segment. During a thunderstorm rain and wind may come from any and all points of the compass, so there is no way of avoiding these by facing a hut entrance in any particular direction.

The floor of a hut is simply the cleared, bare sand. Repeated sweeping to rid the hut of food scraps and other detritus lowers the floor level until it is several inches below the level of the surrounding sand after a week of occupation.

As summer wanes into autumn the shelters built at successive campsites are progressively less substantial, until by winter they are no more than windbreaks, and the annual architectural cycle begins once more.

SPATIAL DISPOSITION

The variety of resources on which the G/wi depend is not uniformly distributed in the reserve. Even within any one of its three main regions, they are relatively concentrated in some areas and sparse in others. The G/wi, in exploiting these resources, are concerned not with the relative richness or poverty of an area in a single item, but with the availability of a nexus of resources which they require to fill a wide range of needs and in all seasons of the year. These are food plants, wet-season waterholes, fodder plants for game animals, and trees and shrubs. There must be an adequate variety and number of food plants to provide for their dietary needs in all seasons. Waterholes, being the only means by which man and animal can directly utilize rainwater, are highly desirable constituents of the resource nexus. Grazing and browsing must be sufficient to attract and to sustain the herbivorous animals which furnish the G/wi hunters with their supply of meat and other useful animal products. Trees provide shade and also fuel for fires to cook food and to give warmth during the freezing nights of winter. The woods of a number of trees and shrubs are also needed for a variety of weapons and other artifacts.

The concentration of resources comprising a nexus is limited, first, by the generally low density of food and other resources in the Kalahari and, second, by the mutually exclusive distribution of some of these resources. Good grazing, for instance, is not found under good shade trees, and few food plants grow on the pans surrounding waterholes. This dispersal requires that a human population should have access to a fairly large area of country if it is to find all of the resources on which it depends. The degree of dispersal should not, however, be too great or an excessive amount of energy will have to be expended on their exploitation. The exploitation potential of a nexus depends on the density of resources, the total amount of exploitable material, and the amount of each resource that is available in its appropriate season.

There is a finite number of resource nexus whose exploitation potential is adequate to the needs of a viable human community. In wresting a living from their environment, the G/wi could choose any of several solutions to the problem. Assuming that any human population will be grouped in communities, the G/wi could choose to migrate from one resource nexus to the next or to stabilize each community about one or more nexus. The first course would permit the development of large communities, but would have the disadvantages of (1) wasting large amounts of energy in the necessarily frequent process of migration, since the resources of each nexus would be rapidly exhausted; (2) possibly engendering energy-wasting competition between communities for the same nexus; and, hence (3), making unpredictable the resources to be found in any nexus because of the possibility of their already having been exploited by a rival community. The G/wi follow the second course, that of stabilizing each community or band about a nexus over which the members of the band have exclusive rights of exploitation. The area containing the resource nexus constitutes the territory or domain of the band.

The sizes of the territories occupied by bands range from less than 200 square miles to more than twice that area. The writer selected a sample of six representative band domains and surveyed them within approximate limits. Their areas, average populations (between 1959 and 1966), and population densities were as follows:

A. 350 square miles,   85 inhabitants,   4 square miles per inhabitant
B. 176   "   "   21   "   8   "   "   "   "
C. 400   "   "   64   "   6   "   "   "   "
D. 300   "   "   50   "   6   "   "   "   "
E. 280   "   "   70   "   4   "   "   "   "
F. 300   "   "   53   "   6   "   "   "   "

The location of these territories is shown on Figure 7-2. There is a noticeable clustering of territories along the axis of the Okwa Valley, contrasting with a tendency to isolation throughout the rest of the reserve. These trends reflect the distribution of resource nexus in the relatively rich Okwa Valley area and in the poorer regions to the north and south of it.

The carrying capacity of the territory sets a limit on the size of the occupying community, but the G/wi, by varying their pattern of occupation according to the exigencies of the seasons, broaden their societal basis by maximizing the size of the community which the territory supports.

There are four patterns of territorial occupation. (1) The band migrates within its own territory as one community (synoecious migration), moving from one campsite to the next as the resources within easy range of the campsite become exhausted. (Figures 7-5 and 7-6 trace the synoecious migrations of a band during two years.) (2) The band temporarily migrates as one community to the territory of an allied band. This synoecious emigration is made during seasons of plenty when conditions permit abnormally large concentrations of people. The motivation of such an emigration is social—to visit an allied band and to enjoy the company of its members. With the highly variable distribution of rainfall in the reserve, it occasionally happens that a small number of territories receive less rain than do their neighbors. These localized droughts also stimulate synoecious emigration out of the afflicted territories into those which have sufficient food for both the host and the emigrant bands. Visits are made

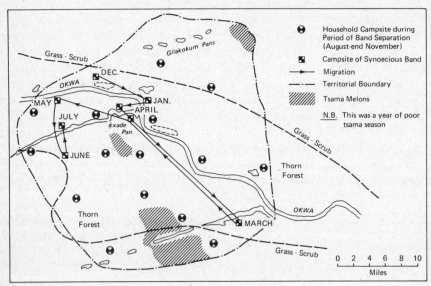

Figure 7–5.   Migration in ≠Xade territory.

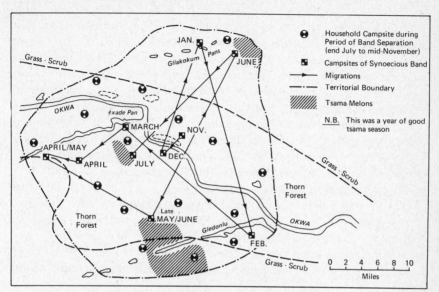

Figure 7–6.   Migration in ≠Xade territory.

only with the hosts' agreement, and never when there is insufficient food in the hosts' territory, for example, in times of widespread drought. (3) The band separates into segments of up to twenty strong when environmental resistance rises in times of prolonged drought and lowers the subsistence density[6] below that which is required by the synoecious band. This pattern is uncommon because of the infrequency of really prolonged droughts. (4) In late winter or early spring of all but the most favorable years, the seasonal drought and frosts reduce the number and variety of available food plants. The subsistence density of the territory drops to a level where the synoecious band rapidly exhausts the food supply around each campsite and is forced to make very frequent moves to fresh supplies. This expenditure of energy on migration and on the search for food becomes excessive and the band responds to this situation by splitting up into units which are small enough to remain sedentary during the period of food scarcity. The population disperses over the domain, which is exploited by small, widely separated groups. In this manner, the density of population and intensity of exploitation are reduced to equal or less than the subsistence density of the territory during the season of scarcity. The units are either nuclear families or small extended families totaling not more than five persons. Each unit goes to an agreed-upon locality in the domain and remains there, isolated from the others, until food again becomes plentiful and the subsistence density rises to a point where the synoecious band can be supported.

This temporary dispersal enables the band to maintain its numerical

strength above that which would be dictated by the seasonally low subsistence density; that is, the band would have to be much smaller if it
were to survive as a permanently synoecious community. At the cost of
losing up to four months of community life each year the band is able
to enjoy the benefits of greater numbers for the remaining months.

The intensity of exploitation of resources obviously varies according to
the pattern of occupation, but is also restricted by seasonal variation in the
density of available resources. For example, the range within which women
are able to gather sufficient food for their families' daily needs depends
on the density of available species. This density varies to some extent
between localities, but, as campsites are selected for their proximity to a
good supply, this variation is not of great significance. The seasonal variation in the number of available esculent species has a great effect, and this
is reflected in the size of the area that women cover while gathering.
Figures 7-7 through 7-11 show the rise in intensity of exploitation (and
corresponding decrease in area exploited) during the course of a typical
summer's gathering by one band of sixteen households containing eighty
people.

In September (Fig. 7-7), when bands are usually split up into isolated,
independent households and there are only four important species of
plant food to be had, the one household represented in the map worked
over a circle of 4-mile radius. The gross rate of exploitation of plant food
resources was then of the order of ⅚ pound per square mile per day.

In December (Fig. 7-8), when the band was again united in one camp,

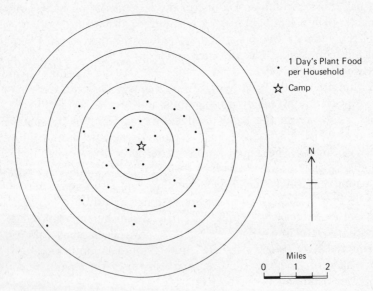

Figure 7–7. Plant food exploitation. September: 20 days' subsistence.

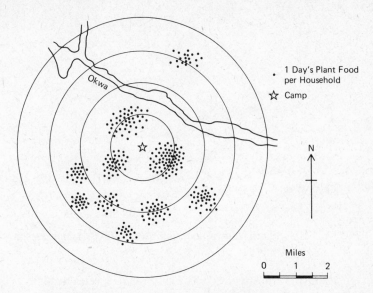

Figure 7–8. Plant food exploitation. December: 20 days' subsistence.

the plant food for all the radius had a gross exploitation rate of 71 pounds
per square mile per day. At this time, and in this locality, Witgat (*Boscia
albitrunca*) berries were plentiful, constituting the main part of the vegetable diet.

In March (Fig. 7-9), the intensity of exploitation was about the same,

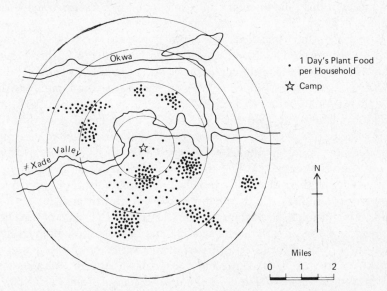

Figure 7–9. Plant food exploitation. March: 20 days' subsistence.

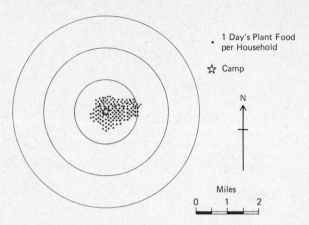

Figure 7–10.   Plant food exploitation. May: prolific tsama season.

although there were nearly twice as many plant species available. There was, however, another important factor operating, namely, the presence of water. The camp was sited about a half mile from the waterhole in the area which had sufficient plant food but somewhat less than other areas. The advantage of good water supply compensated for the extra work entailed in gathering in this poor area.

In May (Fig. 7-10), the tsama melons were superabundant; it was possible for the band to accommodate a visiting band and for both (total population 138) to find their plant food in an area approximately 1 by 1½ miles. In this time of plenty, the exploitation rate increased more than tenfold, to about 736 pounds per square mile per day.

In another year, when there was a poor tsama season, the same month (Fig. 7-11) presented a very different picture. Nevertheless, with the maximum number of 29 esculent species available, gathering was confined to a 25-degree segment of 5-mile radius, and the exploitation rate was 128 pounds per square mile per day.[7]

The availability of food plants is the principle factor governing the band's choice of a campsite. Variations in the distribution of species within the territory result in a differential between the food resources of localities in different seasons. While the distribution of plants is stable from one year to another, the highly variable and patchy distribution of heavy showers of rain gives rise to variations in plant growth and, hence, crop yields, which cannot be predicted before the end of the wet season. There is therefore no fixed pattern of migration and of campsites, although it is usual for a band to spend at least part of the wet season camped near its largest waterholes. Two contrasting years' migrations of ≠Xade band are charted in Figures 7-5 and 7-6. Figure 7-5 concerns one of a series of drought years with severe winters which withered above-ground fruits

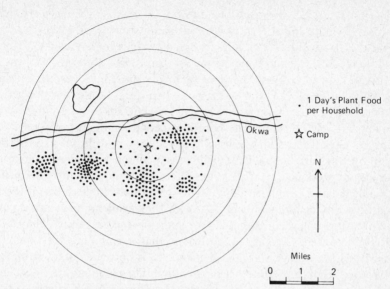

Figure 7–11. Plant food exploitation. May: poor tsama season; 20 days' occupation.

and forced the band into early and prolonged separation into fifteen household units, which remained in isolation until December. In that month, the flushing Yellowwood (*Terminalia sericea*) leaves and a small crop of Witgat berries relieved the near-famine and permitted the band to resume its synoecious life. An early winter again blighted above-ground plant foods and forced the band to separate in mid-July, after having occupied eight campsites in the eight months when food supplies were sufficient to permit the synoecious phase.

Figure 7-6 concerns a happier year of more plentiful food. The band resumed its synoecious phase a month earlier and continued it until the end of July. During that phase it occupied ten campsites, three of which were in patches of tsama. (It was at the first of these that this band was visited by the Easter Pan people, reflected in Fig. 7-9.) The moves to the different patches of melons were motivated by the presence of game animals near them and not by exhaustion of the local tsama crop, which was virtually impossible. The melons were the primary attraction, and the choice among the three patches was governed by the hunters' needs.

In both years the waterholes at ≠Xade Pan itself and at G/edon!u were visited. ≠Xade was the campsite during February and April of the drought year, when the band returned there to drink the water of a late shower. In the good year, when there was more water about, ≠Xade was visited only in March.

It is seldom possible for a band to remain at one campsite for longer than four weeks. After such a long period of exploitation plant food supplies dwindle and it is probable that game animals eventually learn to avoid the area within which hunters operate. G/wi hygiene is not adapted to a long-term sedentary population of band size, and the campsite is eventually fouled by waste portions of food plants, huts become infested by "personal livestock," and in seasons when dung beetles are not active, it is necessary to tread very warily to avoid the human excreta dotted about the outskirts of the camp. The optimum period of occupation appears to be three weeks, and sites are usually selected to provide for at least this length of time, although a band will occasionally make a shorter excursion to a locality to exploit a particular resource, for example, eland caterpillars.

While a band is able to draw on its territorial resources for all of its foodstuffs during normal years, it is clearly dependent upon other communities for imported commodities and for succor during a year of extreme localized drought. It is obvious that a community as small as band B, with a strength of only 21 members, is not indefinitely viable but must have recourse to intermarriage with other communities. The high value that human company has for the G/wi provides additional motivation for band interaction; this is institutionalized in a cross-cutting series of band alliances. Each band has two or more allies which it shares with other bands, to which it may or may not itself be allied (see Fig. 7-12).

Through its allies each band is indirectly in touch with every other band and also with cattle posts, ranches, villages, and trading posts outside the reserve, and it is this network that provides the channels for the importation of such commodities as wire and soft iron for implements and weapons, enamel and ironware, trade beads, and tobacco. The trade balance is maintained principally by the export of cured duiker and steenbok hides, but internal reciprocity (that is, within bands and between members of allied bands in the remote areas of the reserve) involves the exchange of a wide range of goods and services.

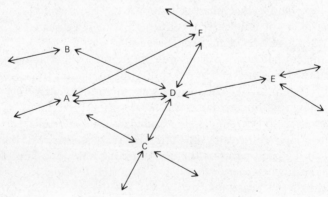

Figure 7–12.   Allied bands.

The large majority of interband contacts takes the form of visits by individuals and small groups (for example, nuclear families) from one band to the synoecious camp of an ally. Frequency and intensity of these contacts is enhanced by the consanguineal and affinal kinship links, which, in turn, result from intermarriage between allied bands. The G/wi custom of a young married couple's living with the wife's parents until the birth of the first or perhaps second child, and then usually returning to the husband's band, means that temporary and permanent change of band membership is a normal consequence of intermarriage between bands.

There is also a certain amount of protracted visiting which can be considered as temporary change of band membership. In some instances this lasts so long as to constitute a permanent change.

The duration of alliances could not be established from informants' statements nor from an analysis of origins of immigrants into bands. A widespread epidemic of smallpox in 1950 and 1951, followed by a lesser epidemic of poliomyelitis, appear to have wrought such dreadful destruction that some bands ceased to exist. Survivors scattered all over the G/wi country and even beyond it. At all events, the alliances that existed between 1959 and 1966 were stable, and it is probable that they normally endure for at least a generation.

There is no enmity between nonallies, who meet quite happily in the territory of a mutual ally. The G/wi explanation of the absence of direct interaction between nonallies is that they find all that they need among their allies who are their "friends and kinsmen, to whom we always go."

Alliances are not marked by any formalities. Visitors from allied bands are welcomed and enjoy the same rights to the resources of the host territory as do its permanent inhabitants. If a whole band temporarily emigrates to an ally's territory, it camps at the same site as does the host band and forms an additional series of segments in that camp. There is even a mingling of segments when close kin of friends move out of their usual segments to others in the host or visiting band. These large-scale visits are not preceded by formal invitations, but by the gossip of individual visitors; "The people at X have good food this year, they long for the people of Y." "The people at Y long to see the people at X." When this pleasant news filters through, there is discussion in Y of the possibility of a visit to X, and the matter is egged on to the climax of a decision by visitors from X. All this is done very delicately and tastefully, but is taken for granted as a matter of course by the bands concerned.

Cooperation between allied bands includes, then, facilitating importation of commodities that are not or cannot be produced from territorial resources; facilitating travel by extending to visitors the use of territorial resources and, through extraband extension of kinship and friendship links, facilitating social interaction. Band intermarriage and the custom of supporting drought-stricken bands by sharing with them the territorial resources of more fortunate bands enhances the chances of survival of individual communities and, hence, of the population as a whole.

Competition between bands is effectively inhibited by the unequivocal allocation of resources through identity of territory and community and by the reciprocity inherent in social relations and their stabilization by such institutions as kinship, friendship, and the band alliances.

SOCIAL FEATURES

SOCIAL ORDER

G/wi society is egalitarian and loosely structured. Within the limits of community size imposed by environmental and technological factors, the social system is flexible and versatile, readily accommodating differences and fluctuations in numbers (up to a maximum of 150 for short periods and up to about 90 for long periods). It is a high-valency society, permitting fusion and fission at many points; it is also an open-ended and informal system in which situations can be met by alternative responses—a system that provides a theme for improvisation rather than a rigid precept or precedent.

Division of Labor The slow processes of maturation and learning impose a division of labor by age, as do the declining powers of the elderly. Division of labor by sex is simplified by the lack of emphasis on masculinity and femininity and the relative paucity of strongly contrasted male and female roles. Among subsistence activities the only generally valid distinction is that women do not hunt or work with bows, arrows, or spears. Most gathering and preparation of plant foods for household consumption is done by women, but men collect their own plant food while out hunting and also help in providing for the household in early summer. In most households women build the shelters and huts at each new campsite, but many husbands habitually help their wives without there being any regularity in the range of tasks of each partner. Similarly, the allocation of the chores of collecting firewood and setting pit-oven fires is a matter settled by each couple.

As hunting is the exclusive province of men, the manufacture and overhaul of weapons and artifacts is also in their hands. This includes the curing and preparation of hides and leatherworking, but here again there are many women who can and do sew and who are able to work with wood and make or repair their own pestles and mortars. Women do not, however, forge iron, although there is no prohibition on their using iron tools such as axes and knives.

Children join in the economic activities of their parents as soon as they are able. Girls go out collecting with their mothers and, by the age of seven or eight, are usually capable of providing for their own households.

Boys take until fourteen or fifteen to learn the more difficult and extensive skills of hunting.

A woman does a little less work as she grows old and weaker, but the nature of her work does not change and she manages to make a useful contribution almost until the day she dies. Men, however, retire from bow and arrow hunting in their mid- or late thirties, when deteriorating eyesight and stamina impair their skill. They still join in "biltong" hunts as helpers, but on their one-day trips from the band's camp, their hunting is confined to small game, to trapping steenbok and duiker and digging up springhares. These less demanding methods of hunting take up the same amount of time, so middle-aged and elderly men do not have more leisure than do the younger, bow and arrow hunters. At this age, men devote more of their time to crafts. They are not specialists and do not make a living from their craftsmanship. With every man having to fend for himself during the phase of band separation, none can afford to depend on a specialist for food or implements. Instead, the G/wi craftsman produces a small quantity of weapons, implements, or leather goods which he gives or lends to others in the band. These favors are reciprocated by gifts of food or the rendering of services which do not significantly add to what a man produces for himself. Every G/wi household is capable of independent subsistence and is forced to rely on its own manpower resources almost every winter and early summer when the band separates. The reciprocal exchange of goods and services in the synoecious band is perhaps therefore more an expression of and a means of sustaining social solidarity than it is an economic necessity. The production of any surplus that might be used for trade or barter is too unpredictable to be the basis of regular exchange of goods and services.

Reproduction G/wi girls marry before puberty, usually between the ages of seven and nine. Boys are usually seven years older when they marry. Premarital pregnancy is therefore not a problem. The G/wi express a preference for cross-cousin marriages, but this is not borne out by an attempted analysis of the kinship status of partners in 25 existing marriages. Only four partners could be definitely identified as being cross-cousins; these were young couples whose parents were still living and among whom siblingship could be confirmed. Other couples were either uncertain of their kinship links or were not cross-cousins.

Informants were unanimous in their view that intending spouses should be well known and well disposed to each other and that their respective parents should also be on friendly and familiar terms. It seems possible that the G/wi, in their expressed preference for cross-cousin marriages, are using a kinship model to illustrate the preferred social arrangements, that is, harmonious familiarity between both spouses and their respective parents. This hypothesis would explain the persistence of the stated preference in the face of (a) the low incidence of actual cross-cousin marriages and (b) the number of partners who had so little interest in their mutual kinship status as to be unable to decide whether or not they were, in fact, cross-cousins. Children of close and old friends will employ fictitious kinship terms, which indicates that the kinship model is used to express extrakinship relationships. The G/wi kinship system classifies parallel cousins as siblings, which, in the next generation, greatly increases the number of classificatory cross-cousins, and the category loses much of its distinctiveness, making it difficult for an individual to distinguish them. These are persuasive but inconclusive arguments in favor of the hypothesis. Informants agreed, but did not volunteer, that marriage partners should be "like cross-cousins," but the writer misgives this answer to what was a leading question.

The arrival of a boy or girl at fitness for marriage generates great interest among adults and young couples in the band, and there is much discussion of who his or her partner should be. The choice is supposed to be made by the parents, with the agreement of the boy or girl, but it seems probable that the more or less subtle suggestions of other band members have a persuasive influence. Premarital roles are not passive, however, and courtship may be initiated by a boy and a girl. There is no defined ritual or formality. If both belong to the same band, they have already seen a good deal of each other, and there is little change in their behavior which an outsider would notice. The gossip preceding and during courtship is a much more obvious indication of what is going on. When a boy seeks a wife in another band (or is attracted by her when he visits her band), his arrival in the girl's band makes courtship only a little more noticeable.

There is much more self-consciousness after marriage, which is without ceremony but is a simple assumption of life together in a shelter or hut next to that of the girl's parents. A young husband is teased by his slightly older friends about his wife's youth and unreadiness for sexual intercourse and about the agonies of frustration that he is supposed to be suffering. In fact, the couple commences sexual intercourse when the girl is still in early puberty, about the time her breasts begin to develop. When she menstruates for the first time, she undergoes a puberty ceremony[8] in the last phase of which she is joined by her husband and the couple is symbolically united and given advice and instruction about the conduct of a happy marriage.

With the completion of the puberty ceremony a girl is said to leave her childhood behind her, but this does not mean that she passes straight into adulthood. She and her husband remain in the tutelage of her parents, continuing to live with them and with the marriage still on something of a probationary basis. The husband must prove himself as hunter and provider and the wife must show that she is able to gather food and otherwise care for a household. Both spouses must show that they are compatible and can live in harmony with the other members of the band. The role of the wife's parents is not that of critical examiners, but of helpful and affectionate advisers and teachers. (See the earlier remarks on cross-cousin marriage.) When the band separates into constituent households the young couple remains with the wife's parents, and it is only after birth of their first or, perhaps, second child that they set up an independent household of their own.

Adolescent sterility is apparently common among G/wi girls, for most do not conceive until reaching sixteen or seventeen. A baby is weaned at about three years, before which time the mother should not conceive as, in the G/wi view, she would have to wean the baby before it is strong enough and she would also be unable to care properly for two small babies. The G/wi are aware of the connection between intercourse and conception, and it is the husband's responsibility to abstain from intercourse until the baby is weaned, for the G/wi have no means of contraception. Considering that most G/wi are monogamous, this hardship is borne with remarkably cheerful fortitude. Children are spaced four or five years apart and most women bear and rear three children. (The average in a sample of 52 women past reproductive age was 2.8 children, the median being 3.)

Although polygamy is permitted, an insignificant number of men have more than one wife. In a band of sixteen households, two had two wives and one man had four. There was one instance of polyandry, which was a compromise reached in dealing with the problem of a woman who divorced her husband and married a close friend of his. The first husband did not want to take another woman as his wife, and the bonds of affection between the woman and the two men were such that, rather than become estranged by the situation, they (with the concurrence—perhaps inspiration—of the band) agreed to the polyandrous solution. This was a success and everyone felt rather pleased with himself for his ingenuity. It was a unique situation, but the band felt that a satisfactory relationship was more important than a "break with tradition."

Divorce is simply the recognition that a man and his wife no longer live together. Band colleagues and kin will try to persuade a couple into reconciliation, but if their differences are insuperable, separation is regretfully accepted and the partners are free to contract other marriages. Children remain with their mothers until four or five years of age and then go to their fathers. Divorced spouses contract other marriages within about a year of divorce; where persistent adultery precipitates divorce, which is commonly the case, the adulterous couple usually marries.

There is a stated preference for widows and widowers to marry their deceased spouse's sibling, in other words, a levirate and sororate. As the only widows and widowers investigated during the survey were middle-aged and older, their sisters- and brothers-in-law were all already married and no data on the operation of the preferences were collected. The fact that parallel cousins are classificatory siblings and mother's sisters and father's brothers are classificatory parents facilitates the operation of the preference.

The relation between partners in successful marriages is one of quiet, undemonstrative affection and an easy, almost automatic cooperation. Most marriages are stable, and G/wi marriage has "fail-safe" mechanisms in the absence of stigma which might attach to divorce and in the early remarriage of divorced partners, widows, and widowers.

Groupings The largest social group identified by G/wi society, and within which regular interaction occurs, is the band. It is a loosely structured series of small, interconnected kin groups and is segmented into a varying number of more or less stable groupings of households of kin and friends.

In the G/wi image, a band is founded by a man and his nuclear or extended family moving into an uninhabited area containing a resource nexus, and thus providing a nucleus around which other families settle. Initially the settlers are drawn from among the kin and friends of the founding family. Later members are, in turn, friends and kin of the settlers. Compatibility of personality is the expressed motive for migration to a band and is the qualification for acceptance of a recruit. Pressure of population on the territorial resources of an established band undoubtedly plays a part in motivating emigration.

The male and female descendents of the founding family are termed the owners, and their permission must be sought to join the band or to visit in its territory. The G/wi have small interest in lineage, and few, if any, adults can trace their ancestry beyond their grandparents. Thus, after three generations, the identity of the founding family is lost in the confusion of numerous descendants with short memories. In practice, the owners are those who have lived longest in the territory. Seeking and granting permission to use territorial resources is unvarying etiquette, and the owners always consult with their band colleagues as a matter of form. "Ownership" is not, therefore, an office with any authority and does not imply leadership.

There is a continued, intermittent trickle of migration between bands occasioned by exogamy and by individuals' changing tastes in company and their consequent move to what is, for them, a more congenial social environment. Membership status is not unchanging, but is established by prolonged residence, during which the immigrant's identification with his old band is gradually replaced by identification with his new group. These changes in personnel are minor, and their effect is countered by the permanency and continuity given to the band by the stability of the larger part of its membership and by the fact that the distribution of resource nexus determines the location of territories which are the foci of habitation.

The segmentation of the band is expressed in the arrangement of huts and shelters in synoecious camps; households comprising a segment are clustered close together, but are still an integral part of the whole camp. In years of exceptional drought, when the depleted territorial resources will not support synoecious camps, segmentation is also expressed in the gathering of households in separate and temporarily independent camps of one segment each. The only apparent criterion of segment composition is the preference that members have for one another's company. There is no stratification by age nor any pattern of kinship bonds; segments are composed of a random range of kin and friends of all ages. The size varies from two households to as many as seven. Membership changes easily and unpredictably; some segments are stable for a succession of several camps before their membership changes, while others may form intermittently. Interaction within a segment is more frequent than with the rest of the band, but is by no means exclusive.

The mechanics of band recruitment and band-endogamous marriage lead to the establishment of direct or indirect kinship links between nearly all band members. Band alliances and marriages between members of allied bands spread the net of kinship beyond the band, and, combined with the extension of the kinship model to close, nonkin relationships, such as friendships, eventually make it probable that any G/wi can trace some sort of kinship with practically every other G/wi with whom he is likely to come into contact. The kinship system is therefore an important factor in the ordering of relationships and in the formation of groups. It is a classificatory system with an inventory of ten terms (each with masculine and feminine equivalents) which identify all kin within the formal scope of the system. Only one term is an isolate; *gje:sa* ("mother"), but this has its classificatory derivative *gje:g/wâsa* (literally "mother-child-female," that is, "little mother," which designates mothers of parallel cousins and great grandmothers). In the vertical dimension, seven generations are distinguished: ego's and three ascending and three descending generations. Horizontally, terminological recognition extends to the sibling group of ego and that of ego's parents and the offspring of both these groups. Affines are not classified in the same way as are consanguines, but each spouse recognizes the whole of the other's kin group. As might be expected from this feature, the same ranges of matrilineal and patrilineal kin are designated; that is, the system is symmetrical, the patrilateral kinship structure being virtually the mirror image of the matri-kin structure (Figs. 7-13 and 7-14).

The unity of the sibling group is expressed in the preferential levirate and sororate of widows and widowers and in the classification of the off-

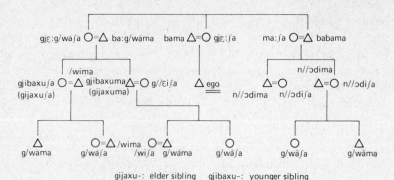

gijaxu-: elder sibling   gjibaxu-: younger sibling

Figure 7–13. Matrilineal kin.

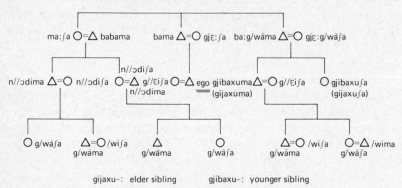

gijaxu-: elder sibling   gjibaxu-: younger sibling

Figure 7–14. Patrilineal kin.

spring of same-sex siblings as children. Parallel cousins are, therefore, classified as siblings. FBr is termed *ba:g/wâma* ("little father"), and MSi is *gje:g/wâsa* ("little mother"). Within ego's group, elder and younger siblings are distinguished, as is sex. Classificatory siblings are similarly differentiated according to sex and to real relative ages; that is, there are no classificatory age differences.

Relationships between kin are categorized as either joking (*ho:khwudi*) or avoidance (*gjiukxekxu*), and an individual distinguishes between those of his kin whom he should *!ao* (fear, respect) and those with whom he may "play." In general, avoidance is expressed by:

1. Not sitting close to the relative and avoiding bodily contact
2. Refraining from loud laughter or noisy conversation, taking care not to swear or to mention sexual or other intimate matters in the relative's hearing, and always speaking softly and politely to him or her
3. Not addressing an avoidance relative by his or her name, but using the honorific plural, aggregate gender pronoun instead

4. Not touching the avoidance relative's possessions without permission and not receiving or passing anything directly from or to the relative, but through the hand of an intermediary.

Behavior toward other kin, the joking relatives, is free of such restraint. Instead, mutual teasing, uninhibited joking and criticism, free use of one another's property, and, between relatives of opposite sex and comparable age, mildly provocative flirting and a certain amount of erotic bodily contact are expected.

All kin are expected to *wiku* (love one another), to behave affectionately to one another and to be helpful and generous.

In the categorizing of kin as joking or avoidance, generations are alternated, so that the generation proximate to that of a joking relative is in the avoidance category, and vice versa. The result is that an individual is on joking terms with the joking kin of his joking partners and must respect his avoidance kin. Were this not so, the embarrassing situation could arise in which B jokes with A's avoidance relative C, and with A simultaneously; for example,

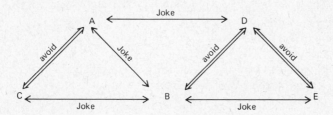

This should not happen; instead, what should be is:

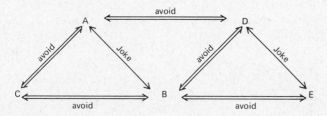

This ordering of relationships might be termed the principle of congruent triangles. There are some situations in which it does not operate, for example, both cross-cousins and their parents are in the joking category, but this is changed if ego marries his cross-cousin, in which case the latter's parents are transferred to the avoidance category.

Avoidance kin are those between whom there exists, or potentially exists, a relationship involving authority and submission; this relationship is extended to kin who, actually or by classification, are in a parent-child relationship with ego or with ego's spouse. Kinship terms coincide with the joking-avoidance categories, and the following terms are applied to people who are in the avoidance category:

> *ba:ma* (father; matri- and patrilateral great grandfather and great grandson, the generation after persons termed *n//odima* or the female equivalent, *n//odisa*)
> *gje:sa* (mother)
> *ba:g/wâma* (FBr, MSiH, great grandfather)
> *gje:g/wâsa* (female counterpart of *ba:g/wâma*)
> *g/wâ* (*-ma* or *-sa*) (ego's children, children of siblings of same sex, grandchildren of sibling of opposite sex, children of parallel cousin of same sex, the generation younger than *n//odima* or *n//odisa*—in which case this term is an alternative to *ba:ma* and *ba:sa*)

The following kin are in the joking category:

> *ba:bama* (patri- or matrilateral grandfather, spouse's grandfathers, FSiH, MBr)
> *ma:masa* or *ma:sa* (female counterpart of *ba:bama*, including FSi, MBrW)
> *n//odima* or *n//odisa* (grandchildren, the generation after *g/wâ*)
> *g/wauma* (WsiH)
> *g/wausa* (WSi, BrW)

Siblings, whether own or classificatory, are avoidance kin if of opposite sex and joking partners if of same sex.

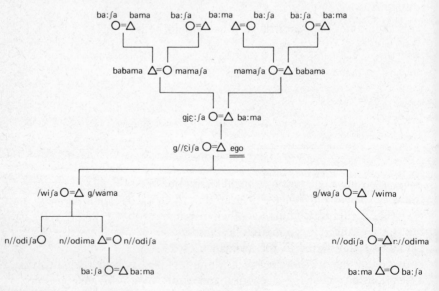

Figure 7–15. Ancestors and descendants.

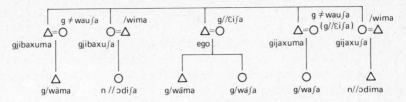

Figure 7–16.   Sibling group and offspring.

The G/wi kinship system is essentially concerned with ordering relationships between ascendants and descendants (Fig. 7-15), between siblings and between their offspring (Fig. 7-16), and between affines.
In the context of band life, this range is usually more than sufficient
to include band colleagues who are also kinsmen and will also include
kinsmen in allied bands, which is the practical limit of the social life
of most individuals. It is a system that permits easy fusion at a number
of points because of its symmetry and nonexclusive nature. At the same
time, its generalized, unspecialized, and nonhierarchical nature permits
fission at almost any point outside the nuclear family. Kin, apart from
those in the nuclear family, do not have particular and peculiar obligations
to one another which might inhibit the division that takes place when
interband migration occurs and when the band separates into constituent
households. Fission is, in any case, attenuated by the system of band
alliances, which maintains links between those who are separated by
distance and seldom see each other.

Ownership—Inheritance   A band's territory and its resources are not
susceptible to ownership by man (despite the institution of owners), but
are the property of the Supreme Being, N!adima. The band is the corporate
holder of exclusive rights of occupation and exploitation, and the owners
might be considered the administrators of this right on behalf of the
band. Ownership by man is confined to exploited resources and their
products (and imported commodities); in short, food, artifacts, and
tobacco. The rights of ownership are encroached upon by the general
pressure toward generosity and sharing and the particular demands of
sharing with joking relatives. Nevertheless, these factors do not erase
ownership; many people may borrow an item of property and, however
little an owner may see of it, it is always identified as belonging to him.

With the exception of beadwork, inheritance of property is precluded
by the custom of breaking all of a deceased person's belongings on his
grave and leaving them there to mark the grave. Beadwork is excluded
and devolves, without formality, on the daughters of the deceased. There
are no grades of status to be inherited, except possibly that of owner,
which has already been discussed.

SOCIAL CONTROL

Transmission It appears to be a fundamental tenet of G/wi philosophy that man is an essentially reasonable being and is well disposed toward his fellows. This belief is consistent with the form that the processes of child training and socialization take.

While the procreation of children is not the principal object of marriage, the birth of a child is nevertheless a joyous event for the parents and the whole band. A baby is named by one of its grandparents or by one of the siblings of its parents in a public announcement. The name usually commemorates some happening or circumstance immediately prior to the baby's birth. Should the parents of a baby leave the band for more than a few days and then return, the baby is welcomed back by each band member in turn, each touching its upper lip and introducing himself or herself, "Halisima, I am the woman !xai!xai. Stay well with us." It is clear that a baby is regarded as a member of the band from the time of the naming ceremony, and probably from birth.

A baby is never left alone, but is carried everywhere on its mother's hip or slung in her cloak. If the child cries, it is given the breast immediately. When the mother is sitting in a group, the baby is passed around and rocked in the arms of anybody old enough to do so without dropping it. Men and boys show the same fondness for babies as do women and girls. Babies are not parted from their mothers at night, but sleep held in their mothers' arms. (The G/wi sleep in a curled position, from which they do not move while asleep, so a baby is in no danger of being rolled on or crushed.) A baby thus spends its first years in the secure affection of attentive band colleagues.

Teaching the child to walk is an enjoyable group activity, which consists of passing the infant from one side to another of a circle, holding him in an upright position on his feet, and at first allowing him to fall gently into the hands of the person opposite. Later, the baby is allowed to fall forward onto his hands, but is encouraged to stand up again. The lesson lasts until the baby grows tired, and there is no hurry or pressure on him to learn quickly. The G/wi have no formulated norms for child development and each baby learns at his own pace with no comparisons being made with other babies. Perhaps because of this method of training G/wi babies do not go through a proper crawling stage. Dance rhythms are instilled into children at the same time as they are taught to walk by holding their hands and beating time with them to the clapping and singing of those seated in the circle. By the time they are able to walk, G/wi babies are able to keep closely approximate time with the complex dance and song rhythms.

Toilet training, if one may term it thus in the absence of any facilities other than the bush itself, is the responsibility not only of the parents but of all the people who play with the baby. Training consists of hastily positioning an empty melon skin or other suitable receptacle whenever the baby relieves itself (babies are naked) and then wiping its bottom clean with a tussock of soft grass. If the receptacle is too late, the ensuing mild commotion communicates to the child the need for control. This "hit and miss" method seems to be entirely satisfactory.

Other tasks of early training are also shared by the band, particularly by the segment in which the parents put themselves in each camp. Initially, the only punishment is the fuss caused by the baby's upsetting behavior, and the slight and short-lived lessening of the warmth of the affection of those who surround him. Later, after his third year, he is admonished to be more gentle and cooperative. When children misbehave, they are told to desist; if the persist, somebody will try to divert them into some more acceptable form of behavior. Physical punishment is rarely used, and then only consists of a slap or tap. To thrash or to beat a child would be regarded as savage and irrational; "if a child won't listen to you when you speak to him, he certainly won't do so when you beat him."

The weaning process is described as "the child's growing tired of the breast." Solids are introduced into the infant's diet at an early stage as supplementary feeding and as material on which to cut emerging teeth. The supplementary component is gradually increased until, before his third year, the child is feeding himself and is given the breast only at fairly long intervals or when he needs comforting. The diminishing nutritional dependence on breast feeding and the desire to imitate older, weaned colleagues are probably the main factors terminating a child's desire for breast feeding. The initiative appears to come as much from the child as from the mother.

After weaning, children no longer accompany their mothers everywhere, but are left in the care of an old man or woman who is camp keeper for the day. The children play together at games which are mostly imitations of adult activities, and also receive from the camp keeper informal instruction and advice on every topic that crops up. Child lore of adult activities is more accurate than is that of European children, and G/wi children's games are an effective part of training for adulthood. By the age of five, a child is expected to know the etiquette of avoidance and joking and no longer to seek bodily contact with parents except in times of emotional stress.

When girls are old enough to manage the long walks, they occasionally leave the camp "school" and go out gathering with their mothers and the other women. They learn the skills involved in gathering food, and their socialization is furthered by listening to the uninhibited gossip and comments of the adult women.

Boys' training in subsistence activities is mainly through playing games involving mock hunts, imitating older boys, and, around the fires at night, listening to the men's conversation about their day's hunting. A father begins to take his son out on training hunts at ten or eleven, although instruction in the making, care, and use of weapons starts much earlier than this. It takes a long time to become a hunter, and a boy continues his training under the care of his father-in-law for several years after marriage.

Initiation of girls at puberty and of boys at any age from thirteen to their early twenties is a dramatic summary of the processes of socialization which have gone on during the whole of the initiates' lives. Girls' ceremonies are individual, their timing determined by the girl's menarche. After a period of seclusion the initiate is introduced to the band, its territory, and resources and, in a series of aphorisms, instructed in the values and ideals of the people.

Boys who are judged to be big enough and mature and determined in their behavior are initiated in autumn or winter in groups of up to ten. The older men take them out into the bush where a special type of hut is built for the occasion. The boys and men remain there for ten days and nights, during which time the boys are taught a secret dance and secret ceremonies. Most of the time, however, is spent in instructing them in hunting and in correct, friendly behavior to one another, to kin and band colleagues, and to strangers. The dances and ceremonies are new information, but the rest is a concise formulation of what they have always been taught. The status of initiates is not altered by the ten days in the bush—they are still only boys or young men and must show by their behavior that they are fit to be considered adults. Individuals are judged by their behavior, as there are no clear-cut grades of status or other categories by which a man may be labeled or a woman stereotyped.

Maintenance The concepts of power and authority are weakly developed among the G/wi. The only institutionalized authority resides in parental status in the context of the parent-child relationship and its classificatory extension, along which it is progressively attenuated by the decrease in frequency of interaction. In other relationships power and authority depend upon prestige and personality and not upon status. Persuasion is the only means of imposing one's will, and this requires expertise in the activity being initiated, a reputation for proposing successful actions, and the ability to elicit favorable responses. This combination militates against any one individual's chances of exercising authority in more than one or two fields of activity. There are no means of acquiring any significant amount of power. Most of the economic resources are either in the hands of the Supreme Being or dispersed almost equally over the whole band. Imported commodities can be obtained from any one of the allied bands, so in the present environment and with the present technology, concentration of wealth or of control of the economy is not possible. Neither the kinship system nor the arrangement of band segments provides a sufficient measure of solidarity for the stabilization of factions that might be marshaled to establish and maintain power. In fact, the number of points at which fission and fusion into another configuration might occur is so great that not even the band structure itself is stable enough for this purpose. The atomizing influence of the annual separation into isolated households is too strong.

Outside the nuclear family, then, authority is ephemeral, rising to deal with specific situations, with power exercised by persuasion, and lapsing again when the response has been executed. Authority lacks any institutionalized recognition and is rewarded only by the continuation of the group's activities and attainment of its goals and, perhaps, by the personal satisfaction of the exercise of skill. In the randomly selected population of the band there is a limited proportion of members who possess the attributes of even this ephemeral leadership; it is thus inevitable that the same individuals repeatedly come forward to deal with situations in which particular ability is required. This does not lead to a centralizing of authority in them nor to the ascription of power to them. Each of these initiators or proposers operates in a limited field of activities; in these he acquires the prestige needed to persuade the group to his point of view more easily, but this power does not overflow into any other field of action.

In this climate of limited personal power and authority, the real power and authority reside in the community as a whole, that is, in public opinion. The absence in the band of strongly cohesive units larger than the nuclear family makes it necessary to canvass each band member in order to mobilize public opinion. Even within a nuclear family, the status of husband and wife are on terms of equality, which precludes any prediction that a husband or wife will follow the lead of the other, and the household cannot, therefore, be regarded as one unit of opinion. In the intimate social life of the band, with its high rate of interaction between members, there is constant awareness of everybody's business, so the mobilization of public opinion by gossip, aided by the uninhibited comment of joking partners, is very effective. In this sensitive environment conflict and tension are detected early in their development and countermeasures can be taken before a matter becomes serious and escapes the rather weak means of control which are available to a community in which there is no one voice of authority. It is not possible for this observer to measure the efficacy of resolution of conflict in its initial stages, since the potential seriousness of situations cannot be reliably predicted. However, some impression may be gained from the rarity of conflicts which progress as far as the public scene of "talking at," in which an aggrieved member airs his difference with another by expounding his grievance to a third party in the hearing of the whole band. His adversary, if he has an answer, pleads his case to a fourth party. In most instances the band comes to judgment after hearing the opening pleas, and, by interjections and comments, band members indicate their views of the matter. The offender sees his fault and comes to the aggrieved colleague and apologizes or makes other reparation, thus ending the affair.

There are few hard and fast rules by which band judgment is guided. Hypothetical instances of incest and murder were immediately and unanimously condemned, but these offenses never occurred. Rape has been known, and here judgment sometimes went to the rapist because he had been provoked, and the girl was criticized for having started something she could not handle. Matrimonial disputes involving accusations of meanness, neglect, and adultery cause the most difficulty, and discussions have gone on for weeks before opinion crystallized.

If the expression of a band's decision against him does not mend an offender's ways and he is impenitent in the face of the barbed comments of his joking partners, he will eventually be eased out of the band by means of a public conspiracy to keep him on the wrong foot. Carefully avoiding any behavior of which the offender could legitimately complain, band members put him through the frustrating treatment, such as not hearing him, misunderstanding what he says, and appearing to anticipate his needs wrongly, thus upsetting his plans. It is oblique and sometimes very subtle, and its effect is to make the offender so disgusted with them that he leaves for another band. It is a means of rejection which does not engender hostility, but only disgust and disappointment, and the offender is not left with a need to even the score or to carry on the conflict. In a new band, removed from the cause of his misbehavior and in a different atmosphere, the offender usually settles down to a normal, peaceful life. A small number of individuals, however, never settle down but move constantly from one band to another at intervals of a season, a year, or a couple of years. Their reputations are known to everybody and it is accepted that each band must have its share of putting up with them.

The early detection of conflict and its treatment by means of a number of tension-relieving processes which reinforce cooperation and harmony reduce the need for elaborate devices of social control which depend on the imposition of sanctions. The versatility of social groupings and the lack of an inflexible set of precedents allow the bands a considerable measure of compromise and improvisation in meeting situations and there are few offenses of the species of crime against custom. There is only a small number of taboos and some of these are backed by a belief that breaking them will incur the wrath of the Supreme Being which could be visited on the whole community or the whole G/wi country. Potential offenders are deterred by their fear of the punishment itself and also by the anger of their fellows for having brought disaster on everybody. This idea of others being punished for the acts of one is also expressed in the doctrine of vicarious liability of parents for wrongs committed by their children (for example, destruction or damage of property) and the liability of one spouse for the other's acts. Group liability encourages group responsibility for the acceptable behavior of its members.

ETHOS

Religion The G/wi believe in a Supreme Being, N!adima, and a lesser being, G//amama. They are not clear whether these two are separate entities or differing aspects of the personality of N!adima. The logical implications of the characteristics and acts of the two favors an interpretation of disparate, rather than dyadic, identity.

N!adima created the universe, life, and all the systems that operate in the universe. All that exists is his to do with as he pleases, within the limits of the systems he ordained. There is no coherent account of the creation in the form of a myth; the story of the creation is part of general knowledge. N!adima is omniscient, omnipresent, and, within the limits of natural systems, all powerful. He is inscrutable and unapproachable by man, who passively accepts his will and seeks only to avoid making him angry. His interest in man is unknown; his anger is expected if some taboos are broken and as a result of certain acts, but is not an invariable consequence. Death and other misfortunes are sometimes attributed to his anger or his capriciously "growing tired of a face," but there is no certainty of his agency. On rare occasions he intervenes directly to help man, for instance, by appearing in dreams and guiding him in the solution of difficult problems. N!adima gives life, quickening the foetus in the womb and the creature in the egg and the plant in the seed when rain falls on it (fertilization and vivification being separate processes). The supply of life is inexhaustible; life is created, *ab initio*, from nothing and no raw material is involved. In punishing or helping man, N!adima can manipulate phenomena; although he cannot transcend his creations by making them act contrary to their natures, his agency can be recognized in the unexpected behavior of phenomena. He cannot, for instance, make rain fall from a clear sky, but he can divert a storm from its previous path.

It is not known why he created the universe or whether esculent, and other useful plants, and game were created for man's special benefit or whether man, with other living things, has been placed in his environment and has to make of it the best that he can. The remoteness of N!adima is such that the G/wi have no prayer, sacrifice, or other forms of worship and direct communication with him. Thunderstorms, the new moon, and the sun are addressed in prescribed formulas which are interpreted by informants as placating N!adima's powerful creations in order to show man's lack of arrogance and thereby to avoid his displeasure.

G//amama's origin is unknown. He has many forms and is eternal, but is not all-powerful. Hostile to man, he is responsible for misfortunes that, like those sent by N!adima, are exceptional in their unexpectedness or in the severity of the results of minor causes. A woman ran a *Dichrostachys* thorn into her finger while digging up a root and developed a blood poisoning which cost her a finger and months of illness and agony. At about the same time a party of hunters was repeatedly attacked by a lion and one man was badly bitten in the thigh, but beat off the lion and made a good recovery. These accidents were believed to be the work of G//amama; had N!adima caused them, the woman and the man would not have survived but would certainly have died. G//amama can be frustrated by the use of medicines and dances which N!adima made—again it is not clear whether for man's special use or whether their innate powers are now known and used as a result of man's serendipity. There are also other medicines that N!adima imbued with curative powers which are used to cure misfortunes which are not sent by G//amama and which have no known origin, for example, common illnesses and a hunter's persistent failure. There is, however, no witchcraft or sorcery. N!adima and G//amama are never seen as coming into direct conflict and sometimes work together to accomplish somebody's death or other misfortune by a series of complementary or contributory acts.

N!adima is regarded with awe and fear, but apparently without love. G//amama evinces fear and a rather malicious delight in frustrating him, but no hatred. The misfortunes they send are rued for their pain, but do not undermine the confidence and security of the sufferers. Both beings are too remote to produce emotional reactions of this sort and their natures are stoically accepted for being what they are.

Man and Beast To a G/wi his fellows in the band are the most important part of his environment. From them he derives companionship, the enjoyment of which is the ultimate motivation of rational acts. Although much time and energy are spent on subsistence activities whose primary object is the provision of the means of living, the object of life is to enjoy good company. The G/wi word *khwe-* means "man" in the general sense and implies possession of the qualities of generosity, friendliness, wisdom, calmness, humor, and good temper. They regard men as being inherently good and, although initially shy and reserved toward strangers and fearful of them, anticipate the development of good relations with further acquaintance. Display of unpleasant characteristics such as anger or meanness is regarded as aberrant and a departure from true nature rather than as symptomatic of underlying evil. They distinguish between themselves, G/*wikhwena* (bush men) and other Bushmen. Their main contact is with the G//ana, whom they consider greedy, but like well enough. The Nharo are believed to have a tendency to quick temper and to taking without giving in return. The ≠âû//ei are feared for their fierceness and violence and their practice of turning themselves into lions and preying on people. The G//olo are cannibals. As the people of the

southern part of the reserve had very little direct contact with anybody
but the G//ana, nobody had experienced the stereotyped shortcomings
of the other peoples.

Their attitude toward a stranger (/xajekhwema, literally "entering
person") is expressed in the instruction given to boys at initiation: "Even
if you visit very far among khwena ("people," here specifically Bushmen)
whom you do not know, you must not keep to yourself and ignore them.
Go out to them and be friendly, for all khwena are good. You must not
fight with them, for they will never fight with you."As nobody expects to
travel so far as to find himself among ≠âû//ei or G//olo people, the
precept is presumably not applicable to such a situation. Non-Bushmen
strangers are not immediately termed khwena, but either ≠ibina (Bantu,
especially Kgalagari) or /ô:xana (Europeans). These terms are not pejora-
tive, but lack the favorable connotations of the word khwena. The stereo-
type attributes of Bantu and Europeans are their unpredictability and
irrationality. When they become known and trusted, individual non-Bushmen are referred to as khwena.

Of the characteristics that distinguish man from beasts, there are the
obvious differences in appearance, but there is also the uniqueness of
human speech. Mammals and birds also have speech, but theirs is different
from that of man and, except for baboons, they do not understand human
speech. Man is alone in the range of artifacts he makes and in the possession of a postmortem spirit (g/ama). However, he does not stand
completely apart from animals. Both are N!adima's creatures and are
subject to his anger and caprice and, to about the same extent, to the
vagaries of the natural environment. Hunting is part of the battle for
survival, and the hunted animal is an adversary in the contest of the hunt,
not something that exists specially for man to prey upon. A man may
not kill more than he needs nor a woman take more plant food than she
needs for her household without angering N!adima.

CHANGE

INTERNAL

The ecological and social factors controlling the G/wi population could
not be measured nor definitively determined by the writer during his field
work (1958–1966). The age pyramid of the population is inconclusive
because of an anomalous bulge above the sixteen-year level. However, it
suggests that there has been a significant acceleration of expansion after
the 1950–1951 smallpox epidemic. There is no indication of a long-term
decline, but rather of a population that had previously been stable or
slowly growing. The writer hypothesizes that the population would normally stabilize about the point of optimum density. Further expansion

would be inhibited by, among other things, the density-dependent and interdependent factors of food scarcity and endemic disease. Catastrophic reductions, such as that caused by the 1950–1951 epidemic, appear to have occurred in the past and would have reduced density, and hence, density-dependent factors of environmental resistance. The long-term decline (Stott 1962:355–476) characteristic of a population that has outgrown its resources and been reduced by mounting environmental resistance would not therefore occur. The population curve would flatten out as a peak is approached and then plunge.

At present, the rate of expansion is high, but the size of the total population is below that at which optimum density would be reached. However, some bands appear to have reached or exceeded optimum density in their territories, and pressure toward fission and emigration of part of the band can be discerned. The symptoms of overcrowding are, first, a realization that food plants around a campsite are not sustaining the band for as long as they used to and that intervals between moves are becoming perturbingly short. The fluctuating annual rainfall and consequent variations in the density of plant food resources masks this state of affairs for two or three seasons. After this time the band has a basis for comparison and can detect, for instance, that this year's plant growth is unmistakably better than that of last season and appreciably better than that of the year before last, but that food runs out after a shorter occupation of a campsite than in previous years and that there are now too many people in the band.

As people begin to feel the discomfort of strained resources, there is an increase in tension and conflicts become more numerous. Tension-dispelling processes are resorted to more frequently and more people make visits to allied bands. In one band, a whole segment went off on a visit and, on its return, decided to set up its own separate camp in its band territory, although it was a good year in which segment separation would not be the normal pattern of territorial occupation. In so doing, the group did not break with the rest of the band, and the separation was not accompanied by any coolness or resentment. Links were maintained by frequent visits between the main camp and the satellite. The tensions in the band relaxed appreciably. In the next stage the segment, with the addition of a few men from the main camp and three households from allied bands, moved south into an unoccupied resource nexus and stayed there for a season. In the winter members returned to their bands and again moved south after the following wet season and remained there for the whole year. This was a new band in the process of formation. The selection of members was on the basis of their fondness for the central figure in the new band, a young man of exceptional ability and intelligence. Some households went "to visit" and stayed; others who joined in the original move returned to their old bands. No hostility, resentment, or rivalries arose and everybody was pleased with the process. From the statements and reactions of informants, and from the behavior of the bands concerned, it was clear that this was an acceptable instance of band meiosis, and it seemed to be representative of the normal operation of the process.

This process of expansion of area occupied by bands and of the network of band alliances and, hence, of the social environment does not amount to much more than a process of repetition. The greater number of contacts and their closer proximity would increase the rate of interaction to some extent, but would not alter its nature until expansion reached a stage necessitating adaptation to encroachment of new bands into established territories. But before this happened, the process of repetition would, if the earlier hypothesis of cataclysmic reduction is correct, be halted. Bands would be reduced in size and number, territories would be abandoned and their link with identifiable bands would be lost; the whole process of meiosis would begin again. The data suggest that this cycle of growth, fission, reduction, and fusion was the pattern in the past.

EXTERNAL

The import of commodities that could not be produced from territorial resources is evidently of some antiquity. Tobacco smoking is a firmly established habit, and the fact that the G/wi word for tobacco, sodisa, is not derived from either a Bantu or European language suggests that tobacco has been part of G/wi culture for a long time. The early European travelers in the Kalahari reported the use of iron by Nharo and other Bushmen to the west of the G/wi. It is probable that this commodity has also been imported for a long time, possibly from the iron-working Tswana along the Botswana-Transvaal border. If these assumptions are correct, the greater range of commodities now imported would not result in profound changes, but would just be the continuation of an old process of replacing older materials and articles with new, more durable, and efficient ones.

The growth of the country's economy, particularly in the 1950s, led to increased attempts to control outbreaks of foot-and-mouth disease among the cattle, the mainstay of the national economy. Among the measures taken was the erection of game-proof fences along the Ghanziland-Ngamiland border and along part of the Ghanziland-Bamangwato border. The fences and the patrols along them were to prevent the movement of game animals which might be infected to and from the districts so separated. The merits of the fences are debatable; certainly Ghanzi cattle remained free of foot-and-mouth, but the fences cut across much of the route taken by migrating game herds at the beginning and end of each summer and, with an increase in hunting, caused a dramatic drop in the numbers of game animals in the Central Kalahari.

At the same time well-equipped hunters started moving into the hitherto undisturbed Central Kalahari, and the extent of their depredations was such that the government declared the 20,115 square miles of the eastern part of the Ghanzi district a game reserve to protect the fauna resources of the G/wi. The tracks made by the Bushman survey party into the Central Kalahari Reserve were followed by Bushmen from the ranches, and those in the remote parts of the reserve were brought into direct contact with Bushmen who had previously been at the other end of a long chain of allied bands. Some G/wi moved out to the ranches on reciprocal visits and, of these, some remained permanently, but the new circumstances did not bring any significant changes in the life of those who remained in the reserve.

The presence of the Bushmen survey team itself, and of the people who periodically accompanied the team, introduced motor vehicles, aircraft, firearms, and other new things. This was new knowledge and led to some change of attitudes, but the only significant changes were in the medical field. New medicines, whether administered on the spot or in the Health Center at Ghanzi, were readily accepted as complementary to the old, and a number of patients who might otherwise have died were successfully treated.

The Botswana government is trying to encourage and facilitate integration of the people of the Central Kalahari into the national economy by establishing training settlements in which families will be trained in a variety of new skills. At the same time the exploitation of game animals as a commercial source of meat is to be researched. If it proves feasible, and early indications are hopeful, Bushmen who have passed through the training settlements will put their hunters' knowledge of game animals to use in the new field and will be smoothly integrated into the wider world of the national market. There will have to be a drastic reorientation of the values of these people, and their cooperative, community-oriented economic system will have to adapt to competition and the concept of profit and loss and a capitalist system of husbanding resources instead of conserving and exploiting them.

NOTES

1. Following the practice of dropping the nominal class prefix of Bantu tribal names, the G/wikhwe ("Bush people") are referred to as G/wi. The second element, -khwe, means "people"; thus G//ana for G//anakhwe, and so on, and G/wi language for G/wikxwisa.
2. See Cole (1955:191–192) for an explanation of verbal extensions. His terminology has been followed where there is coincidence of significance of categories of G/wi and Tswana verbal extensions.
3. The minimum temperature measured by the writer was −13 degrees C (8 degrees F).
4. This is necessarily an estimate; the writer could not observe all households during periods of band separation or during his own intermittent absences from the field. The reliability of the estimate cannot be vouched for, but is as sound as observation and interrogation could make it under the circumstances mentioned.

5. A South African term for sun-dried meat, or jerky.
6. The density of population which the environment can support at subsistence, or bare survival, level. See Dasmann (1966:6).
7. These gross exploitation rates are based on the assumption that gathering is even throughout the area in which plants are collected; this is, of course, not the case, but it was not feasible to measure any more accurately. The figures therefore give no more than a comparison of the seasonal rates of exploitation and fruitfulness of the land.
8. For a description of the ceremony, see Silberbauer (1963).

REFERENCES

Bleek, D., 1928. *The Naron*, Cambridge: Cambridge University Press.
A sketchy and patchy account of the Nharo and adjacent tribes.
Cloudsley-Thompson, J. L., and M. J. Chadwick, 1964. *Life in Deserts*, London: Foulis.
Cole, D. T., 1955. *An Introduction to Tswana Grammar*, Cape Town: Longmans.
Dasmann, R., 1966. *The Relationship of Population Theory to Wildlife Conservation*, University of Adelaide.
Heinz, H. J., 1966. *The Social Organization of the !Kô Bushmen*, M.A. thesis, University of South Africa.
A clear and informative description, mainly of social organization, of the western Bushman neighbors of the G/wi.
Lee, R. B., 1965. *Subsistence Ecology of the !Kung Bushmen*, Ph.D. thesis, University of California, Berkeley.
A closely reasoned description and analysis of the subsistence patterns of the !Kung, destroying the myth that hunter-gatherers constantly live on the brink of starvation and devote all their time and energies to nothing but subsistence activities.
Marshall, L., 1957a. "The Kin Terminology System of the !Kung Bushmen," *Africa* 27 (1).
————, 1957b. "N/ow," *Africa* 27 (3).
————, 1959. "Marriage among !Kung Bushmen," *Africa* 29 (4).
————, 1960. "!Kung Bushman Bands," *Africa* 30 (4).
————, "Sharing, Talking and Giving: Relief of Social Tension among !Kung Bushmen," *Africa* 31 (3).
————, 1962. "!Kung Bushman Religious Beliefs," *Africa* 32 (3).
The first account of professional standard of these aspects of the culture of a Bushman people. Mrs. Marshall was the first person to do systematic and significant field work among Bushmen.
Marshall-Thomas, E., 1959. *The Harmless People*, London: Secker & Warburg.
A popular interpretation of the atmosphere of G/wi and !Kung band life, written with feeling and insight.
Passarge, S., 1907. *Die Buschmänner der Kalahari*, Berlin.
A popular but highly informative account of daily life of north-central Kalahari Bushmen, maily //ai, written by a geologist who was the father of Kalahari exploration.

Silberbauer, G. B., 1963. "Marriage and the Girl's Puberty Ceremony of the G/wi Bushmen," *Africa* 33 (3).

———, 1965. *Bushman Survey Report*, Bechuanaland Government, Gaberones, 1965.
A general and, because of its nature and length, somewhat superficial account of the G/wi in particular, and Botswana Bushmen in general.

Stott, D. H., 1962. "Cultural and Natural Checks on Population Growth," in *Culture and the Evolution of Man*, M. F. Ashley Montagu, ed., Oxford University Press.

Summers, R. (ed.), 1955. *Prehistoric Rock Art of the Federation of Rhodesia and Nyasaland*, Salisbury: National Trust.

Wellington, J. H., 1955. *Southern Africa: A Geographical Study*, Cambridge: Cambridge University Press.

GLOSSARY

!ao: fear, respect

ba:bama: patri- or matrilateral grandfather, spouse's grandfathers, FSiH, MBr

ba:g/wâma: "little father"; designates FBr, MSiH, great grandfather

ba:ma: father, matri- and patrilineal great grandfather and great grandson; the generation after persons termed *n//odima* or *n//odisa*

biltong: a South African term for sun-dried meat; "jerky"

g/ama: postmortem spirit

G//amama: a being of less omnipotence than N!adima

gje:g/wâsa: "little mother"; designates MSi, FBrW, and great grandmother

gje:sa: mother

gjiukxekxu: avoidance relation between kin

g/wâ (-ma or -sa): ego's children; children of siblings of same sex; grandchildren of siblings of opposite sex; children of parallel cousins of same sex; the generation younger than *n//odima* or *n//odisa*, in which case this term is an alternative to *ba:ma* and *ba:sa*

g/wauma: WSiH

g/wausa: WSi, BrW

g/wikhwena: "bush men"; G/wi term for themselves as opposed to other Bushmen

ho:khwudi: joking relation between kin

≠ibina: Bantu

khwe: man, in the general sense

khwena: "people"; used to refer to Bushmen or trusted non-Bushmen

ma:masa or *ma:sa:* patri- or matrilateral grandmother, spouse's grandmother, FSi, MBrW

N!adima: supreme being

n//odima (male) or *n//odisa* (female): grandchildren, the generation after *g/wâ*

/ô:xana: Europeans

pan: a natural basin or depression

sodisa: tobacco

wiku: to love one another

/xajekhwema: stranger; literally, "entering person"

CHAPTER

8

THE !KUNG BUSHMEN
OF BOTSWANA

Richard Borshay Lee

Richard Borshay Lee is currently Associate Professor of Anthropology at the University of Toronto, and received his Ph.D. in anthropology from the University of California at Berkeley in 1965. He held teaching and research positions at Harvard and Rutgers Universities from 1965 to 1972 and has spent a total of three years in field research among the !Kung Bushmen. His investigations have centered not only on human ecology and band organization but also on primate behavior and human evolution. Among his publications is the co-editorship with Dr. Irven DeVore of Man the Hunter.

EDITOR'S INTRODUCTION

The !Kung Bushmen of Botswana number 2000 and comprise, along with the G/wi and other Bushmen groups, a physically and linguistically unique people. The Bushmen are considered to have inhabited all of southern Africa at one point in their history, but most groups have been assimilated or isolated by their encroaching Bantu neighbors or have been killed in wars and epidemics. Much of their final demise has been attributed to recent European movements into the area. The !Kung are the largest and perhaps most isolated of the remaining Bushmen groups, although they have lived in close contact with Bantu ranchers since the 1920s. Today the Bantu pastoralists live in hamlets associated with the permanent waterholes that are frequented by the Bushmen during the driest parts of the year. Some !Kung perform part-time services at these hamlets, but the majority live in independent nearby camps.

The natural domain of the Dobe area is a sandy plain that supports mature open woodland, shrubs, and grasses. Because of the broken nature of the vegetation, however, the area is not frequented by the migratory herds of big game which are available to the G/wi.

The !Kung bands, like those of the G/wi, are flexible in composition. This flexibility is attributed not only to the practical necessity for group fission and fusion but also to the visiting network in which individuals and their families are free to roam from band to band. Lee demonstrates here some of the interrelations between social organization and economic practices and the relations of these to the physical environment. He emphasizes, as Silberbauer does with the G/wi Bushmen, the flexibility of band organization, primarily in light of the minimization of personal conflicts, the importance of congeniality among band members, and, perhaps its corollary, the egalitarian ideal. Comparison of the G/wi and !Kung in these chapters may be most rewarding in emphasizing these bases of Bushmen life in which day-to-day existence is on a face-to-face basis.

Perhaps the most remarkable thing about the Bushmen is the fact of their survival. One would be astonished to discover bands of mounted Indians hunting buffalo on the American plains of the 1960s. Yet the Bushman equivalent of this is what we do find in contemporary Africa. In newly independent Botswana, hundreds of Bushmen are hunting and gathering for a living with bows and poisoned arrows. Elsewhere in the country there are thousands more who have taken to agriculture and stock raising only within the last generation. Altogether there are some 45,000 Bushmen scattered over the territories of Botswana, Angola, and South West Africa, and their numbers appear to be increasing.

When the very numerous Cape Bushmen had been exterminated by the end of the nineteenth century, it was assumed that all the Bushmen were on the way out. Schapera, for example, in his classic *The Khoisan Peoples of South Africa*, tried to salvage what data he could of a way of life that was passing. "There seems little doubt," he wrote, "that the Bushmen are steadily dying out as a race. What relentless persecution at the hands of other peoples has failed to achieve is being slowly accomplished by disease and racial intermixture. Racially pure Bushmen are already in a minority and their ultimate absorption by their neighbors is probably inevitable" (1930:40).

Subsequent events have proved Schapera's obituary to be premature. Mr. and Mrs. Laurence K. Marshall initiated a renaissance in Bushmen studies in 1951 when they began their researches among the 600 full-time hunting and gathering !Kung Bushmen around the Nyae Nyae area of South West Africa. At the same time, Professor Phillip V. Tobias and the Kalahari Research Committee of Witwatersrand University were initiating a series of investigations into the physical anthropology of the Bushmen. Since 1953 new studies have been made by George Silberbauer and Jiro Tanaka on the G/wi of the Central Kalahari; by H. J. Heinz on the !Ko of southwestern Botswana and on the River Bushmen of the Okavango swamps; by Nicólas England on Bushman music; by E. O. J. Westphal on Bushman and Hottentot languages; and by the author and a number of others on several aspects of the Botswana !Kung.[1,2]

In recent years the style of Bushman research has been transformed from a salvage operation to the study of ongoing social and economic systems. This new research has overthrown many of the traditional views of the Bushmen and has played a part in developing a more accurate picture of the hunting and gathering way of life in general, a way of life that was, until 10,000 years ago, the universal mode of human organization (see, for example, Lee and DeVore 1968).

THE CURRENT STATUS OF THE BUSHMEN

Until a few years ago all Bushmen and Hottentots were thought to be included under a single "click" family of languages (Bleek 1929). Due to the linguistic work of Westphal (1963), it is now apparent that at least three and possibly four independent language stocks are present. Although all are characterized by the possession of clicks, or popping tongue sounds produced with an ingressive air stream, the grammars and vocabularies are so different that divisions into independent stocks seem warranted. The distribution of the major groups is shown in Figure 8-1.

The largest division is the Tshu-Khwe group, numbering about 26,000 in northern, eastern, and central Botswana, with outliers in Angola, Zambia, and Rhodesia. The Tshu-Khwe languages show a close genetic relation to classical Nama Hottentot. This resemblance led Westphal to

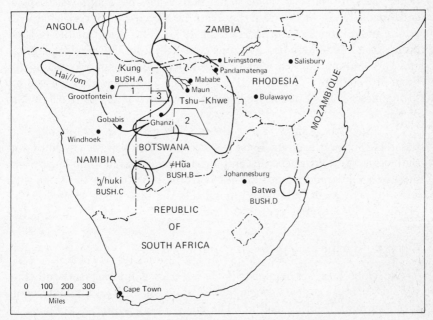

Figure 8–1. Major linguistic divisions of the Bushmen.

label them (erroneously, I think) as Hottentots in spite of the fact that all were hunter-gatherers and lack a tradition of pastoralism in the recent past. Most of the Tshu-Khwe speakers today are independent farmers or workers on European farms and Tswana cattle posts. Especially in the east, they have intermarried with their Bantu neighbors. One Tshu-Khwe group, however, the 3000 G/wi Bushmen of the central desert, is among the most isolated of the remaining hunter-gatherers (Silberbauer 1965).

A second language group is !Xho, called Bush B in Westphal's 1963 classification. Currently numbering about a thousand, the !Xho Bushmen are more or less associated with the cattle posts of the neighboring Kgalahari (Silberbauer and Kuper 1966), although a portion of them maintain hunting and gathering camps for at least part of the year (Heinz 1966).

The third language is N/uhki, or Bush C, of which only six speakers remain, who appear to be the last survivors of the formerly widespread Cape Bushmen (Westphal personal communication). The N/uhki speakers live in the Kalahari-Gemsbok National Park of South Africa and they are the Bushmen that tourists are most likely to encounter. The //Xegwi Bushmen of the eastern Transvaal (Bush D), who number less than one hundred, may also be remnants of the Cape Bushmen. There is a possibility of a remote genetic relation between the Bush B, Bush C, and Bush D languages.

Standing quite apart from other Bush languages and from Hottentot is !Kung, spoken by 13,000 people in northern Botswana, South West Africa, and Angola. Most of the !Kung speakers have been closely associated with Bantu and European farmers since the 1920s. The !Kung of the isolated Nyae Nyae interior, studied by Lorna Marshall, were independent hunters and gatherers until 1960, when a government settlement was set up for them at Tsumkhwe (marked "1" on Figure 8-1). Today they are subject to the direct control of the Department of Bantu Affairs of the Republic of South Africa.

The last of the hunting and gathering !Kung are the 1600 scattered at waterholes in northwestern Botswana between the Okavango swamps and the South West Africa border and around Lake Ngami. The largest and most isolated population in 1963–1965 was the 466 !Kung in the Dobe area, a line of permanent waterholes around the Aha mountains, located at "3" on Figure 8-1.

THE PEOPLES OF THE DOBE AREA

The Dobe area has retained its character as a hunting and gathering stronghold because of its geographic isolation and the unsuitability of its soils and rainfall for agriculture. The eight waterholes are surrounded by a belt of waterless uninhabited country which varies in width from 20–30 miles on the north and west to 60–100 miles on the south and east. The area was unknown to outsiders until the 1880s when European hunters and Tswana pastoralists began to make summer hunting trips to the interior. In 1925 a small colony of Herero cattle herders settled at !angwa, but it was not until nine years later that the British colonial administration made its first official tour of inspection. The Dobe area was relatively peaceful, and since it required no "pacification," little attention was paid to it. In 1946, however, a !Kung Bushman murdered one of the Bantu colonists and this episode resulted in the appointment of a Tswana headman in 1948. Mr. Isak Utuhile has continued to administer justice at his tribal court at !angwa to the present time.

During 1954 the character of the country changed markedly as a large influx of Hereros with several thousand head of cattle entered from the east, having been driven out of the Okavango swamp margin by an outbreak of tsetse fly. Until this date the Dobe area had been in close contact with the Nyae Nyae area forty miles to the west. Visiting and intermarriage between the two populations of Bushmen were common, and many of the Dobe area residents had originally emigrated from Nyae Nyae. Most of the incoming Herero pressed through the Dobe area and built their cattle posts throughout the Nyae Nyae area. The South African Government put an end to this, and for the first time, international politics became a reality to the Dobe area !Kung. The border was surveyed and demarcated, and the Herero were forced to move all their cattle back behind the Bechuanaland frontier. At the present time the Bushmen share their waterholes with some 340 Hereros and Tswanas and several thousand head of cattle, goats, donkeys, and horses.

The pastoralists live in small permanent hamlets of three to ten well-built mud huts arranged in a semicircle around the central kraals where the livestock are penned at night. To some of the hamlets are attached small camps of Bushmen who divide their time between the usual round of hunting and gathering activities and helping the Herero or Tswana cattleowners with herding and milking, for which they receive a daily ration of soured milk, the basic staple of the pastoral diet. Agriculture plays only a minor role in the economy of the Bantu. With a highly variable annual rainfall varying from six to over twenty inches, cultivation is a risky proposition, and crops may be harvested only one year in three.

The majority of the Bushmen (72 percent at the time of the 1964 census) live in independent camps, a quarter to half a mile from the nearest hamlet. The camps consist of a ring of grass huts around a central plaza and dancing ground. These are temporarily occupied for three to five months each winter while the members carry out the complete round of subsistence activities. During the summer months the camps are abandoned as the population moves upcountry to enjoy the resources of the rainy season water points. After the rains, when the group returns to the permanent waterholes, a new winter camp is built at a different site.

The relations between the Bushmen and their neighbors are friendly.

The Hereros are generous, making a point of giving milk, meat, or tobacco to the Bushmen when they come to pay a visit. The Bantu have a healthy respect for the fierce reputation of the Bushmen, and they remember the days when stock theft was a common occurrence. One of the older Tswana residents told me, "I always give tobacco to the !Kung. If you don't, you never can tell when you'll get a poison arrow shot at you."

The principal Bushman-Bantu economic relation is the oral contract in which a young Bushman enters the service of a Herero household as a cowboy. During the one or two years of his contract, the young man shares his meals with the family and is provided with clothing and the use of a donkey or a horse. At the end of the period, he receives a donkey or a goat, or if he has done particularly well, a cow in payment. As late as 1964, cash wages were not known. After marriage, the young man usually returns to the camps and takes up hunting as a full-time occupation, leaving his cow or goat in the herd of his employer. Many of the younger men and women have experimented with agriculture at some point in the past, but because of the unpredictable rainfall, few have succeeded.

In addition, thirteen of the !Kung women have married Bantu and are raising their children as Hereros or Tswanas. A few of the women have adopted the characteristic Victorian dress of the Herero women.

Although the Tswana are numerically few in the Dobe area, their acculturative influence has been more profound than that of any other outside group. Their relation with the Bushmen extends back almost eighty years. Most of the Bushmen speak some Setswana, and dozens of loan words have entered !Kung from Setswana.[3] The outside world is all Tswana and all matters concerning government, modern technology and migrant labor are dealt with in Setswana. The major contribution of the Tswana to Bushmen life from the point of view of Bushmen and Tswana alike is *molao*, the bringing of the law. Ever since the founding of the tribal court at !angwa in 1948, the Bushmen have increasingly preferred to make use of the headman's arbitration rather than attempt to resolve conflicts among themselves. Although homicide occurred at the rate of one every second year before 1948, only two murders have been committed since then, and none at all since 1955.

European influence is still minimal. Government officers are seen in the Dobe area only six to eight times a year and their business is largely with the pastoralists. The Bushmen pay no taxes and receive no services from the colonial administration except for an occasional visit by the medical officer to vaccinate against smallpox.

Knowledge of the outside world has come slowly to the Dobe area. Few of the Bushmen were aware in 1964 that they were citizens of the Bechuanaland Protectorate, and none of the people whom I asked had ever heard of "Africa."

The Dobe area !Kung have absorbed the changes brought by the influx of the Tswana and Herero and have maintained intact the basic institutions of their culture; the language, the subsistence techniques, and the ritual life are particularly strong. The area in which they have been most affected is conflict resolution (see "The Management of Conflict," pp. 359–360).

POPULATION

The life of the Bushmen centers around the eight permanent waterholes. Each person considers himself a resident at one or another of the wells, although all are free to change from one well to another, and each year about 15 percent do. Taking a census of Bushmen is not easy, because a constant flow of visitors makes the size and composition of the camps vary from week to week. In the hut census taken in November 1964, the Bushmen and their neighbors were distributed by waterholes as shown in Table 8-1.

The population of Bushmen at waterholes varies from 10 at !xabe, where a small group is attached to a Tswana cattle post, to 147 at /ai/ai,

TABLE 8-1

THE POPULATION OF THE DOBE AREA BY WATERHOLE, AS OF NOVEMBER 1964

Name of Waterhole and Location Relative to Dobe	Bushmen			Bantu
	Residents	Alternators[a]	Total	
1. Dobe	35	—	35	—
2. !xabe—four miles southeast of Dobe	10	—	10	12
3. Mahopa—seven miles east	33	10	43	65
4. !angwa—thirteen miles northeast (Tswana headman)	45	—	45	72
5. Bate—ten miles east	41	3	44	29
6. !ubi—five miles south	23	25	48	65
7. !gose—twenty-three miles northeast	75	—	75	30
8. /ai/ai—twenty-five miles south	117	30	147	67
9. !gausa—twelve miles north	—	19	19	—
Totals	379	87	466[b]	340

[a] Alternators spend part of the year within the area and part of the year outside it, at Tsum!we, N!aun!au, Nokaneng, or around Lake Ngami.

[b] This total includes 130 persons outside the Dobe area on date of census, but who had been present at various times during 1964. For a head count by waterholes at end of the dry season (November 1964), see Lee 1968:30–31; 1969:57–58.

where seven independent camps are located. Most of the other waterholes support two or three camps with populations of from 35 to 48 Bushmen.

Because of the extremely vague boundaries between subsistence ranges and the frequencies of group changes, it is difficult to specify the population densities at each waterhole. It is more useful to consider the total range utilized by the population in the course of an annual round. This area of roughly 1000 square miles supports the population at a density of forty-one persons per 100 square miles. This is a rather higher population density than has been attributed to desert hunter-gatherers, for whom estimates are in the range of one to twenty-five persons per 100 square miles (Kroeber 1939). The higher figure for the Dobe area is made possible by the abundance of high-quality vegetable foods in the environment: the present level of population does not represent a threat to the resource base.

The breakdown of the population by age and sex and the dependency ratios are shown in Table 8-2. The first point to be noted is the high percentage of old people: 10 percent of the population (forty-six individuals) is over sixty years of age. This should contradict the widely held notion that the hunter's life is so rigorous that people rarely live beyond the age of forty-five. The data suggest that Bushmen who survive childhood may have at least as good a chance of surviving to old age as the average member of tribal and peasant societies.

Among the !Kung the aged hold a respected position; they are the leaders of the camps, the collective owners of the waterholes, and the repositories of traditional ritual-medical skills. Senilicide is rare, and we have observed old people supported by their descendants long after their productive years have passed.

By comparison with other non-Western populations, the percentage of young people is relatively low: 30 percent of the Bushmen are under fifteen years of age, in comparison to 38 percent of the Indian population, 42 percent for Mexico, and 44 percent for the Phillipines. As a result, the economically active section of the population is not heavily burdened by

TABLE 8-2

THE BUSHMEN POPULATION BY AGE AND SEX AS OF NOVEMBER 1964

Age	Males	Females	Total
Old (60 years and over)	17 (7.5%)	29 (11.9%)	46 (9.9%)
Adult (15 to 59 years)	141 (63.5%)	138 (56.8%)	279 (59.9%)
Young (birth to 14 years)	65 (29.0%)	76 (31.3%)	141 (30.2%)
All Ages	223 (100%)	243 (100%)	466 (100%)

Dependency Ratio (the number of young and old per 100 adults) = 67
Child Dependency Ratio (the number of young per 100 adults) = 51

the necessity to support a high proportion of dependents. The young people are not pressed into the service of the food quest at an early age. Adolescents are expected to provide a share of the food only after they are married, and it is not uncommon to see healthy, active teenagers moving from camp to camp while their older relatives provide food for them.

The factors that produce this favorable demographic picture are difficult to define. It seems unlikely that the !Kung women practice a conscious program of fertility control, since they state that children are highly desired and they would like to have as many as they can. Infanticide, for example, is practiced only rarely and under circumstances that the Bushmen consider abnormal, such as the death of the husband during pregnancy, a case of insanity in the pregnant woman, or a congenital defect in the newborn.

There is some indication that the average interval between successive births is four or five years. This long spacing limits the number of pregnancies a woman may undergo during her reproductive span. The women say that it is bad for births to follow one another too closely. They believe that three years is the proper duration of nursing for a normal, healthy child. Another reason they give for this preference is the necessity of carrying infants and young children through the day's activities. Their nomadic life requires that children under the age of five be carried by the mother while she is out gathering food and during group moves. A mother with two-year birth spacing will find at the end of four years that she has a four-year-old, a two-year-old, and a newborn to carry. On the other hand, a woman whose births are spaced five years apart will have only one child to carry at a time.

How often and by what means this ideal pattern is achieved in practice is currently under study by Dr. Nancy Howell, under a grant from the National Institute of Mental Health. Contraception, infanticide, infant mortality, and internal hormonal mechanisms affecting lactation and ovulation are some of the factors that may contribute to the spacing of births.

HABITAT

The Dobe area is part of a level sandy plain stretching from the South West African escarpment in the west to the Okavango swamp in the east. The mean elevation is 3400 feet above sea level. The main topographic feature is the series of fixed dunes running parallel to each other, five to fifty miles in length and oriented roughly east-west. In the spaces between the dunes are an equivalent series of parallel basins or *molapos*. This remarkably uniform pattern is interrupted by several rock outcrops and pans, and in places the landscape is incised by deeper dry-river courses that expose the bedrock.

Digging bulbs in a dried-out pan at the end of the rainy season.

At the winter camps thousands of mongongo nut shells carpet the village floors around the cooking fires.

Cooking in newly imported iron pots goes on side by side with use of the traditional mortar and pestle. There is little direct teaching; this child is using her grandmother's utensils.

A *summer camp in the mongongo nut forests shortly after a rainstorm. The lean-to provides deep shade against the overhead sun and protection against rain.*

The winter dry season camp around the central court. The hut walls are thatched to cut the cold winds and the roof is left open to catch the sunshine. Stretched animal hides hang from the central trees.

A ritual curer, in trance, works over a patient whose leg was caught in a steel trap.

The Tswana headman and his scribe, at desk, hear case brought by Hereros (right) against a Bushman (left, in shadow) for cattle theft, as Bushman women pass by on way to waterhole.

SOILS AND VEGETATION

The soils vary from loose red and white sands on the crests of dunes and higher elevations to grey compacted alluvial soils in the *molapos*. At the lowest elevations, in the exposed beds of limestone, are the eight permanent waterholes. With a highly variable annual rainfall, there are no permanent rivers through the area, but during exceptionally heavy rains the low-lying regions are subject to flooding. Later the flooded areas are reduced to scattered large pools or pans which may hold water for up to six months after the rains have stopped. The direction of drainage is eastward toward the swamps, but all the rainfall is absorbed by the deep sand long before it reaches the Okavango drainage system.

The Dobe area supports a particularly rich vegetation characterized by broad-leaved trees and shrubs on the dunes and flanks and acacias and other thorny species in the *molapos* and river courses. There are twenty species of excellent shade trees, some growing to fifty feet in height. Mature open woodlands with abundant deep shade are more common than are the sparsely wooded open grassy plains that characterize most of the Kalahari Desert.

Apart from the edible species, the habitat provides the Bushmen with an unlimited supply of shade and firewood and a wide variety of fine hardwoods for making weapons, tools, and domestic articles.

CLIMATE

The climatic regime is characterized by hot summers with a four-month rainy season and by moderate winters without rainfall. The Bushmen divide the year into five seasons:

1. *!huma* (spring rains). The Bushman year begins in October or November with the onset of the first rains. These are light convectional thunderstorms which have the effect of triggering growth in plants and reproduction in animals. Overnight the landscape is transformed from a parched dry state to one of lush greenery. The Bushmen take advantage of the water that collects in the hollows of trees by leaving their winter camps around the permanent waterholes and establishing temporary camps in the mongongo nut forests.

2. *bara* (main summer rains). From December to March the heaviest rains fall, bringing with them a season of plenty. In years when flooding occurs, migratory ducks and geese flock to the pans in great numbers while elephant, buffalo, and other wet-country fauna migrate from the swamps into the Dobe area. This is also the period when the major summer plant foods (fruits, berries, melons, and leafy greens) make their appearance. There is standing water at many points in the hinterland and the Bushmen abandon the permanent wells to live upcountry.

3. ≠obe (autumn). A brief autumn occurs in April or May after the rains have ceased but before the onset of cold weather. As the seasonal water points dry out, the Bushmen converge on the main summer pans, which may continue to hold water right into the winter. There is still plenty of food, for the nut harvest is mature and there is still an abundance of the summer berries and melons.

4. !gum (winter). The cold dry season extends from the end of May through August. It is heralded by a sharp drop in nightly temperatures. In 1964, Dobe experienced six weeks of freezing and near-freezing nights. Fortunately, the days are crisp and clear and the temperature always warms up to 24–27 degrees Celsius. The Bushmen fall back on the permanent waterholes or, in exceptionally rainy years, on the largest summer waters, where they build new camps, well stocked with a large supply of firewood to burn through the nights. The diet becomes much more eclectic during the winter. Mongongo nuts and a variety of roots and tubers comprise the staples. The pleasantly mild days are ideal weather for walking, and many people undertake long journeys to visit relatives at distant camps. The fine weather and good tracking conditions encourage more hunting and snaring. Through time, plant foods become increasingly scarce as foods are eaten up in a wider and wider radius around the permanent waterholes.

5. !ga (spring dry season). From late August to the onset of the first rains in October is the most unattractive time of the year. Although the humidity remains low, the days are exceedingly hot, with highs ranging from 35–43 degrees C. in the shade. Working is difficult and the good foods are plentiful only at considerable distances from the camps. It is in this season that the Bushmen make use of the widest variety of plant food species. Fibrous, unattractive roots are dug and eaten without enthusiasm. Hunting is hard work, but the men may go out often, out of boredom with the drab diet more than anything else. It is a time of waiting for the rains to come.

EPIDEMIOLOGY[4]

Because of the relatively high altitude and dry climate, the Dobe area is free from many of the infectious diseases that are endemic in tropical Africa. There is no bilharzia or sleeping sickness in Dobe, although both are found in the swamps ninety miles to the east. The dry sandy soils and the five species of dung beetles solve many public health problems for the Bushmen. The incidence of parasitic infection appears to be low. Gonorrhea, introduced by Bantu men returning from the mines, is the major epidemic disease among the adults. Tuberculosis, rheumatic fever, leprosy, malaria, and trachoma are also present. Colds and chronic sniffles affect the children through the cold winter months.

Fauna

Because of the broken nature of the vegetation, the area does not support the large herds of migratory plains game that are found on the open stretches of the southern Kalahari. Wildebeest, for example, seen in herds of 5000 to 10,000 in the Central Kalahari Game Reserve, are seen in herds of 10–20 in the Dobe area. There has been a diminution of game in the northwestern Kalahari over the past fifty years. Rhino, hippo, and springbok have disappeared completely, while zebra are now rarely seen. Buffalo and elephant were formerly numerous but now are only occasional summer visitors.

Of the forty species of resident larger mammals, the most prominent are kudu, wildebeest, and gemsbok. Giraffe, eland, roan antelope, and hartebeest are also present. Of particular importance to the Bushmen as game are wart hog, antbear, porcupine, steenbok, duiker, and springhare.

The major African predators are all represented in the area, including lion, leopard, cheetah, wild dog, and two species of hyena. The smaller carnivores include caracul, wildcat, genet, jackal, and several species of mongoose.

Unprovoked attacks by wild animals on Bushmen are extremely rare. The people do not regard the bush as threatening or hostile. They sleep in the open without fires when necessary and make no provision to protect or fortify their living sites. The most common threat to Bushmen homes, in fact, comes from the Herero cattle which periodically blunder into camp to browse on the grass huts.

Bird life is remarkably abundant and varied. Some eighty species have been recorded. Ostrich are still common and continue to provide the !Kung with a steady supply of ostrich eggshell water containers and materials for making beads. Only eight species of birds are systematically hunted by the Bushmen for food: guinea fowl, francolin (two species), korhaan, kori bustard, sandgrouse, cape turtle dove, and the red-billed teal.

Some twenty-four species of reptiles and amphibians are named and known by the Bushmen, including five poisonous snakes. Only two reptiles are of any importance as food: the rock python and the large leopard tortoise.

Fish are not present in the Dobe area, but aquatic species such as terrapins, leeches, clams, and snails are found in isolated waterholes, indicating that at some time in the past the area was connected to a river system by flowing water.

Of invertebrates, there is an abundance of scorpions, spiders, ticks, centipedes, and millipedes as well as at least seventy species of insects that are known to the Bushmen. The most important of the latter are the mantises (about whom there is a body of myths), bees (highly prized for their honey), flying ants and click beetles (dietary delicacies), and poison beetles (the sources of Bushman arrow poison).

Almost 500 species of local plants and animals are known and named by the Bushmen. Of these, the Bushmen find some use for 150 species of plants and 100 species of animals. From their virtually exhaustive knowledge of the environment they are self-sufficient, with a single exception. The only item the Dobe area does not provide is iron.

SUBSISTENCE ECOLOGY

The "hunting and gathering way of life" has assumed a misleading connotation in the ethnographic literature. Especially in reference to the Bushmen, the term has come to imply a random precarious existence, one of searching for food and eking out a living of odds and ends. Service, for example, writes of the !Kung Bushmen:

> In utter contrast to the Pygmies of the Ituri forest, the !Kung are a hungry people, their habits oriented around a constant struggle for food and water. Vegetable foods are rare most of the year, as is grass and water that would attract game. The most usual game hunted is a small antelope, birds, rodents, snakes, insects, lizards and the difficult ostrich. Foods gathered include mostly roots and seeds, and in the northern areas fruits and nuts. (1966:100–101)

This description bears almost no resemblance to the !Kung Bushmen of the Dobe area and their neighbors in Botswana.[5] The hunting and gathering Dobe Bushmen have a reliable subsistence based on a systematic strategy of exploitation of abundant food resources. Very little of their food-getting is left to chance. Their knowledge of the local environment, of the habits of game, and of the growth phases of food plants is virtually exhaustive. Information about food is rapidly disseminated through the dense communications network of intercamp visiting. The people know where the food is at each season of the year and how to get it. They do not allow themselves to get into difficult situations, and even during the time of scarcity at the end of the dry season gatherers never come home empty-handed.

What makes their security of life possible? First, they depend primarily on vegetable foods, and these are abundant, predictable, and surprisingly nutritious. Game animals, by contrast, are scarce and unpredictable and the meat is only of secondary importance in the diet. A second factor is the intelligence and sophistication that informs their exploitation of the food resources. And a third factor is the principle of generalized reciprocity that pervades the social life of the Bushmen. Food is shared throughout the camp in such a way that everyone receives an equitable share. This principle extends as well to the relations between camps; local food shortages are always balanced out through the redistribution of population in the visiting network.

THE RESOURCE BASE

The foundation of Bushman subsistence is the over one hundred species of edible plants of the Dobe area. These include thirty species of roots and bulbs, thirty species of berries and fruits, and an assortment of melons, nuts, leafy greens, and edible gums. The most important of the food plants is //"xa, the mongongo or mangetti nut (*Ricinodendron rautanenii*), a superabundant staple which yields both an edible fruit and a kernel. The latter, for example, has a caloric content of 600 calories per 100 grams and a protein content of 27 percent, a level of nutritional value that ranks it with the richest cultivated foods, such as ground nuts and soybeans. Thousands of pounds of these nuts are consumed each year by the Bushmen, yet thousands more rot on the ground for want of eating.

≠m, the baobab fruit (*Adansonia digitata*), is another staple. It yields a delectable and refreshing powdery fruit rich in vitamin C, calcium, and magnesium and a kernel which compares favorably in calories and proteins to domesticated nuts.

//gwe, the sour plum (*Ximenia caffra*), is a delicious tart fruit that enjoys a two-month season in December and January when thousands are havested. The flesh of the fruit is high in thiamin and carotene.

gai, the marula nut (*Sclerocarya caffra*), less common than the mongongo nut, yields an inner kernel which is even more nutritious than mongongo. The nut contains 31 percent protein and extremely high concentrations of calcium, magnesium, phosphorous, sodium, and potassium. At 740 calories per 100 grams, only ten ounces of these nutmeats provide all of an adults's daily caloric requirements.

These are only a few of the more abundant and attractive foods available to the !Kung. The nut species (mongongo, baobab, and marula) are particularly important, since they contain high levels of vegetable proteins of high quality and fats that substitute for meat when game is scarce. Not all the Bushman foods are attractive, however. Some of the larger roots and melons have a decidedly bitter taste and a high proportion of roughage. These the Bushmen eat only when other more desirable foods are depleted.

The vegetable foods are plentiful enough for most of the year that the !Kung can afford to exercise selectivity in their diet. They tend to eat only the most attractive foods available at a given season and bypass the less desirable ones in terms of taste and/or ease of collection. Over the course of a year only twenty-three species of plants make up about

90 percent of the vegetable diet by weight, and one species, the mongongo nut, accounts for at least half of the total (Lee 1968:34).

Game resources are less abundant and less predictable than plants. Meat provides from 20–50 percent of the diet by weight, depending on the season and the number of men hunting in the camp. The general diminution of game in the northwestern Kalahari has not led to the collapse of the Bushman way of life, however, for the hunters have developed their techniques for capturing smaller mammals, and the meat from these kills serves to supplement a diet primarily based on vegetable sources.

At some camps for short periods the amount of game brought in may be much higher. In December 1964, for example, a camp with four hunters killed twenty-nine animals over a seventeen-day period.

The big antelopes, kudu, wildebeest, and gemsbok are regularly hunted with poisoned arrows, but a hunter feels he has done well if he kills as many as six of these in a year. In addition, attention is given to the stalking of wart hogs with hunting dogs. The owner of a well-trained pack of four or five dogs can count on twelve to fifteen of these 100–170-pound animals a year. Duiker and steenbok, small antelopes weighing 20–40 pounds, are next in importance. These are taken with dogs, trapped in rope snares, or, more rarely, shot with poisoned arrows. In the birth season (December to March) the young are often run down on foot or brought down with throwing clubs.

An unorthodox but highly effective hunting technique is the probing of underground burrows. Four important species are taken this way. The springhare is killed with a flexible fourteen-foot pole with a metal hook at the end. These nocturnal animals sleep in long narrow burrows by day. The hunter finds an occupied burrow, probes it with the pole until he has hooked his prey, and then excavates the soft sand until he can retrieve the animal. The large African porcupine (40 pounds) and the antbear (up to 140 pounds) are also underground dwellers. When an occupied burrow is found, the hunters close off the exits and build a fire at the mouth until the half-asphyxiated animal tries to break out. The hunters then finish if off with spears and clubs. Wart hogs are also killed in this way when they have run to ground. There are moments of high excitement here, and when the prey bursts through the flames, dogs and occasionally men are injured in the fracas. The underground species are highly desired because they are very fat, and animal fat is one of the elements most scarce in the Bushman diet.

The game birds, guinea fowl, francolin, and bustard, are captured in ingenious snares when the opportunity arises, as are the small mammals such as hare, bat-ear fox, mongoose, genets, and aardwolf. Occasionally the dogs flush these animals out of the bush and are allowed to eat them. When there is no other meat in the camp, however, the people eat these themselves.

The big leopard tortoise, weighing up to eight pounds, is a great favorite and is easily collected by men, women, and children. It is baked in the shell and can feed a family of four. The nonpoisonous rock python also makes a good meal. Few of the many other snakes, lizards, and amphibians are sought as food. Nor, for that matter, do insects play more than a negligible role in the diet. A species of flying ant has an annual two-day outbreak around December 1 each year, when thousands are collected and roasted, mainly by the young women and children.

By and large, the snakes, insects, and lizards that Service (1962) says are the staples of the Bushman diet are despised by the Bushmen of the Dobe area.

In all, 220 species of animals are known and named by the Dobe area Bushmen. Of these, 54 species are classified as edible, but only 17 species are systematically hunted. These, in the order of their importance, are:

1. wart hog	10. leopard tortoise
2. kudu	11. ant bear
3. duiker	12. francolin ⎱ two species
4. steenbok	13. francolin ⎰
5. gemsbok	14. korhaan
6. wildebeest	15. hare
7. springhare	16. rock python
8. guinea fowl	17. flying ants
9. porcupine	

These seventeen species make up over 90 percent of the animal diet by weight.

THE ORGANIZATION OF SUBSISTENCE

The camp, *chu/o*, is the basic residential unit and is the focus of subsistence activities. It consists of a circle of grass structures with doors facing inward around a central plaza 25 to 100 feet in diameter. The constituent social units are nuclear families related through primary consanguineous and affinal ties and who exploit a common range and share in the products of individual subsistence efforts.

The organization of work is simple. Members move out of camp each day individually or in small groups to work through the surrounding range and return in the evening to pool the collected resources. The sexes are almost always segregated in food-getting activities. The women go out in groups of three to five with a well-defined objective of which species they want to collect. They move to the species area, fill their karoses,[6] and return to the camp, gathering other species along the way to add variety to the evening meal. They are home by mid- or late afternoon and never stay out overnight.

Hunting is a more individualistic activity. Men prefer to hunt alone or in pairs. Game drives are not practiced, and the men see no advantage to putting larger hunting parties into the field. The essence of successful hunting is to cover ground. The density of game is so low that it is necessary to cut a wide swath in a march of eight to fifteen miles through the bush in order to come into contact with fresh spoor. The day's hunting is rather open ended. A man starts with a good lead which determines the opening direction of the march, such as a reported sighting of fresh kudu spoor or a plan to check up on recently occupied ant-bear burrows. Dreams and divination techniques may also give a hunter his lead. But luck plays a major part in the hunt. Men are willing and even delighted to give up the opening lead if a better opportunity presents itself. If nothing turns up, the hunter will usually fill his bag with roots or nuts in order to have something to bring home. In a typical run of days in July 1964, I found that men averaged one kill for every four man-days of hunting (Lee 1968:40).

The men rarely stay out overnight. Even if they have shot an animal in the afternoon they break off tracking and return to the main camp to sleep. Their arrow poison works effectively but slowly, and if the arrow has been well placed, the hunter is reasonably sure that his prey will die during the night. At dawn the next day the hunter makes up a carrying party of two to five men and women and then sets out to track the animal to the place where it has died. It is frequently necessary to drive off lions and hyenas that have gathered in the night before the meat can be butchered and brought home. Kills are sometimes lost to the carnivores in this way, but this is a risk the Bushmen accept. One hunter pointed out that even if he stayed with the prey all night he would still have to leave it exposed to scavengers when he returned to camp to bring back the carrying party.

In the Dobe area the men consistently confined their hunting to within a day's walk of their camps. The long hunting expeditions, such as the four-day giraffe hunt depicted in John Marshall's film "The Hunters" (1956), were rarely observed in the Dobe area, where the men appear to get enough meat close to home.

Within the range men travel more widely than women, and each evening there is a thorough "debriefing" around the campfire as the men relate in detail the latest news of the rainfall, the ripening of fruit and of food plants, and the movements of game. Visitors arriving from other camps add to the discussion what they have observed along the way. In this manner, the members of the camp are kept fully informed about what their environment currently has to offer.

The timing and coordination of the subsistence activities of the camp are difficult to discern. There is no authority such as a headman who directs and coordinates the people's activities. Not even the father of an extended family can tell his sons and daughters what to do. Most people appear to operate on their own internal schedules. On a given day usually between one fifth and one half of the able-bodied members of the camp are out getting food. The others are in camp resting, house cleaning, and making tools, wearing apparel, and jewelry. On most days there are visitors from other camps to entertain and some of the camp members are away visiting relatives at other camps and at the Herero and Tswana cattle posts. A typical week in July for a young mother of two might run as follows:[7]

> *First day*—to the mongongo forests with mother-in-law and sister-in-law; collect enough nuts for three days.
> *Second day*—in camp: rethatch hut in morning, sleep in afternoon.
> *Third day*—visit a married sister at a neighboring camp; stop at Tswana cattle post in the afternoon to ask for tobacco. Return home at dusk.
> *Fourth day*—in camp: youngest child has a cold; visitors arrive in the afternoon bringing the news that a curing dance is to be held at their camp the following night.
> *Fifth day*—to the dance with husband, children, and husband's brother and his wife; stop to collect baobab fruit along the way; dance begins after dark and continues all night.
> *Sixth day*—sleep until early afternoon, return home by evening.
> *Seventh day*—in camp: eat wart hog killed by father-in-law the previous day.

When records are kept on a daily basis of the activities of individuals it becomes apparent that very little time is actually devoted to the food quest (Lee 1968, 1969). In July 1964 the women of the Dobe camp put in only two or three days of work per week. The men tended to work more, but their schedule was uneven. A man might hunt three days in a row and then do no hunting for ten days or two weeks. Since hunting is an unpredictable business and subject to magical control, hunters may experience a run of bad luck and stop hunting for weeks and months at a stretch. Part of the explanation of this stop-and-go rhythm may be that after a run of successful hunting, during which he has played host at several meat distributions, the hunter stops hunting in order to enjoy the benefits of some of the reciprocal obligations he has built up. For example, ≠oma, the best hunter of the Dobe camp, stopped hunting for three months in 1963. He explained that his hunting power was "cold" and that the game "refused" him. He stayed in camp awaiting inspiration while his wife and kinsmen provided food for him. In 1964 his luck returned and he started killing wart hog at the rate of three per month.

The activity diary of the Dobe camp in July 1964 showed that of the eleven men of hunting age in residence, four did no hunting at all while the other seven worked an average of three or four days per week. In 78 man days of hunting, 18 kills were made yielding about 450 pounds of edible meat. Their efforts produced a daily share of about a half a pound of meat for each man, woman, and child in the camp.

FOOD DISTRIBUTION

The net result of the individual subsistence activities is that there is always something to eat in the camp. Food is the property of the man or woman who gets it, yet somehow every member of a camp participates in the evening meal, even on days when only a few of the members have been out collecting. Every evening the Bushman camp is the scene of quiet activity: fires are built up, food is put on to cook, and small portions of foods both cooked and raw are passed from fire to fire. Children are called over to a neighboring fire to have a bite of this or that or to take a handful over to their parents. The men gather at one of the fires to discuss the day's events and, as roasted roots are rolled out of the hot ashes, they stay on for supper.

The sharing of meat is more formally organized than the sharing of vegetable foods. The owner of the meat, usually but not always the hunter who killed the game (see Marshall 1961), is responsible for butchering and distributing the meat.

The style of distribution varies according to the size of the kill. The smallest game, weighing less than ten pounds, such as springhare, hare, game birds, tortoise, and young duiker and steenbok is butchered, cooked, and eaten by the hunter's immediate family and by whoever joins them at their fire.

Game of medium size, such as the adult steenbok and duiker, porcupine, and young wart hog, weighing 20–40 pounds, is usually butchered and cooked by the hunter's family, and portions of the cooked food are distributed throughout the camp.

Larger game, weighing 100–400 pounds, such as antbear, wart hog, kudu, wildebeest, and gemsbok, is butchered and divided into three portions: roughly one fifth remains with the family, one fifth is cut into strips for drying into biltong, and three fifths is distributed to the closely related households in the camp. This latter portion then undergoes a secondary distribution to more distantly related households and to visitors. Each family then cooks part of its allotment at the family fire. On subsequent days when news of the kill reaches neighboring camps, visitors arrive to join in to eat the fresh meat and to receive five or six dried strips to take home with them.

The primary division of meat is carried out with care. The hunter, especially if he is young, calls in older men to advise him, or he may even turn the whole carcass over to his father or father-in-law for division. Due attention is paid to the taboos of each of the recipients, to the size of the family of each recipient, and to the number of secondary obligations they in turn may have to fulfill, and to the current alignments and cleavages within the camp. This latter consideration may involve quite subtle distinctions: for example, if the owner is currently bickering with a brother-in-law, he may tacitly express his disagreement by giving him a slightly less desirable cut or by calling over his spouse to accept the family's portion.

By the end of the fourth day the animal is finished, having been consumed by as many as sixty different people. I never observed hunters set aside a "surplus" of meat for later consumption,[8] although Mrs. Marshall says that the Nyae Nyae hunters do (1961:241). There are two good reasons for this seeming prodigality. The first is that meat spoils quickly in the desert and even carefully dried biltong is often contaminated after 72 hours. The second and crucial reason is that withholding a portion of one's meat would immediately draw the hostility of one's neighbors. On the other hand, the total distribution of meat draws the good feelings of one's neighbors, a feeling that later on will make one a favored guest at the neighbors' distributions. Mrs. Marshall writes:

> The !Kung are quite conscious of the value of meat sharing and they talk about it, especially about the benefit of mutual obligations it entails . . . . To keep meat without sharing is one of the things that is just not done (1961:241).

FOOD AND CONFLICT

Although the meat from every kill is shared, this does not imply that the owner is required to give a portion to *everyone*. When conflicts arise one of the surest indicators of its presence is the apparent overlooking of one of the recipients in a distribution. On one occasion old N!eisi pointedly omitted ≠oma //gwe, his sister's husband and camp mate of thirty-five years, from a wart hog distribution. Only the anthropologist, of course, had the bad manners to ask why. N!eisi replied: "≠oma //gwe can eat from his wife's pot. I gave him his share of all the other ones [that is, previous kills]. This one I want to eat with my friends." Three days later ≠oma //gwe, his wives, and three married sons had left for an extended trip to the mongongo nut forests.

Accusations of improper meat distribution and improper gift exchange are the most common topics of verbal disputes. In many cases they are followed by a group split. Despite their vehemence and the fact that they sometimes break up the camp, these disputes are not as serious as they first appear to be. N!eisi and his brother-in-law have been breaking up for as long as they can remember. Every other year or so one or the other packs up and takes his group off, only to recombine the following season.

Although disputes over food sharing may be symptoms of conflict rather than the root causes, their resolution by group fission serves to underline the basic principle underlying camp life. The camp is regarded by the Bushmen as a unit within which food is shared, and when sharing breaks down, it ceases to be a camp. Persons leave and others come in until the routines of subsistence are reestablished. Absolute sharing is the ideal of camp life but is rarely attained in practice. Fission and recombination of camps are the means by which the Bushmen can combine their search for food with a search for congenial camp mates.

GROUP STRUCTURE

The definition of !Kung living arrangements presents a most challenging problem to the observer. The !Kung commonly live in camps that number from ten to thirty individuals, but the composition of these camps changes from month to month and from day to day.

Intercamp visiting is the main source of this fluctuation, but each year about 15 percent of the population makes a permanent residential shift from one camp to another. Another 35 percent divide their time equally between periods of residence at two or three different camps both in and out of the Dobe area.

The nature of hunter-gatherer social units has recently been the subject of controversy among anthropologists. Service, for example, following Radcliffe-Brown (1930) and Lévi-Strauss (1949), has argued on formal grounds that the basic social unit of hunter-gatherers is the virilocal-patrilocal, territorial, exogamous band. A group of males related through the male line own and exploit a common territory and exchange women with other male-centered groups (1962; 1966:34–38). Recent field studies, however, have shown quite a different picture. The living groups of Pygmies, Eskimo, Dogrib Indians, and Australian Aborigines tend to be open, bilateral, nonterritorial, and flexible in composition (Helm 1965; Hiatt 1962; Lee and DeVore 1968; Turnbull 1965). Many ethnographers would agree that the earlier formulations are inadequate, because they are overly rigid and fail to account for the observed facts. But the problem remains of what to do analytically about the apparent chaos of hunter social arrangements.

The Dobe area !Kung Bushmen are a case in point. Their camps are not "bands" in Service's sense, for they do not consist of a core of males related through the male line. But neither is the camp a random assortment of unrelated individuals whom adverse circumstances have thrown together. What the !Kung camp is, in essence, is a group of kinsmen and affines who have found that they can live and work well together. Under this flexible principle of organization, brothers may be united or divided and fathers and sons may live together or apart. Furthermore, through the visiting network an individual may, during the course of his life, live for a time at many waterholes, since establishing residence at one camp does not require one to relinquish a claim to any other.

The constant circulation of population makes it appear at first that there is no stable basis of residential life and that the !Kung are a mobile people who can live anywhere and with anyone, but in no one place for very long.

The !Kung living arrangements *do* have a stable basis, however, although the underlying principles of association can be discerned only after an extended period of field work. At the center of each camp is a "core" of siblings—both brothers *and* sisters—and their offspring of both sexes, who share a claim to the ownership of their waterhole. These owners, or *K"ausi*, are generally recognized as the "hosts" whom one approaches when visiting at a given waterhole.

The *K"ausi* are simply the people who have lived at the waterhole longer than any others. The camps associated with the waterhole are built up gradually by the addition of inmarrying spouses of the core siblings. These spouses in turn may bring in *their* siblings and their spouses, so that the basic genealogical structure of the camp assumes the form of a "chain" of spouses and siblings radiating from the core, as shown in Figure 8-2. Other means by which the camp is built up are by the incorporation of whole families through primary marriages and of partial families through secondary marriages. At a given time the camp is composed largely of persons related by primary ties: almost every member has a parent, a child, a sibling, or a spouse to link them to the core.

To illustrate the process of group structure, it is useful to examine it from a developmental perspective. Figure 8-3 is the genealogy of the adults

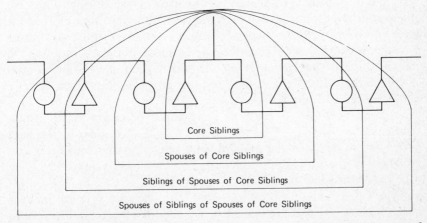

Figure 8-2. The development of a camp by the addition of spouses and spouses' siblings to the core residents.

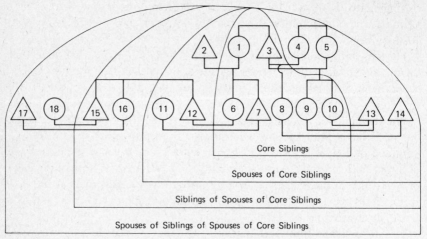

Figure 8–3. Genealogy of the !angwa camp (November 1964). Note two cases of sororal polygyny: 3 married 4 and 5, and 13 married 9 and 10.

of the main camp at !angwa as it was composed in November 1964. The evolution of the camp started around 1910 when //gau (1) married /'ase (2) and brought along her younger brother dam (3), who in turn brought in his two wives, the sisters n!ai (4) and sa//gai (5). The family of /'ase (not shown) died or moved away, leaving (1) and (3) as the core sibling unit at !angwa. When the children of the cores (6, 7, 8, 9, 10) grew up, their spouses (11, 12, 13, 14) moved into !angwa. One of these spouses (12) brought in two of his siblings (15, 16), and these siblings were later joined by their spouses (17, 18).

By 1964, (2), (3), and (5) had died, leaving fifteen adults in the !angwa camp. Of these, one (1) is the only survivor of the original core; five others are the offspring of the core members and constitute the present core. Four others are the spouses of the core, while two are siblings of the spouses and two are the spouses of the siblings of the spouses of the core. The inmarrying sibling group (12, 15, 16) are now in middle age, and since they have lived at !angwa for twenty-five years, they are also considered to be K"ausi of the waterhole.

A second example will illustrate the building of chains radiating outward from core siblings. Figure 8-4 is the simplified diagram of the links in one of the camps at the Mahopa waterhole. The core consists of two brothers and a sister (1, 2, 3) who moved into Mahopa around 1940. Each of them married and brought their spouses in (4, 5, 6). One spouse (4) brought in her brother (7) and his wife (8). The wife, in turn, brought in her brother (9) and his wife (10). Thus Karu (10) traces her link to the core through her husband's sister's husband's sister's husband.

The increasing distance of the married couples to the core is reflected

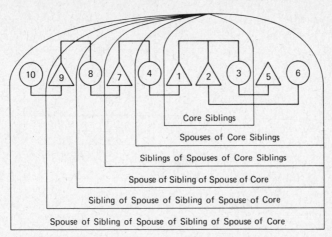

Figure 8–4. Genealogy of a Mahopa camp (1964) illustrating development of groups through chains of siblings and spouses.

in the amount of time they spend at Mahopa. The core siblings and their spouses (1 and 4, 2 and 6, 3 and 5) spend most of the year at the camp, leaving for occasional visits to other waterholes. The couple at the first remove (7 and 8) spend at least half their time away from Mahopa, while the couple at the second remove (9 and 10) spend only a few months each year at Mahopa.

A third case will illustrate a further mode of affiliation: the incorporation of large affinal segments through primary and secondary marriages. The joining of two families through the marriage of their children is one of the important sources of new alliances. But whereas in most societies this alliance is expressed through gift exchange, reciprocal visiting, and mutual interest in the offspring, among the !Kung the marriage may also be the occasion for the entire families of bride and groom to combine in a single camp. The inmarrying spouse may be accompanied not only by his or her siblings and parents but also by grandparents and parents' siblings. In the case of secondary marriages a mature widow or widower may bring in his or her married children and their spouses. These spouses, in turn, may bring in their married siblings.

Each of these processes of group formation is illustrated in the diagram of the Dobe camp in 1964 (Fig. 8-5). The core siblings //oka (1) and her younger brother N!eisi (2) moved into Dobe around 1930. After the former owners died or moved away (1) and (2) became the K"*ausi*. They brought in their spouses (3, 4, 5); the children of these marriages (6, 7, 8, 9) later brought in their spouses (10, 11) to live at Dobe. After n/ahka (11) had been married to 'ase (6) for several years, her entire family joined her at Dobe, including her six brothers and sisters (13, 14, 15, 16, 17, 18), her parents (19, 20), her maternal grandfather

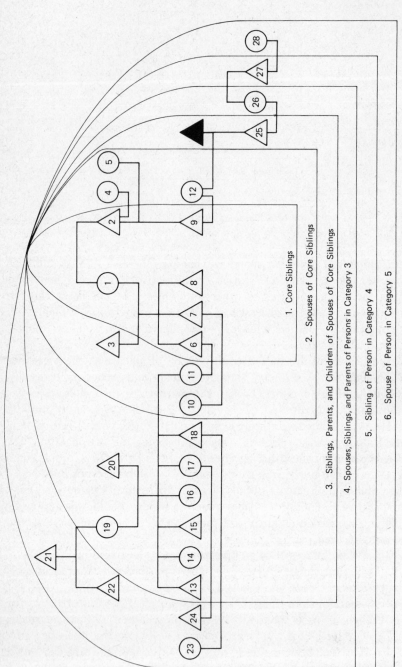

1. Core Siblings

2. Spouses of Core Siblings

3. Siblings, Parents, and Children of Spouses of Core Siblings

4. Spouses, Siblings, and Parents of Persons in Category 3

5. Sibling of Person in Category 4

6. Spouse of Person in Category 5

Figure 8–5. Genealogy of the Dobe camp (July 1964).

(21), and her mother's brother (22). Later, when two of her siblings (17, 18) married, their spouses also came to Dobe (23, 24).

On the other side, in 1955, ≠oma (9) married a forty-five-year-old widow, ≠in!ay (12), who brought her adolescent son (25) to Dobe. Around 1960 the son married (26), who in turn brought her younger brother (27) along. Finally, in 1964 the last link was established when (27) married and brought his wife (28) to Dobe.

Of the twenty-eight persons in the Dobe diagram, six are cores and another six are spouses of cores. Nine more members are the siblings, parents, and children of the inmarrying spouses, and seven are more distantly related. All camp members, however, can trace their relation to the core through the primary ties of sibling, parent, offspring, or spouse.

The closeness to the core is reflected in the amount of time spent at Dobe. For example, six members (17, 18, 21, 22, 23, 24) spent only about three months at Dobe in 1964.

In addition to the camps of one's parents or parents' siblings, one may join a camp by marrying in or by following an inmarrying sibling or an inmarrying child or parent. A married person may join a camp in which his spouse has a sibling, parent, or child in residence. Thus the individual has a considerable scope for choosing a place to live. By one or another of these modes of affiliation people are able to establish a claim at most of the eight waterholes in the Dobe area.

For example, Tsaa is a young man of twenty-five who married n!uhka, a sixteen-year-old in 1965. His mother and a married sister live at !angwa, while another married sister lives at Bate. His wife's parents live at !gausa, and his wife has three married siblings living at !angwa, at Dobe, and at ≠abase (in South West Africa). Tsaa and n!uhka have paid extended visits to each of these five waterholes, spending most of their time at !gausa with n!uhka's parents. It is not yet clear where the couple will settle, but each of these places is possible, and when any of these primary kin shift to other waterholes, additional camps will become available to them.

It is evident from the above that the core units of camps are composed of siblings of both sexes. An analysis of twelve camps showed that a brother and sister formed the core in four cases, two sisters and one brother in two cases, and two brothers and one sister in one case. In addition, four camps had a core composed of two sisters, and one was composed of two brothers. These combinations are to be expected in a strongly bilateral society such as the !Kung, and the results serve to emphasize the futility of trying to establish whether the !Kung have matrilocal or patrilocal residence arrangements.

Related to the bilateral noncorporate nature of the group structure is the relatively short-lived ownership of the waterholes. In all but two of the twelve camps, the present owners of the waterholes were born elsewhere. Typically, the core sibling group moved into the waterhole twenty-five to fifty years ago when one of their number married a girl or boy of the previous core group. The previous cores then died off or moved away, leaving the newcomers in possession of the waterhole.

The causes of the high turnover may be found in demographic factors, particularly in the vagaries of family size and sex ratios of very small populations. Given the small family size and the likelihood of disparities of sex ratios, the probability is extremely small that a family would be able to maintain its numbers at an ecologically viable level if it had to depend solely on natural replacement. For example, if the rule of residence were strictly patrilocal, the waterhole group with all daughters would be quickly put out of business, while the waterhole group with a preponderance of male offspring would have far more hunters on hand than the limited game could support.

A far more adaptive way of maintaining group size and of distributing population with reference to resources is to allow many different avenues of group affiliation. The flexible group structure of the Dobe area is the result. The !Kung do not resort to elaborate fictions to bring living arrangements on the ground into line with an ideal model. They simply leave group and geographic boundaries open and allow the most effective subsistence units to emerge anew in each generation.

KINSHIP AND THE NAME RELATION[9]

If the !Kung had to rely on genealogical reckoning alone, their kin universe would be severely circumscribed. Their genealogical knowledge is of shallow depth; only one or two generations beyond the oldest ascendants are known, and they rapidly lose track of cousins beyond the second degree. This primary kinship system, however, is only the start for an elaborate development of fictive kinship based on the common possession of personal names. There is a limited repertoire of personal names among the !Kung: only thirty-five men's names and thirty-four women's names were in use in the Dobe area in 1964. All names are sex-specific and there are no surnames. Personal names are transmitted from grandparent to grandchild according to strict rules of precedence. There are no "new" names, and the current repertoire appears to have been handed down over many generations. A first-born male is named after his father's father, and a first-born female after her father's mother. The second-born of each sex are named for their maternal grandparents. If further children are born, they are named after siblings of their parents or more distant relatives. A parent may never name a child after himself.

This is only a bare introduction to the many complexities of !Kung naming rules. Readers desiring to go further into the matter are urged to consult Lorna Marshall's classic paper, "The Kin Terminology System of the !Kung Bushmen" (1957).

Their naming system enables the !Kung to extend primary kinship ties far beyond the boundaries of personal genealogical kindreds. In fact, the thousands of !Kung language speakers are connected by name relations into a network of fictive kinship that extends all the way from Angola in the north to Ghanzi five hundred miles to the south in central Botswana. The basic principle is that bearers of the same name have a special affectionate relation with one another, and they use the kin terms "old name— young name" regardless of the actual biological connection. It obtains even in cases where there is no traceable connection at all. The !Kung believe that all persons holding a given name are descended from the original bearer of that name. In the Dobe area, 22 of the 223 men are named ≠oma, and whenever ≠omas meet they enjoy the familiarity of the joking relation. The bonds are particularly strong among men who actually share a common ancestral namesake. For instance, nine of the twelve men named /i!ay in the Dobe area are descended from a single prolific /i!ay. Of him it can truly be said that his name is legion.

This principle is extended widely, so that a person with ego's father's name is treated "like father," bearers of ego's mother's name are "like mother," and bearers of ego's siblings' names are "like brother and sister." It is important for the !Kung to use a kinship term for every person they meet, since the term defines whether a person is in the joking or avoidance category. In establishing a relation with a newcomer or a person at a distant camp, the older of the pair has the right to specify the terms used. He chooses a kin term that he applies to a member of his own kindred with the same name as the newcomer. If no common basis of association can be found, he may turn to his affines or to his sibling's affines to see if the other shares a name with any one of them. With 70 percent of the population using only twenty of the sixty-nine personal names in use,[10] it is almost always possible for a person to establish kinship with another even if he comes from a far distant camp. In fact, there are usually several possible name routes from one person to another. This ambiguity is useful to the !Kung in keeping the kinship system flexible in the face of frequent changes in group structure.

MARRIAGE

The far-reaching ties made possible by the name relation are of particular importance in the arrangement of marriages. The !Kung Bushmen are unusual among hunter-gatherers in that they extend the incest taboo collaterally and forbid marriages between actual cousins. This prohibition sends the young men (and women) far afield when seeking a spouse.

A young man has a wide range of potential spouses to choose from. In addition to his immediate female relatives as far as second cousins, a man may *not* marry a girl with the same name as his mother, his sister, or in the case of second marriages, the same name as his daughter or his mother-in-law. Similarly, a girl may not marry a man whose name is the same as her father, her brother, her son, or her father-in-law. All others not excluded by reason of blood or name-sharing kinship are potential spouses for ego if they are of a suitable age.

The favored marriage is with a woman drawn from the large category that ego addresses by the kin terms *tun* (older) or *tuma* (younger than ego). The *tuns* and *tumas* are the girls with whom ego has a relaxed joking relation, the female equivalent of the cordial "old name—young name" relation. Women classified as //ga, the !Kung say, are "like mothers" and the respect relation holds. Nevertheless, if the //ga in question is not ego's mother's or sister's namesake or a first cousin, he may marry her. Contracting a marriage with a family whose members are already in-laws of one's family is highly desired, and levirate, sororate, and sister exchanges occur fairly commonly.

Men marry between the ages of twenty and thirty, usually after they have served a period as cattle herder for the Herero. Girls marry around the time of menarche, which tends to occur late, between the ages of fourteen and sixteen. Parents try to arrange a match while their children are still young, and one of the more pleasant topics discussed during intercamp visiting is *gau !xom*, or betrothal. Most of these arrangements go by the board, however, since the adolescents of both sexes often have ideas of their own. In current practice there is a period of unstable marriage when young people may have several temporary liaisons before settling down with a lifelong partner. Adolescent sterility makes it possible for girls to experiment sexually without becoming pregnant. Even if a pregnancy occurs, illegitimacy is virtually unknown, since husbands are always found to marry the girl and assume fatherhood of the child.

The qualities a girl's parents look for in a son-in-law are hunting ability and a pleasant, nonaggressive personality. In order to prove himself, the young husband may serve a period of "bride service" in the camp of his wife's parents. However, with the fluidity of group structure, the young couple may spend as much as half of their time living elsewhere, as is illustrated by the example of tsaa and n!uhka (p. 355).

While the Dobe !Kung permit it, they are ambivalent about plural marriage. In 1964 only 5 percent of the marriages in the Dobe area were polygamous. There were six cases of polygyny (and only one man had three wives) and one polyandrous household. Several factors would seem to favor a higher incidence of polygyny. There is no lack of surplus women; in 1964 thirty-five divorcees and widows (16 percent of all women over fifteen years) were living without husbands. Also, the economic burden of a second wife is not great, since it is the women who provide over half of the food for the household. The major obstacle seems to be the attitude of the wives themselves. Many men have said that they desire a second wife, but fail to take one for fear of incurring the wrath of their present wife. Married women threaten to leave their husbands if they bring a second wife into the household; and if a man does, in spite of his wife's objections, she may make life miserable for the junior wife and the husband alike. The women of the Dobe area, at any rate, would not subscribe to Lorna Marshall's statement that "Polygyny is the ideal form of marriage among the !Kung" (1959:345). A marriage to two sisters has the best chance of success, since the girls have grown up in a close cooperative relation: three of the six polygynous unions were sororal in form.

Divorce is common in the early years of adult life. Arranged marriages often fail to prove durable, although the young couple may eventually reunite after a period of traveling around in temporary liaisons. Divorce in both young and older adults is initiated as frequently by the women as by the men. (Lorna Marshall notes seven cases of divorce in the Nyae Nyae region, all initiated by the wives [1959:359].) Wives may pack up and go if the husband is adulterous, if he beats her, or if he insists upon taking a second wife. Divorce is a simple matter, since there is no community property and no bride wealth to dispute about. Children always remain in the "custody" of their mother. In general, divorce does not leave the same quality of bitterness among the !Kung that it often does in our society. Ex-spouses usually maintain extremely cordial relations and may even continue to live in the same camp after one or both have remarried.

After the age of thirty almost all Bushmen settle down to a stable union which lasts until the death of one of the spouses. These unions survive the frequent temporary separations of husband and wife in the visiting network and even such trying circumstances as adultery by either partner, and long periods of hunting inactivity by the husbands. For those who seek it, the Bushman social system offers ample opportunity for sexual experimentation in early adulthood, and this latitude undoubtedly contributes to the stability of marriage in later years.

THE MANAGEMENT OF CONFLICT

Verbal disputes are the common currency of camp life. The !Kung must surely be among the most talkative people in the world. The buzz of conversation is a constant background to the camp's activities: there is an endless flow of talk about gathering, hunting, the weather, food distribution, gift giving, and scandal. No !Kung is ever at a loss for words, and often two or three people will hold forth at once in a single conversation, giving the listeners a choice of channels to tune in on.

A good proportion of this talk in even the happiest of camps verges on argument. People argue about improper food division, about breaches of etiquette, and about failure to reciprocate hospitality and gift giving. The language is peppered with far-fetched analogy and hyperbole. Cases are built up out of an individual's past bad behavior and ancient conflicts are rehashed in minute detail. Almost all the arguments are *ad hominem*. The most frequent accusations heard are of pride, arrogance, laziness, and selfishness. As tempers mount the language and the charges become more and more extravagant.

These disputes are puzzling for their apparent lack of clear-cut outcomes. They flare up and die down without either party giving ground. The bubble of tension is often burst by a joke, which reduces the entire camp, including disputants, to helpless laughter. One is astonished to see two men chatting amicably together who only a few minutes before had been shouting abuse at one another. To a certain extent verbal battles appear to be a game played principally for the fun of laughing about it afterwards.

Not all conflicts are dissipated so rapidly. More rancorous disputes may require the intervention of peacemakers to restore good relations, but several days later one or both parties packs up and leaves the camp. Much of the coming and going observed in Bushman camps can be traced to a recent history of strained relations. When an argument is too serious to be dissipated by rough good humor it is far simpler to split the camp than to stay together and fight it out. Old N!eisi explained it this way: "In the case of arguments in the camp, we sit down and talk it out, and bring in others who know more to listen. But with people like myself who don't want trouble, we will just pack up and go away."

The Bushmen recognize three levels of conflict: talking ($n\neq wa$), fighting (nh!aie), and killing (n!waakwe). They appear to delight in the first level and engage in it at every opportunity. But their dread of the second and third levels is extreme. The word n!waakwe means literally to "kill one another." Fighting as well is to be feared, since the act of homicide is well within the means of all adult men whose poisoned hunting arrows are always close at hand.

The Bushmen are perhaps unusual among human societies in that they attach no value to fighting. They have no ideal of honor or of brave, aggressive masculinity. There are no culturally accepted outlets for physical violence, no wrestling matches, no games of strength, and no ordeals or duels in which a man can "prove" himself. The violent-tempered man and the proud man are sorry misfits among the !Kung, whose heroes are great curers and healers and not fighters.

The extreme fear of violence among the !Kung by and large appears entirely justified: there have been some nasty "punch-ups" in the past and the !Kung have a reputation among their neighbors as fierce fighters. At least twenty-two homicides occurred among the !Kung during the period 1920–1955. The recent introduction of Tswana legal institutions has undoubtedly played an important part in controlling fighting. Today serious disputes are usually brought to the attention of the headman. In one recent case of adultery the aggrieved husband asked a neighboring Herero, "Are you going to take this matter over, or shall I do what is in my heart to do?" The Herero man, of course, interceded and brought the principals to court. My impression is that the Tswana court has proved very successful because the Bushmen have been relieved to have an outside agent take the heavy responsibility of resolving conflicts out of their hands.

THE ECONOMIC BASIS OF !KUNG SOCIETY

Despite the changes that have overtaken them, the !Kung Bushmen of Dobe continue to live as hunters and gatherers without cash, trading posts, wage labor, and markets.[11] One valuable result for the anthropologist is the opportunity to observe how ecological adaptation, social structure, and ideology articulate in a dynamic ongoing system. Because the economy persists, the analyst does not have to rely for his materials solely on a reconstruction of an ethnographic situation that is no longer functioning.

This study has shown, first, that the hunting and gathering way of life is not as rigorous and demanding as it is often made out to be. If we are to understand these societies, we have to go beyond the overly simple argument that hunters are poor because the harsh environment and the crude technology does not allow anything better.

A number of features appear to set the Bushmen and other hunter-gatherers apart from tribal and centralized societies. An important one is their radically different conception of the relation between man and his environment. The wealth of agricultural and pastoral peoples is that which they have been able to develop out of the natural order by careful husbandry and improvement of land, livestock, homesteads, and durable goods. The Bushmen, by contrast, make no sharp dichotomy between the resources of the natural environment and the social wealth. The unimproved land itself is the means of production, and since it is owned by no one exclusively, it is available to everyone who can make use of it. The Bushmen do not amass a surplus, because they conceive of the environment itself as their storehouse. The necessities of the hunter's life are in the bush no less surely than those of the agriculturalists are in the cultivated ground. The Bushmen know everything there is to know about what their environment has to offer. This knowledge is, in effect, a form of control over nature: it has been developed over many generations in response to every conceivable variation in climatic conditions. The Bushmen are not experimenters introducing new crops or domesticated animal species into an unknown habitat. Their adaptation is a conservative one, based as it is on naturally occurring plant and animal species that have been genetically adapted to desert conditions.

Because they know what to expect from the environment, they see little point in bringing the food and raw materials to camp before they are actually needed. The food collected by the members of a camp is distributed and consumed without delay within the boundaries of the camp or by the camp's immediate neighbors. There is no "setting aside" of a portion of the production for consumption at a later date or for distribution to more distant points. This lack of "surplus" requires that a constant level of work be maintained throughout the year. This uniformity of effort stands in sharp contrast to the management of subsistence in agricultural societies, in which an intense period of work (planting and harvesting) is followed by a period of relative inactivity. The actual amount of time devoted by the Bushmen to the food quest is modest, amounting to about twelve to nineteen hours of subsistence effort per adult per week, or about 600–1000 hours a year, a lower level of work than has been observed in some agricultural societies (see Lee 1969).

Another outcome of this relation to the environment is the relatively small investment that the Bushmen make to what may be called the capital sector of their economy. Every adult manufactures and maintains a basic set of utensils considered essential to the tasks of daily life. Lorna Marshall compiled an exhaustive catalog of the material culture in use among the Nyae Nyae !Kung, a list that comprises only ninety-four items in all. With the exception of iron, beads, and pots obtained from the Bantu, all the items of material culture, necessities and luxuries alike, are easily manufactured from locally available materials (Marshall 1961:246–248). Building a house for a rainy-season camp is a day's work; shelters for the dry-season camps are thrown up in a morning. The all-important digging stick can be whittled in an hour, and this will last the user for several months. A complete set of bow, arrows, and quiver takes somewhat longer to make: a man assembles the materials over a period of weeks in the course of normal activities and then spends three or four days manufacturing the kit itself. These weapons will then have a useful lifetime of several years.

Because of the ease with which articles can be made during the abundant leisure time, there is no lack of duplicate items. These are put into circulation through the gift-giving network, called *hxaro*. If an individual receives a valued good such as an ostrich eggshell bead necklace, thumb piano, or a finely carved pipe, he keeps it for several months and then passes it on to a trading partner. Months or even years later his trading partner reciprocates with a similar item. The net effect is to maintain a constant circulation of goods and an equal distribution of wealth among the members of the society. Particularly active participants in the *hxaro* network are not richer than others in the sense of possessing a greater share of the world's goods. Rather, they are the people who have a greater than average number of trading partners and thus a more rapid turnover of goods. Nobody keeps *hxaro* goods for very long.

This lack of wealth accumulation, even though the means for it—free time and raw materials—are at hand, arises from the requirements of the nomadic life. For people who move around a lot and do not keep pack animals, it would be sheer folly to amass more goods than can be carried along when the group moves. Portability is the major design feature of the items themselves. The total weight of an individual's personal property is less than twenty-five pounds and can easily be carried from place to place. When a family is packing, it is remarkable to see all of their worldly possessions—weapons, cooking utensils, water containers, medicines, cosmetics, pipes, musical instruments, childrens' toys, and beads—disappear into a pair of leather sacks the size of overnight bags.

The immediacy of food consumption, the modest investment in capital goods, and the lack of wealth disparities all contribute to the distinctive style of Bushmen social relations. With personal property so easily portable, it is no problem for people to move as often as they do. There is a similar lack of investment in fixed facilities such as village sites, storage places, and fenced enclosures. When parties come into conflict it is simpler to part company rather than remain together and resolve differences through adjudication or fighting.

Although a number of individuals are recognized as the owners of each waterhole, the K"ausi do not represent a land-holding corporate group with fixed membership. Each waterhole has a history of changing occupancy and ownership over the years. No one cares to exercise his authority at a waterhole too strongly, lest his own dubious history of occupation and claim to ownership becomes a subject for searching examination.

Rights of access to food resources, like ownership of real estate, remain open and diffuse. An individual's primary kin and close affines are always distributed at several different waterholes, and through the far-reaching ties of the name relation he may establish close ties at a number of others. The outcome of these multiple options is that an individual may utilize the food resources of most or all the waterholes as long as he observes the elementary good manners of sharing fully with the members of the local camp. Whether an individual will choose to join a given camp depends on the history of his relations with the long-term residents. Many men and women who have a reputation for good humor, industry, or curing skills have standing invitations at many different camps. Even less popular individuals nevertheless have strong primary kinship ties that make them welcome in at least two or three camps and tolerated in the others.

It has become a commonplace in the anthropological and popular literature to regard the hunters and gatherers as living a life of constant struggle against a harsh environment. The nomadic round, the paucity of material goods, and the lack of food surpluses of these people are taken as *prima facie* evidence of the dreadful conditions endured by man in the state of nature. That the hunter's life is difficult is self-evident, the argument runs, for if it were not, surely the hunters would be able to settle down, lay in food reserves, and generally have the leisure time to "build culture."[12]

Data on the !Kung Bushmen of Botswana contradict this view. The people of the Dobe area are full-time hunters and gatherers in an unattractive semidesert environment, yet they appear to work less and live longer than do some peoples with more advanced economic systems. Their subsistence requirements are satisfied by a modest input of labor, on the order of two or three days of work per adult per week. This level of effort is sufficient to support a large proportion of nonproductive young and old people. There is plenty of time to develop the public life of the community. Ritual curing dances with their elaborate trance performances are frequently held, bringing together fifty or more participants from miles around. At some waterholes these all-night dances occur as often as two or three times a week (Lee 1967).

The Bushmen do not have to struggle with one another over food resources. Their attitudes toward ownership are flexible and their living groups open, offering a wide latitude for individuals to choose congenial surroundings. Because the members of the society are not divided into close-knit territorial groupings, defending what they have against outsiders, a major source of conflicts is removed, and it is possible to keep conflicts, both within and between groups, to a minimum by fission. This feature alone sets the !Kung apart from the more technologically developed societies whose very survival depends on their ability to maintain internal order and to control real estate—at the family, tribal, and national levels.

It is precisely this feature that has been and is the fatal flaw in the hunting and gathering way of life, and not its nomadic style and low productivity. In encounters with more aggressive societies, the hunting peoples have always come out second best and have always given up their land base and moved away to avoid or end conflicts with agricultural, pastoral, or industrial peoples. Findings that the hunters of today are largely confined to unattractive marginal areas or to rural slums should not blind us to the fact that the hunting and gathering way of life was a remarkably stable and successful one.

NOTES

1. This paper is based on fifteen months of field work in 1963–1965. Since it was written the author has conducted a further twenty months of Bushman field work. The data from the subsequent research are being published elsewhere. Thanks are due to the National Science Foundation (U.S.), the National Institute of Mental Health (U.S.), and the Wenner-Gren Foundation for their generous financial support. The ethnographic present used throughout refers to the period October 1963 to January 1965.
2. See the list of references up to 1970 at the end of this chapter.
3. Some loan-word examples include *molato*, a case or argument; *molao*, law; *bogosi*, chieftainship; *moloi*, witch. Other loan words have come into !Kung from Afrikaans via Setswana. Some examples are *bereka*, work (from *werke*); *toronko*, jail (from *toronko*); //*orise*, police (from *polisie*); *bankere*, store (from *winkel*).
4. The health and nutritional status of the Dobe area !Kung is being studied by a research group from the University of Cape Town medical school (Truswell and Hansen 1968).
5. In fact, Service may have taken his description of the !Kung from Elizabeth

Marshall Thomas' account of the G/wi, an entirely different Bushmen group living in the Central Kalahari (Thomas 1959). Even for the G/wi, however, his picture of hardship is exaggerated (see Silberbauer 1965).

6. The kaross is a combination garment and carrying device worn by the women, made from a single tanned antelope hide (usually kudu, but sometimes eland, gemsbok, or hartebeest).

7. This is a composite drawn from activity diaries compiled in March, July, and October 1964. A detailed analysis of actual work diaries has been previously published (Lee 1969).

8. An occasional exception is the hide of the animal, which may be consumed as food at a later time when there is no fresh meat.

9. A detailed discussion of Bushman kinship and the name relation will be published elsewhere.

10. Because of differential reproduction, some of the names are far more popular than others. Eight of the men's names have ten or more holders each, while eleven other names each have only one holder in the population.

11. This was the situation as of 1963–1965. In 1967 a trading post was built at !angwa.

12. An interesting discussion of hunter-gatherer economics is found in Marshall Sahlins' "Essays in Stone-Age Economics" (in press).

A NOTE ON ORTHOGRAPHY

/   dental click, produced by drawing the top of the tongue sharply away from the lingual (inside) surface of the upper incisors; makes a sucking sound (for example, *chu/o*—"camp")

≠   alveolar click; the tongue position is the same as for the dental click, but the blade (not the tip) of the tongue is drawn sharply away, producing a flat popping sound (for example, *≠oma*—a man's name)

!   alveolar-palatal click; the tongue tip is pressed against the roof of the mouth and drawn sharply away; a hollow popping sound is produced (for example, *!un!a*—"old name")

//   lateral click; the tip of the tongue is pressed against the alveolar ridge, but the sound is produced by drawing the lateral edges of the tongue away from the lingual surface of the cheek teeth. The sound is similar to that used when urging on a horse (for example, *//gwe*—"sour plum")

'   glottal stop (*/'ase*—a man's name)

"   glottal flap; a glottal stop with a distinctly audible flap of the glottis (for example, *//"xa*—"mongongo nut")

Most other sounds may be rendered approximately as in English. This is a simplified orthography.

REFERENCES

Bleek, D. F., 1929. *Comparative Vocabularies of Bushman Languages*, Cambridge University Press.
A pioneer linguistic classification of the click "family," superseded by Westphal 1963.

Heinz, H. J., 1966. *The Social Organization of the !Ko Bushmen,* M.A. thesis, University of South Africa, Pretoria.
New data on a little-known group; soon to appear in monograph form.

Helm, J., 1965. "Bilaterality in the Socio-Territorial Organization of the Arctic Drainage Déné," *Ethnology* 4:361–385.
An analysis of the bilateral, flexible organization of northern Indians.

Hiatt, L. R., 1962. "Local Organization among the Australian Aborigines," *Oceania* 32:267–281.
Aboriginal organization is reviewed and the universality of the patrilineal horde is put under question.

Kroeber, A. L., 1939. *Cultural and Natural Areas of Native North America,* Berkeley and Los Angeles: University of California Press.
The distribution of ecosystems and cultures of American Indians, many of whom were hunters and gatherers.

Lee, R. B., 1967. "Trance Cure of the !Kung Bushmen," *Natural History,* November 1967, pp. 30–37.
Bushman ritual curing, trance performances, and theory of disease causation.

————, 1968. "What Hunters Do for a Living: or, How To Make Out on Scarce Resources," in R. B. Lee and I. DeVore, eds., *Man the Hunter,* Chicago: Aldine Press, pp. 30–48.
A reappraisal of the hunting and gathering way of life, suggesting that it is not necessarily nasty, brutish, and short.

————, 1969. "!Kung Bushmen Subsistence: An Input-Output Analysis," in A. P. Vayda, ed., *Environment and Cultural Behavior: Ecological Studies in Cultural Anthropology,* New York: The National History Press, pp. 47–79.
Energy and exchange relations of a hunting and gathering society.

————, and I. DeVore (eds.), 1968. *Man the Hunter,* Chicago: Aldine Press.
Fifty contributors discuss the world's hunter-gatherers: their current status, organization, economy, and future; includes results from recent field research.

Lévi-Strauss, C., 1949. *Les Structures Elémentaires de la Parenté,* Paris. Presses Univ. de France.
Classic exposition of the author's theory of kinship, with special attention to Australian Aborigines.

Marshall, J., 1956. Film: *"The Hunters,"* Cambridge, Mass.: Center for Documentary Anthropology.
An epic giraffe hunt by four Nyae Nyae !Kung Bushmen.

Marshall, L., 1957. "The Kin Terminology System of the !Kung Bushmen," *Africa* 27:1–25.
An excellent introduction to the complexities of !Kung kinship and the name relation.

————, 1959. "Marriage among !Kung Bushmen," *Africa* 29:335–365.

————, 1960. "!Kung Bushman Bands," *Africa* 30:325–355.

————, 1961. "Sharing, Talking and Giving: Relief of Social Tensions among !Kung Bushmen," *Africa* 31:231–249.
The central features of Bushman social life and economics.

————, 1962. "!Kung Bushman Religious Beliefs," *Africa* 32:221–252.
!Kung theology and ritual.

————, 1965. "The !Kung Bushmen of the Kalahari Desert," in J. L. Gibbs,

ed., *Peoples of Africa*, New York: Holt, Rinehart and Winston, Inc.
A balanced ethnographic account.

Radcliffe-Brown, A. R., 1930. "The Social Organization of Australian Tribes," *Oceania* 1:34–63; 322–341; 426–456.
The standard exposition of Australian section systems and local organization: his patrilineal horde is now considered a dubious construct by some.

Schapera, I., 1930. *The Khoisan Peoples of South Africa: Bushmen and Hottentots*, London: The Humanities Press.
A compendium of explorers' and early anthropologists' accounts; still useful on religion; out of date on social organization.

Service, E. R., 1962. *Primitive Social Organization*, New York: Random House.
A view of hunter organization that has been superseded by recent field work.

————, 1966. *The Hunters*, Englewood Cliffs, N.J.: Prentice-Hall, Inc.
More up-to-date than the preceding; a useful introduction to the hunters.

Silberbauer, G. B., 1965. *Report to the Government of Bechuanaland on the Bushman Survey*, Mafeking: Bechuanaland Government.
Monograph on the G/wi Bushmen.

————, and A. Kuper, 1966. "Bushman Serfs and their Kalahari Masters," *African Studies* 39:267–277.
A feudal relation in the Central Kalahari.

Thomas, E. M., 1959. *The Harmless People*, New York: Alfred A. Knopf, Inc.
A charming account of the Marshall family's residence among the Bushmen.

Tobias, P. V., 1956. "On the Survival of the Bushmen," *Africa*, 26:174–186.
Recent census shows that the Bushmen are still numerous and many opportunities for anthropological research remain.

————, 1964. "Bushmen Hunter-Gatherers: A Study in Human Ecology," in D. H. S. Davis, ed., *Ecological Studies in Southern Africa*, The Hague: W. Junk, pp. 67–86.

————, (ed.), in press. *The Biology of the Bushmen*, Johannesburg.
A complete catalog of South African medical, genetic, and physiological research.

Truswell, A. S., and J. D. L. Hansen, 1968. "Medical and Nutritional Studies of !Kung Bushmen in North-west Botswana: A Preliminary Report," *South African Journal of Medical Science*, December 28:1338–1339.

Turnbull, C., 1965. *Wayward Servants: The Two Worlds of the African Pygmies*, New York: National History Press.
Contemporary African hunters with a rich food base and flexible social organization.

Westphal, E. O. J., 1963. "The Linguistic Prehistory of Southern Africa: Bush, Kwadi, Hottentot and Bantu Linguistic Relationships," *Africa* 33: 237–265.
A controversial but sound reclassification of the "click" languages.

GLOSSARY

bankere: store (from Afrikaans *winkel*)
bara: main summer rains
bereka: work (from Afrikaans *werke*)

bilharzia: disease characterized by blood loss and tissue damage caused by any of a genus of toematode worms parasitizing the blood vessels; occurs in birds, mammals, and in man; common in Asia, Africa, and South America

biltong: dried meat; "jerky"

bogosi: chieftainship

chu/o: the camp, the basic residential unit

clicks: popping tongue sounds produced with an ingressive air stream

!ga: spring dry season

//ga (older than ego) and *//gama* (younger than ego): kin terms for females; these are females with whom ego has a respect relation

gai: marula nut (*Sclerocarya caffra*)

gau !xom: betrothal

!gum: winter

//gwe: sour plum (*Ximenia caffra*)

!huma: spring rains

hxaro: gift-giving network

K"ausi: the owners of a waterhole; those people who have lived at the waterhole longer than anyone else

≠m: baobab fruit (*Adansonia digitata*)

molao: law

molapos: parallel basins between east-west oriented dunes of the Dobe area

molato: a case or argument

moloi: witchcraft

nh!aie: fighting

n≠wa: talking

n!waakwe: killing

≠obe: autumn

//orise: police (from Afrikaans *polisie*)

toronko: jail (from Afrikaans *toronko*)

tun (older than ego) and *tuma* (younger than ego): kin terms for females; these are females with whom ego has a joking relation

//"xa: mongongo or mangetti nut (*Ricinodendron rautanenii*)

PART
4
ASIA

CHAPTER

9

THE BIRHORS

D. P. Sinha

D. P. Sinha is currently Professor of Behavioral Sciences at the Indian Institute of Management in Calcutta. He received his Ph.D. in anthropology from Southern Illinois University in 1964, and he has conducted field research in central India, the United States Midwest, and the New Guinea Highlands. He has served as a Senior Specialist at the Institute of Advanced Projects, East-West Center (1964–1965) and has taught at universities in India, the United States, and Australia. In 1955 he was awarded the distinction of the Indrajit Singh Gold Medal of the University of Lucknow. Dr. Sinha is the author of several monographs and papers, including his last volume, Culture Change in an Intertribal Market *(1968).*

EDITOR'S INTRODUCTION

The Birhors of the Chota Nagpur plateau of central India are a small group of hunters and food-gatherers, trappers, and rope-makers. They have lived for centuries in close contact, involving primarily trade relations, with agriculturalists, basket-makers, and iron-smelters. Birhor territory is limited to densely forested mountain slopes in a climate characterized by hot summers, cool winters, and rainy monsoon seasons. This climate and the intertribal market on which the Birhors depend for much of their food staples are the controlling influences on their economic activity.

The Birhor socioeconomic unit is the *tanda*, a minimal patrilineage that carries out all social and religious as well as most economic functions. *Tandas* are interrelated through marriage ties, and allied *tandas* cooperate on communal monkey hunts. Monkeys are caught in net traps, and not only is the meat eaten but the hides are sold at the intertribal market. In 1955 the Birhors were moved by the Indian government to agricultural settlements where subsequent adaptive transitions have taken place in their traditional ways of life.

Sinha stresses in this chapter the exploitative techniques of the Birhors as both food-gatherers and hunters and as a people dependent on an intertribal market—a rather uncommon but not unique situation for hunting and gathering peoples. So stable was this situation that it would be difficult to imagine a time in which the Birhors were totally self-sufficient despite the abundant resources of their physical environment.

In contrast to other societies represented here, except perhaps the Mistassini Cree, the Birhors have developed positions of leadership within the *tanda*. Like the Mistassini, this may have been in response to the introduction of extragroup trade. Comparison of the Birhors and the Paliyans indicates two different responses to pressures from outside groups: the Birhors in a cultivation of dependence and to some extent interdependence with other peoples through the intertribal market, and the Paliyans in their fierce individualism and emphasis on avoidance of interaction with other groups.

HISTORY

The Birhors have no recorded history, but they do have folk history which credits them as the first people to occupy the Chota Nagpur plateau. They believe they have continued to practice their aboriginal way of life while some of their tribe incorporated various alien ways of living. This they see as evidenced by their contemporary cognates: the shifting cultivator Birjia; the basket-maker Mahli; the agriculturalist Munda. The Birhors were pushed farther into the forest when the Dravidian Oraon appeared over 2500 years ago and occupied the more hospitable part of the region.

Although there is no record of the origin of nomadism among the Birhors, there are historical evidences of the emergence of sedentary habits among some sections of the tribe. Roy (1925:35) writes that there are some families of the Birhors which have settled down for a comparatively long period, generally on some hilltop or on the outskirts of a jungle. A few Birhors of this class may squat on land near the hillside or clear some land in the jungle for purposes of more or less permanent cultivation, but the majority are landless and live mainly by hunting and by making and selling ropes. Sometimes they rear a scanty crop of maize or beans by burning a patch of jungle, scratching the soil, and sowing seed in the ashes. Even the landed Jaghi Birhors rarely stop at one place for any considerable length of time. Indeed, there is no Jaghi settlement I have known that is more than ten to fifteen years old. Some Jaghi Birhors have also been known to revert to their old nomadic life.

LANGUAGE

Linguistically, the Birhors are related to their Munda-speaking tribal neighbors in Bihar, who in turn form a part of the Austro-Asiatic language group. The dialect of the Birhors is called Birhori. While it is distinct from the Mundari and the Asuri, the other two related dialects spoken in the area, these are mutually understood by the native speakers. Most Birhors are bilingual, also speaking Sadani, a dialect of the Indo-European Hindi, the *lingua franca* of the region.

ETHNIC DESCRIPTION

Racially, along with other aboriginal populations of central India, the Birhors have been classified as proto-Australoid (Guha 1944). They are considered to be one of the earliest aboriginal tribes inhabiting the Chota Nagpur region of Bihar, but it is doubtful if they represent an unmixed racial type. There has been no study, as such, of the racial features of the Birhors. Roy (1925) has described them as roundheaded and broad-nosed, with a protruding face, and of medium build. Their skin is brown and their black hair ranges from curly to wavy. They are short-statured, rarely exceeding 5½ feet. The men have scanty facial hair. These Birhor physical features are shared, in varying degrees, by other aboriginal groups in the region.

OTHER TRIBES

The Birhors settled their country alongside several other aboriginal tribes in the area—primarily the agricultural Oraon, the horticultural Birjia, the basket-maker Turi, and the iron-smelter Asur. Each of these communities has a particular and exclusive ecological niche on which it depends for its livelihood (Fig. 9-1).

THE NATURAL DOMAIN

Terrain and Climate

The country of the Birhors comprises three distinct ecological zones. The hills and plateaus, characterized by rocky upland with small scattered deposits of iron ore and dry forest, make the first. The valley, dominated by a fertile paddy land intersected by rivers and streams, makes the second. The escarpments and slopes, between the first two zones, marked by luxuriant growth of wild trees, bamboos, and other fibrous plants, make the third ecological zone. It is the latter, the forest, that constitutes the ecological niche of the Birhors.

Climatically, the whole region is characterized by severe heat during

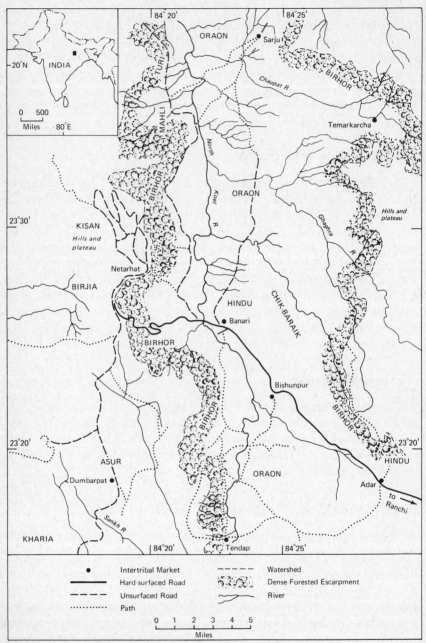

Figure 9–1. Birhor country.

summer (maximum temperature 104 degrees F), cold during winter (minimum temperature 21 degrees F), and heavy rainfall (72 inches during the monsoons). Rainfall, topography, and the drainage pattern markedly influence the vegetation and animal life of the region (Fig. 9-1).

TOTAL ENVIRONMENT

The Birhors live in the forest, where a wide variety of game is found, including elephant, tiger, leopard, hyena, bear, wolf, wild cow, deer, monkey, porcupine, hare, and squirrel. The larger animals are a constant threat to the life of the people who wander in the forest; in fact, such animals are difficult for the Birhors to hunt or trap with their limited technology. Of greatest importance to the Birhors are the animals that can be trapped with nets. The monkey is the biggest animal trapped; its meat is a delicacy and its skin provides the best hide for making drums. Monkey hunts are among the few collective activities of the Birhors. The number of monkeys in a forest is, however, limited, and such hunts are seasonal and infrequent. During winter and spring the Birhors trap porcupine, hare, and rat, whose meat they greatly enjoy. Of necessity, then, the Birhors are hunters and trappers of lower forms of animal life.

The forest supports a tropical vegetation consisting of timber trees like sal (*Sharea Robousta*) and the gambar (*Gomelina Arborea*); wild fruit trees like the jamun (*Eugenia Jampolena*), the bair (*Zezyphus Jujuata*), and the mahua (*Bassia Latifolia*); and several kinds of wild timbers plus bamboos and the *chop*, a fibrous creeper (*Bahemia Scandenes*). Such vegetation has very limited value for Birhor technology, and therefore the people circumscribe their activities mainly to the collection of wild roots and fruits and/or creepers for making ropes for intertribal market.

The natural environment of the Birhors together with their simple technology directly influence the size and composition of their *tanda* (band) encampment and its pattern of mobility. Movement of a *tanda* is caused by depletion of the natural resources in the area. The Birhors also believe that an area must be left unexploited, in a sort of fallow system, for a period of time ranging from one to four years, so that it may regenerate. Whenever the need for movement of a *tanda* arises, scouts are sent in different directions in search of another site of encampment where the resources are plentiful enough to sustain the tanda for at least a year.

A *tanda* on an average stays at a site for one and a half years, although the range of duration of a camp varies from three months to four years. Selection of a new site depends upon four principles: (1) nearness to forest resources; (2) proximity to water supply, streams, or rivers; (3) distance from another *tanda* already located in the vicinity; and (4) proximity to an intertribal market.

SOCIAL ORGANIZATION

A *tanda*, on an average, comprises eight *kumba*, though the number varies from five to twelve. A *kumba* is a conical leaf hut erected from poles and thatched by leaves. It takes less than a day for a couple to erect a *kumba*, which is about 6 feet high at the center with an arched narrow entrance and a base diameter of about 10 feet. One has to crawl to get inside; even for the Birhors it is not possible to stand erect inside except at the center. A *kumba* offers, to the Birhors, a weatherproof and cozy accommodation, of which they often speak proudly.

The population of a *tanda* varies a great deal, from twelve to seventy, with an average consisting of thirty-five persons. The scarcity of the forest resources, especially the availability of *chop* fibers, is the crucial factor in determining the size of a *tanda*. Variation in climate through seasons makes the availability of wild fruits and roots, creepers, and animal resources unpredictable. Monkeys may be so numerous in certain areas that people assemble from several *tandas* to organize a communal hunt; and then it may not be possible to have a communal hunt again in the same area until several years have elapsed. Their ecology, therefore, puts a premium not only on the size of a *tanda* but also on the nature and timing of inter*tanda* cooperation.

The yield of a communal hunt may be enough to support a larger population than a *tanda*, but the absence of preservation and storing techniques has reduced the value of animal products. Were the Birhors able to store the animal and forest products, it is possible that fairly permanent settlements would develop along certain rich forest zones. In the absence of this possibility, the habitation density of the Birhors is limited to a few families and to occasional contacts between *tandas* in the region. The size of a *tanda* is also limited because of the importance of wild roots, which puts a premium upon separation rather than upon cooperation. A small group can collect more wild roots and fruits if it has an area of its own. As in hunting of monkeys, participation of many persons in the collection of wild roots and fruits not only puts a check on increased output but it often decreases it so greatly that small groups of Birhors prefer to remain alone so as not to compete with other *tandas*.

A monkey hunt of this type, when held, yields not only meat, which the Birhors consider a delicacy, but also hides, which make excellent dance drums and fetch a handsome return in the neighboring markets. The only distinctive technological equipment for this hunt is the indigenous rope net. A number of these nets are placed end to end to form a huge semicircle. Some persons stand by the nets quietly and the rest go over a wider area, beating the trees and pursuing the monkeys toward the net. When a number of monkeys come closer to the net, the net is thrown over them. They are thus trapped alive or beaten with clubs and killed.

There are more frequent hunts of monkeys, porcupines, and other animals on a small scale, where only members of a *tanda* participate. Although in these the net yield is less than in the communal hunts, the Birhors prefer to hunt without inviting persons from other *tandas*, in order to conserve the limited game available in the region. Scarcity of game again puts a premium on the development of larger settlements among the Birhors.

In exploring most resources each Birhor *tanda* restricts itself by common understanding to a limited area. As long as it camps at a particular spot, its members occupy forest zones which are exclusively theirs. *Tandas* camp five to ten miles apart and almost never trespass on one another's territory.

The activities of a *tanda* are influenced by the variation in seasons. During spring, summer, and winter months of a normal year, the forest yields a quantity and variety of food which supplies most of the Birhors' dietary needs, but during the three months of the monsoon rains, the Birhors experience a period of scarcity. During the monsoon, the streams, with a sudden rise of water level, are difficult to negotiate; plant food and game are in short supply and the tasks of foraging and trapping become extremely difficult. The monsoon, being the period in which forest vines and creepers grow, also limits the quality and quantity of raw material required for the production of marketable commodities.

With a simple technology a Birhor *kumba* generally owns one or more nets, 30 feet by 6 feet, for hunting monkeys, 6 feet by 2 feet for trapping small animals, one steel net, a sickle, and a knife. The Birhors have developed an efficient ecological adjustment in a complex environment. They experience periods of scarcity but seldom a spell of starvation. Theirs is, however, truly a subsistence economy. Of their harmony with nature, the Birhors often say, "When we skin trees and cut vines we do not hunt them; we help them in their further growth." What the Birhors mean precisely is that they do not exploit nature; they work in cooperation with it.

ECONOMIC FEATURES

The Birhors traditionally undertake a wide range of economic activities or, stated another way, they exploit a wide range of forest resources to obtain their livelihood. The products are either consumed by the household or prepared for sale at an intertribal market. Production for home consumption centers on the gathering of wild fruits, roots, and leaves and the trapping of small animals, including porcupine, hare, rats, and monkeys. Food-gathering is the main task of the Birhor women, while the men do the trapping. Production for the market consists of rope-making, using forest vines; the manufacture of wooden vessels carved from forest timber; and various minor occupations such as collecting honey, bees wax, and wildflowers (used in the fermentation process of beer); and curing monkey hides, used in drum-making.

The two main influences on the economic activities of the Birhors are the climate (season to season and year to year), which affects the supply of raw materials available for home consumption and for production of marketable commodities, and the nature of the market, which dictates the commodities to be produced and the quantities required at any one time.

The Birhors manufacture three types of rope, all from vines collected in the forest. At the present time, they utilize a rope-making machine and raw materials that were unknown until 1961. The first, the *dora*, about 20 feet long, is specifically used in drawing water from wells by bucket. The second is the *pagha*, 6–7 feet long, used for controlling livestock. (There are special *paghas* for cows, calves, goats, bullocks, and so on.) The third is the *sika*, a short web of rope used for suspending storage baskets inside houses. A *dora* lasts about six months if carefully used, but has a short life if used during the rainy season. A *pagha* must be replaced annually, while a *sika* lasts perhaps as long as two years, depending on where it is hung (only six months if hung over the hearth).

Paghas are in greatest demand after the monsoon rains when livestock owners wish to control grazing activities. *Doras* and *sikas* are in demand throughout the year. The demand for *doras* is slack during the wet season and at a maximum in the summer months and sowing seasons.

The Birhors manufacture four types of wooden products. The most important are the *kathout*, a type of basin made in two sizes, and the *kathola*, used as a container for cooked rice. They also fashion wooden drum cases (*dhols*) and a minor number of wooden ladles (*daboos*). A few regional groups do not purchase Birhor *kathouts* and *katholas*, namely, the Asurs, Birjias, and Turi, who make their own vessels. For the rest, most households have an average of two *kathouts* and two *katholas*.

All groups in the region purchase Birhor drums—or rather the components, drum cases and monkey hides. Actually, another group, the Ghansi, finishes the assembly of drums. This drum is used for ceremonial and festive occasions, but more important, it is used by people to drive off wild animals while traveling to and from the market and to scare off animals from standing crops—for example, roving bears that damage the maize crops of the plateau.

Most families have one or more Birhor drums, and those relatively well off have as many as four. Each drum lasts about five years.

The demand for these wooden products is distributed evenly throughout the year, but is slack for all during monsoon season. It is worth noting, though, that the sale of monkey hides for drums is determined as much by the success of trapping expeditions as by the market demand. There is seldom any excess of supply over demand in the market for Birhor drums.

The quantities of honey and beeswax marketed by the Birhors depend on rather irregular collections, which are made incidentally on trips to the forest organized for other purposes. Demand for these products comes partly from the few relatively affluent Hindu neighbors who can purchase in some quantity and partly from other households that customarily wish to have a small bottle of honey on hand for medicinal purposes. An average Birhor family collects about 8–10 pounds of honey and 20–24 pounds of wax annually.

It is worth noting here that a Birhor *tanda* using a particular regional market, such as Banari, monopolizes this market during the period it is located near the market. By agreement, only one *tanda* has the right to sell at this market, except under special circumstances when permission is given for others to enter and sell their produce. By this means, therefore, a *tanda* protects itself against outside competition from other *tandas*.

Food-gathering is the chief task associated with the nonmarket activities of the Birhors, and this is chiefly the women's responsibility. The men contribute directly to the food supply from their trapping work, but most of the men's activities center on the production of marketable goods—ropes, wooden products, monkey hides—and the gathering of saleable produce such as honey and wax and wildflowers.

It is characteristic that within a *tanda* each household produces the same commodities for market and, with minor variations due, for example, to personal differences in abilities and capacities, each household produces somewhat the same quantity of these goods. There is no evidence of any explicit agreement to this effect, but the manner in which tasks are organized suggests that a system of market sharing has become implicit and customary in the Birhor economic system. For example, in rope-making, *tanda* males go out as a group to the forest to cut vines, return together to make the ropes, and then market them at the weekly market. The situation is different only in detail for wooden products. For these, the weekly market demand clearly would not absorb the numbers produced had all the *tanda* males concentrated on these lines at the same time. The *tanda*, apparently recognizing this, splits the members into smaller groups whose total weekly output roughly equals the expected demand in the market. The groups rotate, thus giving all an equal access to the market for these products over the whole year. Such communal rhythms in these activities naturally promote an equalization of economic opportunities within a *tanda*.

Aside from day-to-day subsistence work, economic activities are organized with a view to the weekly market day. In rope-making, the head of the household typically spends one full day in the forest (twelve hours, including traveling time), five days back in the *tanda* manufacturing ropes from vines, and usually one day selling the ropes in the market. The quantity of vines collected during an excursion to the forest varies

A Birhor inside his kumba. Note the belongings on the floor and hanging from the roof.

A Birhor profile.

A kumba, *the Birhor leaf hut.*

A Birhor on the way to a monkey trapping with his net.

A Birhor dance. The participants are dressed in neighboring Hindu costume.

seasonally and ranges from lengths sufficient for five *doras* to enough for ten *doras*, with an average collection sufficient for about seven *doras*.

According to the calculations above, some 10,000 *doras* are sold annually, or about 100 per household, so that about twelve weeks might be absorbed in the manufacture of this type of rope. By the same calculations, the average number of *paghas* made annually per household is probably about 200, and being one third the length of *doras* and involving roughly the same work per foot, they are probably able to make about twenty-five per week. Consequently, about eight weeks are spent annually in this occupation. *Sikas* are shorter in length but more complex to make than the other ropes. Above calculations suggest that a household might produce thirty annually, about four per week, so that about seven weeks might be absorbed for the working time of the adult male Birhor in rope-making.

One informant gave an estimate of eighteen to twenty-two *kathouts* and *katholas* produced per Birhor household per year. In order to produce the vessels, a small group of men from the *tanda* spend about three days continuously in the forest. The group combines to fell trees for each man in the group. Then each man chops his tree into "suitable" lengths from which he generally fashions five wooden vessels of various sizes. The men return to the settlement and spend another three days preparing the vessels for sale at the weekly market. On a twelve-hour-day basis, therefore, they produce five articles in a week's work of seventy-two hours. Thus, with an annual output of about twenty or so *kathouts* and *katholas*, which require about one month's work, and, in addition, about a half-dozen drum cases (*dhols*) and a number of ladles (*daboos*), the Birhor male is probably employed for one and a half months or more annually on production of wooden products.

As mentioned above, collection of honey and beeswax and/or wild-flowers is carried on incidentally to other tasks and absorbs no important or particular portion of the Birhor labor time. The only activity that does demand a significant labor input is the periodic monkey hunt. It is difficult to estimate how often these are undertaken, however. Usually the men of one or more *tanda* spend about three days in the forest on a hunt, and if successful, return to the village to cure the skins, preparing them for the market. From the limited data available, it is possible to estimate that trapping monkeys and other animals involves each male in a month's work per year.

These estimates of activities suggest that a total of nine months or more of the male's working hours are absorbed in the above tasks. This roughly corresponds to the available time in the nonmonsoon months. For the other two-and-a-half months of the monsoon season, the economic activities of the Birhors are severely curtailed and mainly consist of searching for wild fruits and roots. The group still attends the Banari market during this period, mainly to make purchases and not to sell their own products.

The Birhors use a minimum of tools and equipment in the course of their economic activities, and only a portion of these are purchased from other groups. They make their own rope nets for trapping and use their own ropes for various purposes. They purchase iron axes for felling trees and a large chopper knife for slashing jungle growth and for cutting vines for ropes. All of these are purchased from the neighboring Asurs. They also use a balance for transportation and purchase baskets from the Turi, another regional community, to hang from the ropes at either end of the wooden pole.

From the preceding calculations it is possible to provide an estimate of the annual money income which an average Birhor household might earn from the sale of marketable products (Table 9-1). As shown, the total money value of sales amounts to 137 rupees[1] annually, or about 11 per month on the average. It should be remembered that there is a substantial month-to-month fluctuation, and, in particular, for almost three monsoon months the Birhors earn virtually no income at all.

Actually, in the traditional economy, ropes and sometimes *kathouts* and *katholas* were bartered for cereals (paddy or maize). Each *dora* was worth about 3 pounds of paddy, each *pagha* brought 1 pound, and a *sika* could

TABLE 9-1

ANNUAL BIRHOR INCOME PER HOUSEHOLD FROM MARKETED COMMODITIES

Commodity	Average Annual Number	Price per Unit	Total Value (rupees)	Percent of Money Income
Ropes				
dora	100	20 Paise	19	14
pagha	200	13 Paise	25	18
sika	30	50 Paise	15	11
Kathouts				
large	5	2 Rupees	10	7
small	4	1 Rupee	4	3
Kathola	12	20 Paise	2	1
Dhol	6	2 Rupees	12	9
Daboo	15	20 Paise	3	2
Honey	10 lb	1.5 RS/lb.	15	11
Beeswax	24 lb	1.0 RS/lb.	24	18
Monkey hides	8	1 Rupee	8	6
Estimated total annual income			137	100

1. Numbers are based on estimates given by Birhor informants.
2. Prices were average market prices ruling in the Banari market over a three-month period from June to August 1966.
3. There is also a minor income source in wildflowers.

be exchanged for 6 pounds. Thus the paddy equivalent of the annual rope production listed above was approximately 680 pounds. On the assumption that this barter did, in fact, take place, the actual money income would have been only 94 rupees annually, or an average of 8 rupees per month.

If the money equivalent of the ropes is included, some 43 percent of total marketed income stems from rope production, about 22 percent from wooden vessels, and 29 percent from sale of honey and beeswax.

It is possible, both by direct observation and from interviews, to obtain a rough picture of Birhor consumption patterns, particularly in relation to purchases made in the Banari market from other regional groups.

Undoubtedly, the major category of purchases from the market is food. As indicated above, the food supply from the forest appears to provide a reasonable dietary level and balance for about nine months of the year, although the Birhors continually supplement this to some extent with purchased food, for example, paddy or maize, salt, and oil. However, during the monsoon season, forest food is always in short supply and the Birhors find it necessary to rely heavily on purchased food, particularly cereals. Since the monsoon season is also a period when they sell few commodities on the market themselves, the Birhors generally have to spend money saved from other seasons specifically to meet their needs in the period of scarcity. Over-all, they probably spend in excess of 42 percent of their income on cereals alone, since they typically barter their ropes for paddy or maize. Other than cereals, salt, and oil, they purchase only rice beer and tobacco among "food" items.[2]

Their clothing requirements are minimal. The men wear a type of loincloth, and the women dress in a sort of "lap-lap," a wrap-around cloth, both of which are purchased from the Baraik weavers. Each man and woman probably purchases a few combs from the Mahli and some earthenware each year from the Kumhar potters (they make their own wooden vessels for various purposes), and some individuals obtain metal ornaments from the Malhars. Birhor houses are made of wooden poles with leaf thatching and necessitate no purchase items.

It should be clear from the above discussion of the activities and living habits of the Birhors that they lead extremely simple lives in a material sense, with living standards barely above minimum subsistence levels. Furthermore, they appear to have been forced to divide their economic activities between production for home consumption and for the market and to widely diversify their market-production activities in order to reach even this standard. It is likely, for example, that had they not been able to develop and market some specialties such as ropes and wooden vessels and to save at least a portion of the proceeds, the monsoon season would have been a period of near starvation instead of merely a time of scarcity, as it was traditionally.

It is also apparent that the Birhors traditionally exploited the resources of the forest to the fullest to achieve the living standards described above. The clearest evidence of this is the periodic necessity for *tandas* to move to new forest locations as the resources in the old ones became depleted. They seem quite conscious of the need for conservation in order to maintain the long-term yield of the forest. This means, however, that it is difficult to boost production for home consumption or for the market without commencing to damage the long-term regenerative capacity of the forest.

Even if resources have not been fully exploited, it is unlikely that further exploitation could result in any substantial gains in net income and higher living standards for the Birhors. This is primarily due to the apparently inelastic demand for the important marketable commodities. In one direction, the fact that many of their products—for example, ropes for drawing water, tethering animals, and suspending storage containers—are regarded as necessities by other groups is advantageous, and a market is always assured for these commodities, especially since, traditionally, there were no acceptable substitutes. However, the inelasticity also works the other way. Although these commodities are needed in any period of time, they are required in rather invariable numbers; for example, there are only a limited number of wells in the regions, limiting the demand for *doras*, and, additionally, these ropes deteriorate in storage, so there is no point in purchasing beyond immediate requirements.[3] In the same way, the number of *paghas* that can be sold in any period depends on the number of livestock. Price reductions cannot be expected to stimulate sales beyond numbers needed to control these animals. Similar arguments apply to other important commodities marketed by the Birhors.

It could be argued that, with their monopolistic position, particularly with regard to rope production, the Birhors could profitably raise their prices to take advantage of the inelasticity of demand. But here it must be remembered that they too purchase necessities in the form of cereals, required to supplement their own often-inadequate subsistence production. In the nature of the market, it seems highly likely on an *a priori* basis that there would be retaliation by the Oraon rice producers (and others) who would proceed to raise the price of paddy, and so on, and to restore the terms of trade to their original level.

All these arguments suggest that, aside from minor seasonal price variations arising from temporary gluts or scarcities, there is little opportunity for the Birhors to improve their living standards by varying the market supplies in any way. This could, in fact, be the explanation for the stability in exchange values between Birhor commodities and those of other groups, which has been noted in the Banari market (Sinha 1968).

It is clear, in conclusion, that this group is highly dependent on the rest of the region for its subsistence in at least one part of the year and, because of the necessity for saving in the rest of the year to cover the period of shortage, they are dependent year round. By the same token, all groups in the region are highly dependent on the Birhors, particularly for ropes, which they need for subsistence purposes.

The economy of the Birhors hinges on the one hand on the forest and on the other on the intertribal market.

The only place where Birhors come into contact with outsiders is the intertribal market. Of their isolation, Dalton (1870:158) wrote, "They [the Birhors] are seldom seen in the village [of other tribes], but the women frequent the markets to sell their ropes and jungle produce." Another ethnographer, writing in 1888 (Driver 1888:14), states, "their [Birhor] women help them to make chop strong, and also carry this and monkey skins to the village market situated nearest to the jungles, and there, either sell or barter their articles for rice, salt, and oil. The skins of monkeys are used for making kol [tribal] drums." There are other accounts on the tribe (Risley 1911:33; Roy 1925:41) which describe their isolation and also their contacts with other peoples through intertribal markets.

The forest economy of the Birhors creates great physical strain on the group. The collection of roots, fruits, honey, and wax is seasonal, the hunting of animals is uncertain, and cutting wood is a difficult enterprise with their simple axes and adzes. These activities put much premium on their time. Sometimes weeks elapse and, yet, they have hardly any return from their efforts in the forest. In their weekly cycle, it has been observed that they spend four to five days in the forests, one day in the intertribal market, and the rest in camp preparing the marketable commodities. As the Birhors have little time to trade their commodities by visiting neighboring villages, the intertribal market provides them with a ready-made place for trading commodities in a short period of time. It serves as the pivot of their "primitive" economy.

In 1959, several proposals of collective hunts originated at the Banari intertribal market, which I had the opportunity to record.

COMMERCE

A Birhor from the Banari region regularly visits the intertribal market, where he has a fixed zone in the market place. There he sits, and sells or exchanges commodities. The presence or absence of a Birhor, as also the number and kinds of commodities he brings to the market, reflect his economic conditions. On several occasions in the monsoon, it was observed that only four to five Birhors came to the market place. Interviews revealed that others from their *tanda* were still in the forest trying to collect resources that could be exchanged at the market. The seasonal variation in their economy can usually be gauged through the market. They bring for exchange or sale various kinds of ropes and strings and wooden tubs in the summer and honey, wax, and monkey skins in the winter. As the forests do not yield sufficient produce in the monsoon, few of their commodities enter the market. Sometimes when their commodities are not sold at the Banari market, the Birhors walk down to other intertribal markets outside the region. This is necessary, primarily because they do not adjust their prices according to the modern economic principle of supply and demand. In the monsoon of 1958–1959, the Birhors of the Banari market faced a serious crisis. Some of them traveled fifteen to twenty miles on foot to sell their commodities at other intertribal markets. This situation was created by an influx of mass-manufactured ropes by the urban traders at the intertribal market. Virtually at the point of starvation, the Birhors of the region decided to migrate, but in time the state welfare officer intervened. The state purchased all the ropes manufactured by the Birhors for the next few months and eased their difficulties.

MATERIAL CULTURE

The material culture of the Birhors is quantitatively simple. A nuclear family owns one or two baskets or winnowing fans made by the Mahli and Turei of the region; two or three earthenwares made by Hindu potters for storing water, cooking cereals, or fermenting rice beer; a couple of bottles for storing oil; a mirror and a comb; wooden tubs for storing roots, fruits, and cereals; an iron axe or edge for cutting wood; and creepers and several nets for trapping monkeys, hares, and other small animals.

In one *tanda* one Birhor had a spade and a sickle and another had a knife and a pair of scissors, the latter used for cropping hair. Several young girls had tailored blouses, some boys had vests, and a few children had shorts and jackets. In another *tanda*, two young men owned scarves, and three girls had glass bangles and eyeliners. Some women owned nickel ornaments, necklaces, earrings, and rings. Others had earrings made of palm leaves. A quick look at these possessions, however, indicates that most of them were acquired by the Birhors from other tribes and castes at intertribal markets.

The seminomadic Birhors generally do not domesticate animals other than dogs. Occasionally they raise poultry. Some of them stated that in times of need it is easier to sell fowl and eggs than rope and strings at the intertribal market. One Birhor had regular contact with an urban trader to supply eggs weekly. In return he could, at any time, borrow cash or kind from the trader.

The Birhors are considered the most primitive tribe of Chota Nagpur (Roy 1925; Vidyarthi 1958), and yet they are not a self-sufficient community. The list of material equipment of a Birhor family, enumerated earlier, indicates how dependent they are on other communities. This dependence—or, rather, interdependence—is clearly manifested in the Banari intertribal market where a Birhor sells or barters his commodities: ropes, monkey hides, wooden tubs, honey, and wax for rice, maize, and other grains to the agricultural Oraon tribesmen; for clothes to the Chik-Baraik weavers; for earthenware to the Kumhar potters; for baskets to the Mahli and Turi basket-makers; for steel axes and several urban commodities to the urban traders. The occupational speciality of the Birhors gives them a distinctive identity at the intertribal market and brings them into contact with other tribes and castes of the region. Through recurrent economic transactions, some Birhors also establish permanent economic ties with other peoples at the market. Roy (1925:31) has elaborately described how some Birhors have taken to permanent settlement and agricultural occupation at the influence of some agriculturalist tribes and castes. In Banari, I have recorded a half-dozen cases of Birhor young men who worked as laborers during the monsoon for agriculturalist Oraon of the region. Interviews with these individuals revealed that they had established contacts with their patrons at the intertribal market, who offered them employment in the monsoon when their traditional craft produced little result.

SOCIAL FEATURES

Birhor culture is of interest for the nature of its organization as much as for its quantitative simplicity. For all practical purposes, the sociocultural activities of the Birhors are carried out by the *tanda*, which is their term for a settlement and implies a minimal lineage living in comparative isolation from other *tandas*. The patrilineage represented in a *tanda* comprises a group of agnates with a depth of three generations. It is a unit of food quest and is therefore set near a forest and a stream or reservoir, convenient to a market and away from other *tandas*. It has a social organization and is self-sufficient in religious activities. The only point where the Birhors come in frequent contact with outsiders is in the intertribal market, described earlier. Why this is so among the Birhors can be explained largely in terms of their cultural and ecological adaptations.

A typical Birhor *tanda* is more or less an isolate. It works as an independent, self-sufficient unit during the greater part of the year. It carries out most social, ritual, and cultural activities with little assistance from other *tandas*. Yet, a *tanda* has to depend on its counterparts for marital alliances, help with social problems that cannot be solved within the *tanda*, and for joint efforts such as communal, collective hunts.

These collective hunts among the Birhors are their most important form of cooperation. Such hunts are principally for monkeys and are held only when there is sufficient game, when a considerable number of participants assemble, and when an appropriate leadership is available. This, of course, gives better dividends to the participants—much more than what one *tanda* could get by hunting independently.

The monkey hunt of this type is infrequent. When it is held it yields not only meat, which is considered a delicacy by the Birhors, but also skins, which make the excellent drums for dancing and which also fetch a handsome price in the neighboring markets. The only distinctive technological equipment for this hunt is the indigenous rope net. A number of these nets, several hundred feet long, are placed end to end to form a huge semicircle. While some persons stand by the nets quietly, others converge from over a wide area, beating the trees and causing the monkeys to run toward the net. When a number of animals are close to the net, it is thrown over them. The monkeys thus entrapped are beaten with clubs, caught alive, or killed.

Hunt Ritual

This collective hunt is preceded and followed by a series of rituals. The *mati*, the priest, and the *mukhiya*, the headman, are given supreme authority to supervise and direct the activities. They choose an area for hunt, bless the nets while setting out for it, direct the fixation of the nets, regulate the drivers, offer prayers for the game, and distribute the catch according to custom. Since monkeys are trapped under particular nets, their owners receive the forelegs in addition to the usual share, which is apportioned among all the participants equally.

The Nuclear Family

The smallest unit of Birhor society is the nuclear, or biological, family. Individuals who are unmarried, old, or widowed could not think of living isolated in the ecocultural situation, and they are generally attached to a nuclear family. For the same reason, a big congregation cannot possibly emerge at a particular place. The most suitable unit, then, under the Birhors' ecological conditions has been minimal lineage, which makes up a *tanda*. This unit has been able to carry out most of the activities necessary for existence: women gather wild fruit and vegetable foods, care for the home and hearth, and rear the children; men devote most of their time to the forests, collecting *chop* fibers for ropes and wood for vessels and hunting small animals.

The activities of each *tanda* are dictated by the food quest, which takes precedence over all other considerations and works to promote the separatism already noted earlier in this chapter. Marital alliances are fairly enduring and create a strong fabric of close relations which extend from one region to another. Kinship ties thus offer some support and can be banked upon if needed.

Leadership, Law

Every Birhor *tanda* has a *mukhiya* (headman), *mati* (priest and/or witch doctor), and *kotwar* (watchman) who are officials of the settlement. Since Roy wrote on the Birhors in 1925, it appears that the traditional names of the headman (*pradhan*), priests (*naya*), convener of meetings (*digwar*), and witch doctor (*sonkha*) have undergone change. Some of the roles such as that of *kotwar* and *digwar*, have been fused; others have gone out of use. The services of the *mati* in a *tanda* are required on all rituals and religious ceremonies. His supernatural powers make him especially qualified to deal with illnesses, which are presumed to be inflicted by evil eyes or spirits. The *mukhiya*, being always an experienced elder, helps in solving the social problems of the settlers. It is his responsibility to offer sacrifices to Ora Bonga, the lineage deity, for the security and peace of the *tanda*, and in case some calamity occurs, he is accused for not propitiating the deity to ward off the evil.

What distinguishes a patrilineage in a *tanda*, if there are by any chance more than one, is its *bonga ora*, the hut in which the lineage deity resides. A lineage deity represents all dead ancestors, who are supposed to look after the welfare of their descendants. Whenever a *tanda* moves, the *mukhiya*, or head of the *tanda*, carries the *bonga* (deity) and leads the move. It is taken for granted that their *bonga* will lead them to a rich forest and to a safe abode.

In their own dialect, *Birhor* means "the man of the jungle." In fact, the Birhors consider themselves the kings of the jungles. They have a deep sense of rights as people and would like to distinguish themselves from the rest of the tribes. The neighboring tribes, such as the Oraons and the Asurs, have looked at them with despise and praise, exhibiting a sort of ambivalent attitude: despise because they eat flesh of monkeys and lead a nomadic life and praise because they live in forests, face wild animals without fear, and carry on adventurous activities. All the same, the Birhors live a life of interdependence with the Oraons, the Asurs, and other tribes living in close proximity. However, the Birhors are considered socially inferior.

BIRTH AND CEREMONY

Like many other societies, among the Birhors the birth of a child is an occasion of great joy. All the members of a *tanda* celebrate the arrival of a new member on the sixth day, which is called *chhatti*. However, when the resources do not permit immediate festivity, they celebrate the event at any time during the first year. On this occasion it is obligatory for a Birhor to invite maternal relatives of the child and his own paternal relatives. Since a Birhor always lives hand to mouth, trying to accumulate food provisions for the next day, he hardly finds time to visit his relatives or to invite them to visit personally. Here he takes advantage of the intertribal market, from where he sends invitations to relatives by word of mouth. During the winter of 1959, I observed the birth ceremony of a Birhor at Serka *tanda*. Budhua, whose wife delivered a baby, came to the Banari intertribal market on Monday and announced the birth to his tribesmen. He, along with other elders of his *tanda*, decided to celebrate the occasion on the following Monday. He sent word to his relatives through people present at the market, asking them to join in the celebration. On the next Monday, four pitchers of rice beer were prepared by the members of Badhua's *tanda*. In the late afternoon, the Birhors gathered near Ora Bonga and sacrificed chicken. All present drank beer, which was ceremonially offered to Budhua. The mother's brother brought a hand-loomed dress for the child's mother. Other guests brought gifts of rice, pulse, and salt. The ceremony lasted hardly an hour, but the visitors stayed overnight.

MARRIAGE

Marriage is considered the second important event in the life of a Birhor. It takes place only when two persons of the opposite sex decide to build a *kumba* and undertake responsibilities for an independent household.

Marriage serves as an important institution for bringing several *tandas* together. It is essentially a contract and can be solemnized only when the bride price has been paid. A young man is married to a girl when he has accumulated enough resources to afford expenses of the formal ceremony. Although there are contributions made by members of one's *tanda*, a Birhor man has to spend nearly 100 rupees on his wedding ceremony. The bride price comprises about 40–50 pounds of paddy (purchased from the Oraon); an article of clothing for the bride, her mother, and the groom; a necklace, bangles, and ring for the bride; a pitcher (15 gallons) of rice beer (also from the Oraon); a few (Malhar) ornaments; and 10–15 rupees in cash. As celebrating marriage presents a difficult financial problem to a Birhor, he generally marries a girl only after they have lived together several years.

Data on marital alliance revealed that twenty-nine out of thirty-six marriages were performed one or more years after a couple began living together as husband and wife. In most cases, a young man had met a girl at the intertribal market, and after a series of contacts they decided to live together. As long as the rules of clan and *tanda* exogamy are observed, informal permission from the parents is enough for the couple to establish a *kumba*. Cases of elopement of married women with un-married men from the intertribal market are not infrequent among the Birhors. In the course of a year, four such cases were witnessed.

One may illustrate the situation. Somra, a thirty-two-year-old Birhor, was married to an eighteen-year-old girl, Budhni. Somra was lazy; he could not support his wife; consequently, she was unhappy. Budhni met Chatar-pal, a young man from another *tanda*, at the Banari intertribal market. In the course of weeks they developed a strong acquaintance, and one day they met and eloped from the market place. They spent two weeks in the forest. Later, Chatarpal brought her to his *tanda,* and there they lived together. This precipitated conflict between the two *tandas,* which I will discuss later.

Some Birhor marriages are arranged by negotiations between the parents of the bride and groom, but they are exceptions rather than the rule.

Death Rites

Unlike the marriage ceremony, death rites among the Birhors cannot be postponed. Within a week, the news of death has to be communicated to the relatives and members of• the clan inside and outside the region through persons attending the intertribal market. On the ninth day after death, the clan elders assemble at the *tanda* and perform rituals which place the dead in the category of *ora bonga,* the ancestor spirits. Every relative brings gifts in kind: rice, pulse, rice beer, and so forth, which are pooled for the death feast.

Intertribal Relations and Communications

The pattern of nomadism of a Birhor *tanda* is more or less stable, and yet the three thousand Birhors hardly know of all the *tandas* of the tribe. There are less than seventy-five *tandas* in Chota Nagpur, spread in an area 250 miles long, from Hazarlbagh to Singbhum, but the Birhors of Banari know only eight *tandas* outside their region. Ordinarily, a Birhor knows only those of his tribesmen whom he meets at intertribal markets.

A Birhor *tanda* is related primarily to one intertribal market, but occasionally its members visit neighboring markets to sell commodities and meet friends, relatives, and clansmen. Intertribal contacts among the Birhors are maintained through a chain of intertribal markets. The Birhors of Banari sometimes visit the Adar intertribal market, ten miles west. I was told that Birhors from Banari, Tendar, and Palkot, farther west, occasionally meet at the intertribal market and renew contacts.

Although the *tanda* is an independent social entity, when disputes between two or more *tandas* arise, tribal elders from several *tandas* are invited to adjudicate them. In the already cited case of the elopement of Somra's wife with Chatarpal, a meeting of the elders from five neighboring tandas was called by members of Somra's *tanda.* On a scheduled date the tribal elders assembled to settle the dispute. Since Somra insisted that his wife be returned to him, and since his wife was unwilling to return, the dispute could not be resolved. The tribal elders then decided to include people from several *tandas* outside the region to aid in solving the dispute. Two weeks later the meeting was called at the Tendar intertribal market, where it was decided that Chatarpal, who had eloped with Somra's wife, should return to Somra the amount he had spent on her marriage. Soon after the payment was made and the dispute resolved.

A Birhor *tanda* is always located away from other habitations, but the Birhors usually identify their location in relation to the intertribal market they visit. Once when I asked a Birhor chief about the locations of his past settlements, he replied, "I was born here and have since moved to Tendar, Chatakpur, Palkote, Chakradharpur, Adar, Jamti, Manatu, and Mudar." All these names are names of markets, and he thought that settlements could best be identified by the markets associated with them. It is interesting that Birhors tell their life histories with references to the intertribal markets they have known in the past. As the Birhors are preliterate, their important events such as birth, marriage, and death are calculated by their recounting associations with the markets at the time of the incident. The Birhors' knowledge of time and space is greatly influenced by the intertribal markets.

SUPERSTITIONS

Some Birhors of the Banari region are famous as sorcerers and witch doctors. Although they follow their traditional occupation, sorcery and witchcraft fetch them supplementary income as well as prestige among the tribes and castes of the region. The Birhor sorcerers are known for curing men and animals, as well as for inflicting disease on them. In order to make themselves available to the people of the region, the Birhor sorcerers regularly attend the Banari intertribal market. On several occasions I noted Oraon and other tribesmen contacting sorcerers at the market place. In some instances a sorcerer reads an omen for his client at the market; at other times he visits the client at his settlement to diagnose and prognose the ailing individual. Although I have never witnessed any instance of a sorcerer inflicting evil influence on any enemy of his clients, I was told by several persons that the Birhors practiced this art as well. In any case, the intertribal markets help the sorcerer practice his art.

INTERTRIBAL CEREMONIAL FRIENDSHIP

The practice of intertribal ceremonial friendship has been considered by several ethnographers of central Indian tribes as an important means by which the tribesmen insure security and hospitality in an inaccessible region (Roy 1925:269; Tandon 1960:58). Some Birhors of Banari reported ceremonial friendship with Oraon, Birjia, Asur, Mahli, and Hindu castes who live in different parts of the region. In some cases, I was told, such friendships (which are among members of the same sex) gave an individual entry into other tribal groups, which led to intertribal marital alliance. Although tribal elders do not approve of this, in the Banari region one young Birhor man had married an Oraon girl and two Oraon men had married Birhor women.

CHARACTER VALUES

Psychological Components

In the Birhor world an individual is not important. The consciousness of the individual self, which the anthropologist finds so dominating in complex societies, seems to be somewhat lacking among the Birhors. This is rather obvious in life histories, folklore, and in anecdotes of the community (Sinha 1960).

Once Mangra, a Birhor, discovered a rich isolated deposit of fibrous creepers which could have provided him raw material for manufacturing ropes for the whole year. However, he immediately ran to his group and announced the deposit so that others from his *tanda* could share the find. My Birhor informants time and again told me that Mangra could have kept the find to himself, but that is not what a Birhor does.

Another example, of a different order, may be cited here. In 1957 I witnessed the death of an eight-year-old. Sukhram, his father, knew earlier that his son was dying of sorcery inflicted by another Birhor from a neighboring *tanda*, but he did not speak it out until others in his *tanda* had gathered around the ailing boy and suspected sorcery made by Charwa, the sorcerer. A later interview with Sukhram revealed that a Birhor was not expected to initiate an issue, however helpful he might think it to be for himself. A Birhor always leaves his fears and anxieties for his *tanda* to redress. There is an allied incident to attest it.

The wife of Somra, a young Birhor of twenty-four, once disappeared from her husband's house. Budhu was extremely sorry for his wife, and more for the bride price he had paid for her, which he said was extremely difficult to recover. He was helpless. He would not assert himself to his people to fight for him and to get back his wife. None of the settlers showed any anxiety until they realized that it was a threat to the corporate and homogeneous life of the *tanda*.

Personal Life

The Birhors have little worry about their impulses. Though they do lead active sex lives, they do not have problems associated with sex. As long as incestuous relations are avoided, license is given. But the Birhors restrain themselves from excessive acts because of their belief that overindulgence is harmful. They give here an impression of a strong self-confidence, which is also evidenced in their life histories. In contrast to sex, the Birhors have many anxieties about women, especially about their wives. Without a wife a Birhor is scarcely a person. A wife is an asset in many ways. She gives status to her husband and lends help in all his spheres, from economic to ritual. Some important rituals, in fact, require close cooperation between husband and wife. A Birhor is proud to have two wives, and if he happens to get his elder brother's widow, he is considered fortunate. A Birhor, upon marriage, builds a separate hut, but remains in close association with his parents. Sons look after invalid parents, collecting food and fuel for them without reluctance. Usually a daughter leaves her parents after marriage, but if, as in some cases, she stays with her husband in her parents' *tanda*, she has similar obligations to attend to. In such cases, a son-in-law has a role similar to that of a son. Parents, on the other hand, do not interfere with their grown-up sons and daughters. Invalid children are, however, a source of great anxiety to the parents.

For a Birhor, more important than himself is his relation with the people of his *tanda*. All the Birhors in a *tanda* go to the forest together to collect fruits, roots, creepers, and bark. The hunting expedition, which is often undertaken, necessarily warrants a cooperative effort by all the settlers.

The Birhors of a *tanda* face the world together as a single group. When one member is threatened all are expected to come to his support, and usually they do. A *tanda* is a sociocultural unity. In case there is a conflict within the *tanda*, which is again a rare event, the *tanda* splits, and one group moves to another camp.

All this, however, does not deny the extension of the Birhor world, which primarily centers around his *tanda*. A Birhor recognizes his fellow-tribesmen who live in different *tandas* and meets them frequently at market and, occasionally, while on a trip to find a bride or to meet relatives. A Birhor's primary interest, however, lies not in his relations with other men but in his relations with nonman—that is, spirits, both supernatural and natural.

SPIRITUAL LIFE, RELIGION, GODS

The Birhors recognize a mysterious spiritual force or energy behind various animate beings, inanimate objects, natural or artificial, and even in certain immaterial things such as a spoken word, an expressed wish, a name, or a number. Their sense of awe and fear of the unseen spirit world has led them to devise methods by which they expect to enter into friendly relations with the more important spiritual powers. The Birhors have personified these powers as *bongas* (spirits and deities) and have assigned to each of the more important ones a symbol, a habitation, a name, and a suitable periodical sacrifice by which they conciliate and enter into communion with them. In cases of omens and dreams, when the spirit involved is not known, the Birhors seek to protect themselves with the help and advice of the *matis* (witch doctors), who are supposed to know the language of the spirit world.

To the Birhors, the gap between deity spirits and man is very narrow. When a Birhor goes to the forest he is said to carry spirits along with him. He stays day and night in dense forest cutting woods, skinning trees, and making wooden tubs. In a local proverb, the forest is believed to be the home of the Birhors.

Whenever the Birhors move their *tanda* from one place to another they first send two or three people, mostly *matis*, to conduct a pilot survey, choose a place, and determine whether the local spirits will be disturbed by their camp. Only when the conditions are favorable do the Birhors shift their *tanda* along with their *bongas*.

The supreme Birhor god is Singbonga, who does not ordinarily cause harm. Singbonga is invoked when the Birhors go hunting and is offered a white fowl. Burhi Mai, the mother goddess, ranks second. She is supposed to be interested in human welfare and brings good luck, children, and health if properly propitiated. The deity who insures success in hunting is Chandi, and he must be propitiated with sacrifices to achieve success. Bandar Bir ("baboon god") and Hanuman Bir ("monkey god") are other spirits who bring success in catching monkeys.

Besides these supernatural beings, a Birhor propitiates his clan spirits, *manita bhuts*, who are concerned with his welfare and the welfare of his clan. There are many other Birhor tutelary deities and spirits, but mention must be made of the ancestor spirits, described earlier. To the Birhor, death, unless caused by violence, results from the misdeeds of evil spirits and enables the dead to join the ranks of ancestor spirits. But persons dying unnatural deaths make a separate cadre of spirits, the *haproms*. The *haproms* are regularly given food and drink; failure to so pacify them, it is believed, will cause them to prevent success in hunting and, perhaps sickness in the family.

Birhor life is pervaded with supernatural influences. An individual closely observes the rules of the spirits and does not want to work against them but to live in harmony with them. In a sense, the Birhors regard the gods and spirits as their equals, possessing a certain sanctity or sacredness and superior power, but inclined to be friendly in due time if kept in good humor and supplied with food and shelter.

Ecology

The traditional culture of the Birhors indicates the intricate balance they have achieved in their ongoing life situation for at least two and a half millennia. They have developed a symbiotic relation with the flora and fauna of their environment and have worked out their customary ways of life by dealing with their situation as well as they can. In the given situation, that is, with their natural, technological, and social resources, the Birhors are solving their problems and needs by utilizing the limited possible alternatives available to them. Their movement from one forest region to another in more or less cyclic order is geared to protect their natural resources and follows the same principle as rotation of fields in agriculture. Their small *tanda* organization represents a successful solution to their problematic situation, as does the occasional inter*tanda* hunting expedition.

CHANGE

GOVERNMENT INTERVENTION

The evolutionary process that led some of the seminomadic Birhors into a sedentary life in the early decades of this century (Roy 1925) and their frequent contacts with the agricultural communities at the intertribal markets indicate that the Birhors are aware of the socioeconomic activities of the peasants who live in an entirely different ecological zone. But they have never been attracted enough by the peasant economies to incorporate them into their own society. When in 1955 government authorities asked the Birhors to leave their habitat and resettle in the agricultural colony planned by the state, they expressed positive dissatisfaction. They did not want to give up their seminomadic way of life.

Manjira, the Birhor chief, once told me that he did not know how he could keep his *bongas* appeased in the tile-roofed house of the settlement, since they were used to being propitiated beside his leaf-hut *kumba*. After great deliberation, however, the Birhors decided that they had no alternative but to move to the resettlement colony already built for them.

Manjira also informed me that it was a great dilemma for his tribesmen (Sinha 1966). All the *matis* were called to read omens. Some of them were quietly sent to the resettlement site to insure that it was not infested with malevolent spirits. They carried with them complete household gear and two chickens; the former was left unguarded overnight and the latter were ritually sacrificed at the site. The following morning they returned and found everything in order. They were convinced that the site was favorable for human settlement.

The houses appeared attractive and far superior to those of neighboring peasant communities. There were fields nearby, and the extension agents assured them that once they moved to the colony the lands could be reclaimed for cultivation, and they were told that facilities for farming— plows, oxen, implements, seeds, and so on—would be given to them. The forests were near and a stream flowed close by. The government also assured them that they could pursue their traditional occupations side by side; also, they could build leaf-hut *kumbas* for ritualistic purposes. These promised a continuity of the traditional life as well as a better life for the community.

For several days the Birhors discussed the offer among themselves. Those from the Manjira invited headmen from Serka *tanda*, four miles north, Narma *tanda*, ten miles west, and Chatakpur *tanda*, ten miles south, to advise them on the problems of and prospects for a settled life. Most of the persons agreed to accept the invitation, explained and endorsed by the Birhor chief Manjira. Only one Birhor elder differed. But there was no scope for difference. They feared that if they did not agree, the government would forcibly settle them. However, the government's practical problem to develop the scheduled areas and "raise the standard of living" of the tribal people, and its decision to resettle the Birhors—whether they liked it or not—foreshadowed change in the situation of the community. Their cultural and ecological balance disrupted, the Birhors faced new problems.

The first, and perhaps most explicit, problem that emerged when the Birhors moved to the settlement concerned the houses. They were too big and too ventilated. The small leaf huts were warm and cozy; and the new houses created fresh needs: blankets and clothes, which obviously they could not afford from their limited resources. They looked to the government to help them out.

When the resettlement was formally inaugurated in 1956, each Birhor nuclear family head was given a certificate, according to the laws of the state, which conferred title to two or more parcels of land, totaling five acres, to be utilized for homestead and agricultural farming. The preliterate Birhors hardly understood or attached any significance to this piece of paper; the certificate stated that if the land was not reclaimed within three years, the tenant would lose ownership rights.

Five years later, in 1961, the settlers had not reclaimed even half of the land and were faced with the problem, as interpreted to them by the schoolteacher, of whether they still owned the barren land and whether it was worth investing any more labor in it.

The Birhors cannot face the problems associated with farming: some land is not only barren but rocky; agricultural implements, oxen, and seeds did not arrive on time; the dam built for irrigation did not last long; and, above all, agriculture warrants continued cooperation between a number of persons and families, an interaction the Birhors are not accustomed to in their traditional economic activities. They are in a quandary: whether to go to the forest in pursuit of their traditional occupation or to work in the fields to reclaim the land. It is a choice between a culturally fashioned occupation and an innovation which is not immediately rewarding. The Birhors prefer the former, but the aggregation of fifteen families at one place results in quick consumption of the forest resources in the nearby regions which they traditionally used. This, in the absence of timely substitution of agricultural activities, creates fresh problems. The settlers complain that they must go to far-off forests to collect raw materials, and the time they spend doing so is much more than the return they receive. At one point, when they had a threat of starvation, which lessened the promise of a better life in the settlement, the government offered doles to settlers who were willing to work on the land reclamation. But others solved this problem by discovering a new trade of trapping small live monkeys and selling them to agents of the rhesus research laboratories, who contacted them at the intertribal market and paid a handsome price for the animals. The Birhors are, however, afraid that this indiscriminate exploitation will eliminate all the monkeys from the forests in the not-too-distant future.

When the situation worsened and the Birhors were undecided whether to stay at the settlement or leave, the rope-making industry was established. The rope-making machine called for a new habit and used a raw material unknown to the Birhors. Hence, it evoked little enthusiasm and interest. Those who were persuaded to join the rope-making industry did not get the ropes they made—since the raw material was supplied by the government—or the stipend they were assured they would have at regular intervals. All these factors combined to lead two families to run away to the forest. Two young Birhor men were sent for training in weaving, but they could not use the craft on their return to the colony, since they could not afford either looms or the raw material for weaving. Their level of aspiration having been raised, they had to revert to their traditional occupation, and further dissatisfaction was created among the Birhors.

The mode of living at the settlement calls for a new level of social interaction among the settlers. As the government brought two semi-nomadic *tandas*, that is, two distinct social groups, at one place for resettlement, conflicts abound among the settlers during religious festivities, rites and ceremonies, and other social activities. What was anticipated by government authorities to provide administrative convenience and efficiency in development planning has created cleavages within the settlement, along *tanda* lines, precipitating a series of crises, ranging from quarrels to the employment of witchcraft and sorcery (Elwin 1960:227). Disputes and confusion have also arisen regarding the local leadership. In one instance an elder Birhor had to leave the settlement (Sinha 1958). On such occasions, however, the government agent intervenes and makes his decisions and judgments binding upon the people.

THE PRESENT: SUMMARY

The situation of the resettled Birhors is well summarized in the following observations by Elwin (1960:229) in his report to the federal government's committee on special multipurpose tribal blocks:

I was told that the Birhors are now economically much better off and if this is true I cannot imagine what they were before. They are still miserably poor; their houses are unsuitable, dirty and untidy, their health does not appear to be good, and I noticed that the children were very dirty and some

of them were suffering from various eye diseases, their eyes being bunged
up with pus. . . . The Birhors have been a free and an independent people;
today they appear a little crushed. Will we be allowed to do this or that,
they ask; must we have cooperative cooking as well as cooperative farming.
They should be made to realize that they are free men and women, and that
it is not the policy of the government to impose anything on them.

Every time the settlers have new problems they look to the government
to come to their aid. In the early phase of resettlement the government
doled out cash and commodities when the Birhors asked for it; later they
dictated terms for doles and made decisions for them in both economic
and noneconomic activities. These, while making the settlers dependent
on the government, disturb the harmony the Birhors had in aboriginal
days with nature, plants, animals, men, and spirits. The parental attitude
of the government tends to undermine the self-confidence of the Birhors
as a group. In sum, while in aboriginal days the Birhors' problems concerned primarily their relation with their environment—spirits, men,
animals, and plants—in the resettlement their problems primarily concern
their relation with the government.

The Birhors are a tribe in transition. They are of methodological interest,
since they give an example of changing processes of sociocultural life. Because of their cultural-ecological processes, which have been determined by
the necessity for exploitation of their environment by means of the simple
techniques available to them, the *tanda,* which is a grouping based on
minimal lineage, works as the basic and independent unit for most of their
cultural, religious, and economic activities. The few collective activities
like communal hunts, or the contacts with Birhors of other *tandas* at the
markets, have created no permanent inter*tanda* extensions. The wandering
Birhors thus typologically evidence a minimal lineage level of sociocultural integration.

The Birhors are not, it is true, typologically unique. The Korwas of
Palamau and Mirzapur (Majumdar 1944), the Kadars of Cochin (Ehrenfels 1952), and the Shoshonean Indians of America (Steward 1955) are a
few among many who could come under this category. The Birhors, however, may be said to represent a minimal lineage level of sociocultural
integration of a cross-culturally significant type.

The minimal lineage type of organization found among the Birhors
should be considered as characteristic only of the seminomadic Birhors
and not of the society that is developing with resettlement.

NOTES

1. At the current exchange rate, 7.50 rupees equals 1 U.S. dollar.
2. The Birhors claim that both tobacco and beer are in the nature of necessities. They claim that chewing tobacco assuages the pangs of hunger, while

beer, consumed before forays in the forest, sharpens their senses for the tasks ahead.
3. The level of demand in any one time period also, of course, depends on the rate of deterioration of ropes. It might be possible to delay rope purchases somewhat, but there would clearly be limits to this.

REFERENCES

Census Report of Bihar, 1951.

Dalton, E. T., 1812. *Descriptive Ethnology of Bengal*, Calcutta: Superintendent of Government Printing.

Driver, W. H. P., 1888. "Birhor," *Journal of the Royal Asiatic Society of Bengal* 47 (1):12–38.

Ehrenfels, U., 1952. *The Kadars*, Madras: University of Madras Press.

Elwin, V., 1960. *Report of the Committee on Special Multipurpose Tribal Blocks*, New Delhi: Ministry of Home Affairs.

Evans-Pritchard, E. E., 1954. *The Nuer*, London: Oxford University Press.

Grierson, G. A., 1905. *Linguistic Survey of India*, Vol. 4, Calcutta: Superintendent of Government Printing.

Guha, B. S., 1944. *Racial Elements in the Indian Population*, London: Oxford University Press.

Holmberg, A., 1958. "Research Development Approach to the Study of Change," *Human Organization* 17:12–19.

Majumdar, D. N., 1944. *The Fortune of Primitive Tribes*, Lucknow: Universal Publishers.

Malhotra, S. P., 1960. "Birhor Resettlement Scheme," *Journal of Social Research* (Ranchi) 3:69–81.

Mason, L., 1950. "The Bikinians: A Transplanted Population," *Human Organization* 9:5–15.

Risley, H. H., 1915. *The People of India*, London: W. Thacker.

Roy, S. C., 1915. *The Oraons of Chotanagpur*, Calcutta: The Brahmo Mission Press.

———, 1925. *The Birhor: A Little Known Jungle Tribe of Chotanagpur*, Ranchi: London, Probsthain.

Sen, Bijay K., and Jyoti Sen, 1955. "Notes on the Birhors," *Man in India* 35 (3):169–176.

Sinha, D. P., 1958. "Cultural Ecology of the Birhor: A Methodological Illustration," *Journal of Social Research* 1(1):86–96.

———, 1959. "World and World View of a Wandering Tribe," *Adibasi, Journal of Tribal Research Bureau* (Bhubaneshwar).

———, 1960. "Portrait of a Birhor Chief: A Biographical Study in Culture Change," *Journal of Social Research* 3 (2):57–68.

———, 1967. "Socio-cultural Implications of Economic Development in Banari: The case of Birhor Resettlement," *Eastern Anthropologist* 20:2.

———, 1967. "Principles and Problems of Planned Cultural Change," in *Applied Anthropology in India*, L. P. Vidyarthi, ed., Allahabad: Kitab Matial.

————, 1968. *Culture Change in an Intertribal Market*, Bombay: Asia Publishing House.

————, in press. "Resettlement and Applied Anthropology," in *Anthropology and Austronesia*, Donald Marshall, ed.

Stanner, W. E. H., 1953. *The South Seas in Transition*, Sydney: Australasian Publishing Company.

Steward, J., 1955. *Theory of Culture Change*, Urbana: University of Illinois Press.

Tandon, J. S., 1960. "Ceremonial Friendship among the Bhattra of Bagtar," *Journal of Social Research* 3 (1):38–54.

Thompson, L., 1961. *Toward a Science of Mankind*, New York: McGraw-Hill Book Company.

————, 1965. "Applied Anthropology's Role in Developing Science of Man," *Human Organization* 24 (4):277–287.

Turmin, M., *et al.*, 1958. "Values in Action: A Symposium," *Human Organization* 17 (1):2–26.

Vidyarthi, L. P., 1958. "Cultural Types in Tribal Bihar," *Journal of Social Research* 1:1.

————, 1960. "The Birhor: A Study in Ecology, Economy and Wandering," in *Selected Papers of the Fifth International Congress of Anthropological and Ethnological Sciences*, Philadelphia.

Williams, B. J., 1968. "The Birhor of India and Some Comments on Band Organization," in *Man the Hunter*, eds. R. B. Lee and I. DeVore, Chicago: Aldine Publishing Company, pp. 126–131.

GLOSSARY

Bandar Bir: baboon god
Birhor: in their dialect, "man of the jungle"
bonga: spirit or deity
bonga ora: hut where the lineage deity resides
Burhi Mai: second-ranking god—mother goddess
Chandi: deity who insures success in hunting
chhatti: celebration sixth day after the birth of a child
chop: fibrous creeper used in the construction of rope
daboo: wooden ladle
dhol: wooden drum case constructed by the Birhors
dora: form of vine rope, about 20 feet in length, used for drawing water from wells by bucket
Hanuman Bir: monkey god
haproms: spirits of those who die unnatural deaths
kathola: wooden container for cooked rice
kathout: wooden basin, produced in two sizes
kotwar: watchman
kumba: leaf hut which accommodates a nuclear family
manita bhuts: individual clan spirits
mati: priest and/or witch doctor
mukhiya: headman of a *tanda*

Ora Bonga: lineage deity, represents all dead ancestors who are supposed to look after the welfare of their descendants

paddy: cereal product; threshed, unmilled rice

pagha: vine rope, 6–7 feet in length, used for controlling livestock

sika: shortest length of vine rope constructed by the Birhors, used for suspending storage baskets from the ceiling of the houses

Singbonga: supreme god of the Birhors

tanda: band, part of the whole tribe; term for settlement, implies minimal lineage

CHAPTER

10

THE PALIYANS

Peter M. Gardner

Peter Gardner is currently Associate Professor of Anthropology at the University of Missouri, Columbia, and received his Ph.D. from the University of Pennsylvania in 1965. Since his first field work with the Paliyans in 1962–1964, he spent a further fourteen months in India during 1967–1968, concerned with ways of synthesizing materials on Indic culture. His publications include articles on Indian caste and dominance in addition to papers and monographs on the ecology and social structure of the Paliyans. Dr. Gardner has also taught at both the University of Pennsylvania and the University of Texas.

EDITOR'S INTRODUCTION

The Paliyans occupy several ranges of hills in peninsular India and, like the Birhors, have been classified as proto-Australoid in physical type. Their language is a dialect of the Tamil which is spoken by their agriculturalist neighbors. The Paliyans have found it necessary to retreat continuously from the expanding Tamil culture and because of this have maintained an evasive mobile life while retaining some contact for purposes of limited trade. In addition, they have adopted a form of "token assimilation" through the use of Tamil rituals and kin categories in extracultural contexts. The natural domain of the Paliyans is within the rain shadow of the ranges, so that the water supply is somewhat problematic; this environment, however, provides ample faunal and floral resources, allowing the Paliyans to exploit only their preferred foods. Today Indian plantations both destroy their habitat and offer new alternatives in wage labor. The Paliyans' rigid individualism and residential instability, however, have made this transition difficult, and they continue to follow traditional sources of livelihood sequential to or simultaneous to employment as laborers.

Like that of the Bushmen, Paliyan band organization is flexible, allowing high mobility among individuals and families, although normally within a cluster of three to four bands related through intermarriage. Individual autonomy is most highly valued and nuclear families or even individuals are economically self-sufficient. Community-wide interaction takes place in the contexts of great need, in limited hunting activities, such as deer drives, and in recreation and ceremony. The Paliyans as individuals, rather than as a group, create order; they value neither the mechanisms that lead to standardization nor order achieved through social tradition.

Like the Guayaki, the Paliyans have dealt with culture contact primarily through the avoidance of other groups. They are comparable as well in that both are hunters and gatherers who share a history and a language with agriculturalist neighbors.

In this chapter, Gardner is primarily concerned with the relation between social and economic organization and the total environment. Specifically, he emphasizes the workings of the individual ideal within the total system. The Paliyans seem to carry egalitarianism, common to so many simple societies, to an extreme, and in this sense they are unique.

The hunting and food-gathering peoples on the edge of the world—the Australian aborigines, the Eskimos, the Andamaners—attract our attention because of their apparent integrity as aboriginals. The isolation that has allowed their cultures to develop relatively undisturbed not only evokes the interest of the romantic but has a special value for the anthropological theorist as well. To the student of cultural adaptation, food collectors of another kind, those who are to be found in tiny enclaves shoulder to shoulder with the sophisticated peoples of the world, are no less interesting. Their very existence raises fascinating questions about why and how they live as they do. Not the least of these questions is whether their often quite remarkable cultural simplicity represents a persistence of aboriginal patterns or whether it is merely an adaptation to the conditions in which recent history has placed them.

Although India's food collectors have been described ethnographically, we cannot say that they have ever been treated as much more than survivals. Given the rich historical and contextual data that India could provide, this lapse is both unfortunate and unnecessary. In the course of the present ethnographic sketch I think that it will become clear that the culture would be beyond comprehension if excised from its context. For this reason, I begin with a brief look at history, physical anthropology, and language.

The tribal peoples of the hills have been referred to repeatedly in the early descriptions of peninsular India: first in Megasthenes' account in the third century B.C. and then in the classic Tamil Sangam poetry during the first millennium A.D. Tamil Sangam poets were particularly concerned with geographic metaphor. This is a stroke of luck for the ethnohistorian, because Tamil poets not only used a standardized classification of the natural geographic zones but often, in order to elaborate, they went on to discuss the culturally diversified inhabitants of these various zones. The strange result is that our knowledge of India's shy, honey-gathering, yam-digging tribal peoples antedates our knowledge of many of the major elements in the Sangam poets' own society.

Markham, in the nineteenth century, brings us nearer the present by describing silent barter for honey between plainsmen and mountain tribals of Madurai district in the Tamil country (now Madras State, or Tamizho-nadu, India's southernmost state) (Grierson 1903:46). And today, over-looking railways and on clear days within sight of the perennial city of Madurai (once a center of the ancient Tamil Sangam poetry and an active trade partner of Augustan Rome), there are again to be found dispersed bands of nomadic food collectors, the Paliyans.[1]

History allows us, then, to talk of persistence of this cultural type in the region, even though full details and proof of continuity are lacking. There are other food-collecting isolates which appear to have persisted in the same way as the Paliyans and in the same context of almost timeless contact with South Indian civilization, the Malapandaram and Kadar in Kerala on the west side of the very southern ranges which the Paliyans inhabit and the Chenchu and Yanadi of Andhra, several hundred miles to the north.

But what of Paliyan origins? Perhaps these people are nothing more than runaway Indians whose culture is secondarily simple due to the exigencies of flight. Physical anthropology helps us answer the question. Within any one settlement the Paliyans are very heterogeneous physically, a feature noted for other South Indian food collectors. However, the various Paliyan phenotypes fall within the already known range of South and Southeast Asian characteristics formerly termed Negrito, Malid, Ved-did, and proto-Australoid. They particularly parallel those described by Fürer-Haimendorf for the Konda Reddi (1945:35–37) and portrayed in the photographs of the Semang of Malaya (Evans 1937; Schebesta 1927; Skeat and Bladgen 1906). If the Paliyans are runaway Indian plainsmen, then why was it primarily people with these phenotypic characteristics who fled to the hills; why are they also found in other tribal enclaves; and why are there few people with these characteristics in the dominant plains population today? We cannot attribute the physical difference between tribals and plainsmen to diet, when those tribals who have lived on the plain as field laborers for a century, consuming the standard plains diet of rice, almost completely retain their physical distinctiveness. While admit-ting that there is Tamil admixture in every Paliyan community, I am obliged to reject as mistaken Aiyappan's well-intentioned statement that such tribals "cannot be distinguished by any bodily peculiarities from the plains people . . ." (Aiyappan 1948:3).

The extreme alternative to the runaway hypothesis is that these persisting enclaves of shy people possess a relict culture. It is equally untenable. For example, from the viewpoint of language the Paliyans are a standard food-collecting enclave for this part of the world; with the exception of the Semang, Mainland South and Southeast Asian food collectors speak the language of the dominant plains people of their region.[2] All Paliyans speak a dialect mutually intelligible with colloquial Tamil of their area. Divergences from standard Tamil exist mainly in the area of intonation, articulation, and phonology. Only one Paliyan word was encountered which could not be referred to the Southern Dravidian language family to which Tamil belongs. Unless Paliyans have spoken Tamil from prehistoric times and maintained such close contact with other Tamil speakers that their language did not become independent, then one has to think of their having had either fairly intensive cultural contact at some time in the past or else fairly continuous contact of a less intense sort in order for them to have adopted Tamil so completely. Either way, the idea of contact cannot be avoided.

In sum, while there is no physical anthropological or historical evidence indicating that these food collectors are recent runaways from Indian society, neither do the data of history and linguistics allow us to consider them as undisturbed enclaves.

These findings are consonant with the contemporary record of contact between Paliyans and their neighbors. Paliyans in their tiny bands find it necessary to retreat constantly before the virile expanding culture of the Tamils. Yet, at the same time, they maintain an intermittent, tangential contact with outsiders for reasons that are chiefly economic. Most of the Indians with whom they have contact are unsophisticated, domineering, and somewhat exploitative. As the Paliyans themselves put it, they maintain an evasive mobile way of life as a necessary protective maneuver. And so it is that today, although their forest is literally vanishing beneath them, some 3000 scattered Paliyans doggedly orient their life toward the last few zones of refuge. Their sense of constant retreat colors every aspect of their culture, from technology to religion, in ways that will be elaborated in the following description.

ENVIRONMENT

The several ranges of hills which the Paliyans occupy present an imposing face to the plainsmen below. The Palni range rises to 8380 feet, with several peaks of 8000 feet; it constitutes a plateau of 105 square miles at an altitude of over 7000 feet (see Fig. 10-1). Particularly from the south it appears as an unscalable escarpment hung much of the time in cloud and mist. The Anaimalais peak at 8841 feet, but lack the appearance of massive continuity of the former range because of foothills. The hills to the south are a southern extension of the Palni-Anaimalai east-west range

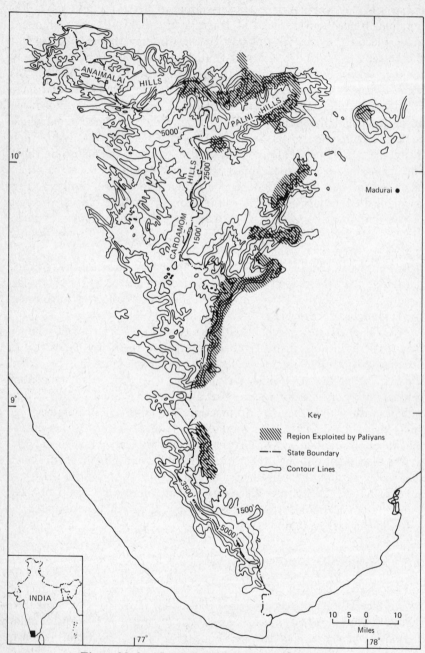

Figure 10–1.   South India, the Paliyans' homeland.

and form two ranges, the Cardamom hills to the west, which average only 3000 feet, and the adjoining eastern range, which is slightly higher, with several peaks of 6000 feet or more. The face of the hills is precipitous from most quarters; because of breaks in the escarpment, the wall is punctuated by valleys. Some of these valleys terminate suddenly, walled in on three sides by near-vertical rock and floored by verdure along the course of swift, cold rivers.

The lower slope is frequently dry, thorn forest, with scattered trees such as *Acacia* and *Albizzia*, spiny bushes such as *Zizyphus*, milk hedge cactus, and seasonal grass (Puri 1960:I 247). Sometimes the ground cover is fairly open and savannahlike, sometimes the thorn bushes are virtually impenetrable. With slightly higher rainfall the lower slope may instead be heavily forested with dry, tropical evergreens, which, though the area is still dry, thorny, and stony, provide a fairly complete canopy in the upper story (Puri 1960:I 246).

Several species of *Dioscorea* yam, which provide the basis of Paliyan subsistence, are found in abundance throughout the lower-altitude botanic zones. Here too are several genera of *Rubiaceae*, bushes with hard wood suitable for making the 10–50-inch digging sticks used in procuring yams. There is a wide variety of fruits (generally in season from May to July), leaves, stems, woods, barks, and roots which are usable for food or manufacture. Some mountain valleys contain bamboo, the young stems of which are edible.

The lower forest is rich in fauna. Mammals include wild pig, elk, red and spotted deer, mouse deer, mountain goat, gaur bison, elephant, wildcat, tiger, leopard, wolf, red dog, jackal, two species of bear, porcupine, otter, rabbit, mongoose, squirrel, field mouse, bat, pangolin, slender loris, and several species of monkey. Birds are not at all numerous, but one sees falcon and eagle, great hornbill, peacock, rock horned owl, woodpecker, forest hen, parrot, bulbul, crow, and dove. Reptiles include two kinds of monitor lizard, chameleon, tortoise, python, various vipers, cobra, and king cobra. Other than black murrel and loach, the fish of the area were not identified. Seven other species are commonly found. A variety of bees manufacture honey in tree holes, on branches, and in three-foot combs on the granite cliffs. The amount of game is particularly striking, considering the claims of older hunters in the area that large-scale poaching has been decimating game in the last twenty years.

Above 3500–4000 feet these dry-forested hillsides tend to become subtropical hill savannah, with trees such as teak standing in the open and various other species forming dense groves along water courses. On wetter hillsides the initial dry zone gives way to heavy, moist, tropical and subtropical forest as low as 2000–3000 feet in altitude. At this intermediate level one finds sago and date palms, both of which have edible pithy stems. And, since the Sangam era, these slopes also have been the home of

A woman and one of her husbands dig in the dry thorn forest for yams. She called him to assist her in levering apart the stones (in background) so that she could reach a large root.

End of the hunt. A small female pig, wounded by a predator sent by the gods, has been tracked for ten hours.

Paliyan houses in a farming village of the plains. They are well-built structures comparable to those of neighboring Tamil villages.

A Paliyan man collecting drinking water from a stagnant pool in a dry river bed.

Social activity in the early morning sun. This hour of the day is spent in the same relaxed way in forest communities and in sedentary villages such as this.

The Paliyan habitat with its light, open forest and seasonal water supply.

aggressive shifting cultivators who have periodically left their millet fields to act as mercenaries for the princes of the plains.

The slopes above 5000 feet, which Paliyans seldom have cause to visit, are cool and wet. Subtropical and temperate forest yields to grasslands above 6000 feet, except along rivers. In contrast with the inhospitable lower slope, these upper zones in the Palni range have black, peaty earth and rich flora.

Rain is a major factor in determining the soil, as well as the flora. Both the time of year at which rainfall comes and the amount of rain vary considerably from range to range. If their orientation is right, some upper slopes pick up large amounts of rain twice annually (June–September and then October–November). But rain-shadow areas are lucky to get even one meager monsoon and sometimes go for many months with no appreciable rain.

Many year-round rivers flow from the upper Anaimalai-Palni ranges which catch rain during both monsoons. Smaller streams in the Palnis and perhaps the majority of the rivers on the eastern side of the smaller ranges to the south tend to dry up seasonally. During the rains water runs off the slope quickly, swelling the rivers, temporarily, into impassable torrents.

Although the Paliyan lives in a habitat which has a problematic water supply, major plant foods which are difficult to obtain, thorny ground cover, and little foliage overhead to protect inhabitants from a tropical sun, discomfort must not be mistaken for inadequacy of resources. While the Paliyan is vocal about each of the difficulties cited above, he finds himself in a forest of relative plenty[3] and faced with no direct competitors for his primary resources.

ECONOMY

The simple food-collecting way of life of the Paliyans could be looked at from the point of view of the classic definition of an economy—as a system of production, distribution, and consumption. But, because of the permissive natural environment and social and ideological emphasis on individual autonomy, it is more to the point to let our description of Paliyan economy revolve, instead, around three of its distinctive aspects: unused resources; pressures for a simple, all-purpose technology; and social aspects of the exploitation of resources. Our description cannot end here, however. It is crucial that we also examine the part played by culture contact in the traditional economy of Paliyans.

During a normal year, Paliyans exploit only a fraction of the food resources in their area. They choose to ignore a number of plants and even more animals for those which they prefer. Nowhere is anything but *Dioscorea* yam found as a staple for those who still dwell in the forest, even though there is a good bit of variation in the foods that are available across the 150 by 80 mile Paliyan region. The roots of the five main species of yam usually weigh between one and ten pounds each. They grow at the base of trailing vines, under and around the great granite boulders, often up to depths of five or six feet. Exploitation, under the best conditions, is a hardship; in dry weather, exposing them with simple, pointed digging sticks becomes substantially more difficult. Informants in more than one area talk of using sago in the past—about a generation ago; for some reason this has generally been discontinued and, at present, a rough estimate by weight is that yams provide 70–80 percent of the food eaten.

While the staple yams are considered "food," there are a number of other vegetable items which do in fact serve as supplements. One could say, for example, that fruits, berries, and nuts are important even though their utilization is by no means proportionate to their seasonal prevalence. There is no regular pattern of exploitation. They are sometimes cooked with other food, brought home as treats for children, or eaten as sweets on the way to and from work, but they are not thought worth leaving a path to pick. Boiled leaves of four species are regarded as somewhat more important, especially during the rainy season. In addition, the durable leaves of *Acacia intsia caesia* (mimosa) serve as an emergency food in times of drought, when yams cannot be dug from the baked earth and even plainsmen come to the forest in search of grass to eat.

Another pursuit, the collecting of honey, is a traditional Paliyan occupation and the one which is best known to outsiders. But the small combs which they occasionally enjoy while working in the forest appear to be of less importance than the large ones, which serve as instruments of barter.

The technology for honey-gathering is fairly complex, the two chief concerns being safety and access. Small bees can be raided without safeguards, and even medium-sized tree-dwelling bees can be driven away merely by crushing a handful of pungent *tarahu* grass, but the giant bees which make combs on cliff faces (or in the highest trees) have to be driven away with smoke. Their sting is severe; dense smoke is the only effective deterrent. Paliyans from four to seventy are agile in the trees. Large, unbranching trunks may, however, require that vine-tied ladders of wood be used—especially to ensure an easy descent. Ladders for descending cliff faces are constructed of interlocked vine loops fastened to a twisted three-strand vine rope, two or three lengths of which are joined together with a modified sheet-bend knot.

It is difficult to assess the degree to which honey is or is not exploited. In the case of hunting, the nonutilization of resources is much more clear-cut. Big game is generally ignored, as is a good deal of small game. Wild pig and deer are the two animals of any size to be hunted deliberately; the usual game is monitor lizard, forest hen, rock horned owl, bat, loris, field mouse, squirrel, rabbit, fish, and other such small animals.

The Paliyans talk about tigers and wild red dogs, which, under the influence of the Paliyan gods, kill and leave large game on their behalf. This supernatural aid may be their most effective tool for the hunt because the Paliyans' own implements are merely pointed sticks, stones (for small animals in trees), iron-tipped spears borrowed on occasion from plains villagers, or billhooks acquired from the barter of honey and other forest produce. Hunting and trapping are sometimes planned: deer are driven across treacherous rocks or into ambush; small game is enticed into simple deadfalls made of large stones propped up with baited sticks. But, more typically, game is encountered accidentally and dealt with on an *ad hoc* basis. Pigs wounded by poachers are spotted and trailed. Rabbits and mice are followed to their burrows and dug out.

Fish are significant, seasonally, as food. Two fish poisons are used in still water; in running water fish can be caught in "nets" of cloth, either by sweeping the cloth through the water or by making a small stone dam which spills its water through a pole-propped cloth.

A list of the resources which Paliyans choose not to exploit would be long indeed. Their natural environment in a good year is bounteous far beyond human need. While this allows them a wide margin of safety in times of distress, conditions do sometimes become so difficult that inter-regional migrations are necessary. In normal times Paliyan men and women spend a bare three to four hours a day in obtaining food and evidence no anxiety whatsoever about its supply. They find the work arduous, to be sure, but this is accepted as a condition of existence.

With the value that they place upon mobility, Paliyans usually maintain only the smallest kit of tools. The preferred implement is all-purpose. Almost every Paliyan adult carries a billhook either in his hand or tucked in his clothing; with its 8–12-inch hooked blade it serves as his chief tool and weapon. Billhooks are so essential today that it is difficult to conjure up a picture of how Paliyans exploited their environment in the past without them. Paliyans may have been able to trade forest goods for ready-made metal implements even centuries ago, as we know the Ceylon Veddas to have done. But before that the picture is unclear. While the few limestone outcrops in the Paliyan area may contain chert, there is no archaeological or historical record as to the sort of technology which pre-existed the Paliyans' use of metal. Of more specific function than the billhook is the digging stick. Its size varies with need and with extent of resharpening. Women straighten their sticks after first heating the bends in a fire and then prepare very fine points on them. In contrast with the women, who keep good sticks and may have two or three on hand, men find it more convenient to manufacture sticks when needed. They seldom carry sticks with them, discarding even a good one after a single use.

The paucity of specialized technology can again be seen in the relative lack of nonsubsistence manufactures. Those things which are made show a good deal of formal variation, a variation which can usually be referred to ecological factors. Houses or shelters provide a good illustration. Some Paliyans spend at least ten months of the year as full nomads, sleeping a night or two at a time in rock shelters, in or under trees, and in comparable places of shelter from sun, wind, and animals; these people build houses, if at all, only during the brief period of rains. Others are more sedentary and construct houses of puddled mud, equal in size and durability to those of peasant Indians. Between these extremes there is a wide range of shelters and houses, variously thatched, walled or unwalled, large or small, that almost defies description in terms of formal modes or norms. Where a structure is made at all, the one regularly occurring feature is a ridgepole to support two sloping sides. Even so, one-sided roofs have been observed and roof pitch itself is a variable. On the sloping sides a variety of thatches is used, from palm leaves to grass. *Tarahu* grass is especially good when available because of its ability to shed water and to adhere to a reasonable slope without being fastened down. But if there is relatively little value placed on one particular form or style of shelter, one would do well to review the situational variables which might have an effect on the form: building materials immediately at hand, local climate, number of persons to be accommodated, manpower available for construction, and degree of permanence intended. Of these, the last consideration overrides the others, because, in order to preserve independence and to avoid unnecessary contact with non-Paliyans, almost any compromise with residential stability is acceptable. Small bands sometimes have only one or two small shelters for all fifteen or twenty persons. In larger groups each house builder constructs his home at a site which is personally convenient, so that the over-all form of settlements is as variable as that of the separate houses.

Paliyan methods of exploiting their natural environment are simple from the social standpoint as well as the material. Although several food-collecting activities benefit from some degree of cooperation between families, the majority of subsistence pursuits entail only individuals or at most nuclear families. Without much hardship at all, one person alone may constitute a unit of production and consumption. Of those activities which do frequently involve extrafamilial cooperation, hunting of deer and pig and honey-gathering are the most important.

A hunting group of five to ten operates in terms of discussion and consensus with no one person obviously dominating the decision-making. Without centralization the group manages, nonetheless, to surround the quarry and to cover escape routes with a conscientiousness proportionate to the value of the animal and the excitement generated. Group-hunted game is dissected into tiny pieces, then apportioned out into piles which contain equal amounts of each part of the animal. When all have agreed that the piles are of equal size, each hunter takes one, whatever his role in the hunt. Cooperation of a similar sort is witnessed also when poisonous snakes are found in the settlement, but coordination of snake hunts is usually not adequate to ensure killing the snake. Gaps in the line and children underfoot reduce the effectiveness of the effort. One might call such activity parallel, rather than joint, and its effectiveness is in direct measure to the motivation of the participants.

Genuine cooperation in the form of coordinated, complementary labor is necessary for exploiting cliff honey. One person descends the cliff on a vine ladder while another is needed at the top to watch the ladder. This is treated as a very special activity. Indeed, one of the few Paliyan "formulas" prescribes the relation between the two participants in this exploitative pursuit—they should be brothers-in-law, or, alternatively, father-in-law and son-in-law. Some informants went on to say that one should never do this with a brother, who would sever the ladder and steal one's wife. If we consider that Paliyans fear rivalry and that rivalry is expressed in terms of sexuality, then it becomes clear that wife's father and wife's brother are appropriate guardians of the ladder. Because they are among the least likely sex rivals in the society, they are maximally trustworthy in terms of Paliyan sociology.

None of the above activities is that of regularly constituted groups, hunting especially being on an *ad hoc* basis. Households, by contrast, persist through time and are the locus of frequent cooperation. Even so, while they are the only durable social units to be characterized by economic cooperation, for them too the cooperation is qualified. To understand this situation we have to refer to conditions which permit and which restrict human behavior in general. First, as has been stated above, although basic subsistence pursuits are arduous, they are usually within the ability of a healthy individual to carry out alone. Second, for social and ideological reasons that will be discussed in full below, Paliyans avail themselves to a great extent of the opportunity for economic autonomy which is permitted them ecologically. The ideological factors which prescribe individual autonomy, are, however, less imperative within the nuclear family, so that one finds husband and wife joining forces in nonobligatory contexts. They work together to lever aside two- or three-ton boulders to obtain the yams below. However, they also share much less demanding tasks than this, perhaps in feeding their children, perhaps just in the spirit of flirtation. If they choose instead to lead parallel lives, each feeding only himself for months at a time, this too is acceptable under the more general rules for interaction. A peripheral member of a household is in a different position. Take the case of a sixty-five-year-old widow who lives with her son's family. If she chooses to go off to the forest alone for two weeks at a time she is not at all an object of concern for her household or her neighbors. She is viewed instead as having the skills and capabilities required for survival just as if she were a thirty-year-old man. Not only is her right to exploit this freedom beyond question, but if she failed to demonstrate such economic self-sufficiency it would actually be held against her. Only infirmity, advanced pregnancy, extreme age, or pyschological disorientation would oblige the family to accept a dependent. This is not to say that an old woman will not care for grandchildren, but she must take the initiative for her own maintenance.

Members of related families frequently go to and from work together, and they even work side by side as work parties. Their labor, once more, is what one could call parallel. If they attempt to remain together, it appears to be for reasons other than effective exploitation of their environment. For example, different work parties or dispersed members of one work party are likely to converse sporadically over great distances by shouting simple messages back and forth in a high-pitched voice. By this means they are able to facilitate communal rest in early afternoon and a synchronized return from work.

In the foregoing discussions there have been several references to culture contact and its effect on Paliyan economics. Far from being an intrusive factor, one that can simply be subtracted in order to reveal a pure food-collecting economy, it is an integral aspect of the economic system to be described. In fact, the systematic consideration of intercultural environment is just as vital to our study of "traditional" Paliyan economics as it would be to the study of a peasant village. The main impact from without will be discussed from three viewpoints: bartered goods, the possibility of inferring aboriginal economic patterns, and recent adjustments to expanding Indian society.

There is a great deal more to external barter than the trading of honey for billhooks. The most isolated Paliyan band is likely to have not only one billhook per family (or per adult) but also a knife or an axe, clothing, simple ornaments, steel and quartz for fire-making, and cooking pots. Consumables also find their way into Paliyan hands: salt, chilies, rice, tobacco, snuff, betel, and areca. These items will have been acquired by trading honey, medicinal roots and barks, resins, elk horn, hemp fiber, captured young animals (such as the loris, valued medicinally), soap nuts, and so on. The exchange may instead be for services—Paliyans guide pilgrims to forest temples in return for cooking pots, clothing, or cash; they tend cattle or goats seasonally in the forest for plainsmen in return for small periodic payments.

One cannot really talk about any of the existing economic patterns as being aboriginal. The most isolated nomadic bands are responding through mobility and dispersal to their intercultural environment. Under culture-contact pressure the premium which Paliyans have learned to place upon self-sufficiency has in turn put limits on the nature of exploitative groups and on the kinds of resources which it is practical to exploit. Thus, paradoxically, the first and foremost phenomenon that has to be interpreted with reference to intercultural relations is simplicity in the economy of isolated Paliyans.

A precontact aboriginal pattern is impossible to infer. The present-day population density of up to two persons per square mile suggests that, in absence of intercultural pressure, the Paliyans would have been permitted a more sedentary existence, settlements would have been larger than the usual present size of eighteen to thirty, and ways of exploiting their natural environment would have been wholly different. There are innumerable obstacles to our drawing these conclusions. Almost no elements of the present ecological situation can be extrapolated into a precontact past. This would entail looking back a very long way. And, not only do the Paliyan "resources" which permit the present population density include the efficient items of technology obtained through barter, but there is no particular reason to locate unharassed food collectors in the narrow zone of inhospitable, dry thorn forest in the first place.

In recent years India's tremendous need for wood and the expansion of plantations into the forest have been working together with other factors to destroy the Paliyan habitat on the one hand and to offer alternative sources of income on the other. The last half century, and particularly the last twenty years, has seen an increasing number of Paliyans move into more or less regular labor on plantations, achieving closer contact with Tamils, while at the same time retaining their customary habitat. Families move from one sphere into the other as needs arise, or they exploit both simultaneously. The next step has been for Paliyans to become day laborers outside the forest, but few have done it and then only with much vacillation and hesitancy. Emergence from the forest has been helped, however, by the appearance of benevolent agents (welfare workers, malarial eradication crews, Block Development Officers, and teachers) in the period since Indian independence (1947). They have shown Paliyans that all Indians do not "bully" in the manner of so many forest contractors, forest guards, and police; their superiority has been more subtle and less difficult to rationalize. The new jobs provide Paliyans with wages that are lower than those of their plainsmen co-workers, but Paliyans are rarely as productive or reliable as Tamil laborers because of their continuing residential instability and noncompetitive attitudes. For the moment their wages mean newly acquired luxuries and social enfranchisement, even though most of the pay must go for low-grade rice. These recent developments will all be considered in more detail at the end of the chapter.

SOCIAL STRUCTURE

Paliyans place particular emphasis upon individuals. Because of the way in which a group compromises the autonomy of an individual, it is both important and interesting in characterizing Paliyan social structure to pay attention to social aggregates. After a look at the household, the band, and some less formalized intermediate groupings, we shall turn our attention to patterns of interaction and, finally, to mechanisms of cultural transmission and maintenance.

GROUPS

A Paliyan band is made up of a number of households, which are as distinctive socially as they are economically. In most cases households consist of complete nuclear families or nuclear families which lack one adult, but they may also be made up of lone individuals or small, loosely knit, extended families. Since most Paliyan households revolve about a marriage, it is appropriate to begin our description with a look at this institution. Detailed discussion of the position of children in the household will be kept for the section on socialization.

At a given time, most adult Paliyans in a settlement are cohabiting and cooperating economically with one or more persons of the opposite sex. It is quite frequent, especially in first partnerships, for the union to have been solemnized with the exchange of betel leaves and salt and a promise of lifelong fidelity. Though it may endure only a matter of days, a public union, with or without such ceremony, is considered a legitimate marriage. While many marriages last for life, the usual situation is one of fragile, often serial, unions, terminated quickly by the offended party when conflict arises. Previous marriages are sometimes resumed, often after one or more intervening unions (see Figs. 10-2 and 10-3). Additional forest liaisons with lovers punctuate each life history.

Paliyans generally prefer a monogamous union with a person of the same age. However, to meet special needs three alternate arrangements exist. First, old people who are unmarried often form unions with very young partners. Sixteen out of 153 marriages recorded are of this type; more complete data might reveal still other cases in the sample. These pedogamous[4] unions originate in two ways. Some children are adopted at about six to eight years of age and make a quick but gradual transition from the status of son or daughter to that of husband or wife. Conjugal relations may be initiated before parent-child kin terms are given up; they certainly precede puberty. The other sort of pedogamous arrangement entails marriage with a stepchild, specifically, the child of a former spouse in the fashion of "Lolita." Two examples are shown in the upper left-hand corner of Figure 10-3. In a population of sixty, simultaneously three men were courting mother and daughter pairs. Each of these cases looked like the beginning of new Lolita arrangements. The advantage of pedogamous marriage is expressed in terms of sexual satisfaction and malleability— young partners can be "brought up to behave properly." There seems to be a suggestion that compatibility is more certain where marriage is built upon the foundation of a parent-child relationship. Such unions have a

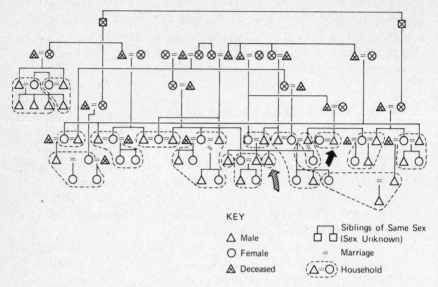

KEY

△ Male
○ Female
△ Deceased (shaded)

⊡ ⊡ Siblings of Same Sex (Sex Unknown)
= Marriage
(△=○) Household

Figure 10–2. Households among three related Paliyan bands that have recently settled together near a plantation. Deceased persons and former spouses are shown only where they clarify present relationships; relatives residing elsewhere are not shown. The black arrow indicates the headman and the shaded arrow the sibling group whose marriages are represented in Figure 10–3.

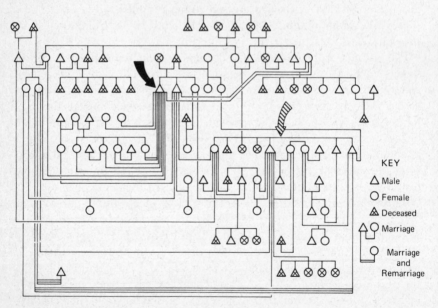

KEY

△ Male
○ Female
△ Deceased
△○ Marriage
△○ (vertical) Marriage and Remarriage

Figure 10–3. Paliyan marriages. Most living individuals are those portrayed in Figure 10–2. Marriages of a headman (black arrow) and of a sibling group (shaded arrow) are shown as completely as possible.

durability which is above average, as if to bear out the judgment of the contracting parties. Informants expressed no interest in the latent economic value of these arrangements, that is, as insurance for the aged, but then planned dependence is antithetical to Paliyan mores.

The second variant form of marriage, polygyny, is less common. Four cases were recorded, only two of these on the basis of firsthand evidence. One of the cases I knew directly involved three sisters who were married on and off, sometimes simultaneously, to the same man. They had a joint household when living as co-wives. This case is the only one known to be sororal, but like the two which were known from indirect sources, it involved a "headman," a fact which deserves further treatment below. In the other case I observed, the co-wives were not related. Instead of there being a joint household, one of the women lived separately with another husband.

No purpose could be elicited for the polygynous unions, which is of interest in itself. The third variant marital arrangement, polyandry, has an explicit rationale. In the two instances I recorded, a woman remained in economic and residential union with an ill and therefore (reputedly) sexually incapable first partner while enjoying stable and publicly acknowledged sexual relations with another man. These were long-term arrangements which the original husbands resented but tolerated to avoid insulting and losing their wives. In each case other people termed both men husbands and showed acceptance of the situation by tracing kinship relationships through both of the marriages without hesitancy. One of the arrangements involved residential unity and a degree of economic cooperation between the men; in neither case were the men brothers.

While exceptional marital arrangements have helped make clear the limits of a household, the normal situation also warrants close study. In most instances a monogamously married pair constitutes the core of a residentially, sexually, procreatively, and economically distinct family group. Although the household is the only unit of Paliyan society characterized by any degree of cooperation, this attribute should not be overemphasized. The cooperation is not at all marked, either in the form of division of labor or joint labor. For example, in one instance a couple that lived together in outward harmony had exchanged no food in four months. Each spouse had provided his or her own food, though both had helped feed their children. One should note, however, that if the husband or the wife had been unable to work, then cooperation would have been expected.

Within a nuclear family, there is no clear line between individual and joint property, except as defined by needs of the moment. Items such as a plate, a billhook, or food, which are of value to both husband and wife, should be given away or bartered only by mutual agreement. There might be an exception if the item is surplus and if a person gives it to a relative who is not a competitor for the spouse's attention. The criterion of surplus is important; for a man to give food to his needy grandchild when food for his own household is short is a distinct violation of his wife's rights. Though preference should in general not be shown, if anyone does have the right to preferred treatment it is the husband, wife, or immature child. When an item such as a piece of clothing, used by only one person, is given away by that person, there can be little difficulty, unless giving of the gift suggests that there has been a breach of the conjugal rights of the spouse. Husband and wife have exclusive, mutual sex rights, except where plural marriages occur. And, even in the latter instance, sexual jealousy may be a significant disruptive factor. Since an injured party is expected to leave, there is little actual redress possible when conjugal rights have been violated.

The simplest and most comprehensive way of phrasing the various sorts of personal rights which are relevant to family structure is in terms of authority. Independence of authority is a treasured right. Neither spouse can order the other and neither, by virtue of sex or age, is entitled to a greater voice in matters of mutual concern. Thus, whether a problem is individual or shared, it should be settled on the basis of equal rights of spouses. As we shall see below, the rights of older children are expressed in a similar fashion.

While economic independence of household members is permitted, and, while their autonomy is deemed a right, the household gains considerable coherence from dyadic bonds of affection. Affection may be expressed merely by proximity at work and during rest; grooming and playful light teasing represent an upper limit for its overt expression in public. Most couples are discreet and undemonstrative before others. Ties of affection appear also to form the explicit basis of extended family aggregates where these exist. Aging persons, especially widowed women, live near or with affectionate married sons and daughters. And young men and women who have lost their parents but who are not married are likely to attach themselves to the households of those married siblings with whom they feel close. In just one case, that of a very old woman, was the additional party observed to be economically dependent. A residential unit is seldom more than a socially coherent group that engages in parallel economic and recreational behavior. There may be some activity of mutual benefit (gathering fish together) and some mutual help (especially with infants or in time of sickness), but it is evident that the main ties are companionship with the trusted and close.

The membership of a Paliyan band is always in flux, since individual as well as group mobility is great. Yet, one can say with assurance that movements are far from random. A man is not likely to go to live with a band in which neither he nor his wife have primary relatives or, at least, near kin. In a big settlement of sixty, nearly half the marriages are group endogamous; in a usual-sized nomadic band of eighteen to thirty persons, most marriages are between related adjacent bands. In either case marriage tends only to compound the kinship bonds of an already closely inter-related group instead of creating new networks of relationship. And this means that the movements of a family usually do not transcend a cluster of three or four bands. If the actual composition of a band is difficult to define from the point of view of formal structure, at least the basis for membership is clear.

Members of unrelated or distantly related bands may be thrown together by interterritorial movements in times of stress and by the economic ad-vantages of living near large plantations. It is usual, under these circum-stances, for not one person but a group of relatives, such as a sibling group with their spouses, to migrate. Immigrant groups in larger settlements are reserved or aloof at first; but children's play groups and intermarriage eventually generate broader feelings of community.

Community-wide interaction takes place in the contexts of emergency, hunting, recreation, and ceremony. Games in which adults participate and dancing are evening entertainment. Recreation groups of this kind are made up of people of the same sex, but with ages varying from about seven to thirty or forty; membership crosscuts all kinship lines. The dances are mainly circle dances with simple steps upon which individual dancers elaborate. Any drums or wind instruments which have been acquired from non-Paliyans give a rough accompaniment. Men play a version of "prisoner's base," for which they give the "rules" in the form known to plains Tamils. They have transformed the game, however, by eliminating the elements of cooperation and competition. The game for them is a ballet with as many primadonnas as participants. No one catches anyone else and, in fact, no player expresses much interest in another's performance.

Probably nothing brings a whole band or settlement together as effec-tively as a wedding or funeral. Virtually everyone is present and no one considers going to work if there will be a feast (toward which all con-cerned parties contribute, if able). Funerals of children are quiet affairs, but those of mature persons affect the whole community deeply; there is a clear sense of obligation to be present. Indeed, for the funerals of the elderly both relatives from distant bands and representative delegations from adjacent groups may try to be present. Other kinds of rituals do not always lead to the same physical unification of the group. For example, patterns of attendance at annual festivals to the local deities or "first fruit" ceremonies for yams are highly variable from region to region. In some bands, first fruit rites are celebrated individually by households at times of their own convenience; one band, by contrast, had full attendance for the ceremony. In another region, an annual festival to the seven locally recognized deities was performed at a shrine a mile from the settlement with only a third of the community present. But all of the absentees except a Christian convert, a very old woman, and a recent immigrant had primary relatives present.

Intermediate, between the household and the band, are groupings which form along kinship lines, but which have no permanent definition. Those people with whom one sits in the early morning sun or after dinner, with whom one walks to work or to fetch water, and to whom one extends aid in emergencies are normally of such a group. While we could think of them as constituting small kindreds, this is only approximately correct: interaction diminishes rapidly among tertiary and more distant relatives and, purely from the point of view of interaction, certain consanguines within this range (for example, a man's brother) are excluded from the group while certain affines (for examples, a man's brothers-in-law or a woman's daughters-in-law) are included. The Paliyans' own term, *sonda-kārar* (roughly, "relative"), which is usually used with about this scope, does, however, include a man's brother.[5]

Paliyan communities and kin groups have little of the coherence and few of the corporate functions with which students of folk culture are familiar.

PATTERNS OF INTERACTION

Patterns of interaction are of two sorts, those which are characteristic of interpersonal relations in general and those which are particular to the kinship realm. They will be dealt with in this order.

The Paliyans were portrayed in the preceding discussion as highly individualistic people, uncomfortable either cooperating or competing. To put this in their terms, they are quick to condemn as disrespectful any sort of behavior in others which interferes with their autonomy as individuals. The term which I translate "to be disrespectful" means more literally "to lower or diminish status"; in the context of egalitarian ideals it constitutes an interesting way of phrasing the loss of autonomy that can result from cooperation or competition.

The Paliyan avoidance of cooperation is nearly as complete as it can be if society as such is to be retained. That this orientation ramifies widely has been shown already by numerous examples of the way in which it shapes economic interaction and the formation of social groups. Behavior in these two spheres and others appears to be influenced by an underlying but consciously felt need to avoid unnecessary dependence. Dependence involves two things: an abdication of one's own sovereign rights and dependence on the resources of others, which amounts to a violation of their sovereign rights as well. Without concerning ourselves for the moment about how individual Paliyans might develop their desire for personal autonomy, it is worth noting that emotional ties of all sorts are kept down in a manner suggesting that autonomy is of psychological as well as social significance to the Paliyans.

Helpful and friendly behavior have observable limits which help us to demarcate the circle within which emotional interaction is to be found. An effective sense of obligation to extend aid beyond the household in emergencies is usually limited to certain primary relationships: brother-sister, sister-sister, and parent-grown child. Anyone will come to the aid of a child that is hurt or afraid, but then a child is allowed to be dependent. Warm, friendly interaction is not often observed, except within the nuclear family and surreptitiously between lovers. Between members of a household or members of primarily related households (such as grandparent and grandchild, mother-in-law and daughter-in-law, or brothers-in-law) friendship is acceptable though not effusive. Intimacy beyond the immediate circle of kin is something else. For one thing, extrafamilial friendship between persons of opposite sex implies for the spouse of either party a violation of marital rights. This is so even if the friendship is with a kinsman; the very narrow definition of incest employed by Paliyans and their demonstrated preference for intragroup marriage allow little freedom between the sexes that could be judged innocuous. And, in one acknowledged case of friendship between two young married men who were unrelated, the smiles which followed enquiry about their relationship and informants' statements that they "go to the forest together" connote a sexual component to their interaction. Whether or not they were meant in fun, the smiles and comments suggest that Paliyan friendship is largely a conjugal matter.

Regarding their avoidance of competition, it is of first importance that Paliyans assert an explicit code of nonviolence. One man expressed it thus in his first interview: "If struck on one side of the face, you turn the other side toward the attacker." But it is avoidance of overt aggression in a much broader sense that is meant by this rule. As has already been brought out, they extend their injunction against competition even to games.

Paliyans appear to believe that competitiveness arises from a desire to rival, a desire for superiority, influence, and control. Even in its mildest form, this would be a denial of the egalitarianism and autonomy which every adult preserves so jealously. Paliyans are self-conscious about receiving anything which sets them off from others. For example, when it was noted that Virappan had gathered far more soap nuts than anyone else for a forest contractor and would be paid more, he squirmed uncomfortably and denied it. Then he smiled, placed his hand on the next man's shoulder and in effect said that tomorrow the other man would collect more than he. In this and other cases the discomfort appears to be over the implication of rivalry. There is considerable motivation to minimize or deny social or economic differences. In this context the status of headman bears close examination. A band usually has one or two people who are designated by a term (shared with plains Tamils) which translates literally as "headman." In some instances there is no headman; there may be up to three.

Forest contractors invariably designate still other men, industrious men, as leaders, hoping thereby to facilitate their exploitative enterprises. But Paliyans, by introducing these quasi-foremen to other outsiders as "headmen," do not necessarily imply that these men meet their own expectations of headmanship. To the contrary, often just the opposite is true because their criteria for intracommunal headmanship are specific and quite independent of the criteria contractors use. In a society in which, ideally, authority or power statuses are symmetric (the only legitimate exception being the complementary statuses of parents and immature children), the resolution of social conflicts is greatly furthered if skilled people voluntarily act as conciliators. Whether they use calm words or the distraction of wit, their intervention can be of great advantage without violating the rights of those in conflict. However, headmen may come to appreciate the influence which derives from their subtle but legitimate manipulation of others; they are graced with titles and sometimes with limited ritual prerogatives as well. It should not be a surprise to find that some headmen are not the best representatives of their culture's norms, that some of them manifest a slight arrogance or officiousness. It should be equally understandable that other men are hesitant to acknowledge any additional "rights" of headmen such as that of polygyny. When confronted with the fact that three of my four cases of polygyny involved headmen, informants uniformly denied any possible connection. But these denials were almost too emphatic to be convincing and they were offered by the same men who reported dreaming that they, but not other men (including the headman), could fly. Could this not indicate at least an unconscious interest in achievement of power and a resentment of those who have openly achieved it? In addition, since rivalry is usually expressed in sexual terms, might not some headmen have violated the norm of monogamy as an expression of their feeling of superiority over others? The questions are not farfetched. The only polygynous headman known directly by me did indeed have an awkward position in the community. Though he was a masterful wit, I eventually began to hear oblique criticism of his assertiveness and a questioning of his stature as a headman. One might say that the Paliyan cultural maps at this point are capable of leading skilled men off the accepted path. Past rewards for correct performance tempt headmen to push toward actual leadership.

The Paliyan classification of relatives is distinctive in having two underlying patterns, not one.[6] Each classification is applicable to a particular context: one to the intracommunal context in which no non-Paliyans are present and the other to the extracommunal context. As communication with an ethnographer takes place in the latter context, it was only due to informant error that the intracommunal kinship system became known to me.

I first became aware of variability of usage when I found that informants were actually uncertain of which terms to use for close relatives. Initial interviews revealed a fairly straightforward Dravidian terminology, yet 15 percent of the terms given were at variance with the rest. Furthermore, informants frequently "changed their minds" about the appropriate terms even for tertiary and secondary kin. And sometimes Paliyans passing by would "correct" informants. When they introduced the notion of "correctness," it became quite clear that the high rate of "errors" was itself a phenomenon to be studied. In many cases Paliyans are related to each other in two, three, or more ways, because of their close marriages. When such cases were omitted from the sample an analysis of the remaining body of errors showed that there were really only two kinds of mistakes. And these tallied with kinship terms that I was beginning to hear used when my presence was not obvious.

Intracommunally, kin terms differentiate male from female. Second, kin are distinguished from affines. Third, among kin, the kin terms differentiate generations in a regular fashion. Fourth, affines are designated by a special set of terms which are skewed a generation depending on whether the linking affines are male or female. This skewing is best explained with the help of an example. The term *atte* (which in extracommunal context would refer to MoBrWi, FaSi, and WiMo) refers intracommunally to two quite different groups of relatives: (1) women of the second ascending generation who are related through one's wife or brother's wife and (2) women of one's own generation related through one's husband or sister's husband. This sort of skewing is entirely regular. The skew is used somewhat less regularly for the children of skewed individuals where the children are not themselves affines. For example, ego's brother's wife is an affine and, although her son is also ego's brother's son, he may be given a skewed term in the same manner as his mother. This skewing is reciprocated so that brother's son and father's brother use terms for each other which in the extracommunal context are used for males separated by two generations. Thus, except that affinal terminology is given this skew, the kinship terms used privately among Paliyans are patterned in a way that is usually called generational or Hawaiian.

When non-Paliyans are present, the criteria for differentiating kin are quite different. Sex and generation of ego's relatives are still taken into account, but the essential patterning is provided by two other criteria—bifurcation and relative age.

Bifurcation denotes a distinction between (1) those relatives who are linked to ego by a cross-sex sibling relationship or a single affinal bond, on the one hand, and (2) ego's lineal relatives plus those who are linked to ego by a same-sex sibling relationship (plus those who are affines of affines, affines of "cross" relatives, and so on), on the other. It is the so-called cross-parallel distinction.[7]

Distinguishing terms are used for kinsmen of one's own generation who are older or younger than oneself and for first ascending generation parallel kinsmen who are older or younger than one's parents. This sort of distinction, by relative age, is shared with the plains Tamils, as is bifurcation.

The problematic kin terms that I first elicited were from the extracommunal kinship system, with about 15 percent interference (that is, accidental intrusions) from the intracommunal terminology. These errors were almost all either in the form of generational terms or affinal skew.

To move now from the area of kin terminology to kinship behavior, we find a repetition of the same double patterning. And the variation, once more, is not that between ideal and real but that between two independent sets of principles, each appropriate in its own context.

Paliyans insisted that they marry cross-cousins and cross-nieces exclusively—actual ones, not classificatory—and that they are barred from unions with parallel cousins and nieces. While compliance with their stated norms is impossible for statistical reasons, the real nature of their marriage pattern is such that it could not have been predicted from those norms: 22 percent of marriages are with the prescribed cross-kin; 19 percent are with the supposedly forbidden parallel kin. Once I got outside the interview situation and overheard old women talking about the potential matches of adolescents, it became clear that the cross-relative ideal for marriage was never voiced as an intracommunal ideal. To the contrary, for purposes of marriage, a sort of bilateralism prevailed: cross- and parallel relatives were held to be functionally equivalent and, if anything, genealogical propinquity was the basis for preference. This aspect of the double patterning was borne out by other data. During a marriage ceremony, I was informed that the bride's mother's only brother would be the first recipient of a salute, after the parents of the couple had been honored. I missed this part of the ritual (meaning that no outsiders were present at the time), but made inquiries immediately afterwards. Although family relations were excellent, the salutation had not taken place, and neither had there been protest or comment. Again, the ideal of preferential treatment of a cross-kinsman as verbalized to an outsider was not actualized in intracommunal behavior.

In trying to understand the Paliyan emphasis upon bilateralism in intracommunal kinship we should recall their principle of social symmetry or egalitarian respect. This is the first rule of Paliyan social interaction. I find that when Paliyans talk about bilateralism they do so in terms of egalitarianism. They act as if they are afraid of the possible consequences of favoritism toward certain classes of relatives; I expect they are.

The very absoluteness of the principle invites us to ask whether there are no exceptional or privileged relationships among Paliyans. There are. Affines stand out clearly from the otherwise bilateral, egalitarian matrix. In many instances there is open friendship between brothers-in-law, between father-in-law and son-in-law, and between mother-in-law and daughter-in-law without any indication that it bears seeds of social disruption. These affines are treated by one another with more intimacy than their genealogical position would lead us to expect. The special status of affines finds its most explicit expression in the ritualistic context of honey-gathering on the cliffs. The guardian of the vine ladder must be father-in-law or brother-in-law; it may not be one's brother. Paliyans explain this formalization of roles in terms of rivalry: "Your brother will kill you for your wife." The implication is that one may trust those who are unlikely sex rivals (unless incestuously or because of lovers in common). As echoed by the emphasis upon complementation in kin terms, one's relationship with the guardian of the ladder is a complementary relationship par excellence. Dependence could hardly be more real.

Kinship behavior is part of the neatly patterned double kinship system which was revealed by the study of kin terms. In the one sphere there is bilateralism and affinal relationships are distinct, and in the other, cross-parallel distinctions are of great importance. It is tidy indeed that Paliyans use the same set of kin terms for affines as for cross-relatives, but then this equivalence is already part of the Dravidian kinship system.

TRANSMISSION AND MAINTENANCE

We are able, to some extent, to identify the means by which basic patterns in Paliyan culture are transmitted from one generation to the next; we can also isolate a hierarchy of the mechanisms by which they are maintained in the face of the conflicts and difficulties which are inevitable in human society. These two aspects of perpetuation of the Paliyan cultural system will be dealt with in terms of the following four topics: socialization, social controls, order and the supernatural, and systemic needs.

During the first stage of Paliyan child-training indulgence is very prominent. Initial indulgence is so extreme, in fact, that it is beyond that of any culture in the large world sample of Whiting and Child (1953).[8] This lack of restraint is illustrated by the following examples.

The child spends most of its sleeping and waking hours in direct physical contact with its mother's body. In the daytime, it rests on her left hip in a sling formed from a swath of her upper sari cloth. At night, it sleeps by her side. The mother gives her breast to the child at the slightest whimper, as often as four or five times an hour; denial even at night would be inconceivable, because, as they put it, the child's throat would become dry. Infants over a year old ask regularly for these night feeds. There is a great deal of maternal warmth during the first two years, and much concern is expressed for the infant. Unless a child is ill, prolonged crying is unlikely. Outbursts of anger are rare; they are averted or appeased quickly, if possible. The most inappropriate elimination accidents, such as on the mother's clothing or in a grandparent's fireplace, provoke little or no annoyance. The mother coos softly to the child as she cleans up the mess. Normally a child is simply held away from the mother as it relieves itself. There are no sexual restraints in the early years; there is no clothing, no segregation of the sexes, and no punishment or disapproval of interest in or manipulation of the genitals of self or others. The initial period of indulgence is more prolonged in the sexual sphere than in others.

The comforting world of the child undergoes a series of rapid changes at the time of weaning at about two or two and a half years of age. The mother not only denies the child her breast or deters it with bitter paste on the nipples, but she puts it down now for increasingly long periods. It may even be left (with playmates, older siblings, a grandmother, or someone who is staying behind) when the mother goes to work. Facing situations without continuous maternal guidance for the first time, the child is suddenly introduced to new kinds of experiences—misbehavior and punishment. For example, the child may stray into somebody's pot of food or it may strike another child. Although the punishment will not go beyond an angry word or at most a mild slap, this is a distinct change of tone, especially if it comes from the mother. During this period the mother frequently attempts to ignore her child's demands. When it presses for attention it is a common sight to see the mother busy her hands, tighten her lips, and avert her eyes. If the child is not already crying, it becomes enraged at its mother's lack of response; it cries spasmodically, pulls its hair, and stamps its feet. During this performance the child remains in a squatting position, which reminds one of its position and range of movements on the mother's hip. Alternatively it curls up on its side and sobs. A grandmother or aunt may on occasion pick the child up and take it off to be pacified, but it seldom calms down in less than ten to twenty minutes. Such tantrums continue until the child is four or five; in one case the episodes persisted until ten years of age.

The move into adulthood progresses steadily from here on, with independence in the different behavioral spheres being achieved at different ages. Emotional independence comes first, possibly as a result of the mother's treatment. Thus, by about four years of age the child seldom violates the basic social rules; certainly by the time it is five it plays quietly without fighting with its playmates; it is reticent but it gives the impression of being socially skilled and self-confident. Soon afterwards there is maturation in technological skills. Nobody pays attention to a two- or three-year-old who runs about with a razor-sharp billhook or who climbs on a house top. A five-year-old is permitted to make fires for preparing food. But a child is usually about seven before it is in control of basic technology. Social independence finally comes at eight or nine, or perhaps ten, after which time the child is beyond parental punishment and is, in fact, beyond the authority of any person other than itself. Frequently, a young adult is not fully independent economically before thirteen or fourteen so that families may contain several people who are socially mature. On the other hand, these same young people will for several years have been free to contract employment where they please or to marry a person of their own choosing.

The marked features of child-training are initial indulgence; then sharp discontinuity at the age of two and a half in the areas of feeding, independence, and control over aggression; and, finally, after a turbulent transition period, an early, smooth assumption of adult roles. Probably more as a response to subtle pressures for autonomy than due to formal indoctrination, the Paliyan child learns to be self-sufficient and to leave others alone.

Yet, no training is perfect and, as in all societies, interpersonal tensions and other violations of order are inevitable. Adult Paliyans require means of resolving conflicts which accord with the basic rules of their way of life. Censure of a person, which originates either from the group or from a single leader, does not so accord; it is a breach of that person's sovereignty. Moreover, joint group-administered controls call for a social coherence which cannot be expected of Paliyans. Order can, however, be maintained or restored without violating the rules. And this can be done by means of a hierarchy of personal, social, and supernatural mechanisms. The personal and social mechanisms are five in number, several of them having been mentioned in the course of describing Paliyan society.

The first personal mechanism, quite simply, is the exercise of self-restraint. Besides suppression, which is a conscious withholding of expressions of hostility, there may also be repression of angry feelings, but it was beyond the scope of my study to determine the extent to which this unconscious sort of self-restraint is practiced. So as to insure self-restraint in themselves, Paliyans employ at least two conscious safeguards. First, drinking of alcohol is carefully avoided. Paliyans say that it is alcohol which makes their neighbors so overtly aggressive; although this is not a realistic appraisal of Tamils, Paliyan phrasing of the matter shows what they think would be unleashed in themselves were they to become intoxicated. The other safeguard is an agent which dissipates anger and tranquilizes a person when he applies it to his forehead. It is called *sirupani pu*, "laughing flower."

A second personal mechanism is that of redirecting aggressive feelings. It is not uncharacteristic of self-controlled people to have fantasies about aggression; Paliyans commonly dream of power over others, and those on plantations who have been so exposed particularly enjoy the violent aspect of Tamil-language films. This sort of fantasy, which is discussed in more detail below, presumably constitutes a safe outlet for pent-up feelings.

When open friction between people does arise, the first social mechanism frequently comes into operation. Those people known as headmen step forward with their jokes and soothing words, attempting to conciliate unobtrusively. Without mandate to punish, order, arbitrate, or even suggest, they affect their ends subtly indeed. In my quiet attempts to hold a group together long enough to work with it (after my first community ran away!) I often assumed the role of conciliator and should have been less surprised than I was to hear myself referred to subsequently as a headman.

Sometimes conciliation is not available, and sometimes attempts at it are unsuccessful. If conflict is not suppressed or averted, the two parties must separate. This second social mechanism for resolution of conflict is widely used, as the following examples show.

One morning a mother struck her seven-year-old son firmly three times for taking food which belonged to his aunt. Another woman who was not in any way a relative and who had several dependents of her own came directly over and led the boy by the hand back to her house. She let him stay the rest of the day and fed him with her own children. This case and one or two others of a similar nature stand out as extraordinary examples of actual cooperation between persons not members of the same household. Perhaps this is meant less as "cooperation" than insurance that minors exercise their basic rights for separation, with circumstances being complicated by their dependence.

Spouses separate at the first quarrel, which results in the serial marriages already described. One girl of fifteen rotated between three men, moving after each quarrel; she had experienced eight unions, each of which was referred to as a marriage. A man of thirty-five had had thirteen marriages and innumerable love affairs, a figure which even the Paliyans felt to be a bit high. His separations were above criticism—it was only their combined effect which drew a half-amused, half-critical response.

What began as joking between two groups that worked for forest contractors at different rates of pay led to bitter words and the formation of factions. Half the community left that evening. When they returned two weeks later the wounds were not entirely healed so the other half left for a week.

Paliyan discretion has traditionally dictated the avoidance of outsiders through nomadism whenever necessary. Again, this is the same mechanism. It is unnecessary to invoke "whim" (Ehrenfels 1952:127) or "instinct" (Fürer-Haimendorf 1943:44) in order to explain the residential instability of India's food collectors, be they Kadar, Chenchus, or Paliyans. On every level, when separation is used as a means to avoid conflict, it is the person or group who has been injured or offended who is expected to take leave. The mechanism is, in effect, a self-imposed ban against retaliation.

The final social mechanism which aids the control of behavior has its basis in the alleged manipulation of supernatural power. During eighteen months in the field I heard four accusations of sorcery and I was able eventually to collect fairly specific information on its technology. Though there is no direct evidence that sorcery has been used, fear of it does help create properly circumspect behavior. In the nonsororal polygynous family which I observed, one woman had a difficult birth. She told me privately afterwards that her barren co-wife had caused this out of jealousy—but she made no public protest. In another instance, a man upset by the factional split (described above) was accused by an informant of bringing an epidemic on the village magically. This allegation was months after the event and my field record showed that the "resulting" epidemic had preceded, not followed, the supposed social injury.

There are, then, human ways of effecting orderly society, the first, third, and fourth being hierarchic in relation to one another. The fifth and last device is of a different kind—fear of covert revenge reinforces other pressures for correct behavior, but it does not in itself constitute a direct problem-solving mechanism.

Social order is tied up with the supernatural in much more intimate ways than man's magical manipulation of impersonal powers. Each Paliyan village has several deities who are of immediate concern to man. These vary in number from two to seven in the communities studied and they are different from one area to the next, but it is uniformly true that they possess and speak through the living. Some Paliyans call them *tāta*, or grandfather; some say that they are parentlike. However it is phrased, they are usually thought to be fairly immediate beings. Frequently they are the spirits of Paliyan men or women who fell and died when gathering honey. Others are forest gods who are named but about whom little appears to be known. Still others are the deities of forest shrines, worshipped in common by Paliyans and Tamil plainsmen.

Whatever their origin or identity, they are called, as a class, "the gods," and they are treated alike. What concerns us here is that they are asked for advice and protection both at times of personal problems and when the entire community faces crises. For instance, when an unknown party attacked one village at night, throwing large granite stones out of the darkness, one of which injured a woman, the deities were called. Several possible origins had already been proposed for the mysterious stones, but one man held fast to the idea that two tigers were throwing them. He said he had seen them that afternoon at a spot less than 100 yards from the settlement—great tigers such as sorcerers use. The stones finally stopped, but three men began to chant, petitioning the deities to descend upon them to speak. After an hour two female deities descended, one on the man with the tiger explanation, then, five minutes later, another on his wife's brother. The third petitioner, who had been the proponent of another explanation, did not become possessed. The possessed men ran from the village unarmed and screams were heard. Eventually, after a twenty-minute silence, they returned to report that they had discovered and fought off the two tigers. For the next hour they diagnosed illnesses, prescribing cures. And to those who asked they promised protection from spirits.

Possession takes place in a wide variety of contexts: drought, illness, a girl's attainment of puberty, and so on. It may be spontaneous or induced (singing with held breath, drumming), and it may last from five minutes to over three hours. In most communities about one person in eight (that is, about one adult in five) becomes possessed quite frequently. Men fill this role somewhat more often, but both men and women are possessed by both male and female deities, and members of both sexes develop familiar relations with individual supernaturals. Possession is valued; it seems not to be regarded as dangerous, as has been reported in other areas.

A good bit of the man-god relation is divinatory. Besides showing the diagnosing of illness, the tiger episode gives an example of supernatural resolution of a difficult social question: who was right about the source of the stones? An authoritative verification of one point of view was provided in a manner which did not conflict with the Paliyan abhorrence of social authority differences. This tiger episode also reveals the other component of the man-god relation, that of reliance upon the gods for protection and reassurance. This was seen when the deities protected the people from the tigers. But it was also seen when they promised protection from the attacks of spirits, the beings which are often said to cause illness. Paliyans who actually are ill are also in need of protection. Their response to a severe boil, for instance, is one of exaggerated weakness; the patient staggers about with a stick for support and an anguished expression. Patients will lay their heads on the feet of the gods in acts of subordination foreign to Paliyan patterns of social self-reliance.

One could say that gods are "on call" to provide the Paliyans with the benefits of hierarchy when problems arise, but that this is usually at the Paliyans' pleasure. The hierarchy does not assert its authority of its own accord, except when the rare spontaneous possession occurs or when the gods on their own initiative punish incest, theft, or murder with an accident or illness. Several informants noted, for example, that a forest guard who is alleged to have shot a Paliyan to steal his wife died a week later with severe stomach pains. This sort of direct supernatural intervention might be added to the list of control mechanisms.

Not all problems are resolved for Paliyans by means of social and supernatural controls. Even the most smoothly running society has its ambiguities due to unavoidable rigidities in the system. We can refer to this sort of problem as structural or systemic. The examples which follow are all concerned with the problems of complementation of roles.

As noted earlier in the chapter, Paliyans have a fantasy sphere concerning power and violence. Besides dreaming of everyday events (work, sexual relations) and of unusual difficulties in the forest (falling in holes, meeting bears, storms), they admit to dreaming of flying and of beating the would-be lovers of their wives. After a number of men had mentioned flying over the village, a young married man related this: "I dream of flying in the air, and challenging others to fly like myself. The others would be unable to fly." He then named a headman and two other young hard-working men. The headman had the same dream and said, "I take it as an ill omen, and it brings me trouble." He then proceeded as an apparent *non sequitur* to talk about accidents such as Paliyans associate with punishment for incest, murder, or theft by the deities. Nowadays there is the added fantasy sphere of the cinema. Those who have been to the theaters tend to recount the contents of a film in terms of the violent episodes even though they are peripheral to the plot. As one man put it, "It is very exciting to see people fighting and so we like those pictures." These examples show the continuing concern which Paliyans have for complementation in terms of power.

Another sort of complementation is that of sex. Although there is minimal division of labor, except that women care for children and men are prominent in hunting and honey-gathering, there is unavoidable complementation inherent in the sex difference itself. This is expressed by Paliyans in terms of clothing and gait. During evenings of dance, some men and women adopt the dress of members of the other sex. This is greatly enjoyed and it makes possible mixed dancing, which is otherwise judged improper. Similarly, a married couple occasionally exchange clothes amidst the approving cheers of their fellows, to go off thus for the day's work.

Prominent and absolute is the complementation of god and man. This may be a special sort of relation, but it is not without ambiguity. One rainy morning, a sixty-five-year-old woman clowned and danced on and off for three quarters of an hour. Bystanders were doubled up with laughter at her ecstatic dance and unintelligible prophesying, but they especially enjoyed it when one of the usual vehicles for deities came and grasped her from behind as is done to support those in real possession. At another time three men stood as gods with mango net helmets and goat fodder garlands while a young man made them offerings of flowers, ash, and water. Two headmen were at the front of an amused cluster of onlookers. These occurrences allow us to put in context replies such as "go to hell" when the gods request too large an offering, and commands made to the gods in a grammatic form which would be impolite and condescending even to children.

Despite the rigid Paliyan insistence on egalitarianism and individual autonomy, there are several areas in which social complementation exists by necessity or creeps in unavoidably. The structural difficulties caused by conflicting imperatives appear to invite release through behavior which either inverts the social order or denies in a ritual context the basic assumptions of the culture.

SYMBOLIC STRUCTURE

The care and delicacy with which Paliyans maintain correct forms of social interaction contrast markedly with the casual treatment they accord to form of ritual, knowledge, belief, and artifact.[9] We shall examine this aspect of their culture from the various standpoints of ritual and practice, styles of thought, and the assessment of worth.

Paliyan ritual can be described in three different senses by the term "optional." First, we find the same dual systematization on the basis of context as existed in the area of kinship. Second, Paliyan ritual within either of these contexts is changeable or irregular in form. Third, ritual is often dispensed with altogether. A review of the main Paliyan rituals will demonstrate the range of variation found.

In front of outsiders Paliyans put on a display of ritual which is both different in content and richer in form than that which they use purely among themselves. The ethnographer's presence thus generated a continuous and expensive need to maintain ritual forms appropriate to this extracommunal sphere. Similarly, plantation Paliyans who have no privacy from outsiders perform elaborate and expensive weddings, funerals, and female puberty rites. As an example of contextual variation, at one such wedding, gifts and decorations were purchased in town and consultations were held with outsiders as to correct roles and procedures. On the wedding day a marriage hut was built before the bride's house and decorated with palm fronds and flowers. The wedding was off to a good start from any visitor's eyes. Alone, at midnight, the Paliyans performed the ceremony their own way. The role of the headman as ritual leader became submerged in the practicalities of preparing the feast. The marriage hut never assumed the function it would have had in the plains, as a sacred spot in which to formalize the marriage; it remained, instead, a convenient porch for sleeping children and festive adults. The bride's mother's brother did not play the part which prior discussion had established as his. A shrine was visited and saluted twice, then twice more for the added fun; it was circumperambulated once by some, twice or three times by others, with no sense of precise form and none of the compulsion which usually characterizes ritual.

It is interesting to compare this ceremony with the exchange of salt, betel, and a vow which is done in the forest, or with the unceremonialized unions which are still more common.

The situation at funerals is the same. Elaborate but disorganized ritual is found in the culture-contact sphere; in the forest all is simple. The young men from one village of plains Paliyans bathed carefully when returning from a burial ground. Asked the reason for their actions, the young men replied variously; no one cited repurification, but several commented on the general hygienic value of bathing. In the forest context, bathing appears not to be part of the ritual.

When a girl attains menarche she is isolated in a small thatched hut for fifteen days. At night she stays in the hut in the company of her friends, but during the day they hide her in the forest. No man should see her until she has been bathed by the older women at the end of her isolation. If this event is combined with her marriage, she is bathed with her fiancé and they are then isolated together in a house for an additional day or two until the wedding. But, as in the case of a wedding or funeral, the puberty ceremony can be simplified. In one case, a man absconded with a girl during her initial isolation and they returned to the village a week later as man and wife. There was no marked disapproval. If a girl has been married while still a child, then the isolation is arranged by her husband, and it is reported to be a simpler business. I did not witness this, however.

Apart from (female) puberty rite, wedding, and funeral, Paliyans make claim to just one other life-cycle ritual, a brief ceremony at the time an infant is named. I have never seen this performed, even in abbreviated form, but I suspect, nonetheless, that it belongs entirely to the extra-communal sphere. Religious ritual having to do with other than the life cycle is limited to only a few kinds of intracommunal rites: calling the gods to come and speak to men; an annual worship of the gods found in some Paliyan bands (this ritual may be elaborate in the extracommunal context); a first-fruit ceremony in December in thanks for the ripening yams; and brief prayers of gratitude when game has been caught.

Comparative data make abundantly clear what the reader will already have inferred, namely, that the special extracommunal culture of Paliyans, both kinship and ritual, is intended as imitation of plains Tamil culture. But the copy is only of outward form, not of rationale; for this reason I have termed the extracommunal culture "orthoprax" (Gardner 1966a). It should also be clear that Paliyans have not borrowed elements of Tamil ritual to replace their own, but rather that they have taken them to be a parallel set, choice between the two being a function of context. For, to a great extent, these alternative cultural forms are kept distinct, in stable dualism. Close examination of the borrowed set suggests strongly that to Paliyans their exact content is of less importance than the fact of their rather elaborate existence. If intracommunal ritual is unelaborate by contrast, we have only to look at Paliyan economy, settlement pattern, and multifaceted individualism to understand why. Only some Paliyan rituals, mainly those of the life cycle, have extracommunal variants. But they are the ones with the most clear-cut Tamil equivalents, the ones in which Tamil plainsmen would be interested.

The ideational sphere, which includes belief and knowledge, is much more private than the sphere of ritual. Not surprisingly, the dual patterning of the highly visible cultural forms has no clear parallel in the realm of Paliyan thought. Instead, we run into another kind of variation in form, variation in belief and knowledge from individual to individual.

Having witnessed several Paliyan rituals, such as the possession ceremony the night we were attacked by stone-throwing tigers, I was able in each instance to elicit as many different explanations of certain elements of the rituals as I had informants. In the same way, when I asked five informants about the fate of a soul after death, they gave me the following answers: "How can we know that?"; "It merges with the air"; "It goes up"; "It goes to another world"; "Some go to the sun, some to the moon." These cases are similar to those I reported on in an earlier paper (Gardner 1966b), for example, the time that three Paliyans gave me three different names for a healthy bush from which they derive one of their five digging stick woods. They argued among themselves briefly, because the terms they gave me were not synonymous, then one of them laughed, turned to me, and said, "Well, we all know how to use it!" There was again the same degree of disagreement over terms for the few species of lethal viper in the area.

The explanation of individualized taxonomy and idiosyncratic belief may be more clear if we look at another kind of datum. It is usually impossible to elicit from Paliyans valid statements about behavioral modes or norms. They are not disposed, for example, to articulate rules about either the preferred place of residence for a young couple after marriage or the usual practice or range of practices in this regard. The statements which Paliyans offer are invalid as generalizations, because, although informants speak as if generalizing, their words reflect only what they or their immediate family have most recently done. A young man who had just recited for me an elaborate prayer to the gods balked at repeating it because, he maintained, "How can I remember what I said? We just speak." Songs are spontaneous; the most serious rituals are *ad hoc* in design. Again and again one runs into what is perhaps not so much a lack of order as a lack of concern for standardized formalization. Individuals rather than the group create order. That is, order is not taught. There is little conscious accumulation or transmission of generally accepted bodies of knowledge, no concern for traditional usage, and no appeal to precedent. Furthermore, Paliyans are very uncommunicative verbally, and gossip is generally avoided; discussion about major events in the village is also avoided. Because of this situation, collation and systematization of the sum of the experiences of those in a group are limited severely. It is the deviant who is verbose, but he is disregarded. Knowledge is something personal; it *should* be something personal, because to seek advice is to submit oneself to an undesirable dependency. Not only are the mechanisms that would lead to standardization relatively ineffectual but standardization and social tradition are, in most spheres, little valued as such.

"Memorate" is an appropriate term for individualized knowledge, "the result of personal experience and individual analysis, rather than being derived from group opinion or tradition" (Gardner 1966b:390). And the term will apply both to content and to organization. Memorate thinking is a part of every culture, but seldom so large a part as in the culture of Paliyans. This is not to say that there is no resemblance between the beliefs and taxonomies of different Paliyans, but the degree of divergence is considerable.

Any hierarchy of Paliyan values would certainly be capped by insistence on individual autonomy in all of its expressions. Self-sufficiency, respect for others, self-control, placation of hostile parties, and mobility are desirable; dependence, loss of self-control, unnecessary contact with strangers, and provocative behavior are to be avoided. These values are tempered, however, by an indulgent attitude toward children. Paliyans also believe deeply that certain acts should not be committed, such as murder, incest, and theft. Important, but on a much lower order than the imperatives noted above, are their high valuation of the kinship group and, more especially, the nuclear family.

Paliyans, in evaluating human behavior, give greater attention to actual or probable outcome than to ideal form. It is for this reason that a promise or plan is only a statement of probability. After all, one cannot predict future circumstances, and accordingly one should not be bound by unrealistic preplanned responses. All that can really be predicted is that whatever the circumstances, each individual Paliyan will attempt to reason out his responses as he is called upon to do so. This lends a sense of fluidity to the Paliyan way of life—an atmosphere of constant change and adjustment.

If esthetics is defined as a concern with form as such, Paliyan disinterest should almost be predictable. But our expectations are not wholly borne out by the data; dance and music are enjoyed immensely by men and women alike. It is true that this is their only area of great esthetic development, and it is also true that much of the resulting form is improvization. Some of it is no more than autocommunicative, but the enthusiastic performances and grinning faces during a night of dance speak eloquently for its importance.

In view of what has been said about economic and social institutions, it must be admitted that there *is* a style to the Paliyan way of life. For all the fluidity and variability which is found in specific cultural forms, the individualism which overrides all else gives a distinctive tone to the culture as a whole. And this brief review of the symbolic and abstract side of the culture brings us somewhat closer to understanding what underlies the production of characteristic or traditional Paliyan behavior.

CONTEXT FOR CHANGE

It has been impossible to describe the traditional culture of the Paliyans without phrasing it in terms of culture contact and adaptation. This is so because, as historical sources will attest, basic features of the all-important intercultural ecology of the region have been stable for centuries or even millennia (Gardner 1965). There are actually several situational factors which have worked together to create the social pluralism that has traditionally prevailed between Paliyans and Tamil plainsmen. After reviewing them briefly it will be interesting to look back at some of the ways in which this intercultural situation has affected Paliyan culture. Today a set of new pressures is acting upon the Paliyans, undermining the old equilibrium. Again a brief review is in order. The chapter will conclude with the question of whether Paliyans and their neighbors are at present forging a new equilibrium that will have any lasting meaning.

Four situational factors appear to have operated together in the development of stable social pluralism between plains Tamils and Paliyans: the Tamil treatment of a caste group; unavailability of intergroup justice; existence of a refuge area; and a psychocultural response to chronic intercultural pressure.

In South Indian culture, including that of the Tamils, groups which are endogamous and which have distinctive attributes are treated as separate social and legal communities with sovereign rights over internal laws and the maintenance of group traditions. Tribes are considered to be such communities, distinctive because of their adaptation to the forest and hills. As such they are granted the same immunities and privileges as "castes" of the plains; they are free to pursue customs and maintain intra-communal law of their own design. The Paliyans are not likely to have been treated as other than a "caste" in their recent history.

In the plains it is a village or town (with or without satellite hamlets or villages) which is the source of legal institutions that mediate the relations between members of different social communities—as between Paliyans and others. This is a world of power as well as principle, and it is unlikely that those not immediately associated with a village could bring a concern before a village council, let alone find satisfaction. Paliyans are sufficiently peripheral in power as well as in space that their interaction with others is covered neither by the law nor by any other mechanism of justice.

However, where legal institutions fail, the dry-thorn forest, which one finds on the lower slope of the high ranges, provides a very basic form of protection. The discomfort of the lower forest is enough to keep away all but the ascetic, the pilgrim, the fugitive, and the most intrepid entrepreneur. If the Paliyans can stay beyond their reach, then intergroup difficulties can be solved before they begin. One botanist holds that the present thorn forest is "clearly the result of biotic features of browsing by sheep, goat, . . . etc." (Puri 1960:I 247). This means that, against the time scale of South Indian ethno-history, the forest may be fairly recent in its present inhospitable form. On the other hand, the forest-plain boundary, as a cultural boundary, is not at all recent, and the forest, though perhaps formerly more attractive in its flora, may still have provided some sort of protection for tribal people. For example, big game have always constituted a fairly significant barrier to farmers, herders, and other sorts of visitors.

The attitude of superiority which colors Tamil interaction with simple tribal peoples (superiority in power, "purity," and level of sophistication) has given rise to a wide range of abusive behavior. Besides being a casual resource, the tribal people seem to serve as a general scapegoat against whom hostility can safely be vented. One encounters repeated cases of harassment, from light ridicule to unprovoked group murders, that would not have been directed toward a less helpless people. If South Indians who are on pilgrimage to forest shrines treat Paliyans as holy because of their life of abstinence and simplicity, and if Tamils are the source of several needed items in the Paliyan economy, this does not wholly undo the effect of chronic exploitation and humiliation. The balance sheet of intergroup relations is badly skewed. I have argued elsewhere that the most reliable solution which seems to have presented itself in the past is withdrawal, not just in the sense of the sociogeographic retreat from contact but also in the sense of suppression (or repression) of hostility when there is contact (Gardner 1966b:406–408). Other psychological processes are taken to be ancillary. External factors thus add to and reinforce the Paliyan childhood experiences that incline them to seek individual autonomy. Ironically, these protective mechanisms of withdrawal put Paliyans under considerable psychological and social stress while, at the same time, giving them a deceptive outward appearance of whimsical, carefree independence. It may also be said of their adaptation that, when it comes to actual protection, the forest offers immediate freedom and refuge, but it leads Paliyans further and further from alternatives. A vicious circle is created, because, in combination, the emotional and social forms of retreat increase the vulnerability of Paliyans. They cause the Paliyans to rely more and more upon their own resources as individuals and they make it increasingly certain that men of the forest will not seek legal recourse through the nearby villages.

This ecological situation has affected Paliyan culture in several ways. First, just as peasants confronted by gentry, the Paliyans live in a polarized world: we-they; insider-outsider; weak-powerful; good-bad. When geographic retreat is impossible or when the Paliyans are willing to compromise their prized independence and safety in order to obtain needed commodities from the outside,[10] then they try to avoid antagonizing those people who stand essentially as their masters. All efforts are bent toward appearing nonhostile, respectful, and respectable. They say "yes sir" as they grit their teeth. In this context they generate their orthoprax behavior as a protective screen to reduce interference. Sometimes it is only a superficial device which facilitates smoother exploitation of critical resources from the outside world; much less commonly there seems to be a degree of actual conviction that there is something superior about the Tamil way. It is notable that their gods have stepped in and asked them to avoid contact with beef and leather.

Second, in the same way that we have to refer to refugee status in order to understand the full scope of Paliyan psychological and social individualism, so also must we recognize that their memorate culture is part of this wider complex of retreat. Paliyans as individuals are mobile and residentially unstable, they are economically and socially self-sufficient, and they are generally disaffected from other persons. These characteristics work together effectively to reduce the general level of communication among Paliyans. And, of course, the inhibiting of communication is fundamental to the formation of memorate phenomena.

There are many other observations that could be made in summing up the impact of traditional intercultural relations on Paliyan culture, such as the effect of their residential instability on their technology and economics. But these are much less in need of being spelled out. The one important topic which remains to be treated is that of recent environmental change.

The basic features of the changing situation are four in number. First, under great pressure for the resources of the forest, Tamil plainsmen are virtually flooding into the Paliyan habitat. They bring herds of goats and cattle in search of food and water even into reserved forest. They come in, both under legal contracts and illegally, to remove wood for fuel and precious woods for sale—even the teak which the forestry department has planted is stolen before it matures, the trunks for roof timbers and the leaves by the thousands for plates. Astute forest guards stationed by the path can make 7 to 10 rupees a day just from woodcutters alone. In many areas they have no effect at all on the rate of exploitation. Poaching of game is all but unchecked. At night in the forest one might meet one hunter a mile equipped with ancient muzzle loaders. Farmers near the forest encourage them because of the damage which wild pigs do to their crops; there is no question that they are a serious factor in the depletion of many forms of game. Besides purposeful exploitation of forest products there has probably been greater accidental destruction as well, for the general increase in the transient forest population will have contributed to the number of forest fires.

The second changing feature is the transformation of forest into plantations. While Paliyans have in the past been employed sporadically to tend herds or to help forestry officials remove sandalwood, plantations are quite another matter. For one thing, year-round employment is available; for another, a permanent pacification of the forest takes place—roads, shrines, wells, canals, malaria eradication, regularly employed outsiders, and so on. Plantations may be found at all altitudes, but their increasing appearance in the lower valleys has brought them into intimate contact with Paliyans. For every Paliyan band that has had fifty or sixty years of such contact, there are many which have had this sort of experience only in the last five to twenty years. As noted above, Paliyans are paid less than their co-workers on plantations, but treatment of them varies from bullying and contempt on the one hand to a gentle paternalism on the other. Some plantation owners seem genuinely fond of their quiet forest wards and indulge their cultural peculiarities. This, of course, has practical advantages as it aids in recruitment and ensures a more reliable labor force. Foremen do not always exhibit the same degree of tolerance, however.

This introduction of benevolent agents is the third aspect of recent change. Besides the occasional kindly plantation owner, there are many others who have come to the forest with good will. A private welfare van reaches some Paliyans regularly with simple medicines, blankets, and food. Malaria eradication crews, if they actually patrol their forest areas, usually appear as pleasant, helpful people. Some Block Development Officers (these civil servants are in charge of development of roads, schools, water supply, and so on, for population areas or "blocks" of about 60,000 people) are quite ignorant of the existence of their forest charges; others have arranged for tidy concrete houses to be built or for the creation of special Paliyan schools at which the children get meals and a course of training oriented toward acculturation. It is too early to evaluate the full impact of these programs, but not too early to note that they may bring about a swift change in the attitudes Paliyans hold toward outsiders. Paliyans, even well treated, remain somewhat wary of newcomers, but trust builds more rapidly than in the past after such positive experiences.

Probably of at least as much significance as the loss of forest or the introduction of new sorts of agents of contact is the lure of material advantages. Paliyans, especially young men and women, find it difficult to give up for any length of time movie films, plastic combs, metal utensils, quality tools, and clothing. They are always ready to take temporary leave of these things, but the new affluence compensates increasingly for the difficulties of culture contact.

If a man goes off to dig yams in a tailored shirt with cigarettes in his pocket, it is not so clear that his son and grandson will be so comfortable astride the two worlds. It is as if the vicious circle of defenselessness leading to flight leading to increased vulnerability is being broken once and for all. One can get a preview of the new intercultural equilibrium which might come about by looking at a village of Paliyans who moved to the plains for regular farm labor over a century ago. They still live near the forest, maintain a high valuation of self-sufficiency and egalitarianism, look to the forest for occasional yams and meat, and think of themselves as forest people. Yet, for all intents and purposes they are a voting, wage-earning community of Indians: they call village meetings to rebuke those who resort to violence after the model of caste councils; their village officers are conspicuous and even inherit their posts patrilineally, if they are capable; and they are more assertive in their dealings with non-Paliyans. Problem areas exist, however. For example, caste council notwithstanding, hostile feelings and actual violence are very difficult for them to cope with now that they resort less to flight. Another touchy subject is the relation of Paliyan women with outsiders; the women have lost their shyness but not their independence, and Paliyan men in the name of orthopraxy are less and less happy about the sexual freedom of their wives, sisters, and daughters.

Those Paliyans who are undergoing the more rapid recent change, with the help of schools and privileged treatment, may well end up differently from this agricultural village which made a slow transition. For one thing, their expectations are higher. This could mean greater frustration when as adults they have to compete actively in Indian society to maintain the standards they set for themselves as schoolchildren, for they shall certainly end up primarily as laborers. In addition, having made a sharp break with the past, they cannot be expected to maintain for very long their identity as forest people. One thing is definite, however. Soon neither they nor their fellows will have a forest retreat. And when that day comes, "Paliyan" can never mean the same.

NOTES

1. Field work on the Paliyans was undertaken from 1962 to 1964 under a fellowship granted by the Ford Foundation and administered by the Joint Committee of the Social Science Research Council and the American Council of Learned Societies. An extension of this grant and a later grant from the University of Texas, University Research Institute provided time and facilities for analysis of the field data. While the assistance of those foundations is gratefully acknowledged, all statements and conclusions are the responsibility of the author alone.

   Nine months were spent with a settlement in Ramnad district, which was in the process of emerging from the forest for plantation work. Six more months were spent with a Paliyan village in Madurai district which has been involved in stable agricultural labor for at least a century. Short periods with more nomadic groups bring the total number of communities studied to twelve. All personal names have been changed. But actual genealogical charts and village names are available to scholars on request. Paliyan is a regional dialect version of Paraiyan, "the ancient." Although "Paliyar" is somewhat more respectful as a term for the tribe, it is in the plural form. For simplicity's sake I have used "Paliyan" in this paper. It is properly both a singular noun and an adjective, and it permits use of an Anglicized plural.

2. The Phi Tong Luang are another partial exception in that they speak Laotian while retaining a language of their own.

3. This represents a different interpretation from that which I offered in my earlier description (Gardner 1969).

4. "Gerontocracy," a more usual term for marriage of persons whose ages are significantly different, suggests great age on the part of one spouse, putting emphasis in the wrong place. Its suffix is also inappropriate, if what is meant is a form of marriage; in the Paliyan case it is particularly inappropriate. I prefer the term "pedogamy," because, while the elder party may be only middle-aged, what is regular—one could even say necessary—for this marital type is the youth of the other.

5. The term *sondakārar* has a broader range of use than this. It may be used to refer only to one's half-dozen nearest relatives or to all members of two or three related bands. In this regard, because there was a term applied to such an aggregate of related bands, I took this aggregate at first to be a territory. Data on adjoining bands showed that they too married into the two or three adjacent bands along the range of hills, creating almost endless chains of relatedness rather than discrete territories. There were some disjunctures.

6. Other cases of this are reviewed in Gardner (1966a); see especially Turnbull (1965).

7. This is considered to be the main diagnostic feature of the kin terminology of South Indian Dravidian speakers. There are good grounds, however, for thinking that the usual model which Dravidians themselves employ is not cross versus parallel relatives at all but father's patriline versus mother's patriline (or father's line versus the line into which father's line marries). Paliyans, as Westerners, look at Dravidian kin-term patterning with a bilateral bias and tend to emphasize the equation of parallel kin with lineal kin. This cross-parallel model provides just as efficient a description of the pattern as does the Dravidian model which emphasizes patrilines. However, from an objective viewpoint, both models are equally culture bound.

8. Whiting and Child (1953) have studied initial indulgence and severity of socialization in five areas: oral, anal, sexual, dependence, and aggression.

9. When an ethnographer suggests a cultural "disinterest" such as this there is quite properly a heavy burden upon him not only to demonstrate but also to explain his contention. Because I have put forward my explanation in an earlier paper (Gardner 1966b), I shall restrict myself here mainly to descriptive materials.

10. The silent barter noted by Markham is, of course, an alternative—if it can once be established (Grierson 1903:46).

REFERENCES

Aiyappan, A., 1948. *Report on the Socio-Economic Conditions of the Aboriginal Tribes of the Province of Madras*, Madras: Government Press.
A government report with brief but up-to-date descriptions of the present condition of many South Indian tribes.

Ehrenfels, U. R., 1952. *Kadar of Cochin*, Madras: University of Madras Press.
An ethnography of the food-collecting people who, with the Malapandaram, are most closely akin to the Paliyans. The study was based upon very brief field work.

Evans, I. H. N., 1937. *The Negritos of Malaya*, Cambridge: University Press.

Fürer-Haimendorf, C. von, 1943. *The Chenchus: Jungle Folk of the Deccan*, London: Macmillan.
A substantial *Kulturkreis* ethnography of food collectors several hundred miles north of the Paliyans. It is the most complete and most useful account so far published of a peninsular Indian tribe having this type of economy.

———, 1945. *The Reddis of the Bison Hills: A Study in Acculturation*, London: Macmillan.
A description of another peninsular Indian tribal people who combine food-collecting and shifting cultivation.

Gardner, P. M., 1965. *Ecology and Social Structure in Refugee Populations: The Paliyans of South India*, unpublished Ph.D. dissertation, University of Pennsylvania, Philadelphia. (Also, University Microfilms, Ann Arbor, Mich.)

———, 1966a. "Orthopraxy and the Double Kinship Systems of Refugees," paper presented at the American Anthropological Association Annual Meeting, Pittsburgh, Pa.

———, 1966b. "Symmetric Respect and Memorate Knowledge: The Structure and Ecology of Individualistic Culture," *Southwestern Journal of Anthropology* 22:389–415.

———, 1969. "Paliyan Social Structure," *Contributions to Anthropology: Band Societies*, Ottawa: National Museums of Canada (*Bulletin No. 228*).

Grierson, P. J. H., 1903. *The Silent Trade*, Edinburgh: William Green and Sons.
His quote from Markham is of special interest.

Puri, G. S., 1960. *Indian Forest Ecology*, Vol. I, New Delhi: Oxford Book Company.

Schebesta, P., 1927. *Among the Forest Dwarfs of Malaya*, London: Hutchinson.

Skeat, W. W., and C. O. Blagden, 1906. *Pagan Races of the Malay Peninsula*, London: Macmillan.

Turnbull, C. M., 1965. *Wayward Servants: The Two Worlds of the African Pygmies*, Garden City, N. Y.: Natural History Press.
An ethnography of the Mbuti that brings out particularly well the double life of refuge area food collectors. The author's earlier, more popular, account, *The Forest People* (New York: Simon and Schuster, 1961), is also useful.

Whiting, J. W. M., and I. L. Child, 1953. *Child Training and Personality*, New Haven, Conn.: Yale University Press.

GLOSSARY

atte: (1) extracommunal context: MoBrWi, FaSi and WiMo; (2) intracommunal context: (a) females of second ascending generation who are
related through one's Wi or one's BrWi, (b) women of one's own generation related through one's Hu or SiHu
billhook: a small hooked machete
extracommunal: of or pertaining to contact between Paliyans and others
intracommunal: of or pertaining to relations within an exclusively Paliyan group
memorate: knowledge and belief resulting from individual experience and
analysis rather than from group opinion or tradition
orthoprax: correct in behavior; this term is coming into currency in order that
a distinction between proper form in behavior and belief can be made
Paliyan: regional dialect version of *Paraiyan*, "the ancient"
sirupani pu: "laughing flower"; believed to dissipate anger and tranquilize
sondakārar: in Paliyan, "relative"; a small group of cooperative kinsmen; term
may be extended to all the members of two or three related bands
tarahu: a type of pungent grass
tāta: "grandfather"; also applied to village deities

CHAPTER

11

THE AINU

Hitoshi Watanabe

Hitoshi Watanabe is Associate Professor of Anthropology at the University of Tokyo and received his D.Sc. from that university. He has been the recipient of numerous grants which have allowed him to conduct field research in both archaeology and ethnography. His publications include articles on the prehistory of Japan and Palestine, historical reconstruction and ethnology of the Ainu, and ecology of the Ainu and other northern food gatherers. Dr. Watanabe is a member of professional organizations in both Japan and Great Britain and has been a participant in many international conferences on archaeology, ethnology, and human ecology.

EDITOR'S INTRODUCTION

The Ainu, like the Bushmen a linguistically and physically unique people, live on Hokkaido, an island north of the mainland of Japan and now part of Japan. They exploited their rich environment, paralleled perhaps only by the northwest coast of North America, through hunting, fishing, and gathering. Despite historical contact with the Japanese, the culture of the mainland had little impact upon the lives of the Ainu until Japanese colonialization and introduction of agricultural programs in the late nineteenth century. This chapter is an historical reconstruction of the Ainu life style just prior to their change from traditional subsistence patterns to agriculture.

The natural domain of the Ainu is one of wooded mountain ranges and river valleys. Their faunal resources include salmon, which run in the streams from early summer to midwinter, and big game, such as bear and deer. Floral resources offer ample opportunity for food-collecting. All exploitation of their physical environment was tightly interwoven into their ideological system of Kamui deities, as all plant and animal resources were considered to be representatives of deities in temporary guises. In this context, all exploitation involved ritual and every household was the center of religious as well as economic activities. Communal, or local group, activity took the form of bear and deer hunts and salmon fishing and trapping, while the bear ceremony was the only occasion for activity outside the local group.

Central to this chapter is the author's interest in the spaciotemporal structures of human activity systems and their relations to habitat, with the aim of understanding man's place in nature in terms of ecology. In the case of the Ainu, this involves a complete understanding of their ideological system, which served to directly link groups and individuals to nature.

Comparison of the Ainu with other groups indicates that ritual as the intervening link between man and nature is not unique. Of the groups represented here, formalization of man in nature is paralleled by the Australian Aboriginal myth and ritual cycles, which also served to place man in harmony with, rather than in opposition to, his physical environment.

The Ainu are an aboriginal people living in Hokkaido, southern Sakhalin, and the southern part of the Kurile Islands. The term "Ainu" means "men" or "humans." The population of the Hokkaido Ainu was estimated in 1940 at about 16,300, a figure which has remained almost stable since 1854 (see Table 11-1).

PHYSICAL APPEARANCE

The Ainu are characterized by such physical features as medium stature; abundant facial and body hair; light brown skin; general tendency toward longheadedness; wavy black hair; broad face; and low frequency of Mongolian eyefold. Resemblances are on the one hand toward the Mongoloid, on the other toward the Caucasian. Owing to those characteristics, their relation with Caucasian or Australoid has long been discussed, but their racial classification remains doubtful.

TABLE 11-1

POPULATION

Date of Population Census		Number of Ainu Homes	Ainu Population
1822	Sakhalin	357	2,571
	Hokkaido	4,749	21,149
1854	Sakhalin	373	2,669
	Hokkaido	3,407	16,136
1873	Hokkaido	3,599	16,272

LANGUAGE

The Ainu are distinct in their language as well as in their physical type. Some scholars find a grammatical similarity between the Ainu language and the languages of Palaeo-Asiatics, but any definite genetic relation has not been demonstrated between them.

HABITAT

Hokkaido is an island of about 46,740 square miles, situated north of the Japanese mainland between about 41 degrees, 30 minutes north and 45 degrees, 30 minutes north and between about 140 and 146 degrees east. The northern tip of the island is about 24 miles away from Sakhalin, and to the northeast of the island the Kurile Islands stretch toward Kamchatka. From north to south, through the center of the island, runs a range of hills and mountains in which the main rivers of Hokkaido have their sources (Fig. 11-1). In most rivers of Hokkaido there are successive runs of salmon from early summer to early or mid-winter. The island is well wooded: the southwestern part is rich in latifoliate trees represented by beech, while the northeastern part abounds in coniferous forests, the representative species being firs. Among larger land mammals on the island are brown bear and deer. The Ainu exploited these resources by hunting and fishing and also collected wild plants. The annual mean temperatures for the years 1921–1950 vary from 5.2 degrees C to 8.5 degrees C in different areas in Hokkaido. There is a long season of snowfall from October to May. The monthly mean temperatures in the island for the years 1921–1950 indicate below 0 degrees C for the four months from December to March. Apart from some local differences, this is roughly the period of base snow which covers the ground through the winter. This climate affects the ecology of biotic species and, in turn, the life of the Ainu.

HISTORY

Ainu contact with the Japanese, their southern neighbors, is of long standing. Before 1599, the contact must have been limited. But in that year the Japanese Matsumae clan, which was subordinate to the Tokugawa Shognate, was established with its headquarters in the southwestern end of Hokkaido, and with adjacent area as clan territory. Japanese civilians were prohibited to live outside the area, that is, in the Ainu territory. The Matsumae had exclusive trading rights with the Ainu and established trading and fishing posts along the coast. During this period, the Ainu continued to retain their independence. But in 1799, this part of Hokkaido came under the direct control of the Tokugawa Shognate. The

Figure 11–1.   Rivers of Hokkaido and old administrative divisions.

Japanese established a limited administrative organization over the Ainu territory, but did little to interfere in their internal affairs. Trading continued as before. In 1821, the Matsumae resumed the administration of the territory and continued the same policy. Ainus were seasonally summoned by the Japanese to compulsory service at the coast. Those employed at the coastal posts were mainly adolescent and adult males, but sometimes women and children were included. Later, Ainus responsible for supporting a family were exempted from shore service. Some Ainus, who lived on the upper courses of the larger rivers or in regions with poor fishing grounds, were free from the service. In 1854–1867, the territory again came under the direct control of the Tokugawa Shognate. However, it seems quite reasonable to state that until 1867, the Japanese had relatively little effect upon the life of the Ainu, except through the distribution of Japanese goods. The "basho" system, represented by the network of coastal fishing posts and the seasonal employment of the Ainu, was abolished in 1869 by the Japanese government, shortly after the establishment of the colonial government for development of Ezo Island. In 1868, Hokkaido came under the administration of the Japanese government, the island became a part of the territory of Japan, and colonization was started. With this began a process which greatly changed Ainu life, so that today the Ainu language is rarely spoken, and then only by the aged; full-blood Ainus are about to become extinct; and the whole system of their subsistence has been profoundly altered. The most sudden and significant change in their mode of life occurred in 1883, when the new government started carrying out its program of encouraging the Ainu to take up farming. The following descriptions are of the Ainu as they lived their autonomous life.

METHOD

Field trips were made to collect data in Hokkaido during a period between 1951 and 1959. The main portion of the original data incorporated in this paper was collected in the upper Tokapchi, Otopuke, and Azuma valleys (Fig. 11-1). The intention of the author was to understand the make-up and working of the Ainu groups of a preceding generation in relation to their habitat; accordingly, some special caution in handling the technique was necessary, namely, determination of a time horizon and indirect observation.

The date chosen for the study is that immediately preceding the period of great changes brought about in Ainu group life by Japanese interference (the introduction of new farming systems under Japanese guidance and superintendence) following the agricultural-land–allotment program and the free distribution of farming tools and plant seeds by the Japanese government. The period dates after 1883, although there are some regional variations, that is, from 1886 in the Tokapchi Valley and from 1888 in the Azuma Valley. At this time there occurred throughout Hokkaido wholesale migrations of settlement groups, with attendant dispersions and aggregations. For instance, as far as the present study is concerned, the Nitmap group on the Tokapchi River moved from their old home to a new site allotted downstream; the Ainu on the Otopuke, a tributary of the Tokapchi, were suddenly transformed from a subsistence based entirely on gathering to a new farming subsistence. This visible and sudden change brought on the Hokkaido Ainu was vividly imprinted in the memory of those who experienced it as an epoch-making event in their life histories, the fact which enabled the writer to segregate data pertaining to the Ainu groups prior to the transition. As a necessary procedure to studying groups at the given time horizon, it was important to get into contact with informants who experienced the life of the groups themselves as members and who also were competent to supply information of that life. Three Ainu informants who satisfied these conditions were available to the author.

It must be remembered that the simple fact that an informant belonged to a group at the given date is no guarantee that his or her information pertains to the particular group at the particular time horizon. With a view to restricting the information sought to the desired group at the desired date, interviews were conducted by focusing on the visible and concrete activities of that group to which the informants belonged at the date. This means indirect observation by which the investigator may examine the actual and concrete working of the group through descriptive information about the actual daily behaviors and activities of the informant himself, in the group, and of his fellow-members and neighbors. From this concrete but fragmentary information the investigator may extract relations existing between those activities. This process was of particular importance, because by interview technique there would be the danger of the informants supplying their own generalized and theorized explanations in place of information about the concrete activities from which the investigator is to deduce some relations. Actually, there exists such a strong tendency which might lead the researcher to false interpretation. In this chapter a comparison is made of the relations thus observed in different Ainu groups at the time horizon and a generalized description is given of those relations which are common to all the groups. Where there is some important variation found in any group, a note is included.

It should be noticed that besides the firsthand information supplied by the three key informants, a considerable amount of data was obtained from at least twenty Ainu informants who belonged to younger generations than the other three. These latter could supply information only about life experiences and observations made at periods later than or immediately following the date under survey and about hearsay from their older generations. This type of data is referred to only on necessary occasions.

HOKKAIDO IN THE 1880s

The time horizon for the Ainu life, as treated in the present study, is coeval with the final stage of the intermediate period, between the abolishment of the "basho" system and the beginning of the agricultural program for the Ainu. During that period the Ainu, especially those in the interior regions, still led their social life of independence based on gathering activities, with a minimum of interaction with Japanese through trading and fishing labor. The "basho" system, abolished in 1869, was temporarily replaced in some areas by direct government control, and in others, including Tokapchi, by the new system of fishery holding, whereby fishing in each district was consigned to some person, who was placed concurrently in charge of the postal service in the area. In 1876, these temporary measures were all formally abolished, but a period of transition seems to have prevailed for some time afterward.

In Tokapchi, for instance, which forms a main subject area for the present study and where Japanese immigration and settlement came later than in other districts, practically no Japanese immigrants were found in about 1874. It was in 1882–1883 that a small party of Japanese settlers came to settle near Obihiro, in the middle part of the Tokapchi River valley. In the upper Tokapchi area, surveyed by the author, not a single Japanese settler was found, even at the outset of the land-allotment and the agricultural-coaching program launched in that area in 1886. As a result, the Tokapchi Ainu continued their gathering activities and remained free from Japanese pressure and influence until a comparatively later period.

According to the author's informants, relating their own experience, the social intercourse between the interior Tokapchi Ainu and the Japanese at the time horizon chosen for the study was as follows. Conditions in the Azuma Valley seem to have been much the same. Every year in the spring Japanese agents came by boat to the interior Ainu settlements in order to hire natives for employment at coastal fishing grounds. The selection of persons to go was decided at the *ukosanio*, an assembly of the headman and houshold heads of the local group. Such negotiations with Japanese were generally conducted by a representative called *ottena*, an old title conferred by the feudal clan on native officers under the "basho" system and still used among the Ainu after its abolition by the Japanese government. Sometimes the title ottena was held concurrently by the traditional headman himself; sometimes it was held by someone else. Ainu hired labor at the Japanese fishing grounds consisted mostly of young men, but included some women. Women's work, such as drying sea tangles, was sometimes over in a relatively short period; but the work of the men, chiefly salmon and sardine fishing, usually lasted well into autumn. On returning home, the men had to immediately go hunting with fellow-members. In reward for their labor at the fishing grounds, they received Japanese wine and foodstuffs, such as rice and salt. In the spring, Japanese fur traders also came to their settlements to exchange deer and bear skins, bark clothes, and other products for articles of clothing, such as cotton fabrics, and food, such as wine, tobacco, rice, and salt. The southwestern and coastal Ainu, who had been in long and frequent contact with the Japanese, were already in the initial stage of using guns. The use, however, was still quite limited; on the upper Tokapchi, in particular, the native Ainu continued to depend on their traditional hand and spring bows with accompanying poisoned arrows.

GROUP STRUCTURE: THE HOUSEHOLD

The Ainu had permanent dwellings which formed their settlements and served as their bases of social life. The dwelling house was built for permanent use, wooden-framed, rectangular in plan, and single-roomed. All the occupants of each house constituted one household, sleeping, cooking, and eating together around a fireplace at the center of the room. The occupants, that is, the household, usually consisted of the nuclear family, the composition varying to some extent. Table 11-2 shows the variation in the upper Tokapchi Valley.

TABLE 11-2

HOUSEHOLD TYPES

Total number of households identified	59
Simple family	48
Widow plus her eldest son's family	2
Widow plus her unmarried children	2
Widow (? plus her unmarried children)	2
Widower plus his eldest son's family	1
Widower (? plus his unmarried children)	1
Unmarried woman	1
Unmarried man	1
Unmarried siblings	1

It is difficult to understand Ainu life without seeing its conditioning by its supernatural environment. Social solidarity between Ainu and nature, which is symbolized by their system of beliefs and rituals of *kamui* deities, is a basic principle underlying their social life and a central post supporting their social structure. The principle is amply shown even in their home life. Dwelling houses were built so that the sacred window faced the upper stream of the river of the settlement. The orientation scheme of working sites and associated structures around the dwelling house was based on the location of the sacred window and the fireplace (Fig. 11-2). According to their belief, the fireplace was the abode of the fire *kamui*. Without the mediation of this deity, the Ainu could not communicate with other *kamui*. For this reason all the *kamui* rituals began with the ritual for the fire *kamui* by the fireplace. The sacred window had a function specified for the communication between the fire deity and the other *kamui* deities outside. The window was used to bring in and out the head of the bear killed in the bear ceremony. This was a ritual to show that the bear *kamui* visited the Ainu house to present its host with the bear skin and the bear meat it brought. Outside the sacred window, toward the upper stream, stood the altar; between this altar and the window was erected the cage for the bear cub. The orientation scheme is based on Ainu

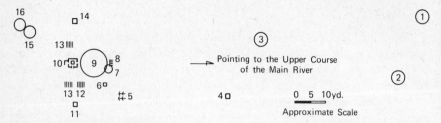

Figure 11–2. The reconstructed plan showing the arrangement of an Ainu house and associated structures and sites in Tokapchi. (1) Skinning spot. (2) Skin dump. (3) Bone dump. (4) Storehouse for tools and crafts. (5) Dead trees set up for drying fresh meats and skins. (6) Cage for the bear cub. (7) Ash dump. (8) Outdoor altar. (9) Ground for the bear ceremony. (10) Dwelling house. (11) Storehouse for meat. (12) Drying frames for meat. (13) Drying frames for fish. (14) Storehouse for fish. (15) Site for drawing water. (16) Site for the preparation of fish.

belief that their important *kamui* resided on the upper reaches of the river along which they lived. Fields of their domestic activities extended outside the house. Around the house there was a site for drawing drinking water and one for preparing fish; a skinning spot; open-air drying frames for meat and fish; a storehouse for tools and crafts; storehouses for fish, meat, and other foods; and sites for dumping ashes, bones, and spoiled furs. These buildings, structures, and sites were arranged according to a prescribed pattern, on both sides of an axis formed by the fireplace, the sacred window, and the altar and pointing up the stream flowing past the settlement. According to the Ainu view, all animal and plant resources were *kamui* deities in their temporary guises, and every topographical feature, such as a hill and river, was their activity field. In consequence, all Ainu activities in exploiting natural resources implied social intercourse with *kamui* and could not be done without ritual observance. For this reason, all the above sites were sacred and were set in with *inau*, offering sticks for *kamui* deities; these offering rituals took place periodically or on every occasion of work. The Ainu house was the base of ritual activities, and it was the male household head who observed and controlled the members.

The most fundamental problem in the daily life of the Ainu was exploitation of various resources, especially food resources. The Ainu household was the most important unit in food production. Their technique of gathering did not require any large-scale cooperation; some important techniques required only a single person, while most of the others needed no more than a few individuals to carry them out. A few families were industrially self-contained units, gathering independently all the materials of living, whether the family lived with other families in a

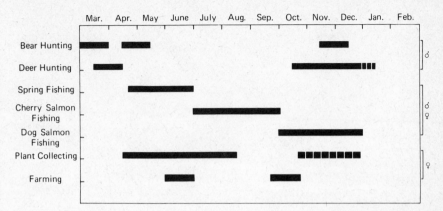

Figure 11–3. Seasonal cycles of gathering activities and sex divisions of labor. Farming was not practiced by some upstream groups.

single settlement or singly in a settlement by itself. Another important mechanism in Ainu food production was the division of labor by sex (Fig. 11-3). Men hunted deer and bear while the women collected plant foods. Fishing was done by men and women, although the techniques of the men were different from those of the women. Hunting was done in two seasons, spring and autumn. During those seasons, male household heads and other male members migrated to hunting huts in the hills and mountains. When they moved, their wives and young children were left behind. The remaining household members had various jobs to do, the most important being the collection of edible plants. Women played as great a role as men in food production; nevertheless, their status was lower. The basic reason for this was that exploitation of resources required symbolic control, and its means and rights were exclusively in the hands of the men.

THE SETTLEMENT

The place where the dwelling house, as the base of Ainu social life, stood was called *kotan,* "the settlement" (Fig. 11-4). The number of houses constituting a settlement varied from one to more than ten, although, usually there were less than ten. Settlements were distributed along river courses. The distance between two adjacent settlements varied from about 1½ to more than 4 miles, the usual being 2½ to 4 miles. The distance between dwelling houses next to each other in the same settlement varied from about 110 yards to 550 yards, and some might be even farther apart. Sites for settlements were chosen with a view to being near sources of drinking water and fishing and hunting grounds. The most important factor was usually the spawning grounds of dog salmon. The

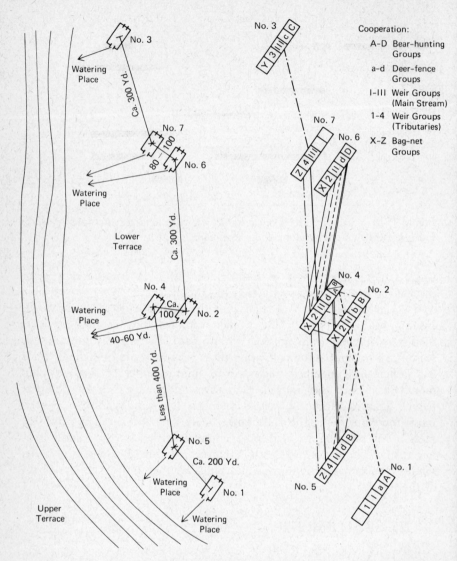

Figure 11–4. *Spatial arrangement of Ainu dwelling houses in the settlement Nitmap in the former half of the 1880s and cooperation between the households. The house numbers are given in order of birth among the household heads who are full siblings. Number 4 was occupied by a widow and her unmarried children, number 7 by an unmarried woman living alone, and the rest each by a simple family. Number 2 was the headman's.*

spawning beds were well developed and aggregated in concentrations in the main stream, near the junctions of tributary streams. The settlement itself was usually situated on the river terrace near the spawning ground and was usually named after the stream near which it was located.

COOPERATION

Settlements are classified into two types, according to size and cooperative function. Settlement type I is composed of three households or less forming a single cooperative unit for some fishing and hunting activities. Settlement type II is composed of more than three households not forming a single cooperative unit for any gathering activities. The maximum size of a cooperative unit was three households from the same settlement. Cooperative gathering activities clearly identified are bear hunting, deer hunting, weir fishing, and bag-net fishing (Fig. 11-4). The members of the bear hunting group were patrilineally close kinsmen, usually within the category of male siblings and their sons; but cooperative groups in other types of gathering tasks sometimes comprised men of different patrilineal descent and/or their families. These cooperative groups acted under the leadership of the most capable person in the given group. The settlement group formed an economic unit in the sense that they habitually exploited a common spawning ground or grounds of dog salmon. These spawning grounds, regularly exploited by settlement groups, were named and controlled by local groups. In cases where a single settlement group formed a local group, the group was a unit of exploitation of the spawning ground and the body that controlled the ground as its territory.

DEFINITION OF LOCAL GROUP

The settlement group did not always constitute a sociopolitically integrated territorial unit, that is, a local group. The local group as a politically autonomous group could either consist of several settlement groups or of only a single settlement group (Fig. 11-5). The Ainu local group is classified into two types: type A, the monosettlement local group; and type B, the multisettlement local group. Type A is further classified into two subtypes: subtype (a) with settlement type I; and subtype (b) with settlement type II. Type B is also classified into two subtypes: subtype (a) with settlement type I; and subtype (b) with settlement types I and II mixed. The local group of type B with only settlement type II, however, has never been encountered. A common type is A. B is mostly with settlement type I. In some valleys either A or B was predominant.

The local group, the principal corporate group, was characterized by a common headman, collective ownership of spawning grounds of dog salmon, cooperation in housebuilding, and a collective ritual, that is, the dog salmon ceremony. For all economic purposes the local group was self-sufficient. Ainu technology did not require the cooperation of a unit larger than the local group. In fact, the family was often self-sufficient in this respect; although members of a few families sometimes joined together for certain activities, such as bear and deer hunting and weir and bag-net fishing. Social intercourse beyond the local group seems to have been rare,

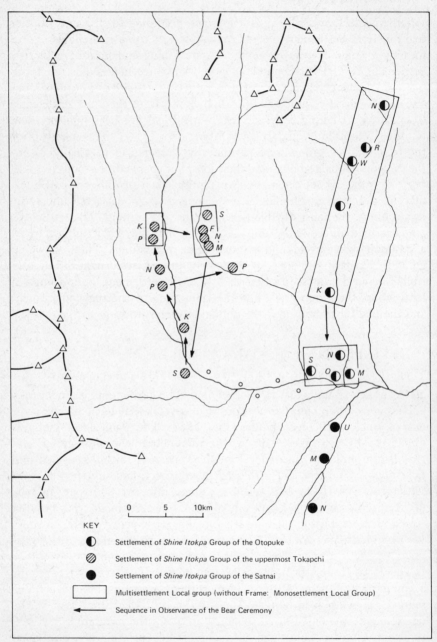

Figure 11–5. Distribution of the Ainu settlements, their local groups and shine itokpa groups in the upper Tokapchi area.

although there had been a certain degree of intermarriage. The principal occasions for Ainus to meet members of other local groups were at the bear ceremonies in winter.

HEADMAN

The headman was leader of a local group and head of a patrilineal kin group of males, which constituted the core of the local group. His main function was religious-ritual regulation of the group. He was in charge of such external or intergroup affairs as observance of rituals for affiliation of a newcomer to his group; ritual sanction of a trespasser; ritual permission to nonmembers to exploit resources; and negotiation of interlocal group affairs and such internal or domestic affairs as leading the observance of the dog salmon ceremony and keeping informed of the areas where hunting with spring bows and poisoned arrows was taking place and of the people engaged in it. He also supervised the observance of rituals and taboos by individuals of his group, protected individual families who were short of food, and gave advice to individuals of his group in practical and moral matters, which varied from production techniques to medicine. He did manual work himself, but from the above point of view he was respected and was always given an honored position on such occasions as the bear ceremony.

KINSHIP ORGANIZATION

Each local group had its core, which was held to be a group of male patrilineal kinsmen descended from a common male ancestor and from which the headman was drawn. The kin group was known as *shine ekashi ikiru*, "one and the same male-ancestor descent." The overt expressions of membership of this group were the possession of a common male-ancestor mark, *ekashi itokpa*, to be engraved on the offering stick for *kamui* deities, and the observance of common rituals for these deities. The kin group might be and was usually divided, each section belonging to a different local group in the same river valley.

The local group often included a few males semiadopted to the core *ekashi ikiru* group. Virilocal marriage was preferred, but was not a strict rule. A man of a different *ekashi ikiru* might take up uxorilocal residence and was thus affiliated with the local group. If a male of a different *ekashi ikiru* wanted to come to live with the local group as one of its regular members, he had to marry a patrilocally residing daughter of a male of the core *ekashi ikiru* so that he could obtain the right to perform the *kamui* ritual associated with the ancestor mark of the core *ekashi ikiru*, and he had to observe these rituals on some necessary occasions. The bear ceremony was certainly one, but the others cannot be identified. The transmission of the mark and the associated ritual had to be performed by the headman of the daughter's father's local group. The newcomer was thus affiliated with the local group of his wife's father; but he continued to hold his own ancestral mark, inherited from his father, and to observe the ritual associated with it. Thus, he was not fully adopted to the core *ekashi ikiru* but was semiadopted. This was not the case with his sons, however. The first son was affiliated with his father's *ekashi ikiru*, being expected to return to live with the local group, to the core of which his father belonged. All sons except the first were expected to live with the local group in which they were born. However, whether the senior son or others, they might be affiliated with either their father's *ekashi ikiru* or their mother's father's, that is, the core *ekashi ikiru*. Which of the above *ekashi ikiru* they were to be affiliated with was determined under the direction of their headman. All the procedures concerned had to be followed under the direction of the headman of their local group, and the transmission of the ancestor mark and associated rituals had to be observed by him.

In some Ainu local groups there were found besides regular members a certain number of persons in the category of *anun utari*, "foreign people." By *anun utari* it is meant observers of nonlocal *kamui* rituals, or of *kamui* rituals other than those of the core of the local group. They fall under two classes. To one class belonged those from other places who, relying on some affinal kinship with a local member, had come to stay as a sort of guest of his or her side. With the aid of the members and the headman, they would remain for a year or two, or even four to five years, enjoying hunting and fishing with regular members, and then go home again to their native areas. They were usually married and were with their families. To the other class belonged those who had no relatives among the local group members, but pressed by certain narrow circumstances had to come for aid. After passing certain questionings by the headman, these foreign people were taken in and then, whether married or single, male or female, were temporarily housed (for the first year or two) by the side of the headman's residence. Such housing may have been under the floor of the headman's elevated storehouse built on piles, for instance. These visitors were provided with food and clothing by the headman and in return helped with the manual work in the local group, under the supervision of the headman. Eventually, the headman, if convinced of their good intention and attitude, gave permission for the *anun utari* to build and live in a house of their own somewhere in the area, according to his direction. Nevertheless, they remained *anun utari* just as before. In subsistence activities they were under supervision at all times so as not to behave wrongly and ignore the *kamui* deities venerated by the local members. If they were single, the headman usually arranged marriage for them with some local woman with whom they would make a home in the area. No longer *anun utari*, they were then counted as regular members.

SHINE ITOKPA GROUP

Neighboring local groups were aggregated into larger territorial groups. The larger group was called *shine-itokpa ukokoru utaru*, "one and the same ancestor mark jointly possessing people," or, in abbreviation, *shine utaru*, "one and the same people." The present author calls it *shine itokpa* group. The group usually consisted of several local groups situated next to each other along a river distinguished by the Ainu (Fig. 11-5). Some of the groups might have consisted of a single local group, and actually there is one such example. The cores of the member local groups were held to be a group of patrilineal kinsmen, *shine ekashi ikiru*, descended from an ancient common male ancestor of local origin. It was the *ekashi itokpa*, the male-ancestor mark, of this ancestor which was possessed by every member of the *shine itokpa* group, whether obtained by birth or adoption. In some valleys, all the local groups were divided into several *shine itokpa* groups. The ancestor mark, *ekashi itokpa*, instead of being a mere family crest for showing lineage, was the very mark of ancestry to be incised on such objects as the *inau* sticks offered to *kamui* deities. It is the symbol of the social solidarity between Ainu and *kamui* of the river valley in which they lived. The only collective action of the group as a whole was the bear ceremony. It provided the only occasions for meetings with relatives and friends who resided outside the local group.

THE RIVER GROUP

An aggregation of all the local groups which lived along a river as distinguished by the Ainu constituted the river group. It was called by the name of the river. The group regarded the river valley as its own territory, claiming exclusive rights to exploit all its resources; however, in normal times, there was no single authority controlling the group as a whole. The main bond which linked the people of a river seems to have been based not only on economic interests but also on a deeply rooted cosmological background. There is evidence that each river, as distinguished by the Ainu, was associated with one or several particular *ekashi itokpa*. It was the *shine itokpa* group which had one of those aboriginal *itokpa*. Only the people having the aboriginal *itokpa* associated with the river, observing the associated ritual for local deities, and living in the river valley were regarded as the real people of the river and thus were entitled to be guardians of the river valley and of the deities that were believed to

Typical Ainu house. (Photo from Frederick Starr, The Ainu Group, *Chicago: Open Court Publishing Company, 1904)*

Outdoor altar showing a cluster of inau *with bear skulls. (Photo from Frederick Starr,* The Ainu Group, *Chicago: Open Court Publishing Company, 1904)*

Bear cage and feeding trough. (Photo from Frederick Starr, The Ainu Group, *Chicago: Open Court Publishing Company, 1904)*

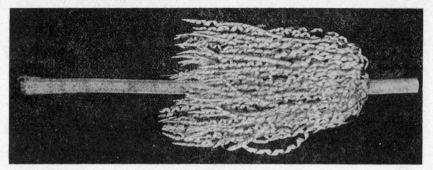

Inau, *offering stick for a* kamui *deity. (Photo from Frederick Starr,* The Ainu Group, *Chicago: Open Court Publishing Company, 1904)*

Storehouses. (Photo from Frederick Starr, The Ainu Group, *Chicago: Open Court Publishing Company, 1904)*

Ritual killing of a bear cub. The cub is shot with blunt, decorated arrows. (Photo from Frederick Starr, The Ainu Group, *Chicago: Open Court Publishing Company, 1904)*

live there and look after them. The members of the river group were potential collaborators in case of defense of their territory and a single unit in case of collective ritual against a catastrophic natural phenomenon.

MARRIAGE

The most notable of the Ainu habits concerning mate selection, might have been the avoidance of coupling the matrilineally related. Matrilineally related women were called *shine huchi ikiru*, "one and the same ancestress descent." The implication of the avoidance is that men should not marry women of the same *huchi ikiru* as their mothers. Those women assisted each other in marriage, childbirth, illness, and death on the basis of the person-to-person relation of *huchi ikiru* kinship, but there is no evidence that they were a corporate kin group. Data concerning inter-marriage is meager. In such a large *shine itokpa* group as that in the upper Tokapchi Valley, endogamy within the *shine itokpa* group was predominant; but, in the case of a smaller *shine itokpa* group in the neighboring valley, marriages beyond the *shine itokpa* group were quite frequent. All of the available data suggest that the Hokkaido Ainu were perhaps divided into several geographical groupings which were separated by the central range of hills and its major branches, which may approximately correspond to the maximal sphere of their intermarriage. The geographical division seems to correspond to the old administrative division of Hokkaido, which is reported to have been established according to the traditions of the Ainu. Among those regional groups, perhaps nine or ten in total in Hokkaido, there were often feelings of hostility and even serious conflicts.

SUBSISTENCE

The Ainu had two major cycles of gathering activities: a leisurely winter season of about two months and a work season of about ten months from spring to fall (Fig. 11-3). During the work season, Ainu labor was devoted to two to three months of hunting by the men, to five to six months of collecting by the women, and to eight to nine months of fishing (mostly salmon) by men and women. The cycle of Ainu subsistence activity corresponds to the seasonal change of climate and associated change of the distribution of biotic species. The most significant factor is the base snow, which remains on the earth's surface throughout the winter. It divided the Ainu year into two major phases. Deer retreated from the fields to their winter quarters before the base snow covered the food plants. At about the same time, the bear also began to retreat upstream into the interior of the mountains, where they went into hibernation, and the salmon stopped running. Then the Ainu, whose techniques were adapted to such ecology, stopped their gathering activities to remain inactive until the next spring. During the wintering period, the Ainu had to live on stored provisions, consisting chiefly of dried dog salmon and venison. In the areas of the Pacific side of Hokkaido, the wintering season was roughly from late December to late March, the climax of which was a period of two months from January to February. During those months, festivity thrived among all the Ainu and relatives and friends were invited from different local groups to join the bear ceremony. Early in March when the snow in the mountains hardened, bear hunting began. Then, as the base snow on the fields started disappearing, plant-collecting began. In summer, the Ainu devoted themselves to fishing for cherry salmon and collecting edible plants. In autumn, when the dog salmon ran in place of the cherry salmon and the meat of the deer grew greasy, their food-gathering activity became most intense. It was during this season that the Ainu prepared and stored their main food supply for the winter. Animal food supplies came chiefly from deer and salmon. These were the staple foods of the Ainu and the main food for wintering. The plant food, though essential and varied in kind, played rather a subsidiary part in the Ainu diet. The longest season of food-getting activities was that of river fishing, going on throughout the year except for their winter months. Six months, or nearly two thirds, of the fishing season were devoted to catching cherry salmon and then dog salmon.

FISHING

In fishing, both men and women had an important part to play, but the chief techniques of men differed from those of women. Generally, men speared the fish and women trapped them. Among the major fishing devices, which were fish spear, basket trap, bag net and weir, the first two were made and used by each family, while the other two were constructed and manipulated by cooperative groups consisting of the members of three or less families in the same settlement. For the most part, the dog salmon was taken in and around the spawning grounds near the settlement. The methods and the sites of fishing changed as the season wore on (Fig. 11-6). Before the beginning of spawning in the spawning ground near the settlement, Ainu men speared fish with *marek* at the peep huts set up on the running course. When spawning began in the spawning grounds near their own settlement, the Ainu started spearing fish at sunset and in the early morning. All the spawning and running activities of the fish usually become brisk at night between sundown and daybreak. In the daytime, the spearers went around spearing salmon hiding in the bank-side hollows and under driftwood. In this season, the basket trap was set effectively to catch fish moving up and down around the spawning grounds. Toward the beginning of the winter, when there was a variety of dog salmon, all the Ainu began spearing salmon at night by torchlight.

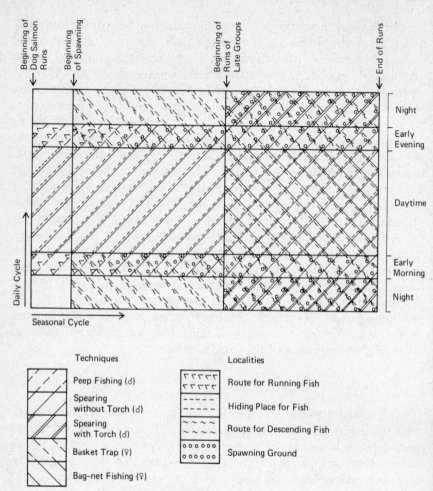

Figure 11–6. *Daily and seasonal cycles in dog salmon fishing.*

This method was employed most effectively in spawning grounds and for running fish. In the daytime, women came out to take part in bag-net fishing to supplement the spearing activities of the men. During the cold season, the older men were occupied with catching running salmon in peep huts. Torchlight or night fishing and bag-net fishing were prohibited for the earlier runs. The greater part of the dog salmon needed by the natives was obtained during the period of the earlier runs, between October and November, and was sun-dried for storing. Salmon caught during the cold season in December were made into a sort of frozen fish. Well-developed spawning grounds or concentrations of spawning beds of dog salmon annually recur in practically the same sites. Those were maintained by Ainu local groups as their territories. Each settlement was usually situated near one of the grounds of their own local group.

Fishing gear and techniques for cherry salmon were somewhat the same as those for dog salmon, but owing to the difference in ecology of the fishes, fishing sites for cherry salmon were different from those for dog salmon. Dog salmon generally spawn in large main streams, while cherry salmon spawn mostly in smaller streams and glens. When cherry salmon appeared in the river near the settlement, the Ainu immediately set up the weir. The fishing was carried out by the cooperative group of three or less families from the same settlement. The weir was used effectively during the night when the runs became active. By day, men speared fish hiding in pools and under driftwood. Fish that were missed or driven out were captured by partners, usually women using the bag net. When the cherry salmon began to spawn, they moved their major fishing grounds from the river to small tributaries. Some local groups migrated regularly to the same streams at some distance from their settlements and lived in huts, which served as their fishing bases. Part of the female population, especially housewives, remained at home collecting edible plants.

HUNTING

Men played the leading part in hunting. It is true that young men, helped by hunting dogs, occasionally hunted deer with a rope or wooden stick, but it was taboo for Ainu women to use hunting weapons. In spring and autumn, men of each cooperative hunting group were divided into two parties, the bear-hunting party consisting of younger and more active hunters and the deer-hunting party of older and less able men. The autumn bear party was generally smaller in size than the spring one, for in that season deer hunting and dog-salmon fishing were of special importance for securing winter foods. The members of the bear-hunting group were patrilineally close kinsmen, usually within the category of male siblings and their sons; but cooperative groups in other types of gathering tasks sometimes comprised men of different descent and/or their family members.

Deer were hunted in two separate seasons, spring and autumn. Autumn deer were as important a source of winter food to the Ainu as were dog salmon. Autumn hunting of the deer extended into winter and was divided into two successive phases. Of the two phases, the first one of field hunting was the more important, for in this period a more or less sufficient quantity of venison could be secured to last the winter. This phase started when the deer's fur began to change for the winter and the meat began to get greasy and continued until the base snow covering the food plants for the deer caused the animals to retreat from the fields to their winter quarters. The Ainu set spring bows and poisoned arrows to the

deer fences. These fences were usually located in fields at the foot of a
hill or on the gentle slope of a lower hill. They frequented the fence
usually from their homes in the settlement or while engaged in salmon
fishing in the river. On the way to and from the fence they also hunted
deer with bows and arrows. Hunting with hand bows came into full
swing with the arrival of mating time, when the animal was decoyed with
the deer whistle. In the second phase, the scene of deer hunting shifted
from the fields up to the hills. When the base snow came and all the
deer tracks had disappeared from the fields, the animals gathered at their
winter quarters on the wooded valley slopes. The hunters stayed at their
huts in the river valleys down from the winter quarters, chasing their
game with hounds and with hand bows and poisoned arrows. They usually
returned home when the snow was too deep for themselves and the dogs
to walk in. The hill hunting was performed by only part of the hunters,
to supplement field hunting. Deer hunting was resumed by hunters back
at their huts near the winter quarters in the spring, when the surface of
the snow on the hills thawed by day and hardened again at night. Early
in the season, the Ainu shot the animals after driving them into glens
filled with snow. As the snow began to disappear, deer passing by way
of ridges where the snow had melted earlier gradually came down in
herds to the lower plain in search of fresh plants. The Ainu continued
hunting by means of spring bows set along the migration tracks, as well as
with hand bows, until the base snow disappeared from the fields and the
downward migration was completed. Spring hunting was important for
securing deer skins.

The Hokkaido species of bear grows to a large size and is of a ferocious
nature. The Ainu were most probably the only people to use bows and
arrows as chief weapons for hunting this bear. Moreover, it seems that no
people in the neighboring areas ever hunted the bear with such a degree
of active, organized effort as the Ainu. Furs of the animals were the most
important item of barter with the Japanese, and bear cubs were a necessity
for the Ainu bear ceremony. But as a part of the Ainu food economy, the
bear was not as important as deer or salmon. The spring hunting of bear
began about the time the mountain snow became hard enough to walk in
and bear cubs had been born in dens. Early in the season, the Ainu
carried out raids on the dens while the inmates still lay in hibernation.
As the mountain snow began to melt, the hunters by means of spring
bows set on the tracks started hunting bears which were coming out of their
dens, located mainly on the ridges where the snow melts earlier. The
season of autumn bearhunting covered a period between the time when
the bears began to retreat to their dens and the time when almost all the
bears were in hibernation. Spring bows were set on the tracks, usually along
the small glens, where food for the bear, nuts and berries, was plentiful.
The animals were hunted with hand bows as well, and some hunters even

chased bears to their dens. The hibernation centers of the bear were distinct from the winter quarters of the deer, even in the same river valley. The tracks for the seasonal and local migration of the bear were more concentrated, mingled, and permanent on the ridges and the small glens near the hibernation centers. With full knowledge of the game, the Ainu selected bear-hunting grounds in those source areas of the rivers where there were hibernation centers. On each ground a hut was built for hunters to pass each season.

COLLECTING OF PLANTS

In collecting edible plants, no cooperation between families was attempted. Neighboring women of the same settlement would invite one another along and go in one group, gathering edible plants, but usually each woman collected for her own family. In spring, when the snow had disappeared from the plains, the Ainu set to work collecting wild plants. The work continued incessantly and with persistence until dog salmon began ascending the rivers. Most of the plants collected were dried and stored away in sufficient quantities to last the winter. During spring and summer, all varieties of plants with edible leaves, stalks, or roots were taken. In summer, roots of a species of *Cardiocrinum* were chiefly collected and made into starch for storage. Those groups of Ainu who did some farming gathered the roots with less frequency and in smaller quantity. In autumn, certain kinds of nuts, fruits, and berries were collected, though not in such quantities as would last any great length of time.

CULTIVATION OF PLANTS

Before the land allotment to the Ainu by the Japanese government, the Ainu in the Otopuke Valley and half of the member households of the local group in Kuttaraushi, who lived farthest upstream on the Tokapchi, and at least one household in Pipaushi, farther downstream, had done no farming; but other Ainus in the Tokapchi Valley, as well as those in the Azuma Valley, had done some small-scale farming. The old techniques were simple and the farm work was usually performed by women. The main crops were a variety of *Panucum* and a variety of millet. Preparation of fields and sowing was done in early summer, after storing of the chief varieties of wild leaves was finished. Suitable plots on the river bank near Ainu settlements were cleared and leveled with small wooden picks, which were also used for digging wild roots. Sowing of seeds followed without making any ridges in the soil. The crops were harvested by picking the ears with an implement made of a moluscan shell, collected in the river, then dried and stored.

ECOLOGICAL ZONES

Each river valley inhabited by the Ainu is divided into the following ecological zones (Fig. 11-7):

1. The river and its tributaries: fishing.
2. River banks: plant collecting; cultivation of plants.
3. River terraces: deer hunting (autumn); plant collecting; Ainu settlement.
4. Hillsides along the river courses: deer hunting (early winter and spring); bear hunting (occasional or subsidiary).
5. Riverhead mountain region: bear hunting (periodical and intensive); collecting of Ulmus bark.

Systematic and organized bear hunting in zone 5 was performed only by specified bear hunters from part of the Ainu families. Deer hunting in zone 3 was indispensable for the Ainu to secure meat for wintering. Zones 1–3, providing the Ainu with all the essential food resources, were distributed around each one's own settlement and were exploited from a single center, the settlement. Dog salmon were taken for the most part in and around the spawning grounds near the settlement. Although the cherry salmon in the small tributaries and glens were not concentrated around each settlement during the spawning season, most Ainu fished within

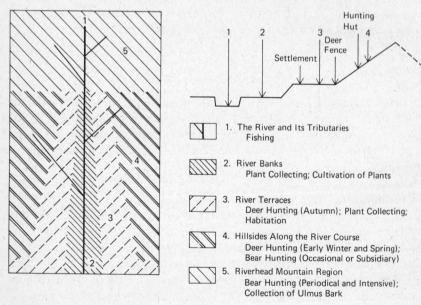

Figure 11–7. Diagram representing a river valley as the territory of a river group and its ecological zones.

their own settlement areas. Venison was obtained chiefly from around the settlement, where deer fences were set with spring bows, and hand-bow hunting was also conducted. All the edible plants were usually gathered from around each settlement. The outermost zones, 4 and 5, were hunting fields, each being exploited from a different hunting hut. Neither area was important as a part of Ainu food economy. Zone 5 was utilized only by specialized bear hunters from part of the Ainu families and by some collectors of Ulmus bark for clothing. Zone 4 was utilized only by deer hunters in early winter and spring. Hunting in early winter was carried out by some Ainu in case the winter store of venison obtained in autumn was scarce. The spring hunting was chiefly for skins. The zones were distributed parallel to the river course, usually at a distance within reach of one day's trip from the settlement. The Ainu gathered foods in these ecological zones from a single center, the settlement, having centrifugally brought in and stored food in their homes (Fig. 11-8). Distribution of their essential food resources within these zones was so stable that the Ainu could maintain permanent settlements without ever turning to nomadic life. Huts were arranged in hunting and fishing sites far from the settlement. Among those, the most popular were bear-hunting huts in zone 5 and deer-hunting huts in zone 4. Some families or local groups had cherry-salmon fishing huts near the spawning grounds in smaller tributaries. Those hunting or fishing sites were so stable that each hut was usually occupied by the same cooperative group of families every season. The cooperative group or hut group in hunting or fishing usually consisted of members of three or less families from the same settlement. The seasonal migrations to hunting huts were undertaken by part of the members of each family. When they moved, their wives and children were left behind; the remaining family members had work such as collecting edible plants. The periodic migrations occurred each spring and autumn; men moved to the same huts to stay for about one month each season. Thus men shifted residence usually twice every year. However, the total period of their stay away from their homes was only about two to three months. The permanent dwelling houses in the settlement were occupied by the whole family for nine to ten months of the year and by housewives and their children nearly all year.

TERRITORY

Staple foodstuffs of the Ainu were gathered from a relatively narrow area surrounding their settlement and covered three ecological zones—the river along which they settled, its river banks, and river terraces. Main hunting and fishing sites were fixed in location owing to the adaptability of their techniques to migrative habits of animals. Under these conditions, the Ainu were able to maintain permanent settlements in spite of their

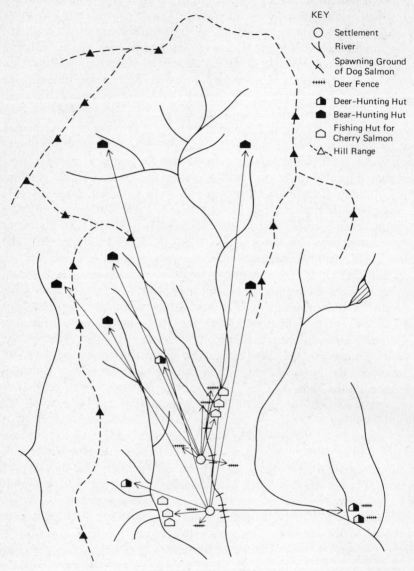

Figure 11–8. Exploitation of ecological zones by the settlement groups and the distribution of hunting and fishing huts (upper Tokapchi area).

dependence upon a hunting-gathering subsistence. The river valley occupied by each river group constituted a nearly or completely self-sufficient
unit of Ainu habitat. The Ainu had seldom to overstep the territorial
boundaries of their own river group for gathering purposes. As regards
the staple items in particular, such as deer, dog salmon, cherry salmon,
and edible plants, every river group was at normal times sufficiently sup-

plied from resources found within its own territory. Within this larger area there were territories of minor categories, which were seasonally maintained by such smaller groups as the local group, the cooperative group, and the individual household. These might be hunting or fishing sites, which were exploited by means of fixed devices, or concentrations of certain specific resources which annually recurred at the same places (see Table 11-3).

Except for such specified localities, the entire area within the river-group territory might be utilized freely by any member belonging to the group. In this open area, any person, male or female, could freely open up a new ground for spring-bow hunting or trap fishing, go hunting with hand bow, or go about collecting plants. Even the aforesaid specific localities were open to anyone in the same river group when they were not seasonally assigned for a particular locality. Despite the presence of the free-gathering areas within the river-group territory, the Ainu were usually able to obtain most of their necessary supplies from the immediate surroundings of each settlement without having to go great distances for gathering. All the Ainu territories were defended and protected for the natural resources therein. Ainu claim to resources on land, however, was activated not only by their economic interest but also by their cosmological relation with their habitat.

TABLE 11-3

TYPES OF TERRITORY

Territory Maintained by River Group	Territories Maintained by Smaller Groups within River Group	Controlling Body	Condition of the Place
River basin	Site for peep hut	Simple nuclear family	Unstable
	Site for fish trap		
	Site for weir	Cooperative group	Stable
	Place for setting bows		
	Place for deer fence		
	Spawning grounds of dog salmon	Local group	Very stable

BELIEFS AND RITUALS

All animals and plants were seen by the Ainu as *kamui* deities in their temporary guises, or as *kamui* appearing in front of the Ainu with gifts to them. The earth's surface, covered with fauna and flora, was seen by the Ainu as the abode and activity field of the *kamui* deities. From this point of view, the Ainu divided the whole of their land into a number of *iworu* on the basis of their system of classifying streams. The Ainu distinguished different streams by different names and classified individual streams into rivers and glens. Each named river or glen was believed to be the dwelling of, and was owned by, a *kamui* deity. The river-owning *kamui* was believed to be the chief or head of the deities which lived in and owned streams flowing into the river. The basin or valley of a river or glen was named by adding the suffix *iworu* to the name of the stream. Each *iworu*, that is, the area drained by a stream, was believed to be the area which the *kamui* of the stream kept its eyes on. The *iworu* of a river was also inhabited by a number of *kamui* as represented by individual plants and animals. The chiefs among them, as well as the chief water *kamui*, or the river-owning *kamui*, were held to reside in the upper reaches of the river.

The Ainu believed that the *kamui* deities, which lived in the *iworu* of the neighboring river, looked after them. The inhabitants of a river, that is, the river group, claimed exclusive rights to exploit the resources in the river basin. Outsiders were allowed no access to those resources except by permission. The permission was obtainable from the headman of any local group in the river valley by going through a certain ritual procedure for the local *kamui* deities. If someone wanted to fish at the spawning grounds owned by another local group, he had to ask permission of the headman of that group. Under the direction of the headman, the applicant observed a proper ritual for the fire *kamui* and the river-owning *kamui* and offered *inau* sticks made by him to the spawning grounds. Among the member local groups of the same river group, permission was usually given without fail. Fishing in areas of a river outside of the named spawning grounds and private sites was freely done as occasions demanded by the people of the same river, that is, by the members of the same river group. However, in order to prevent fishing by outsiders without permission, by custom every fisherman gave information of his coming to the people of the nearby settlement. In case of gathering, either fishing, hunting, or collecting, in the territory of a different river group, one had to get permission from any one of the headmen in the river valley, regardless of the method of one's hunting or fishing. Such permission was usually (but not always) given on the performance of a ritual for local *kamui* deities, because assurance was required that the fisherman or hunter would be faithful to the local *kamui* deities. The discoverer of any trespasser must bring him to his headman or some headman available at hand in the river valley to make the transgressor apologize as soon as possible to the local *kamui* deities of the river concerned. Also, the discovery of evidence of trespassing, such as salmon bones thrown in the *iworu* of the river, was a cause for serious issue, for it meant a grave violation to the *kamui* deities of the river, from which the people of the river received exclusive favor and which they guarded with greatest caution. The Ainu expressed the maintaining of their territory by the words "the guard of our *iworu*-owning *kamui*." Their territoriality was actually activated not only by economic interest but also by their system of social solidarity.

BEAR CEREMONY

The greatest of the Ainu *kamui* rituals was the winter bear ceremony. It was the only group action available for the expression of the solidarity of the *shine itokpa* group, the local patrilineal descent group. It provided the Ainu with the principal occasions to meet members of other local groups. As mentioned previously, Ainu hunters entered deep mountains in early spring when mountain snow hardened and began hunting bears and their cubs in hibernation. When cubs were taken, they were either allotted for rearing among the member families or taken on in one lot by the leader's family, all the other families contributing necessary feed. Rearing of a cub usually took nearly a year, or in some cases two years, at the end of which period the animal was killed ritually. The ritual killing of the cub, *iomante*, "sending off the bear *kamui*," took place in January, or at the latest, in February before the spring bear hunting set in once again. The ritual was the only peacetime collective activity participated in with regularity by the *shine itokpa* group as a whole and the greatest of the Ainu peacetime collective actions. The purpose of the ceremony was to send the bear *kamui*, as a visitor to the Ainu, back to their homeland, which was believed to be in the upper reaches of their own river. The bear *kamui* had its kinsmen and its headman. The headman was believed to be the big bear that lived in a large house on the lofty mountain top at the river head. The headman was never known to move outside of its abode, but in spring, on its orders, its people put on the bear's form ready for their visits to the Ainu. When they went, they took with them bear meat and bear skin to give to the Ainu. When they set out of their land, the headman gave notice to the fire *kamui* who resided in the house of each Ainu hunter. The messenger of the fire *kamui* was the bear hound that conducted the Ainu to meet the visitor. The bear, then, was not hunted by the Ainu but came to visit them. When the visitor arrived, it entered the hunter's house by the sacred window, presenting the host with the bear skin and the bear meat it brought. In return, it received all the hospitality due an honored guest. After accepting the treasured *inau*, shaved wooden sticks, the visitor, again in human form, went back to the river head to his headman. On its return home, the bear *kamui* was received by the headman and its fellow-people, who all shared with it the gift brought back from the Ainu. If the bear was treated with due attention, the headman was pleased to send more of its people to visit with the same host again next year.

Prior to the ceremony, the headmen of the member local groups of the *shine itokpa* held a meeting at the house of one who, by custom, came first in order among them to fix dates for the ceremonies at their respective settlements (Fig. 11-5). Whether cubs were killed individually at the keeper's house or collectively at the headman's where they were all brought together, the rituals were performed in a fixed order of households in each local group. First came the headman's. He had exercised a custodianship over all the cubs kept within the group. It was not until the initial killing had been performed by the headman on his own cub that other cubs in the same group were killed ritually by other keepers. In a certain local group the headman was followed by others in the order of seniority, but in another the order was in the nearness of kin to the headman. The ritual killing at each keeper's house in a local group was finished in a day, and it went around among all the keepers' houses in the group until all had finished. Generally, a couple of days were left between the last day of ritual killing in one local group and the first in the next group. Thus, in case of a larger *shine itokpa* group, the entire period required by the whole group extended well over a month.

The ritual in each keeper's house was also participated in by the headman and others. The leading part, however, was played by the keeper. He offered to his bear cub the *inau* sticks marked with his own ancestral patrilineal mark. If he was a man of a different *ekashi ikiru*, semiadopted through marriage as a member of the core *ekashi ikiru* of the local group, he had to offer the *inau* stick bearing his wife's father's ancestral mark. Attendants of the bear ceremony seem to have been mostly, or almost exclusively, members of the *shine itokpa* group. At the season of the ceremony, people often stayed away from home for more than ten days, attending one ceremony after another in the member settlements of their *shine itokpa* group. Some of the senior members, it seems, were away even for a whole month.

Dog Salmon Ceremony

According to the Ainu view, the dog salmon was the subordinate of the *kamui* in the sea and had a human form like the Ainu. There were a number of leaders among salmon deities, who ran up different rivers to visit the Ainu, leading their own group of salmon deities under the direction of the chief *kamui* of the sea. When visiting the Ainu, they brought with them meals of salmon meat for the Ainu. After giving this meat to the Ainu and being entertained by them, each salmon deity assumed a human form and went back by boat to its home in the sea. Which river they ran up depended upon the direction of the *kamui* in the sea. The salmon deity would forward plenty of salmon to the river along which the Ainu who lived there respected and welcomed them in the proper way. The fire *kamui* told the river-owning *kamui* how the salmon that were caught were treated by their captors, the Ainu. The river-owning *kamui* communicated this to the *kamui* in the sea.

The dog salmon ceremony was held by the local group as a unit and was not associated with such a festivity and feast as accompanied the bear ceremony. The salmon ceremony consisted of three stages: the prefishing ritual; the first salmon ritual; and the postfishing ritual. Before the arrival of dog salmon, each local group observed a prefishing ritual to ensure their coming up the river. The male heads of each household of the local group participated in the ritual, which was organized and directed by the headman. Prayers and offering sticks, *inau*, were given to the fire *kamui* and the river-owning *kamui*. The *inau* bore the ancestor mark of the headman, that is, of the patrilineal male-kin group which constituted the core of the local group. After the collective ritual at the headman's house, each household head made *inau* offerings and set these up at the prescribed spot near the spawning ground habitually exploited by his own settlement group and controlled by his own local group. The members of each settlement, who caught the first salmon, sent it to his headman. Besides this gift, the first fisherman in each settlement invited the people to eat together from his first catch, which was cooked in his house for the first time in the season. The first dog salmon to be eaten for the first time in each house, either in the first fisher's house or in any other's, had to be offered to the fire *kamui* of each household, and the ritual cutting had to be performed by a male with his man's knife, the *inau* scraping knife. When the spawning of dog salmon ended at the spawning grounds of each local group, each headman called together all the male household heads to his house and observed a postrun or postfishing ritual to "see off salmon deities" and to pray for a plentiful next run. The ritual procedure seemed to have been much the same as that for the prefishing ritual, except that on return from the headman's house, each household head threw special offering sticks, "boat *inau*," laden with all the mandibles of the dog salmon eaten in his house during the year, into the river at a prescribed spot near the spawning ground most frequented by the people of his settlement.

Supernatural Beliefs

The Ainu world was full of divine visitors: all the natural resources exploited by them were *kamui* deities in temporary guises. In consequence, all their gathering activities implied social intercourse with *kamui*. Thus, there was a close interdependence between Ainu and *kamui*, and their ritual and taboos were an expression of this relation. The relation, that is, the social solidarity between the Ainu and the *kamui*, was established on the principle of coresidence or local contiguity. Ainu cosmology emphasized its component of spatial orientation; nature, that is, *kamui*, were ordered on local bases. The effective ritual relation between those spatially oriented *kamui* and the Ainu was in the hands of the patrilineal kin group of males, which formed the basis of the Ainu local organization.

PRESENT LIVING CONDITIONS

The living conditions of the Ainu change ceaselessly. Fragmentary remnants of their old customs, which have narrowly been maintained in their daily life, may be lost completely in several years. Informants who have knowledge about things Ainu will cease to be in the near future. Physically the Ainu are not likely to become extinct so soon, but the Ainu as a cultural group are just on the brink of extinction, leaving various unsolved problems behind.

The Ainu language has now been dead for a long time. Some Ainus still keep it in memory; however, its complete extinction is in view with the death of such individuals. Ainus under forty years of age seldom understand their own language, beyond a handful of words learned from someone. Those able to make short sentences in their own language are said to be few in number in Hokkaido.

The traditional structure of their habitation has nearly disappeared. Houses of present-day Ainu usually have nothing to remind us of their old life, although a few of them still retain the traditional type of roofing. Ainu live in wooden houses of the Japanese style popular in Hokkaido. Even their furniture and utensils are Japanese. The only exceptions still in use in some localities are Ainu baskets made of local plant fibers; however, younger Ainus tend to dislike using them. Sites for their home dwellings were traditionally chosen with a view to proximity to sources of drinking water and fishing and hunting grounds. The most important factor in this respect was usually the spawning grounds of dog salmon. Thus, the houses were usually situated on or near the edge of a river terrace near the spawning grounds. They were specially arranged according to traditional cosmological principles. But those patterns and arrangements of Ainu houses were fast discarded with their conversion to agricultural life, which started in 1883. The Hokkaido government moved the Ainu to more favorable areas, desiring, at the same time, to bring their hitherto scattered settlements together into smaller areas for the convenience of supervision and instruction in farming. The land-allotment program caused splitting and mixing of Ainu settlement groups and other serious disturbances of their traditional organizations. Modern Ainu dwellings are generally distributed in or near the new settlements established in that period.

No reservation system, such as seen among the American Indians, has been applied to the Ainu, and no legal or administrative distinction has been made between them and the Japanese. But there is still a tendency for present-day Ainu to maintain their own communities, living in settlements more or less separated from those of the Japanese. Those settlements consisting chiefly of Ainu, are found concentrated in the Hitaka district, especially in the valleys of such rivers as the Saru, the Mukawa, and the Shibuchari. In other districts, such settlements (the so-called

Ainu settlements, or *kotan*) are much fewer and more scattered, noticeable among them being Shiraoi near Tomakomai (Iburi district), Fushiko near Obihiro (Tokachi district), Harutori and Tohro near Kushiro (Kushiro district), Akan and Kutcharo (Akan National Park), Bihoro near Kitami (Abashiri district), Naibuchi near Nayoro (Teshio district), and Chikabumi near Asahikawa (Ishikari district). Of these, Shiraoi, Akan, and Chikabumi are now popular tourist centers for seeing Ainus. Many Ainus in these places are engaged in commercial activities related to tourism. But the Ainu in other localities usually have nothing to do with tourists in general. Their occupations vary from stock farming to local transportation, but the commonest one appears to be agriculture, or agriculture plus seasonal labor for wages in such industries as forestry. The standard of living among the Ainu varies to a great extent among different households, although they seem to be generally poorer than their Japanese neighbors. There seem to be many unmarried Ainus working in towns and cities in Hokkaido and for various industrial enterprises in places more distant from their homes. The only opportunity for their homecoming, in general, comes at the *bon* season in summer, the traditional Japanese holiday season (based on Buddhism) for observing an ancestor ceremony. It is in this season that present-day Ainu observe their own ancestor ritual, although the form seems to have been influenced by Buddhism.

Since their transformation into agriculturalists, the Ainu system of *kamui* cult has rapidly collapsed and its formal aspect has been only partially retained in the ancestor ritual, *shinnurappa*. A significant fact concerning the practice, at present, is the shortage of Ainus who are able to observe the ritual properly. The author once saw an old male Ainu acting as a kind of professional specialist priest for the ancestor ritual, visiting round houses and settlements in a river valley. The so-called bear ceremony of the Ainu, in its traditional form, is only barely preserved among present-day Ainu hunters, even with whom the event has ceased to function socially as it did in the past. Every Ainu house in the past had an outdoor altar with a cluster of various *inau* sticks standing in a row; nowadays the altar is seldom seen near their houses.

The clothing habits of the Ainu have completely changed; today no Ainu ever wears traditional dress. Even traditional objects of personal decoration have disappeared from their daily life. The transition of subsistence from hunting and gathering to agriculture radically changed their food habits. The traditional foods, salmon and deer, have been replaced by cultivated food plants. All their animal food supplies now come from local dealers. Wild plants have also ceased to be of importance to the Ainu. Cultivation and stock farming have devastated patches of wild edible plants, once so important in their daily diet. Ainu food habits today show little appearance of difference from those of neighboring

Japanese, although no reliable scientific data has been made available on the current conditions.

The current educational system makes no distinction between the Ainu and the Japanese. By 1909, twenty-one primary schools had been established exclusively for the Ainu children, but from 1910 onward, these were gradually abolished. In spite of educational and administrative efforts made by the Japanese government, there still remains a sociopsychological barrier between the Ainu and the local settled Japanese in general. Intermarriage between the two people has taken place rather frequently, but it seems that there are still a few Ainus of "pure blood."

REFERENCES

Batchelor, J., 1901. *The Ainu and Their Folklore*, London.

Chiri, M., 1959. "Ainu no Sake-ryō: Horobetsu ni okeru Chōsa" (Dog Salmon Fishing of the Ainu: An Investigation in Horobetsu), *Hoppō Bunka Kenkyū Hōkoku*, Sapporo [14]:245–265.

Habara, M., 1939. *Ainu Shakai-keizai-shi* (A Socioeconomic History of the Ainu), Tokyo.

Hayashi, Y., 1958. "Ainu no Kōun Gijutsu" (Cultivation Techniques of the Ainu), *Hoppō Bunka Kenkyū Hōkoku*, Sapporo, [13]:175–203.

Hikita, H., 1956. "Hokkaido-Engan oyobi Kasen de torareru Taiheiyō Keison-rui" (Pacific Salmon, Genus: Oncorhynchus, Known to Occur in Coasts and Rivers of Hokkaido), *Hokkaido Suisan Fuka-jyō Shiken Hōkoku*, Sapporo, [11]:25–44.

Hokkaido-chō (Hokkaido Government) (ed.), 1917. *Nopporo Kokuyūrin Yasei Shokubutu Chōsa Hōkoku-sho* (Scientific Report on Wild Plants in the Nopporo National Forest), Sapporo.

——— (ed.), 1937. *Hokkaido-shi* (A History of Hokkaido), 7 vols., Sapporo.

Hokkaido Nōji Shiken-jyō (Experimental Farm of Hokkaido) (ed.), 1931. "Hokkaido ni okeru Shokuyō Yasei Shokubutsu" (Edible Wild Plants in Hokkaido), *Hokkaido Noji Shiken-jyō Ihō*, Sapporo [52].

Hokkaido Sake Masu Fuka-jyō (Hokkaido Salmon Hatchery), 1956. *Sake Masu Tennen Sanran Jyōkyō Chōsa Keikaku-sho* (Scheme for Survey of Natural Spawning-beds of Salmon). Official circular.

Inukai, T., 1942. "Tensai ni okeru Ainu no Taido" (Ainus' Attitudes towards Natural Disasters), *Hoppō Bunka Kenkyū Hōkoku*, Sapporo, [6]:141–162.

———, 1952. "Hokkaido no Shika to sono Kōbō" (On the Deer in Hokkaido, Its Decrease and Coming Back), *Hoppō Bunka Kenkyū Hōkoku*, Sapporo, [7]:1–45.

———, 1954. "Ainu no Sake-ryō ni okeru Matsuri-goto" (The Salmon Ceremonialism among the Ainu), *Hoppō Bunka Kenkyū Hōkoku*, Sapporo, [9]:79–90.

———, and T. Natori, 1939. "*Iomante* (Ainu no Kuma-matsuri) no Bunka-shi-teki Igi to sono Keishiki," I (On the Significance of the Bear Festival, *iomante*, in Ainu Culture and Its Local Forms, I), *Hoppō Bunka Kenkyū Hōkoku*, Sapporo, [2]:237–271.

—— and ——, 1940. "Iomante (Ainu no Kuma-matsuri) no Bunka-shi-teki Igi to sono Keishiki," II (On the Significance of the Bear Festival, iomante, in Ainu Culture and its Local Forms, II), Hoppō Bunka Kenkyū Hōkoku, Sapporo, [3]:79–135.

Izumi, S., 1951. "Saru Ainu no Chien Shūdan ni okeru Iworu" (The Iworu and the Territorial Group of the Saru Ainu), Minzokugaku Kenkyū, Tokyo, [3–4]:29–45.

Kintaichi, K., 1944. Ainu no Kenkyū (Studies on the Ainu), 3d ed., Tokyo.

Kōno, H., 1934. "Ainu no Inau Shiroshi" (Inau Shiroshi of the Ainu), Jinruigaku Zasshi, Tokyo, 49 [1]:12–24.

——, 1936. "Ainu to Totem-teki Ifū" (The Ainu and a Totemism-like Custom), Minzokugaku Kenkyū, Tokyo, 2:45–53.

Kubodera, I., 1951. "Saru Ainu no Sorei Saishi" (Ancestor Cult of the Saru Ainu), Minzokugaku Kenkyū, Tokyo, 16 [3–4]:46–61.

——, 1956. "Hokkaido Ainu no Sō-sei—Saru Ainu wo Chūsin to shite" (The Antiquated Funeral Customs of the Hokkaido Ainu with Special Reference to the Saru Ainu), Minzokugaku Kenkyū, Tokyo, 20 [1–2]:1–35.

Mihara, T., S. Ito, T. Hachiya, and M. Ichikawa, 1951. "Hokkaido ni okeru Keison Gyokyō no Hendō ni kansuru Kenkyū," I (Studies on the Change of Fishing Conditions of Salmon in Hokkaido, I), Hokkaido Suisan Fuka-jyō Shiken Hōkoku, 6 [1–2]:27–133.

Natori, T., 1940. "Kezuribashi Soin Sokei Sogen oyobi Shushin yori mitaru Saru Kawasuji no Ainu" (The Origin of Gods and the nusa cluster of inau, in the Bear Festival of the Saru Ainu), Hoppō Bunka Kenkyū Hōkoku, Sapporo, [4]:35–112.

Sarashina, G., 1942. Kotan Seibutsu Ki (Ethnobiological Notes on an Ainu Settlement), Sapporo.

Sugiura, K., 1951. "Saru Ainu no Shinzoku Soshiki" (Kinship System of the Saru Ainu), Minzokugaku Kenkyū, Tokyo, 16 [3–4]:3–28.

Takabeya, F., 1939. "Ainu Jyūkyo no Kenkyu." (Studies on Ainu Dwellings), Hoppō Bunka Kenkyū Hōkoku, Sapporo, [2]:1–124.

Takakura, S., 1942. Ainu Seisaku-shi (A History of Ainu Policies), Tokyo.

——, 1957. "Meiji-izen no Hokkaido ni okeru Nō-boku-gyō (Agricultural History of Hokkaido before the Introduction of European Techniques), Hoppō Bunka Kenkyū Hōkoku, Sapporo, [12]:13–41.

Watanabe, H., 1951. "Saru Ainu ni okeru Tennen-shigen no Riyō" (Utilization of Natural Resources by the Saru Ainu), Minzokugaku Kenkyū 16 [3–4]: 71–82.

——, 1953. "Ainu ni okeru Yumi" (Bows among the Ainu), Jinruigaku-kai Minzokugaku-kyokai Rengō Taikai Kiji, Tokyo, 6th Session, pp. 129–132.

——, 1954. "Ifuri Ainu ni okeru Suisan Shigen no Riyō" (Utilization of Aquatic Resources by the Ifuri Ainu), Jinruigaku-kai Minzokugaku-kyokai Rengō Taikai Kiji, Tokyo, 7th Session, pp. 43–48.

——, 1955. "Kisetsuteki Ijyū Gijutsu Shigen. Ainu ni okeru Seitaiteki Ichi-sokumen" (Seasonal Migration, Technology and Natural Resources. An Ecological Aspect of the Ainu), Jinruigaku-kai Minzokugaku-kyōkai Rengō Taikai Kiji, Tokyo, 8th Session, pp. 62–63.

——, 1963. "Ainu no Nawabari to shiteno Sake no Sanran-kuiki" (Spawn-

ing Grounds of Dog Salmon as the Territory of the Ainu Local Group),
Minzokugaku Note, Tokyo (Oka Kyōju Kanreki Kinen Ronbun-shū), pp.
278–297.

————, 1965. "Ningen to Shizen no Shakai-teki Ketsugo Kankei. Ainu Nihon-
minzoku Tungus no Kyōtsūsei" (Social Solidarity between Man and Nature.
Features Common to the Ainu, the Japanese and the Tungus), Minzokugaku
Kenkyū 29 (3):297–298.

Yoshida, I., 1955. "Higashi Hokkaido Ainu Koji Fudoki Shiryō" (Ethnographical Materials on the Ainu in Eastern Hokkaido), *Obihiro-shi Shakai
Kyōiku Sōsho,* Obihiro [1].

————, 1956a. "Higashi Hokkaido Ainu Koji Fudoki Shiryō (Ethnographical
Materials on the Ainu in Eastern Hokkaido), *Obihiro-shi Shakai Kyōiku
Sōsho,* Obihiro [2].

————, 1957. "Higashi Hokkaido Ainu Koji Fudoki Shiryō" (Ethnographical
Materials on the Ainu in Eastern Hokkaido), *Obihiro-shi Shakai Kyōiku
Sōsho,* Obihiro [3].

————, 1958. "Higashi Hokkaido Ainu Koji Fudoki Shiryō" (Ethnographical
Materials on the Ainu in Eastern Hokkaido), *Obihiro-shi Shakai Kyōiku
Sōsho,* Obihiro [4].

GLOSSARY

Ainu: "men" or "humans"

anun utari: "foreign people"; persons not of one's *ekashi ikiru*

basho system: system of seasonal employment of Ainu at Japanese coastal
fishing posts on Hokkaido in the nineteenth century

ekashi itokpa (or, *itokpa*): the common male ancestor mark which was the
overt expression of membership in a particular *ekashi ikiru* and *shine itokpa*

inau: offering sticks for *kamui* deities

iomante: "sending off the bear *kamui*"; the ritual killing of a bear cub

iworu: the area of a specific stream's drainage which is watched by the stream-
owning *kamui.*

kamui deities: all deities of the Ainu ideological system

kotan: the Ainu settlement; consisted of one to ten dwelling houses

marek: a fish spear

ottena: title conferred by the Japanese on Ainu officers of the "basho" system

river group: the aggregate of all local groups which lived along one river

shine ekashi ikiru (or, *ekashi ikiru*): "one and the same male-ancestor descent";
a group of male patrilineal kinsmen which formed the core of a specific local
group and the related neighboring local groups (the *shine itokpa* group)

shine huchi ikiru (or, *huchi ikiru*): "one and the same ancestress descent";
applied to matrilineally related women

shine-itokpa ukokoru utaru; (or, *shine itokpa*): "one and the same ancestor
mark jointly possessing people"; an aggregate of patrilineally related neighboring local groups, or, in some cases, a single local group

shinnurappa: an ancestor ritual; the only formal retention of the *kamui* cult
since the Ainu's adoption of agriculture

ukosanio: an assembly of the headman and household heads of the local group

INDEX

Wati Warumala, 222
Weaning, 41, 259, 307, 315, 335, 430
Wellington, J. H., 276
Wentworth, W., 264
Western Desert Culture (Australia), 177–216
  kinship and cultural variation, 196–198

Pitjandjara, 217–268
  subsection system, 194–198
  themes in, 191–192
  tribal composition, 180–181
Westphal, E. O. J., 328, 329, 330
Whiting, J. W. M., 429
Wolmeri (*see* Walmadjeri)